A DICTIONARY OF
AUSTRALIAN COLLOQUIALISMS

A DICTIONARY OF
AUSTRALIAN
COLLOQUIALISMS

G. A. Wilkes

ROUTLEDGE & KEGAN PAUL
London and Henley

This book is funded by money from
THE ELEANOR SOPHIA WOOD BEQUEST

First published in Great Britain in 1978
by Routledge & Kegan Paul Ltd
39 Store Street,
London WC1E 7DD and
Broadway House,
Newtown Road,
Henley-on-Thames,
Oxon RG9 1EN
Set in Monophoto Apollo
Printed in Great Britain by
Thomson Litho Ltd,
East Kilbride, Scotland

British Library Cataloguing in Publication Data

Wilkes, Gerald Alfred

A dictionary of Australian colloquialisms.
1. English language in Australia—Dictionaries
2. English language in Australia—Spoken
English
I. Title
427'.9'94   PE3601.Z5

ISBN 0 7100 8930 9

Introduction

While on study leave in Oxford in 1968, I was asked by an English scholar whether there were any distinctively Australian proverbs. My first response was that there were not, although I could think of expressions like *game as Ned Kelly, the biggest liar this side of the black stump,* or *we've got two chances, ours and Buckley's,* that might be difficult for anyone other than an Australian to understand. Some of them might be found in dictionaries, but others – expressions of stoic resignation such as *I suppose it's better than a poke in the eye with a burnt stick,* or *If it was raining palaces, I'd get hit on the head by the dunny door* – almost certainly would not. Having always been interested in Australian idiom, I began to note such expressions when I encountered them, encouraged as I went on by the view of the Oxford authority on proverbs, the late Professor F. P. Wilson, that a man may value an occupation that 'keeps him busy and interested when he is too tired to do anything else'.[1]

As the list of 'proverbial' expressions grew, it became increasingly difficult to explain them without first explaining the colloquial vocabulary they depended upon. *Humping the drum* calls for an explanation of *drum,* which carries a different meaning in *give someone the drum* (or in *run a drum* in racing parlance), and means something else again in a reference to a Cairo *drum* in an Australian war novel. The need was for a collection of Australian colloquialisms.

Colloquialisms are a particular area of Australian English, not the whole field. A dictionary of colloquialisms omits much that a general dictionary of Australian English would include – the names of most plants, animals, trees and fish, for example – while giving more scope to informal usage than a standard dictionary can normally allow. The indispensable pioneer survey of Australian vocabulary in the nineteenth century, Edward E. Morris' *Austral English*[2] is not strong in colloquialisms, partly because it was being compiled in the years just before the vernacular idiom of writers like Lawson and Furphy had become established, and partly because of the compiler's preoccupation with flora and fauna at the expense of other things. The balance was redressed in the twentieth century in the work of Sidney J. Baker, from his early *A Popular Dictionary of Australian Slang*[3] to the revised edition of *The Australian Language*[4]. It is a matter for regret that Baker did not digest all his findings into a comprehensive dictionary of Australian English. The indexes to his books provide alphabetical lists, and *The Drum*[5] includes a dictionary of a kind, but we do not have in tabular form both the words and the supporting quotations needed as a guide to

[1] 'The Proverbial Wisdom of Shakespeare' in *Shakespearian and Other Studies*, Oxford 1969, p. 144.
[2] *Austral English A Dictionary of Australasian Words Phrases and Usages*, London 1898, facsimile reprint Sydney 1972.
[3] *A Popular Dictionary of Australian Slang*, Melbourne 1941.
[4] *The Australian Language*, Sydney 1966.
[5] *The Drum Australian Character and Slang*, Sydney 1959.

their usage and currency. All later workers in the field must nonetheless owe a substantial debt to Baker.

What is a colloquialism? It has its existence in familiar speech rather than in the language of the printed page, but the border between the two is constantly shifting. It is obviously a colloquial usage to say *nong* rather than 'simpleton', *come the raw prawn* instead of 'impose upon', *shickered* instead of 'drunk' or *shouse* instead of 'lavatory'. (Colloquialisms are not only less formal, but often also less respectable than 'standard' English.) But the boundaries remain inexact. The word *squatter* (imported from America) began life in Australia as a colloquial term for an unauthorized occupant of land, became 'standard' and respectable when it was defined in government regulations, and in the later nineteenth century asserted itself as a colloquialism again as a slightly hostile way of referring to a 'pastoralist' or 'grazier' – the hostile implication lingers in *squattocracy*. The history of *bushranger* is similarly complex. A dictionary of colloquialisms would not include *kangaroo* or *bandicoot*, which are standard terms, but would include the verb *kangaroo* for the jerky movement of a car and the verb *bandicoot* for stealing potatoes while leaving the surface soil apparently undisturbed, besides such expressions as *kangaroos in the top paddock* and *like a bandicoot on a burnt ridge*. Given that rigid divisions are not enforceable, I have tended to include rather than reject, just as in choosing citations I have not discarded any because they seemed amusing.

The difficulty of deciding what is colloquial is matched by the difficulty of deciding what is 'Australian'. As the example of *kangaroo* indicates, the discovery of Australia added some new words to the English language. The first 'Australianisms' were the words taken over from the Aborigines. Allowing that *bandicoot* is an Indian word, *emu* is Portuguese, and that *piccaninny* is West Indian, there is no difficulty in accepting terms like *boomerang, billabong, corroboree, bingey, humpy, gibber, mulga* and *warrigal* as Australian English, especially as all have been adopted colloquially by whites. Other terms arose as a patois evolved in attempts at communication between black and white – the 'pidgin' to which might be assigned *walkabout, mary* (for a woman), *sugar bag* (wild honey) and other words (e.g. *monaych, nanto*) which no lexicographer seems to have picked up.

As English experience of Australian conditions expanded during the nineteenth century, this stock of words was augmented by the necessity to describe the new circumstances encountered – hence *southerly buster, running a banker*, going *on the wallaby track*. The use of *cockatoo* as a sentinel no doubt arose from observing the habits of cockatoos, as perhaps did *cockatoo* for a small settler. A *pure merino* became someone insistent on his social status; *post-and-rails* was a nickname for a coarse bush tea. The *government stroke* had been observed by the mid-nineteenth century, as had the institutions of *smoko* and (later) *heading them*. The development of the vocabulary becomes a partial record of social history as this process goes on. I have found no record of *bottle-oh* until the turn of the century; *susso* belongs to the Depression; the *toastrack tram* and the *six o'clock swill* occur between the wars; the *brown bomber* and the *reffo* come a little later, and the *Pitt Street farmer* later still – though all may now seem *as Australian as a meat pie*.

Other terms are identifiable as Australian because they derive from persons or place-names, or from figures in Australian folklore. Examples would include *Jacky Howe* (for a sleeveless shirt), *furphy, doing a Melba, up there Cazaly, Hay or Hell or Booligal,* the *Barcoo spews* or the *Barcoo salute.* A particular expression like *Sing 'em muck* is associated with Dame Nellie Melba, just as *tall poppies* was given currency by J. T. Lang. We approach the region of folklore with *Buckley's chance, beyond the black stump, Blind Freddie* and *Jimmy Woodser,* although in each case historical evidence has been adduced. There are also a number of rather synthetic Australian expressions fostered by comic strips (e.g. *stiffen the lizards*) or by entertainers (e.g. *Cop this, young 'Arry*) which have become part of colloquial usage as life imitates art. The most recent example is the vocabulary of Barry McKenzie (e.g. *go for the big spit*), described by its inventor as a pastiche in which 'words like *cobber* and *bonzer* still intrude as a sop to Pommy readers, though such words are seldom, if ever, used in present-day Australia'.[6]

Indigenous expressions, wherever they can be certified as such, are the first category of colloquialisms within Australian English. A second consists of terms that did not so much begin life in Australia as find a new life here. Words like *dinkum, bowyangs* and *damper,* as W. S. Ramson has shown, had their origin in England, but have so fallen into disuse there that an Englishman encountering them in Australia may have to ask their meaning. They are most often dialect words, sometimes surviving in parts of England, but in Australia having no restriction of class or region. When the twelve-volume Oxford dictionary was completed in 1928, the word *skerrick* was not included. When the first *Supplement* appeared in 1933, *skerrick* was entered as '*Austral. colloq.* A small fragment' with a citation from Ion L. Idriess. It had already been recorded in the *English Dialect Dictionary* in 1905, with citations going back to 1863, in exactly the '*Austral.*' sense: 'a particle, a morsel, scrap, atom', and it was this dialectal usage which had become established in Australia. Australian English may have no particular claim to *skerrick,* still used in parts of England, although its use in Australia is more widespread. But it indicates how the currency of a word, rather than its point of origin, may persuade a lexicographer how to classify it. Terms that pass completely out of currency in Britain may eventually survive as part of Australian English alone. This may already have happened with *dinkum* and *bowyangs,* and words like *shanghai, larrikin* and *ringer* have a similar history.

Sometimes the source is not so much a dialect as the language of a particular class. The convicts brought with them the thieves' slang of England, which instead of remaining the property of criminals often passed into general use – for example *plant* in the sense of 'hide', *school* for a collection of gamblers, or *skinner* for a betting coup in racing. The practice of *scaling*

[6] Barry Humphries, 'Barry McKenzie', *Times Literary Supplement,* 16 September 1965, p. 812.

a ride on trams may have gone out with the Sydney trams themselves, but a character in a Patrick White play still uses *shake* in the sense of 'steal'. Similarly the technical language of gold-mining, much of it brought from America, has made *pan out* an expression that no one would now connect with the wash-dish, just as the adjective *nuggety* (itself of dialectal origin) would not now recall the goldrush of the 1850s. The practice of *chiacking*, apparently the prerogative of costermongers in nineteenth-century England, is in Australia available to all.

To the same general category belong words of overseas origin which in Australia have undergone a change or extension of meaning. The use of *bail up* for securing a cow for milking derives from the English word *bail*, but in Australia *bailing up* came especially to be applied to the activities of bushrangers, while a city-dweller even now may run the risk of being *bailed up* in the street by a talkative acquaintance. *Swag* was originally an English word for the booty of a thief; in Australia it is extended to the legitimate baggage of an itinerant. *Spell* is commonly used in England for a turn of work; in Australia it is more commonly used for an interval of rest. *Bastard* in England either imputes illegitimacy or serves as a general term of insult; in Australia it can be an affectionate mode of address.

All these words have therefore acquired particular Australian senses, not shared by the linguistic community from which they came. The same holds for words of foreign derivation absorbed into Australian idiom. *Swy* (for 'two-up') is from the German *zwei*, as *spieler* is from *spielen* and *shicer* from *scheissen* (possibly mediated through English and American slang); *shickered* and *put the moz on* are from Yiddish; *donah* and *bimbo* are from Spanish and Italian, though probably not directly; *hoot* (for 'money') has been traced to Maori and *donga* to South African. All have developed meanings here not found in the original language, much as the original language may help to explain them.

The second general category of Australianisms therefore consists of words of overseas origin which have either survived here while becoming obsolete elsewhere, or else have undergone semantic change. The third category is the most uncertain. It consists of words which do occur in the same sense in other linguistic communities, but on which the information is lacking that would establish priority or relative currency. *Swamper* is recorded in American English in 1850 as a 'road-breaker, who is constantly employed in keeping the roads open', especially in logging operations, and in 1870 as 'a man who goes with the driver of a 10, 12 or 14 – mule team as his assistant'. This sufficiently antedates the Australian use of the word (which again develops in a slightly different way) to establish that *swamper* came into Australian English from North America. The same would apply to *corduroy, rouseabout* and *shinplaster*. But what of *knock* in the sense of 'disparage'? It is recorded in Australia in 1892, in America in 1896, in Canada in 1906 and thereafter in England. It has a general currency in Australia, and has been taken as referring to a national characteristic (a book was published in 1972 with the title *Knockers*), but it is not an Australianism of the same order as the other two categories I have distinguished. For a modern colloquialism, *knock* is comparatively well documented: for dozens of other terms there is hardly any guide at all, except that Partridge, Mathews or other chroniclers of slang elsewhere do not record them. Is *go for the doctor* used in racing parlance outside Australia? Did the advice *bum to mum* really originate with sporting coaches in Victoria? Did the ironical expression *That'll be the day!* arise first in New Zealand, and then find its way to the United States? The colloquial language is not well enough documented at present for these questions to be answered. One can only record the occurrence of the expressions in Australian English for the benefit of researchers elsewhere.

The problem of what to include or exclude is complicated by the ephemerality of colloquialisms themselves. We no longer use *logs* for gaol, offer *flash your dover* as an invitation to eat, or refer to canned meat as *tinned dog*. As these expressions may be encountered by readers of Marcus Clarke or Henry Lawson, a dictionary of colloquialisms should explain them. A reader born since World War II may be mystified by *the man outside Hoyts*, *more arse than Jessie*, or *like a pakapoo ticket* (as a synonym for untidiness). The future biographer of Prince Charles will no doubt be able to understand his reported remark at an Australia Day dinner in 1973 that 'all the faces here this evening seem to be bloody Poms', but may be puzzled by the Prince's joke about having his name linked romantically with 'the naughty Nullarbor nymph'. Even so short-lived a phenomenon as *the Nullarbor nymph* has found its way into the colloquial language, and so should be recorded.

The value of any survey of colloquialisms will rest finally on what it records. This dictionary is planned, in a modest way, 'on historical principles'. It seeks to record the history of each word, through examples of usage. The citations are the most important part of the dictionary, as the evidence on which it rests. To have simply listed the words themselves, with definitions, would have been to risk giving them all the same status. It is important to see that examples of *bonzer* fall mainly between 1900 and the 1940s, and that by 1969 the word is being described as 'an anachronism'. On the other hand *beaut* has gained in popularity, with its allied expressions *you beaut!* and *beauty* (pronounced *bewdy*, and conveying full agreement or approval). Any historical record of usage is uncertain, as the first occurrence of a term is usually beyond recovery, and the printed evidence on which one has to rely is always in arrears – thus *root* (for intercourse) was used in speech long before it came to be recorded in print. But it is possible to gain some impression from the quotations given of the period to which *brickfielder* and *humping the drum* chiefly belong, when *compo* and *sickie* came into vogue, how *bush telegraph* and *crawler* developed different meanings.

I have not attempted to distinguish levels of colloquial usage in the way that was still possible for Partridge in his invaluable dictionary of slang, by the use of terms like 'low' or 'vulg.'. At a time when the four-letter words are gaining common acceptance, the exercise has little point. More sensitivity is now attached to terms like *abo*, *boong* and *poofter*, and I have found a continued usefulness in the old-fashioned labels *derogatory* and *jocular*. Thus *reffo* and *silvertail* would have a *derogatory* implication; examples of *jocular* usage would be found in expressions of interstate rivalry: *the coathanger, the only river in the world that flows upside down, Bananalander, sandgroper*. Most colloquial terms for non-Australians are derogatory, although the gradations are subtle. A *Pommy bastard* is viewed with disfavour, but one who comes to be described as *not a bad poor bastard* has won grudging acceptance.

All dictionaries are tentative, and a colloquial dictionary is most tentative of all. Comments and further information from readers will be welcomed, and may contribute to the full *Dictionary of Australian English* being prepared by the Australian Language Research Centre at the University of Sydney. I am indebted to the expertise of my research assistant, Miss E. Morrell, at an important stage in the assembling of material, and for help at other stages to Miss Jennifer Urquhart and Mrs Jan Kociumbas. A draft of the entries from H to Z, as it then stood, was deposited with the *Oxford English Dictionary Supplement* in May 1975, when the *Supplement* editor, Mr R. W. Burchfield, generously provided access to the material in his charge – a courtesy that has continued in correspondence since. For the deficiencies that remain in the present text, I am of course responsible alone.

University of Sydney   G. A. WILKES

Abbreviations

Acland	L. G. D. Acland, 'A Sheep Station Glossary' (1933) in *The Early Canterbury Runs*, Christchurch 1951.
Baker 1941	Sidney J. Baker, *A Popular Dictionary of Australian Slang*, Melbourne 1941.
Baker 1943	Sidney J. Baker, *A Popular Dictionary of Australian Slang*, 2nd edn, Melbourne 1943.
Baker 1945	Sidney J. Baker, *The Australian Language*, Sydney 1945.
Baker 1953	Sidney J. Baker, *Australia Speaks*, Sydney 1953.
Baker 1959	Sidney J. Baker, *The Drum Australian Character and Slang*, Sydney 1959.
Baker 1966	Sidney J. Baker, *The Australian Language*, Sydney 1966.
Barrère and Leland	A. Barrère and C. G. Leland, *A Dictionary of Slang, Jargon and Cant*, 2 vols, Edinburgh 1889–90.
EDD	*The English Dialect Dictionary*, ed. Joseph Wright, 6 vols, Oxford 1898–1905.
Franklyn	Julian Franklyn, *A Dictionary of Rhyming Slang*, 2nd edn, London 1961.
Grose	Francis Grose, *A Classical Dictionary of the Vulgar Tongue*, London 1785, 1788, 1790, 1811.
Hotten	John Camden Hotten, *A Dictionary of Modern Slang, Cant and Vulgar Words*, London 1859, 1860, 1864.
HRA	*Historical Records of Australia*, Series I, 33 vols, Sydney 1914–25.
HRNSW	*Historical Records of New South Wales*, 7 vols, Sydney 1892–1901.
Lawson *Prose*	Henry Lawson, *Collected Prose*, ed. Colin Roderick, 2 vols, Sydney 1972.
Lawson *Verse*	Henry Lawson, *Collected Verse*, ed. Colin Roderick, 3 vols, Sydney 1967–9.
Mathews	M. M. Mathews, *A Dictionary of Americanisms*, Chicago 1966.
Morris	Edward E. Morris, *Austral English A Dictionary of Australasian Words Phrases and Usages*, London 1898; facsimile reprint Sydney 1972.
O'Brien and Stephens	S. E. O'Brien and A. G. Stephens, 'Materials for a Dictionary of Australian Slang 1900–1910', Sydney, Mitchell Library MS Q427.9/0.
obs.	obsolete
OED	*The Oxford English Dictionary*, 13 vols, Oxford 1933; *Supplement*, 2 vols to date, 1972–.

Partridge	Eric Partridge, *A Dictionary of Slang and Unconventional English*, 2 vols, London 1970.
Ramson	W. S. Ramson, *Australian English An Historical Study of the Vocabulary 1788–1898*, Canberra 1966.
SND	*The Scottish National Dictionary*, 10 vols, Edinburgh 1932–76.
Turner	G. W. Turner, *The English Language in Australia and New Zealand*, 2nd edn, London 1972.
Vaux	'A Vocabulary of the Flash Language' (1812) in *The Memoirs of James Hardy Vaux*, ed. Noel McLachlan, London 1964.
V.F.L.	The Victorian Football League

A

abo *n.* & *a.* Australian Aboriginal. Not always intended as derogatory, but now increasingly taken to be so [abbr.]
1922 *Bulletin* 5 Jan. 22: I was sheltering from a hailstorm under the verandah of the pub, and among my fellow refugees was an abo. who had been to the mission school.
1934 Jean Devanny *Out of Such Fires* 18: 'Wouldn't take long to get back to the abo state. A few hundred years, perhaps?'
1944 *Salt* 8 May 19: 'Abo Paints his World' [article on Albert Namatjira]
1958 Gavin Casey *Snowball* 118: 'You wait till he gets a bit older. Them abos always go t' the pack,' a cynic told him.
1966 Peter Mathers *Trap* 185: 'You're sure it's not La Perouse, the Abo settlement, you want?'
1970 Barry Oakley *A Salute to the Great McCarthy* 79: 'What ya do out there? Play in bare feet, like the abos?'

abos, give it back to the As for 'give it back to the blacks' q.v.
1951 Dymphna Cusack and Florence James *Come in Spinner* 126: 'This house is a hundred years old.' 'Then it's time they gave it back to the Abos.'

ace, on one's Alone, left to one's own resources [? f. *ace* the score of 'one' in dice; or associated with *arse*]
1906 Edward Dyson *Fact'ry 'Ands* 298: 'Would yeh believe it, that tin was tickin' like forty watches, 'n' when Sniff stirred it, you'd think it was full iv live dried peas, 'n' was rattlin' on its ace.'
1908 E. G. Murphy *Jarrahland Jingles* 58: Brim's in London on his 'ace'.
1934 Archer. Russell *A Tramp Royal* 213: 'They're capable of a good work at times,' said a 'boss cattleman' to whom I had applied for his opinion of the merits and demerits of the aboriginal as stockman, 'but you've got to be with them. Send 'em out "on their ace" and they'll probably "go camp" under the first shady tree they come to.'

1953 Baker 131: *ace, on one's* On one's own. [as prison slang]

ace it up Stop it: *rare* [unexplained]
1965 Graham McInnes *The Road to Gundagai* 164: 'Hey, ace it up Bill, that hurts.' Bill grinned and loosened the tourniquet slightly.

acid, to put the ~ on To make the kind of demand (for money, information, or sex) that will either yield results or eliminate that possibility [f. *acid test*]
1906 Edward Dyson *Fact'ry 'Ands* 215: Evidently it was Mr Cato's intention to try the acid on Feathers again. Ibid. 210: ' 'E [the Toucher] puts ther acid on so't yeh think it's the milk iv 'uman kindness.'
1919 W. H. Downing *Digger Dialects* 40: *To put the acid on* (1) Ask. (2) Test. (3) Put a stop to.
1925 Arthur Wright *The Boy from Bullarah* 16: 'He owes me anything up to a score of quids ... I'm going to put the acid on.'
1942 Leonard Mann *The Go-Getter* 234: Somehow they had learned Carkeek's share in this business, but when they had put the acid on him they had found he could not help them.
1948 Ruth Park *Poor Man's Orange* 165: 'I'll tell every feller I know she's easy, and she won't be able to go down the street without having the acid put on her.'
1966 Patrick White *The Solid Mandala* 147: 'And a woman like that, married to such a sawney bastard, she wouldn't wait for 'em to put the acid on 'er.'
see **hard word**

acre (acher) Buttocks, backside [? f. appearance]
1938 Heard in conversation.
1966 Baker 169: *acre* the anus. [as World War II slang]
1971 Frank Hardy *The Outcasts of Foolgarah* 18: Wiping between his toes [after a shower] and falling on his acre. Ibid. 94: 'I'll give you a free kick up the acher if you're not careful.'
1973 Roland Robinson *The Drift of Things* 164: Because they used to surf

in the nude and lie among the flowering tea-trees on the sides of the valley sunbathing, one shack dweller ... called his shack 'Sunburned Acres.'

Acre, the Dirty Half see **Dirty Half Acre**

act, to put on an To indulge in a tantrum, make a fuss (esp. with an implication of pretence or overstatement) [f. *act* (a role)]
1945 Margaret Trist *Now That We're Laughing* 96: She groaned agonizingly. 'Get her something, quick,' cried Joyce. 'It's only Daffy putting on an act,' said Pearl.
1949 Lawson Glassop *Lucky Palmer* 60: 'You should have seen me put on an act when they gave me a rocking horse for Christmas.'
1957 Judah Waten *Shares in Murder* 58: 'Don't put on an act,' he said half pleading, half angry.
1962 Criena Rohan *The Delinquents* 113: 'Do you think she's stacking on an act?' asked the younger cop. 'Or do you think she's sick, or in the D.T.'s?'

adjective, the great Australian see **Australian**

aerial pingpong Australian Rules Football: *jocular* [f. the long kicks and high leaps which are features of the game]
1965 Frank Hardy *The Yarns of Billy Borker* 43: Melbourne Mick would say, 'Australian Rules draws bigger crowds in Melbourne than Rugby in Sydney.' 'What?' Sydney Sam would say, 'that's not football, mate, it's aerial ping-pong.'
1973 *Sun* 4 Apr. 93: Aussie Rules, or aerial pingpong as it is sometimes called, is being telecast live from Melbourne by Nine.

aerialist
1970 Barry Oakley *A Salute to the Great McCarthy* 30: The high and mighty MacGuinness, the aerialist who drew the crowds and then fell.

after Afternoon, superseded by 'arvo' q.v. [abbr.]
1933 Norman Lindsay *Saturdee* 193:

'So what price comin' a walk with me this after?'
1939 Leonard Mann *Mountain Flat* 242: 'This after we'll go for a swim.'

Akubra (ōō) Hat [brand name]
1930 *Bulletin* 23 Jul. 16: Hamlet himself stirs pity in the soft-hearted boy, who is overheard to remark that the 'Prince is taking a bit of a risk getting about in the cold without his Akubra.'
1972 Patrick White *The Eye of the Storm* 450: The solicitor was looking at her from under the brim of his Akubra.
1977 *Southerly* 51: He ... took his leprous Akubra from a table near the door, perched it on top of his straggling grey hair.

alas! milfissed the balfastards see **balfastards**

Albany Doctor A cool and refreshing breeze [place-name in W.A.]
1922 Edward Meryon *At Holland's Tank* 162: The south breeze, better known in those parts as the Albany Doctor, had arrived.
1937 A. W. Upfield *Mr Jelly's Business* 57: The 'Albany Doctor' people called it, because the strong cool wind from Albany way swept clear the bodily and metal languors brought on by the heat of the long day.
see **Fremantle doctor**

Alberts, Prince Rags wound about the feet in place of socks [f. the alleged poverty of Prince Albert before he became Victoria's consort: listed by Partridge as nautical]
c. 1888 'Sam Griffith' *Old Bush Songs* ed. Stewart and Keesing (1957) 203: I knew his feet were blistered / From the Alberts that he wore.
1903 Joseph Furphy *Such is Life* (1944) 39: Unlapping from his feet the inexpensive substitute for socks known as 'prince-alberts', he artistically spread the redolent swaths across his boots to receive the needful benefit of the night air.
1912 G. H. Gibson *Ironbark Splinters*

44: 'Prince Alberts' ain't the fashion now, / The shearers all wears socks.
1949 John Morrison *The Creeping City* 112–13: 'I once walked all the way from Nar-nar-goon to Thargomindah with nothing on me feet but Prince Alberts!'

alec, aleck A stupid fellow, an ass [f. *smart alec* U.S. 1865 Mathews]
1944 Lawson Glassop *We Were the Rats* 168: 'I reckon if I got stomach ache all you alecks would know almost before I did.'
1946 Margaret Trist *What Else is There?* 90: 'If a man goes on the booze and belts you up, you know where you stand. But when they start in preachin' I kind of feel a big aleck.'
1962 Alan Seymour *The One Day of the Year* 64: 'He looked such a big aleck, marching along as though he'd won both wars single-handed.'
1962 Stuart Gore *Down the Golden Mile* 96: 'Don't be an aleck!' the other returned brusquely. 'There haven't been any boongs – not real myalls – around here since Adam was a boy!'

Alf The uncultivated Australian (the opposite to *Roy* q.v.) now being superseded by *ocker* [see quot. 1965]
1960 Murray Sayle 'As Far As You Can Go' *Encounter* May 28: The Australian worker, the 'Alf' as we call him.
1965 E. Morris 'Reliques of Sope' [Neil C. Hope, d. 1964] *Nation* 27 Nov. 21: Middle-class 'Roys' in sports cars and yachting jackets, and red-necked 'Alfs' who want to fight those who swear in front of ladies. (It was Sope who invented the now-ubiquitous term.)
1968 Craig McGregor *People, Politics and Pop* 163: Alf is always someone else, the bloke in the bungalow, Fred down the road, dead from the neck up, a talking beer gut from the neck down.
1974 *Australian* 23 Nov. 21: He does not want to show his films in the film workshop-co-op settings and they are too way out for your ordinary Alf.
Alf-land Australia
1971 Craig McGregor *Don't Talk to Me about Love* 130: 'We're all expatriates here, living an expatriate life in the middle of Alf-land.'

Alfred, Royal An elaborate swag [? f. Alfred, Duke of Edinburgh who toured Australia 1867–8]
1902 Henry Lawson 'The Romance of the Swag' *Prose* i 501–2: The weight of the swag varies from the light rouseabout's swag, containing one blanket and a clean shirt, to the 'Royal Alfred', with tent and all complete, and weighing part of a ton.

Alfreds, Prince As for 'Prince Alberts'
1896 Henry Lawson 'Stragglers' *Prose* i 92–3: Occasionally someone gets some water in an old kerosine tin and washes a shirt or pair of trousers, and a pair or two of socks – or foot-rags – (Prince Alfreds, they call them).

Alice, the Alice Springs N.T.; more recently 'Alice'
1901 F. J. Gillen *Diary* (1968) 92: I was sleeping on a canvas covered stretcher which I procured at the Alice.
1933 R. B. Plowman *The Man from Oodnadatta* 140: 'I just dropped on them quite unexpectedly. I didn't know they had left the Alice.'
1953 *The Sunburnt Country* ed. Ian Bevan 75: When, years ago, I first visited that part of the world, a journey to 'the Alice' was a journey indeed.
1959 Lyndon Rose *The Country of the Dead* 159: 'I'll let them know in at Alice and out at the mission.'
1961 Jack Danvers *The Living Come First* 16: 'I met them in Alice a while back.'

alkie An alcoholic [abbr.]
1964 Bruce Beaver *The Hot Sands* 16: Ben Tickell, the regular night porter, was an alkie if ever she had seen one.
1971 Rena Briand *White Man in a Hole* 31: Kind-hearted, he'd share ... his last cigarettes with the alkies at the Front Bar.
1975 Elizabeth Riley *All That False Instruction* 126: 'Tried to think what I'd feel like if I was a sixty-odd alkie.'

all alone like a country dunny see

alley A marble [f. *alley* a choice marble or taw OED 1720–1865]

1 *To pass (toss) in one's alley* To give in, die

1916 C. J. Dennis *The Moods of Ginger Mick* 109: But if I dodge, an' keep out 'uv the rain, / An' don't toss in me alley 'fore we wins.

1924 *Truth* 27 Apr. 6: *Alleys, to toss in the* To give in.

1933 Norman Lindsay *Saturdee* 23: 'This book says a bloke kicked the bucket, an' Bill says it means a bloke pegged out, so what's it mean?' 'Means a bloke passed his alley in.'

1937 Vance Palmer *Legend for Sanderson* 31: 'Too much beer over the weekend, wasn't it, Neil? First time I've known you to toss in the alley.'

1960 Jack McKinney *The Well* in *Khaki Bush and Bigotry* ed. Eunice Hanger (1968) 228: 'Don't sling in yer alley, missus. There's a good time comin'.'

2 *To make one's alley good* To make the grade, improve one's status or prospects

1924 C. J. Dennis *Rose of Spadgers* 160: That 'e 'ad swore to get me one uv those / Fine days, an' make 'is alley good with Rose.

1952 T. A. G. Hungerford *The Ridge and the River* 109: 'That's all right,' Shearwood said soberly. 'It makes Wilder's alley good, but it doesn't win any popularity stakes for you.'

1964 *Sydney Morning Herald* 10 Aug. 2: 'Hey, Tom! Joe is making his alley good with Nelly Bli down be th' crik.'

1975 Xavier Herbert *Poor Fellow My Country* 362: Berated Pat for taking up the cause of a scab in order to make his alley good with a designing female.

see **marble**

amster, ampster Confederate of the manager of a sideshow, with the task of attracting custom [rhyming slang *Amsterdam* = *ram* q.v.]

1941 Kylie Tennant *The Battlers* 181: As soon as the showman begins to shout: 'All right, the show is commencing Roll up! Roll up!' . . . the amster rushes eagerly up to the ticket window and says: 'Right-o, mister, I'll have a ticket.' He pretends to pass his money over, and is handed a ticket. His brother-amsters form into an impatient queue behind him and file into the tent at the head of the multitude who, like sheep, will follow the leader, but will not be the first to pay their money.

1975 Hal Porter *The Extra* 244: A shady Soho club patronised by dips, amsters, off-duty prostitutes.

angora sc. goat, usually in the phrase 'act (play) the angora': *obsolescent*

1899 *Truth* 8 Oct. 5: Refrain from playing the giddy ox, the antic angora, and the cowardly, foul-mouthed dirty devil generally.

1908 Henry Fletcher *Dads and Dan between Smokes* 61: But ther cove wot piles up a big fortchin fer others ter spend is a double-barrelled angora.

1922 Henry Lawson 'The Last Rose of Winter' *Prose* i 906: He had that lovable expression of a Bushman admiring his mate making a giddy angora of himself.

1937 Vance Palmer *Legend for Sanderson* 27: 'Don't be an angora, Leo. What d' you take me for?'

1945 Cecil Mann *The River* 142: 'And you, Clarkey – you, you great angora – standing there, leaning on the rail, scared stiff.'

animal A term of contempt, esp. since World War II

1892 William Lane *The Workingman's Paradise* 80: 'There we were, poor, ragged, hungry wretches . . . and that animal ran up a great wall in our faces so that we couldn't see the grass.'

1945 Baker 156: *animal* A term of contempt for a person. [World War II slang]

1946 K. S. Prichard *The Roaring Nineties* 317: 'To hell with Sir John Forrest and any other animals like him!'

1955 John Morrison *Black Cargo* 19: 'I had mates starved in that strike, and that animal . . .'

1959 Dorothy Hewett *Bobbin Up* 57: 'I've never met a copper yet was any good. They're all a lotta animals.'

1968 Geoffrey Dutton *Andy* 58: 'Where

did you two animals come from? Anybody'd think we were in the bloody Army.'

1974 David Ireland *Burn* 141: I reckon he knew about the other officers tossed overboard on the way home for their bastardry . . . Paid in full for the animals they were.

Anzac As the code address adopted by General Birdwood in Egypt for the Australian and New Zealand Army Corps in 1915, and used by him in naming the landing-place at Gallipoli 'Anzac Cove', 'Anzac' is not a colloquialism. There is more of a colloquial colour in its application to members of the Gallipoli expedition, to that operation as a whole, to Australian servicemen in later wars, and to an Australian 'tradition' sometimes heroically and sometimes ironically regarded.

1916 Tom Skeyhill *Soldier Songs from Anzac* 26: But it's different 'ere at Anzac;/Mr Turk! 'e ain't arf slick.

1916 Let. in Bill Gammage *The Broken Years* (1974) 156: So three cheers for the Anzac and the early ending of this sinful game.

1919 Edward Dyson *Hello Soldier* 18: Little Abdul's quite a fighter . . . /But the Anzacs have him snouted.

1936 Miles Franklin *All That Swagger* 447: They remain incapable of instructing the rising generation that the glories of Anzac were as empty as all military glory down the centuries, symbolised by a tattered flag or a suit of rusty armour in a silent museum.

1943 *Khaki and Green* 107: Greetings such as 'You'll do me, you big bronzed Anzac' are not encouraged.

1957 Randolph Stow *The Bystander* 21: 'It's just the way I am. The lean bronzed Anzac type. Don't you agree?'

1965 Eric Lambert *The Long White Night* 8: Most of them had come to the hall straight from the pubs. They were dinkum diggers and bronzed Anzacs all over again. They were perpetuating the Australian Myth.

1970 Richard Beilby *No Medals for Aphrodite* 169: 'Get on the big, bronzed Anzac, will yer!' Darcy mocked.

1974 *Sun-Herald* 15 Sep. 43: Although tarnished over the years, the Australian image of the healthy, bronzed Anzac still lingers as part of our folklore.

see **bronze gods**

Apple isle, the Tasmania [f. crops]

1965 *Australian* 10 Feb. 14: Smallest state in the Commonwealth – the 'Apple Isle' of Tasmania.

1971 *Sunday Australian* 13 Jun. 7: Apple Isle dumps a million bushels.

apples, everything's In good order, under control [? f. *apple pie order,* or rhyming slang *apples and spice = nice*]

1952 T. A. G. Hungerford *The Ridge and the River* 44: 'How's it going, Wally? Everything apples?'

1961 Frank Hardy *The Hard Way* 132: 'For Pete's sake keep mum about it.' 'She's apples,' the worker replied, with another demonstrative wink.

1966 Hal Porter *The Paper Chase* 251: 'Listen, mate, here's the problem. Mascot at five thirty. Passport photographs first – here's the address. While that's happening, can you collect my luggage at Usher's, buy me sixty cigarettes, and pick me up at the photographer's?' Sydney taxi-drivers are the world's best. 'She'll be apples, mate.'

1975 *Sydney Morning Herald* 24 Jun. 6: No one reckons it's 'apples' in the battle for Bass.

see **sweet, jake**

aristocracy, bunyip see **bunyip**

arse 1 Effrontery, 'cheek', as in the phrase 'more arse than Jessie' q.v. [? f. 'hide']

1963 John Cantwell *No Stranger to the Flame* 76: 'The johns'd never have the arse to frisk every house in a dump like this – people'd feel their word was being doubted.'

2 Equivalent to 'tail' (U.S.): sexual access to women; the good fortune this implies

1958 Frank Hardy *The Four-legged Lottery* 188: 'See all the snooker balls going the pockets – he had more arse than a married cow playing snooker, I can tell you.'

1963 Frank Hardy *Legends from Benson's Valley* 73: 'They've had the luck of Eric Connolly all night,' Darky said sheepishly. 'Our turn for a bit of arse.'
1972 John Bailey *The Wire Classroom* 145: He used to have as many as twenty of them in his room stark naked romping all over him. The natives didn't mind it, of course. A bit of arse comes naturally to the blacks.

arse, get the; be arsed out To be dismissed
1966 Baker 366: *Got the arse at Bulli Pass* [as one of a number of sayings based on place-names]
1969 William Dick *Naked Prodigal* 19: 'What's up?' I asked. 'They give me the arse,' he answered loudly.
1974 John Powers *The Last of the Knucklemen* 50: 'I'm not worth a day's pay a week. I'm lucky Tarzan doesn't give me the arse out of the place.'

arsehole, to To dismiss someone peremptorily
1965 William Dick *A Bunch of Ratbags* 153: 'It's orright when yuh young, but when yuh get a bit old and yuh can't keep up . . . they'll arsehole yuh!'
1974 David Ireland *Burn* 125: They want to clear us right out. Arsehole us completely.

Arthur or Martha, not to know whether one is A state of confusion
1957 D'Arcy Niland *Call Me When The Cross Turns Over* 52–3: 'Don't try the Barcoo spews. A cow of a thing. Get a feed into you, and then you want to chuck it up again. You chuck it up and you're right as pie till you eat again. And so it goes on. You don't know whether you're Arthur or Martha.'
1965 John Beede *They Hosed Them Out* 104: 'Probably freeze your knackers off,' said Bill sceptically. 'I only tried swimming once over here and didn't know if I was Arthur or Martha when I came out.'
1971 Frank Hardy *The Outcasts of Foolgarah* 76: 'The boys don't know

whether they're Arthur or Martha, what with all this talk about Red plots, there, and the latest telegram from Judge Parshall.'
see **bored or punched**

artist Expert, specialist, addict, esp. in expressions like 'bull artist', 'booze artist' [f. *artist* an adroit rogue; a skilful gamester U.S. 1890 OED]
[1895 Cornelius Crowe *The Australian Slang Dictionary* 4: *Artist* a cunning thief or gamester.]
1919 W. H. Downing *Digger Dialects* 9: *Artist* 'One-star artist' – a second lieutenant.
1938 Xavier Herbert *Capricornia* 379: 'We'll take a couple of bottles with us. Joe's a champion booze-artist.'
1941 Baker 14: *Bull artist* A braggart, an empty-headed blitherer.
1946 Rohan Rivett *Behind Bamboo* 395: *Bash artist* guard always beating up P.O.W.s.
1951 Dal Stivens *Jimmy Brockett* 49: Bill was fond of telling us he'd be able to retire in a few years, but he'd always been a bull artist.
1960 Murray Sayle 'As Far As You Can Go' *Encounter* May 27: Education, if he [the Australian worker] thinks of it at all, seems to him a childish trick whereby the 'bullshit artist' seeks to curry favour with the boss and thus get a better job.
1970 Patrick White *The Vivisector* 456: Decent people left the two derelicts plenty of room to pass; drunks, or more probably, metho artists.
see **merchant**

arvo Afternoon [abbr.]
1927 *Sunday Sun* 9 Oct. 'Sunbeams' 1: I told young 'Ocker' Stevens to come up and say that so I could go shooting with him with his new pea rifle this arvo.
1958 H. D. Williamson *The Sunlit Plain* 41: 'Going up to see the cricket match this arvo?' Hattie asked, yawning.
1965 Patrick White *Four Plays* 121: 'Later on this arvo I'm gunna take Ernie out and buy him a good time.'
1973 Ward McNally *Man from Zero* 65:

'See you this arvo,' he said, turning and walking towards the docks.

Aspro Associate-professor, in academic slang [abbr.]

Auntie The Australian Broadcasting Commission [f. nickname of the BBC]
1972 *Australian* 1 Jul. 12: 'Auntie turns 40'. [heading to an article on the fortieth anniversary of the ABC]
1975 *Sydney Morning Herald* 23 Aug. 1: That wicked act which aborted the Third Test produced one clear winner – the A.B.C. . . . Tuesday's abandonment of play saved Aunty some $16,000.

Aussie *n. & a.* 1 An Australian, usually with nationalistic overtones, as in phrases like 'a dinkum Aussie', 'a dinky-di Aussie' [abbr.]
1918 *Aussie The Australian Soldiers' Magazine* 18 Jan. 1: In short, make him a dinkum Aussie.
1934 Steele Rudd *Green Grey Homestead* 191: He's sure she's selected the right man for her husband – 'a good, industrious, God-fearing dinkum young Aussie.'
1940 Arnold Haskell *Waltzing Matilda* 164: Unlike so many who find success, she [Melba] remained a 'dinkum hard-swearing Aussie' to the end.
1951 Dal Stivens *Jimmy Brockett* 80: We would show them that a dinkum Aussie was worth ten of anyone else.
1971 Hal Porter *The Right Thing* 51: 'Both of them [the housekeepers] fell for dad, first the Pommy one, and then a dinky-di Aussie one.'
2 Australia
1918 *Aussie The Australian Soldiers' Magazine* 18 Jan. 1: To the Australian Soldier the name Aussie stands for his splendid, sea-girt, sun-kissed Homeland, and his cobbers are always Aussies.
1928 Arthur Wright *A Good Recovery* 110: And together they had set out for Aussie.
1974 *Australian* 15 Aug. 10: 'Cheers from A Sunburnt Country!' the advertisement trumpets. 'Toast your Pommie mates with a gift from good old Aussie!

Great beers, Hardy's fine wines, and Vegemite for the kids!'

Aussie Rules Australian Rules Football (first played in 1858)
1963 R. and E. Wordley *How to Play Aussie Rules.* [book title]
1973 Max Harris *The Angry Eye* 63: Aussie Rules remains in its condition of benign stagnation.

Australia for the Australians A catchphrase of the 1880s and later, and the motto of the *Bulletin* from 21 April 1888 (following the anti-Chinese issue of 14 April) to 30 April 1908, reflecting the nationalistic spirit of the time
1888 *The Republican* 8 Feb. 5: Australia for the Australians. [article on the Australian Republican league, which advocated the abolition of the office of Governor, nationalization of the land, federation of the colonies under republican rule]
1889 A. B. Paterson *Australia for the Australians.* [pamphlet opposing the concentration of land in the hands of a few, and advocating protective tariffs]
1902 A. G. Stephens 'Australia for the Australians' *Bulletin* 25 Jan. Red Page [article questioning the influences of the British in Australia: 'Let young Australia come to the front with the motto of Australia for the Australians. This question of independent national development overshadows all others.']
1908 C. H. S. Matthews *A Parson in the Australian Bush* 307: How did the Roman Catholics reply? By an immediate appeal to the popular Australian catchword, 'Australia for the Australians.'
1911 E. M. Clowes *On the Wallaby Through Victoria* 172: Australia . . . needs to open its arms, to enlarge its sympathies, and to get rid, once for all, of that 'precious only child in the world' idea by which it seems each year to grow more completely engrossed – I mean the 'Australia for the Australians' ideal.

Australia for the White Man Motto of the *Bulletin* from 7 May 1908 until

30 November 1960, indicating support for the White Australia policy

Australian adjective, the great Bloody q.v.

1894 *Bulletin* 18 Aug. 22: The *Bulletin* calls it the 'Australian adjective' simply because it is more used, and used more exclusively by Australians, than by any other allegedly civilised nation.
1899 W. T. Goodge *Hits! Skits! and Jingles!* 115: '—!'/(The Great Australian Adjective!) [poem title]
1939 *Daily Telegraph* 23 Jan. 7: Legal opinion upholds the ruling of Mr Atkinson S. M. that the Great Australian Adjective is sometimes offensive but not indecent.
1944 *Daily Telegraph* 7 Jul. 8: The great Australian accent, and the greater Australian adjective, are two of the best advertisements Australia has in other parts of the world.

Australian as a meat pie see **meat pie**

Australian novel, the great The novel that is always still to be written, or identified
1941 A. J. A. Waldock *Southerly* Nov. 34: Do people still muse on 'the great Australian novel' for which we wait? Casey, I believe, has it in him to write it.
1948 A. W. Upfield *An Author Bites the Dust* 133: 'Her work is much appreciated by the discerning and we are still expecting her to produce the Great Australian Novel.'
1966 Hal Porter *The Paper Chase* 70–1: The result is, of course, to be the Great Australian Novel.
1970 Patrick White *The Vivisector* 112: 'Well, good luck to you, kid! I'm going to write the Great Australian Novel.'

Australian salute The movement of the hand in brushing away flies
1972 Ian Moffitt *The U-Jack Society* 65: I flopped a hand at the flies (the Australian salute).
1976 *Australian* 9 Mar. 3: A sexually-mutated blowfly developed by CSIRO scientists in Canberra could lead to the demise of the great Australian salute.

see **Barcoo salute**

Australia's national game see **national game**

awake see **wake up**

axe-handle A unit of measurement, in country areas: *obsolescent*
1977 *Australian* 11 Apr. 6: A big woman, but not a big man, would be described as being 'two axe handles across the arse'.

B

babbler, babbling brook Cook, esp. one cooking for a number of men, as in the army or in the outback [rhyming slang]
1919 W. H. Downing *Digger Dialects* 9: *Babbling Brook*; *Babbler* An Army cook.
1924 *Truth* 27 Apr. 6: *Babbling brook* A cook.
1932 Leonard Mann *Flesh in Armour* 96: The new tins hadn't been properly cleaned out by the babbler.
1940 Ion L. Idriess *Lightning Ridge* 59: We were craftily diplomatic in our dealings with the Babbling Brook. All bush cooks are touchy.
1956 Ruth Park and D'Arcy Niland *The Drums Go Bang!* 71: The shearers ... drew as their lucky last a wizard cook from Sydney who could throw cream-puffs together with one hand and carve the roast with the other, while he washed up with his feet. Or so it seemed. He was voted one of the best babbling brooks in the business.
1964 *Sydney Morning Herald* 25 Apr. 11: 'If I keep this pretty woman babbler on my books next year I'll have to get an older team.'
babbling
1962 *Sydney Morning Herald* 24 Nov. 12: Gaily aproned women do the 'babbling' (cooking) now instead of cranky, gingery-whiskered old blokes.

bachelors' hall Another term for 'barracks' q.v.: *obs.*

1881 A. C. Grant *Bush-Life in Queensland* i 56: The fourth side [of the square of buildings at the head-station] was filled up by the building John had dined and slept in, and which was called 'The Bachelors' Hall'.

bachelor's tart An improvised bush delicacy: N.T.
1951 Ernestine Hill *The Territory* 426: Dessert was ... 'bachelor's tart' – damper and jam.

back block 1 A block of land further from water or grass, and so less favourable to settlement
1872 Anon. *Glimpses of Life in Victoria* 31: We were doomed to see the whole of our river frontage selected and purchased ... The back blocks which were left to us were insufficient for the support of our flocks, and deficient in permanent water supply. [Morris]
1874 Rolf Boldrewood *My Run Home* (1897) 265: 'A regular "back block", if ever there were one – all rock and mountain.'
2 *The blackblocks* Regions remote from settled areas
1888 Overlander *Australian Sketches* 65: Jim Brandon's Christmas on the Back Blocks and what came of it [story title]
1902 Henry Lawson 'The Shearer's Dream' *Prose* i 312: They were part of a theatrical company on tour in the Back-Blocks.
1908 Mrs Aeneas Gunn *We of the Never-Never* (1966) 140: 'Back blocks!' he said in scorn. 'There ain't no back blocks left! Can't travel a hundred miles nowadays without running into somebody!'
1925 Seymour Hicks *Hullo Australians* 198: 'You haven't seen Australia if you haven't seen the back blocks.'
1944 Gilbert Mant *You'll be Sorry* 31: Bill was a gawky lad from the backblocks who had this day seen Sydney for the first time.
1970 Barry Oakley *A Salute to the Great McCarthy* 78: 'Where ya from, kid? The backblocks? Flash boy from the paddocks?'

back blocker An inhabitant of the back blocks
1870 *Argus* 22 Mar. 7: 'I am a bushman, a back blocker, to whom it happens about once in two years to visit Melbourne.' [Morris]
1898 David W. Carnegie *Spinifex and Sand* 149: Strong and hard, about thirty-five years of age, though, like most back-blockers, prematurely grey.
1907 Alfred Searcy *In Australian Tropics* 125: If a crowd of overlanders and backblockers happened to be present, things would be made lively, for ... they would hardly give up all the liquor without a strong protest.
1957 Sydney Hart *Pommie Migrant* 161: He would ... brew up his old billy-can on one of the furnace fires – a regular back blocks veteran, who preferred his own way to that of the moderns.

back country The areas remote from settlement, usually further inland [U.S. 1746 Mathews]
1863 Samuel Butler *A First Year on Canterbury Settlement* 116: Blocks ... are frequently bought with a view to their being fenced in and laid down in English Ear grasses. In the back country this has not yet commenced, nor is it likely to do so for many years.
1888 Overlander *Australian Sketches* 1: 'You want to know how I first took to the roads and the back country, do you?'
1893 Simpson Newland *Paving the Way* 198: I presume you will continue the examination of the back-country with all the hands available, it is useless trying to track her in that thick scrub.
1903 Joseph Furphy *Such is Life* (1944) 34: 'I wish you could talk to him. Lots of information in the back country that never gets down here into civilisation.'
1911 C. E. W. Bean *The Dreadnought of the Darling* 98: This back country along the Darling produces some of the very best wool in the world.
1921 K. S. Prichard *Black Opal* 69: His father, James Henty, had taken up land in the back-country, long before

opal was found on Fallen Star Ridge.

1945 Tom Ronan *Strangers on the Ophir* 58: It was a feature of the development of the Back Country [of western Queensland] that when a man reached the frontier his past and all it signified were forgotten.

1956 A. W. Upfield *The Battling Prophet* 140: 'Us people from the Back Country can always look after ourselves. How long have you been in Australia?'

bag To disparage, 'knock'

1975 *Australian* 11 Nov. 10: 'He [the TV critic] said his wife loved the show and I said yeah but you're always bagging it and he said, yeah but we've got to sell papers somehow.'

bag, get a Reproach to a cricketer who has dropped a catch

1925 Seymour Hicks *Hullo Australians* 246: If a man who is fielding misses a catch they tell him to get a bag.

1969 Leslie Haylen *Twenty Years' Hard Labour* 70: When annoyed at some bad play Evatt yelled out 'Get a Bag'.

1975 Xavier Herbert *Poor Fellow My Country* 1239: 'Sometimes you'd think you were listening-in to a commentary on a cricket-match or something, and expect someone to yell *Get a Bag!*'

bagarup see **bugger**

bagman 1 An itinerant carrying his possessions with him. This is the broadest sense of the word, covering both the tramp (cf. *swagman*) and the traveller on horseback (*bagman²*).

1904 Henry Lawson 'The Last Review' *Verse* ii 63: Thought he [Steelman] was an honest bagman.

1910 C. E. W. Bean *On the Wool Track* 220: When a man says he met a 'traveller' or a 'bagman' in the bush he does not mean a commercial traveller. He means a man making his way from station to station, probably a man on horseback with his kit in his bag.

1941 Kylie Tennant *The Battlers* 19: 'Well, this (*adjective*) song was about an (*adjectival*) bagman who was getting

himself a bit of meat ... The busker nodded somewhat contemptuously. 'Waltzing Matilda, the Australian National Anthem.'

1971 Keith Willey *Boss Drover* 45: You were likely to find a bagman anywhere. Some of them walked right around the country.

2 A mounted swagman: esp. in N.T. and W.A.

1911 E. S. Sorenson *Life in the Australian Backblocks* 72: Two terms that are often confused one with the other are swagman and bagman. The first is a footman, the other a mounted man who may have anything from one to half a dozen horses. Though both are looking for work, they move on very different planes; the latter is considered a cut above the former, and looks down with a mildly contemptuous eye on the slowly plodding swagman.

1951 Ernestine Hill *The Territory* 429: In those vast distances where no man could foot walk, the swagman became a bagman with a riding-horse, a pack-horse and couple of spares, travelling from station to station, from creek to creek.

1966 Tom Ronan *Once There Was a Bagman* 31: The bagmen, the horse-borne wanderers, the one purely unique type Australia ever produced.

3 An unemployed itinerant in the depression of the 1930s

1935 Kylie Tennant *Tiburon* 19: Mrs Malloy, who had made herself the council's curse for many years by her generosity to that 'undesirable element', the travelling unemployed. It was she who had built the sheltershed, and ... it had saved many a bagman from lying stiff with rheumatism under a bridge.

1962 Ron Tullipan *March Into Morning* 11: The bagman sprawled out in the shade ... waiting for the mixed goods and passenger train that went through there twice a week.

1965 Frank Hardy *The Yarns of Billy Borker* 49: 'I joined the army when war broke out. Came straight off the track. The sixth Divvy was made up mainly of bagmen, first steady job we ever had was getting shot at.'

Bagman's Gazette A fictitious publication containing news and rumours; graffiti left by itinerants [f. *bagman*²]

1954 Tom Ronan *Vision Splendid* 266: 'If the Bagman's Gazette,' decided Mr Toppingham, 'was an actual news sheet and not just a figure of speech, I'd advertise for the old beggar in the agony column.'

1957 W. E. Harney *Life Among the Aborigines* 183–4: We passed the windmills and tanks that stretch along the way to water the herds as they travel, and on the big black iron sheets of the squatters' tanks one could read the 'Bagman's Gazette' which is the escape channel for the grievances of the travellers as they go by ... Each tank we passed had its 'news', and only when a boss passed by and saw his name in a headline would he get the tank re-tarred.

1968 *The Barry Humphries Book of Innocent Austral Verse* 130: Bagman's Gazette. [poem title]

bag system, the In the depression of the 1930s, the issue of a bag of groceries each dole day to the unemployed

1963 Frank Hardy *Legends from Benson's Valley* 176: Ernie Lyle read two of the small signs 'Work not Charity', 'Down with the Bag system'. A chord in his heart responded: bags of groceries at Ambler's store, margarine, bulk tea, the cheapest brands thrust into your hand without choice or ceremony.

bags, rough as Uncouth, to outward appearance

1919 W. H. Downing *Digger Dialects* 42: *Rough as bags* See 'Rough stuff'. *Rough stuff* An undisciplined, reckless, indecent, disorderly or disrespectful person or thing.

1929 K. S. Prichard *Coonardoo* 22: 'Ted was as rough as bags,' Geary said; 'a good-looking, good-natured bloke who could neither read nor write.'

1938 Eric Lowe *Salute to Freedom* 318: 'Rough as bags. Cleared his throat – you know the way he does – and spat, just missing a pile of ribbons.'

1948 Patrick White *The Aunt's Story* 34: Tom Wilcocks was as rough as bags. His neck was red and strong. The pollard had caked hard on his hard hands.

1955 John Morrison *Black Cargo* 184: 'Only a few acres here and there settled at all – berry-farming and wood-cutting. Everything rough as bags.'

bail, I'll go Equivalent to 'I warrant' or any other expression guaranteeing the credibility of a statement: *obsolescent* [listed as a characteristic Irish expression in P. W. Joyce *English as We Speak it in Ireland* (1910) 9–10. ? f. *bail* = security]

1832 *The Currency Lad* 6 Oct. 4: 'I'll go bail she will be better.'

1847 Alexander Harris *The Emigrant Family* (1967) 47: 'Only leave it in their way, and I'll go bail you never clap eyes on it again.'

1870 Marcus Clarke *His Natural Life* ed. S. Murray-Smith (1970) 411: 'I'd cut the biggest iron you've got with this; and so would he and plenty more, I'll go bail.'

1880 Rolf Boldrewood *The Miner's Right* (1890) 43: 'There's something in that lead, I'll go bail.'

1928 Miles Franklin *Up the Country* (1966) 142: 'I'll go bail it's some of the mean things he's always saying about other people that are making him bilious.'

bail up All the senses illustrated seem to have been current simultaneously, although 3 gained more currency as 'bailing up' came to be associated more with highways

1 'To secure the head of a cow in a "bail" while she is milked ... *Austral*. and *N.Z*.' (OED 1847–1950)

2 In bushranging, to hold the victims under guard, confine them or tie them up

1843 *Sydney Monitor and Commercial Advertiser* 21 Jan. 2: On last Wednesday week, two armed bushrangers went into Grovenor's public house ... they pulled out pistols, 'bailed up' the whole of the family and proceeded to plunder

the house ... about 10 o'clock, Mr Grovenor was enabled to free himself.
1843 John Hood *Australia and the East* 178: Bailing up is the term used to express their usual mode of proceeding in these occasions; which is this ... one of them goes in with his gun pointed and cocked, his finger upon the trigger, and with the muzzle disagreeably near your person, invites you to retire into the corner, while his companion inspects your property, and helps himself to anything which you may happen to have and he to lack.
1843 'Billy Barlow' *Old Bush Songs* ed. Stewart and Keesing (1957) 53: But by bushrangers met, with my traps they made free, / Took my horse, and left Billy bailed up to a tree.
1844 Louisa Meredith *Notes and Sketches of New South Wales* 132: The plan usually pursued by the bushrangers in robbing a house ... is to walk quietly in, and 'bail up' *i.e.* bind with cords, or otherwise secure, the male portion, leaving an armed guard over them, whilst the rest of the gang ransack the house.
1852 G. C. Mundy *Our Antipodes* i 179: The coachman was then compelled to take his horses off, the passengers were ordered severally to get out and to 'bail up' like cows prepared for milking at the fence side.
1862 Horace Earle *Ups and Downs* 82: A plan at that time not unusual amongst bushrangers in their dealings with their victims, namely 'baling them up', or securing them to trees, and leaving them thus to starve.
1863 R. Therry *Reminiscences* 2nd edn 125–6: We had still a further ordeal to pass through, which is termed *'baling up'*. This sort of ordeal consisted in our being grouped together on the roadside, whilst one of the three bushrangers was placed as a sentinel over us, with instructions from the captain to shoot the first man that stirred without permission.
3 Equivalent to the highwayman's 'Stand and deliver'
1852 G. C. Mundy *Our Antipodes* i 179: 'Bail up – or you're a dead man,'

resounded from behind a thick tree, through a fork of which a double-barrelled gun covered the driver's head.
1853 Mrs C. Clacy *A Lady's Visit to the Gold Diggings of Australia in 1852–53* 127: I cannot quite realise the terrified passengers being driven through the Black Forest, but can picture their horror when ordered to 'bail up' by a party of Australian Turpins.
1895 Rolf Boldrewood *The Crooked Stick* 6: As the coach came abreast of them the man on the grey turned towards it, and, with a raised revolver in his hand, shouted, 'Bail up!'
4 More generally, to hold at bay, arrest the progress of, 'corner'
1859 Henry Kingsley *Recollections of Geoffry Hamlyn* iii 152: And they [the bushrangers] were bailed up in the limestone gully, and all the party were away after them.
1870 Rachel Henning *Letters* ed. D. Adams (1963) 239: [The creek] had risen so that he could not get back, and was 'bailed up' in Stroud for two days.
1908 Henry Fletcher *Dads and Dan between Smokes* 127: He'll bail up ther fust bottle-oh he meets an' ask him who lets out vans.
1919 W. K. Harris *Outback in Australia* 3: Five miles further on ... a road maintenance man bailed me up. 'The mailman said he saw your roan colt tied up near my shanty. Did you have a feed?'
1949 Ruth Park *Poor Man's Orange* 91: Brought up in Surry Hills, she felt there wasn't a drunk in the district she couldn't have handled if he bailed her up.

baker, floury see **floury baker**

balfastards, alas! milfissed the An exclamation indicating the failure of some action, from an anecdote 'A hulfunting we will golfo' current among Australian soldiers in World War II (communicated by L. Bottomley). Another version is given in Baker (1945: 274).

c. 1944 A rififleman jumped into a trulfuck with his gulfang to shoot dulfucks swilfimming on the walfater, he raised his rififle and ailfaimed at the dulfucks. Balfang! balfang! went the rififle. Flalfap! flalfap! went the dulfucks. 'Alas! milfissed the balfastards!' said the rififleman.

ball of muscle, style [analogous to *ball of fire* OED 1821]
1939 Kylie Tennant *Foveaux* 160: Rolfe was again 'a ball of muscle', as he termed it, working on the Slum Abolition Committee.
1945 Cecil Mann *The River* 137: Spider Hayes, who's a ball of muscle, one of the fittest of the whole bunch.
1947 Margaret Trist *Daddy* 171: 'The missus isn't ready yet,' he greeted his mother-in-law. 'She'll be a ball of style when she's through, if you can count on the preparations.'
1951 Dymphna Cusack and Florence James *Come In Spinner* 251: 'Hullo,' he said pleasantly, 'you look a ball of muscle tonight.'
1960 Ron Tullipan *Follow the Sun* 30: 'This old bus isn't exactly a ball of style, but it's handy while I'm building.'
1965 Patrick White *Four Plays* 239: 'That Miss Scougall's a ball of ego.'

Balt An immigrant to Australia from the Baltic countries (and Poland and Holland) after World War II: *derogatory* [f. *Balt* a native or inhabitant of one of the Baltic states OED 1878: not used pejoratively]
1953 T. A. G. Hungerford *Riverslake* 32: A dozen of them, six Poles and the rest a mixture of Lithuanians and Ukranians and Latvians and Estonians, big and small, old and young, dark and fair, but indistinguishable now in their terrible nonentity. Balts.
1957 Randolph Stow *The Bystander* 134: 'Will she mind so much, that a bloody Balt marries her cousin?'
1959 Dorothy Hewett *Bobbin Up* 150: 'Look at them bloody Balts, all with their heads down and their arses up,' old Betty grumbled ... 'They'll never be Aussies while they keep that up. They'll work us all outa a job.'

1963 Bruce Beaver *The Hot Summer* 32: 'You're taller than most of those Balts' ... He knew she meant the migrant construction gangs working on an electrification project there.

Bananaland Queensland: *jocular* [f. crop]
1893 Henry Lawson 'Hungerford' *Prose* i 106: The post office is in New South Wales, and the police barracks in Bananaland.
1946 *Sunday Sun* 4 Aug. Suppl. 15: They reckon as he [Captain Cook] sailed away he gave one look back at the coast of Bananaland and said: 'Strewth, I'm glad to give that dump back to the blacks.'
1973 Patrick White *The Eye of the Storm* 185: 'Don't yer remember that, Florrie, from Banana land?'

Bananalander Queenslander: *jocular*
1887 *Bulletin* 26 Feb. 67: He made all the arrangements for being married on that day, and his friends rallied up to congratulate him, and see him through, after the custom of the simple Bananalanders.
1911 E. S. Sorenson *Life in the Australian Backblocks* 66: The Bananalander's[1] pet [swag] is short and plump. [1]Queenslander's.
1968 Kit Denton *A Walk Around My Cluttered Mind* 3: 'I c'n tell a bananalander any time. I c'n pickem. You come from Queensland 'n' I *know it*!'
Banana man, Banana city, Bananabender
1886 Percy Clarke *The 'New Chum' in Australia* 66: A Queenslander is ... distinguished by the title of 'bananaman'.
1893 J. A. Barry *Steve Brown's Bunyip* 181: He had, he flattered himself ... been making rapid progress with the damsels of the Banana city.
1976 Robert Drewe *The Savage Crows* 61: 'Banana-benders of course, look at that mob of classic Queenslanders over there in the shade.'

bandicoot *n.* Used in phrases suggesting misery or destitution [f. the animal]
1845 R. Howitt *Impressions of Australia*

Felix 233: 'Poor as a bandicoot,' 'Miserable as a shag on a rock,' & c.; these and others I very frequently heard them make use of.

1859 Henry Kingsley *Recollections of Geoffry Hamlyn* iii 83–4: 'That Van Diemen's bush would starve a bandicoot.'

1877 Rolf Boldrewood *A Colonial Reformer* (1890) 442: He hadn't had a soul to talk to for three weeks, since the muster began, and was as miserable as a bandicoot.

1885 *The Australasian Printers' Keepsake* 75: I crouched beside him 'as miserable as a bandicoot.'

1900 Henry Lawson 'Joe Wilson's Courtship' *Prose* i 546: I mooched around all the evening like an orphan bandicoot on a burnt ridge, and then I went up to the pub and filled myself up with beer, and damned the world.

1934 Steele Rudd *Green Grey Homestead* 18: 'Spring Gully!' he'll snarl. 'That country is no good for you; 'twouldn't feed a bandicoot!'

1946 K. S. Prichard *The Roaring Nineties* 81–2: 'Was as miserable as a bandicoot, felt like chucking up prospecting and trying to get a job . . . on the mines.'

1951 Dymphna Cusack and Florence James *Come In Spinner* 22: 'Hiya, Blue?' she said, stepping in. 'Miserable as a bandicoot.'

1969 Osmar White *Under the Iron Rainbow* 111: At first he looked as miserable as a bandicoot.

bandicoot *v.* To remove potatoes from below the surface, leaving the top of the plant intact [f. the animal's burrowing habit]

1898 George Dunderdale *The Book of the Bush* 102: 'You bandicooted my potatoes last night, and you've left the marks of your dirty feet on the ground.'

1916 Joseph Furphy *Poems* 15: You may forgo your stylish duds, / And trade away your pin and studs, / To live on bandicooted spuds; / But you Must Never Whine.

1944 M. J. O'Reilly *Bowyangs and Boomerangs* 2: There was a general rule in our district . . . that swagmen might be allowed to go into the paddocks and 'bandicoot' potatoes. The interpretation of 'bandicooting' is that the swaggie could scratch a hole round the potato plant, pick out a few big ones, and hill up the plant again to allow the remainder to mature.

bandy, knock someone To worst completely, leave flabbergasted [listed by Partridge as 'tailors': from ca. 1860']

1899 W. T. Goodge *Hits! Skits! and Jingles!* 165: 'You can talk about yer sheep dorgs,' said the man from Allan's Creek, / 'But I know a dorg that simply knocked 'em bandy!'

1908 E. S. Sorenson *Quinton's Rouseabout* 88: 'Joe was reg'lar knocked bandy.'

1934 F. E. Baume *Burnt Sugar* 59: 'You're seventeen, and could knock me bandy.'

1948 Ruth Park *Poor Man's Orange* 174: 'If I hear you slinging off at her again, I'll knock you bandy, honest to goodness I will!'

1968 Craig McGregor *People, Politics and Pop* 43: What do most of his [the taxi-driver's] passengers feel about the heat? 'Why, it knocks 'em bandy,' he says.

bange, banje (j) *n.* & *v.* Rest: *obs.* [f. *benge* to lounge lazily EDD Fr. *baigner*]

1847 Alexander Harris *Settlers and Convicts* ed. C. M. H. Clark (1954) 105: Stray hands wandering back were already dropping in every now and then at some of our pits for a few days' 'bange' (rest) on their way to Sydney.

1850 B. C. Peck *Recollections of Sydney* 98: Having scrambled down the rocks we may enjoy a quiet 'bange' on the greensward.

1873 J. C. F. Johnson *Christmas on Carringa* 16: So Sunday, Monday, Tuesday / I jogs upon my way / With a little banje* or whaling / To just fill up the day. *Banjing is bush slang for sleeping or lying full length under a tree.

bangtail *v.* To dock the tails of cattle or

horses

1908 Mrs Aeneas Gunn *We of the Never-Never* 160: He ... suggested bang-tailing the cattle during the musters.

bangtail muster See quots 1888, 1938
1888 W. S. S. Tyrwhitt *The New Chum in the Queensland Bush* 61: Every third or fourth year on a cattle station, they have what is called a 'bang tail muster'; that is to say, all the cattle are brought into the yards, and have the long hairs at the end of the tail cut off square ... the object of it is, to take a census ... unless marked in some way, it would be impossible to distinguish those that have been through the stockyard from those that have not.
1901 *The Bulletin Reciter* 157: And the day we got the buster was just after bangtail-muster.
1938 Francis Ratcliffe *Flying Fox and Drifting Sand* 331 n.: In a bangtail muster every beast rounded up has the tuft of its tail docked to prevent its being counted twice. This is the only way of getting an accurate tally on an unfenced run several hundreds or thousands of square miles in area.
1951 Ernestine Hill *The Territory* 391: 'We're sellin' Merryfield, an' now the buyers have asked for a bang-tail.'
1957 R. S. Porteous *Brigalow* 187: I had decided to make this a bangtail muster, a form of stocktaking where the brush was cut from the tail of every beast before it was passed down the dip crush to be dipped and tallied.

banje see **bange**

Banjo, the The pen-name of A. B. Paterson (1864–1941), used in his contributions to the *Bulletin* from 12 June 1886; nickname of anyone surnamed Paterson
1896 *Bulletin* 3 Oct. Red Page: An English weekly declares that Becke is popularly known as the Kipling of the Pacific. 'Banjo' and Lawson have also been identified as more-or-less Kiplings.

banjo 1 A frying pan [f. shape]
1900–10 O'Brien and Stephens: *Banjo* a bush name for a frying pan.
2 A shovel
1919 W. H. Downing *Digger Dialects* 10: *Banjo* – a shovel. *Swing the banjo* – dig.
1924 *Truth* 27 Apr. 6: *Banjo* a shovel.
1942 Gavin Casey *It's Harder for Girls* 224–5: All his mother's big ideas, and mine, too, wouldn't keep him off the handle of a banjo if that was what he was suited for.
1973 Donald Stuart *Morning Star Evening Star* 110: He was alongside me swinging his banjo.
3 A shoulder of mutton
1919 W. K. Harris *Outback in Australia* 146: Called at his particular station for the proverbial free . . . 'banjo' (shoulder) of mutton.
1925 *Sydney Worker* 3 Jun. 13: The mutton was not of super-excellent quality, but Johnny was rarely known to part with a 'banjo' without getting good value in return.

banker A river with the water up to or overflowing its banks, esp. in the expression 'run a banker'
1848 W. H. Haygarth *Recollections of Bush Life in Australia* 129: Now that I take a second glance at the river, its waters look very muddy, which is a sure sign of its being high, not to say a 'banker'.
1868 C. Wade Brown *Overlanding in Australia* 19: Nothing but a large river, running a 'banker' can stop them, and that they are soon made to swim.
1877 Rolf Boldrewood *A Colonial Reformer* (1890) 410: The river was high, had come down a 'banker', and any further rainfall might bring down a flood such as the dwellers in those parts had not seen for many a day.
1889 Henry Lawson 'The Ballad of the Drover' *Verse* i 27: Till the river runs a banker / All stained with yellow mud.
1927 Steele Rudd *The Romance of Runnibede* 88: The Station Creek rose to a banker – rose till it spread itself a quarter of a mile on either side, carrying down logs and uprooted trees and the

carcases of dead bullocks.

1934 Thomas Wood *Cobbers* 27: 'That night she was running a banker, with sheep, trees – Oh anything you like coming down, and the water a mile wide.'

1956 Kylie Tennant *The Honey Flow* 209: Cobberloi Creek was running a banker.

1963 A. W. Upfield *The Body at Madman's Bend* 17: 'It's going to run again soon ... Going to run a banker?'

half-banker

1925 E. S. Sorenson *Murty Brown* 59: In a few minutes he was baulked by the creek, which was running half a banker.

1951 Ernestine Hill *The Territory* 444: *Half-banker* A river in half flood.

bar, can't stand (won't have) a ~ of Can't tolerate on any terms [? f. *bar* in music]

1945 Margaret Trist *Now that We're Laughing* 25: 'I can't stand a bar of these people that visit you and must have a bath every day to show you how clean they are.'

1954 T. A. G. Hungerford *Sowers of the Wind* 1: 'You're right, I couldn't stand a bar of the animal myself.'

1962 Gavin Casey *Amid the Plenty* 149: 'Not that I'd have a bar of a bloke who'd lie to his mates, but it's different with that other mob.'

1973 *Australian* 4 May 2: Dr Arnold said that doctors would be violently against direct billing. 'They won't have a bar of it,' he said.

barb A breed of sheep-dog [see quots 1908, 1945]

1908 W. H. Ogilvie *My Life in the Open* 162: The barb is a larger dog. Perfectly black in colour, stout and square in build, he too has the best points of the kelpie; the broad, almost bulldog forehead, the small feet and the short smooth hair. The barb dogs are all prick-eared and have a peculiar crouching and watchful carriage. They too are wonderfully enduring, though they are heavier dogs than the kelpies ... This breed is supposed to have originated from a black dog given to one

of the early squatters on the Lachlan River by a blackfellow, and is supposed to be related to the wild dogs or dingoes.

1915 Vance Palmer *The World of Men* (1962) 30: During the day ... he spent the time talking to his dog, a black and white barb that sat all day near the door, watching him out of its sleepy eyes.

1926 K. S. Prichard *Working Bullocks* 262: Mark remembered dog-fights he had seen. Blue barbe and bull-terrier, that was the fight stuck in his mind.

1945 Baker 73: One of these pups [of a kelpie] was given to a stockman who named him *Barb* after the 1866 winner of the Melbourne Cup. He proved such an excellent sire that he, also, gave his name to a breed.

1952 *Sydney Morning Herald* 29 Mar. 7: The kelpie proper is generally used in the open, the barb for penning and yarding.

barbie A barbecue [abbr.]

1976 *Australian* 14 Aug. 20: He propounded the natural and national virtues of the Aussie beach barbie with beer and prawns, and the big chunder.

Barcoo challenge See quot. [f. river and district in Queensland]

1933 Acland: *Barcoo challenge* (1) To scrape the points of the shears on the floor or wall, or (2) to throw the belly over another shearer's head, indicating a challenge for the day's tally.

Barcoo rot A skin ulceration similar to scurvy

1870 E. B. Kennedy *Four Years in Queensland* 46: Land scurvy is better known in Queensland by local names, which do not sound very pleasant, such as 'Barcoo rot', 'Kennedy rot', according to the district it appears in. There is nothing dangerous about it, it is simply the festering of any cut or scratch on one's legs, arms or hands. [Morris]

1886 Percy Clarke *The 'New Chum' in Australia* 302: One of the most extraordinary features attendant on such a state of the body is the skin complaint known as the 'Barcoo rot'.

1903 Joseph Furphy *Such is Life* (1944)

201: The backs of his hands were pretty bad with the external scurvy known as 'Barcoo rot' produced by unsuitable food and extreme hardship.
1933 F. E. Baume *Tragedy Track* 45: A case of oranges . . . was decided on as an antidote for scurvy which, in its barcoo rot form, was playing havoc with any tiny wounds on face, body or limbs.
1968 Walter Gill *Petermann Journey* 57: He has broken out in clusters of sores on hands and wrists. 'Barcoo rot' undoubtedly.

Barcoo salute See quot. 1973
1973 Patsy Adam Smith *The Barcoo Salute* title page: 'I see you've learnt the Barcoo salute,' said a Buln Buln Shire councillor to the Duke of Edinburgh. 'What's that,' said His Royal Highness, waving his hand again to brush the flies off his face. 'That's it,' said the man from the bush. [quotation dated 1953]
1974 *Sydney Morning Herald* 23 Apr. 6: The humble, if ubiquitous, bushfly is not only responsible for our national habit, the Barcoo salute, but is also the feature of Australia most often commented on by overseas visitors.
see **Australian salute**

Barcoo sickness (spews, vomit) See quots
1898 Morris: *Barcoo Vomit* painless attacks of vomiting, occurring immediately after food is taken, followed by hunger, and recurring as soon as hunger is satisfied.
1925 E. S. Sorenson *Murty Brown* 56: 'I've had the barcoo, an' other upheavals.'
1927 M. M. Bennett *Christison of Lammermoor* 62: One of the great hardships of those days [the 1860s] was the sickness brought on by the monotonous food and bread made from tainted flour, every settler supposed it peculiar to his district, and named it accordingly Burdekin, or Belyando, or Barcoo sickness.
1935 H. H. Finlayson *The Red Centre* 50: A gastric disorder, known to the settlers by the crude but expressive term 'barcoo spews' is common in summer.
1966 *Australian* 3 Jan. 6: The unending irritations of the shearer's life . . . barcoo spews and purgatorial insects.

bardie An edible wood grub [*Bardistus cibarius*] which figures in the exclamation 'Starve the bardies!' (a variant of 'Starve the lizards!') more often encountered in lists of Australianisms than in actual conversation
1941 Baker 8: *Bardies! Starve the*: A popular W.A. ejaculation, synonymous with 'Stone the crows!'
1946 K. S. Prichard *The Roaring Nineties* 200: Kalgoorla brought her toasted bardies to eat. Sally recognized the fat white grubs Maritana used to devour with such relish.
1969 *Pocket Oxford Dictionary* 1020: *Starve the bardies!* excl. of surprise or disgust.

bark, short of a sheet of As for 'a shingle short' q.v.
1885 Mrs Campbell Praed *Australian Life* 199: He had always understood that Richard Murray was short of a sheet of bark – the Australian equivalent of 'a tile loose'.

Barker, a Bishop A long glass of beer [f. Frederick Barker, Bishop of Sydney 1845–81, 6′ 5½″ in height]
1886 Frank Cowan *Australia: A Charcoal Sketch* 32: Long sleever, Bishop Barker, and Deep-sinker, synonyms of the Yankee Schooner.

Barlow, Billy The inexperienced immigrant who meets with misadventures in the colony [f. the ballad 'Billy Barlow': see *Old Bush Songs* ed. Stewart and Keesing (1957) 53–5]
1843 'Billy Barlow' *Maitland Mercury* 2 Sep. 4: When I was at home I was down on my luck, / And I yearnt a poor living by drawing a truck; / But old aunt died and left me a thousand – 'Oh, oh / I'll start on my travels,' said Billy Barlow / Oh dear, lackaday, oh; / So off to Australia came Billy Barlow.

Barn, the Old The Sydney Stadium (closed in 1970)

1973 *Sydney Morning Herald* 13 Feb. 15: It would never have happened at the Old Barn.

see **Tin Shed**

barney *n*. An argument, disagreement, fight [f. *barney* A disturbance, dispute, altercation EDD 1891]

1858 Charles Thatcher *Colonial Songster* 68: A barney first commences/ With a little bit of 'skiting',/But calling names is not enough,/And so it ends in fighting.

1875 Rolf Boldrewood *The Squatter's Dream* repr. as *Ups and Downs* (1878) 12: 'Well, we had a sair barney, weel nigh a fight, you might be sure.'

1893 Henry Lawson 'Brummy Usen' *Prose* i 77: 'She was just as self-opinionated as the neighbours, and many a barney she had with them about it.'

1938 Xavier Herbert *Capricornia* 379: 'Joe always plays tunes like that when there's been a barney with the men.'

1942 Sarah Campion *Bonanza* 45: That started such a hullabaloo and general barney among one and all.

barney *v*. To argue, dispute

1876 Rolf Boldrewood *A Colonial Reformer* (1890) 183: 'If you go barneying about calves, or counting on horses that's give in, he'll best ye, as sure as you're born.'

1888 E. Finn *Chronicles of Early Melbourne* i 85: The queer old Crown Prosecutor ... used to be very loud in his talk at times to those about him, and one day he and Chief-Constable Sugden were 'barneying' about some hitch in a criminal case. Their recrimination attracted the attention of the judge.

1947 Vance Palmer *Hail Tomorrow* 63: 'No more barneying with pannikin bosses about the length of a smoko or whether the sheep's wet or dry.'

Barney's bull see **bull**

barrack 1 To indulge in noisy comment; to subject to banter; to ridicule, jeer at [f. *barrack* to brag, to be boastful at one's fighting powers N. Irel. EDD. Quot. 1878 may be from *baragouin* (*barrikin*) language so altered in sound or sense as to become generally unintelligible; jargon, 'double-Dutch' OED 1613]

1878 T. E. Argles *The Pilgrim* iv 39: Douglass mumbled over a 'petition' intended for presentation to Parliament, for the edification of assembled toughs and larrikins, but it was received with noisy insult and cries of 'cheese your barrickin'' and 'shut up'.

1885 *The Australasian Printers' Keepsake* 121: The same old rubbishy gibes that had been vogue for centuries were raked up again ... the customers enjoyed the barracking.

1893 Henry Lawson 'For'ard' *Verse* i 259: There's a broken swell amongst us – he is barracked, he is chaffed.

1907 Nathan Spielvogel *The Cocky Farmer* 29: Grant had been barracking Joe about some girl.

1915 C. J. Dennis *The Songs of a Sentimental Bloke* 22: Me! that 'as barracked tarts, an' torked an' larft,/An' chucked orf at 'em like a phonergraft!

1934 Vance Palmer *Sea and Spinifex* 285: He had never liked being barracked, he was beginning to lose his temper.

2 In sport, to interject in favour of one side or against the other; to support

1891 Henry Lawson 'At the Tug-of-war' *Verse* i 114: It gave the old man joy/To fight a passage through the crowd and barrack for his boy.

1903 Joseph Furphy *Such is Life* (1944) 34: 'Toffs is no slouches at barrackin' for theyre own push.'

1913 John Sadleir *Recollections of a Victorian Police Officer* 278: They yelled and shouted, some 'barracking' for Jack, some for the sergeant.

1924 C. J. Dennis *Rose of Spadgers* 91: ''Oo was it tried to stoush that rat-face mutt?/'Oo was it barracked for me in the fight?'

1934 Tom Clarke *Marriage at 6 a.m.* 200: When Arthur Gilligan's Test Team came out he 'barracked' for Australia.

1969 William Dick *Naked Prodigal* 93: 'He barracks for the Magpies though, same as me.'

1971 David Ireland *The Unknown Industrial Prisoner* 135: This was great fun for the audience, who barracked loudly for the two men after each trick was done.

barracker One who 'barracks'

1892 G. L. James *Shall I Try Australia?* 129: In Victoria also, the people are 'football mad', and the youths wear the colours of their favourite club, in a profusion which is apt to mystify the new arrival, these are the 'barrackers', the verb 'to barrack' meaning to audibly encourage their own favourites, and comment disparagingly upon the performance of their opponents, a proceeding which frequently leads to an interchange of compliments between the 'barrackers' themselves.

1910 Henry Lawson 'Roll up at Talbragar' *Prose* i 751: Maybe some of the big, simple souls had a sort of vague idea that the departed would stand a better show if accompanied as far as possible by the greatest possible number of friends – 'barrackers', so to speak.

1914 Arthur Wright *In the Last Stride* 8: She followed the games, and with the colours of her favourite club pinned to her breast, graced the ladies reserve at all the big matches, applauding her champions at times to such an extent as to be in danger of being classed as a 'barracker'.

1925 Seymour Hicks *Hullo Australians* 246: A place they call the Hill is occupied by thousands of barrackers, not soldiers, but fellows who are sure they understand cricket better than the umpires.

1933 Norman Lindsay *Saturdee* 34: A prominent barracker for the local team, and deep in its polemics.

1969 Alan O'Toole *The Racing Game* 169: 'Like the football days, eh, Bill? You can't beat having a few barrackers.'

barracks Building on a station for the accommodation of the jackeroos, etc., and marking a division in the social hierarchy

1876 Rolf Boldrewood *A Colonial Reformer* (1890) 100: At a short distance from 'the house', Mr Jedwood's cottage, or hut, as the residence of the proprietor was indifferently designated, stood a roomy, roughly finished building known as the 'barracks'. Here lived the overseer ... Three of the numerous bedrooms were tenanted by young men ... neophytes, who were gradually assimilating the lore of Bushland. To the barracks were also relegated those just too exalted for the men's hut, while not eligible for ... 'the cottage'. Such were cattle dealers, sheep-buyers, overseers of neighbouring stations, and generally unaccredited travellers whose manners or appearance rendered classification hazardous.

1903 Joseph Furphy *Such is Life* (1944) 254: Being a little too exalted for the men's hut, and a great deal too vile for the boss's house, I was quartered in the narangies' barracks.

1942 Jean Devanny *The Killing of Jacqueline Love* 3: A hundred yards from the house the low wooden barracks, the home of the overseer and jackeroo and occasional workmen, stood with its back to ... the edge of the scrub.

barrakin see **barrack**

barrel To fell or 'flatten', esp. in a football tackle

1966 Baker 169: *barrel*, to shoot and kill [from army notebook of 1940–5]

1972 John de Hoog *Skid Row Dossier* 106: 'I'll barrel her ... The only thing that stopped me shovin' her through the window was a charge of assault.'

1973 Alexander Buzo *Rooted* 84: 'Remember that last football match, the grand final when Davo got barrelled?'

1975 *Bulletin* 26 Apr. 46: 'Some mug picked Punchy for a mark and barrelled a king at him at the bar.' ... (Barrelled; to throw a punch. A king is a king hit; a punch thrown without warning.)

Barrett's twist A chewing or pipe tobacco [f. brand name]

1885 *The Australasian Printers' Keep-sake* 84: Ever and anon extracting from a cavernous pouch a huge roll of Barrett's twist, like a bludgeon, from which he would bite off a Gargantuan quid.

1898 Alfred Joyce *A Homestead History* ed. G. F. James (1969) 106: The tobacco [in 1847] was always of one kind, Barret's twist, in long square twisted sticks, sixteen to the pound.

barrow To start or finish off a sheep for a shearer, as a way of learning to shear [? f. Gaelic *bearradh* shearing, clipping]

1904 E. S. Sorenson *A Shanty Entertainment* 94: It's a good while since we started, you and me, to get a shed; / 'Ow you barrowed that first year for Marty Kell.

1933 Acland: *Barrow* To shear or partly shear a sheep for a shearer. 'No barrowing allowed on the board' was at one time a rule which the Shearers' Union got into the award. Boys often finish or begin a sheep for a shearer, who, of course, is responsible for its being properly shorn.

1964 H. P. Tritton *Time Means Tucker* 39–40: On the advice of the boss of the board, I spent most of the afternoon watching and 'barrowing', that is, finishing off. Bill would shear a sheep to the 'whipping side' then pass it to me and as it was straight going, seven or eight blows would complete the job ... Soon I was holding my own with the other learners.

1975 Les Ryan *The Shearers* 126: 'Though I had done only a bit of barrowing here and there, I fluked a learner's pen.'

bart A girl: *obs.* [unexplained]
c. **1882** *The Sydney Slang Dictionary* 1: *Bart* A girl, generally applied to those of loose character.

1899 W. T. Goodge *Hits! Skits! and Jingles!* 150: And his lady love's his 'donah', / Or his 'clinah' or his 'tart' / Or his 'little bit o' muslin', / As it used to be his 'bart'.

1941 Baker 8: *Bart* A girl. Now prac-

tically obsolete.

bash, have a, give it a Make an attempt at (as 'give it a burl')
1959 David Forrest *The Last Blue Sea* 183: 'Yair, it's somebody else's turn to have a bash,' said Lincoln.

1969 William Dick *Naked Prodigal* 179: 'Reckon you'll be able to do it? I mean it's pretty hard.' 'I hope so. I'm gonna give it a bash, anyway.'

1972 Richard Magoffin *Chops and Gravy* 106: *give a bash* have a go, give it a trial, attempt.

1973 Max Harris *The Angry Eye* 106: They did have a bash at the weather, I remember.

bash the ear To harangue, talk incessantly [f. *earbasher*]
1971 Rena Briand *White Man in a Hole* 26: Other days I'd ... drown my sorrows at the Front Bar and bash Johnny's ear with my tale of woe.

1975 Xavier Herbert *Poor Fellow My Country* 30: 'They told me that I'd be lucky if you talked to me at all ... and just as unlucky if you did' ... 'They mean you'd regret it, because then I'd bash your ear?'

bastard None of the senses distinguished is exclusively Australian, but all are so much a part of the colloquial language as to be remarked upon by overseas visitors
1 Derogatory, but not necessarily suggesting illegitimacy
1892 Henry Lawson 'The Captain of the Push' *Verse* i 187n: 'Here's the bleedin' push, me covey – here's a bastard from the bush! / Strike me dead, he wants to join us!' said the captain of the push.

1929 A. B. Piddington *Worshipful Masters* 46: *Digger* [paraded before an English officer trying to discover who called the regimental cook a bastard] 'You keep on asking us who called that cook a bastard; what we want to know is, who called that bastard a cook?'

1939 Kylie Tennant *Foveaux* 170: 'A man ought to heave the bastard out on his ear.'

1958 H. D. Williamson *The Sunlit Plain*
128: 'Have you ever heard of a bloke
being one of Nature's gentlemen?' I
says. 'Why, yes,' he says, grinning all
over his fat mug. 'Well,' I says, 'you're
one of Nature's bastards.'
1960 Donald McLean *The Roaring Days*
199: 'I want a few quid for th' school
tonight, so don't be a bastard.'
1974 E. G. Whitlam [addressing the
Canberra branch of the ALP] *Sunday
Telegraph* 9 Jun. 2: 'I do not mind the
Liberals, still less do I mind the Country
Party, calling me a bastard. In some
circumstances I am only doing my job
if they do. But I hope you will not
publicly call me a bastard, as some
bastards in the Caucus have.'
2 Compassionate, indicating a grudging
acceptance
1903 Joseph Furphy *Such is Life* (1944)
31: 'Seen better days, pore (fellow),'
observed Cooper sympathetically, as
the ripple of water into the pannikin
indicated that the whaler was at the tap.
1931 William Hatfield *Sheepmates* 269:
'I've knocked around a bit in my time,
and I'll tell them that don't know him
he's a decent sort of a poor bastard.'
1934 F. E. Baume *Burnt Sugar* 249:
'And not a bad old bastard either. Been
here twenty-two years.'
1953 T. A. G. Hungerford *Riverslake*
24: 'Not such a bad sort of a poor old
bastard, but the grog's got him.'
1962 Stuart Gore *Down the Golden
Mile* 159: Conlon . . . replied casually:
'Ah, he's not such a bad poor bastard.'
3 Friendly, affectionate
1882 A. J. Boyd *Old Colonials* 62:
'Now then, Harry, you old —, what
the — is it going to be? Give it some —
name or other!'
1944 Lawson Glassop *We Were the Rats*
168: 'G'day, ya old bastard,' said Jim,
and I was amused again that the
Tommies could never get used to our
main term of endearment.
1964 H. P. Tritton *Times Means Tucker*
[recalling period 1905–6] 109: A short-
necked man, with a chest like a barrel,
and arms reaching to his knees, forced
his way through the crowd, put his
hand out and said, 'Frank, you bloody

old bastard!' . . . They pumped his hand,
smacked him on the back, swore at him
and each other, then took possession of
most of the bar.
1969 Patsy Adam Smith *Folklore of the
Australian Railwaymen* 218: There was
a Welsh fellow with us, a lay preacher,
and . . . a ganger called him a Welsh
bastard. It was friendly you know. But
Taffy didn't know and told us that he
had evidence of the marriage of his
parents. The ganger got heated and
said if he himself didn't mind being
called a bastard why was this Welsh
bastard complaining and with that
Taffy up and jobbed him.
1974 *Sydney Morning Herald* 13 Mar. 7:
The Charmhaven Branch of the Australasian Order of Old Bastards will
meet tonight.
4 Impersonal
1915 Ion L. Idriess, diary in Bill
Gammage *The Broken Years* (1974) 77:
Of all the bastards of places this is the
greatest bastard in the world.
1944 Lawson Glassop *We Were the Rats*
169: 'It's like one of your mates going
out on patrol and not coming back.
It's a bastard, but you can't do anything
about it.'
1962 Alan Marshall *This is the Grass*
128: Sometimes a man began with a
question seeking an explanation of my
crutches: 'What's wrong with you?'
'Paralysis.' 'Bastard, isn't it . . . ?'
1974 John Power *The Last of the
Knucklemen* 11: 'The air-conditioner's
. . . on the blink. Bastard's not worth
two bob.'
see **Pommy bastard**

bastard from the bush, the An uncivilized interloper who imposes himself
on the society he enters. [f. Lawson's
poem 'The Captain of the Push' and
variants of it; the lines most often
quoted are not by Lawson: 'Will you
have a cigarette, mate?' said the Captain
of the Push / 'I'll have the flaming
packet!' said the Bastard from the Bush.]
1892 Henry Lawson 'The Captain of
the Push' *Verse* i 187n: Till he gave
an introduction – it was painfully
abrupt – / 'Here's the bleedin' push, me

covey – here's the bastard from the bush!/Strike me dead, he wants to join us!' said the captain of the push.
1962 Stuart Gore *Down the Golden Mile* 216: 'Don't think they'd have a bar o' me any other place, I suppose. Not cultured, eh? The bastard from the bush!'
1964 Dan Reidy *The Road to Tabuggerie* (1967) 79: 'Things get lively here at times when all the bastards from the bush come in and get tanked up.'
1975 Xavier Herbert *Poor Fellow My Country* 1079: 'It's you're the bastard ... The Bastard from the Bush. Get back where you belong!'

bastard, happy (lucky) as a ~ on Father's Day Unhappy, unlucky
1958 Frank Hardy *The Four-Legged Lottery* 128: 'I've got about as much luck as a bastard on Father's Day.'
1967 Frank Hardy *Billy Borker Yarns Again* 20: 'The Parrot would be happy being talked out of seven winners in succession?' 'Happy as a bastard on Father's Day. Tears his ticket into confetti.'
1974 *Sunday Telegraph* 9 Jun. 30: Those words of the Bank of NSW's Russell Prowse – 'bankers are as miserable as a bastard on Father's Day' provided a touch of humour not normally associated with banks.

bastardization Term applied to initiation ceremonies at colleges, schools etc.
1969 *Australian* 20 Sep. 5: Mr Barnard also asked if the terms of reference of the board of inquiry into Duntroon were wide enough to look into whether 'bastardisation' at the college was condoned by some of the permanent military staff.
1971 *Sydney Morning Herald* 29 Oct. 10: The report said: 'Organised initiation ceremonies, a formal pattern of bastardisation or any form of patterned violence or misbehaviour have never been a part of the program, official or otherwise, at Leeuwin.'
1972 *Sunday Telegraph* 27 Aug. 1: A brutal bastardisation ceremony at Australia's oldest public school has forced a boy to leave school only two months before his matriculation examination.

bastardry See quot. 1945 [f. *bastard*[1]]
1945 Baker 156: *bastardry* Ill-treatment, injustice, anything unpleasant, especially when done at the whim of a superior officer [World War II slang]
1948 Summer Locke Elliott *Rusty Bugles* in *Khaki Bush and Bigotry* ed. Eunice Hanger (1968) 95: 'You see ... bastardry all the way along the line.'
1950 *Meanjin* 222: Bastardry, Bastardry, Bastardry [review of Frank Hardy's *Power without Glory*]
1953 T. A. G. Hungerford *Riverslake* 2: They even acknowledged a perverted sort of pride in the sheer virtuosity of his bastardry, telling each other about things they had seen him do.
1962 David Forrest *The Hollow Woodheap* 195–6: 'As one expert to another, Mr Lucas, I have to admire your particular brand of bastardry.'
1974 David Williamson *Three Plays* 165: 'Now come on! That's just plain bastardry.'

bastards, run over the Reported instruction of the N.S.W. premier, Mr R. Askin, when demonstrators lay on the road before President L. B. Johnson's motorcade in Sydney in 1966
1968 *Sydney Morning Herald* 24 Jul. 4: Mr Askin was clapped and cheered yesterday when he told a luncheon meeting [of the American Chamber of Commerce] that he had advised a policeman to run over demonstrators trying to block President Johnson's motorcade in Sydney in 1966. He had turned to the policeman and had said 'Run over the bastards.'
1971 *Sydney Morning Herald* 20 Mar. 3: Mr D. Chipp [Minister for Customs and Excise, reported addressing a dinner of the American Chamber of Commerce in Canberra] 'I would like to think that men of goodwill of my generation have more in common with the agonised student movement than with some of the extreme nigger-flogging reactionaries of the establish-

ment complete with their "run-the-bastards down" philosophy.'

bat the breeze To engage in idle talk [cf. U.S. *fan the breeze*]
1945 Baker 154: *to bat the breeze*, to gossip or talk. [World War II slang]
1957 T. A. G. Hungerford *Riverslake* 75: 'I've got no time to stand here batting the breeze with you.'
1963 Jon Cleary *A Flight of Chariots* 246: 'What have you two been batting the breeze about?'

batch To do one's own cooking and housekeeping (of a man) [f. *bach* abbr. of *bachelor* U.S. 1870 Mathews]
1892 G. L. James *Shall I Try Australia?* 116: Boarding-houses soon spring up, where he can be very well fed at about 2/- daily; but if he elects to 'batch'* himself, I have heard many declare they can live well for 7/- weekly. *A common expression for finding yourself in food, derived perhaps from the word 'batchelor'.
1896 Henry Lawson '"Dossing Out" and "Camping"' *Prose* i 164: He had a partner. They batched in the office, and did their cooking over a gas lamp.
1908 E. S. Sorenson *Quinton's Rouseabout* 61: 'Batching in a lonely wilderness for twenty-five bob a week!'
1911 E. M. Clowes *On the Wallaby through Victoria* 234: I remember one beautiful young man 'batching' there for years – cooking his own dinner, doing the housework, such as it was, washing up the dishes and working meanwhile like fury on his little fruit farm.
1936 William Hatfield *Australia Through the Windscreen* 235: Rooms in which men 'batch' with all the untidiness of men to look after themselves in single blessedness.
1947 Margaret Trist *Daddy* 163: 'Now this poor young man, his brother is dead and he batches with his father.'
1955 *Sydney Morning Herald* 6 Sep. 1: 'When I'm batching,' he writes, 'I put on the electric kettle, cook the eggs in it, make the tea, shave and wash up with the same water.'

1971 David Ireland *The Unknown Industrial Prisoner* 278: 'How are you getting on, batching? You going to get married again?'

bathers Swimming costume
1936 H. Drake-Brockman *Sheba Lane* 91–2: He appeared, as he had threatened, in his bathers, and was greeted with cries of 'Bright idea' from everybody.
1942 Gavin Casey *It's Harder for Girls* 152: Most of them were wearing trunks, and my old bathers were baggy as well as out-of-date.
1972 Richard Magoffin *Chops and Gravy* 49: I mean the style of bathers – like bikinis and the such.

battle (battling) 1 To struggle for a livelihood; to work in low-paid employment (usually with an implication of praiseworthiness or self-congratulation)
1907 Henry Lawson 'The Strangers' Friend' *Prose* i 731: 'The fellers as knows can battle around for their bloomin' selves, but I'll look after the stranger.'
1923 Jack Moses *Beyond the City Gates* 128: When you're cockyin' and battlin' and live on what you grow.
1939 Kylie Tennant *Foveaux* 178: All her life Mrs Thompson had been what she called 'battling for a crust.'
1959 Dorothy Hewett *Bobbin Up* 58: 'Battled all me life Al and for what . . . a humpy on the Lachlan.'
1969 Alan O'Toole *The Racing Game* 156: 'That money would make all the difference between battling and being comfortable.'
1973 Max Harris *The Angry Eye* 32: Ideas come into the realm of the settled refinements of life, and 'battling', the Australian *modus vivendi*, is conducive to athletic greatness only.
2 To cadge, subsist by hawking homemade artifacts; used esp. of itinerants. Not derogatory, from respect accorded those down on their luck or able to live by their wits.
1902 Henry Lawson 'On the Tucker Track' *Prose* i 227: They were tramping along the track towards Bourke, they

were very hard up and had to 'battle' for tucker and tobacco along the track.
1941 Kylie Tennant *The Battlers* 75: 'I'm going back to battle for some more rum.'
1944 Alan Marshall *These Are My People* 157: 'I'd been on a bad track and I knew this town was a hard town to battle, so I pulled up a bo and asked him if he knew where I could get a hand-out.'

battle, on the Working as a prostitute
1944 Lawson Glassop *We Were the Rats* 93: The girl was still staring. Perhaps she was, as Eddie would say, 'on the battle'. I had been told some of those girls hung about this lounge.

battler 1 A toiler, one who struggles for a livelihood. Anyone so styling himself asserts his apartness from the affluent class
1896 Henry Lawson 'Stiffner and Jim' *Prose* i 127: I sat on him pretty hard for his pretensions, and paid him out for all the patronage he'd worked off on me . . . and told him never to pretend to me that he was a battler.
1911 E. S. Sorenson *Life in the Australian Backblocks* 100: He was dressed like an ordinary battler, swinging a billy can.
1949 Lawson Glassop *Lucky Palmer* 150: 'I'm no big shot,' he had said. I'm a battler. Just a battler having a good trot.'
1958 Frank Hardy *The Four-Legged Lottery* 164: Sparks was a typical Australian battler, tall and angular, a sardonic wit, a kindly cynic who favoured the underdog . . . Tom Sparks had tried every way known to man of making a 'more or less honest quid', from gold prospecting to inventing gadgets. Now he eked out a living punting horses and, during a bad trot, 'turned over a quid' as a salesman.
1964 Donald Horne *The Lucky Country* 25: Australians love a 'battler', an underdog who is fighting the top dog, although their veneration for him is likely to pass if he comes out from under.

1967 John Yeomans *The Scarce Australians* 24: She and her husband owned no land anywhere, she explained. They were, in Australia's expressive slang, battlers – people for whom life is a daily battle . . .
1975 *Australian* 12 Aug. 9: There are no signs that the forthcoming Federal Budget will give any help to the small Aussie battler.
2 Someone making a living, not just by toil, but by ingenuity [f. *battle*[2]]
1935 F. D. Davison and B. Nicholls *Blue Coast Caravan* 157–8: We met two members of the genus 'battler' . . . they were side-show artists, travelling from one country show to another.
1941 Kylie Tennant *The Battlers* [book title]
3 A prostitute
1898 *Bulletin* 17 Dec. Red Page: A *bludger* is about the lowest grade of human thing, and is a brothel bully . . . A *battler* is the feminine.
1956 Ruth Park and D'Arcy Niland *The Drums Go Bang!* 142: The landlord shrugged casually. 'We got a battler in there,' he said. A battler is Sydneyese for prostitute.
4 See quots
1895 Cornelius Crowe *Australian Slang Dictionary* 7: *Battlers* broken-down backers of horses still sticking to the game.
c. **1914** A. B. Paterson 'Racehorses and Racing in Australia' in *The World of 'Banjo' Paterson* ed. C. Semmler (1967) 310: A battler is a turf hanger-on who has not capital enough to be a backer, not personal magnetism enough to be a successful whisperer, and not sense enough to get work.
1922 Arthur Wright *A Colt from the Country* 118–19: Professional punters and racetrack battlers, who manage to make a living of sorts out of the game.

Bay, the 1 In N.S.W., Long Bay Gaol
1918 J. Vance Marshall *Jail from Within* 16: 'If yer lucky yer might get a bite at the Bay tonight,' said the officer with brutal unconcern.
1939 Kylie Tennant *Foveaux* 350: 'They can't send you out to the Bay

on a Sunday, so you spend Sunday yarning with the chaps at Central and then Monday morning at six you get out to the Bay and put in your week.'
1967 B. K. Burton *Teach Them No More* 169: 'You could serve the whole five years, and you could do the lot at Grafton, or the Bay.'
1971 Frank Hardy *The Outcasts of Foolgarah* 34: The waterfront police [inquired] why his attic was full of smuggled transistors, and gave him a seaside holiday at the Bay.
2 In Victoria, Port Philip Bay
1915 C. J. Dennis *The Songs of a Sentimental Bloke* 81: We're honey-moonin' down beside the Bay.
1934 Vance Palmer *The Swayne Family* 1: Hurrying over breakfast so that they should not miss a moment of the slow approach up the Bay.

Bazza-land Australia, as represented by Barry (Bazza) McKenzie, hero of the comic strip by Barry Humphries
1973 *Sunday Telegraph* 25 Nov. 89: The losers: the Australian composers we won't hear now, the ticket holders, and above all Bazza-land itself.
1974 *Sydney Morning Herald* 23 Nov. 11: Who's who and who's not in Bazzaland. [review of *Who's Who in Australia*]

bear, teddy see **teddy bear**

Bears, the 1 The North Sydney Rugby League team [f. club emblem]
1975 *Sydney Morning Herald* 18 Aug. 9: Gallant Bears skinned.
2 The police, in the argot of long-distance road hauliers [U.S.]
1976 *The Sun* 28 May 7: Bear Policeman. *Wall-to-Wall Bears* High concentration of police.

bear up, do a To pay court to a woman: *obs.* [OED 'U.S. colloq.' n.d.]
1899 Henry Lawson 'The Hero of Redclay' *Prose* i 297: 'I'd been getting on all right with the housemaid at the Royal . . . I thought it was good enough to do a bit of a bear-up in that direction.'
1942 Sarah Campion *Bonanza* 208: 'I

was all set to lay another fiver on your chances o' gettin' hooked – you looked to be bearin' up proper, an' no mistake.'

beaut 1 Applied to something which is exceptional in its class, and therefore usually deserving admiration; vague term of commendation [abbr. *beauty* U.S. 1866 Mathews]
1905 Randolph Bedford *The Snare of Strength* 223: At the sound all the stallion's senses were . . . bent in his direction. 'He's a bute,' said Dunphy. 'Quick as a flash; his nerves are all on ball-bearings.'
1907 Nathan Spielvogel *The Cocky Farmer* 42: 'Them's Piggy Howe's cows. Best milkers on the plains. That big Allerney gives a heap of milk a day. She's a beaut.'
1911 Edward Dyson *Benno and some of the Push* 123: 'Ain't he a beaut?' vociferated Benno. 'Good man, Brophy! It's twenty t' one on yeh!'
1930 L. Lower *Here's Luck* 266: 'An all I get out of it is a black eye. Look at it!' 'What a beaut!' exclaimed Stanley admiringly.
1944 *Coast to Coast 1943* 156: Everything had been beaut that spring.
1969 Thomas Keneally *The Place at Whitton* 214: 'I'm a specialist in loneliness. Your mate down there's a beaut as far as loneliness goes.'
1973 Alexander Buzo *Rooted* 46: 'It was a beaut design . . . He did this incredible white obelisk anchored into a beaut welter of blue streaks on a sheet of black strips with this incredible screen of pink flecks on a beaut steely surface.' 'Sounds beaut.'
1976 *Sydney Morning Herald* 6 Aug. 3: 'It's been beaut,' the Prime Minister, Mr Fraser, said yesterday of his four-day fishing holiday.
2 In the phrase 'You beaut!', as an interjection of approval
1944 Lawson Glassop *We Were the Rats* 212: 'You beaut!' I cried. 'You bloody beaut!'
1951 Dal Stivens *Jimmy Brockett* 184: 'You beaut!' he said. 'There's a fortune in it.'
1962 Gavin Casey *Amid the Plenty* 206:

'I've got a job,' he said. 'You bloody little beaut!' the grocer roared.

2 Indicating reproach or disapproval
1909 Arthur Wright *A Rogue's Luck* 35: 'You're a beaut,' he said, 'leavin' 'er cobber like that.'
1948 H. Drake-Brockman *Sydney or the Bush* 201: 'Mum,' his reproach met her, 'you're a beaut. Wher've you been?'
1953 T. A. G. Hungerford *Riverslake* 238: 'You must've thought I was a beaut, not sticking with you.'

beaut, the you ~ country Australia [f. *beaut²*, and the 1961 series of paintings by John Olsen called *You Beaut Country*]
1964 *Australian* 3 Oct. 15: The pale sunniness of the Heidelberg painters . . . will undoubtedly prevail and celebrate 'you beaut country'.
1971 Craig McGregor *Don't Talk to Me About Love* 18: 'Australia? She's the You Beaut Country. It's so You Beaut even Olsen has to get out of it every year or so.'
1972 Germaine Greer *Sun-Herald* 23 Jan. 103: Notwithstanding, if you are poor in the 'You Beaut' country, it is your fault.

beauty Expression of full agreement and approval, often pronounced 'bewdy'
1974 *National Times* 15 Apr. 6: It is not unfair to see Mr Snedden . . . thinking to himself at the beginning of this campaign, 'I shall ask the people to give me the opportunity to lead Australia to greatness.' And the answer he would want from the electorate is 'Bewdy, Bill.'

Bedourie shower see **shower**

beer-up See quots
1919 W. H. Downing *Digger Dialects* 10: *Beer-up* A drunken orgy.
1924 *Truth* 27 Apr. 6: *Beer-up* A drinking bout.
1941 Kylie Tennant *The Battlers* 314: 'If he's on a real proper beer-up,' the Stray whispered, 'he may go on for days.'
1971 Frank Hardy *The Outcasts of*

Foolgarah 200: 'He moved in today and they're havin' a big beer-up tonight to celebrate.'

Bee's Nest See quot.: N.T. and W.A.
1951 Ernestine Hill *The Territory* 424: The Pleiades are the Bee's Nest.

beggars in the pan, on the coals Small damper (see quots): *obs.*
1846 G. F. Angas *Savage Life and Scenes in Australia and New Zealand* i 161: Our cook had not been idle: there were 'dampers', 'dough-boys', 'leather-jackets', 'johnny-cakes', and 'beggars-in-the-pan'.
1848 Charles Cozens *Adventures of a Guardsman* 140–1: There is another sort of bread made when in a hurry, called 'beggars-on-the-coals' which is made very thin like our girdle bread, and merely placed in the hot ashes, and afterwards turned, about five minutes will suffice to make it.
1908 Giles Seagram *Bushmen All* 94: Over the grilled chops and 'beggars-on-the-coals' the probability of meeting wild blacks was discussed.
1934 P. H. Ritchie and H. B. Raine *North of the Never Never* 164: I decided to make some johnny cakes, commonly known by most old bushmen as 'b – s on the coals'.
see **devils on the coals**

behind In Australian Rules football, a kick that does not pass cleanly through the goal posts, or that goes between the goal post and the behind post: worth one point
1880 'The Opening Ball' *Comic Australian Verse* ed. G. Lehmann (1975) 2: 'Forward Carlton!' is now the cry, / And we rush it like the wind, / A roar from ten thousand throats go up, / For we've kicked another behind.

behind, further ~ than Walla Walla see **Walla Walla**

behind like Barney's bull, all see **bull**

Beliander (Belyando) spew See quots [f. place-name]

1889 C. Lumholtz *Among Cannibals* 58: Beliander is also a common disease in Queensland, without the slightest apparent cause, a person is suddenly seized with vomiting, but is relieved just as suddenly.
1918 C. Featherstonhaugh *After Many Days* 58: All the ills that flesh is heir to in a new and tropical country ... fever and ague, Moreton Bay rot (skin scurvy), Belyando Spue (pyrosis or water brash), sandy blight, bungy eyes, and dysentery.
see **Barcoo sickness**

bell sheep A sheep taken from the pen just as the bell rings to signal the end of a shift (important to a shearer trying to increase his tally)
1900 Henry Lawson 'A Rough Shed' *Prose* i 464: He [the shearer] is not supposed ... to take a sheep out of the pen *after* the bell goes (smoke-ho, meals, or knock-off) but ... he times himself to get so many sheep out of the pen *before* the bell goes, and *one more* – the 'bell-sheep' – as it is ringing ... The shearers are racing each other for tallies.
1911 E. S. Sorenson *Life in the Australian Backblocks* 245: There is also hard cutting among greedy persons for a bell sheep (the one caught just as the bell is about to ring off.)

Benghazi Handicap (Derby) See quots
1944 Lawson Glassop *We Were the Rats* 135: The confusion that was the retreat to Tobruk early in 1941 – we always called it the Benghazi Handicap – has rarely been equalled in the history of a war full of confused retreats.
1952 Eric Lambert *The Twenty Thousand Thieves* 103–4: The Ninth Division and the remnants of a British armoured division reached Tobruk. The Benghazi Derby was over. In Tobruk they turned to stand before Rommel.

berley *v.* & *n.* To scatter bait on the surface of the water to attract the fish; the bait so thrown [unexplained]
1855 G. C. Mundy *Our Antipodes* i 388: Anchoring the boats in about thirty feet of water, the first operation was

the baiting of the spot – locally termed 'burley-ing' with burnt fish, and with the eggs of sharks when any have been caught.
1882 J. E. Tennison-Woods *Fish and Fisheries of New South Wales* 75: It is usual to wrench legs and shell of the back [of the crabs], and cast them out for berley.
1907 Ambrose Pratt *The Remittance Man* 9: 'They don't seem to be biting this morning,' said the boy. 'You should give 'em some burley.'
1937 Vance Palmer *Legend for Sanderson* 124–5: They had burleyed all their favourite fishing-grounds, mixing a sardine paste and scattering it over the sea-floor.
1965 Thomas Keneally *The Fear* 160: The man had worked considerably closer to us, and was hunting blood worms with a sugar-bag full of berley.

Berries, the The Canterbury-Bankstown (N.S.W.) Rugby League team
1974 *Sydney Morning Herald* 9 Sep. 11: Berries just pip Sharks.
1975 *Sunday Telegraph* 15 Aug. 44: Berries' bliss. Form back with a vengeance.

bet like the Watsons see **Watsons**

bib, to stick one's ~ in To interfere, intrude
1952 T. A. G. Hungerford *The Ridge and the River* 57: Here was Wilder, almost a schoolboy amongst them, sticking in his bib.
1960 Jack McKinney *The Well* in *Khaki, Bush and Bigotry* ed. Eunice Hanger (1968) 265: 'What's it got to do with you? Who asked you to stick yer bib in?'
1974 *Sydney Morning Herald* 28 Dec. 8: 'Sayings of the Year'. Sir Robert Askin: I would thank Mr Chipp and his pussyfooting Victorians to keep their bibs out of N.S.W.
1975 Xavier Herbert *Poor Fellow My Country* 523: 'You, eh, Delacy, stickin' your bib in.'

Bible, the Bushman's see **Bushman's**

bible-basher A clergyman, missionary or any devout person: *derogatory* [variant of *bible-banger, – pounder, – puncher*]

1944 Lawson Glassop *We Were the Rats* 124: 'I doan want any bible-bashing bastard who's never seen me before mumblin' any bull– over me.'

1975 Xavier Herbert *Poor Fellow My Country* 254: 'The bigger the case, the more the publicity. That's what the Anthrops and the bible-bashers want.'

1976 Alan Reid *The Whitlam Venture* 58: The National Country Party Premier of Queensland, Joh Bjelke-Petersen, whom Whitlam in a fit of petulance described publicly as that 'Bible-bashing bastard'.

Big Fella, the J. T. Lang (1876–1975) Labor Premier of N.S.W. 1925–7, 1930–2 [? f. nickname given to Michael Collins, Irish republican hero, and the height and presence of Mr Lang]

1971 *Sydney Morning Herald* 5 Jul. 3: 'Big Fella' rejoins ALP after 28 years.

1975 *Sunday Telegraph* 28 Sep. 2: John Thomas Lang known to his friends and enemies as the Big Fella, died in St Joseph's Hospital, Auburn, after being admitted ten days ago for a rest.

big-note man A bookmaker or punter placing or handling large bets

1950 *Australian Police Journal* Apr. 111: *Big-note man* Wealthy.

1956 J. T. Lang *I Remember* 115: When he was not in Macquarie St, he was operating at Randwick. He became a 'big note' man. At one stage he was a bookmaker's agent, laying-off bets for one of the leviathans of the day. At other times, he acted as a betting commissioner, placing bets for wealthy patrons.

big-note oneself, come the big-note To attempt to inflate one's status or achievements

1953 Kylie Tennant *The Joyful Condemned* 23: 'Morton the bustman!' Rene sneered. 'Listen to him big-note himself. He's going to do a bust.'

1959 Dorothy Hewett *Bobbin Up* 137: 'You've made a career out of the Party.

You don't give a bugger about the workers. You're just big-notin' yourself, carving out a slice of your own particular glory.'

1967 B. K. Burton *Teach Them No More* 127–8: Terry had often laughed with the other workers at the attempts of George to big-note himself, to make himself appear bigger in character and experience than he really was.

1970 Barry Oakley *A Salute to the Great McCarthy* 65: 'Don't come the big note with me, Fortune, your next sarcasm may be your last.'

1974 John Powers *The Last of the Knucklemen* 21: 'This gives him a chance to big-note himself.'

bike A promiscuous woman, usually in such expressions as 'the town bike', 'the office bike' [f. *ride* for the male role in intercourse]

1945 Baker 123: A willing girl is sometimes described as an *office bike, a town bike* etc.

1951 Dal Stivens *Jimmy Brockett* 178: 'I might have known you were the bloody town bike.'

1965 Leslie Haylen *Big Red* 186: Murgatroyd, whose wife now had openly become the 'village bike'.

1972 David Williamson *The Removalists* 36: 'Turned out the tart was the biggest bike in the district.'

bike, to get off one's To appear to be losing control of oneself

1938 Xavier Herbert *Capricornia* 565: 'I tell you I saw no-one.' 'Don't get off your bike, son. I know you're tellin' lies.'

1952 Jon Cleary *The Sundowners* 237: 'I'm sorry. I didn't mean to get off me bike like that.'

1962 Alan Seymour *The One Day of the Year* 24: Alf (*yelling from kitchen*) Where the bloody hell are you? Mum (*yelling back*) Awright, don't get orf yr bike!

1963 Randolph Stow *Tourmaline* 115: 'You make me sick,' she cried again. 'Don't get off your bike,' he said.

Bill and Jim Typical outback Australians in the 1890s, and typical soldiers in World War I: *obs*.

1896 *Bulletin* 31 Oct. Red Page: The harrowing tale of the lost Bill or Jim in the Australian desert whose eyes are picked out by the crows almost before his death-struggle ceases.

1899 Henry Lawson 'Jack Cornstalk' *Prose* ii 44: And so out back, to the land of Bill and Jim, where we carried swags together.

1911 E. S. Sorenson *Life in the Australian Backblocks* 14: Bill and Jim have lapses at long intervals, they go on a roaring bender for a week or two weeks, after which they do not touch a drop of liquor for months.

1916 Joseph Furphy *Poems* 29: Better we were cold and still, with famous Jim and Bill, / Beneath the interdicted wattle-bough, / For the angels made our date five-and-twenty years too late, / And there is no Up the Country for us now.

1919 W. J. Denny *The Diggers* 171: The freedom with which 'Billjim' spends his pay not unnaturally adds to the warmth of his welcome.

billabong, on the Out of work and camped on a waterhole: esp. N.T. and W. A. [f. Ab. *billabong* waterhole]

1954 Tom Ronan *Vision Splendid* 16: The north has got better men than you, better men than me. When it gets a man it generally throws him on the Billabong and leaves him there.'

billabonger One of those 'on the billabong'

1883 John Farrell 'My Sundowner' *How He Died* (1913) 63: Sam, the Billabonger.

1954 Tom Ronan *Vision Splendid* 217: They dispensed tactfully casual invitations for lunch or tea to billabongers who hadn't eaten a really square meal for months.

billabong whaler see **whaler**

billet A post, job, appointment (at first including lodgings): *obsolescent* [f. *billet* order providing quarters for a soldier OED 1644]

1846 L. W. Miller *Notes of an Exile to Van Dieman's Land* 343: 'What in the name of common sense do you want to get into the *wash-house* for?' I asked. 'Oh, it is a *billet*. The work is light, and performed under cover; and the men get tobacco, and enough to eat into the bargain.'

1865 J. F. Mortlock *Experiences of a Convict* (1965) 101: Mr Jones used his influence to get me made clerk (being one of the best 'billets' for which I was eligible).

1885 *The Australasian Printers' Keepsake* 64: Up-country billets oft are loss; / Work for tucker – trust the boss.

1890 *Bulletin* 4 Oct. 12: 'Why,' says the layman, 'you give all the best billets to men from Scotland [when appointing clergy] and think Australians only fit for the back bush blocks.'

1892 William Lane *The Workingman's Paradise* 14: 'I've got a pretty good billet. A pound a week and not much lost time.'

1902 Henry Lawson 'The Story of "Gentleman-Once"' *Prose* i 535: 'He got a billet in the Civil Service up-country ... He commenced to drink again, and went on till he lost his billet.'

1941 Baker 10: *Billet* A position or job.

1950 *Coast to Coast 1949–50* 191: 'H'm,' he says, 'You'll have to take care of your billet.'

bill-poster, as busy as a one-armed ~ in a high wind Extremely busy or harassed ['As busy as the devil in a high wind' Grose 1811]

1951 Dal Stivens *Jimmy Brockett* 214: I was as busy nowadays as a one-armed bill-sticker in a gale.

1971 Frank Hardy *The Outcasts of Foolgarah* 216: 'I'm in more trouble than a one-armed bill-poster in a high wind.'

Billy Barlow see **Barlow**

Billy, King see **King Billy**

billy, boil the To make a cup of tea, not necessarily with a billy-can; to stop for refreshments [f. *billy-pot* cooking utensil SND c.1828]

1956 A. W. Upfield *The Battling Prophet* 5: 'Glad to meet you. Come on in and we'll boil the billy.' [an electric jug]
1958 H. D. Williamson *The Sunlit Plain* 5: Except for a break at noon to boil the billy, they had been on the move since dawn.

bimbo Term applied to a young tramp in the depression of the 1930s, usually with an implication of homosexuality [? f. It. *bambino*]
1966 Elwyn Wallace *Sydney and the Bush* 144: 'That "mate" as you call him is a queer,' Paddy explained. 'You know, a queen. I think they're called "Bimbos" on the track.'
1973 Frank Huelin *Keep Moving* 139–40: The older man claimed the younger as his nephew ... but we concluded there was also a more intimate sexual relationship – that the younger was the older man's 'bimbo'.

bindi-eye *Calotis cuneifolia*, a weed noted for its prickles or burrs [? Ab.]
1910 C. E. W. Bean *On the Wool Track* 226: Often the only sign that tells you he is a shearer at all is the scar made by binde-i or some other burr in the fleece on the back of his hand.
1937 Ernestine Hill *The Great Australian Loneliness* 304: Walking thirty or forty miles in the day, her feet impervious to the scalding sand or the torture of the bindi-eyes.
1959 C. V. Lawlor *All This Humbug* 62: The bindi-eye burrs had sent the little feet back to the comfort of the dust on the track.
1963 Bruce Beaver *The Hot Summer* 113: Continue on her way bare-footed, the blue-metal chips and bindy-eyes presenting less of a trial to her broad toughened feet.
1971 Rena Briand *White Man in a Hole* 32: Our shower clogs were a poor protection against burrs from small, brittle plants which grew profusely. 'Bindy-eye', the miners called them.

binghi n. & a. White term for an Aboriginal: *derogatory* [Ab. word for 'brother']
[1847 Alexander Harris *Settlers and Convicts* ed. C. M. H. Clark (1954) 173: 'Poor fellow you, binghi (brother).']
1930 *Bulletin* 5 Feb. 23: Binghi was on his way to join the mob in a corroboree, having been summoned by smoke signals.
1936 H. Drake-Brockman *Sheba Lane* 167: 'And yer need ter be mighty careful not ter fall fer a binghi tart.'
1944 Lawson Glassop *We Were the Rats* 5: 'He stopped the abo in three last Saturdee. What a punch! It was a bloody beaut. I leaves me cart outside and sneaks in just in time to see Jerry knock Binghi as cold as a Polar bear's backside.'
1964 Mary Durack *The Rock and the Sand* 212: Before long every white family in Broome had acquired a mission educated 'binghi' couple.
see **boong, Jacky**

bingle A car crash, a 'prang' [? *bingle* a hit in baseball U.S. 1902 Mathews]
1953 Baker 169: *bingle* A skirmish. [as World War II slang]
1966 Baker 253: *bingle* a dent or fracture in a surfboard.
1966 Roger Carr *Surfie* 122: There was this clang of metal on metal and both cars lurched over the shoulder and we nearly went for a bingle.

bingy (j) Belly [Ab.]
1832–4 Joseph Larmer 'Native Vocabulary 1832–4' (MS Mitchell Library) 24: 'Binje' in that neighbourhood is a word applied to the stomach.
1859 Henry Kingsley *Recollections of Geoffry Hamlyn* ii 94: 'Don't fret your bingy, boss.'
1887 *Tibb's Popular Songbook* 27: He's not much about the bingey,/But on legs he's standing high.
1889 Carl Lumholtz *Among Cannibals* 305: There are now a number of such words which are in vogue throughout the civilised part of the continent – for example, yarriman, horse; dillibag, basket; kabra, head; bingee, belly.
1908 *The Australian Magazine* 1 Nov. 1251: Two or three aboriginal words

...are now found in standard dictionaries ... but others have remained, and are likely to remain in the category of slang, such as bingy (bin jee), stomach.

1911 Steele Rudd *The Dashwoods* 111: Big-bingied, stiff-backed old fogies who did nothing all the week but smoke cigars.
1919 Edward Dyson *Hello, Soldier!* 31: Son pussied [crawled] on his bingie.
1924 *Truth* 27 Apr. 6: *Bingy* The stomach.
1931 William Hatfield *Sheepmates* 243: A well earned poke in the bingie.

bird, blue, bower see **bluebird, bowerbird**

bird, a dead A certainty, esp. in horse-racing [see quot. 1898]
1889 *The Arrow* 20 Jul. 1: A school-teacher recently asked his class 'What is a moral!' and with one accord came the answer 'A dead bird, sir.'
1898 Morris: *Dead-bird* In Australia, a recent slang term, meaning 'a certainty'. The metaphor is from pigeon-shooting, where the bird being let loose in front of a good shot is as good as dead.
1941 Baker 22: *Dead bird* A certainty.
1951 Dal Stivens *Jimmy Brockett* 47: It was betting on a dead bird. We had waited nearly a year for a killing like this.

birds, box of see **box**

Biscay, Bay of ~ country Country with a very uneven surface for travelling: *obs.* [f. reputation of the Bay of Biscay for rough seas]
1854 C. H. Spence *Clara Morison* (1971) 376: The jolting ... caused by a bad gully or an awkward piece of 'Bay of Biscay ground'.
1926 Alfred Giles *Exploring in the Seventies* 116: We proceeded five miles over Bay-o'-Biscay country which we found sticky as glue, and boggy.
1941 Charles Barrett *Coast of Adventure* 111: A low expanse of greyish sandstone, flaked and heaped fantastically; Bay of Biscay country, as easy to walk

over as the ruins of a bombed stone building.
1951 Ernestine Hill *The Territory* 443: *Bay o'Biscay* Tumbled country, hills and hollows as of a rough sea.

Bishop Barker see **Barker**

bite, put the ~ on To seek a loan, scrounge money or food [? f. *bite the ear* borrow OED 1879]
1919 W. H. Downing *Digger Dialects* 11: *Bite* (*n.* or *v.*) (1) A borrowing, to borrow, (2) an attempt to borrow.
1935 Kylie Tennant *Tiburon* 120: 'An' the perlice is only makin' themselves more work, see, puttin' chaps off the dole, so they 'ave t'bite people, see?' Ibid. 164: He watched the group stream down the road to 'bite' Tiburon and spread the tale of their hardships.
1949 Lawson Glassop *Lucky Palmer* 35: 'Can I bite you for a few quid, Lucky?'
1957 Ray Lawler *Summer of the Seventeenth Doll* 98: 'Your money's runnin' out, you know you can't put the bite on me any more, and so here's the new champion, all loaded and ready.'
1963 Alan Marshall *In Mine Own Heart* 164: 'Have you got any tucker with you or will we have to go in and bite the town?'
1969 Alan O'Toole *The Racing Game* 132: He pulled out a battered packet of cigarettes, bit the gentleman next to him for a light, and focussed his attention on the start.

bitser A mongrel dog
1941 Baker 10: *Bitser*: Anything made of bits and pieces; a mongrel animal.
1949 John Morrison *The Creeping City* 36–7: He called the dog Bitser because, as he candidly confessed to anyone who asked its breeding, it was 'just bits of this and bits of that'.
1958 A. W. Upfield *The Bachelors of Broken Hill* 212: 'Had one [dog] once, though. Black an' tan bitser.'
1968 *Australian* 4 Apr. 20: He lives with two bitser dogs that belonged to his mother.

bitumen, the 1 A tarred road

1953 Baker 137: *one for the bitumen*, a final round of drinks, i.e. 'one for the road'.

1972 W. A. Winter-Irving *Beyond the Bitumen* [book title]

1974 John Morrison *Australian by Choice* 118: It lay three miles off the bitumen, two miles of dirt road and one mile of winding track.

2 *The Bitumen* The highway between Darwin and Alice Springs

1965 *Australian* 28 Jan. 10: Maps may tell you the thousand miles long black ribbon linking Darwin with Alice Springs and the south is the Stuart Highway. But up here it is 'the Track' or 'the Bitumen'.

1969 Osmar White *Under the Iron Rainbow* 160: 'We used to get a lot of commercials there, travelling up and down the Bitumen.'* *The Bitumen: The sealed highway from Darwin to Alice Springs.

bitumen blonde Aboriginal girl

1943 Baker 10: *Bitumen blonde* An aboriginal girl or woman.

black hat A newly arrived immigrant, inexperienced in the ways of the colony i.e. still wearing city clothes: *obs.*

1876 Rolf Boldrewood *A Colonial Reformer* (1890) 21: 'A "black hat" in Australian parlance means a new arrival.'

1881 Mrs Campbell Praed *Policy and Passion* 277: 'You remember that 'ere long chap from England as wur stopping here? Lord! if I were Mr Dyson Maddox I'd never let it be said that a *black hat* has cut me out sweetheartin'.'

black prince A variety of cicada [f. colour]

1951 Dymphna Cusack and Florence James *Come In Spinner!* 106: 'Mine's a Floury Baker ... and mine's a Black Prince.' Young Jack and Andrew held up their fists for her to peep at frosted fawn body and tan-and-black.

1959 Anne von Bertouch *February Dark* 124: Through the shimmer of heat and the drilling song Helen saw the beautiful cicadas of childhood, the Black Prince, the Greengrocer, the Yellow Monday, held on a child's small hand.

1974 Ronald McKie *The Mango Tree* 18: He had talked to her about his first puppy, a Black Prince and the Double Drummer he had caught in the garden.

Black Saturday 10 December 1938, a day of severe bush fires in N.S.W.

Black Stump 1 An imaginary last post of civilization. There have been country properties so called, including one near Coolah N.S.W. dating from 1826, and another at Merriwagga N.S.W. (see *Sun-Herald* 22 Feb. 1970) but these names may have derived from the currency of the expression.

1954 Tom Ronan *Vision Splendid* 264: 'You're looking,' he boasted, 'at the best bloody station bookkeeper this side of the black stump.' [spoken in Adelaide]

1959 Eric Lambert *Glory Thrown In* 146: 'You're the greatest lurk-artist this side, or any bloody side of the black stump.'

1962 Criena Rohan *The Delinquents* 151: 'Good old, sweet old, wholesome, pure little Brisbane, best little town this or any side of the Black Stump.'

1971 Frank Hardy *The Outcasts of Foolgarah* 42: Moss was about the best bloody listener this side of the Black Stump.

1975 Xavier Herbert *Poor Fellow My Country* 1149: 'I've been played for the biggest mug this side o' the Black Stump.'

2 The State Offices block in Sydney [f. appearance]

1970 Jon Cleary *Helga's Web* 263: His office was in the State Government block, a beautiful dark grey tower that the citizens, with the local talent for belittling anything that embarrassed them with its pretensions, had dubbed the Black Stump.

Black Sunday 6 February 1938, the day of a record number of rescues by lifesavers at Bondi beach, when five lives were lost

Black Thursday 6 February 1851, a day of bushfire devastation in Victoria
1855 William Howitt *Land, Labour and Gold* i 68–9: The great bush-fire of what is called Black Thursday, or Thursday the 6th February, 1851 ... raged fiercely in these parts.
1885 J. Jenkins *Diary of a Welsh Swagman* (1975) 139: This, the 6th of February, is the anniversary of 'Black Thursday' of 1851, when one half of the state of Victoria was on fire.

blacks, they should give it back to the Expression of disgust at any inhospitable feature of Australia [? f. U.S. 'hand it back to the Indians']
1946 *Sunday Sun* 4 Aug. Suppl. 15: They reckon as he [Captain Cook] sailed away he gave one look back at the coast of Bananaland and said, 'Strewth, I'm glad to give that dump back to the blacks.'
1952 Jon Cleary *The Sundowners* 153: 'Give me the coast, and I'll give the rest of Australia back to the blackfellers.'
1969 Christopher Bray *Blossom Like a Rose* 75: 'They should give it back to the blacks: 'What's that?' asked Jake. 'The bloody north,' said Tom.
1971 Colin Simpson *The New Australia* 213: Robin Boyd begins by saying that he often feels that Melbourne should be given back to the blacks.

black taxi A Commonwealth government car, providing free transport for politicians and public servants
1973 *Sun-Herald* 25 Nov. 112: Fred Daly ... has ordered a crackdown on official use of the 'black taxis'. He has warned MPs that the long black official limousines will not wait outside flats and hotels if those who ordered them aren't ready.
1975 *Sun-Herald* 3 Aug. 48: Commonwealth cars (flippantly known as 'black taxis' to those new to power) were used to ferry junior aides to lunch.

black velvet Aboriginal women, as

sexual partners [listed by Partridge as English military slang in the nineteenth century]
1899 Henry Lawson 'The Ballad of the Rouseabout' *Verse* i 360: I know the track from Spencer's Gulf and north of Cooper's Creek – / Where falls the half-caste to the strong, 'black velvet' to the weak.
1929 K. S. Prichard *Coonardoo* 79: 'You're one of these god-damned young heroes. No 'black velvet' for you, I suppose?' 'I'm goin' to marry white and stick white,' Hugh said.
1938 Xavier Herbert *Capricornia* 24: He began to take an interest in native women, or Black Velvet as they were called collectively, affairs with whom seemed to be the chief diversion.
1958 Gavin Casey *Snowball* 17: 'Did you see the girls, when you were out there? ... The sort of black velvet that makes me sometimes wish I wasn't a policeman.'

blades, the The hand shears, used before the introduction of machine shearing
1964 H. P. Tritton *Time Means Tucker* 47: Conimbia was having its last season with the blades and was starting next day.

Blake, Joe see **Joe Blake**

Blamey, a Lady See quots [wife of General Sir Thomas Blamey]
1945 Baker 157: *Lady Blamey* A beer bottle, from which the neck has been removed, used as a drinking vessel. [World War II slang]
1972 *Sydney Morning Herald* 28 Oct. 8: During this time she gave her name to the 'bottle' drinking glass used by thousands of Diggers. She taught them to slice an empty bottle cleanly in half with the aid of kerosene-soaked string. The string was wound round the bottle, and set alight. When the bottle was hot it was plunged into water and would break cleanly. The men used the lower part for drinking.

Blind Freddie see **Freddie**

Bliss, Johnny A piss [rhyming slang]
1973 Alexander Buzo *Rooted* 77: 'I couldn't bear to watch it, so I ducked out for a Johnny Bliss.'

blister A debt, bill [f. *blister* a summons OED 1903]
1888 E. Finn *Chronicles of Early Melbourne* ii 546: As far as the bushmen were concerned, they might certainly be styled 'blisters', for they burned their pockets while they had them. [The term 'blister' wrongly applied to 'shinplasters' q.v.]
1934 Vance Palmer *Sea and Spinifex* 14: 'Well, they need every quid they can rake together,' McVeagh defended. 'There's a blister on that boat that won't be worked off unless they strike a few good patches.'
1951 Ernestine Hill *The Territory* 431: [In the bush] never carry a 'blister', a bill or an account ... A rider passing by was an honoured guest, and he couldn't be hounding a man down with bills.

block, do the To make a fashionable promenade, in Melbourne along Collins Street between Swanston and Elizabeth Streets, in Sydney in the area bounded by George, King and Pitt Streets: *obs*.
1869 Marcus Clarke *The Peripatetic Philosopher* 12: The 'doing the Block' is doubtless worthy of censure, 'Collins-street Folly' is foolish enough to be visited with the severest blame.
1887 Fergus Hume *The Mystery of a Hansom Cab* (1971) 58–9: It was Saturday morning and of course all fashionable Melbourne was doing the Block. With regards to its 'Block', Collins Street corresponds to New York's Broadway, London's Regent Street and Rotten Row, and to the Boulevards of Paris. It is on the Block that people show off their new dresses, bow to their friends, cut their enemies, and chatter small talk.
1892 Henry Lawson 'The Drover's Wife' *Prose* i 50: She takes as much care to make herself and the children look smart as she would if she were going to do the block in the city.

1902 Ambrose Pratt *The Great 'Push' Experiment* 278: I strolled down King Street to do the block.
1910 H. H. Richardson *The Getting of Wisdom* 134: They were going to 'do the block', Tilly explained, and would meet Bob there.

block, do (lose) one's Of the various expressions in which 'block' is used as 'head' (OED 1635), such as 'knock your block off', the most 'Australian' seems to be 'do your block' i.e. lose rational control from rage, excitement, falling in love. The converse is to 'use your block' i.e. apply all shrewdness and judgement.
1907 Charles MacAlister *Old Pioneering Days in the Sunny South* 19: At this Mr Donovan 'lost his block' completely. 'Clear out of my sight, ye skunks,' he screamed.
1915 C. J. Dennis *The Songs of a Sentimental Bloke* 47: I done me block complete on this Doreen, / An' now me 'eart is broke, me life's a wreck!
1934 Thomas Wood *Cobbers* 159: 'When I've had five double whiskies I do me block[1], but when I've had six I'd tackle anything.' [1]lose my head.
1959 A. W. Upfield *Bony and the Mouse* 133: 'Not much of a bushman!' 'Good enough, if he uses his block, to get a long way.'
1963 Randolph Stow *Tourmaline* 63: 'Don't think you're the first bloke that ever did his block with Byrnie in this bar.'
1970 Patrick White *The Vivisector* 586: 'Orright! Don't do yer block! What else?'

blockee, blocker The owner of a block of land on which grapes are grown [listed by Baker as peculiar to S.A., but also encountered in Victoria]
1945 Baker 197: *blocker* an owner of a vineyard, specifically, a block of land on which grapes are grown.
1948 *Coast to Coast 1947* 229: He stooped and straightened and thrust under the vines ... even when the blockie gave him a row to himself and kept the others working in pairs, he outstripped them.

1973 Frank Huelin *Keep Moving* 62: 'Th' blockees want us here f'r th' pickin' ... It's no good after the harvest. They couldn't care less then, but now they want us alive and fit to snatch their bloody grapes.'

Bloke, the 1 The man in charge, the boss [f. naval slang for a ship's commander OED 1914]
1966 Tom Ronan *Once There Was a Bagman* 2: Kelly the Nip [imagined giving advice to Ronan, about to lunch on the royal yacht *Britannia*] 'See if you can work me in for a yarn with the Bloke. I'll bite him if you won't.'
2 The hero of C. J. Dennis' *The Songs of a Sentimental Bloke* (1915)
1939 R. H. Croll *I Recall* 163: The Bloke has passed: Oh, dip the lid!
1967 R. D. FitzGerald *Southerly* 261: Remember too that when the one and only Bloke was presented with a son ... Dennis makes the Bloke say: 'Doreen she says 'e's got a poet's eyes;/ But I ain't got no use for them soft guys.'
3 *The Old Bloke* God [outback slang]
1958 Russel Ward *The Australian Legend* 98: I was one of a party of four, driving an old truck through the Musgrave Ranges ... One of my companions gushed considerably over the beauty of the mountain sky-line, silhouetted against the sunset. An elderly stockman answered drily. 'Yes. The Old Bloke makes a good job of them up this way.'

blonde, bitumen see **bitumen**

blonde, bushfire see **bushfire**

bloodhouse A public house with a reputation for brawls, gambling
1938 Heard in conversation.
1953 Dymphna Cusack *Southern Steel* 138: 'Ought to have more sense than to go to the Seven Seas – nothing but a bloodhouse. Always blues there.'
1956 Tom Ronan *Moleskin Midas* 51: 'Try the bloodhouse – I mean, Silman's – next hotel down the street.'
1963 Frank Hardy *Legends from Benson's Valley* 104: He stopped to study

the defences of the hotel – not such a bloodhouse as the Royal Oak, but nevertheless addicted to after-hours trading.
1971 Hal Porter *The Right Thing* 91: 'She toils in the Kilkenny blood-house, mother. Where father used to drink like a fish.'

Bloods, the The South Melbourne V.F.L. team, now the Swans

bloody The 'great Australian adjective' q.v. is by no means distinctively Australian, but has always been conspicuous enough in the colloquial language to be seen as such by overseas visitors
1833 Trial before the Supreme Court, 9 and 10 December, in *True Patriots All* ed. G. C. Ingleton (1952) 149: John Larnack, being duly sworn, said; on the morning of the 5th November last, I went to the river to superintend sheepwashing; between 12 and 1 o'clock I heard a voice exclaiming – '*come out of the water every bloody one of you, or we'll blow your bloody brains out!*'; on looking behind, I saw three men advancing towards me with guns.
1847 A. Marjoribanks *Travels in New South Wales* 57–8: The word bloody is a favourite oath in that country. One man will tell you that he married a bloody young wife, another, a bloody old one, and a bushranger will call out, 'Stop, or I'll blow your bloody brains out.'
1855 William Howitt *Land, Labour and Gold* ii 76: The language of the diggings is something inconceivable in its vileness, and every sentence almost is ornamented with the word bloody. That word they seem to think the perfection of phraseology; it is the keystone and topstone of all their eloquence, it occurs generally in every second or third sentence; and, when they get excited, they lard every sentence with it profusely ... Two diggers passing our tent one day, saw the thermometer hanging on the post: – 'What d – d, blasted, bloody thing is that now?' said one to the other. 'Why I'm blowed if it ain't a d – d, blasted,

bloody old weather glass,' replied his mate.

1875 A. J. Boyd *Old Colonials* (1882) 107: 'I'll put my (adjective) fist where I (adjective) well please. I've a mind to knock yer (adjective) head off.'

1899 W. T. Goodge '—!' (The Great Australian Adjective!) in *Hits! Skits! and Jingles!* 115: The sunburnt—stockman stood, / And, in a dismal—mood, / Apostrophised his—cuddy; / 'The—nag's no—good, / He couldn't earn his —food – / A regular—brumby.

1942 C. Hartley Grattan *Introducing Australia* 193: When I asked an old 'cove' when he first arrived in Darwin, he replied, 'Young man, in nineteen bloody eight!'

1951 Dymphna Cusack and Florence James *Come In Spinner* 306: 'Got in a troop train . . . after a fortnight comin' down from Broome across the Trans-contibloodynental.'

1969 Patsy Adam Smith *Folklore of the Australian Railwaymen* 218: One of the witnesses, a fettler, came into the inquiry room and tripped on a mat and said, 'What stupid bastard put that bloody mat there?' And he slung it out the door. 'Bull' Mitchell on the inquiry board said to him, 'None of your bloody swearing here, you just remember that you're at a bloody inquiry and bloody well behave yourself.'

1973 Mr C. Jones [Federal Minister for Transport] *Sydney Morning Herald* 18 Aug. 2: There is going to be some bloody mammoth changes – some mammoth changes which the Budget will disclose. Bloody mammoth changes, that is the only way you can describe them. I think Frank [Crean] has done a bloody good job to stand up to the pace. Bloody oath, he has done a marvellous job in standing up to the bloody pace.

blot Anus, buttocks
1945 Baker 156: *blot* The posterior or anus. [World War II slang]

1965 William Dick *A Bunch of Ratbags* 262: He pushed me away and he gave me a kick up the blot.

1968 Frank Hardy *The Unlucky Aus-* *tralians* 67: As a parting gesture, sticks his fingers up the dog's blot.

1974 David Ireland *Burn* 146: Maybe he'll grab this last chance for some action after sitting on his blot all these years.

blow v. 1 'To boast, brag (chiefly dial.)' OED c. 1400–1873: *obsolescent*
1857 *Thatcher's Colonial Songster* 35: About your talents blow, / Mind, that's the regular caper.

1873 Rolf Boldrewood 'The Fencing of Wanderowna' *A Romance of Canvas Town* (1901) 31: 'Well, I thought he seemed a blowin' sort of fool.'

1887 *Tibb's Popular Songbook* 24: The squatters blowed they'd cut the price / To seventeen and six.

1924 *Truth* 27 Apr. 6: *Blow* To boast.

1945 Gavin Casey *Downhill is Easier* 41: Ordinary rouseabout labourers don't get many chances to blow out their bags about what good men they are, unless they tell lies.

2 To lengthen in odds, the opposite to 'firm' (horse-racing)
1922 Arthur Wright *A Colt from the Country* 129: 'Ain't Lobitout fav'rit?' he gasped . . . 'No!' snapped the stranger. 'Got blown right out.'

1949 Lawson Glassop *Lucky Palmer* 63: 'I've got the commission for it this end of the ring, and I'm trying to blow the price out.'

1977 *Sun-Herald* 9 Jan. 47: The book-makers blew Gold Spring's odds to 10–1, but the mud did not dull her speed.

blow n. 1 Bragging, boasting: *obsolescent* [f. *blow* v.[1]]
1868 C. Wade Brown *Overlanding in Australia* 18: He seldom carries out his threats, it is more 'blow' (bounce) on his part than anything.

1885 *The Australasian Printers' Keepsake* 162: A European type, working in Sydney, was grievously galled by the 'blow' of the Cornstalks.

1893 Francis Adams *The Australians* 149: The drawling 'blow' (Anglice, boasting) of the competitive bushman borders on an anger which is so high-strung as to threaten insanity.

2 A stroke of the shears in shearing
1870 Rolf Boldrewood 'Shearing in
Riverina' *In Bad Company* (1901) 309:
Every 'blow' of the shears is agony to
him, yet he disdains to give in.
1878 G. H. Gibson *Southerly Busters*
180: My tally's eighty-five a day – / A
hundred I could go, / If coves would
let me 'open out' / And take a bigger
'blow'.
1885–1914 'Click go the Shears' *Old
Bush Songs* ed. Stewart and Keesing
(1957) 254: The ringer looks around
and is beaten by a blow, / And curses
the old snagger with the blue-bellied
'joe'.
1911 E. S. Sorenson *Life in the Australian Backblocks* 233: The blades are
pulled back and the knockers filed
down, so the shears will take a bigger
blow.
1964 *Sydney Morning Herald* 6 Apr. 2:
The two men evolved a style which
cuts out some fifteen blows (shearing
strokes) a sheep and allows shearers
to increase their tally.

blow, strike a To start or resume work
1974 Sir Robert Askin *Australian* 18
Dec. 9: 'I think it's bad that people
can live on high interest rates, like 15
per cent, and can get enough money
to live on them without striking a
blow.'

blow through As for 'shoot through'

blowie A blowfly [abbr.]
1945 Gavin Casey *Downhill is Easier*
204: 'There was clouds o' blowies.'
1973 *Australian* 7 Jul. 16: I love this
ripper country / Of funnel webs and
sharks / With blowies big as eagles /
Where your car gets booked by narks.

blow-in A casual arrival: *derogatory*
1953 T. A. G. Hungerford *Riverslake*
195: A couple of blow-ins from the
Causeway, with loud-mouthed women.
1962 Dymphna Cusack *Picnic Races*
19: 'Lotta jumped-up blow-ins putting
on more guyver than the Governor's
wife.'

bludge *n.* A job requiring no exertion
[f. *bludger*²]
1943 Donald Friend *Gunner's Diary* 18:
'I've been three weeks in hospital with
measles.' 'Ah – that's not a bad bludge.'
1949 Lawson Glassop *Lucky Palmer*
154: 'A man's got to earn a living and
this is a good bludge.'
1962 Stuart Gore *Down the Golden Mile*
53: 'What a smart bludge he's on, eh?
At six thousand a year or whatever it
is he gets.'

bludge *v.* **1** To live on the earnings of
a prostitute [a verb inferred from
*bludger*¹, but not encountered]
2 To avoid effort and live by someone
else's exertions; to acquire something
without payment
1919 W. H. Downing *Digger Dialects*
12: *Bludge on the flag* To fail to justify
one's existence as a soldier.
1931 Vance Palmer *Separate Lives* 264:
'I've stood you too long already, loafing
around here, and bludging on your
mother.'
1957 Ray Lawler *Summer of the Seventeenth Doll* 37: 'I won't bludge. I'll get
a job or somethin'.'
1964 Donald Horne *The Lucky Country*
26: Covering up for an incompetent
mate is the usual thing as long as he is
considered to be trying and not simply
'bludging'.
1975 Richard Cornish *The Woman Li-
lith* 25: We cleaned the house, painted
the walls . . . bludged some furniture.

bludger **1** Someone living on the earnings of a prostitute: *obs.* [f. *bludgeoner*
OED 1842]
1898 *Bulletin* 17 Dec. Red Page: A
bludger is about the lowest grade of
human thing, and is a brothel bully.
1904 Henry Lawson 'The Women of
the Town' *Verse* ii 54: And they profit
from the brewer and the smirking
landlord down / To the bully and the
bludger, on the women of the town.
1924 *Truth* 27 Apr. 6: *Bludger* A man
who lives on the proceeds of prosti-
tution.
1946 K. S. Prichard *The Roaring Nineties* 388: Bill led an attack on the

French bludger who kept three or four Japanese women in miserable shacks at Kanowna.

1959 Dorothy Hewett *Bobbin Up* 115: 'But what about libel? "There's a name for a man who lives off women!" Can't you get pinched for callin' a man a bludger?'

2 See quot. 1900–10

1900–10 O'Brien and Stephens: *Bludger* The word has come to be applied to any person who takes profit without risk or disability or without effort or work.

1945 Gavin Casey *Downhill is Easier* 15: 'They don't put many on here, but they don't put many off either, unless they're dinkum bludgers.'

1958 H. D. Williamson *The Sunlit Plain* 21: 'You and your rotten, boozy cobbers! Think I don't see enough of 'em in this place to know what they are? Dirty, greasy mob of bludgers!'

1971 *Sydney Morning Herald* 6 Aug. 1: The only people who would benefit from full pay on workers' compensation would be 'genuine loafers, shirkers or bludgers', the Chief Secretary, Mr Willis, said in the Legislative Assembly yesterday.

3 Affectionate, when addressed to friends, like *bastard*[3]

1965 William Dick *A Bunch of Ratbags* 216: 'Don't be scabs, yuh pack of bludgers, all youse ever think of is money,' Argles laughed.

bludger, dole see **dole bludger**

blue (bluey) 1 A summons, esp. for a traffic offence [f. colour of paper]

[**1895** Cornelius Crowe *Australian Slang Dictionary* 58: *Piece of blue paper* a summons.

1899 Henry Lawson 'Jack Cornstalk' *Prose* ii 50: He gets on the spree and into a row, and so into trouble that merits the serving on his person of what he calls 'a piece of blue paper'.]

1939 Kylie Tennant *Foveaux* 348: 'Take a look at these blues.' With a flourish he produced a wad of grey summonses which he shuffled like a pack of cards.

1965 Graham McInnes *The Road to Gundagai* 242: A uniformed John Hop with a tall patent leather helmet rang the bell and handed me the dreaded 'bluey', the summons for riding a bike without lights.

1974 *Sydney Morning Herald* 5 Nov. 1: After half a century the era of the 'bluey' is over. From now on, thanks to Dataprint, the Police Department's new $66,000 computerised traffic system, offending motorists will receive 'whiteys'. The blue summons paper has been replaced by white computer paper.

2 A quarrel, brawl, particularly in expressions like 'bung (stack, turn) on a blue', 'pick a blue'

1943 *Khaki and Green* 105: The 'blue' started, and you knew you'd be going up. Not the whole reinforcement draft, first time.

1946 Rohan Rivett *Behind Bamboo* 395: *Blue* A row, trouble.

1957 Judah Waten *Shares in Murder* 58: 'Want to stack on a blue?' he said looking at her strangely.

1963 Jon Cleary *A Flight of Chariots* 178: 'That's one advantage to being a big bastard – people think twice about picking a blue with you.'

1974 David Ireland *Burn* 28: 'You tryin' to bung on a blue? I'll give you a smack in the chops in a minute.'

3 A blunder, mistake [f. *bloomer*]

1941 Baker 11: *Blue* (2) An error or mistake; a loss.

1957 Randolph Stow *The Bystander* 187: 'I reckon you ought to tell your missus she made a bit of a blue.'

1969 D'Arcy Niland *Dead Men Running* 189: 'I still think they made a blue.'

4 Nickname for a red-headed person

1932 Leonard Mann *Flesh in Armour* 37: Blue McIntosh, No. 1, red in the head, a League footballer.

1950 Brian James *The Advancement of Spencer Button* 267: Two single ones . . . became just Flora and Blue (she had red hair).

1961 Patrick White *Riders in the Chariot* 252–3: Hair – a red stubble, but red . . . 'Blue is what he answers to.'

Bluebags, the In N.S.W., the Newtown

Rugby League team [f. colours]
1976 *Sunday Telegraph* 6 Jun. 56: Hail the Bluebags! Gallant win over Tigers.

blue bird The police 'paddy-waggon' [f. colour]
1939 Kylie Tennant *Foveaux* 415: The two-up school on the corner took no notice of Bramley and Kingston. The only thing that really disturbed the streets was 'the blue-bird', the police car on its rounds.

blue duck Anything which does not come up to expectations; a dud, a 'write-off'
1895 Cornelius Crowe *The Australian Slang Dictionary* 10: *Blue Duck* No good; no money in it.
1902 Mrs Campbell Praed *My Australian Girlhood* 21: 'One evening as he sits smoking outside the hut, without a moment's warning he finds a spear in his chest. 'Dam'd, but he would have been a blue duck if I hadn't ridden up at that very moment and scared the natives off.'
1911 Edward Dyson *Benno, and Some of the Push* 111: In the language of the flat Susie 'got nothing' for the next hour or two. As the pasters worked they exercised their ingenuity in reminding Miss Gannon of what she had lost ... 'Wot price th'opera 'n' the fam'ly jewels,' said Harrerbeller. 'They're a blue duck fer Susie.'
1917 A. B. Paterson *Three Elephant Power* 131: Time and again he had gone out to race when, to use William's own words, it was a blue duck for Bill's chance of keeping afloat, and every time did the gallant race pony pull his owner through.
1926 L. C. E. Gee *Bushtracks and Goldfields* 4–5: His sharp eyes could detect the smallest speck of gold in any of the stone given to him ... and his discards of 'blue ducks' saved much time in the examination of samples.
1954 Tom Ronan *Vision Splendid* 252: 'If they'll step up my expense account to include a stenographer, the secretary's job is yours. Otherwise I'm afraid it's a blue duck.'

blue monge An improvised bush delicacy: N.T.
1951 Ernestine Hill *The Territory* 426: 'blue-monge' of cornflour and currants.

Blue Orchid A member of the R.A.A.F. in World War II, considered to have a more glamorous uniform than the other services: obs.
1943 George Johnston *New Guinea Diary* 76: In the hearing of a Port Moresby digger never call a R.A.A.F. pilot [giving much needed air support] 'Blue Orchid'!
1946 Rohan Rivett *Behind Bamboo* 395: *Blue Orchids*, Army chaffing for air force.

Blues, the 1 In N.S.W., the Newtown Rugby League team (see Bluebags) [f. colours]
1977 *Daily Telegraph* 25 Jan. 30: Newtown ... are ready to shake off their tag of the 'Battling Blues'.
2 The Carlton V.F.L. team
1975 *Sunday Telegraph* 6 Jul. 42: Blues win as Dons brawl.
3 A team representing N.S.W. in state competition
1976 *Sunday Telegraph* 21 Nov. 72: Red faces is order of the day for the Blues.

blue-tongue A shed-hand, rouseabout, or other unskilled worker [f. (*blue-tongue*) lizard]
1943 Baker 12: *Blue tongue* A station rouseabout.
1968 L. Braden *Bullockies* 119: He did not have an off-sider with him; he always drove by himself – they used to call off-siders Fridays or blue-tongues.
1975 Les Ryan *The Shearers* 124: 'Righto, you blue-tongues!' he bellowed out. 'Get stuck into it!'

bluey 1 A blanket [f. colour]
1891 Henry Lawson 'Harry Stephens' *Verse* i 409: Another bushman found him with his 'bluey' wrapped around him.
1918 Bernard Cronin *The Coastlanders* 181: We'd our blueys to cover us.

1924 *Truth* 27 Apr. 6: *Bluey* A blue blanket: a swag.
1936 Archer Russell *Gone Nomad* 61: I was ever ready to roll my bluey* and travel the roads again. *Blanket.
1941 Sarah Campion *Mo Burdekin* 209: To bed they went, wrapped as before in their blueys on the rain-loud verandah.
1958 *Coast to Coast 1957–8* 208: To the pack his wife held ready he added a piece of ground-sheet, a roll of newspaper, a bluey, and a heavy pullover.
2 The swag rolled in the blanket
1886 John Farrell 'My Sundowner' *How He Died* (1913) 60: His swag, the orthodox horse-collar 'bluey'.
1905 A. B. Paterson *The Old Bush Songs* 25n: To hump bluey is to carry one's swag, and the name bluey comes from the blue blankets.
1933 Acland: *Bluey* Swag.
3 A hard-wearing jacket for outdoor work
1977 *Sunday Telegraph* 5 Jun. 27: A tough, all-wool weatherproof jacket could become the new 'uniform' of Sydney wharfies. The jacket is the Tasmanian bluey, first made in Hobart in 1905.
4 A cattle dog
1941 Baker 11: *Bluey* Colloquial name of a cattle-dog widely used in Australia.
5 Nickname for a red-headed person
1918 Harley Matthews *Saints and Soldiers* 48: Bluey's face went as red as his hair.
1944 Lawson Glassop *We Were the Rats* 277: I did not bother to ask which Bluey. Every fellow in the A.I.F. with ginger hair was called Bluey.
1965 Patrick White *Four Plays* 172–3: 'I don't like the red, freckly man!' 'Don't go much on the blueys meself.'
1975 Xavier Herbert *Poor Fellow My Country* 1120: They were calling her *Bluey*, from the copper curls popping out of her maroon cap.

bluey, to hump To carry one's swag, take to the track [f. *bluey*[2]]
1890 Henry Lawson 'Possum' *Verse* i 81: He 'umped his bluey ninety mile

an' kum to Bunglelong.
1906 A. B. Paterson *An Outback Marriage* 147: 'I've got to hump my bluey out of this, and take to the road like any other broken-down old swagman.'
1911 E. M. Clowes *On the Wallaby through Victoria* 278: An expression used for what in England we call 'tramping' is 'going on the wallaby', otherwise, 'humping the swag', or 'the bluey', or 'sundowning'.
1919 W. K. Harris *Outback in Australia* 146: All the ... celebrities of the day were 'on the wallaby', 'humping bluey', and called at his particular station.
1934 Tom Clarke *Marriage at 6 a.m.* 46: *Hump your bluey* – pack up, move on.
see **drum, swag**

board The floor of the wool-shed on which the sheep are shorn
1873 Anthony Trollope *Australia* ed. P. D. Edwards and R. B. Joyce (1967) 156: The floor [of the wool-shed], on which the shearers absolutely work, is called 'the board'.
1908 W. H. Ogilvie *My Life in the Open* 36: A raised floor called 'the board', on which the shearers shear the sheep.

board, boss over the The man supervising the shearing, the contractor
1899 Henry Lawson 'A Rough Shed' *Prose* i 464: And worse words for the boss-over-the-board – behind his back.
1910 C. E. W. Bean *On the Wool Track* 177: The wool-classer, the 'boss-of-the-board', and one of the 'experts' were strolling across to their cottage.

Bob, staggering A newly born calf, hence veal ('bobby veal' in N.Z.) [E. dial. *Staggering Bob* ... A calf just dropped, and unable to stand, killed for veal in Scotland Grose 1785]
1873 Charles de Boos *Congewoi Correspondence* 157: Well, there wasn't nothing handy afore I'd cooled down, and so master Staggerin Bob got orf that time, and I was saved from makin a fooler myself.
1877 Rolf Boldrewood *A Colonial Re-*

former (1890) 343: 'I showed 'em how their cattle was falling off, and at last they offered the lot all round at eight and sixpence – no calves given in, except regular staggering Bobs.'
1917 A. B. Paterson *Three Elephant Power* 51: The very youngest calf, the merest staggering Bob two days old.
1959 Mary Durack *Kings in Grass Castles* 246: They had been forced to dispose of no less than thirteen hundred new-born calves during the trip. It was a complete waste, for stockmen were oddly squeamish about eating veal or 'staggering Bob' as it was known in the cattle camps.

bob (two-bob) in, a See quot. 1931
1931 William Hatfield *Sheepmates* (1946) 172: A bob-in [referring to an episode described thus at 72–3: 'There's too big of a mob fer one man to shout the house on his pat at a zack a pop, so you shove in a deaner a nob and flip the rats an' mice, see? An' the winner clouts on the centre an' weighs in fer the shicker, then rams the bunce down south – that is to say, I forgot you were a new chum – in his kick.' Atherton wondered why someone couldn't have said – 'We subscribe a shilling each, dice for the pool, winner paying out of that for drinks.']
1964 Tom Ronan *Packhorse and Pearling Boat* 178: No one shouted the drinks. The poker dice and box were on the counter and it was 'two bob in and the winner shouts for the mob'.
1969 Lyndall Hadow *Full Cycle* 232: After another bob-in, Buller and Nugget . . . went home.
1975 Les Ryan *The Shearers* 71: 'Well, what's it to be? . . . Two bob in?'
see **Tambaroora**

boco, boko A horse with one eye
1901 'Boko' *The Bulletin Reciter* 157: With his single eye to guide him, very few could live beside him.
1906 A. B. Paterson *An Outback Marriage* 243: 'I'm going to ride the boco.' * *One-eyed horse.

bodger, bodgie *a.* Inferior, worthless, false, counterfeit [f. *bodge* to patch or mend clumsily OED 1552]
1945 Baker 156: *Bodger* Worthless, second-rate (this term is apparently related to English dialect in which *bodge* means to botch or work clumsily). [World War II slang]
1950 *Australian Police Journal* Apr. 111: *Bodger* Unreal, worthless, a fraud.
1951 Frank Hardy *Power Without Glory* 383: This involved the addition of as many more 'bodger' votes as possible.
1965 William Dick *A Bunch of Ratbags* 64: For having accepted the bodgie coin, he would be obliged to come good out of his pay at the end of the day.
1972 John de Hoog *Skid Row Dossier* 106: 'Oh, I gave a bodgy (false) name, and a bodgy last employer – the whole bloody form I filled out was a bodgy.'

bodgie *n.* The Australian equivalent of the Teddy boy: see quots
1950 *Sunday Telegraph* 7 May 47: 'This youth frequents King's Cross milkbars with other young hoodlums and known prostitutes,' Vice Squad Constable Thompson said . . . [The accused] stood in the dock dressed in the bizarre uniform of the 'bodgey' – belted velvet cord jacket, bright blue sports shirt without a tie, brown trousers narrowed at the ankle, shaggy Cornel Wilde haircut.
1958 A. E. Manning *The Bodgie: A Study in Psychological Abnormality* [book title]
1966 Bruce Beaver *You Can't Come Back* 5: A would-be bodgie from Redfern, Sam. About five feet five of tight blue jeans, pea-jacket, long black side-levers, and a bit of the Presley look.
1970 Barry Oakley *A Salute to the Great McCarthy* 65: 'This clean-living country lad! I don't want him ruined by any of your pimply office bodgies, you understand.'

bog see **flybog**

bog in To start energetically on any task; to start to eat with a will ('Two, four, six, eight; Bog in, don't wait' is a mock 'grace')

1916 *The Anzac Book* 164: Vaulting the parapet and bogging into a dinkum bayonet charge.
1920 *Bulletin Book of Humorous Verses* 115: He'd say, 'Bog into Shakespeare, Syd;/He has the English style, no kid.'
1941 Baker 11: *Bog in, to* To eat (2) To take direct action, tackle a job with a will.
1941 Kylie Tennant *The Battlers* 88: 'There's plenty o' stoo', the Stray offered bountifully. 'Bog in for all you're worth.'
1951 Dymphna Cusack and Florence James *Come in Spinner* 360: He ... motioned them to the tray. 'Bog in, it's all on the house.'
1975 Les Ryan *The Shearers* 45: Clarrie stood nearby, munching a lamington, apparently disapproving of the two, four, six, eight, bog in don't wait, business going on.

Bogan shower see **shower**

bogey, bogie (ō) *v. & n.* Bathe, swim [Ab. 1788: Ramson 105]
1830 Robert Dawson *The Present State of Australia* 166: I at length told him we must go, when he said 'Top bit, massa, bogy', (bathe) and he threw himself into the water, where he enjoyed himself as long as I could stay.
1847 Alexander Harris *Settlers and Convicts* ed. C. M. H. Clark (1954) 132: In the cool of the evening has a 'bogie' (bathe) in the river.
1894 G. N. Boothby *On the Wallaby* 246: Then an hour's sharp tennis ... prepared the body for the evening bathe, or bogie as it is usually called, after which comes dinner.
1911 E. S. Sorenson *Life in the Australian Backblocks* 122: It is common to see the whole troop, blacks and whites, marching down to the river with towels for a 'bogey' after their day's ride.
1933 R. B. Plowman *The Man from Oodnadatta* 107: While the team went on the white men remained behind to have a bogey.
1957 R. S. Porteous *Brigalow* 222: I called 'Bogie dogs. Bogie.' The water-hole was only fifty yards away.

1973 Donald Stuart *Morning Star Evening Star* 60: Drinking tea, after a bogey and a good feed.

boggabri 'Fat hen' (*Chenopodium*) a kind of wild spinach valued as anti-scorbutic [see Morris under *Fat-hen*]
1892 Henry Lawson 'The Bush Undertaker' *Prose* i 52: 'We'll get dinner,' he added, glancing at some pots on the fire; 'I can do a bit of doughboy, an' that theer boggabri'll eat like tater-marrer along of the salt meat.'
1910 Henry Lawson 'Native Fruit' *Verse* iii 323: The way to live away from home/That all Bush children know./Cress, boggabri, sap of stringy bark,/And many a leaf and root.
1966 Patrick White *The Solid Mandala* 43: 'Boggabri or red-leg.'

bogghi, boggi (ī) The handpiece of the shears [? f. resemblance to shape of the *bogghi* lizard]
1952 *People* 13 Feb. 12: *Boggi* Handpiece of shears.
1957 D'Arcy Niland *Call Me When the Cross Turns Over* 47: A time in those summers past when a man could take a bogeye and shear two hundred a day.
1963 *Sydney Morning Herald* 17 Aug. 11: For the last ten years Darky's ... renunciation of the 'bogghi' (shearing handpiece) has become a stock joke among his shearing mates.
1975 Les Ryan *The Shearers* 45: 'A man needs a bloody axe, not a boggi.'

boilover An unexpected result in racing, esp. from the favourite not winning
1878 Rolf Boldrewood *An Australian Squire* repr. as *Babes in the Bush* (1900) 175: How often is the favourite amiss or 'nobbled', the rider 'off his head', the certainty a 'boil over'!
c. 1882 *The Sydney Slang Dictionary* 1: *Boilover* Favourites not winning Bookmakers and sporting men out in their calculations.
1904 Nat Gould *In Low Water* 149: The members of Tattersall's has a wholesome dread of 'one of Hickin's hot pots', and were not as a rule inclined to deal speculatively in the hopes of a 'boil-

over'.

1924 *Truth* 27 Apr. 4: One of the biggest boil-overs in the rowing world was Queensland's meritorious win in the interstate eights for the King's Cup at Adelaide yesterday.

1965 Baker 237: *boilover*, a win by a long-priced entrant in a horse or greyhound race, a series of such wins at a race meeting.

1974 John Powers *The Last of the Knucklemen* 21: 'I've seen too many boil-overs to get sucked into mug bets any more.'

1975 *Sunday Telegraph* 8 Sep. 48: Roosters plucked in semi boilover.

boko see **boco**

bolter 1 Runaway convict, bushranger
1844 Louisa Meredith *Notes and Sketches of New South Wales* 132: During our stay at Bathurst, a party of the mounted police went in search of a very daring gang of bush-rangers, or, as they are sometimes called, 'bolters'.

c. **1845** James Tucker *Ralph Rashleigh* (1952) 187: At length one of the bullock-drivers asked what the prisoners were charged with, and McCoy replied, 'They are *bolters* (runaway convicts). They belonged to that mob of Foxley the bushranger's.'

1865 J. F. Mortlock *Experiences of a Convict* (1965) 221: Three or four 'old hands' were pointed out to me as Tasmanian 'bolters', who had made their escape to England and been for another crime again transported.

2 An outsider (applied more recently to one who wins or succeeds)
1941 Baker 35: *Hasn't the bolter's* Used of a person or race-horse that has no chance at all in a contest or situation.

1973 *Sydney Morning Herald* 17 Sep. 1: A South Coast publican who continually spurns the big money of Sydney Rugby League was the 'bolter' in the Australian team announced last night to tour France and England.

1975 *Sun-Herald* 14 Sep. 42: Books cheer as 'bolter' gets home.

bomb An old or dilapidated motor-car

1950 *Australian Police Journal* Apr. 110: *Bomb, A* A dud – usually refers to second-hand motor vehicles in poor mechanical shape.

1958 Christopher Koch *The Boys in the Island* 69: 'Jake's gunna go out – taking his old bomb, so we'll get a free ride.'

1962 Gavin Casey *Amid the Plenty* 58: The car, they called it! Well, he never wanted to be seen in that old bomb, that was for sure.

1970 Patrick White *The Vivisector* 470: Italians from Temora who are here in a bomb they bought, they want to take us for a ride.

bomber, brown see **brown bomber**

Bombers, the The Essendon V.F.L. team [f. proximity to aerodrome]

bombora (o͞r) A submerged reef, esp. near the foot of a cliff [Ab.]
1933 *Bulletin* 24 May 27: 'Bombora' is an aboriginal word applied to the high-crested wave which breaks ... over submerged rocks near the coastline.

1945 Baker 224: *bomboora* ... a dangerous reef of rocks usually found at the foot of cliffs.

1975 *Sydney Morning Herald* 1 Dec. 2: Five men were tossed about in the darkness on a small liferaft for two hours yesterday after their yacht struck a reef and later sank. The mishap occurred about 3 a.m. when the yacht ... struck a bombora about a kilometre off Norah Head.

Bondi, to give someone To beat someone up: *obs.* [? f. a fracas between larrikins and the police at Bondi on Boxing Day 1884]
1890 *Truth* 19 Oct. 3: Suppose a live policeman is on the ground while the gay and festive members of a 'push' are 'giving him Bondi'. Ibid. 16 Nov. 7: The scribe ... accepted a hint to take his bloomin' hook. The hint was the picking up by one of the young gentlemen of an empty bottle, and the somewhat uncertain attitude of two or three others, who looked fully competent and

perfectly willing to give him Bondi at a moment's notice.

1951 Dal Stivens *Jimmy Brockett* 67: Then Snowy got Maxie in a corner and began to give him Bondi.

1973 Ruth Park *The Companion Guide to Sydney* 415: 'Bondi' also means the heavy warrior's club, and the word was incorporated in a now-forgotten fragment of larrikins' cant – 'I'll give you Bondi!' meaning a severe bashing.

Bondi tram, to shoot through like a To make a speedy departure [f. trams running from Sydney to Bondi beach, discontinued in 1961]

1951 Seaforth Mackenzie *Dead Men Rising* 53: He called the rolls . . . looked up to check the inevitable comments from the ranks: 'Shot through like a Bondi tram.' 'Not 'ere today, Sar'Major.'

1956 Kylie Tennant *The Honey Flow* 151: 'We collected Mike from where he and Hertz was mixing it, and we went through like a Bondi tram.'

1962 John Morrison *Twenty-Three* 192: 'He shot through like a Bondi tram the minute the telegram arrived.'

1972 Geoff Morley *Jockey Rides Honest Race* 65: I punched him in the mouth and shot through like a Bondi tram.

1974 *Sunday Telegraph* 29 Sep. 11: The catch-phrase to 'shoot through like a Bondi tram' will have a fresh meaning when Sydney restores its city tramway system.

bone, to (point the bone) 1 In aboriginal 'magic', to will an enemy to die 2 Among whites, to place a 'jinx' or hoodoo on someone, single someone out with this purpose

1943 Donald Friend *Gunner's Diary* 21: The bone is pointed at myself and a few others. We are to be transferred to a draft battery.

1951 Dymphna Cusack and Florence James *Come In Spinner* 367: 'I just thought you been off the last coupla mornin's, you mightn't be too good like.' Guinea poked her in the ribs. 'Pointing the bone at me are you, you old witch?' [implying pregnancy]

1965 *Daily Telegraph* 27 Apr. 2: Harold

Wilson has pointed the bone at the House of Lords. If they don't pull their heads in, he'll chop them off.

1970 Barry Oakley *A Salute to the Great McCarthy* 28: 'I am a bit older and I do understand. You're in no position to point the bone.'

1974 Morris West *Harlequin* 15: When you tell a banker that there are anomalies in his accounts, it is as if you point a bone at him or chant a mortal curse over his head.

bonfire night As for 'cracker night' q.v.

1976 *Sydney Morning Herald* 12 Jun. 36: Police had warned against the misuse of firecrackers at traditional Queen's Birthday bonfire night celebrations tonight.

bong see **bung**

bonzer Excellent, deserving admiration: *obsolescent* [origin uncertain]

1904 *Bulletin* 14 Apr. 29: A bonser or bonster is comparatively superior to a bons.

1906 Edward Dyson *Fact'ry 'Ands* 246: 'He had er dull eye, 'n' er vacant face, 'n' no chin, his face jist slippin' off where his chin should iv come in, but 'e had er bonzer nose.'

1915 C. J. Dennis *The Songs of a Sentimental Bloke* 13: The air is like a long, cool swig o' beer, / The bonzer smell o' flow'rs is on the breeze.

1919 W. H. Downing *Digger Dialects* 12: *Bonzer* Good.

1925 Seymour Hicks *Hullo Australia* 88: 'Strange sayings the Australians have, sir, don't they? I asked Davis this evening what the weather would be like when we reached the other side and he said "Bonser".'

1934 Vance Palmer *Sea and Spinifex* 117: 'A bonza night!' she said with drowsy enthusiasm.

1947 John Morrison *Sailors Belong Ships* 72: 'I've got a bonzer little joint not ten minutes from the station.'

1969 Hal Porter *Southerly* 11: For me an anachronism mars all. An author should not have . . . 1957 Australian children saying, 'Bonzer!'

bontoger, bontosher, bonzarina (almost nonce-words)
1904 *Bulletin* 14 Apr. 29: A bontosher is a real slasher ... A bonsterina is a female bonster. Ibid. 5 May 29: 'Bonster' is a corruption of 'Bontojer', pronounced Bontodger, and 'Bontojer' is a corruption of the two French words *bon* and *toujous.*
1934 Thomas Wood *Cobbers* (1961) 212: 'She was a little bonzarina.'
see **boshter**

boo-eye, the The remote rural areas: a New Zealandism, rarely encountered in Australia, equivalent to the Australian 'Woop Woop' or 'never never'
1955 D'Arcy Niland *The Shiralee* 67: Could have been worse. He could have been out there in the boo-eye, thrusting his body into the wind and rain, getting blown about like an old moll at a plonk party.

Booligal Town in western N.S.W. given a place in folklore by A. B. Paterson's poem 'Hay and Hell and Booligal'
1901 *The Bulletin Reciter* 193: Hot? Great Scott!/It was Hell, with some improvements, worse than Booligal a lot!
1902 A. B. Paterson *Rio Grande's Last Race* 40: 'Oh, send us to our just reward/In Hay or Hell, but, gracious Lord,/Deliver us from Booligal!'
[1916] Oliver Hogue *Trooper Bluegum at the Dardanelles* 58: It was generally thought that he had spent some time in hell, or Booligal, so familiarly did he speak of the infernal regions.
1953 *Caddie A Sydney Barmaid* 172: He told me he'd just come from Booligal, and asked me if I knew where it was ... 'Surely you've heard of Hay, hell and Booligal?' I remembered then. It was a place of heat, dust and flies.
1955 John Morrison *Black Cargo* 11: We've cursed the Federation from Hell to Booligal for all the muck they've tossed out at us.

boomah, boomer 1 A very large kangaroo (*Macropus giganteus*) [f. *boomer* anything very large of its kind EDD]
1830 *Hobart Town Almanack* 110: We saw a huge kangaroo. ... What did we not feel when Juno [the hound] snapped the boomah's haunches and he turned round to offer battle.
1845 R. Howitt *Australia Felix* 273: A boomer, or large forester Kangaroo.
2 Anything of exceptional size
1843 Charles Rowcroft *Tales of the Colonies* iii 97: 'There's one! and there's another! he's a regular boomah!' [describing a flea]
1896 Edward Dyson *Rhymes from the Mines* 102: It was said that a nugget – a boomer – / Had been found by the Chows in our shaft.
1926 'Alpha' *Reminiscences of the Goldfields* 21: 'What do you make of her?' said the skipper. 'Oh, sir, she is a boomer,' said I, 'she's 500 feet long.' [describing a whale]
1936 Miles Franklin *All That Swagger* 413: 'Old Robert's overdraft must be a boomer.'
1956 Tom Ronan *Moleskin Midas* 114: 'Fights you're talking about! Well, I just seen a boomer!'
1974 *Sydney Morning Herald* 5 Jun. 17: The English Rugby League centre kicked several goals from the 25 metre mark on the sideline, and one boomer from right on the halfway mark.

boomerang To move like a boomerang; to recoil
1901 Henry Lawson 'The Mystery of Dave Regan' *Prose* i 327: He said that to the horse as it boomeranged off again and broke away through the scrub.
1945 Kylie Tennant *Ride on Stranger* 63: Money must boomerang back to his hand or it never left it in the first place.
1956 J. T. Lang *I Remember* 181: In the end bigotry boomeranged on its chief sponsor.

boomerangs, he could sell ~ to the blacks A persuasive personality
1974 Peter Kenna *A Hard God* 23: 'He's a first class con man. He could sell boomerangs to the blacks.'

boondy A stone, pebble (W.A.); a throwing stick (N.S.W.) [Ab.]

1952 T. A. G. Hungerford *The Ridge and the River* 94: 'See that bastard, practising grenade-throwing with bits of boondies?'

1957 Randolph Stow *The Bystander* 132: 'He's chucking boondies on the roof!'

1964 W. S. Ramson *The Currency of Aboriginal Words in Australian English* 15: In New South Wales, *boondee* or *bundy*, a throwing stick.

boong An Australian aboriginal; New Guinea native; any Asiatic: *derogatory* [Ab.]

1941 Kylie Tennant *The Battlers* 123: 'These boangs are all too matey,' Thirty-Bob grumbled. 'If a bit of trouble starts, it's a case of one in, all in.'

1943 George Johnston *New Guinea Diary* 186: The boys from the Middle East called them [the natives] 'wogs' at first, because it was their name for the Arabs. Soon they learnt the New Guinea army term, which is 'boong'. Before they have been there long they are calling them 'sport', which seems to be the second A.I.F.'s equivalent for 'digger'.

1946 Rohan Rivett *Behind Bamboo* 395: *Boong* Any Asiatic or coloured person. *Boongs with boots on* Japs.

1959 Xavier Herbert *Seven Emus* 58: 'He might have a lot of boong in him, but he's also got a lot of the white man.'

1966 Peter Mathers *Trap* 131: For several seconds she stared at him. Was it proper for her to serve a boong?

1976 Dorothy Hewett *Bon-bons and Roses for Dolly* 53: 'Give it back to the Boongs, me ol' Dad useta say.'

boot, chewy on see **chewy**

boot, put in the To kick an opponent when he is down; to be ruthless in pressing an advantage

1915 C. J. Dennis *The Songs of a Sentimental Bloke* 42: 'It's me or you!' 'e 'owls, an' wiv a yell, / Plunks Tyball through the gizzard wiv 'is sword, / 'Ow

I ongcored! / 'Put in the boot!' I sez. 'Put in the boot!'

1923 Steele Rudd *On Emu Creek* 174: They ... butted into him, played havoc with his clothes, threw him heavily every time he tried to rise, and put the boot into him.

1939 Kylie Tennant *Foveaux* 247: 'Give it to 'em! Put in the boot, boys!' the onlookers encouraged.

1946 Dal Stivens *The Courtship of Uncle Henry* 75: Anyone could see he was as mad as a cut snake about everything and wanting to put the boot in.

1950 Jon Cleary *Just Let Me Be* 67: He didn't want trouble, but he couldn't turn his back on savagery – a fight was anybody's business when someone started to put the boot in.

1962 Gavin Casey *Amid the Plenty* 79: 'You stand up to my old lady a bit, if you have to. If you let her get you down she'll put in the boot, don't you worry.'

1975 *Guardian* [London] 5 May 6: Anti-Marketeers put financial boot in.

boots and all An all-out effort; 'no holds barred'

1953 Dymphna Cusack *Southern Steel* 260: 'When you do a thing you go into it boots and all.'

1968 *Australian* 4 Apr. 8: On this view, 1969 would see a rejuvenated LBJ in power and an American boots-and-all war in North Vietnam.

1974 John Power *The Last of the Knucklemen* 72: 'You lift your arse off that floor, mate, an' I'm gonna come wadin' into you – boots an' all!'

1975 *Sydney Morning Herald* 3 Jan. 6: His political opponents see him [Sir Robert Askin] as an old-style 'boots-and-all' political fighter, but his image with those who have worked under him . . . is of a tolerant boss.

bo peep, have a Take a look at

1944 Lawson Glassop *We Were the Rats* 79: 'Let's take a bo peep at what they got in the canteen.'

borak, borack Nonsense, gammon, humbug [Ab.]

1845 Thomas McCombie *Arabin, or, The Adventures of a Colonist* 273: *Borack*, Gammon, nonsense.
1885 *The Australasian Printers' Keepsake* 124: Oh, we were bad – no borack, mind, boys.
1961 Tom Ronan *Only a Short Walk* 111: The chief steward was full of borack . . . He wasn't a very good liar, this steward.

borack, to poke ~ at To ridicule, make fun of
1885 *The Australasian Printers' Keepsake* 75: On telling him my adventures, how Bob in my misery had 'poked borack' at me, he said – 'You were had.'
1893 J. A. Barry *Steve Brown's Bunyip* 21: 'They're always a-poking borack an' a-chiackin' o' me over in the hut.'
1915 Louis Stone *Betty Wayside* 268: 'If I catch anybody poking borack at my get-up, they'll hear some fancy English!'
1936 William Hatfield *Big Timber* 245: 'Poke borack at me, would you?' he snarled.
1947 Vance Palmer *Hail Tomorrow* 47: 'For God's sake, leave me alone, Jim. You're always poking borak at me!'
1962 Dymphna Cusack *Picnic Races* 22: 'Makes me ropeable that feller does, poking borak every time he gets a chance.'
1975 Xavier Herbert *Poor Fellow My Country* 349: 'The old boy had been poking borak at him about anthropology.'
see **mullock**

bore it up them Equivalent to 'sock it to them' [Army slang from World War II]
1951 Eric Lambert *The Twenty Thousand Thieves* 178: 'A provost I got into a blue with in Tel Aviv was barkin' the orders. Christ! Did that bastard bore it up me?'
1952 T. A. G. Hungerford *The Ridge and the River* 198: 'Listen to that strafing. Bore it up 'em, you little beauties!'
1959 David Forrest *The Last Blue Sea* 84: 'Into it!' he yelled at Three Platoon.

'Bore it into them!'
1963 Lawson Glassop *The Rats in New Guinea* 128: 'Stand fast, Aussies, and bore it up 'em.'

bore-casing Macaroni: N.T.
1951 Ernestine Hill *The Territory* 426: 'Bore-casing', macaroni.

bored or punched, he doesn't know if he's A state of stupidity or confusion [Australian version of English and Canadian 'he doesn't know if his arsehole's bored or punched': Partridge]
1952 T. A. G. Hungerford *The Ridge and the River* 120: 'They didn't know whether they were punched or bored, after that, until we got out again at the crossing, where you marked on the map.'
1959 Dorothy Hewett *Bobbin Up* 125: 'You're just a mad militant Snow. You wouldn't know if you was punched, bored or . . .'
1962 Stuart Gore *Down the Golden Mile* 301: 'The noise and the bloody flash . . . he won't know whether his stern's bored or countersunk!'

Borroloola sandwich See quot.: *jocular* [f. place-name in N.T.]
1951 Ernestine Hill *The Territory* 426: A 'Borroloola sandwich' was a goanna between two sheets of bark.

boshter, bosker Equivalent to bonzer, but never attaining the same currency: *obs.*
1906 Edward Dyson *Fact'ry 'Ands* 1: This was the fifth time Benno had declaimed on the 'boshter' qualities of the unknown.
1908 Henry Fletcher *Dads and Dan between Smokes* 50: Oh the North is a bosker country.
1915 C. J. Dennis *The Songs of a Sentimental Bloke* 14: The little birds is chirpin' in the nest, / The parks an' gardings is a bosker sight. Ibid. 13: Soft in the moon; such *boshter* eyes!
1916 *The Anzac Book* 36: 'A boshter* night for a walk', I remarked. *Bosker, boshter, bonzer – Australian slang for splendid.

1925 Arthur Wright *A Good Recovery* 52: 'What a bosker pair of earrings they'll make.'
1959 Gerard Hamilton *Summer Glare* 53: 'Gee, it's bosker, ain't it?' [set in 1920s]

boss cocky see **cocky**

boss over the board see **board**

bot *n.* A sponger, persistent borrower [? f. the bot-fly, which 'bites']
1919 W. H. Downing *Digger Dialects* 13: *Bott* (1) A cadger; (2) a useless person; (3) a hanger-on.
1924 *Truth* 27 Apr. 6: *Bott* Person who borrows.
1942 Leonard Mann *The Go-Getter* 124: 'Get out, you bot.' Chris ordered him [the beggar] and got up.
1960 A. W. Upfield *Bony and the Kelly Gang* 108–9: 'He says that only five per cent of first-class travellers going overseas pay their own fares. Says the other ninety-five per cent have their fares paid by the tax-payers. They're just bots. Politicians and top civil servants and marketing board people.'
1965 Eric Lambert *The Long White Night* 136: 'He had nothing left to buy schooners for bots like you.'

bot *v.* To borrow, sponge on
1934 *Bulletin* 7 Nov. 46: 'How many's that, sir?' He gazed rheumily into space. 'Six it is; that's three beers I owe y'. Settle up when I sell me next picture.' The notebook went back into his pocket and he sighed with relief. 'Well, that's settled. Never did like *botting* on a bloke.'
1944 Alan Marshall *These Are My People* 174: 'If you get plenty later I'll bot a cigarette off the lot of you.'
1962 Criena Rohan *The Delinquents* 105: Lola, she said, was a botting, bludging little bastard.
1965 John Beede *They Hosed Them Out* 156: To prove that she wasn't on the bot she bought me a drink.

Botany Bay Name applied in the eighteenth and earlier nineteenth century to the penal settlement in Australia (actually Port Jackson), and to Australia as a whole [f. the landing place named by Cook in 1770]
c. 1790 'Botany Bay, A New Song' repr. in Hugh Anderson *Farewell to Old England* (1964) 35: Who live by fraud, cheating, vile tricks, and foul play, / Should all be sent over to Botany Bay.
1819 Barron Field *First Fruits of Australian Poetry* (1941) 3: 'Botany-Bay Flowers' [poem title]
1859 John Lang *Botany Bay, or True Stories of the Early Days of Australia* [book title]

bottle-oh An itinerant dealer in empty bottles [f. the cry]
1906 Edward Dyson *Fact'ry 'Ands* 217: Half-a-dozen of them would have died for the bibulous comp. despite the bottle-o's stock garnered in the trouser fringe at his boot heels.
1908 Henry Fletcher *Dads and Dan between Smokes* 127: He'll bail up ther fust bottle-oh he meets, an' ask him who lets out vans.
1913 Henry Lawson 'Benno and his Old 'Uns' *Prose* i 803: Benno, a Sussex Street bottle-o . . . was an angry bottle-o that day.
1917 A. B. Paterson *Three Elephant Power* 138: Sometimes out in the back yard of their palatial mansion they hand the empty bottles, free of charge, to a poor broken-down bottle-O.
1935 Kylie Tennant *Tiburon* 7: Battered old motor-trucks, bottle-oh carts . . . paused here for the night.
1943 Margaret Trist *In the Sun* 99: A bottle-o followed him, crying cheerily, 'Bottles, bottles, any empty bottles, bottles, bottles, any kind of bottles.'
1962 Criena Rohan *The Delinquents* 278: They packed their clothes and sold the mattresses to the Bottle-oh who made his weekly round that afternoon.
1970 Patrick White *The Vivisector* 39: Tommy Sullivan said that Hurt Duffield was the son of a no-hope pommy bottle-o down their street.

bottler Someone outstanding in his class, for good qualities or bad [cf. the expression 'His blood's worth bottling']

1876 Rolf Boldrewood *A Colonial Reformer* (1890) 95: 'He's a bottler, that's what he [a horse] is, and if you ever go for to sell him, you'll be sorry for it.'

1952 T. A. G. Hungerford *The Ridge and the River* 122: 'The old bastard! The old hooer! What a bloody bottler!'

1969 Osmar White *Under the Iron Rainbow* 142: 'He's a little bottler astride a horse is that bloke,' he said, 'but he's a bloody poor manager.'

1972 Alexander Macdonald *The Ukelele Player under the Red Lamp* 33: The theatre rang with cries of 'Good on yer, Mo!' 'You little bottler!' and other endearments.

1975 Rodney Hall *A Place Among People* 109: 'I might get drowned in this weather.' 'Yes, it's brewing up for a real bottler.'

bottling

1957 Ray Lawler *Summer of the Seventeenth Doll* 35: 'They made Dowdie ganger in his place, and what a bottling job he done.'

bottom In mining, to reach the level at which either gold will be found, or the mine will prove a failure; to succeed or fail in any enterprise

1853 John Sherer *The Gold Finder of Australia* 181: Having bottomed our hole (the bottom is generally pipeclay), we pick up a good deal of gold – suppose four ounces – and return to our tent satisfied with our day's work.

1864 James Armour *The Diggings, the Bush and Melbourne* 8: We ... arrived too late for anything better than an uphill claim, which we bottomed at about one third of the depth that gold might be expected at.

1880 Rolf Boldrewood *The Miner's Right* (1890) 55: 'Bottomed a duffer, by gum, not the colour itself, no mor'n on the palm o' my hand.'

1903 Joseph Furphy *Such is Life* (1944) 261: Bottoming on gold this time, she buried the old man within eighteen months, and paid probate duty on £25,000.

1942 Sarah Campion *Bonanza* 210: 'But there's lots o' fellers as hasn't bottomed on payable dirt.'

1969 *Southerly* 61: Towards the end of his life he must have had the feeling that he had 'bottomed on mullock'.

bounce, the The beginning of an Australian Rules game, equivalent to 'the kick-off' in other codes [because the umpire starts the game by bouncing the ball]

Bourke, back of Beyond the most remote town in north-west N.S.W.; in the remote and uncivilized regions generally

1898 W. H. Ogilvie *Fair Girls and Gray Horses* 161: 'At the Back o' Bourke' [poem title]

1919 R. J. Cassidy *The Gipsy Road* 88: 'I could dump you into the desert at the Back o' Bourke, and you'd be only a speck.'

1933 A. B. Paterson *The Animals Noah Forgot* (1970) 33: The Boastful Crow and the Laughing Jack / Were telling tales of the outer back: / 'I've just been travelling far and wide, / At the back of Bourke and the Queensland side.'

1959 Gerard Hamilton *Summer Glare* 89: I took the attitude that if girls didn't like to dance with me ... they could go to Bourke or buggery.

1961 G. R. Turner *A Stranger and Afraid* 95: 'To you there is the City, and all else is back o' Bourke.'

1970 Alexander Buzo *The Front Room Boys* in Penguin *Plays* 38: 'I helped open up the bush, mate, I was out the back o' Bourke when you were a dirty look.'

Bourke, no work at see **Tallarook**

Bourke Street, not to know whether it's Tuesday or The Victorian equivalent of not knowing (in N.S.W.) whether it's Pitt Street or Christmas q.v.: a state of confusion or stupidity

1952 T. A. G. Hungerford *The Ridge and the River* 4: 'You waste too much time on the dope. He don't know whether it's Tuesday or Bourke Street.'

1971 Ivan Southall *Josh* 119: 'I told

you he was dumb. He doesn't know whether it's Tuesday or Bourke Street.'

bovril Euphemism for 'bull': *obs.* [f. trade name for a beef extract]
1937 *Bulletin of Australian English Association* July 2: A few years ago most young men here said Bovril! whenever they found anything unimpressive, and University students certainly made good use of a song, 'It all sounds like Bovril to me.'
1950 Brian James *The Advancement of Spencer Button* 273: 'Bovril, if you ask me,' said Mr O'Leary ... 'Hooey!' said Mr Mooney complacently. 'Eye-wash!' said Mr Sterling bitterly.

bower bird A person with the habit of collecting and treasuring odds and ends [f. the bird's habits]
1941 Kylie Tennant *The Battlers* 233: George the Bower-bird ... had the habit of searching camps for discarded trifles or bits of rubbish ... old boots or clothes that the travellers threw away he gathered up as though they were priceless treasures.
1953 *Sydney Morning Herald* 3 Jan. 6: Those eccentric bower birds, the students of Australiana, are uttering shrill little chirrups of joy.
1955 Mary Durack *Kings in Grass Castles* 293: 'The Bowerbird', a quaint old kleptomaniac ... who filched odds and ends from the miners' tents that would be tactfully retrieved when he was not at home.
1966 Bruce Beaver *You Can't Come Back* 164: He put it back in his pocket, just like the old bower-bird he was.
1973 Patrick White *Southerly* 139: All my novels are an accumulation of detail. I'm a bit of a bower-bird.
bower birding
1941 Kylie Tennant *The Battlers* 386: 'I don't want him bower-birding round this camp,' Mrs Tyrell complained.
1951 Ernestine Hill *The Territory* 443: *Bower-birdin'* Picking up unconsidered trifles for one's own use or camp.

Bowral, the boy from Sir Donald Bradman [b. Cootamundra, but his cricketing career began in Bowral N.S.W.]
1962 R. J. Hoare *The Boy from Bowral* [title of biography]
1968 *The Barry Humphries Book of Innocent Austral Verse* 43: The boy from Bowral hits four after four.

bowyangs 1 A string tied round the trouser-leg below the knee [f. *bowy-yanks* leather leggings EDD]
1893 *Warracknabeal Herald* 22 Sep.: The two straps used to hitch the lower part of labourers' trousers are 'boyangs'. [OED]
1907 James Green *The Selector* 10: His moleskin trousers were tied below the knee with boyangs of string.
1924 *Truth* 27 Apr. 6: *Bowyangs* straps or string tied below the knee, outside the trousers, to give the leg freedom.
2 Applied derisively to anything rustic, clownish, out-of-date
1945 *Southerly* ii 14: The story is Romeo and Juliet in bowyangs, set in the Australian countryside.
1969 Don Whitington *The House Will Divide* ix: Menzies ... was aided by the stubborn and intransigent attitudes of Labor leaders like Evatt, Ward and Calwell when it became obvious that Labor's bowyang days were past.
1972 A. A. Calwell *Be Just and Fear Not* 257: Anti-Labor parties have their troubles, too, but being composed of well-bred, middle-class, properly educated people who are concerned with the preservation of the status quo, they are better able to reconcile their personal and other difficulties that those possessing what conservatives have called 'bowyang' mentalities.

box see glory box

box *n.* 1 The female genitals [listed by Partridge as 'low English and Australian: C20']
1949 Alan Marshall *How Beautiful Are Thy Feet* 150: 'I believe Leila's running hot in the box,' said Sadie.
1972 Geoff Morley *Jockey Rides Honest Race* 38: 'Say, she's not real bad after all.' 'Nice big boobs.' 'Nice big box, too, I bet.'

1974 David Ireland *Burn* 60: 'Post Office? I know where she gets to and it's no post office. She's got the box and they all post with her.'
1975 *Australian Graffiti* ed. R. Ellis and I. Turner [32]: I've lost me virginity. Never mind long as you've got the box it came in!
2 The protector worn by sportsmen, the 'rupture box'
1974 Keith Stackpole *Not Just for Openers* 45: Once, I was hit in the box during a one-day match; an agonizing blow that left me crook for four days. A supporter for the opposing team shouted, 'Weak Australian sod, get up.'
3 A mixing of flocks of sheep which should be kept separate; a blunder, esp. in the expression 'make a box of'
1870 Rolf Boldrewood 'Shearing in Riverina' *Town and Country Journal* 29 Oct. 10: This distinguished them from other sheep in the neighbourhood, in case of a 'box' or mixing of flocks, not always to be avoided where so many thousands and tens of thousands are on the march.
1941 Baker 13: *Box* A mistake or confusion, e.g. 'to make a box of something': to muddle.

box *v.* To mix flocks of sheep which should be kept separate; to make a mess of something
1873 Rolf Boldrewood 'The Fencing of Wanderowna' repr. in *A Romance of Canvas Town* (1898) 69: Great was the bleating and apparent confusion – two flocks incontinently 'boxed', or mixed together.
1903 Joseph Furphy *Such is Life* (1944) 282: 'Tell him a lot o' his sheep was boxed with ours in the Boree Paddick.'
1905 *The Old Bush Songs* ed. A. B. Paterson 70: If the heavenly hosts get boxed now, / As mobs most always will, / Who'll cut 'em out like William, / Or draft on a camp like Bill?
1919 W. K. Harris *Outback in Australia* 154: The boundary rider must take heed to his fences ... or trouble may result in the straying of sheep or the 'boxing' of flocks.
1934 Mary Gilmore *Old Days: Old Ways* (1963) 97: In the unfenced states of the newly settled country sheep boxed and then had to be sorted out.
1960 *Sydney Morning Herald* 19 Jul. 1: Thurber's moral is Those who live in grass houses shouldn't stow thrones. Emily boxed it.

box of birds Equivalent to 'in good spirits': N.Z. rather than Australian
1951 Dal Stivens *Jimmy Brockett* 120: I was feeling as happy as a box of birds.
1955 D'Arcy Niland *The Shiralee* 122: 'I had a mate, but he got himself pinched. And just quietly, I been a box o' birds ever since.'
1966 G. W. Turner *The English Language in Australia and New Zealand* 136–7: A young English woman who had just arrived in New Zealand shared a cabin on an inter-island ferry with a woman whose conversation in the evening consisted only of the words, 'I feel a bit crook.' In the morning, asked how she was, the stranger replied, 'Oh, box of birds, now.'

box (bag), out of the Exceptional, outstanding
1926 *Sun* 29 Jul. 1: Two out of the box. These Siamese cats are just looking at the world from the box in which they travelled on the Comorin. [caption to photograph]
1941 *Coast to Coast* 63: 'You talk about it as if 'aving kids is somethin' out of the box.'
1953 Dymphna Cusack *Southern Steel* 29: Come to think of it, both his brothers were something out of the box.
1961 Tom Ronan *Only a Short Walk* 135: She was something out of the bag, was Hetty.
1975 *Sun-Herald* 9 Nov. 111: To be frank, the novel is nothing out of the box, and neither is the movie.

box seat, in the In the most favoured position (to succeed, control the situation) [f. the driver's seat on a coach]
1949 Lawson Glassop *Lucky Palmer* 116: 'I jumped him away smartly and

had him in the box seat all the way. Cantering just behind Lovely Rose and Murragum at the turn, he was.'

1957 Judah Waten *Shares in Murder* 117: 'They'll do Fenton-Lobby favours now and again, and Fenton'll repay them when he's in the box seat.'

1977 *Australian* 4 Jan. 6: With 15 overs and 56 runs required to win, Australia was in the box seat.

break it down A plea to desist from or to moderate some action; an expression of disbelief or disagreement; i.e. 'Give over', 'Come off it'

1944 Lawson Glassop *We Were the Rats* 193: 'There's no other bastard in the world can talk to me like that. For Christ's sake break it down or I'll lose me grip on meself. I'm tellin' ya now. Break it down, see.'

1955 D'Arcy Niland *The Shiralee* 60: 'I'd have been just asking for more trouble and it would have been signing your death-warrant.' 'Ah, break it down,' Macauley said.

1961 Hugh Atkinson *Low Company* 58: The barman was worried about the noise and kept saying uselessly, 'Now, now, blokes, break it down,' and 'Fair go there, fellars.'

1966 Betty Collins *The Copper Crucible* 18: 'You're not going to refuse to talk to everyone who doesn't agree with your political beliefs?' 'Break it down, mate.'

break out Used of the discovery of a goldfield and the 'rush' following

1856 Frederick Sinnett *The Fiction Fields of Australia* ed. C. H. Hadgraft (1966) 36–7: South Australia, at the time when the Victorian gold fields 'broke out', as the common phrase runs, presented a most remarkable social aspect.

1882 A. J. Boyd *Old Colonials* 130: 'I was out prospectin' on the Palmer just after it broke out.'

1901 Rolf Boldrewood *In Bad Company* 30: Labour was scarce, owing to the Coolgardie goldfield having broken out.

Breaker, the Harry Morant (1865–

1902): a pen-name derived from his skill as a horseman and horse-breaker

breeze, bat the see **bat the breeze**

breezer A fart (juvenile)

1973 Patrick White *The Eye of the Storm* 380: 'And lets breezers, as if he didn't know there was anybody else in the room.'

1974 Gerald Murnane *Tamarisk Row* 91: Barry Launder has ordered every boy to write in his composition *at the picnic I let a breezer in my pants,* or else be bashed to smithereens after school.

brick £10 Used most often in gambling, and esp. in the expression 'London to a brick' q.v.

c. **1914** A. B. Paterson 'Races and Racing in Australia' in *The World of Banjo Paterson* ed. C. Semmler (1967) 324: 'Pop it down, gents, if yer don't put down a brick you can't pick up a castle.'

1949 Lawson Glassop *Lucky Palmer* 103: 'Tiger' ... slipped a ten pound note into his hand. 'Here's a brick,' he said in his lifeless voice.

1963 Frank Hardy *Legends from Benson's Valley* 151: Col took the ten bricks down to the Unemployed Workers headquarters and gave it to Tom Rogers before his thirst got the better of his principles.

1975 Les Ryan *The Shearers* 69: Moody flashed a roll of notes, peeled one off and handed it to Tricum. 'Put this brick on for me.'

brickfielder A wind carrying dust with it, originally from Brickfield Hill in Sydney. Confused by Morris with the 'southerly buster' or 'southerly' q.v.

1833 W. H. Breton *Excursions in New South Wales and Van Diemen's Land* 293: It sometimes happens [in Sydney] that a change takes place from a hot wind to a 'brickfielder', on which occasions the thermometer has been known to fall ... from above 100 degrees to 80 degrees! A brickfielder is a southerly wind, and takes its local name from the circumstances of its blowing over, and bringing into town the flames of a large brickfield. [Morris]

1839 W. H. Leigh *Reconnoitering Voyages, Travels, and Adventures in the new Colony of South Australia* 184: Whirlwinds of sand ... come rushing upon the traveller, half blinding and choking him ... The inhabitants [of Sydney] call these miseries 'Brickfielders', but why they do so I am unable to divine, probably, because they are in their utmost vigour on a certain hill here, where bricks are made. [Morris]

1843 John Hood *Australia and the East* 71: A sudden storm had arisen; we were quite unprepared and everybody [on board ship] was alarmed. It was one of the violent and dangerous squalls so frequent off this coast, which are called brickfielders, and came suddenly right off the land without warning. Ibid. 72: The sun this morning shines through a thick dust, which, as well as the wind which sets it in motion, is called a brickfielder.

1853 C. R. Read *What I Heard, Saw and Did at the Australian Goldfields* 38: The weather towards December, [on the Turon goldfields, N.S.W.] and for two or three months following was overpoweringly hot, and from the number of people travelling to and fro, together with the stuff thrown up from the holes caused one continual dust, and when the 'brickfielders'* came on, they could hardly be faced from the sharp quartz and gravel that was flying about nearly blinding you; this was generally followed by a tremendous thunderstorm, with a deluge of rain. *Heavy squalls.

1859 Frank Fowler *Southern Lights and Shadows* 87–8: The 'Southerly Buster', as this change is called, generally comes ... early in the evening. A cloud of dust – they call it, in Sydney, a 'brickfielder' – thicker than any London fog, heralds its approach ... In a minute the temperature will sink fifty or sixty degrees.

1861 H. W. Wheelwright *Bush Wanderings of a Naturalist* 231: In Melbourne a hot-wind day is called a 'brickfielder', on account of the dust,

which darkens the sky.

1865 Henry Kendall 'A Death in the Bush' *Poetical Works* ed. T. T. Reed (1966) 85: So comes the Southern gale at evenfall /(The swift 'brickfielder' of the local folk)/About the streets of Sydney, when the dust/Lies burnt on glaring windows.

1891 Francis Adams *Fortnightly Review* Sep. 393: Sometimes the Antarctic gives Sydney, as it does Melbourne, its stormy 'change' – the dust-clouds of the 'brickfielder' ending in the tempestuous showers of the 'southerly buster'.

1935 H. H. Finlayson *The Red Centre* 21: A desert ... whose chief function is to provide material for the 'brickfielder' dust-storms which occasionally cloud the towns.

1962 Stuart Gore *Down the Golden Mile* 192: Behind him ... the sky looked forbidding, no longer pink but red, charged with a threat of dust straight from the desert heart. 'It's going to be a brick-fielder, Dad!'

bride's nightie, off like a Making a quick departure; acting promptly
1969 Christopher Bray *Blossom like a Rose* 26: 'Come on youse blokes!' he shouted. 'We're off like a bride's nightie!'

Bridle Track, the The Milky Way: N.T.
1951 Ernestine Hill *The Territory* 425: The Milky Way is the Bridle Track, or sometimes the Hopple Chain.

brinny A stone of the size thrown by children: *rare*
1943 Baker 14: *Brinny* A stone.
1977 Phil Motherwell *Mr Bastard* 43: I slowly crouch to pick up two brinnies from the ground.

Bris, Brizzie Brisbane [abbr.]
1945 Cecil Mann *The River* 117: Up in Bris he gets himself shaved at the Barber's down the lower end of Queen Street.
1965 Patrick White *Four Plays* 149: 'Reckon I'll catch the evenin' train to Brizzy.'

Brisbane Line Name given to a military plan to concentrate on the defence of vital areas of Australia, put to the Curtin government in February 1942, which led to claims that the abandonment of Australia north of Brisbane was contemplated (Paul Hasluck *The Government and the People 1942–1945* (1970) 711–17). The plan was attributed to the Menzies government by its political opponents.

1951 *The Calamitous Career of Dictator Bob* [Communist pamphlet] 4: Rather than wage a people's war against fascism Menzies devised the Brisbane Line to give Nth Australia to the Japs!

1951 Dymphna Cusack and Florence James *Come in Spinner* 307: 'All I got against the politicians and their flamin' Brisbane Line is that they didn't give the bloody place away.'

1965 Thomas Keneally *The Fear* 36: There were vacancies, the corset factories told her, but they were all above the Brisbane line, and if the country was invaded, the Government might abandon the North.

1967 R. G. Menzies *Afternoon Light* 20: This legend did not prevent the notorious 'Eddie' Ward from concocting a story, months later, that we had prepared plans to base Australia's defence against Japan on a so-called 'Brisbane Line' . . . and that we were prepared to retreat . . . to the extent of surrendering the northern part of Australia!

Britt, Edgar As for 'Jimmies', 'Jimmy Britts' q.v.

1970 Alexander Buzo *The Front Room Boys* in Penguin *Plays* 22: 'Then he raced out to the john for an Edgar Britt.'

bronze (bronza) Backside

1953 Baker 105: *bronzo*, anus (a variation of *bronze*, used similarly).

1959 D'Arcy Niland *The Big Smoke* 164: He roared laughing and gave her a slap on the seat. 'The biggest bronza in the world – and just think, you're all mine.'

1968 Geoffrey Dutton *Andy* 262: 'Some bloody boomers, boy, be in it. But some hairy nosed dumpers as well. One

of them set me right on my bronze on the bottom.'

1970 Barry Oakley *A Salute to the Great McCarthy* 75: 'Hear this: this is the last day you spend sitting on your bronzes in the sun.'

1975 Les Ryan *The Shearers* 104: 'Go and sit on your bronze while we give scabs your jobs.'

bronze gods See quot. 1946: *jocular*

1946 Rohan Rivett *Behind Bamboo* 395: *Bronze gods* A.I.F. 8th Division. Term was used by a woman journalist visiting Malaya, and subsequently derisively. *Bronzie* member of the 8th Division. Used by officers to indicate other ranks, by British to indicate Australians.

1952 T. A. G. Hungerford *The Ridge and the River* 31: 'Oh, you big bronzed bastard, you! What you do in the war, daddy?' Ibid. 186: 'You big bronzed Anzac!' A bitter smile flickered at the corners of Malise's mouth.

1959 Eric Lambert *Glory Thrown In* 83: 'You can start getting yourself in the mood for the role of a drunken bronzed Anzac thirsting for sheilas and *alicante*.' see **Anzac**

bronzewing A half-caste aboriginal: N.T. and W.A. [f. colour of bronzewing pigeon]

1956 Tom Ronan *Moleskin Midas* 161: 'If there is a few bronzewings being born about my place, there's nearly as much chance of your being their daddy as me.'

brook, babbling see **babbler**

broomie A broom-hand in a shearing shed

1910 C. E. W. Bean *On the Wool Track* 203: There still remain the burry pieces which were skirted from the fleece at the wool-rolling tables and are lying on the floor. A boy, the 'broomy', sweeps them.

1933 Acland: *Broomie* A boy who keeps the board swept of locks, etc., at shearing.

1964 H. P. Tritton *Time Means Tucker* 64: Sam was expert, boss of the board,

wool classer, tar boy and broomie, musterer and penner-up.
1975 Les Ryan *The Shearers* 142: 'That stupid broomie . . . oh, Gawd! . . . what a scream?'

brothel Any untidy, crowded or disreputable place
1953 T. A. G. Hungerford *Riverslake* 148: 'Always drunk. He does his work, in a way – enough to get by in a brothel like this. But in normal times he wouldn't be tolerated in a boong's kitchen.'

brown A penny: *obs.* [f. *brown* a copper coin OED 1812; a halfpenny]
1865 *Queenslanders' New Colonial Camp Fire Song Book* 21: Most others are hard up for browns.
1871 Dogberry Dingo *Australian Rhymes and Jingles* 10: We think it sad to want a pound. / A shilling or a 'brown'.
1885 *The Australasian Printers' Keepsake* 24: We found no change in him – no, not a brown.
1895 Cornelius Crowe *The Australian Slang Dictionary* 12: *Brown* a copper.
1913 Henry Lawson 'The Kids' *Prose* i 806: But for the chartering of the aforesaid craft . . . there must be 'browns', or 'coppers'.
1946 *Sunday Sun* 20 Oct. Suppl. 25: Everybody's jumping about like a double-headed brown had been found at a swy game.

brown bomber In N.S.W., a parking policeman [f. colour of uniform]
1954 *Sun* 8 Jun. 1: New name for the Brown Bomber boys is Walkie-Chalkies.
1959 Baker 95: *brown bomber* A parking policeman in some cities.
1970 Jon Cleary *Helga's Web* 160: He found a parking ticket on his car, put it in his pocket and swore at a parking policeman, one of the Brown Bombers in their khaki uniforms.
1975 *Sun-Herald* 23 Nov. 5: New uniform to boost new image for the Brown Bombers . . . The long-standing, long-suffering brown is out. A new bluish-grey is 'in' for the city's parking squads.

see **grey ghost, grey meanie**

brownie A bush cake made with currants and brown sugar
1883 J. E. Partington *Random Rot: A Journal of Three Years Wanderings* 312: It was an amusing sight to see the three of us, each with a huge hunch of 'browny' (bread sweetened with brown sugar and currants) in one hand.
1886 P. Clarke *The New Chum in Australia* 193: She makes 'browney', a sort of sweet currant cake for her customers.
1901 Henry Lawson 'Joe Wilson's Courtship' *Prose* i 541: 'Here's some tea and brownie' . . . Jack took a cup of tea and a piece of cake and sat down to enjoy it.
1903 Joseph Furphy *Such is Life* (1944) 80: In another hour . . . I was having a drink of tea and a bit of brownie in the men's hut.
1919 W. K. Harris *Outback in Australia* 49: Damper, beef and tea sweetened with coarse brown sugar, was the usual fare, with an occasional 'brownie' cake to vary the menu.
1951 Ernestine Hill *The Territory* 443: *Brownie* A bush cake, damper with sugar and currants.

brown land, the wide see **wide brown land**

brownout A partial blackout in World War II
1942 A. G. Mitchell 'A Glossary of War Words' *Southerly* i 12: *Brownout* A partial blackout.
1946 Dal Stivens *The Courtship of Uncle Henry* 32: They pushed through the glass doors and went down the steps to George Street. The street was browned out and they couldn't see clearly for a minute.
1953 Dymphna Cusack *Southern Steel* 81: She hated the brown-out. It would have been better had they blacked-out the city, instead of this half-way business of restrictive light and deceptive shadow.
1961 *Sydney Morning Herald* 1 Jun. 1: Victoria Faces Brownout [report of electricity restrictions]

1970 Sumner Locke Elliott *Edens Lost* 115: She waited for the King's Cross tram in the brownout winter twilight. Cars went by sluggishly with their muffled headlights and overhead the filtered street lamps gave out a weak gingery light. [describing wartime Sydney]

1975 Hal Porter *The Extra* 207: The skylights, browned-out during World War II, are still painted over.

brumby 1 A wild horse [Ab. *booramby* wild Ramson 120]

1880 *Australasian* 4 Dec. 712: These our guide pronounced to be 'brumbies', the bush name here [Queensland] for wild horses. [Morris]

1892 Gilbert Parker *Round the Compass in Australia* 44: Six wild horses — warrigals or brombies, as they are called — have been driven down, corralled, and caught.

1899 Steele Rudd *On Our Selection* 40: Not that she had any brumby element in her — she would have been easier to yard if she had.

2 A person with such attributes

1911 L. St Clare Grondona *Collar and Cuffs* 98: They were a brumbie lot of rotters, all swagmen, and to all appearances at least, considerably down on their uppers.

1936 Miles Franklin *All That Swagger* 444: 'I'm only a brumby compared with you.'

1940 K. S. Prichard *Brumby Innes* [play title]

1974 *Sydney Morning Herald* 16 Aug. 7: He [Dr Cairns] gave long allegiance to the Victorian Executive when it was the brumby of the ALP and the despair of ALP voters who wanted to see Labor back in power.

brush A woman; women collectively [Partridge suggests derivation from pubic hair]

1941 Baker 14: *Brush* A girl or young woman.

1965 William Dick *A Bunch of Ratbags* 226: We were all hanging out of windows, whistling up some of the bits of 'brush' (sheilas) that were walking along.

1967 Kylie Tennant *Tell Morning This* 16: 'Always be leary of the brush. There's many a man thought he was going to stand over some little lowie and now he's either looking through bars or else he's mowing the lawn for her.'

1975 Elizabeth Riley *All That False Instruction* 229: 'Beer first. Brush later.'

brusher A small wallaby noted for its brisk movement; anyone with these characteristics [? f. *brush-kangaroo* an early name for the wallaby Morris 1802]

1882 *Freeman's Journal* 30 Sep. cit. *Australian Dictionary of Biography* iv 207: To 'Cassius' in the *Freeman's Journal*, 30 September 1882, he [W. J. Foster] was a 'fussy little brusher'.

1898 Morris: *Brusher* n. a Bushman's name, in certain parts, for a small wallaby which hops about in the bush or scrub with considerable speed.

brusher, give To abscond without paying one's debts, abandon a task: *obs.*

1878 T. E. Argles *The Pilgrim* 2nd Series No. 10, 5: He subsequently victimized Mr Weber, Post Office Hotel ... indeed anywhere this penniless Hebrew obtained admission he never failed to give 'brusher' to the confiding boniface.

c. 1882 *The Sydney Slang Dictionary* 2: *Brusher (to give anyone)* To obtain or borrow something and not pay for it or return it.

1898 Morris: 'To give brusher' is a phrase ... used in many parts, especially of the interior of Australia, and implies that a man has left without paying his debts. In reply to the question, 'Has so-and-so left the township?' the answer, 'Oh yes, he gave them brusher', would be well understood in the above sense.

1904 Henry Fletcher *Dads Wayback: His Work* 20: 'I s'pose I may as well give it brusher fer ter-night,' replied Dan, as he wiped his scythe and walked with Dads to the house.

1914 Baker 14: *Brusher, give a* To go off without paying one's debts.

brusher, to get To be rejected, 'brushed off'

1911 Edward Dyson *Benno, and Some of the Push* 33: Mr Dickson, mindful of the ignominy due to the man who gets 'brusher', thought he was combining airy indifference. . . .

buck, buckjump, buckjumper *v. & n.* See quots [U.S. 1869 Mathews]

1838 Stephen Black let. in Baker (1966) 65: I bought a colt . . . I was vain enough to think I could ride him, but in a week he convinced me of the fallacy of this idea by sending me up in the air like a sky-rocket by buckjumping.

1848 H. W. Haygarth *Recollections of Bush Life in Australia* 78: Australian horses have a vicious habit known as 'buck-jumping', or as it is more familiarly called, 'bucking'.

1853 C. R. Read *What I Heard, Saw and Did on the Australian Goldfields* 120: My animal, having a peculiar dislike to spurs, commenced . . . 'buckjumping', I soon measured my length on the ground.

1867 J. R. Houlding *Australian Capers* 223: [He] would rather be crossing Bogie Plains on a buckjumping horse.

1898 David Carnegie *Spinifex and Sand* 98: 'Wait till you make your evening feed off mulga scrub and bark – that'll take the buck out of you!'

1908 W. S. Ogilvie *My Life in the Open* 83: Some are old and noted buckjumpers, hopeless rogues whose names and reputations are known far beyond the station yards.

1926 K. S. Prichard *Working Bullocks* 47–8: Brumbies he had caught who bucked until they bucked their brands off.

1936 Ion L. Idriess *The Cattle King* 246: It was Albert who rode the notorious outlaw until it 'bucked its brands off'.

bucker A horse that bucks

1856 G. Willmer *The Draper in Australia* 122: No sooner had we put the tackling on, than he unfortunately escaped from us, and being a first-rate 'bucker', as they term them in this country, it elicited many hearty laughs from all of us.

buck, give it a See quots: mainly N.Z.

1941 Baker 15: *Buck, give it a* Make an attempt at (something); to try.

1956 Ruth Park and D'Arcy Niland *The Drums Go Bang!* 103: 'Okay, pardner,' he said. 'We'll give it a buck.'

bucket, do a ~ job, drop a ~ See quots

[1950 *Australian Police Journal* Apr. 112: *Drop the bucket* Drop the responsibility on to someone else.]

1971 Alan Reid *The Gorton Experiment* 242: In Australian political argot to 'turn a bucket' means to attack someone on personal grounds, usually of a slightly scandalous nature.

1974 *Australian* 1 Apr. 6: While it might be valid to find Brisbane lacking in Adelaide's grace or Sydney's vigor or Melbourne's dignity, it is not valid to bucket it in total just because its authorities finger *Playboy* with distaste or fall into a faint at the sound of a fourlettered obscenity from the stage.

Buckley, who struck See quot. 1873

[1873 Hotten 99: 'Who struck Buckley?' a common phrase used to irritate Irishmen. The story is that an Englishman having struck an Irishman named Buckley, the latter made a great outcry, and one of his friends rushed forth screaming, 'Who struck Buckley?' 'I did' said the Englishman, preparing for the apparently inevitable combat. 'Then' said the ferocious Hibernian, after a careful investigation of the other's thews and sinews, 'then, sarve him right.']

1885 'The Broken-hearted Shearer' *Old Bush Songs* ed. Stewart and Keesing (1957) 266: She would turn and twist about, saying, 'That slews *you*, old chap'; / 'Sold again and got the money'; 'Who struck Buckley such a rap?'

1903 Joseph Furphy *Such is Life* (1944) 149: I found myself overflowing with the sunny self-reliance of the man that struck Buckley.

Buckley's chance (show, hope) A forlorn hope, no chance at all [Origin obscure. Connections have been sug-

57

gested with 'the wild white man' William Buckley, the convict who absconded from Port Phillip in 1803 and lived for thirty-two years with the natives. He gave himself up in 1835 and lived until 1856. Another suggested derivation is a pun on the name of the Melbourne firm of Buckley and Nunn.]

1898 W. H. Ogilvie *Fair Girls and Gray Horses* 70: But we hadn't got a racehorse that was worth a dish of feed, / So didn't have a Buckley's show to take the boasters down.

1903 Joseph Furphy *Such is Life* (1944) 339: Brummy . . . . . doesn't require to stoop at all – and *his* show is little better than Buckley's.

1908 E. G. Murphy *Jarrahland Jingles* 16: You've done the rattler in today, you ain't got Buckley's 'ope.

1915 C. J. Dennis *The Songs of a Sentimental Bloke:* I knoo / That any other bloke 'ad Buckley's 'oo / Tried fer to pick 'er up.

1936 H. Drake-Brockman *Sheba Lane* 164: 'We ain't got Buckley's chance of a deal, if that's the case,' he commented.

1944 Lawson Glassop *We Were the Rats* 44: I've got two chances, 'I said. 'Mine and Buckley's.'

1953 T. A. G. Hungerford *Riverslake* 150: 'We've got two chances of making this immigration business work – our own and Buckley's.'

1963 John Cantwell *No Stranger to the Flame* 156: 'He won't stand Buckley's with that mob.'

1974 David Ireland *Burn* 18: 'You got two chances of cookin' this fish: your own and Buckley's. Git away before I knock yer block off.'

bugger *n.* Like 'bastard' and 'bloody', bugger (noun, verb and extensions) is not distinctively Australian, but it is remarked upon by visitors as a feature of Australian speech. Intensive uses like 'bugger-all' and 'burnt to buggery' may be more characteristically Australian than the others. The noun is used as an equivalent to 'bastard' in all its senses; as an equivalent to 'damn' ('I don't give a bugger for that'); and in 'bugger all' as meaning 'nothing' [f. *bugger* 2b a coarse

term of abuse or insult OED 1719]

1833 Trial before the Supreme Court 9 and 10 Dec. in *True Patriots All* ed. G. C. Ingleton (1952) 149: There was a general cry among the party coming down to me, of '*shoot the bugger.*'

1944 Lawson Glassop *We Were the Rats* 79: 'Wilson or Macduff. Who cares?' 'I don't give a bugger,' said Eddie.

1951 Dal Stivens *Jimmy Brockett* 294: I felt crook in the guts and miserable as buggery.

1952 Jon Cleary *The Sundowners* 153: 'Look at those plains, will you? Miles and miles of bugger all.'

1960 John Iggulden *The Storms of Summer* 121: 'You'd have bugger all chance of that!'

1964 Tom Ronan *Packhorse and Pearling Boat* 35: She had started life at Beagle Bay Mission and on the Bishop's arrival proudly informed him: 'Me properly bloody Catholic bugger, all the same you.'

1973 John O'Grady *Survival in the Doghouse* 63: 'An hour and a half to cook pork chops? They'll be burnt to buggery.'

bugger *v.* 1 Used most often as an equivalent to 'damn'; also (with *up*) 'to make a mess of'; and (with *off*) 'to depart'

1942 C. Hartley Grattan *Introducing Australia* (1944) 171–2: The word bugger is used in numerous forms and contexts. 'Oh, bugger it all.' 'I'll be buggered.' 'Buggered if I will.' 'Bugger him.' 'Oh go to buggery,' 'The silly bugger.' 'I'm all buggered up.' And triumphantly combining all the favorite words, 'bugger the bloody bastard'. English people profess to find Australian men foul-mouthed.

1957 D'Arcy Niland *The Shiralee* 14: 'But one time I fell off the train and buggered my insides up.'

2 In the pidgin term 'bagarup'

1975 *Australian* 19 Sep. 1: Prince Charles broke into Pidgin at the end of his speech [in Papua New Guinea] saying 'Af de ren I bagarup mi nau arait' which meant 'Unfortunately rain caused me some inconvenience yesterday, but now everything is all right.'

bull *n.* 1 A Torres Islander: *obs.*

1934 Vance Palmer *Sea and Spinifex* 29–30: The proffered notes were too much for Charlie, a tough little Torres Islander ... 'Those bulls'll take on anything [McVeagh commented] if they're shown a few quid.'

2 A wharf labourer unfairly favoured for employment: see quots 1961, 1973

1957 Tom Nelson *The Hungry Mile* 80: The employers ... indulging in illegal trafficking of 'bulls' to suit their own ends. Ibid. 77: The battle to end the bull system is unsurpassed in the history of Australian unionism.

1961 *Sydney Morning Herald* 22 May 2: Under the 'bull' system, wharfies had to front the stevedore, and only the 'bulls' (company men or men who would sling to the foreman) could be sure of catching his eye.

1973 *Sydney Morning Herald* 2 Aug. 7: 'Bulls were tough, strong, hardworking men known to the bosses and, when the wharfies gathered outside the gate looking for work, the foreman would point his finger 'You, and you and you' – always to the 'bulls'. The old, the not so strong and the militants always got the dirtiest, most obnoxious jobs, or were ignored to trudge along the mile to the next gate.

3 Nonsense, pretence, deceit. 'Bull' in a sense close to this is recorded in the OED from 1630, and later in U.S. slang. It would be taken in Australia as an abbreviation of 'bullshit' q.v. and 'bull artist' and 'bull dust' q.v. would have the same implication.

[1871 W. H. Cooper *Colonial Experience* (MS, Mitchell Library) ii 3: *Joe* Oh talk as much Bullock as you can. *Alfred* Bullock? *Joe* Yes, back yourself to ride anything that was ever foaled, tell any amount of crammers about Buckjumpers.]

1905–12 Joseph Furphy *The Buln-Buln and the Brolga* ed. R. G. Howarth (1948) [Title of a novella previously called 'The Lyre Bird and the Native Companion']

1939 Kylie Tennant *Foveaux* 168: 'I never had any luck with the fair,' Mr True said sentimentally. 'They kid you along, and what does it all amount to, these blandishments? ... Bull, it's all bull.'

1941 Baker 14: *Bull* Nonsense, senseless chatter. cf. 'bullsh'

1951 Dal Stivens *Jimmy Brockett* 171: The old man was always talking about England and calling it the Mother Country and Home, but it sounded all bull to me.

1959 D'Arcy Niland *The Big Smoke* 56: 'I come here to get the truth out of you, and no bull. See?'

1969 William Dick *Naked Prodigal* 204: As I walked along the street I wondered if she really was in Heaven or whether it was just a lot of bull.

1973 Alexander Buzo *Rooted* 78: 'You might be an arty sort of bloke, but ... you don't bung on the bull like a lot of these blokes you see around the place these days.'

see **confetti**

bull artist see **artist**

Bullamakanka An imaginary place which is a byword for remoteness and backwardness, like Woop Woop q.v.

1953 T. A. G. Hungerford *Riverslake* 230: 'Hitch out to Bullamakanka and live with the blacks.'

1976 *Australian* 18 Dec. 22: Bullamakanka Premium Dry Red [mock wine label].

1977 *Southerly* 48: 'We've heard you say he lives in Bullamakanka because he likes being a big frog in a little puddle.'

bull, Barney's A phrase suggesting clumsiness or incompetence [? f. *Barney's bull* a worthless person or thing OED 1908; influenced also by *bull*³]

1930 Vance Palmer *The Passage* (1944) 59: 'By hell, we've got 'em. Trapped like Barney's bull!'

1957 Ray Lawler *Summer of the Seventeenth Doll* 17: 'What do they call him Barney for, anyway?' 'Barney's bull, I think. His right name's Arthur.'

all behind like Barney's bull Delayed and confused; with outsize buttocks

1941 Baker 9: *Behind like Barney's bull,*

all Late backward, delayed.

Bulldogs 1 In Victoria, the Footscray V.F.L. team
1974 *Sunday Telegraph* 11 Aug. 100: Bulldogs chase off the Blues.
2 In N.S.W., the East Sydney Australian Rules team
1975 *Sunday Telegraph* 6 Apr. 66: Bulldogs select top Tasmanian recruit.

bull dust 1 Fine sand or dust
1935 H. H. Finlayson *The Red Centre* 126: The loam proved unexpectedly heavy, having a rather spongy texture, like the intumescent clays of the Lake Eyre basin, known locally as 'bull dust'.
1945 George Johnston *Pacific Partner* 148: And there were vast areas of fine drift sand – the troops called it 'bull-dust' – that would make other deserts look positively glacial.
1967 John Yeomans *The Scarce Australians* 122: Bulldust is the superfine red-grey dust which develops on the northern roads. Sometimes this lies in drifts, perhaps axle deep.
1971 Rena Briand *White Men in a Hole* 11: Deep holes filled with bulldust were booby traps for travellers unfamiliar with the road.
2 As for 'bull', 'bullshit'
1951 Ernestine Hill *The Territory* 443: *Bull dust* False promises, empty talk.
1953 T. A. G. Hungerford *Riverslake* 121: 'I suppose Bellairs told you that bit of bulldust about there being spies?'
1965 William Dick *A Bunch of Ratbags* 169–70: One bloke reckoned he dressed up as a bodgie and lived, ate, slept and ran with a pack of us for twelve months while he made notes. We reckoned it was a lot of bull-dust.
1966 H. F. Brinsmead *Beat of the City* 104: 'People are invariably happy,' said Uncle Stefan, 'when they are good.' 'Bulldust!' said Raylene.
1971 Frank Hardy *The Outcasts of Foolgarah* 23: No man is so gullible when it comes to a bit of bulldust sprinkled on the old national ethos than the Australian, who really believes the sun shines nowhere else except out of his arse and his beer is really the best.

bullock To toil as strenuously as a bullock
1875 Rolf Boldrewood *The Squatter's Dream* repr. as *Ups and Downs* (1878) 240: 'Let other fellows, if they're fools enough, do all that bullocking. Wise men buy their work afterwards and cheap enough too.'
1894 Henry Lawson 'The Lost Souls' Hotel' *Prose* i 155: Take a selector who has bullocked all his life to raise crops on dusty, stony patches in the scrubs.
1904 Steele Rudd *Sandy's Selection* 69: And talk about work! Sandy rarely rested. He would begin hard at daylight, and bullock till he couldn't see – bullock till the stars came out and blinked and blazed.
1911 E. M. Clowes *On the Wallaby through Victoria* 14: Carried apparently with so little exertion, and absolutely no bullocking.
1936 Miles Franklin *All That Swagger* 415: He would now have been in a comfortable school instead of having bullocked himself into an early grave.
1948 H. Drake-Brockman *Sydney or the Bush* 201: Now, what chance was there of giving Dick or Phil or Wally even half the things she'd bullocked for?

bullocky 1 A bullock-driver, teamster
1869 Marcus Clarke 'The Language of Bohemia' repr. in *A Colonial City* ed. L. T. Hergenhan (1972) 162: *bullocky* (a teamster).
1876 Henry Kendall 'Bill the Bullock Driver' *Poetical Works* ed. T. T. Reed (1966) 167: Poor bullocky Bill! In the circles select / Of the scholars he hasn't a place.
1891 Henry Lawson 'Song of the Old Bullock-Driver' *Verse* i 162: The bullocks lay down 'neath the gum trees and rested – / The bullockies steered for the bar of the inn.
1905 Randolph Bedford *The Snare of Strength* 210: The bullocky went round the team and recovered the pole-pin.
1926 K. S. Prichard *Working Bullocks* 11: Red Burke was the youngest bullocky in the Karri to own his team, and one of the best drivers.
1941 Sarah Campion *Mo Burdekin* 143:

The bullocky ... stooped to yell at them as they drew level, cursing in the same breath all his plodding oxen.

2 The language of the bullock-driver

1916 *The Anzac Book* 103: Above it all we were certain we heard fragments of language, of the category known in Australia as 'bullocky'.*

*Bullocky – stands both for the bullock driver and for his chief gift.

bullocky's joy Treacle

1933 Acland: *Bullocky's Joy* Golden syrup or treacle.

1934 Archer Russell *A Tramp-Royal in Wild Australia* 202: Luncheon and supper are much the same, except that damper and 'bullockys' joy' (treacle) take the place of porridge.

1951 Ernestine Hill *The Territory* 176: 1 case treacle, bullocky's joy.

bullsh, bullshit *n.* As for *bull*[3]. Not an Australianism in origin, although very common in the colloquial language; the shortening to 'bullsh' is euphemistic

1919 W. H. Downing *Digger Dialects* 14: *Bullsh* 1) Insincerity; 2) an incorrect or insincere thing; 3) flattery; 4) praise.

1938 Xavier Herbert *Capricornia* 377: 'That's all bulsh about trouble if he takes on a coloured man.' Ibid. 395: 'This talk of invasion by the Japs is all plain bulsh.'

1951 Dal Stivens *Jimmy Brockett* 65: He'd kick up a bit of a shindy at first and talk a lot of bulsh about his reputation as a good and fair ref.

1959 D'Arcy Niland *The Big Smoke* 159: 'We won't be able to get out for the bullsh in a minute,' jibed the lumberman. 'Look at it – it's up to me knees now.'

1965 Eric Lambert *The Long White Night* 23: 'It's an intangible thing, a sort of veneration for an idea for its own sake. It's hard to put into words. You'd probably call it bullshit.'

1974 John Powers *The Last of the Knucklemen* 96: 'I just want to see if all this "knuckleman" stuff's for real – or bullshit.'

bullshit *v.* To talk 'bull', esp. in seeking

to delude or impose

1965 John Beede *They Hosed Them Out* 196: 'Don't bullshit to me – I know how I look.'

bum to mum See quots: Victorian sporting

1972 Ian Moffitt *The U-Jack Society* 146: Australian Rules, in Victoria, is, of course, a religion which divides man and wife ('Bum to mum' is the standard order for players forbidden intercourse before the big games).

1973 *Australian* 7 Apr. 17: Like the coach [in V.F.L.] who told his team on Fridays, 'well, it's bum to mum tonight boys', because they might wear themselves out in sexual activity.

bumper *n.* A cigarette butt, esp. in the expression 'not worth a bumper'

1900–10 O'Brien and Stephens: *Bumper* a cigarette or cigar stump or butt.

1916 *The Anzac Book* 47: One mornin' early while we was standin' to arms 'e lights up a bumper.

1924 *Truth* 27 Apr. 6: *Bumper* butt of cigarette.

1947 Margaret Trist *Daddy* 164: 'My old man's not going to be worth a bumper that day.'

1960 Ron Tullipan *Follow the Sun* 90: 'By midday it won't be worth a bumper to you anyway.'

1974 David Ireland *Burn* 44: 'You're not worth a bumper,' Joy says. 'You couldn't fight your way out of a paper bag.'

bundle, drop one's To give up, lose one's nerve, surrender one's responsibilities

1900–10 O'Brien and Stephens: *Bundle* for a competitor to collapse or 'turn it up' is called dropping his bundle.

1906 Edward Dyson *Fact'ry 'Ands* 241: 'He gives er sad cry, 'n' drops his bundle, 'n' goes pluckin' at his 'air.'

1915 C. J. Dennis *The Songs of a Sentimental Bloke* 23: I carn't tell *wot* it is; / all I know / I've dropped me bundle – an' I'm glad it's so.

1924 *Truth* 27 Apr. 6: *Bundle, to drop the* To show cowardice.

1936 H. Drake-Brockman *Sheba Lane* 279: Kent seemed to have come to the end of his tether. He'd dropped his bundle.

1942 Gavin Casey *It's Harder for Girls* 212: 'He dropped his bundle,' said Tom. 'No doubt about it, Sim was right. If they drop their bundles they're gone a million.'

1959 David Forrest *The Last Blue Sea* 96: 'Something happened to him there before the war. He just dropped his bundle. Properly.'

1972 Thomas Keneally *The Chant of Jimmie Blacksmith* 138: 'Panic?' Mort asked. 'Drop your bundle,' McCreadie explained.

bundy The 'clock' by which workers 'clock on' and 'clock off', esp. in the expression 'punch the bundy' [f. trade name]

1936 J. L. Ranken *Murder Pie* 73: 'I remember glancing at the bundy clock as I got in.'

1949 G. Farwell *Traveller's Tracks* 16: There are no bitumen roads back there, hardly an up-to-date picture show, no rush hours or bundies to turn life into a milling ant-heap.

1957 D'Arcy Niland *Call Me When the Cross Turns Over* 161: Thousands of men filing down a track ... to the ship-yards ... Through the gates. Punching the bundy.

1961 Mena Calthorpe *The Dyehouse* 140: 'I want you to make sure every man bundies off.'

1971 David Ireland *The Unknown Industrial Prisoner* 81: There had been another break at a State detention centre, one of those where men couldn't bundy out each day.

1974 *Bulletin* 3 Aug. 13: Relief for the Bundy punchers?

bung it on, to To put on 'side'
1963 Alan Seymour *The One Day of the Year* 48: 'Well, she bungs it on a bit, don't she? ... that young lady's too lah-dee-dah for us.'

1969 William Dick *Naked Prodigal* 187: These flash bastards ... give you the shits bunging on side like they do.

1973 Alexander Buzo *Rooted* 78: 'When I had my one and only exhibition in an art gallery, there was a whole lot of scientists there, bunging it on.'

bung (bong), to go Originally to die, then to break down, go bankrupt, cease to function [Ab. *bong* dead]

[1847 J. D. Lang *Cooksland* 430: A place called *Umpie Bung*, or the dead houses, where there had once been a Government Settlement, now long abandoned.]

1857 F. Cooper *Wild Adventures in Australia* 58: I asked him what had become of 'Solomons'? 'Boung!' said he, making use of the Cameleroi term for dead.

1875 A. J. Boyd *Old Colonials* (1882) 73: Sometimes you've got a horse as is good an' don't suit you, an' you sells him, but just afore you hands 'im over and gets the money, he goes bung* on you. *Dead.

1885 *The Australasian Printers' Keepsake* 40: He was importuned to desist, as his musical talent had 'gone bung', probably from over-indulgence.

1890 *Truth* 19 Oct. 1: The 'National (?) Club appears to have gone bung. No wonder. It is the last retreat of the greedy, grasping bastard Toryism.

1901 Henry Lawson 'Telling Mrs Baker' *Prose* i 416: The world might wobble and all the banks go bung, but the cattle have to go through – that's the law of the stock-routes.

1911 Louis Stone *Jonah* 146: 'The firm's gone bung.'

1933 R. B. Plowman *The Man from Oodnadatta* 122: 'I heard that their well has gone bung, and their garden is completely ruined.'

1946 Dal Stivens *The Courtship of Uncle Henry* 109: 'The radio's gone bung again and I'm just fixing it.'

1951 Dymphna Cusack and Florence James *Come In Spinner* 329: 'What's wrong with 'er? The bank gone bung?'

bung-eye Sandy blight or similar infection [cf. *bunged up* OED 1622]
1892 G. L. James *Shall I Try Australia?* 242: One pest of the bush and plains is

'Sandy blight' or inflammation of the eyes ... It is also known as 'bung-eye', because ... in the morning, the lids are tightly closed, and require no small amount of fomentation to get them open.
1903 Joseph Furphy *Such is Life* (1944) 353: 'Butler, he's laid up with the bung blight in both eyes.'
1934 Archer Russell *A Tramp-Royal in Wild Australia* 172: Bung-eyes, flysickness accompanied by severe vomiting, dysentery in its worst form, and Barcoo Rot ... become the lot of the human.
1946 E. L. Grant Watson *But to What Purpose?* 127: He mentioned a kind of opthalmia, known locally as 'bung-eye', which was very common both amongst natives and whites.

bunny A 'muggins', dupe, person with no mind of his own; in cricket, a player who is no batsman [f. the timidity and helplessness of the rabbit]
1943 Baker 16: *Bunny* A simpleton or fool, an easy victim for exploitation.
1950 Jon Cleary *Just Let Me Be* 14: 'But you wait and see I'm not gunna be like all them bunnies over there for the rest of my life.'
1952 T. A. G. Hungerford *The Ridge and the River* 31: White often wondered why Shearwood had never got his commission when he could run rings round so many of the bunnies who had.
1959 Dorothy Hewett *Bobbin Up* 196: 'We're only the poor old unskilled mugs. The bunnies!'
1965 Wally Grout *My Country's Keeper* 41–2: Once again, at Johannesburg, in the fourth match of the tour, I was one of the 'bunnies'.

bunyip Monster of Aboriginal legend, supposed to haunt water-holes; any freak or impostor [Ab.]
1848 W. Westgarth *Australia Felix* 391: Certain large fossil bones ... have been referred by the natives ... to a huge animal of extraordinary appearance, called in some districts the Bunyup ... It is described as of amphibious character, inhabiting deep rivers, and permanent water-holes, having a round head, an elongated neck, with a body and tail resembling an ox.
1852 G. C. Mundy *Our Antipodes* ii 18–19: Did my reader ever hear of the Bunyip? (fearful name to the Aboriginal native!) a sort of half-horse, half-alligator, haunting the wide rushy swamps and lagoons of the interior ... a new and strong word was adopted into the Australian vocabulary. Bunyip became, and remains, a Sydney synonyme for *impostor, pretender, humbug*, and the like.
1903 Joseph Furphy *Such is Life* (1944) 244: 'He heard "Hen-ree! Hen-ree!" boomin' and' bellerin' back an' forrid across the bend in the dark, an' he thought the boody-man, an' the bunyip, an' the banshee, an' (sheol) knows what all, was after him.'
1956 A. D. Hope *Sydney Morning Herald* 16 Jun. 15: 'The Bunyip Stages a Comeback'. The bunyip of Australian literature is the mythical great Australian novel.
1975 *Bulletin* 9 Aug. 44: Literary gentlemen have tended to call the great Australian novel the bunyip, the monster that has never been revealed.

bunyip aristocracy D. H. Deniehy's derisory description of W. C. Wentworth's plan for a colonial peerage in 1853
1853 *Sydney Morning Herald* 16 Aug. in *Select Documents in Australian History* ed. C. M. H. Clark (1955) 342: [Report of speech by D. H. Deniehy on the proposal to establish a colonial peerage] Here they all knew the common water mole was transformed into the duck-billed platypus, and in some distant emulation of this degeneration, he supposed they were to be favoured with a bunyip aristocracy.
1960 *Sydney Morning Herald* 8 Aug. 3: The A.L.P. in N.S.W. is building up a bunyip peerage of his own [a class of hereditary legislators], even if the bunyips aren't titled, and sit in the Lower, not Upper, House.
1976 *Australian* 14 Jun. 7: The grafting of knighthoods on ... the Order of Australia is a laughable concession to

bunyip snobbery.

Burdekin duck See quots 1945, 1951
[f. river and district in Queensland]
　1945 Tom Ronan *Strangers on the Ophir*
39: A meat fritter known in the Kimberleys as a 'Burdekin Duck', and on
the Burdekin as a 'Kimberley Oyster'.
　1951 Ernestine Hill *The Territory* 426:
'Burdekin duck', meat fritters.
　1961 George Farwell *Vanishing Austra-*
lians 72: His damper, johnny-cakes,
brownie and Burdekin duck were all
evolved from simple materials.

Burdekin vomit See quot. [f. river and
district in Queensland]
　1918 C. Fetherstonhaugh *After Many*
Days 272: What I called the Belyando
Spue was a most trying ailment . . . The
Western fellows called it 'the Barcoo
sickness', the Northern men the 'Burdekin vomit'.

burglar, gin see **gin burglar**

burl, give it a To make a trial of, risk
an attempt [f. *birl* a rapid twist or turn
EDD 1892]
　1924 *Truth* 27 Apr. 6: *Burl* To try
anything.
　1935 Kylie Tennant *Tiburon* 72: 'Come
on,' Kahn mumured to Johnny as the
crowd increased, 'give it a burl!'
　1937 Vance Palmer *Legend for Sander-*
son 79–80: 'Give it a burl, Leo,' Neil
was pleading. 'You can't lose by it.'
　1952 T. A. G. Hungerford *The Ridge*
and the River 3: He pointed upwards
to the threshing palm-fronds. 'Give it
a burl?'
　1964 George Johnston *My Brother Jack*
34: 'Even if you know you can't bloody
win you still got to have a go. You'll
always be pissin' into the wind, but
that don't mean it isn't worth givin'
it a burl.'

burst (bust) A spree, prolonged drinking bout, esp. in the phrase 'on the burst'
[cf. *burst* an outburst of drinking EDD
1861; *bust* U.S. 1843 Mathews]
　1852 *Select Committee on the Manage-*
ment of the Goldfields 97: One-third of

the miners are incorrigible drunkards
. . . they frequently fall into good
claims, and make large hauls in the
course of the week, they then go 'upon
the burst' as they call it, and drink
until all their earnings are 'knocked
down', and then go to work again.
　1865 Henry Kingsley *The Hillyars and*
the Burtons 146: Any corn-stalk cockatoo who might have treed his section
on the burst, and come back to the
shed.
　1868 Marcus Clarke 'Night Scenes in
Melbourne' repr. in *A Colonial City* ed.
L. T. Hergenhan (1972) 102: Walking
up the street, we meet a knot of station-
men from the Murray with cattle. They
have just put up their horses preparatory to 'goin' on the bust'.
　1880 Rolf Boldrewood *The Miner's*
Right (1890) 222: 'If your theory is
right about his having a craving for
drink, it will all come out the first time
he has a "burst".' Ibid. 254: A note
. . . that Mr Bulder had been 'on the
burst' for several days, and that someone . . . ought to come down and look
after him.
　1899 W. T. Goodge *Hits! Skits! and*
Jingles! 64: They'd long been chums in
fights and frays, / Together 'on the
burst' for days.
　1911 E. M. Clowes *On the Wallaby*
through Victoria 106: Men still go 'on
the bust', cheques are planked down,
and 'shouting' – the Australian equivalent for 'treating' – indulged in till
all the money is finished.
　1932 Leonard Mann *Flesh in Armour*
140: 'The chap who looked as if he'd
been on the bust?'
　1942 Gavin Casey *It's Harder for Girls*
98: 'He was a real damn nuisance, allus
in arguments an' stayin' on th' burst for
as much as a fortnight at a time.'
2 A sudden spurt by a football player
　1976 David Ireland *The Glass Canoe*
145: Danny's on the burst and swerves
just before taking a pass from the half.

burster, buster see **southerly**

bush *n.* The 'woods' or 'forest'; the
unsettled or sparsely settled areas gen-

erally; the country as distinct from the towns [f. Dutch *bosch*]

1803 *Sydney Gazette* 17 Apr. 3: Upon perusing a paragraph in one of your Papers, which suggested the propriety of converting the Rocks into an Academy for *Tumblers,* I rather conceived that you might, with an equal promise of success, recommend some parts of the Bush for an improvement in the talent of *Dancing,* as there much instruction might be expected from the assistance of the accomplished *Kangaroo.*

1826 James Atkinson *An Account of the State of Agriculture and Grazing in New South Wales* 64: Very few of the stock owners have sufficient land to support the whole of their stock, and are therefore obliged to have recourse to the unoccupied tracts in the interior . . . they go into the interior, or *bush,* as it is termed, beyond the occupied parts of the country, usually procuring the assistance of some of the black Natives, as their guides.

1833 W. H. Breton *Excursions in New South Wales* 46: The only convenient way of travelling in the 'bush'* is on horseback. *Bush is the term commonly used for the country *per se:* 'he resides in the Bush', implies that a person does not reside in, or very near, a town. It also signifies a forest.

1848 H. W. Haygarth *Recollections of Bush Life in Australia* 10: That hackneyed expression, 'the bush' . . . the resident in Sydney would be apt to consider it any place beyond the suburbs of the town, the Hawkesbury or Illawarra farmer would place it between 30 and 100 miles from the capital; while the distant settler, the *bona fide* bushman, would smile at such fireside notions, and from his dwelling, 300 miles from Port Jackson, he still talks of 'going into the bush', which in his sense of the term implies his own lonely out-stations, or regions yet untrodden by the white man, in short any place beyond the boundaries of his own homestead, and 'on this side sundown'.

1853 S. Mossman and T. Banister *Australia, Visited and Revisited* 62: The term 'bush', as it is used in Australia, is indiscriminately applied to all descriptions of uncleared land, or to any spot away from a settlement, as a person in England would speak of the country when they are out of town.

1892 Henry Lawson 'The Bush Undertaker' *Prose* i 57: And the sun sank again on the grand Australian bush – the nurse and tutor of eccentric minds, the home of the weird, and of much that is different from things in other lands.

1950 Brian James *The Advancement of Spencer Button* 134: 'What's the good of your degree if they are going to send you to the bush?'

bush *v.* In the expression 'to bush it', to camp out in the bush; put up with the hardships of bush life

1827 W. J. Dumaresq in *Fourteen Journeys* ed. G. Mackaness (1950–1) 99: Not being provided for *bushing it,* in these early forests, we made up our minds to return. [OED Suppl.]

1838 T. Horton James *Six Months in South Australia* 157: A young man, not afraid of bushing it.

1845 D. Mackenzie *The Emigrant's Guide* 187–8: Were he [the innkeeper] to refuse cheques in payment of his bills, he would soon lose half his customers, who would in that case be obliged to 'bush it' every night.

bush, to go Used of an Aboriginal disappearing from his habitat, and so jocularly of anyone 'making himself scarce', with variants like 'head for the scrub', 'take to the mallee', 'take to the tall timber' qq.v.

1926 K. S. Prichard *Working Bullocks* 110: 'Duck Hayes told us you had gone bush. And that's the last we heard about you till a couple of months ago.'

1934 P. H. Ritchie *North of the Never Never* 157: He had not seen them since the cows and bull had gone bush eighteen years before.

1961 Patrick White *Riders in the Chariot* 383: Alf Dubbo now went bush, figuratively at least, as far as other human beings were concerned.

bushed Lost in the bush; having lost one's bearings generally

1844 *Georgiana's Journal* ed. Hugh McCrae (1966) 124: Even with the aid of his compass, Captain Reid thinks we ran the risk of being bushed for the night.

1845 C. Griffith *Present State of Port Phillip* 63: Some people never succeed in becoming good bushmen; and there have been instances of persons *being bushed* (that is, having to spend the night al fresco), within a mile of their own doors.

1849 Diary in L. Braden *Bullockies* (1968) 24: Very nearly bushed but we found our way at last and camped about 7 o'clock after a hard day's work over bad roads.

1870 Marcus Clarke *His Natural Life* ed. S. Murray-Smith (1970) 620: It seemed that the streets were endless, and that once entangled in that maze, he would be 'bushed' indeed.

1887 *All the Year Round* 30 Jul. 68: 'To be bushed', of course, simply meant at first to be lost in the bush, but now it is applied to a person in any mental or physical difficulty or muddle.

1930 Vance Palmer *The Passage* 245: 'It wasn't her fault the youngster strayed off like that and got bushed.'

1941 Charles Barrett *Coast of Adventure* 83: You can easily get bushed there; missing the creek's way through the maze.

1965 Patrick White *Four Plays* 344: 'We reckoned on following the track down Hermit Valley ... but got a bit bushed.'

bush, the bastard from the see **bastard**

bush, Sydney or the see **Sydney**

bush, take the 1 To abscond (of convicts); jocularly 'to decamp'

1827 P. Cunningham *Two Years in New South Wales* ii 190–1: Indeed without the aid of that magic care-killer, the pipe, I believe the greater portion of our 'pressed men' would 'take the bush' in a week after their arrival.

1847 Alexander Harris *Settlers and Convicts* ed. C. M. H. Clark (1954) 187: This luckless hutkeeper of Mr —'s was flogged in the five months I lived near the station no less than three times ... and but for my persuasion he would certainly have taken the bush.

1897 Thomas Archer *Recollections of a Rambling Life* 100: I jumped out of one of the back windows and 'took the bush', hiding behind a big gum tree.

2 To become a bushranger

1844 Louisa Meredith *Notes and Sketches of New South Wales* 59: They do frequently evade the vigilance of their guards, and, 'taking the bush', that is, running away into the forests, they often become formidable in their attacks on travellers in the lonely roads up the country ... Several parties of bushrangers were out at the time of our journey.

1859 John Lang *Botany Bay* 156: The career of these men, who took to the bush ... was a very remarkable one. There was not a road in the colony ... upon which they had not stopped and robbed travellers.

1875 Rolf Boldrewood *The Squatter's Dream* repr. as *Ups and Downs* (1878) 165: 'Well, they say taking to the bush is a short life and a merry one,' grumbled out Redcap.

1899 G. E. Boxall *The Story of the Australian Bushrangers* 252: Before 'he took to the bush' he was known as a steady, industrious, kind-hearted young man.

bush bellows (see quot. 1856), **bush carpenter** (a rough and ready carpenter), **bush lawyer** (see quot. 1926), **bush liar** (a teller of tall stories), **bush oysters** (see quot. 1971), **bush pickles** (see quot. 1962), **bush trifle** (see quot. 1951)

1856 G. Willmer *The Draper in Australia* 155: We had much trouble to light our fire, and but for our perseverance in puffing away with the bush bellows (our hats) for an hour, we should have been compelled to go without supper.

1859 C. Calvert *Cowanda* 5: Every room boasted some three or four doors, beneath which – for bush-carpenters never manage to make things fit – the winter's winds whistled in chorus.

1882 Rolf Boldrewood *Robbery Under Arms* (World's Classics 1949) 10: It was a snug hut enough, for father was a good bush carpenter, and didn't turn his back to anyone for splitting and fencing, hut-building and shingle-splitting, he had had a year or two at sawing, too.
1868 C. Wade Brown *Overlanding in Australia* 68: He summoned us because he was put up to it by the old hand, who is a bit of a bush lawyer.
1926 James Vance Marshall *Timely Tips for New Australians: Bushlawyer* A man who gratuitously voices legal opinions although possessing no qualifications for doing so.
1934 F. E. Baume *Burnt Sugar* 179: 'You go off this ship at the Port. I'll have no bush lawyers here. I'll have no Red Feds on my ship.'
1955 Mary Durack *Keep Him My Country* 222: Bush lawyers appeared from all directions and a great deal of contradictory 'evidence' was advanced.
1967 Frank Hardy *Billy Borker Yarns Again* 135: In the old days in the bush, there were no registered lawyers, so some half-shrewd mug, usually a barber, would set himself up to advise all and sundry. So now anyone who throws around a lot of free advice is called a bush lawyer.
1893 Henry Lawson 'Stragglers' *Prose* i 93: Every true Australian bushman must try his best to tell a bigger outback lie than the last bush-liar.
1936 Archer Russell *Gone Nomad* 46: Probably the most dramatic Bush liar I met with on the tablelands ... was 'Longbow'—.
1957 R. S. Porteous *Brigalow* 83: As a yarn spinner and bush liar Wagga had no equal.
1971 *Bulletin* 27 Nov. 48: Eating bull's testicles, or 'bush oysters' as they're known.
1962 J. Marshall and R. Drysdale *Journey Among Men* 170: Bush pickles ... are made by stirring a bottle of Worcester sauce into a large tin of plum jam.

1951 Ernestine Hill *The Territory* 426: Dessert was 'bush trifle' – johnnie cakes, jam and condensed milk.
see **bushranger, bush telegraph, bush week, bushwhacker**

bushfire, get on like a Applied to a rapidly developing friendship, or to any project that proceeds apace [variant of *like wildfire*]
1942 Sarah Campion *Bonanza* 184: They get on like the proverbial bushfire.

bushfire blonde See quot.: World War II slang
1943 Baker 17: *Bushfire blonde* a red-haired girl.

bushman, Piccadilly see **Piccadilly**

Bushman's Bible The *Bulletin* (pre-World War I)
1903 P. F. Rowland *The New Nation* 204: A backblocks' shearer once told him that 'if he only had 6d left, he would buy the *Bulletin* with it.' Whatever may be thought of the anti-religious and separatist principles of this 'Bushman's Bible', it must be conceded to have done a very real service to Australia.
1908 C. H. S. Matthews *A Parson in the Australian Bush* 283: The *Sydney Bulletin*, the cleverest of Australian papers, and so widely read as sometimes to be called the 'Bushman's Bible', ceaselessly caricatures John Bull.

Bushman's clock The kookaburra, whose laugh is heard at dawn and sunset
1846 C. P. Hodgson *Reminiscences of Australia* 165: Laughing Jackass ... is well and truly stiled the Bushman's clock.
1853 John Sherer *The Gold Finder of Australia* 102: With the first peep of dawn we were roused by the laugh of the jackass-bird – an extraordinary creature, which passes by the name of the Bushman's Clock, and which is rarely heard to give utterance to its merry note at any other hour of the

day.
1861 H. W. Wheelwright *Bush Wanderings of a Naturalist* 128: The laughing jackass is the bushman's clock.
see **settler's clock**

bushranger 1 A man with some official task or responsibility in the bush (the English 'ranger')
[**1798** Matthew Flinders *Voyage to Terra Australis* (1814) cxxxv: This little bear-like quadruped is known in New South Wales, and called by the natives, *womat*, *wombat*, or *wombach*, according to the different dialects, or perhaps to the different rendering of the wood rangers who brought the information.]
1805 G. Caley to Sir Joseph Banks *Banks Papers* vol. 20 cit. Ramson 142: If the Bush rangers will always bring plants from the remote parts of their tours, I can form a good idea of what distance they have been.
2 A law-abiding citizen skilled in bushcraft, a bushman
1825 *Australian* 17 Feb. 1: We regret much that ever Mr Hume allowed such a person as Mr Hovell, who knows so little of the interior of the country, and possessed of such poor abilities as a bushranger, to be of his party.
1843 John Hood *Australia and the East* 176: I confess I was again induced to wish that my boys had remained at home in Britain instead of becoming bushrangers in New Holland.
3 A runaway convict trying to survive in the bush, not always by preying on others
1801 James Elder MS Journal cit. *Australian Literary Studies* Jun. 1966, 214: One of these Bushrangers [concerned in stealing a boat] was Williams.
1805 *Sydney Gazette* 17 Feb. 2: On Tuesday last a cart was stopped between this settlement and Hawkesbury, by three men whose appearance sanctioned the suspicion of their being bushrangers ... they did not, however, take anything out of the cart ... from whence it may be hoped they prefer the prospect of being restored to society to any monetary relief that might be obtained from acts of additional imprudence that could at best but render their condition hopeless.
1819 Let. in *True Patriots All* ed. G. C. Ingleton (1952) 82: Men at this settlement reduced to the last stages of despair, frequently run into the woods and live upon what nature in her uncultivated state affords the wild productions of the forest ... A man of the name of Creig, actually asserts, that ... he beheld, leaning against a tree, a skeleton of a man, with a musket by his side, also against the tree, and which he supposes to be a *bushranger*, like himself. Many are compelled from hunger to give themselves up, and very frequently so starved that they can scarce crawl upon their hands and knees.
1823 *Godwin's Emigrant's Guide to Van Diemen's Land* 51: *Bush Rangers* are runaway convicts, who, absenting themselves from the settlements, resort to the woods, where there is plenty of game, which enables them to subsist, and renders them independent so long as they have a supply of ammunition. From 1808 to 1817 they increased in numbers, and were guilty of robberies, murders, and every species of atrocity.
1838 John Curtis *The Shipwreck of the Stirling Castle* 81: During his journey he fell in with a 'bush ranger' (that is a runaway convict) who had escaped from the penal settlement at Moreton Bay several years before, and had now united himself with a tribe of natives.
4 One who evades the law by keeping to the bush, and maintains himself by robbery (whether an escaped convict or not), usually a member of a gang: the commonest sense
1806 *Sydney Gazette* 16 Nov. 1: BUSH-RANGERS. As the daring spirits of these desperate offenders occupies much serious attention at the present moment, we enter into the following particulars ... Five sheep have disappeared in the course of one night, notwithstanding every vigilant exertion of the stock keepers and guards ... Night and day they have been harassed by their daring visitors, their huts plundered as well as their flocks, & their provi-

sions carried off.
1816 *Hobart Town Gazette* 23 Nov. 1:
Soon after, the party were alarmed by
the appearance of the Bush rangers,
headed by *Michael Howe,* & his gang
of 8 runaways.
1856 G. Willmer *The Draper in Australia* 107: I availed myself of the
opportunity to deposit some gold,
rather than carry it with me any
longer, at the risk of being plundered
of it by bush-rangers.
1867 J. R. Houlding *Australian Capers*
380: Bushrangers who stopped them,
then rifled the coach and passengers'
pockets, and read all the letters in the
mail bags that were interesting to them.
1880 J. C. Crawford *Travels in New
Zealand and Australia* 6: About this
time I had occasion to go to Yass, and
on my return was, as they say, 'stuck
up' by two bush-rangers.
1899 G. E. Boxall *The Story of the
Australian Bushrangers* [book title]
5 A business enterprise exploiting the
public
1951 Dymphna Cusack *Say No to Death*
52: 'Bushrangers, aren't they? Ned
Kelly was a gentleman compared with
most of the landlords around here.'
1954 *Coast to Coast 1953–54* 160:
When she overheard Sam [a junk
dealer] described as a bushranger she
spun round aggressively ready to do
battle for her husband's honour.

bushranging
1823 *Godwin's Emigrant's Guide to Van
Diemen's Land* 52: The Sydney Gazette,
of October 4, 1817, contains the above
particulars; but since that period little
has been heard of Bush-ranging.
1827 P. Cunningham *Two Years in New
South Wales* i 194–5: Some [convicts]
disgusted with restraint and steady
labour, will occasionally take to the
woods, and subsist by plundering the
settlers around, with whose convict-
servants they are frequently leagued.
This method of robbery is denominated
'bush-ranging'; it has been a severe
scourge in Van Dieman's Land.
1939 Kylie Tennant *Foveaux* 425: Bud
Pellager ... had taken to a mild and
lucrative form of bushranging as owner

of a garage on the Main Western Highway.

bush telegraph 1 An informant alerting
bushrangers to the movements of the
police
1878 *Australian* i 507: The police are
baffled by the false reports of the con-
federates and the number and activity
of the bush telegraphs. [Morris]
1882 A. J. Boyd *Old Colonials* 175: In
Queensland we have no bushrangers.
There are no convict shepherds – no
bush telegraphs – none of the thousand
and one conveniences for securing the
safety of these gentry.
1899 G. E. Boxall *The Story of the
Australian Bushrangers* 238: The Press
... continued to urge the necessity for
suppressing the 'bush telegraphs' and
other sympathisers of the bushrangers.
2 The passing of information (not illicit)
by unofficial channels e.g. word of
mouth; any message so received
1895 Henry Lawson 'Black Joe' *Prose*
i 255: The nearest squatter's wife ...
arranged (by bush telegraph) to drive
over next morning with her sister-in-
law and two other white women in the
vicinity, to see Mary decently buried.
1961 Patrick White *Riders in the
Chariot* 381: She had acquired a numerous clientele, through her dealings
in bottles, as well as by bush telegraph.

bushwhacker A backwoodsman; someone lacking in social graces or in acumen
1900 Henry Lawson 'Joe Wilson's
Courtship' *Prose* i 544: He said I'd
spoilt the thing altogether. He said that
she'd got an idea that I was shy and
poetic, and I'd only shown myself the
usually sort of Bush-whacker.
1900–10 O'Brien and Stephens: *Bushwhackers* applied to uncouth, rawboned
or unmannerly country people.
1903 Nat Gould *The Three Wagers* 271:
'You'll find it a trifle different riding
against us ... we are not a lot of
bushwhackers down here, let me tell
you.'
1930 L. W. Lower *Here's Luck* 159: 'I
wasn't goin' to have these city blokes
pickin' me for a bush-whacker so I

filled in a coupon for a complete rig-out from Sydney.'

1938 Xavier Herbert *Capricornia* 384: 'You've been readin' newspapers, which from start to finish are only fit for the purpose we bushwhackers use 'em for when we've read 'em.'

1951 Dymphna Cusack *Say No to Death* 170: He wasn't such a bushwhacker that he didn't know quality when he saw it.

1959 Gerard Hamilton *Summer Glare* 68: She was only sixteen, a real bush-whacker, short, buxom and stupid, with little or no education.

1967 K. S. Prichard *Subtle Flame* 38: 'Now, if you'd only grown a beard, you'd look a regular bushwhacker.'

1971 Rena Briand *White Man in a Hole* 17: 'It's the smallest dugout in Coober,' he said, 'but good enough for an old bushwhacker like me.'

bushwhacking Living in the rough conditions of the bush

1935 H. H. Finlayson *The Red Centre* 24: To Giles the Englishman – after weeks of bush-whacking in the mulga farther north – these views appealed with special force.

bush week In the expression 'What do you think this is, bush week?' as a protest or complaint

1945 Baker 76: The time honoured chant of derision, *What's this, bush week?*

1949 Lawson Glassop *Lucky Palmer* 37: 'I get smart alecks like you trying to put one over on me every minute of the day. What do you think this is? Bush Week?'

1951 Seaforth MacKenzie *Dead Men Rising* 53: 'Fall in! Snap into it you lot of old women. Pull your fingers out, now! What do you think this is – bush week?'

1958 Tom Ronan *The Pearling Master* 309: 'What's the strong of pulling up in the middle of a block? What do you think this is? Bush week?'

1966 H. F. Brinsmead *Beat of the City* 26: 'You can just nail it back on again proper. What do you think this is, bush week?'

1975 Les Ryan *The Shearers* 74: 'What do you think it is – bush week?'

bushy, bushie (bush-head) An uncomplicated bush-dweller, as distinct from a townsman

1887 *Tibb's Popular Song Book* 1: 'Bushy in Town'. Have you noticed in the city, / With the Sydney going push, / How they often stare and giggle, / At us chaps from down the Bush?

1900 Henry Lawson 'A Gentleman Sharper and Steelman Sharper' *Prose* i 226: 'We're two hard-working, innocent bushies, down for an innocent spree.'

c. 1914 A. B. Paterson 'Racehorses and Racing in Australia' in *The World of 'Banjo' Paterson* ed. C. Semmler (1967) 318: He saw a genuine bushman, bearded, cabbage-tree-hatted, sunburnt, and silent. Bearing down on the old bushie he told him the old tale.

1949 John Morrison *The Creeping City* 241: 'I'm only a bush-head. I'm not supposed to have the intelligence to put two and two together.'

1955 Mary Durack *Keep Him My Country* 114: He never tried to swear the hardened bushies off the drink.

1973 Max Harris *The Angry Eye* 70: Warm-hearted, open-minded bushies are thin on the ground.

buster, southerly see **southerly buster**

but Used with the force of 'however' or 'though' at the end of a sentence

1957 Gerard Hamilton *Summer Glare* 112: 'Gee, they're lucky but, ain't they?'

1962 Stuart Gore *Down the Golden Mile* 218: 'I always seem to miss th' bastards ... I've given a couple of 'em a bloody good fright but.'

1972 Turner 95: We congratulated him on the Sydney climate. He agreed it was good, then added 'We've got central heating, but.'

butcher A measure of beer [see quot. 1898]

1898 Morris: *Butcher* n. South Australian slang for a long drink of beer, so-called (it is said) because the men of a certain butchery in Adelaide used this refreshment regularly.

1945 Baker 168: *Butcher* is Adelaide slang; in the early days it was used for a glass containing about two-thirds of a pint. In modern times the size has dropped to about half a pint.

1958 A. W. Upfield *The Bachelors of Broken Hill* 130: He ought to be in this pleasant saloon bar reading a paper and enjoying the best cigarettes with long 'butchers' of beer.

1971 Rena Briand *White Man in a Hole* 108: Johnny grinned and ordered three butchers.

buttinski An inquisitive or interfering person: *obs.* [U.S. 1903 Mathews]

1924 *Truth* 27 Apr. 6: *Buttinski* An intruding person.

1926 J. Vance Marshall *Timely Tips for New Australians*: *Buttinski* A slang word frequently used to describe an inquisitive person.

1947 H. Drake-Brockman *The Fatal Days* 120: 'What you wanter speak t' young Ed for? You're a butinski.'

1966 Baker 222: *buttinski* a term used among telephone mechanics for the hand telephone used for cutting in on private phone calls.

buy into, to To involve oneself, esp. in trouble or conflict

1962 Alan Seymour *The One Day of the Year* 56: 'You fight your own battles. I'm not buyin' into any arguments. I get enough of 'em around here.'

B Y O (G) Bring your own (grog): legend on informal invitations to a party, notice in restaurants without a liquor licence

1975 *National Times* 23 Jun. 5: B Y O diplomat. The Australian Government last week paid for itself to be a 'guest' at a cocktail party given by the Japan-Australia Society . . . in Tokyo.

C

cab, (first) ~ off the rank The first to take advantage of an opportunity

1977 *Australian* 19 Jul. 10: It is unlikely the Ranger partners will agree to new terms without concessions, such as being first cab off the rank if, as expected, the Government agrees to limited mining.

1977 *Australian* 5 Feb. 19: Yet the last cab on the rank – Reid's, *The Whitlam Venture* – promises to outshine all of these, both in money and numbers per month.

Cabbage Garden (Patch) The colony or state of Victoria: *jocular* [f. size and crops]

1889 J. H. Zillman *Australian Life* 30: 'The cabbage garden', old cynical Sir John Robertson, of New South Wales, once called Victoria. [Morris]

1903 Joseph Furphy *Such is Life* (1944) 43: 'You are a native of the colonies, I presume?' 'Yes, I come from the Cabbage Garden.' Ibid. 124: I slid gently into the water, and paddled for the Cabbage Garden shore.

1916 Macmillan's *Modern Dictionary of the English Language* 776: *Cabbage Garden* the State of Victoria, in allusion to its small size, and also to its exportation of vegetables to Sydney.

1934 Thomas Wood *Cobbers* 144: People in other States call Victoria, rudely, the Cabbage Patch, and make a show of looking for it on the map with a magnifying glass. Victorians smile a stiff smile.

1939 R. H. Croll *I Recall* 153: The old New South Wales joke that Victoria was merely a 'cabbage garden'.

1970 *Australian* 31 Oct. 3: 'Cabbage patch history' was the way a leading historian yesterday described the Victorian Government's bicentenary awards – now the centre of a growing literary row.

cabbage-gardeners

1908 Henry Lawson 'His Coloured Country' *Prose* i 786: 'You can blanky well secesh and go in with the blanky Cabbage-gardeners.'

cabbage-tree mob Precursors of the larrikin q.v. [f. *cabbage-tree hat*]

1852 G. C. Mundy *Our Antipodes* i 53–4: There are to be found round the doors of the Sydney theatre a sort of 'loafers', known as the Cabbage-tree mob ... These are an unruly set of young fellows, native born generally ... Dressed in a suit of fustian or colonial tweed, and the emblem of their order, the low-crowned cabbage-palm hat, the main object of their enmity seems to be the ordinary black head-piece worn by respectable persons, which is ruthlessly knocked over the eyes of the wearer as he passes or enters the theatre.

1894 James T. Ryan *Reminiscences* 223: Ned Sadler, bootmaker, of Sydney, was a wonder; he was a great politician, and belonged to the 'Cabbage Tree Mob', as they were then called.

1907 Charles MacAlister *Old Pioneering Days* 178: He earned the enmity of the 'Cabbage-tree Hat' mob on account of the part he took in securing the conviction of the Myall Creek (Aborigines) massacre in 1838.

cactus, back to the To return to one's familiar haunts, usually away from the city: catch-phrase of the comedian 'Mo' (Roy Rene) in the McCackie Mansions series of the 1930s

1945 *Coast to Coast 1944* 174: He got in the car and started the engine. 'Well, it's back to the cactus,' he said.

1945 Roy Rene *Mo's Memoirs* 120: Mo is very nostalgic and dying for the end of his honeymoon: 'Oh to get back to the cactus. Just dying to get a saw in me hand.'

calabash A promissory note issued by bush-storekeepers and others: see quots. The name suggests that the calabash had the same brittleness as the 'shin plaster' q.v., as though inscribed on the shell of a gourd.

1917 R. D. Barton *Reminiscences of an Australian Pioneer* 159: Everyone was paid by orders, 'calabashes' we used to call them, drawn on himself by the person paying.

1938 *Smith's Weekly* 12 Nov. 6: Mention of 'shinplasters' recently in 'Smith's Weekly' suggests a mention of 'Calabash'. This was a form of cur-

rency in the early days, and was originally an order for a small amount, drawn upon some agent of the drawer and payable at various dates after presentation. Finally a calabash became an IOU for sums under one pound.

call To broadcast a race description

1949 Lawson Glassop *Lucky Palmer* 247: 'There's no better race caller in Australia than "Lucky" Palmer. When he was only fourteen he used to call the races from the verandah of a house.'

1977 *Sun-Herald* 9 Jan. 67: He's calling the dogs on 2UE on Fridays from Richmond and on Saturdays from Wentworth Park.

camp down To go to bed; to die

1887 *All the Year Round* 30 Jul. 66: 'To go to camp', by a transference from its original meaning, now signifies, in the mouth of a dweller in houses, simply 'to lie down', 'to go to bed'.

1898 Henry Lawson 'Dust Thou Art' *Prose* i 325: 'I can imagine ... the chaps rubbing their hats off, and standing round looking as if it was their funeral instead of mine, and one of 'em saying, maybe, "Ah well, poor Jack, he's camped down at last!"'

1898 *Bulletin* 1 Oct. 14: When he's buried he has 'pitched his camp'.

canary 1 A convict; his yellow clothing [f. *canary bird* a jailbird, or person kept in a cage OED 1673]

1827 P. Cunningham *Two Years in New South Wales* ii 117: Convicts of but recent migration are facetiously known by the name of *canaries*, by reason of the yellow plumage in which they are fledged at the period of landing.

1840 J. Pitts Johnson *Plain Truths* 56: Prisoners ... are commonly denominated 'the canary birds', so called from their dresses being yellow.

1843 Charles Rowcroft *Tales of the Colonies* ii 218: 'Your description of their dress,' said Mr Marsh, 'accounts for a jeering expression I have heard, and could not understand ... my bullock-driver called out to him [the prisoner] 'Going to be caged, my

canary-bird?'
1870 Marcus Clarke *His Natural Life* ed. S. Murray-Smith (1970) 548: We can't bring him off . . . in his canaries. He puts on these duds, d'ye see.'
2 A gold coin [f. *canary bird* guineas Grose 1785]
1853 Mrs C. Clacy *A Lady's Visit to the Gold Diggings of Australia in 1852–53* 91: For the sake of the uninitiated, I must explain that, in diggers' slang, a 'canary' and a half-sovereign are synonymous.
1895 Cornelius Crowe *The Australian Slang Dictionary* 14: Canary Bird a convict; a gold coin.
3 One hundred lashes
1859 John Lang *Botany Bay* 40: There were slang terms applied to these doses of the lash: twenty-five was called a 'tester'; fifty, a 'bob'; seventy-five, a 'bull'; and a hundred, a 'canary'.

carby The carburettor [abbr.]
1973 H. Williams *My Love Had a Black Speed Stripe* 71: 'He's been pumping the accelerator . . . Flooding the carby.'

carrion A term applied to bullocks, horses, most often collectively: *derogatory* [f. *carrion* poor, wretched or worthless beast OED 1634 *Obs.*]
1835 *Colonist* 22 Jan. 28: Passing the hut of a poor settler . . . he heard the man's wife addressing an old scarecrow of a mare in some such terms as the following;- 'Bad luck to you, you old rottern carrion!'
1901 Henry Lawson 'The Little World Left Behind' *Prose* i 376: The same sunburned, masculine women went past to market twice a week in the same old carts and driving much the same quality to carrion.
1903 Joseph Furphy *Such is Life* (1944) 7: 'Where did you stop las' night? Your carrion's as full as ticks.' Ibid. 15: 'Now, chaps, round up yer carrion, an' shove 'em in.'

Carruthers, Go for your life, Lady A catch-phrase from the 'Gay Paree' sketch by Roy Rene ('Mo')
1972 Alexander Macdonald *The Ukelele*

Player under the Red Lamp 239: Mo asked Lady Carruthers how she herself was enjoying her stay in Gay Paree. To which she replied, coyly. 'I've got something to confess, Mr McCackie – I've been here for a fortnight and I haven't once visited the Louvre.' . . . Her next line was an exit-throwaway. 'But now I must go, I must go!' To which one night, with an expression of obscene sympathy, Mo added – 'Oh yes, go! Go! Go for your life, Lady Carruthers!'

caser Five shillings: *obs.* [f. Yiddish *kesef* silver: also English and U.S.]
1849 Alexander Harris *The Emigrant Family* (1967) 104: 'A caser (a dollar) if you give him a night of it; and four if he gets what'll make him quiet.' ·
1901 Henry Lawson 'Send Round the Hat' *Prose* i 471: He rolled the drunkard over, prospected his pockets till he made up five shillings (or a 'caser' in Bush language), and 'chucked' them into the hat.
1924 *Truth* 27 Apr. 6: *Caser* Five shillings.
1950 *Australian Police Journal* Apr. 112: *Caser* 5s.

cashed up Well supplied with money
1930 L. W. Lower *Here's Luck* 163: 'Straight from the Never-Never by the look of him. Is he cashed up?'
1959 D'Arcy Niland *The Big Smoke* 200: 'One of these days when I'm real cashed up like, I'm gonna get myself one of them trombones. They're great.'
1973 John Morrison *Australian by Choice* 127: I . . . came back to Melbourne well cashed up, and for a few leisurely weeks lived well.

cast, make a To make a sweep from a given point to pick up lost tracks; also used (mainly N.Z.) of a dog, so trained to muster sheep
1876 Rolf Boldrewood *A Colonial Reformer* (1890) 205: I wasted no time in the camp but made a cast around, to pick up the tracks of the fugitive. Mayboy, eager as a bloodhound, was soon on the trail.

castor A hat: *obs.* [f. *castor* a hat of beaver or rabbit fur OED 1640–1849; *castor* a hat Grose 1785]
1812 Vaux: *Castor* a hat.
1899 W. T. Goodge *Hits! Skits! and Jingles!* 151: When a 'castor' or a 'kady' / Is the name he gives his hat.

castor, on the castor Similar to 'jake', 'sweet': *rare* [?f. *castor* sugar hence 'sweet']
1945 Baker 156: *castor* Good, excellent. [as World War II slang]
1950 *Australian Police Journal* Apr. 111: *Castor* O.K.
1963 John Cantwell *No Stranger to the Flame* 103: 'How is he today?' 'Castor, now you've arrived,' Max said easily.
1967 Kylie Tennant *Tell Morning This* 283: 'Why am I on the castor with them?' 'Oh that.' Harold's face cleared. 'Soon's they knew you was in with Numismata, they all want to piss in your pocket.' Ibid. 438: 'We've got an eighteen foot stick,' Harold bragged . . . 'She's castor.'

cat, whip (flog) the To give way to feelings of chagrin, frustration, regret; to reproach oneself [OED records *whip (jerk, shoot) the cat* to vomit 1609–1830. This expression seems closer to 'kicking the dog' as a way of venting spleen.]
1847 Alexander Harris *Settlers and Convicts* ed. C. M. H. Clark (1954) 193: And now it was my turn to 'whip the cat'.
1878 G. H. Gibson *Southerly Busters* 68: Though William by the 'cat' was whipped, / He never 'whipped the cat'.*
*To 'whip the cat' signifies, in native parlance, to weep or lament.
1901 Henry Lawson 'A Double Buggy at Lahey's Creek' *Prose* i 595: I 'whipped the cat' a bit, the first twenty miles or so, but then I thought, what did it matter?
1903 Joseph Furphy *Such is Life* (1944) 7: 'Evil-natured beggar, that,' he continued. 'He's floggin' the cat now, 'cos he laid us on to the selection in spite of his self.' Ibid. 20: 'Gosh, you had that bloke to rights. He's whippin' the cat now like fury.'

1919 W. H. Downing *Digger Dialects* 53: *Whip the cat* Experience chagrin.
1932 K. S. Prichard *Kiss on the Lips* 184: 'I been whippin' the cat, thinkin' I'd missed seein' the mare do her gallop.'
1944 Alan Marshall *These Are My People* 137: 'I whipped the bloody cat all the way in the bus.'
1951 Dal Stivens *Jimmy Brockett* 255: Then I started whipping the cat for not having thought of it before.

Cats, the The Geelong V.F.L. team
1976 *Sunday Telegraph* 11 Apr. 74: Olsson has Cats on rampage.

Cazaly, up there A cry of encouragement or congratulation, commemorating the V.F.L. player Roy Cazaly (1893–1963), noted for his high-marking
1943 Baker 85: *Up there, Cazaly!* Used as a cry of encouragement. (Cazaly was a noted South Melbourne footballer, whose specialty was high marking.)
1955 John Morrison *Black Cargo* 231: 'Up there, Cazaly!'
1957 Ray Lawler *Summer of the Seventeenth Doll* 30: 'Up there Cazaly, lots of love – Nance.'
1965 *Daily Telegraph* 18 Feb. 42: The other states and the Northern Territory play football – 'Up there, Cazaly'.
1973 Frank Huelin *Keep Moving* 97: The audience roared approval. Someone, evidently an ardent football fan from Melbourne, yelled 'Up there, Cazaly'.

Centre, the Central Australia, sometimes the Red Centre
1901 F. J. Gillen *Diary* (1968) 149: She has a somewhat pleasant face of a type not common amongst the natives of the Centre.
1936 W. Hatfield *Australia through the Windscreen* 119: Throughout the whole of the Centre not a spot of rain fell between 1923 and 1930.
1974 *Australian* 18 Oct. 20: How red the Centre this summer?
Centralia
1930 *Bulletin* 8 Jan. 19: Some cattle on a Centralian station.

century, go for the To try to shear 100 sheep in a day

1905 'Another Fall of Rain' *The Old Bush Songs* ed. A. B. Paterson 28: For some had got the century who'd never got it before.

1957 'The Backblock Shearer' *Old Bush Songs* ed. Stewart and Keesing 258: 'Tomorrow I go with a sardine blow / For a century or the sack.

1964 H. P. Tritton *Time Means Tucker* 92: Dutchy went for the 'century' and just failed. [recalling 1905–6]

chain, drag the To lag behind: used first in shearing, but now most commonly of a drinker who does not keep up with his group at the bar

1933 Acland: *Drag the chain, to* To be the slowest shearer in a shed.

1941 Baker 25: *Drag the chain* To be slow, to be inferior, to 'tail' the field in any work or contest.

1954 Tom Ronan *Vision Splendid* 124: 'Pass the bottle, Top, you're draggin the chain.'

1961 Mena Calthorpe *The Dyehouse* 156: 'Maybe they could take it easy. Drag the chain just a little.'

1968 Geoffrey Dutton *Andy* 146: 'Rooster here's way behind; dragging the bloody chain. He's due to set 'em up.'

chair, to be in the To be the one responsible for a round of drinks

1966 Baker 230: *to be in the chair* to be the person who pays for the next round of drinks (the pertinent question is often *Who's in the chair?*)

1972 Geoff Morley *Jockey Rides an Honest Race* 18: 'Just to show you what sort of a fellow I am, I'll go first in the chair.'

1974 John Powers *The Last of the Knucklemen* 78: 'Who's in the chair?' 'Me. My shout.'

chalkie A schoolteacher

1941 Baker 17: *Chalk-and-talker* A school-teacher.

1953 T. A. G. Hungerford *Riverslake* 29: 'I was a chalky before the war – just couldn't settle down to it again, after.'

1972 Richard Magoffin *Chops and Gravy* 46: Kev is a bushie too, although he's a chalkie. He teaches at a boarding school in Charters Towers.

1973 Max Harris *The Angry Eye* 229: The quiverful of clerical chalkies who instructed us in the subject.

Challenge, Barcoo see Barcoo

champagne, Northern Territory see Northern

charity moll (dame) An amateur prostitute who does not charge a professional rate; any woman who thus deprives the professional of trade

1953 Baker 125: An amateur harlot or one who undercuts regular professional prices, with little thought for the consequences of this deflationary activity, is called a *charity dame* or a *for-free*.

1962 Criena Rohan *The Delinquents* 104: 'Remember,' she warned, 'no charity moll capers with my men.'

charlie A girl [f. rhyming slang *Charlie Wheeler* = *sheila*. Perhaps related to *charlies*, English slang for breasts.]

1949 Lawson Glassop *Lucky Palmer* 41: 'Charlie?' asked Eric. 'What do mean by Charlie?' 'Your Charlie,' repeated Max. 'Your canary.' 'Canary?' 'Ay, don't you speak English? Your sheila!'

1951 Dal Stivens *Jimmy Brockett* 102: The stocky little Charlie Wheeler said to me, 'I'm having a party soon and you must come along.'

1972 Geoff Morley *Jockey Rides an Honest Race* 61: There's plenty of charlies over here. The town is built for tourism and this has caused an influx of waitresses, barmaids, chambermaids, housemaids and other assorted frilly trillies.

Charlie, Slippery (Circuitous) Sir Charles Cowper (1807–75), Premier of N.S.W. on five occasions

1859 Frank Fowler *Southern Lights and Shadows* 71: Mr Charles Cowper, the Premier . . . is commonly called 'Circuitous Charley', from Mr Lowe's saying of him, that if he saw the gate of heaven opened, he would not walk in straight, but would *wriggle* in like a worm.

1934 Hugh McCrae *Georgiana's Journal* 148: On dissolution of the old council, he was elected from Camden to the new, defeating 'Slippery Charlie' Cowper by a mere hatful of votes.

chase up a cow see **cow**

cheque The total sum received, esp. for work done by contract, or from the sale of some crop

1857 F. Cooper *Wild Adventures in Australia* 66: Drawing my 'cheque' from Wilder, I felt my exchequer sufficiently strong to allow of my embarking in another career, namely, that of an overlander.

1875 Rolf Boldrewood *The Squatter's Dream* repr. as *Ups and Downs* (1878) 93: The shepherd hands his cheque across the bar – and till every shilling, purchased by a year's work, abstinence and solitude, disappears, drinks – madly drinks.

1901 Henry Lawson 'His Brother's Keeper' *Prose* i 517: He was 'ringer' of the shed at Piora Station one season and made a decent cheque.

1922 Herbert Scanlon *Bon Jour Digger* 31: I myself was taking a trip on the results of my huge wool cheque.

1936 Archer Russell *Gone Nomad* 68: So was our mob delivered at last. The drover received the cheque that was due to him and Moleskin, Pilot and I were paid off.

1949 *Coast to Coast 1948* 162: 'If we make any sort of a cheque out of the crop this season you might make a trip to the States.'

1962 Tom Ronan *Deep of the Sky* 6: Calico Hat went for his private horses; at breakfast he asked for his cheque.

1975 *Sydney Morning Herald* 20 Dec. 19: Australia's wool cheque for the first half of the 1975–76 wool selling season is estimated at $367.2 million.

chequed up Well supplied with funds in the form of a cheque

1940 Ion L. Idriess *Lightning Ridge* 126: They'd reappear again in six months time, 'chequed up' and smiling.

1966 Tom Ronan *Once There Was a Bagman* 84: 'You fellows should be well chequed up and if you don't speculate you won't accumulate.'

see **cashed up**

cherry Virginity [listed by Partridge as the hymen; also U.S.]

1959 Dorothy Hewett *Bobbin Up* 158: 'And don't bank on your sailor boy comin' home to you . . . I lost me cherry on the kitchen table to a sailor once. I was fifteen.'

1970 Germaine Greer *The Female Eunuch* 194: The Poison Maiden of *An American Dream* is called, appropriately enough, Cherry. She is pure, to all intents virgin as her name implies.

1974 Robert Adamson *Zimmer's Essay* 46: 'My tip is, do it easy. You have a good time in there. They'll have your cherry before you know it.'

chewy on your boot See quots: Victorian sporting

1966 Baker 370: *Hope you have chewie on your boot!* Used to express a wish that a football player kicking for goal misses because there is chewing gum on his boot.

1975 *Sydney Morning Herald* 8 Nov. 4: Mr Hawke puzzled the crowd when he described their reaction to the Khemlani disclosure as 'You were wrong, chewy on your boot.' He did not seem to realize that he had used an Australian Rules cat-call.

chiack, chiacking *n.* (chī'ack) Good-humoured banter; jeering, esp. collective [1859 Hotten: *Chi-ike,* a hurrah, a good word, or hearty praise; term used by the Costermongers who assist the sale of each other's goods by a little friendly though noisy commendation.]

1853 C. R. Read *What I Heard, Saw and Did on the Australian Goldfields* 148: The 'skyhacking'* to which the police were subject when sent round to inspect people's licenses, was brought up principally by their own individual overbearing conduct . . . It no doubt was

extremely vexing to be shouted after, but their own conduct and language rendered them obnoxious and encouraged people to shout. *Blackguarding
1869 Marcus Clarke 'The Language of Bohemia' in *A Colonial City* ed. L. T. Hergenhan (1972) 159: The hissing of gallery, or the gods, is called *chy-ike*.
1885 *The Australasian Printers' Keepsake* 154: One toff, who fancied himself, still kept poking borack, but Steve stopped his chyacking pretty quick, for he hauled off and let him have it.
1915 C. J. Dennis *The Songs of a Sentimental Bloke* 20: I felt as if I couldn't get that fur, / 'An start to sling off chiack like I used . . . / *Not intrajuiced* !
1959 Gerard Hamilton *Summer Glare* 96: The boys made a few unhelpful suggestions and quite a bit of chyacking went on.

chiack *v.* To 'chaff', tease; to ridicule
1893 J. A. Barry *Steve Brown's Bunyip* 21: 'They're always a-poking borack an a-chiackin' o' me over in the hut!'
1896 Henry Lawson 'Across the Straits' *Prose* i 200: There were several pretty girls in the office, laughing and chiacking the counter clerks.
1908 Henry Fletcher *Dads and Dan between Smokes* 2: Don't walk about; it's tirin'; stand at street-corners and spit – besides, that's ther best place ter see life and chyack the girls.
1931 Vance Palmer *Separate Lives* 14: 'They've been chiacking me about my cold feet.'
1948 Ruth Park *Poor Man's Orange* 105: The milk-carters . . . sloshed the milk into the cans, chyacked Dolour about her goggles, and charged out again.
1967 K. S. Prichard *Subtle Flame* 105: The rowdy bodgie youths kept seats near this group, chiacking the buxom, brassy-haired waitress as she rushed around with a tray-load of dishes and lively back-chat.

Chink, Chinkie A Chinaman: *derogatory*
1876 A. J. Boyd *Old Colonials* (1882) 233: Our colonialised 'Chinkie', as he is vulgarly termed (with the single

variation 'Chow').
1887 *Tibb's Popular Songbook* 7: And educate a Chinkie / To import some thousands more.
1891 Henry Lawson 'The Cambaroora Star' *Verse* i 159: 'Get a move upon the Chinkies when you've got an hour to spare.'
1896 Edward Dyson *Rhymes from the Mines* 101: Here, I state that all Chinkies are vicious / And I hate them like fever and snakes.
1939 Kylie Tennant *Foveaux* 85: 'Went to a herbulist . . . He give me something that took it away. Wonderful them Chinks are.'
1951 Dal Stivens *Jimmy Brockett* 90: We've got the best country in the world and the best people, and we don't want any Chinks or other foreigners butting in on us.
1969 William Dick *Naked Prodigal* 5: He didn't seem a bad bloke for a chinky-chink.
see **chow**

chips, to spit see **spit chips**

Chloe, drunk as Very drunk [listed by Partridge as an English slang expression from c. 1850]
1892 Barcroft Boake 'How Polly Paid for her Keep' *Bulletin* 6 Feb. 10, repr. in *Where the Dead Men Lie* (1897) 69: Drunk! with my loved ones on board, drunk as Chloe!
1941 Baker 17: *Chloe, drunk as* Exceedingly drunk.
1945 Cecil Mann *The River* 43: Drunk as Chloe on the potent cognac of that green and pleasant isle.
1948 A. W. Upfield *An Author Bites the Dust* 140: 'I never seen a bloke stand up to it like he did. If you seen him coming like a parson to a funeral you could bet he was as drunk as Chloe.'
1950 Brian James *The Advancement of Spencer Button* 97: 'An old chap skittled – drunk as Chloe – walked right under it.'
1956 Kylie Tennant *The Honey Flow* 188: They would get as drunk as Chloe and probably end up in a fight somewhere.

choco 1 See quot. (World War I slang)

1919 W. H. Downing *Digger Dialects* 16: *Chocs* The 8th Brigade ('Tivey's Chocolate Soldiers'). Originally an abusive name; now an honourable appellation.

2 A member of the Militia, which did not serve outside Australia and its territories (World War II slang)

1942 *Salt* 14 Sep. 35: 'You labelled him a 'choco', because he did not fight / You thought he didn't have the guts to stick up for the right.'

1944 Lawson Glassop *We Were the Rats* 261: I told myself that I had misjudged the chocos.

1959 David Forrest *The Last Blue Sea* v: Militiamen (Chocolate Soldiers, Chokos) were mostly wartime conscripts, led by a mixture of pre-war militia officers and N.C.O.'s, and of A.I.F. officers with overseas battle experience during 1940–41.

choke down 1 To subdue an unbroken horse

1926 K. S. Prichard *Working Bullocks* 59: He [the brumby] threw himself down, the rope choking him, lay a moment, then scrambling to his feet tugged and pulled again until it looked as if he would break his neck. He choked himself down.

1962 Ron Tullipan *March into Morning* 6: He felt the rope burns caused by the fighting brumby old Riley and he had choked down and fitted with a bridle.

1975 Xavier Herbert *Poor Fellow My Country* 634: You choke down a calf or a micky-bull or some animal with a rope when he gets too tough.

2 To yield to the effects of alcohol

1945 Tom Ronan *Strangers on the Ophir* 131: Artesian Lake, for the first time on record, had, in the vernacular of the country, 'choked down'.

chook A domestic fowl; a woman (*jocular*); nickname of anyone called Fowler [f. *chook* a call to pigs, or occas. to poultry EDD]

1855 William Howitt *Land, Labour and Gold* ii 139–40: They overtook a huge and very fat hen ... they tied chucky

up in a handkerchief, and rode on.

1900 J. C. L. Fitzpatrick *The Good Old Days* 71: A game rooster that could massacre twenty of your neighbours' domestic chooks in as many minutes.

1911 Louis Stone *Jonah* 126: 'Me name's Fowles – Arthur Fowles,' replied Chook.

1915 C. J. Dennis *The Songs of a Sentimental Bloke* 80: 'She's too young – too young to leave 'er muvver's nest!' / 'Orright, ole chook,' I nearly sez.

1935 Kylie Tennant *Tiburon* 33: 'Chook! Chook! Chook!' she called to the fowls.

1951 Dal Stivens *Jimmy Brockett* 247: Miss Helen Bascombe was engaged to a cove called John Graham, who had no more go than a hypnotised chook.

1959 D'Arcy Niland *The Big Smoke* 45: 'Funny old chook. I can get on all right with her, I think.'

1960 Nancy Cato *Green Grows the Vine* 180: The waiter's name was Feathers, and the other waiters called him Chook.

1967 Len Beadell *Blast the Bush* 141: 'Chook' Fowler, driving the old D7, heaped up a barrier of dirt.

1974 L. Oakes and D. Solomon *Grab for Power* 171: 'A lot of them [former Liberal ministers] wandered around like headless chooks for a long time, not having departmental heads to call on, and people to arrange their itineraries, and I think some of them had even forgotten how to use a telephone!

chookyard

1942 Gavin Casey *It's Harder for Girls* 126: 'I've seen one [willy-willy] take the roof off my front verandah an' land it in th' chookyard at the back.'

choom An Englishman: *jocular* [f. dialectal pronunciation of 'chum' as a mode of address]

[**1916** *The Anzac Book* 31: 'Have you got any baadges, choom?']

1919 W. H. Downing *Digger Dialects* 16: *Choom* An English soldier.

1946 *Sunday Sun* 18 Aug. Suppl. 15: That's how the Chooms came to send out Governor Macquarie.

1952 Jon Cleary *The Sundowners* 134: 'The Chooms have been telling us

what's wrong with us ever since they come out here with the First Fleet.'
1962 Stuart Gore *Down the Golden Mile* 24: 'Me old pal the choom. And how would you be, Squire?'
1974 *Sun-Herald* 9 Jun. 17: Chooms make a few blues over Strine.

chop Share, allocation, esp. in phrase 'get in for one's chop' [f. *chop* slice, cut OED 1640]
1919 W. H. Downing *Digger Dialects* 16: *Chop* Share. 'To hop in for one's chop' – to enter in, in order to secure a privilege or benefit.
1949 Lawson Glassop *Lucky Palmer* 104: 'Ginger's chop was twenty-six quid.'
1952 T. A. G. Hungerford *The Ridge and the River* 212: 'There's got to be leaders, so hop in for your chop. Think of the dough and the privileges.'
1966 D. H. Crick *Period of Adjustment* 21: 'Tell him his quid today'll be worth ten bob tomorrow, so he better get in for his chop.'

chop, no No good [f. *first, second chop* OED 1823]
1864 J. F. Mortlock *Experiences of a Convict* (1965) 23: I was in Australasia, dragging a hand-cart (reckoned 'no chop') when informed of it.
1882 Rolf Boldrewood *Robbery Under Arms* (World's Classics 1949) 13: There's good and bad of every sort, and I've met plenty that were no chop of all churches.
1955 John Morrison *Black Cargo* 174: 'I've heard he's no chop, Rory.' 'No chop? – he's a bastard.'

chop, not much Unimpressive, inferior
1849 Alexander Harris *The Emigrant Family* (1967) 369: 'Oh, he's not much of a chop, I must say.'
1903 Joseph Furphy *Such is Life* (1944) 9: 'Mac's no great chop.'
1928 Miles Franklin *Up the Country* (1966) 13: 'That old parson is not much chop, I don't reckon,' he confided.
1944 Lawson Glassop *We Were the Rats* 180: 'We only had those three morning raids. None of 'em were much

chop, apart from hitting H.Q.'
1957 Ray Lawler *Summer of the Seventeenth Doll* 125: 'What I'm offering is not much chop, but – I want to marry you, Ol.'
1962 J. Marshall and R. Drysdale *Journey Among Men* 146: 'How did you like the Big Smoke?' we asked ... 'She's orright, but she's not much chop fer an 'oliday.'
1973 Alexander Buzo *Norm and Ahmed* 25: 'They've improved a lot, these clubs. Twenty years ago they weren't much chop, just a place to go when you wanted to get out on the grog.'

Chow A Chinaman: derogatory [f. *chow-chow* OED 1845]
1864 *Thatcher's Colonial Minstrel* 72: 'The Chinaman's Fate'. Chow Chow his hands with glee did rub.
1876 A. J. Boyd *Old Colonials* (1882) 233: Our colonialised 'Chinkie', as he is vulgarly termed (with the single variation 'Chow').
1880 Rolf Boldrewood *The Miner's Right* (1890) 196: 'Here's these cursed Chows working away and rootin' out the gold like spuds.'
1908 Henry Fletcher *Dads and Dan between Smokes* 4: 'Give out yer washin' to a Chow.'
1921 K. S. Prichard *Black Opal* 59: 'Michael says he works like a chow.'
1945 Tom Ronan *Strangers on the Ophir* 115: The Chow would think the big fellow was sick and try to doctor him up with Chinese herbs.
1970 Patrick White *The Vivisector* 77: Like one of the Chinese beans the Chow had given them at Christmas.

christening, like a moll (streetgirl, gin) at a To be ill at ease, flustered, confused [variant of the English 'As demure as an old whore at a christening' Grose 1811]
1954 Bant Singer *Have Patience, Delaney* 114: You got me floundering like a street-girl at a christening.
1962 Gavin Casey *Amid the Plenty* 124: 'I've had a very nice evening, Mr Mayhew.' 'No you haven't ... you been looking like a moll at a christen-

ing.'
1965 Thomas Keneally *The Fear* 192:
'Come on, Cec' the gunner roared to his
mate. 'Talk about a gin at a bloody
christening!'
1970 Richard Beilby *No Medals for
Aphrodite* 31: 'Why don't you get
going? You're mucking around like a
moll at a christening.'

Christmas hold See quots
   1953 Baker 132: *Christmas hold* A hold
applied by grabbing an opponent's
testicles (a 'handful of nuts') [prison
slang]
   1956 Tom Ronan *Moleskin Midas* 115:
'I'll do my time willin' if I can get a
Christmas hold on him for half a minute
first.'
   1964 Tom Ronan *Packhorse and Pearling Boat* 125–6: Joe came in low,
looking for that grip which the west
coast black fellow learned from that
other clean fighter, the Jap: The
Christmas hold (the handful of nuts).

Christmas, what else did you get for
Derisory retort to a motorist sounding
his horn at another (as though playing
with a new toy)
   1976 Used in a T.V. commercial.

chromo A prostitute: *obs.* [? variant of
crow]
   1938 *Smith's Weekly* 31 Dec. 12: As
Tilly remarked, 'Wot can you heckspect
from a chromo, whose forefathers was
never married.'
   1944 Lawson Glassop *We Were the Rats*
103: 'Not bad for chromos, are they?'
   1949 Ruth Park *Poor Man's Orange*
200: The chromo next door got her
money easy in dark doorways.
   1953 Kylie Tennant *The Joyful Condemned* 166: 'He's one of those big
he-men that go sneaking around the
park waiting to snitch some chromo's
handbag. Just a pie-eater.'
   1959 D'Arcy Niland *The Big Smoke*
152: That old chromo from Campbell
Street: the wrinkled face flaring with
rouge and floury with powder.
   1975 *Bulletin* 4 Oct. 4: It is a pity the
word 'chromo' is old Australian slang

for prostitute (I never knew why). It
would be an apt term for a colour
television addict.

chuck off As for 'throw off' q.v.
   1915 C. J. Dennis *The Songs of a Sentimental Bloke* 22: Me! that 'as barracked
tarts . . . 'An chucked orf at 'em like a
phonergraft!
   1922 Arthur Wright *A Colt from the
Country* 140: 'What y' chuckin' off
about?' he growled.
   1958 A. E. Manning *The Bodgie* 76:
Your friends 'chuck off' at you for
being a 'goodie-goodie'.
   1959 Dorothy Hewett *Bobbin Up* 150:
She waddled away . . . grinning at the
good-humoured chucking off from the
spinners and reelers.

chunder To vomit; a term given currency by the Barry McKenzie comic strip
[variously explained as an abbreviation
of 'watch under' (see quot. 1965) and as
rhyming slang *Chunder Loo = spew* from
Chunder Loo of Akin Foo, a cartoon
figure in a long-running series of advertisements for Cobra bootpolish in the
Bulletin from 8 Apr. 1909]
   1950 Nevil Shute *A Town Like Alice*
76: 'The way these bloody Nips go on.
Makes you want to chunda.'
   1953 Baker 169: *chunder* To vomit,
whence, *chundering*, vomiting; also
chunder, a noun, vomit. [World War
II slang]
   1965 Barry Humphries 'Barry McKenzie' *Times Literary Supplement* 16 Sep.
812: His favourite word to describe
the act of involuntary regurgitation is
the verb to chunder. This word is not
in popular currency in Australia, but
the writer recalls that ten years ago it
was common in Victoria's more expen-
sive public schools. It is now used by
the Surfies, a repellent breed of sun-
bronzed hedonists who actually hold
chundering contests on the famed
beaches of the Commonwealth. I understand . . . that the word derives from a
nautical expression 'watch under', an
ominous courtesy shouted from the
upper decks for the protection of those
below.

1973 Alexander Buzo *Rooted* 91: She put a plate of rissoles down in front of me the other night and I chundered all over them.

cigarette swag A very thin swag, indicating desitution
1943 Baker 20: *Cigarette swag* A small swag carried by a tramp when he comes to a city.
1955 Alan Marshall *I Can Jump Puddles* 158: 'He was humping a cigarette swag,' explained The Fiddler. 'We all dodge blokes with a swag like that. They never have anything. They bot on you for the lot.'
1959 Donald Stuart *Yandy* 16: He had been camped in the river, with a cigarette swag* and almost no tucker. *A swag slim as a cigarette; a poverty swag.
1966 Tom Ronan *Once There Was a Bagman* 235: I was in my twenties and at least did have a couple of horses and some gear. Hughie was well in his sixties, with nothing but a cigarette swag.
1973 Frank Huelin *Keep Moving* 178: *Cigarette swag* One blanket, change of clothes and chaff bag.

circular saw, like being caught in a Metaphor for female promiscuity
1956 Tom Ronan *Moleskin Midas* 236: 'And gins never know properly who fathers their kids. It'd be like getting your hand caught in that circular saw ... and saying what tooth it was that cut you.'
1962 J. Marshall and R. Drysdale *Journey Among Men* 136: 'Oh, Norah,' she said quietly, 'it's happened again. Who was it this time?' 'Mrs South,' replied Norah, 'if you'd been cut by a circular saw, would *you* know which tooth did the damage?'

clancy An overflow [f. A. B. Paterson's poem 'Clancy of the Overflow']
1971 David Ireland *The Unknown Industrial Prisoner* 77: They'd had a clancy ... He had dozed off with the water running, and there was water slopping everywhere.

clinah, cliner Girlfriend, sweetheart: *obs.* [? f. G. *kleine* little]
1895 *Bulletin* 9 Feb. 15: I'm ryebuck and the girl's okay. / Oh, she's a good iron, is my little clinah.
1899 W. T. Goodge *Hits! Skits! and Jingles!* 150: And his lady-love's his 'donah' / Or his 'clinah' or his 'tart'.
1913 Henry Lawson 'The Old Push and the New' *Verse* iii 82: They were faithful to a clinah, they were loyal to a pal.
1916 C. J. Dennis *The Moods of Ginger Mick* 72: Wiv me arm around me cliner, an' me notions far frum wrong.
1924 *Truth* 27 Apr. 6: *Cliner* A young girl.
1928 A. W. Upfield *The House of Cain* 79: 'I 'elped to get 'is clinah out of quod for what she and 'im did for me.'
see **kleiner**

clip, the 'The whole quantity of wool shorn in any place, or in one season' (OED 1825–67)
1840 T. P. MacQueen *Australia as she is and may be* 34: The clip will be from 1469 head at 3lb each.
1850 B. C. Peck *Recollections of Sydney* 22: The clip this season, in New South Wales, falls very short of the average of many years past.
1925 C. E. W. Bean *On the Wool Track* 229: But every Australian State except Western Australia now has it own sales, and at which nearly the whole of the Australian clip is now disposed of.
1933 Acland: *Clip* The whole body of wool for the year (off a station, or belonging to a man).
1948 K. S. Prichard *Golden Miles* 32: She ... heard about the fine property Bill owned: how many sheep it ran and how well their clip had sold at the last wool sales.
1975 *Sydney Morning Herald* 20 Dec. 19: Australia's wool clip sells for $367.2m

clippie A bus conductress [f. clipping tickets]

clock To strike, hit in the face or head
1941 Baker 18: *Clock, to* To strike with the fist.

1956 F. B. Vickers *First Place to the Stranger* 135: 'Somebody will clock that bastard one day.'
1966 Bruce Beaver *You Can't Come Back* 7: 'You're no mate of mine. I very nearly clocked you back there, but I don't want to fight you or anyone else.'
1973 *Sun-Herald* 25 Mar. 108: Dick Woolcott, 46, the man whom Mr McMahon clocked with a squash racquet in America last year.

clock, bushman's, settler's see **bushman, settler**

clucky Pregnant (used by women only) [f. broody hen]
1941 Baker 18: *Clucky* Pregnant.

coach, who's robbing this Equivalent to 'Don't interrupt' or 'Don't interfere'
1945 Baker 250–1: Disapproval or disagreement is indicated by ... *who's robbing this coach?* * *Reputed to be associated with bushranging days, this expression is equivalent to 'mind your own business!'
1951 Eric Lambert *The Twenty Thousand Thieves* 206: Chip's boom shattered the sudden tensity of feeling among them. 'Who's robbing this coach? Do you want to hear the news or not?'
1963 Hal Porter *The Watcher on the Cast-Iron Balcony* 108: 'Shut up, you great lazy beasts,' the aunts cry back to the uncles. 'Who's robbing this coach, anyway?'

coach, coacher Docile cow or bullock used as decoy to attract wild cattle
1874 W. H. L. Ranken *Dominion of Australia* 110: To get them [the wild cattle] a party of stockmen take a small herd of quiet cattle, 'coaches'.
1898 Roland Graeme *From England to the Backblocks* 203: The inferior riders were left in charge of a lot of quiet cattle, or, as they are called, 'coachers'.
1906 A. B. Paterson *An Outback Marriage* 165: 'The way we get wild cattle hereabouts is to take out a mob of quiet cattle, what we call coaches, and let

'em feed in the moonlight alongside the scrub ... When the wild cattle come out, they run over to see the coaches, and we dash up and cut 'em off.'
1929 K. S. Prichard *Coonardoo* 71: 'Got the rest of the mob next evening,' Hugh drawled. 'Most of them, at any rate. But we had to turn in some coaches.'
1947 W. E. Harney *North of 23°* 28: We would find the small wild mobs, in mustering which, coachers – decoy cattle – would be used.
1967 John Yeomans *The Scarce Australians* 37: The docile cattle are called coaches, or coachers, because they coach the wild cattle in the right behaviour.

coat, on the 1 In disfavour, getting 'the cold shoulder'
1941 Baker 18: *Coat, on the* (of a man) To be sent to Coventry.
1949 Alan Marshall *How Beautiful Are Thy Feet* 219: 'Girls that are too easy are on the coat with me,' went on Ron.
1953 Kylie Tennant *The Joyful Condemned* 92: 'I happened to say something about that old hag Jess ... and she's had me on the coat ever since.'
1973 Fred Parsons *A Man Called Mo* 47: He stepped back a pace, and fingered his lapel. It was the 'He's on the coat' sign, a gesture of supreme contempt.
2 Used of a bet that is not genuine, made by arrangement to alter the odds
1949 Lawson Glassop *Lucky Palmer* 66: He held the lapel of his coat between his right thumb and forefinger and shook it. 'On the coat, them bets of mine, of course, Norm,' he said, making it clear they were not genuine.

coat, pull the coat Not to make a genuine effort
1977 *Sunday Telegraph* 2 Jan. 45: Although there are many who believe he pulls the coat in Sheffield Shield, that's as far from the truth as you can get.

Coathanger, the The Sydney Harbour Bridge: *jocular*
1946 *Sunday Sun* Suppl. 20 Oct. 15: The day the coathanger opens, Isaac Isaacs the G G polishes up his topper

and bowls through the smoke to the bunfight with a big cavalry escort.
1957 Sydney Hart *Pommie Migrant* 51: 'Ah,' I countered, jestingly, 'that's what the Melbourne folk call the 'coat-hanger', isn't it?'
1975 *Sun-Herald* 5 Jul. 19: In one of the sketches Hogan returns to the Harbour Bridge, where he used to work as a rigger. This time he's not on the heights of the coat-hanger itself, but in a toll collector's booth.

cobar A penny, a copper: *obs.* [f. name of copper-mining town]
1898 *Bulletin* 1 Oct. 14: A penny is a 'Cobar'.
1911 E. S. Sorenson *Life in the Australian Backblocks* 36: When Jack makes anything for the pet creation you can bet your bottom Cobar he will put all his ingenuity into it.

cobber Friend, mate: *obsolescent* [f. *cob* to take a liking to anyone EDD]
1895 *Bulletin* 9 Feb. 15: Oh she's a good iron, is my little clinah;/She's my cobber an' I'm 'er bloke.
1899 W. T. Goodge *Hits! Skits! and Jingles!* 150: And a bosom friend's a 'cobber'.
1900–10 O'Brien and Stephens: *Cobber* confidant, closest friend, mate or chum.
1910 Henry Lawson 'The Rising of the Court' *Prose* i 660: For the sake of a friend – of a 'pal' or a 'cobber'.
1916 *The Anzac Book* 151n: *Cobber* – Australian for a well tried and tested pal.
1933 F. E. Baume *Tragedy Track* 178: 'Can you imagine your old cobber on the talkies?'
1942 Gavin Casey *It's Harder for Girls* 15: It's only through the years, after a cobber or two has been unlucky ... that it begins to wear you down.
1965 Barry Humphries 'Barry McKenzie' *Times Literary Supplement* 16 Sep. 812: His vocabulary is borrowed from a diversity of national types, and words like 'cobber' and 'bonzer' still intrude as a sop to Pommy readers, though such words are seldom, if ever, used in present-day Australia.

cobber up
1923 Jack Moses *Beyond the City Gates* 29: 'Oh, fair,' said Jimmy, cobbering up in true Australian style.
1928 Arthur Wright *A Good Recovery* 21: 'I cobbered up there with another bloke what was on th' rocks.'
1954 T. A. G. Hungerford *Sowers of the Wind* 51: I thought I might cobber up with them, but ... they don't even know that I'm alive.

cobbera (cobra) Skull, head: *obs.* [Ab.]
1793 J. Hunter *An Historical Journal* ed. J. Bach (1968) 271: *Caberra*, The head.
1832 G. Tipsmill 'The Snake' *Old Bush Songs* ed. Stewart and Keesing (1957) 33: The helpless frogs must rin and quake/When they behold their foe, the snake;/They wish a stick effect would take/Upon your cobra.
1867 J. R. Houlding *Australian Capers* 204: The savage cobbler, who, with a volley of oaths and slang, said he would crack Christopher's 'cobbera'.
1881 A. C. Grant *Bush-life in Queensland* i 31: The black fellow who lives in the bush bestows but small attention on his 'cobra', as the head is usually called in the pigeon-English which they employ.
1899 George Boxall *The Story of Australian Bushrangers* 243: Gilbert dismounted, turned over Parry's body, and remarked coolly, 'He got it in the cobbera. It's all over with him.'
1904 Laura M. Palmer-Archer *A Bush Honeymoon* 348: *Cobra* Head (aboriginal term).

cobbler 1 The sheep left to the last in shearing, as the roughest to shear [f. pun on *cobbler's last,* ? and 'cobbled' appearance of the fleece]
1870 Rolf Boldrewood 'Shearing in Riverina' *In Bad Company* (1901) 315: The 'cobbler' (or last sheep) was seized.
1887 *Tibb's Popular Song Book* 11: But I struggled thro' Nekarboo, boys,/And saw the cobbler cut.
1910 C. E. W. Bean *On the Wool Track* 193: There is gradually left a bunch of animals with wrinkles stiffer than door

mats. The stiffest, wrinkliest, is 'the cobbler', because he sticks to the last.
1961 George Farwell *Vanishing Australians* 96: Its name is The Cobbler – a term which, in sheep talk, means the sheep that is hardest to shear.
2 The cobbler-fish, with long rays like a cobbler's strings [OED]
1937 K. S. Prichard *Intimate Strangers* 154: When it was a cobbler, he called to the children to keep back until Prospero had hacked off the ugly brown head with its poisonous sting.

cock it up Used of a woman offering herself sexually
1961 Xavier Herbert *Soldiers' Women* 202: 'He's waitin' out there, and lookin' that nervous that if you cocked it up to him he'd put his hat over it and run.'
1963 Don Crick *Martin Place* 164: 'If they cock it up, what do they expect?'
1975 Richard Beilby *The Brown Land Crying* 210: 'You thought you had something on me, didn't you? You thought I'd cock it up to you.'

cockatoo *n.* 1 A sentinel or lookout, usually acting for those engaged in some illegal activity [f. belief that a flock of cockatoos when feeding posted a sentry to warn of approaching danger]
1828 P. Cunningham *Two Years in New South Wales* (2nd edn) ii 288: It being a common trick [among convict work gangs] to station a sentinel on a commanding eminence to give the alarm, while all the others divert themselves, or go to sleep. Such are known here by the name of 'cockatoo-gangs', from following the example of that wary bird.
1859 Henry Kingsley *Recollections of Geoffry Hamlyn* ii 141: Many a merry laugh went ringing through the woodland solitudes, sending the watchman cockatoo aloft to alarm the flock.
1949 Lawson Glassop *Lucky Palmer* 2: Snedden, the 'cockatoo', a little rat-faced unshaven man with stooped shoulders, whose job was to watch for the police.
1959 Dorothy Hewett *Bobbin Up* 159: The cockatoo kept watch outside the

dirty house in Reservoir Street, where Thomos two-up school did a roaring, open trade.
2 A small farmer, usually with some overtone of disparagement, because of the cockatoo's inferiority to the squatter or because of his ingrained habits of thrift [see quots 1853, 1867, 1876]
1853 William Howitt *Land, Labour and Gold* (1855) i 320: We were also very near being led into a dilemma by a mischievous cockatoo settler. Most agricultural settlers are thus styled by the squatters, because, I suppose, they look upon them, with their enclosures, as plunderers and encroachers on their wild woods, settling down upon them, as the cockatoos do on the ripening corn.
1865 Henry Kingsley *The Hillyars and the Burtons* 325: The small farmers, contemptuously called 'cockatoos', were the fathers of fire, the inventors of scab, the seducers of bush-hands for hay-making and harvesting, the interlopers on the wool-growers' grass.
1867 Lady Barker *Station Life in New Zealand* 110: These small farmers are called cockatoos in Australia by the squatters or sheep-farmers, who dislike them for buying up the best bits on their runs, and say that, like a cockatoo, the small free-holder alights on good ground, extracts all he can from it, and then flies away.
1873 A. Trollope *Australia* ed. P. D. Edwards and R. B. Joyce (1967) 647–8: The farmers of South Australia are usually called 'cockatoos' . . . the name has been given as a reproach, and in truth it has been and is deserved. It signifies that the man does not really till his land, but only scratches it as the bird does.
1876 A. J. Boyd *Old Colonials* (1882) 32: Why cockatoos? . . . It might have originated with ticket-of-leave men from Cockatoo Island; or it may possibly have been a term of reproach applied to the industrious farmer, who settled or perched on the resumed portions of a squatter's run, so much to the latter's rage and disgust that he contemptuously likened the farmer

to the white-coated, yellow-crested, screamer that settles or perches on the trees at the edge of his namesake's clearing.

1883 R. E. N. Twopeny *Town Life in Australia* 244: A 'cockatoo' is a selector who works his piece of land out in two or three years, and having done nothing to improve it, decamps to select in a new district.

1892 Henry Lawson 'The Ballad of Mabel Clare' *Verse* i 167: There dwelt a hard old cockatoo/On western hills far out.

1954 Miles Franklin *Cockatoos* 3: Both had fallen to the rating of cockatoos, or farmer-selectors, through inability to keep on the higher ledge of squatto-cracy.

3 A convict from Cockatoo Island (see *cockatoo n.²*, quot. 1876): *obs.*

1870 J. L. Burke *The Adventures of Martin Cash* 123: He's the bravest man that could choose from Sydney men or Cockatoos*. *This name was applied to a body of desperate men, who were imprisoned on Cockatoo Island.

1888 J. C. F. Johnson *An Austral Christmas* 49: In the bush in those days, when so many old 'Derwenters' and 'Cockatoo Islanders' were to be met with.

see cocky

cockatoo fence (improvised from crude materials), **cockatoo gate** (see quot. 1934), **cockatoo's weather** (ensuring the longest working hours)

1867 Charles de Boos *Fifty Years Ago* 101–2: She ... sheltered herself as well as she could under the rough logs of the cockatoo fence.

1884 Rolf Boldrewood *Old Melbourne Memories* 155: There would be roads and cockatoo fences ... all the hostile emblems of agricultural settlement.

1899 Steele Rudd *On Our Selection* 15: A cockatoo-fence was round the barley, and wire-posts ... round the grass-paddocks.

1934 Thomas Wood *Cobbers* 140: They [the cockies] work a few hundred acres apiece, and give their name to a gate made from two bits of stick and a

length of barbed wire. A maddening structure. It falls down when you open it and will not stand up to be closed.

1933 Acland: *Cocatoo's weather* Fine by day and rain at night; or, sometimes, fine all the week and wet on Sunday.

cockatoo *v.* 1 To take to the life of a cockatoo²

1875 Rolf Boldrewood *The Squatter's Dream* repr. as *Ups and Downs* (1878) 245: A farm! Fancy three hundred acres in Oxfordshire, with a score or two of bullocks, and twice as many black-faced Down sheep. Regular cockatooing.

2 To perch on a fence

1876 Rolf Boldrewood *A Colonial Reformer* (1890) 224: The correct thing, on first arriving at a drafting yard, is to 'cockatoo', or sit on the rails, high above the tossing horn billows, and discuss the never-ending subject of hoof and horn. Ibid. 227: The cockatoo stockman ... safely on the fence.

Cockeye Bob Sudden squall in N.W. Australia

1894 *The Age* 20 Jan. 13: On the approach of an ordinary thunderstorm or 'Cock-eyed Bob' they [the natives of the north-west of W. A.] clear off to the highest ground about.

1921 E. L. Grant Watson *The Mainland* 218: Often the silent heat of midday was disturbed by fierce gusts of wind known locally as 'Cock-eyed-Bobs'. These swifts and currents of air, not more than a yard or two in width, rush roaring across the levels, carrying a cloud of red dust with them and whirling along broken boughs.

1936 W. Hatfield *Australia through the Windscreen* 219: Only a few luggers were in [Broome] for the long 'lay-up' during the season of the treacherous 'willy willies' or 'Cock-eye Bobs' that come roaring out of a calm sea in those north-western waters anytime from December till March.

1964 Tom Ronan *Packhorse and Pearling Boat* 36–7: One Sunday evening they were in residence when a 'Cock-eyed Bob' blew up. This is a sort of localized cyclone which comes from nowhere, without warning, rarely lasts more than a few minutes, and causes havoc.

1969 Osmar White *Under the Iron Rainbow* 157: 'Only wind. It blew my truck off the road the other side of Bustard Creek. It was the biggest Cock-eyed Bob I've ever been in.'

1973 Patsy Adam Smith *The Barcoo Salute* 151: Then the rain stopped as suddenly as it had begun. The air became deadly still and chilled. 'It's a cockeye-bob following up,' Paddy said. 'Cut into the house quick.'

cockrag Loincloth worn by Aboriginals
1964 Tom Ronan *Packhorse and Pearling Boat* 46: Joe, clad in Malay style sarong, with a grey flannel shirt hanging down outside it ... at night put on the cockrag and joined the blacks in their corroboree.

1971 Keith Willey *Boss Drover* 144: 'Proper naked buggers – not even cock-rag.'

cocktail hour See quot.
1964 *Sydney Morning Herald* 25 Apr. 11: Shearers, avid readers of the women's papers, refer ironically to their beer and rum sessions after work as the cocktail hour.

cocky A cockatoo farmer, usually with an overtone of disparagement, from the sometimes wretched existence led by the cocky, from his reputation for exploiting hired help, from the contempt of the grazier or the stockman for those who scratch the earth [*cockatoo* n.²]

1877 Rolf Boldrewood *A Colonial Reformer* (1890) 262: 'If it wasn't for these confounded cockies,' said Mr Windsor, 'that big flat would be a first-rate place to break 'em into.'

1887 *Tibb's Popular Songbook* 25: Says the cocky then to plough a bit / I think I'll stop at home.

1892 William Lane *The Workingman's Paradise* 165: 'Father a "cocky", going shearing to make both ends meet, and things always going wrong.'

1900 Henry Lawson 'An Incident at Stiffner's' *Prose* i 117: A tall, freckled native (son of a neighbouring 'cocky'), without a thought beyond the narrow horizon within which he lived.

1900–10 O'Brien and Stephens: Cockatoo or cockie, which form is mostly used – has become fixed as an epithet for small farmers. Among bushmen a 'cockie' is synonymous with everything poor and mean. A cockie's clip, in shearing, is equivalent to shaving a sheep ... Though 'cockie' practically covers every settler under the status of squatter, it more especially applies to the small selectors who hold from forty up to one hundred and fifty acres of land ... On many cockies' farms poultry, milk, butter and eggs are either unknown or positive luxuries.

1910 C. E. W. Bean *On the Wool Track* 64n: A 'cocky' is a small farmer. He usually selects himself a three-hundred or five-hundred acre holding, clears it, fences it, pays for it, ploughs it, sows wheat in it – and then goes to bed to wait for his crop. The next morning he gets up and finds the paddock white with cockatoos grubbing up his seed. He is there to plough and sow and reap – cockatoos. And that, they say, is how he got the name of a cockatoo farmer – a cocky.

1926 J. Vance Marshall *Timely Tips for New Australians: Cocky* A small agriculturalist employing labour apart from the members of his own family.

1936 William Hatfield *Australia through the Windscreen* 241: Up in the saddle a man conceives a lofty disdain for grubbing in the soil ... What? Get down and drive a plough? Be a miserable cocky? – Not on your life!

1957 Sydney Hart *Pommie Migrant* 163: He had been a 'Cocky' – which means he had owned a small farm in the open country.

1963 Frank Hardy *Legends from Benson's Valley* 15: He looked what he was: a taciturn recluse, the meanest of all the mean cockies in Bungaree.
cow cocky, fruit cocky, spud cocky, tobacco cocky, wheat cocky (referring to main source of income)

1914 Henry Lawson 'A Reconnoitre with Benno' *Prose* i 833: Cobb and Co's coaches ... ran from Mudgee to Wallerawang nearly as fast ... as the miserable cow-cocky train ... The district ... grows nothing now save cows and rabbits, and breeds nothing save increasingly hateful and well-to-do cow-cockyism.

1934 F. S. Hibble *Karangi* 37: The only difference the Sabbath made ... on all surrounding cow cocky places, was that apart from the two milkings, calf and pig feeding, no other outside work was done.

1963 Hal Porter *The Watcher on the Cast-Iron Balcony* 131: A middle-aged cow-cocky's wife in a scarred and dirty Chevrolet.

1941 Kylie Tennant *The Battlers* 351: 'Some of these fruit cockies down on the irrigation might come at it.'

1949 *Coast to Coast 1948* 161: For a fruit cockie, just nicely getting along, I should have been a very contented man.

1973 Frank Huelin *Keep Moving* 36: 'When we get among the spud cockies you can make a wagga from spud bags.'

1971 *Bulletin* 15 May 68: Australia's powerful tobacco cockies.

1941 Kylie Tennant *The Battlers* 7: 'My father was one of those half-starved wheat-cockies out from Temora.'

cockying Following the life of a cocky
1923 Jack Moses *Beyond the City Gates* 128: When you're cockyin' and battlin' and live on what you grow.

1942 Eve Langley *The Pea Pickers* 236: 'I'm cow-cockying now, Steve, and I don't get any days off.'

1947 Vance Palmer *Hail Tomorrow* 6: 'Cockying, eh? Kill a pumpkin every Saturday night to keep you and your family in food for next week.'

1973 Patsy Adam Smith *The Barcoo Salute* 140: I was cockying until then, but with the depression and the drought I went broke like lots more.

cocky, boss A person eminent among nonentities; someone enjoying the exercise of petty authority, usually with some element of assertiveness implied [1890 Tasma *A Sydney Sovereign* 129: The well-intentioned workers on the way to their selections, whose highest aim in life was probably to establish themselves on their 320 acres as 'boss cockatoos'.]

1900–10 O'Brien and Stephens: It is only the 'boss cockie' who is anything more than a wheatgrower.

1905 Joseph Furphy *Rigby's Romance* (1946) 49: A grazing paddock, consisting of frontage land, purchased or stolen by a squatter in the good old times, and now rented by a local boss-cockie.

1926 J. Vance Marshall *Timely Tips for New Australians*: Boss-cockie A small farmer who works himself but also employs labour.

1945 Tom Ronan *Strangers on the Ophir* 138: 'The mob was with Nolan tonight. Why? Because I've been Boss Cocky too long.'

1965 Hal Porter *Stars of Australian Stage and Screen* 281: A country which has already driven out its most gifted actors and actresses, thus leaving English directors who were not good enough to make the grade in England to act boss-cocky to those Australians not good enough to make the grade in England.

1973 Max Harris *The Angry Eye* 131: Bob Hawke, the boss cocky of the ACTU, is a colourful force in the Australian social scene.

cocky's friend Fencing wire
1930 K. S. Prichard *Haxby's Circus* 239–40: Dan and the boys with hammer, nails and fencing wire, 'the cockie's friend', mended seats and fixed up stakes.

cocky's joy Golden syrup [see quot. 1911]
1910 C. E. W. Bean *On the Wool Track* 64: Cocky's joy is golden syrup in 2 1b tins, costing sevenpence – four times as cheap as jam and six times as portable.

1911 C. E. W. Bean *The 'Dreadnought' of the Darling* 293: Golden syrup goes by the name of 'cocky's joy' because it is cheaper than jam and is therefore supposed, not without reason, to be the delight of the cockatoo farmer.

1918 N. Campbell and L. Nelson *The Dinky-di Soldier* 28: And they'll do you well on cocky's joy, an' damper, an' the rest.

1952 *Sydney Morning Herald* 12 Dec. 1: A customer asked for a tin of golden syrup. 'You know, Cocky's Joy'.

1965 Leslie Haylen *Big Red* 49: Cocky's joy or golden syrup was good on home-made bread smoking hot from the camp oven.

coffee, hot A state of anger or indignation: *obs.*

1885 *The Australasian Printers' Keepsake* 121: He was an Englishman – one of the worst sort – overbearing, ignorant, and impudent – and between him and me there was usually hot coffee.

1901 Rolf Boldrewood *In Bad Company* 13: 'Why, Bill what hot coffee you're a-gettin', all over a little joke.'

coit see **quoit**

collar, soft An easy job: *obs.*

1903 Joseph Furphy *Such is Life* (1944) 225: 'Soft collar we got here – ain't it?'

collect To be hit by, collide with, 'cop'

1945 Roy Rene *Mo's Memoirs* 51: I can remember someone aiming half a brick at him. It just missed. You were liable to collect anything in those times.

1965 William Dick *A Bunch of Ratbags* 268: 'Yuh rotten mug', screamed Ritchie at the driver of an oncoming car who hadn't dipped his lights and practically collected us.

1971 Johnny Famechon *Fammo* 158: I was parked at the traffic lights . . . when a big truck hurtled around a corner and collected me on the passenger side, crumpling up the body work and giving me a terrible fright.

Collins, Tom See quots

1895 Cornelius Crowe *The Australian Slang Dictionary* 86: *Tom Colins*, a fellow about town whom many sought to kill for touching them on 'sore points'; he was said to frequent the hotels, he always managed to vanish before his destroyer, as he was imaginary.

1903 [Joseph Furphy] *Such is Life Being Certain Extracts from the Diary of Tom Collins* [book title]

1951 R. G. Howarth *Southerly* 72: The pseudonym 'Tom Collins', which Furphy adopted as a contributor in the nineties to the Sydney *Bulletin* derives from a mythical bush character who was reputed to start all the idle rumours and taradiddles heard in the Riverina country.

Collins St grazier, farmer The Victorian equivalent of a 'Pitt St farmer' q.v.

1971 Barbara Vernon *A Big Day at Bellbird* 114: 'Unfortunate farmers like Atkins forced off their land so that Collins Street graziers can take over!'

1974 *Australian* 16 Jan. 10: Pitt and Collins Streets farmers are costing Australia between $10 and $15 million a year in lost tax, according to the Bureau of Agricultural Economics. What a surprise.

colonial, a long A long glass of beer of colonial brewing: *obs.*

1893 Henry Lawson 'The Darling River' *Prose* i 90: 'Wal, I reckon you can build me your national drink. I guess I'll try it.' A long colonial was drawn for him.

colonial boy, a wild The bushranger of the ballad 'The Wild Colonial Boy' (*Old Bush Songs* ed. Stewart and Keesing (1957) 39); anyone sharing the same characteristics

1958 Russel Ward *The Australian Legend* 153: To the pastoral workers, to the free-selectors, to lower-class people in general, and usually to themselves, they [the bushrangers] appeared as 'wild colonial boys', Australians *par excellence*.

1959 A. W. Upfield *Bony and the Mouse* 108: 'A wild colonial boy, no woman was ever going to tame him. So he said a million times.'

colonial experiencer, colonial experience man A young Englishman of good connections sent out to gain 'colonial experience', viewed with some cynicism by native Australians because he is an amateur in his work, and not really of their world

[1862 Rachel Henning *Letters* ed. David Adams (1963) 111: He is up here 'to get colonial experience', though Biddulph pays him.

1867 John Morison *Australia As It Is* (1967) 216: That much vaunted 'colonial experience', extolled as the foundation of success.

1870 Rolf Boldrewood 'Shearing in Riverina' *In Bad Company* (1901) 299: Young gentlemen acquiring a practical knowledge of sheep-farming, or, as it is generally phrased, 'colonial experience', a comprehensive expression enough.]

1876 Rolf Boldrewood *A Colonial Reformer* (1890) 95: 'You've really hired yourself to drive travelling sheep! Not but it's a sensible enough thing to do, still you're the first 'colonial experience' young fellow that it ever occurred to.'

1886 P. Clarke *The New Chum in Australia* 295: I remember on one occasion a planter put a new 'colonial experience'* man on to 'boss' a gang of black ladies. *Colonial experience is equivalent to apprenticeship of the new chum.

1893 J. A. Barry *Steve Brown's Bunyip* 208: 'I never did care much about these colonial experience fellows. They generally give a lot of trouble, especially when they're well connected.'

1903 Joseph Furphy *Such is Life* (1944) 347: The well-educated, well-nurtured and, above all, well-born, colonial experiencer, fresh from the English rectory.

1908 E. S. Sorenson *Quinton's Rouseabout* 93: Allan Banford's status on the squattage was summed up ... as a 'colonial experience fellow'. He was a city-bred young man, and blessed with a rich father who carried on business as a wool-broker in Sydney.

1938 Francis Ratcliffe *Flying Fox and Drifting Sand* 122: 'When I was in Bundaberg forty years ago there was a "colonial experience" named Thompson.'

colonial oath, my Emphatic affirmation or agreement [euphemism for 'My bloody oath']

1859 Frank Fowler *Southern Lights and Shadows* 24: Your thorough-bred gumsucker never speaks, without apostrophising his 'oath', and interlarding his diction with the crimsonest of adjectives.

1870 Marcus Clarke *His Natural Life* ed. S. Murray-Smith (1970) 413: 'There ain't a dodge going that he ain't fly to.' 'My colonial oath!' says Tom.

1882 Rolf Boldrewood *Robbery Under Arms* (World's Classics 1949) 381: 'My colonial oath, Dick, you're quite the gentlemen.'

1893 Henry Lawson *Prose* i 78: 'His Colonial Oath' [story title]

1903 Joseph Furphy *Such is Life* (1944) 22: 'My (ensanguined) colonial!' assented Dixon and Bum, with one accord.

colour, the sc. of gold or opal: the indication of success to the miner

1859 W. Kelly *Life in Victoria* i 222: They had not, to use a current phrase, 'raised the colour'.

1882 A. J. Boyd *Old Colonials* 130: He could manage to get 'the colour', *i.e.*, small grains of gold, almost anywhere he tried, but only very rarely did he get anything approaching payable gold.

1897 Barcroft Boake 'The Digger's Song' *Where the Dead Men Lie* 66: Bah! there's not a colour in the bottom of the dish!

1944 Brian James *First Furrow* 44: The last shaft he'd sunk ... A rank duffer – not a colour in it.

1950 *Coast to Coast 1949–50* 137: I worked hard for three months, and I never saw a sight of colour.

combo A white man co-habiting with an Aboriginal woman: N.T. and W.A.

1896 W. H. Willshire *The Land of the Dawning* 72: The *Sydney Bulletin* holds the proud sway over all Australian print productions. It not only reaches the combos and stockmen of Central Australia, but it reaches lepers on isolated islands, lighthouse keepers that are difficult to approach, and wild aboriginals have used its red cover as the salient point of their costume.

1905 Arthur Bayldon *The Western Track* 56: The combo sucked of soul and sense, a mooning hopeless wreck.
1926 K. S. Prichard *Working Bullocks* 47: 'Combo, I call him, gin shepherder . . . combo's what they call a man tracks round with a gin in the nor'-west.'
1931 A. W. Upfield *The Sands of Windee* 99: The stockman . . . in danger of becoming a 'combo', or a white man who is married – more or less – to a lubra.
1935 Mary and Elizabeth Durack *All-About* 68: He never had a lubra of his own, and was once known to have thrown a rug away because he was told a gin had slept in it. ('No b—Combo 'bout me').
1938 H. Drake-Brockman *Men Without Wives* (1955) 24: 'Some fellows simply don't seem to be able to help living with the gins. Going combo, we call it.'
1958 Gavin Casey *Snowball* 51: 'You know what combo means?' 'Joker that lives with black-gins, ain't it it?'
1971 Keith Willey *Boss Drover* 46: The trouble was that the travelling combo was always on the lookout to snaffle somebody else's lubra.

commando, cut-lunch see **cut-lunch**

commie Someone living in a rural commune

compo Worker's compensation: payment for time lost from an injury at work, or for a permanent disability so caused [abbr.]
1941 Kylie Tennant *The Battlers* 373: 'They've got nice rest-rooms for them who faints, and if you do slice your hand, they put you on compo . . . Compensation money while it heals.'
1969 William Dick *Naked Prodigal* 130: Brian had worked at the brick works once and had gotten burnt and was off on compo for a six week spell.

1974 *Australian* 26 Sep. 4: Compo plan changes will cost millions.

Condamine 1 The Condamine bell, with a distinctive note, used with stock [f. place of manufacture in Queensland]
1926 K. S. Prichard *Working Bullocks* 295: Duck Hayes tinkled the condamine he was carrying round to start events.
1955 Alan Marshall *I Can Jump Puddles* 173: 'The Condamine sends a horse deaf. It's too high a note. You bell a horse regular with a Condamine, he goes deaf.'
1962 Tom Ronan *Deep of the Sky* 109: A Condamine bell is one turned out of a cross-cut saw, which has a light but unmistakeable note.
1975 *Australian* 9 Oct. 2: 'He is like the Condamine bell. He has a great tongue and a head full to nothingness.'
2 The drovers' name for Sirius: N.T. and W.A.
1951 Ernestine Hell *The Territory* 425: Sirius, ringing a steady note in the music of the spheres, is the Condamine Bell.

confetti, cowyard, farmyard, Flemington See quot. 1941
1941 Baker 22: *Cowyard confetti* as for 'bullsh'. Ibid. 31: *Flemington confetti*: Rubbish, piffle, 'bullsh'. [from the Flemington stockyards]
1951 Dal Stivens *Jimmy Brockett* 230: You could pull the wool over his eyes if you talked enough Flemington confetti about the woes of the working class.
1973 *Sun-Herald* 30 Dec. 35: Lots of farmyard confetti has been spoken and written about this young man's selection.

Connolly, the luck of Eric A noted punter (d.1944) and a byword for luck in betting
[**1949** Lawson Glassop *Lucky Palmer* 149: 'They're hard to pitch all right . . . Eric Connolly reckons he's known only one certainty in his life and that got beaten.']
1958 Frank Hardy *The Four-legged Lottery* 134: Jim Roberts announced his amazing win of approaching two

hundred pounds . . . and Tom Roberts said: 'Well, I'll be damned. We've got an Eric Connolly in the house!'
1963 Frank Hardy *Legends from Benson's Valley* 73: 'They've had the luck of Eric Connolly all night,' Darky said.

contract A difficult assignment
1954 Tom Ronan *Vision Splendid* 157: 'It would be a contract to put bullocks up that hill with the morning freshness on them. They'd never face it to-night.'

cooee, within In easy reach of; (negatively) nowhere near [f. *cooee* as an Aboriginal call to someone at a distance]
1876 A. J. Boyd *Old Colonials* (1882) 284: 'When you are starved, and are not within cooey of a meat-safe or a bread-bin.'
1887 *All the Year Round* 30 Jul. 67: A common mode of expression is to be 'within cooey' of a place. Originally, no doubt, this meant to be within the distance at which the well known 'cooey', or bush cry, could be heard; now it simply means within easy reach of a place.
1891 Henry Lawson 'The Shanty on the Rise' *Verse* i 155: And I mind how weary teamsters struggled on while it was light, / Just to camp within a cooey of the Shanty for the night.
1908 Henry Fletcher *Dads and Dan between Smokes* 43: But ef we's within cooee o' conquerin' space an' distance, we's nigh handy to abolishin' time.
1928 Arthur Wright *A Good Recovery* 63: Within cooee of the house, covering a patch of cleared country, stood the shearing shed.
1934 H. H. Richardson *The End of a Childhood* 72: No living thing but themselves moved on the miles of desolate beach; not a neighbour was within cooee.
1950 W. M. Hughes *Policies and Potentates* 43: Darling Harbour – the goods depot within cooee of the present Central Station.

Cook, Captain A look [rhyming slang]
1932 Leonard Mann *Flesh in Armour* 179: 'Take a captain cook at love's

young dream.'
1946 Dal Stivens *The Courtship of Uncle Henry* 70: I took a Captain Cook at him then and seen he had on a white coat like a dentist.
1951 Dymphna Cusack and Florence James *Come in Spinner* 310–11: Lofty stuck a knobbly fist under his nose. 'Take a Captain Cook at that, buddy. One more squeak out of you and I'll knock yer bloody block off.'

Coolgardie A Coolgardie safe: see quot. [f. place-name in W.A.]
1945 Elizabeth George *Two at Daly Waters* 32: To keep food cool we had a home-made Coolgardie – a frame covered with hessian, and with long strips of flannel hanging over the sides and resting in water to syphon and keep the hessian wet and cool.

cop, silent see **silent cop**

Cop this, young 'Arry A catch-phrase of Roy Rene ('Mo') in the McCackie Mansions sketches, before giving Harry a clip under the ear. The expression could now be used jocularly by someone passing a cup of tea.
1962 John O'Grady *Cop This Lot* 99: 'Cop that, young Harry,' Dennis said.
1976 *Australian* 15 Jan. 2: The script [for the Roy Rene revival] apparently is incomplete. Hence Spears' cheeky inscription on hand-bills advertising the Adelaide production: 'Cop this young Harry'.

coppertail The opposite to the 'silver-tail' q.v.
1890 A. J. Vogan *The Black Police* 116: The genus termed in Australian parlance 'silver-tailed', in distinction to the 'copper-tailed' democratic classes.
1898 Joshua Lake *Australasian Supplement* to *Webster's International Dictionary: Copper-tail* One belonging to the lower classes of society, as distinguished from *silver-tail*.
1905 Randolph Bedford *The Snare of Strength* 317: Charley Byers, being merely a clerk, danced at the Mechanics' Institute with the Coppertails.

1941 Baker 20: *Coppertail* A member of the proletariat, one of the hoi polloi.

corduroy *n. v. a.* To bed a road with logs to make it passable in wet weather; a road so constructed: *obsolescent* [f. the ribs in the fabric U.S. 1822 OED]

1860 Mrs A. McPherson *My Experiences in Australia* 292: The well-known though somewhat apocryphal tale of a traveller on a Canadian Corderoy road, whose right of treasure trove in a hat which he observed moving about on the surface of a bog by the roadside, was disputed by its submerged wearer.

1867 J. S. Borlase *The Night Fossickers* 159: They talk of *corduroy* roads in America, but I should like to show a Yankee a mile or two of the one we that day travelled over.

1880 J. C. Crawford *Recollections of Travels in New Zealand and Australia* 250: We passed Wallace-Town, and drove through a bad road cut through the bush to Invercargill. Part of this road was 'corduroy'.

1889 J. I. Hunt *Hunt's Book of Bonanzas* 71: The course of true love began to partake of the nature of a 'corduroy' road in the wet season.

1911 E. S. Sorenson *Life in the Australian Backblocks* 183: One teamster I remember 'corduroyed' a bog on the Tatham Road with smothered bullocks.

1938 Eric Lowe *Salute to Freedom* 359: Robin slowed the car down to take the corduroy crossing of Beni creek.

1968 L. Braden *Bullockies* 122: In those days we used to corduroy the roads (lay logs across the soggy spots) and sometimes the spars would wear through in places.

corn, on the In prison [f. the hominy diet]

1949 Lawson Glassop *Lucky Palmer* 76: 'We look like doing three months on the corn.' 'The corn?' 'Yeah. The prison porridge.'

Corner, the (the Corner Country) The area at the junction of the borders of N.S.W., Queensland and S.A.

1932 William Hatfield *Ginger Murdoch*

1: Birdsville, Bedourie, and Betoota ... form a rough triangle and The Corner proper, and its border, unlike the arbitrary State divisions, is flexible and undefined, so that folk as far away as Goyder's Lagoon down in South Australia and even at Innamincka on Cooper's Creek may claim without dispute to belong to The Corner.

1949 Ion L. Idriess *One Wet Season* 147: 'The Corner', meaning the 'corner' country where the borders of southwest Queensland, north-west New South Wales, and the north-east of South Australia join.

1963 A. W. Upfield *The Body at Madman's Bend* 136: 'He was working out in Yandama, up in the Corner, when we won a pretty good prize in a lottery.'

Cornstalk 1 A native-born Australian youth (as distinct from an emigrant) especially if tall and slender: *obs.*

1827 P. Cunningham *Two Years in New South Wales* ii 116: English and Colonial born, the latter bearing also the name of *corn stalks* (Indian corn), from the way in which they shoot up.

1834 George Bennett *Wanderings in New South Wales* i 341: The Australian ladies may compete for personal beauty and elegance with any European, although satirized as 'corn-stalks' from the slenderness of their forms.

1852 G. C. Mundy *Our Antipodes* (2nd edn) i 45: Cornstalk is the national nickname of the Australian white man.

2 Someone born in N.S.W., as distinct from the other states: *obsolescent*

1885 *The Australasian Printers' Keepsake* 162: A European type, working in Sydney, was grievously galled by the 'blow' of the Cornstalks.

1887 *All the Year Round* 30 Jul. 67: A native of New South Wales is known as a 'cornstalk', because the men generally grow tall and thin.

1897 Hume Nisbet *The Swampers* 179: They spent two days in Melbourne, going about and looking at everything with the prejudiced and disparaging feelings of all true-bred cornstalks towards things Victorian, and decided with gleesome alacrity that its days were over.

1899 Henry Lawson 'Jack Cornstalk' *Prose* ii 42: I regard the settled, or agricultural belt of New South Wales as the birth-place and home . . . of Jack Cornstalk.
1903 Joseph Furphy *Such is Life* (1944) 44: 'When anybody calls him a Port Philliper . . . he comes out straight: "You're a (adj.) liar," says he, "I'm a Cornstalk, born in New South Wales".'
1926 J. Vance Marshall *Timely Tips for New Australians: Cornstalk* A New South Welshman.
1957 Sydney Hart *Pommie Migrant* 51: 'Never say that to anyone in New South Wales, or you'll be laid out as flat as a pancake!' he warned me . . . Couldn't the Cornstalks take a joke?

corroboree A gathering or celebration: *jocular* [f. corroboree as Aboriginal dance]
1859 W. Kelly *Life in Victoria* ii 62: I derived a wicked enjoyment in the corrobborie [a colonial ball] as far as I was personally concerned.
1867 J. R. Houlding *Australian Capers* 134: A policeman danced a 'corroboree' in the roadway with his arms working.
1885 *The Australasian Printers' Keepsake* 98: There was a corroboree next day of bosses, clickers, and readers.
1926 J. Vance Marshall *Timely Tips for New Australians: Corroboree* An aboriginal dance. Commonly used in the colloquial to describe a noise or uproar.

cossie A swimming costume [abbr.]
1926 J. Vance Marshall *Timely Tips for New Australians: Cossie* A sea-side term applied to a swimming costume.
1941 Baker 20: *Cossie* A swimming costume.
1959 Dorothy Hewett *Bobbin Up* 30: He imagined them lying on the dark sand behind the rocks at Bondi, undoing the straps of her cozzie, his hands full of her breasts.
1975 Les Ryan *The Shearers* 76: 'Oh!' she hesitated. 'Haven't got a cossie.'

cot case Someone incapacitated, esp. by drink: *jocular* [f. hospital term for patient needing to be confined to bed]

1932 Leonard Mann *Flesh in Armour* 219: Sergeant Burke was boozing and often no better than a cot case.
1946 Kylie Tennant *Lost Haven* 196: Better sooth him, Cherry decided, or he'd be a cot-case.
1949 Ion L. Idriess *One Wet Season* 189: Before closing-up time they were cot cases.
1958 Vince Kelly *The Greedy Ones* 213: 'You're tougher than I thought . . . I expected you to be a cot-case for quite a few hours.'

cove This is a term from English thieves' slang (OED 1567); the two senses of it derived in Australia are given by Vaux in 1812: 'the master of a house or shop, is called *the Cove*; on other occasions, when joined to particular words, as a *cross-cove*, a *flash-cove*, a *leary cove* &c, it simply implies a man of these several descriptions.'
1 The proprietor, station-manager, man in charge
1845 Thomas McCombie *Arabin* 47: He asked if it was far to the home-station of his master. 'Not very far,' replied the shepherd. 'Will the gentlemen have retired?' inquired Dr Arabin. 'Let me see – will the cove have gone to bed, Jim?'
1847 Alexander Harris *Settlers and Convicts* ed. C. M. H. Clark (1954) 150–1: 'Our cove never allowances his men, lad!' Ibid. 34: 'You must go with us and show us your cove's farm; we want to see what he's got in his stores.'
1882 Rolf Boldrewood *Robbery Under Arms* (World's Classics 1949) 114–15: 'To put up a yard at the back of a man's run, and muster his cattle for him! . . . But suppose the cove or his men come across it?'
1916 Joseph Furphy *Poems* 42: 'Are you the Cove?' He spoke the words / As freeman only can. / The squatter freezingly inquir'd, / 'What do you mean, my man?'
see **bloke**[1]
2 A chap, fellow; at first as in thieves' slang, but later without any of the associations of this fraternity
1849 Alexander Harris *The Emigrant*

Family (1967) 66: 'I thought it was some swell cove.'

1875 Rolf Boldrewood *The Squatter's Dream* repr. as *Ups and Downs* (1878) 165: 'I'm thankful we ain't shed any blood, leastways not killed any cove as I knows of.'

1885 *The Australasian Printers' Keepsake* 24: Coves smoked, and 'Will you come and have a drink?' / Was asked by them persistently and oft.

1915 C. J. Dennis *The Songs of a Sentimental Bloke* 34: A cove 'as got to think some time in life / An' get some decent tart, ere it's too late.

1930 *Bulletin* 30 Dec. 24: Bonifaces that would grudge a cove his bit of counter-lunch.

1938 *Smith's Weekly* 19 Nov. 10: A cove I know in Wagga wants a truck driver.

1946 Margaret Trist *What Else Is There?* 260: George watched Denis covertly. 'I don't like that cove,' he thought.

1961 George Farwell *Vanishing Australians* 28: 'The city's mighty lonely for a cove without mates.'

1965 Patrick White *Four Plays* 105: 'Any of you know if a cove name of Boyle lives anywhere around? Ernie Boyle.'

cow 1 Anything disagreeable or deserving vilification. The more intensive form is 'a fair cow' [?f. the English *cow* as an insult to a woman]

1864 *Thatcher's Colonial Minstrel* 14: Called each one of them [the bullocks] an old cow, / Whilst blows thick and fast he kept dealing.

1897 Hume Nisbet *The Swampers* 205: 'Police after him too . . . Me know them, the blooming cows.'

1902 Henry Lawson 'Lord Douglas' *Prose* i 497: 'I vote we kick the cow out of the town!' snarled One-eyed Bogan.

1914 *Bulletin* 1 Jul. 47: Then he jerked his head back at the weather outside. ''S goin' to be a cow of a day.'

1917 A. B. Paterson *Three Elephant Power* 51: In Australia the most opprobrious epithet one can apply to a man or other object is 'cow'. In the whole range of a bullock-driver's vocabulary there is no word that expresses his blistering scorn so well as 'cow'.

1925 E. S. Sorenson *Murty Brown* 143: 'He's a cow of a feller.'

1933 R. B. Plowman *The Man from Oodnadatta* 248: 'It's not so bad coming down the river . . . But it's a fair cow going up.'

1939 Kylie Tennant *Foveaux* 236: 'And when I went back to get it,' he mourned indignantly, 'some cow had pinched it.'

1942 Gavin Casey *It's Harder for Girls* 13: The girls about the place were pretty uppish, and she must have had a cow of a time.

1959 Dorothy Hewett *Bobbin Up* 92: 'I starched your petticoat stiff as a board, and it was a cow to iron.'

1964 George Johnston *My Brother Jack* 121: 'How's the job with the baker?' 'It's a fair cow,' he said.

1965 Patrick White *Four Plays* 270: 'You're a cow of a goat at times.'

2 An object of compassion, as in the phrase 'the poor cow'

1933 Norman Lindsay *Saturdee* 164: Peter was sure the poor cow had never had a sit with girls in all his life.

1938 Francis Ratcliffe *Flying Fox and Drifting Sand* 194: 'Smith, our neighbour on the east, missed it [the rain] altogether, the poor cow.'

1945 *Coast to Coast 1944* 167: 'That poor cow's in a bad way.'

1947 Gavin Casey *The Wits are Out* 42: Sometimes, when misfortune overtook him . . . people felt sorry for him, and decided he wasn't such a bad old cow, after all.

1948 K. S. Prichard *Golden Miles* 89: A bogger working near Dally on the Perseverance had been killed by a fall of earth. 'The poor silly cow,' he said tremulously.

1959 D'Arcy Niland *The Big Smoke* 164: 'Kind of the old cow,' Ocker said.

cow, hunt (chase) up a To find a dry patch in the bush, usually with a sense of sexual opportunity

1957 John O'Grady *They're a Weird Mob* 144: 'Gunna be a bastard tryin' to find a dry spot.' 'Hunt up a cow.'

1959 Gerard Hamilton *Summer Glare* 80: We delighted in following couples at night when they went 'chasing up a cow', as courting was commonly called, for couples mostly began their night's love-making by wandering around looking for a sleeping cow that they could disturb to claim the warm patch of earth where it lay.

cow, Malley's see **Malley's**

cowal See quot. 1910 [Ab.]
1910 C. E. W. Bean *On the Wool Track* 251: If one got bogged in a creek or cowal (which is a small tree-grown, swampy depression often met in the red country).
1934 Jean Devanny *Out of Such Fires* 220: They [the horses] could be trusted not to move far from the little shade afforded by the cowal.

crab-hole A hole supposedly burrowed or inhabited by a land-crab: mainly Victorian
1848 Let. in G. Goodman *The Church in Victoria* (1892) 72: Full of crab-holes, which are exceedingly dangerous for the horses. These are holes varying in depth from one to three feet, and the smallest of them wide enough to admit the foot of a horse ... These holes are formed by a small land-crab and then gradually enlarged by the water draining into them. [Morris]
1855 William Howitt *Land, Labour and Gold* i 308: Crab-holes, or Frog-holes, as they are called in some districts from land crabs and frogs frequenting them when they hold water, are small pools or quagmires some few yards across.
1903 Joseph Furphy *Such is Life* (1944) 16: Price and Cooper, being cooks, had kindled an unobtrusive fire in a crab-hole, where three billies were soon boiling.
1944 Charles Fenner *Mostly Australian* 102: In central Victoria there are wide, treeless, basalt plains ... Such areas have a curious surface, consisting of shallow depressions with intervening low ridges ... The depressions are miscalled 'crab-holes', a name which

appears to have been commonly transferred from moist river flats, where crabs really did make holes.
1967 Len Beadell *Blast the Bush* 49: Having been there with the blackfellow and driven about the clearing, I knew it was free of crab holes or hidden ruts.
see **gilgie**

crabs, draw the To attract unwelcome attention, esp. enemy fire [?f. *crab* as abbr. of 'crab-louse', or *crab* to interfere (Vaux 1812)]
[1919 W. H. Downing *Digger Dialects* 17: *Crabs* shells, shelling]
1932 Leonard Mann *Flesh in Armour* 144: 'The Tommies told us this was a quiet sector, but it's lively enough now, what with the Stokes chucking their muck and running, and leaving us to collect the crabs.' Ibid. 260: The Tommy captain lit a cigarette and I lit my pipe [in an air raid]. The young wench reckoned we would draw the crabs.
1942 *Salt* 25 May 8: *To bring the crabs around* To expose yourself to enemy fire. [reported as having come back 'with the AIF recently returned from the Middle East']
1959 Dorothy Hewett *Bobbin Up* 41: 'And we don't like 'em under age, draws the crabs'. [police]
1974 *Bulletin* 16 Mar. 17: When Prime Minister Whitlam last week told rural members of the Federal Parliamentary Labor Party that they should have expected the abolition of the superphosphate bounty because it was 'in the Coombs report', he really drew the crabs.

crack a fat see **fat**

crack hardy To put on a brave front in misfortune
1915 C. J. Dennis *The Songs of a Sentimental Bloke* 66: A fool 'oo tried / To just crack 'ardy, an' 'old gloom aside.
1919 Edward Dyson *Hello, Soldier!* 49: Always dressin' up the winder, crackin' hardy, though we felt / Fearful creepy in the whiskers, very cold beneath the

belt.

1924 *Truth* 27 Apr. 6: *Crack hardy* To suppress feelings.
1946 K. S. Prichard *The Roaring Nineties* 147: Living from day to day in the heat and glare as if you were withering and drying up inside, but must crack hardy and joke about it to show your grit.
1961 *Australian Stories of Today* ed. C. Osborne 14: Our father stood there, wan and cracking hardy in his flannel and his cold despair.

crack it To succeed in some enterprise, esp. sexual [f. 'cracking a safe', 'cracking a code', etc.]
1941 Baker 23: *Crack it* To record success in an amorous affair.
1948 Sumner Locke Elliott *Rusty Bugles* in *Khaki, Bush and Bigotry* ed. Eunice Hanger (1968) 61: 'Hello, Darky . . . so you cracked it again I hear.'
1953 *Caddie A Sydney Barmaid* 255: 'Romped home with flying colours in his accountancy exams, but like me, he's never been able to crack it for a decent job.'
1963 Lawson Glassop *The Rats in New Guinea* 115: 'You wouldn't even crack it with a nymphomaniac.'
1973 Alexander Buzo *Rooted* 78: 'Keep on with your art, mate. You'll crack it one day, I'm sure of it.'
1975 Les Ryan *The Shearers* 75: 'What are you so bloody cocky about?' said Lofty . . . 'Cracked it, did yer?'

cracker 1 The tip of a stockwhip
1905 Randolph Bedford *The Snare of Strength* 256: 'Ere's a cracker, Daven, for your whip; them spiders make the best crackers in the world.'
1908 W. H. Ogilvie *My Life in the Open* 6: Let the heavy stockwhip fall; fourteen feet from keeper to cracker it lies out along the sand.
2 A worn out horse, sheep, bullock
1950 *Sydney Morning Herald* 21 Jul. 1: A puzzled reader asks 'What is a cracker?' He sends a report of a cattle sale which says . . . 'stores from £7 to £10; crackers sold for less.' Well, this sort of cracker is a worn-out cow –

bottoms in the cattle world.
1965 E. O. Schlunke *Stories of the Riverina* 63: 'Ever seen such a bunch of old crackers?' he said, laughing contemptuously [at the sheep]. 'Fit for nothing but the meat cannery.'
3 A brothel
1963 John Naish *That Men Should Fear* 143: My Aunt Helen worked in a cracker in Munro Street. Worked as a madam or a moll.

cracker, not worth a, haven't got a No evidence has been found for Baker's identification of a 'cracker' with a one pound note (adopted in the OED Suppl.) The word 'cracker' is used for a worn-out cow, and for an attachment to the end of a stockwhip, but neither of these is a likely explanation. The U.S. 'cracker' (a biscuit) would have been unfamiliar to Australia until after World War II. As 'cracker' is found only in negative expressions – cf. 'skerrick' and 'razoo' – it may not refer to anything positive i.e. there is never a report of anyone who *does* have a cracker or *is* worth a cracker. Not to have a cracker is to be completely out of funds, not to be worth a cracker is to be worth nothing at all.

Vaux records 'cracker' in 1812 as 'a small loaf, served to prisoners in jails, for their daily subsistence', but there is no other occurrence of the word in this sense in Australian English.

1934 W. S. Howard *You're Telling Me!* 300: 'What about money?' shade number two asked doubtfully. 'We haven't got a cracker.' [OED]
1942 Gavin Casey *It's Harder for Girls* 162: 'He's got guts, anyway,' said Sayers. 'I didn't think he was worth a cracker.'
1944 Lawson Glassop *We Were the Rats* 83: 'I walked into a country hotel in Queensland without a cracker but with my fur coat and black homberg on.'
1957 Judah Waten *Shares in Murder* 29: 'I've heard her husband didn't give her a cracker when he divorced her.'
1963 Randolph Stow *Tourmaline* 65: 'It doesn't matter a cracker to me.'
1973 Ward McNally *Man from Zero*

110: 'I better clear outa the Northern Territory now – my life won't be worth a cracker if I don't.'

cracker night The night of Empire Day (24 May) celebrated with a bonfire and fireworks; later transferred to Commonwealth Day and then Queen's Birthday, and now fading out with legal restrictions on fireworks
1953 Ruth Park *A Power of Roses* 184: 'Just twenty-seven years ago I met me missus on Cracker Night.'
1963 *Sydney Morning Herald* 17 Apr. 1: A state Government Committee will urge local councils and the general public to discourage public bonfires on 'cracker night' this year.
1976 *Sun-Herald* 30 May 38: Cracker night accidents were avoidable if fireworks users followed simple safety rules, an expert said this week.

crawl To ingratiate oneself with those in authority: *derogatory*
1881 A. C. Grant *Bush-Life in Queensland* ii 45: He had crawled his way up in 'the foorce' to his present distinguished position from obscurity.
1908 Giles Seagram *Bushmen All* 31: He, being free from 'side' and from any suspicion of toadyism or 'crawling' was generally liked by the men.
1933 Frank Clune *Try Anything Once* 168: I was accused of 'crawling to the Pott's Pointers.'
1939 Kylie Tennant *Foveaux* 140: 'Not 'cause you're payin' me. I ain't ever crawled to anyone for that.'
1950 Brian James *The Advancement of Spencer Button* 155: Accusations of 'crawling to the boys' to get them to work.
1965 Eric Lambert *The Long White Night* 22: 'Trying to do a good job!' mimicked Clancy. 'He's crawling for his third [stripe], you mean.'
1969 William Dick *Naked Prodigal* 247: I didn't crawl to him . . . I wouldn't crawl to no bastard for nothing.'

crawler 1 A sheep, cow or other animal that is laggard, weak or docile: *obs.*
1853 *Letters from Victorian Pioneers* ed.

McBride and La Trobe (1898) 270: On this run, out of 1,500 head of cattle, all had been driven off but about 30 'crawlers'. It was many weeks before they were re-mustered.
1868 C. Wade Brown *Overlanding in Australia* 2: Many [sheep] die, particularly such as are old, or weak, technically termed out here the 'crawlers'.
1876 Rolf Boldrewood *A Colonial Reformer* (1890) 321: 'Well, they're a middling lot of quiet cattle for one thing, they're regular crawlers.' Ibid. 217: The well-bred station 'crawlers', as the stockmen term them for their peaceable and orderly habits.
1896 N. Bartley *Australian Pioneers and Reminiscences* 26: Mr Kirby came up and counted them (the sheep), and found them to be 9,924 . . . with 6 crawlers left on the road.
1911 E. S. Sorenson *Life in the Australian Backblocks* 167: The stragglers or crawlers (as the weak ones, doddering miles behind, are called).
2 A shepherd, from the slowness of his activities, and from the contempt of those who worked on horseback: *obs.*
1853 S. Mossman and T. Banister *Australia Visited and Revisited* 64: As we approached him [the shepherd] at a walking pace, we could not but contemplate his peaceful occupation, so much in accordance with the stillness of the Australian wilderness . . . you find him a long-bearded, bronze-featured 'crawler', as he is termed in the colony.
1857 F. Cooper *Wild Adventures in Australia* 50: Fit only for shepherding – the one employment despised by all classes in a country where the strongest reproach was to be a 'crawler.'
1867 John Morison *Australia As It Is* 221: The pastoral life, following flocks of sheep . . . was much more agreeable . . . to them than clearing land and working at farms under a scorching sun. They are now scattered all over the occupied interior, and are mostly debilitated old men, to whom the settlers gave the name of 'old crawlers'.
1875 Rolf Boldrewood *The Squatter's Dream* repr. as *Ups and Downs* (1878)

67: 'Do I look like a slouching, 'possum-eating, billy-carrying crawler of a shepherd? I've had a horse under me ever since I was big enough to know Jingaree mountain from a haystack, and a horse I'll have as long as I can carry a stock-whip.'

3 A 'slowcoach', loafer, shirker; also unspecific term of contempt: *obs.*

1837–8 *Report from the Select Committee on Transportation* ii 75: The clever knaves among the convicts very seldom fell into such an unfortunate predicament as these refuse of the convicts get into on road-parties. The cant name for these among the prisoners themselves was 'the crawlers'. They were scarcely able to work, people whom no settlers wished to employ.

1849 Alexander Harris *The Emigrant Family* (1967) 32: 'You'll have the pick of a score every day; shepherds, tradesmen, and men that never were men yet; good men and crawlers.'

1867 J. R. Houlding *Australian Capers* 186: These colonies are not good places for old folks to come to . . . for few persons care to employ 'old crawlers' (as they are called by the natives) when there are lots of young men and women to be had.

1883 Rolf Boldrewood *Robbery Under Arms* (World's Classics 1949) 607: 'Haven't you served those drinks yet, Bob? . . . I never saw such a slow-going crawler as you are.'

1901 Henry Lawson 'Telling Mrs Baker' *Prose* i 418: 'You're surely not crawler enough to desert a mate in a case like this?' Ibid. 548: 'You're a damned crawler, Romany!' I said.

1924 Rann Daly *The Outpost* 80: 'They're to protect the crawlers who come here to make easy money.'

1931 Miles Franklin *Back to Bool Bool* 265: 'Flaming crawlers!' he commented . . . 'I don't know what to make of the young people to-day. They're born dead.'

4 Someone who toadies to the boss, or any superior

1892 William Lane *The Workingman's Paradise* 104: 'And you'd get more inclined to humour the boss every time you had to try again [for a job].' 'Naturally. That's how they get at us. No man's a crawler who's sure of a job.'

1902 Henry Lawson 'Lord Douglas' *Prose* i 494: 'As for turning blackleg – well, I suppose I've got a bit of the crawler in my composition (most of us have), and a man never knows what might happen to his principles.'

1939 Miles Franklin and Dymphna Cusack *Pioneers on Parade* 140: Albert . . . pondered on what a crawler love could make of a man, though he had never grovelled so with Lizzie.

1945 Kylie Tennant *Ride on Stranger* 22: 'A crawler . . . Ready to do anything as long as he's a good fellow.'

1953 *Caddie A Sydney Barmaid* 135: 'I'm sick of working amongst that mangy lot of crawlers. I'm satisfied they've got legs on their bellies.'

1965 John Beede *They Hosed Them Out* 82: 'You've got to be a crawler to get the odd gongs that are going.'

1973 Roland Robinson *The Drift of Things* 92: 'Don't try to get in good with the boss. He knows what "crawlers" are.'

cray Crayfish, usually regarded as a delicacy

1916 C. J. Dennis *The Moods of Ginger Mick* 46: 'An we'll 'ave a cray fer supper when I comes marchin' 'ome.'

1941 Baker 21: *Cray* A crayfish.

1959 Dorothy Hewett *Bobbin Up* 13: 'Crays and a bottla beer. It's the drunks' special for Saturdee night.'

creamie 1 A cream-coloured horse

1887 *Tibb's Popular Songbook* 28: He likes all lively hacks, / He's very partial to the creamies, / And he'll mate up with the blacks.

1902 Henry Fletcher *The Waybacks in Town and at Home* 105: 'Der yer mind Jack Clark comin' ter our place er ridin' er bag o' bones he called a creamy?'

1945 Baker 71: *creamy*, a white or cream-coloured horse.

2 A quarter-caste Aboriginal girl; any girl of apparently mixed blood (see quot. 1887 above)

1943 Baker 23: *Creamy* A quarter-caste aboriginal.
1951 Ernestine Hill *The Territory* 444: *Creamies* Quarter-caste girls.
1962 Criena Rohan *The Delinquents* 12–13: The other children called her the Creamy. She had come from Singapore with her mother early in '42.
1963 John Naish *That Men Should Fear* 87: 'Reckon a man's a mug to go chasin' a creamie?' [half-caste girl]
1975 Xavier Herbert *Poor Fellow My Country* 52: 'I'm using the term Black Velvet not simply to apply to full-blooded women, but any of obvious aboriginal strain, 'yeller girls', or 'creamy pieces', as they're called, half and quarter.'

cringe, the cultural The phrase invented by A. A. Phillips to describe the denigration by Australians of their own culture, and their attitude of subservience to the culture of overseas countries
1950 Arthur Phillips 'The Cultural Cringe' *Meanjin* 299: Above our writers – and other artists – looms the intimidating mass of Anglo-Saxon culture. Such a situation almost inevitably produces the characteristic Australian Cultural Cringe.
1971 *Australian* 14 Oct. 10: [editorial on the appointment of the Duke of Edinburgh as President of the Australian Conservation Foundation] The cause of Australian conservation deserves better than to be set back into the mould of the great Australian cultural cringe.
1973 *Sydney Morning Herald* 25 Aug. 10: The public will not suffer, tomorrow, the kind of cultural cringe it once felt when confronted by the home-created product.

cronk Out of order, unsound; dishonest, fraudulent; also 'run cronk' (run a dishonest race), 'go cronk' (go wrong, break down): *obs.* [f. *crank* one that is sick or ill OED 1567; G. *krank* sick, ill]
1889 Rolf Boldrewood *Nevermore* (1892) 271: 'From the look of him ... I shouldn't be surprised if there was something "cronk" about him, for all

his gold-buying.'
1894 Henry Lawson *Letters* 57: Things went cronk shortly after my arrival in Sydney.
1903 Joseph Furphy *Such is Life* (1944) 129: 'When a girl's gone cronk, like you, she must expect to see white things darting about.' Ibid. 287: 'It paid us to give him two notes to run cronk.'
1934 F. E. Baume *Burnt Sugar* 58: 'It all sounds pretty cronk to me.'
1958 Jack Lindsay *Life Rarely Tells* 213: 'Not that I believe in doing anything cronk.'

crook Defective, unsatisfactory, disagreeable; (of persons) sick [see prec.]
1898 *Bulletin* 17 Dec. Red Page: *Krook* or *kronk* is bad.
1915 Let. in Bill Gammage *The Broken Years* (1974) 44: Sand in your tucker, in your ears, nose, everywhere, and anywhere, it was real crook.
1915 C. J. Dennis *The Songs of a Sentimental Bloke* 88: 'An then, I sneaks to bed, an' feels dead crook. Ibid. 111: Times I 'ave though, when things was goin' crook.
1924 *Truth* 27 Apr. 6: *Crook spin* Run of bad luck.
1934 Thomas Wood *Cobbers* 19: 'Tell the Gov. I can't come today; I'm crook in the guts.'
1945 Roy Rene *Mo's Memoirs* 107: All through our tour to North Queensland I was feeling crook, but I certainly never realised just how crook I was.
1955 Patrick White *The Tree of Man* 185: 'Are the burns bad? We must dress them. Tell me,' she said, 'do they feel crook?'
1962 Jon Cleary *The Country of Marriage* 76–7: 'Are you feeling crook?' Crook: now there is a good Aussie term. It describes me perfectly: sick, hollow, head aching.
1969 William Dick *Naked Prodigal* 22: 'He's been drivin' her mad since he's been off with his crook back.'

crook, go To upbraid, abuse
1911 Louis Stone *Jonah* 190: 'Yer niver 'ad no cause ter go crook on me,

but I ain't complainin',' cried Chook hoarsely.

1915 C. J. Dennis *The Songs of a Sentimental Bloke* 113: Goes crook on life, an' calls the world a cheat.

1919 W. H. Downing *Digger Dialects* 26: *Go crook* Become angry or abusive.

1929 Herbert Scanlon *Old Memories* 17: 'I wasn't going crook ... I was only barraking you.'

1944 Lawson Glassop *We Were the Rats* 207: 'Then I thinks she'll go crook on me for speakin', seein' that we ain't been introduced.'

1965 Patrick White *Four Plays* 150: 'Dad says Mr Masson is liable. He went real crook.'

crooked maginnis see **maginnis**

Crooked Mick see **Mick**

crooked on Hostile to, averse to

1949 Lawson Glassop *Lucky Palmer* 87: He shuddered when he said 'working'. 'That work,' he said. 'I'm crooked on that.'

1959 Xavier Herbert *Seven Emus* 101: 'It's no good talking religion to Bronco. He's dead crooked on it.'

1962 Alan Seymour *The One Day of the Year* 73: 'Now, if Alf was you he'd have a reason to be crooked on the world.'

1966 Elwyn Wallace *Sydney and the Bush* 52: 'The cops have ... a whole lot more work with no extra money. That's why they're real crooked on dolies.'

croppy 1 An Irish convict (from the rebels of 1798, who had their hair cut short in sympathy with the French Revolution)

1800 *HRA* I ii 581: That he hath often been in company with Holt when drinking inflammatory and seditious Toasts – 'Success to the Croppies' and other improper Expressions were made use of by Holt, that he had asked the Witness if there was a rising of the Irish if he would not join them ... that Holt then said 'You are an Irishman, Kennedy, and we will all go home in one ship together.'

2 A convict; a runaway convict; a bushranger

1809 *HRNSW* 216: It is high time that some fresh Governor should have arrived here before this as such doings was never known – pardons to the worst of characters, Croppeys, and thieves.

1830 Robert Dawson *The Present State of Australia* 294: I said to the natives, as I often had done before, 'You look out, you know, and take care croppy (convict) no crammer (steal).' Ibid. 302–3: Not knowing the persons of the white men, the natives concluded that they were 'croppies,' who had run away from the penal settlement at Port Macquarie.

1883 W. H. Breton *Excursions in New South Wales* 234: The settlers are allowed to be present, but not the convicts, whom they call croppies, of course a word which they [the natives] have learnt from the whites.

1848 H. W. Haygarth *Recollections of Bush Life in Australia* 9: Robbed of his horse, valise ... by the well-known 'croppies' – 'Black Joe' or 'Irish Tom'.

1849 Alexander Harris *The Emigrant Family* (1967) 378: 'He says he'll shear off our hair – and make croppies of us.'

Cross, the King's Cross, Sydney

1946 Dal Stivens *The Courtship of Uncle Henry* 184: 'What a dump,' Jack said. 'The Cross will look good after this.'

1951 Dymphna Cusack and Florence James *Come In Spinner* 58: 'Us girls have got a flat together up at the Cross.'

1966 Elwyn Wallace *Sydney and the Bush* 138: People in Sydney ... always say 'Down the 'Loo' or 'Up the Cross'.

Cross, when the ~ turns over When the Southern Cross has tilted from an eastern to a western orientation, indicating the end of a drover's watch (see *Southerly* 1975 33–7)

[**1881** A. C. Grant *Bush-Life in Queensland* i 217: 'Hadn't you better turn in?' suggests Sam. 'We've good three hours yet by the Southern Cross.']

1951 Ernestine Hill *The Territory* 425:

'Call me when the Cross turns over,' you will hear the drovers say, or 'when the Pointers are clear.'

1957 D'Arcy Niland *Call Me When the Cross Turns Over* 124: 'You know what the drovers say, Mrs Anderson – Call me when the Cross turns over, they say. The Cross turns over for everybody. It marks for some the end of a sleep, for some the beginning.'

crow 1 A woman who is old or ugly: *derogatory*

1925 H. H. Richardson *The Way Home* 84: Between ourselves it makes me feel a proper old crow.

1949 Lawson Glassop *Lucky Palmer* 60: She's no crow, he thought. A real good-looking filly, this one.

1953 T. A. G. Hungerford *Riverslake* 220: 'Those old crows in the office get high and mighty ideas about themselves. They want taking down a peg or two.'

1965 Hal Porter *The Cats of Venice* 112: Surprised at the old Pommy crow's interruption he spares a glance.

1970 Jon Cleary *Helga's Web* 21: She would have been quite a looker. 'Why do they kill the good-looking ones? There are plenty of crows around.'

1974 *Sunday Telegraph* 3 Nov. 9: Mrs Whitlam lashed out at some of the critics who blasted her show. 'I don't mind if they call me an old crow, but you naturally think they're unfair if they attack something you think went very well.'

2 A prostitute (phonetically the same as 'cro', abbr. for 'chromo')

1950 *Australian Police Journal* Apr. 111: *Crow* Prostitute.

1953 Kylie Tennant *The Joyful Condemned* 47: 'She's in with all the higher-ups. And what does she do? Slugs a guy like a cro on a beat.'

1965 Eric Lambert *The Long White Night* 80: 'That big café down on the waterfront. The Universal. The crows hang round it there in droves.'

crow, draw the To come off worst in any allocation [f. the anecdote about sharing out the day's shooting, the bag

containing a number of table-birds and one crow, so that someone would 'draw the crow' in his share]

1944 Lawson Glassop *We Were the Rats* 113: 'That poor bloke drew the crow.' Ibid. 207: 'I reckon with sheilas I always draw the crow.'

1952 T. A. G. Hungerford *The Ridge and the River* 75: 'Oh, all right.' Sweet's tone was resigned. 'I always cop the bloody crow.'

1970 Richard Beilby *No Medals for Aphrodite* 169: 'I knew we'd drawn the crow as soon as I seen this place!'

1975 Les Ryan *The Shearers* 44: 'What a bastard – period,' Sandy said ... He had drawn the crow.

crow (eagle), when the ~ shits Payday

1974 *Southerly* 408: 'Ah well, the crow shits tomorrow ... Pay-day,' he explained, placing it with his lips, 'we get our dough tomorrow.'

1977 Jim Ramsay *Cop it Sweet* 33: *Eagle shits, when the* When the pay-master comes around; Pay day.

Croweater A native of South Australia: *jocular, obsolescent*

1900–10 O'Brien and Stephens: *Crow-eater* An epithet applied to the natives or citizens of South Australia.

1903 Joseph Furphy *Such is Life* (1944) 123: The wire parted, and Pup and I were deck passengers, ong root for the land of the Crow-eater.

1919 W. K. Harris *Outback in Australia* 8: The one exception, a long, typical 'crow-eater' (as South Australians are called).

1934 Thomas Wood *Cobbers* 144: So let this mob of Cornstalks, Crow-eaters, Sandgropers, and Banana-landers[1] go on yapping, say Victorians. [1]New South Welshmen, South Australians, Western Australians, and Queenslanders.

1973 Frank Huelin *Keep Moving* 29: 'South Aus. is the worst State in th' country – bloody crow-eaters!'

crows, stone the Expression of surprise, regret, or disgust. Sometimes 'stiffen the crows', or 'stone the crows and stiffen the lizards', occurring most frequently in comic-strip Australian [listed by Partridge as Cockney]

1918 Harley Matthews *Saints and Soldiers* 116: 'Starve the crows,' howled Bluey in that agonised screech of his.

1924 C. J. Dennis *Rose of Spadgers* 110: 'I'm sorry, sonny. Stone the crows! It's sad / To see yer face so orful cut about.'

1930 L. W. Lower *Here's Luck* 189: 'Stone the crows!' exclaimed Stanley indignantly.

1934 Vance Palmer *Sea and Spinifex* 155: 'Stone the crows, how can a man hit a crawler like that? He'd never get the stain off his hands.'

1942 Eve Langley *The Pea Pickers* 321: 'Stone the crows,' he said faintly. 'What is it?'

1952 T. A. G. Hungerford *The Ridge and the River* 24: 'Stiffen the crows! . . . One thing I don't like, it's mucking around in ambushes.'

1964 Jon Cleary *A Flight of Chariots* 72: 'Stone the bloody crows, you don't know what you've missed!'

crows, where the ~ fly backwards to keep the dust out of their eyes One of the attributes of Woop Woop q.v. or any similar locality

1899 W. T. Goodge *Hits! Skits! and Jingles!* 6: 'The Oozlum Bird'. It's a curious bird, the Oozlum, / And a bird that's mighty wise, / For it always flies tail-first to / Keep the dust out of its eyes!

1936 Ion L. Idriess *The Cattle King* 153: 'I couldn't see the township', growled Bill, 'let alone a mob of cattle. No wonder they call this the place where the crows fly backwards to keep the dust out of their eyes.'

1971 Rena Briand *White Man in a Hole* 137: Posters covered the walls, and there was a sign proclaiming that, 'this isn't the Waldorf, therefore no complaints, please – even the crows fly backwards in these parts.'

cruel (the pitch) To spoil someone's chances [f. *queer the pitch* thieves' slang]

1915 C. J. Dennis *The Songs of a Sentimental Bloke* 16: But wot's the use, when 'Eaven's crool'd 'is pitch?

1922 Edward Dyson *The Grey Goose Comedy Company* 69: 'If I said anythink lars night, I'd only have cruelled everythink. We must think out a plan.'

1928 Arthur Wright *A Good Recovery* 179: 'We found that two men were coming to town who were likely to cruel our chances with you girls.'

1938 Xavier Herbert *Capricornia* 374: 'Do you think the Southern graziers'll stand bein' taxed to bring down beasts to cruel the market for 'em?'

1941 Baker 21: *Cruel, to* To spoil or ruin (something), e.g. a person's chances of success.

1951 Dal Stivens *Jimmy Brockett* 142: Things were going well with Sadie and myself and I didn't want to cruel anything.

1971 David Ireland *The Unknown Industrial Prisoner* 83: He never made it. His eagerness for overtime and promotion cruelled him.

cruiser Name sometimes given to 20 oz. beer glass in N.S.W., as the size larger than the 'schooner'

crumpet, not worth a Utterly worthless

1944 Lawson Glassop *We Were the Rats* 153: 'He won't be worth a crumpet in action, not worth a bloody crumpet.'

1962 Alan Seymour *The One Day of the Year* 73: 'Ballyhoo. Photos in the papers. Famous. Not worth a crumpet.'

crust, a A livelihood

1908 Henry Fletcher *Dads and Dan between Smokes* 116: 'Common labor, battlin' fer a crust, is willin' ter graft fer a crust.'

1910 Henry Lawson 'The Rising of the Court' *Prose* i 660: Police-court solicitors . . . wrangling over some miserable case for a crust.

1918 Bernard Cronin *The Coastlanders* 115: 'I'll bet a new bridle he's earned his crust in the country some time or other.'

1924 *Truth* 27 Apr. 6: *Crust* Livelihood.

1939 Kylie Tennant *Foveaux* 312: 'What's y'r old man do for a crust?' Curly asked . . . 'Driver a taxi.'

1946 K. S. Prichard *The Roaring Nine-*

ties 211: 'He goes around cadging old clothes ... as if he were a poor boy willing to do anything for a crust.'
1962 Stuart Gore *Down the Golden Mile* 65: 'Still, a man has to earn a crust somehow.'
1974 Jack Hibberd *Dimboola* 39: 'What do you do for a crust?' 'I'm a reporter.'

cuffs and collars The insignia of those set apart from the manual workers, esp. in the bush; a jackeroo or 'dude'
1895 Henry Lawson 'The Grand Mistake' *Verse* i 405: You bushmen sneer in the old bush way at the new-chum jackeroo,/But 'cuffs-'n'-collers' was out that day and they stuck to their posts like glue.
1911 Leo St Clare Grondona *Collars and Cuffs, The Adventures of a Jackeroo* [book title]
1935 Kylie Tennant *Tiburon* 66: 'I sees this young lady walkin' in an' I says, "There's one of the bourgeoisie, if y' like. One of the real middle-class cuff-an'-collar team." An' then she turns out to be a friend of Will ... who taught me all the finer points about workin'-class politics.'

cultural cringe see **cringe**

cundy A stone [Ab.]
1941 Baker 21: *Cundy* a small stone.
1962 Stuart Gore *Down the Golden Mile* 113: 'Look, mine friendt, you are scouting roundt for some big coondies, stones, you know?'
see **boondy**

Cup, the The Melbourne Cup
1889 J. Jenkins *Diary of a Welsh Swagman* (1975) 177: This year the Cup was won by a horse named 'Bravo', and he started as third favourite.
1895 A. B. Paterson *The Man from Snowy River* 3: There was Harrison, who made his pile when Pardon won the Cup.
1896 Nat Gould *Town and Bush* 127: At Cup time Melbourne is not the most moral city on the face of the globe. There is an influx of undesirable citizens from all parts of the colonies.

1918 C. J. Dennis *Backblock Ballads* 115: 'I'll lay you ten to one in quids he'll say: 'Wot's won the Cup?'
1975 *Sun-Herald* 2 Nov. 1: Record $25m gamble hangs on the Cup.

currency 1 The local money used in the colonies, as distinct from sterling (OED 1755)
1813 *Sydney Gazette* 27 Nov. 1: Whereas divers Victuallers, Publicans, and others ... altered the then subsisting Rate of Exchange between the Bills drawn for the Public Service, and the Promissory Notes issued by different Individuals, known by the Name of Currency, by means whereof great Confusion has been introduced into all Private Dealings and Transactions. Ibid. 2: The above [advertised commodities] to be had wholesale and retail, for sterling money, or negotiable currency bills.
1817 *HRA* ix 216: On the 30th of June, 1810, I [Governor Macquarie] issued a strong Proclamation ... prohibiting under severe penalties the further issue of Notes of Hand, other than such as expressed in specific terms, *payable in Sterling Money* only, wherein our ... object was to check the destructive issue of what was termed *Currency* Notes, the nature of which was such that the depreciation of the relative Value, when in comparison with Sterling Money, actually became the Chief source of profit and advantage ... to the Issuers of these Notes.
1826 James Atkinson *An Account of the State of Agriculture and Grazing in New South Wales* 132: In the early periods of the Settlement ... every trader constituted himself a Banker, and issued his promissory notes, which were denominated *currency* of various values ... When it was required therefore to exchange the Colonial currency against sterling bills ... the former was always exchanged at a discount.
2 The native-born as distinct from the English immigrant, usually as 'currency lads' and 'currency lasses'
1824 *Sydney Gazette* 26 Feb. 2: Owing to this successful issue, the currency

lads are in great glee.

1827 P. Cunningham *Two Years in New South Wales* i 54: Educating twenty of our young *currency* females in all the requisites necessary to constitute good servants. Ibid. ii 53: Our colonial born brethren are best known here by the name of *Currency,* in contradistinction to *Sterling,* or those born in the mother-country.

1832 *The Currency Lad* [title of newspaper running from 25 Aug. 1832 to 18 May 1833]

1845 Thomas McCombie *Arabin* 134: Nearly all of the species known as 'currency' are matter-of-fact men, with very few elements of originality in their composition, and ignorant of the pleasure to be derived from the fine arts.

1861 H. W. Wheelwright *Bush Wanderings of a Naturalist* 247: As for the young 'currency lads', they are more precocious than the youth at home.

1877 Rolf Boldrewood *A Colonial Reformer* (1890) 342: 'You're a regular Currency lass, Tottie,' laughed Mr Banks, 'always thinking about horses.'

Curry, the Cloncurry, Queensland

1934 F. E. Baume *Burnt Sugar* 234: 'Name's Bert Cross. Whaddayer like for Satdy? Come from the Curry.'

1959 Mary Durack *Kings in Grass Castles* 237: From 'the Curry' the route ran over a deep crossing where the cattle were forced to swim.

1975 Robert Macklin *The Queenslander* 143: They had lost all their money in a pontoon game at the 'Curry's billiard saloon.

curry, to give someone To make it 'hot' for him, assault verbally or physically

1941 Baker 21: *Curry, to give someone* To abuse, reprove, express anger at a person.

1944 *Coast to Coast 1943* 124: She was trying to think up what she was going to say from the platform. 'I'm going to give those old tarts a bit of curry tonight, Ron.'

1970 Alexander Buzo *The Front Room Boys* in Penguin *Plays* 53: 'Let's give

the ratbags a bit of curry. Here, tip some rubbish on them.'

1977 Jeff Thomson *Sunday Telegraph* 30 Jan. 48: My old mate Lennie Pascoe gave the Bananalanders some curry yesterday . . . he shattered the first four wickets for only 16 off seven overs.

cut A stroke of the cane

1900 Henry Lawson 'The Master's Mistake' *Prose* i 252: 'Just a couple of cuts with the cane and it'll be all over.'

1902 Ambrose Pratt *The Great 'Push' Experiment* 12: 'Mr Collins frowned and administered six cuts on each of my hands.'

1933 Norman Lindsay *Saturdee* 144: 'Hold out!' Five apiece they got . . . cuts which extinguished them in a purple mist of anguish.

1965 William Dick *A Bunch of Ratbags* 142: He locked the door and got out his strap and gave me four cuts of it.

1974 Gerald Murnane *Tamarisk Row* 91: She gives them each two stinging cuts and sends them back to their class.

cut-lunch commandos See quot. 1953

1944 Keith Attiwill *Cut-Lunch Commandos* [title of a novel on the public service]

1952 T. A. G. Hungerford *The Ridge and the River* 123: 'Come on! Think I got nothin' to do but wait for a bunch of cut-lunch commandos.'

1953 Baker 170: *cut-lunch commandos* Soldiers serving with a home base unit.

cut out *v.* 1 To separate selected cattle from the herd

1844 *Georgiana's Journal* ed. Hugh McCrae (1966) 127: Mr Jamieson was able to identify some of his own bullocks . . . whereupon, he and Captain Reid, with much shouting and cracking of whips, proceeded to 'cut them out' from the mob.

1873 Anthony Trollope *Australia* ed. Edwards and Joyce (1967) 415–16: I went out one morning at four a.m. to see a lot drafted out of a herd for sale. 'Cutting out' is the proper name for this operation.

1876 Rolf Boldrewood *A Colonial Re-*

former (1890) 222: Riding in pairs, and separating or 'cutting out', as the cattle station phrase is, divers excited animals . . . from the herd.

1897 Barcroft Boake 'Jack's Last Muster' *Where the Dead Men Lie* 7: Thrice Jack with a clout of his whip cut him out.

1918 Bernard Cronin *The Coastlanders* 66: 'He's the best hand at cutting out in a muster that I ever saw.'

1955 Mary Durack *Keep Him My Country* 350: *Cut out* To divide certain beasts from the main mob.

2 Used of the completion of a contract job, either of the work coming to an end or of the worker finishing his labours

1882 Rolf Boldrewood *Robbery Under Arms* (World's Classics 1949) 28: 'You and George can take a turn at local preaching when you're cut out' [referring to a fencing contract] Ibid. 83: Jim and I stopped at Boree shed till all the sheep were cut out.

1892 G. L. James *Shall I Try Australia*? 97: The day before we start to 'cut in' – which is the term for commencing to shear (when we have finished we are said to have 'cut out') – is a busy day.

1905 *The Old Bush Songs* ed. A. B. Paterson 24: Oh, we started down from Roto when the sheds had all cut out.

1919 W. K. Harris *Outback in Australia* 141: Last month, they were in full swing, to-day they will be 'cut-out'.

1936 Ion L. Idriess *The Cattle King* 52: The shearers and rouseabouts were there, freshly 'cut out' from Mount Gipps and Corona.

1941 Kylie Tennant *The Battlers* 364: In a little over a week the job [bag sewing] cut out and they went on again.

1958 H. D. Williamson *The Sunlit Plain* 24: He had rested a week since the fencing contract had cut out.

1960 Donald McLean *The Roaring Days* 124: Mansfield's Reward turned out to be only a small field . . . but a few fossickers stayed on for a year or two after it cut out – like they always do.

1973 Roland Robinson *The Drift of Things* 102: In those days a man who arrived in town after a long spell of bush work would throw his cheque

down on the bar, and say to the publican 'Let me know when that's cut out'.

cut out *n.* The completion of shearing, or other rural work

1911 E. J. Brady *River Rovers* 187: North Yanco shearing shed, where 53,000 sheep were destined to leave their wool before the 'cut out'.

1962 *Sydney Morning Herald* 24 Nov. 12: Later, after the cut out . . . the rep. admitted the sheep were as dry as a punctured water bag.

D

D, dee 1 A detective, or policeman in plain clothes. Also an abbr. for 'demon' q.v.

1877 T. E. Argles *The Pilgrim* i 4: After my name and occupation had been entered in a ledger by the educated sergeant, I was searched. The pitiless 'D.' took all my property away.

c. 1882 *The Sydney Slang Dictionary* 3: *Dee* (D) A detective policeman. 'The D's are about, so look out!'

1894 *Bulletin* 18 Aug. 14: The inevitable result will be that each private 'D' will keep his own corroborator on the premises.

1924 C. J. Dennis *Rose of Spadgers* 77: ' 'E's bein' chased,' she sez, 'by Ds, I've 'eard.'

1930 L. W. Lower *Here's Luck* 152: 'These two gentlemen,' she repeated, 'are private detectives.' 'D's!' shouted Woggo.

1945 K. S. Prichard *Golden Miles* 23: Detective Sergeant Kavanagh and a staff of dees were sent up to investigate.

1965 William Dick *A Bunch of Ratbags* 210: 'Crikey, look at the coppers,' I said as I saw the police-sign up on the front of the Ford. 'They're Dees, too.'

1973 Ward McNally *Man from Zero* 109: 'Those bloody Dees were each over fourteen stone.'

2 A D-shaped loop or clip on a saddle [f. *dee* metal loop in harness OED 1794]

1888 W.S.S. Tyrwhitt *The New Chum in the Queensland Bush* 59: On the solitary occasion when it was my lot to swim a flooded creek, my horse did it so well that my lunch in a pouch hanging behind me from the D's of the saddle, was kept perfectly dry.

1911 E. S. Sorenson *Life in the Australian Backblocks* 207: Novices and others who lack proficiency use ... a monkey (a strap looped between the D's for the right hand to grip).

1931 Miles Franklin *Back to Bool Bool* 280: Each saddle had a quart pot or something else on the dees, and tucker and oil-coats on the pommel.

1959 Desmond Martin *Australia Astride* 194: A leather strap or binding through the pommel D's.

Dad and Dave Title of a radio serial of the 1930s and later, derived somewhat remotely from characters in Steele Rudd's *On Our Selection:* now a byword for a humorous version of unsophisticated rural Australia before World War II

1943 Manning Clark *Meanjin Papers* ii 340: What are we to do about Dad and Dave, about this ideal ... which embarrasses the élite and sustains the vulgar?

1943 Maurice Clough *We of the A.I.F.* 44: Like 'Dad and Dave' of 'hayseed' jokes.

1974 Geoffrey Blainey *Australian* 4 Oct. 8: On the farmlands the trees were ringbarked in their hundreds of thousands, and behind post-and-rail fences they often stood in their pale cemeteries for five or fifteen years before Dad and Dave burned them down.

1977 *Sydney Morning Herald* 14 Jan. 1: Javed Miandad, the Pakistani cricketer, pronounces his name, Me-an'-dad. So what have the Australian test players nicknamed him? Dave, of course.

see **Dave and Mabel, Snake Gully**

daddy The supreme instance, esp. in the phrase 'the daddy of them all' [also English and U.S. ? f. expressions like 'the father of a hiding']

1898 W. H. Ogilvie *Fair Girls and Gray Horses* 54: Though shaky in the shoulders, he's the daddy of them all; / He's the gamest bit of horseflesh from the Snowy to the Bree.

1902 Henry Lawson 'A Droving Yarn' *Prose* i 357: 'Billy was the daddy of the drovers.'

1923 Jack Moses *Beyond the City Gates* 105: There were many who wondered that night how Clinker, the daddy of all horsemen, would come out of the battle.

1932 Myrtle Rose White *No Roads Go By* 135: Then we came to the big sandhill, the 'Daddy of the lot'.

1942 Jean Devanny *The Killing of Jacqueline Love* 154: 'She was the daddy of all liars.'

1954 Bant Singer *Have Patience, Delaney* 77–8: I been in a lot of wild mix-ups in my time ... but this is sure the daddy of the whole flaming lot.

1961 Ion L. Idriess *Tracks of Destiny* 80: Of the Territory pioneer women perhaps the 'daddy' of the lot is Mrs Phoebe Farrar.

dag 1 See quot. 1933

1878 G. H. Gibson *Southerly Busters* 179: I'm able for to shear 'em clean, / And level as a die; / But I prefer to 'tommy hawk', / And make the 'daggers' fly.

1899 W. T. Goodge *Hits! Skits! and Jingles!* 42: With leathery necks and dags galore, / A bad machine and a slippery floor, / And how could a shearer want for more?

1933 Acland: *Dag, dags* hard or soft dung hanging from the breech of a sheep. Cutting this off the sheep with an old pair of shears is called dagging.

1971 Frank Hardy *The Outcasts of Foolgarah* 2: Sir Percival Dagg, the sheep millionaire.

2 A would-be dashing and stylish fellow (the sense replaced by 'lair' q.v.); a humorist, wag, eccentric

1916 *The Anzac Book* 47: Yes; 'Enessy was a dag if ever there was one!

1918 *Aussie* 18 Jan. 14: The Dag – on leave [cartoon of nattily turned out soldier with a self-satisfied expression]

1924 *Truth* 27 Apr. 6: *Dag* A funny fellow.

1932 Leonard Mann *Flesh in Armour* 57: Johnny Wright, a solicitor from a country town, now a bit of a dag, with

the habit of going on a real bender now and then. Ibid. 299: They could imagine that whimsical grin. There he was, just the same old dag.
1937 Vance Palmer *Legend for Sanderson* 33: 'He was a dag, old Chris.'
1946 Kylie Tennant *Lost Haven* 351: He had to be the Alec who was 'a bit of a dag', who always had a joke.
1963 Hal Porter *The Watcher on the Cast-Iron Balcony* 110: Partly to give Uncle Y, the wit, the funny-man, the sad case, the dag, the trimmer, the one-never-lost-for-a-smart-come-back, a further opportunity to set them giggling and squealing.
3 A conventional youth, 'a square'
1975 *National Times* 13 Jan. 40: The surf has a glamour the ordinary boy lacks. 'They're dags,' says Colleen Field, of Kellyville, of ordinary boys. Despite the repulsive tag, dags are the sort of boy every mother would like her daughter to bring home. At least she knows, by the medium-long haircut, that he is a boy. His clothes are tidy, he wears shoes and is known to wear a tie.

damper The form of bread best known to the workforce of outback Australia in the nineteenth century and later, hence used colloquially in phrases like 'worth your damper', 'earn your damper'. [f. *damper* A luncheon, or snap before dinner: so called from its damping, or allaying, the appetite Grose 1785]
1827 P. Cunningham *Two Years in New South Wales* ii 190: The farm-men usually bake their flour into flat cakes, which they call *dampers*, and cook these in the ashes.
1834 George Bennett *Wanderings in New South Wales* i 260: 'Damper' is merely a cake of flour and water, or milk, baked in the ashes; it is the usual mode of bread-making in the bush.
1848 J. C. Byrne *Twelve Years' Wanderings in the British Colonies 1835–1847* i 364: The traveller ... gathers some wood, kindles a fire, boils a pot of tea, and with a lump of damper*, and a cut of salt meat soon satisfies his appetite.
*The word damper signifies bread

unleavened, baked in the ashes, about a couple of inches thick.
1855 E. P. R. *A Romance of the Bush* 52: The next two days' stages were to the meanest of roadside houses and of accommodation, where beef and damper* was all that could be procured.
*Flat cakes of flour and water, without yeast, used as bread.
1867 J. S. Borlase *The Night Fossickers* 46: We ... lit a fire, made tea in our billies, baked some damper in the embers, and sat down to our supper.
1895 A. B. Paterson *The Man from Snowy River* 14: They wouldn't earn much of their damper / In a race like the President's Cup.
1903 Joseph Furphy *Such is Life* (1944) 327: You're not worth your damper at this work.
1961 Patrick White *Riders in the Chariot* 382: 'You are not worth your damper,' she said at once, 'layin' around!'

dark 'un See quot. 1957: wharf slang
1957 Tom Nelson *The Hungry Mile* 81: Some 25 years back a gang of us refused an order of the Union Co. to come back after the breakfast break for four hours, after doing a 'dark-un' (24 hour shift).
1961 *Sydney Morning Herald* 22 May 2: One reason for rank-and-file militancy is that many of those who remember the bad days – the jostling for jobs and the 24-hour 'dark-'uns' – are still in the industry.
1977 *Sunday Telegraph* 6 Mar. 7: 'For 12 years as foreman I worked a weekly 'darkun' – a 24-hour shift. These shifts were inhuman'.

Darling Pea *Swainsonia galegifolia*, a plant which when eaten by cattle sends them mad [f. Darling river and districts]
1889 T. Quin *The Well Sinkers* 101: 'The man's mad!' he said ... 'No ... he's got a touch of what we call the Darling Pea.'
1904 Laura M. Palmer-Archer *A Bush Honeymoon* 349: Darling Pea Madness.
1918 N. Campbell and L. Nelson *The Dinky-Di Soldier* 29: When the Darlin'

pea is drivin' men an' cattle off their chump.

Darling pie See quot: N.T. and W.A.
1951 Ernestine Hill *The Territory* 426: 'Darling pie', baked rabbit and bindi-eyes with scurvy grass for greens if you were diabetic or dietetic.

Darling shower see **shower**

Darlo Darlinghurst, N.S.W. [abbr.]
1941 Baker 22: *Darlo* The district of Darlinghurst, Sydney.
1967 Donald Horne *Southern Exposure* 125: The surfies hang five at the beaches; the beats grow their hair long at Darlo.
1971 Craig McGregor *Don't Talk to Me about Love* 64: Those incorruptible eagle-eyed and pinioned defenders of the Majesty of the Law, the Darlo plainclothes squad.

dart Some especially favoured object; a cherished plan or scheme: *obs.*
[1859 W. Kelly *Life in Victoria* i 218: *Dart* [in gold-mining] is the designation of stuff worth washing, as contra-distinguished from that considered useless.]
c. 1882 *The Sydney Slang Dictionary* 3: *Dart* Object of attraction, or enticing thing or event, or a set purpose.
1882 Rolf Boldrewood *Robbery Under Arms* (World's Classics 1949) 46: The great dart is to keep the young stock away from their mothers until they forget one another, and then most of the danger is past.
1893 Daniel Healey *The Cornstalk* 77: 'You see it's a blooming good dart. We hook on to a cove or a gal that has some friends with a little spons, and is some-what inclined to be givey.'
1902 Ambrose Pratt *The Great 'Push' Experiment* 77: 'Then, ye see, when ye stand for member later on, you'll get respectable, all-round support as well as from the Push. See my blimey dart?'
1911 Louis Stone *Jonah* 60: 'Your dart is ter be King of the Push, an' knock about the streets.'
1924 C. J. Dennis *Rose of Spadgers* 84:

'Wot's yer dart?'

Dart, the old see **Old Dart**

date (dot) Backside, anus
1959 D'Arcy Niland *The Big Smoke* 41: He said, 'Shove it up your black dot,' and went down the stairs.
1961 Mena Calthorpe *The Dyehouse* 214: 'In your bloody date! What do you think we are?'
1973 *Snatches & Lays* 25: The Austra-lian lady emu, when she wants to find a mate, / Wanders round the desert with a feather up her date.
date *v.* To 'goose' someone
1976 Dorothy Hewett *Bon-bons and Roses for Dolly* 52: 'I was up on a chair fixing the new curtains and he comes up behind and dates me. Large as life. Without a word of a lie. He dates me. Cheeky mug.'

Dave and Mabel Characters in the radio serial 'Dad and Dave' q.v., and hence a byword for unsophisticated rural Aus-tralians before World War II
1973 Frank Huelin *Keep Moving* 39: The boss's daughter – a girl in her early teens – who played Mabel to Stan's Dave.
1975 Hal Porter *The Extra* 212: Their table manners pass muster, their accents aren't affectedly Dave and Mabel.
see **Dad and Dave, Snake Gully**

day, that'll be the An ironical rejoinder meaning 'That would be worth waiting for' or 'That will never happen.' Accepted by Turner 134 as a New Zealand coinage, but often heard in American films.
1941 Sidney J. Baker *New Zealand Slang* 50: *That'll be the day!* used as a cant phrase expressing mild doubt following some boast or claim by a person.
1952 T. A. G. Hungerford *The Ridge and the River* 46: White's derisive laughter sounded through the gloom of the fox-hole. 'That'd be the day!'
1957 D'Arcy Niland *Call Me When the Cross Turns Over* 125–6: 'I've got a waiting list.' He smiled. 'Any time you want to go down at the top just say

the word.' 'That'll be the day.'
1963 Anthony Coburn *The Bastard Country* 12: 'He reckons he's stayin' on. Says Dad'll let him.' 'That'll be the day.'

dead bird see **bird**

Dead Heart The interior of Australia, from J. W. Gregory's book of 1906
1906 J. W. Gregory *The Dead Heart of Australia* [book title]
1936 Archer Russell *Gone Nomad* 47: 'Dead Heart' though this region may be to some, it was never so to me. To know the gibber lands you must go and live amid their silence.
1961 Kenneth Cook *Wake in Fright* 6–7: Further out in the heat was the silent centre of Australia, the Dead Heart.
1974 David Ireland *Burn* 110: 'I'll tell you where the dead heart of Australia is. It's right back there in the cities. Not out in the sand and the mulga and the stones burning hot under the sun.'

dead horse, working (off) a Working for a return that is immediately consumed in the payment of a debt, and thus for no personal benefit [OED 1638; To work for the dead horse; to work for wages already paid Grose 1785]
1847 Alexander Harris *Settlers and Convicts* ed. C. M. H. Clark (1954) 181: Endeavour on the part of the labourer, after having largely overdrawn his account, to get rid of the debt; they call working out such a debt, *riding the dead horse*.
1863 Samuel Butler *A First Year on Canterbury Settlement* 146: They will come back possibly with *a dead horse to work off* – that is, a debt at the accommodation house – and will work hard for another year to have another drinking bout at the end of it.
1898 *Bulletin* 17 Dec. Red Page: *Working dead horse* is working to pay off a back debt; or, as a teamster would say, 'This trip has got to pay for a horse that I lost last trip; £20 to make up to pay for the new horse.'
1907 Alfred Searcy *The Australian Tropics* 21: Having incurred certain liabilities in forming the home at Croker Island, Robinson undertook to work them off. This he did, and effectually buried the 'dead horse' at Port Essington.
1932 William Hatfield *Ginger Murdoch* 38: 'I'm hobbled here workin' orf a huge dead horse.'
1945 Tom Ronan *Strangers on the Ophir* 37: I've got a dead horse at McGarry's that is as big as an elephant.

deadhouse Room attached to a hotel in which the drunks could sleep it off [f. *deadhouse* morgue]
1876 Rolf Boldrewood *A Colonial Reformer* (1890) 133: I remember coming to myself in the dead-house of a bush inn.
1888 E. Finn *Chronicles of Early Melbourne* ii 547: Another usage grew up with the old hotels . . . the attaching of a littered room or deadhouse – not the dreary-looking ghostly morgue, where suicides or accidentally made corpses are laid in state, but a secure, unwindowed, comfortably strawed exterior apartment, into which the bodies of those who got dead-drunk by day or night were stowed away, and suffered to rest in peace and sleep off the debauch.
1900 T. Major *Leaves from a Squatter's Notebook* 131–2: [The shearer] might be seen for weeks or days . . . swilling the fiery, poisonous stuff called 'real' Jamaica rum, until, unable to sit or stand, the shanty-keeper carried or dragged him to the 'dead-house' – a shed so named, built near the shanty – and there, on a bunk or on the ground, he slept the sleep of stupefaction.
1922 Arthur Wright *A Colt from the Country* 114: 'Another pint, as you say, and it'd be me f'r th' dead-house.'
1962 Alan Marshall *This is the Grass* 46: 'He has no money and when he goes out to it they toss him into the dead house beside the stable.'

dead marine An empty bottle (of beer or spirits) [?f. *dead men* empty bottles OED 1700; Grose 1785]
1885 J. Brunton Stephens *Convict Once*

109

and *Other Poems* 308: We had filled a dead marine, sir, at the fam'ly water-hole.
1892 Henry Lawson 'Jones's Alley' *Prose* i 41: A small bony horse, which, in its turn, dragged a rickety cart of the tray variety, such as is used in the dead marine trade.
1911 Louis Stone *Jonah* 74: Borrowing a dead marine from the heap of empty bottles, shuffled off to the hotel to get it filled.
1932 Myrtle Rose White *No Roads Go By* 202: All the dead marines from previous festivities were resurrected and a great bottle-washing competition entered into.
1948 K. S. Prichard *Golden Miles* 375: 'Wood-cartin's not the game it used to be, neither is collectin' dead marines.'
1952 *Coast to Coast 1951–1952* 193: Sitting at that bit of a table with a bottle, and bottles on the floor, dead marines.
1973 John Morrison *Australian by Choice* 128: Carry out the dead marines and stack them in the yard.

dead men's graves See quots
1855 William Howitt *Land, Labour and Gold* i 309: Akin to these Crab-holes are Dead-men's Graves. They are oblong heaps of earth distributed over certain extents of these low, volcanic plains, which for all the world present the appearance of a graveyard.
1901 Rolf Boldrewood *In Bad Company* 482: I was walking the horses over a curious formation of small mounds, provincially known as dead men's graves.

dead-un A horse not ridden to its full capacity, to ensure better odds when it next races [cf. U.S. and English *stiff 'un*]
1977 *Sun-Herald* 24 Jul. 57: No matter how you analyse the performance of a suspected dead-un there is really only one person who knows absolutely for sure – the man holding the reins.

Dean Maitland see **Maitland**

death seat The seat next to the driver of a car (as the occupant is the one most liable to injury in an accident) [also U.S.]
1971 Craig McGregor *Don't Talk to Me About Love* 149: Paula, feet braced against the Mazda floor in case of a head-on smash, in which case she, being in the death-seat, would have the chance for neither mistakes nor regrets.

deener Shilling (before the introduction of decimal currency in 1966) [OED 1839]
c. 1882 *The Sydney Slang Dictionary* 3: *Deaner* A shilling.
1901 Henry Lawson 'At Dead Dingo' *Prose* i 452: 'Stumped?' inquired Jim. 'Not a blanky, lurid deener!' drawled Bill.
1923 Con Drew *Rogues and Ruses* 22: 'We couldn't afford a deener to see an earthquake.'
1937 A. W. Upfield *Mr Jelley's Business* 146: 'If I 'ad lorst a deener I'd have got hell for a week.'
1942 Gavin Casey *It's Harder for Girls* 55: 'My dad's got plenty of money ... I can get a few deeners from him easy enough.'
1965 William Dick *A Bunch of Ratbags* 19: One thing about him, though, he knew how to make a deener on the side.

Deep North see **North**

deep sinker A long glass of beer: *obs.*
1877 T. E. Argles *The Pilgrim* vi 64: These misguided mortals spend in 'deep sinkers' ... that money which their landladies are daily sighing for – and sighing for in vain.
1886 Frank Cowan *Australia: A Charcoal Sketch* 32: Long-sleever, Bishop Barker, and Deep-sinker, synonyms of the Yankee Schooner.
1898 Joshua Lake *Australasian Supplement to Webster's International Dictionary* 2021: *Deep sinker* A kind of tall drinking glass; also, the drink which it contains; so called from the fancied resemblance of the glass to the shaft of a deep mine.
1899 W. T. Goodge *Hits! Skits! and Jingles!* 162: 'Can't yer give us a deep-sinker? / Ain't yer got a cask o' beer

behind the screen?'

deli A delicatessen [abbr.]
1973 Max Harris *The Angry Eye* 164: The deli owner would have to employ a bloke with a pencil and paper classifying every sale.
1975 *Australian* 11 Oct. 25: It was the same with Dean's, a pacesetter in the delicatessen world, operating a 'deli' before anyone really had heard the term.

delo Delegate, in trade union parlance [abbr.]
1961 *Sydney Morning Herald* 20 May 2: The boys had been battling for gloves, so I went up to the foreman, I'd cut me fingers and that. The pano said 'See your delegate!' So the delo fronted him and said 'If we don't get gloves we'll walk off!'

demon A policeman, esp. in plainclothes; a detective [? f. *dee*. The OED Suppl. derivation from Van Diemen's Land is unlikely]
1889 Barrère and Leland: *Demons* (Australian) prison slang for police.
1900–10 O'Brien and Stephens: *Demons* detectives, i.e. plainclothes generally (from D's).
1919 J. Vance Marshall *World of the Living Dead* 71: They say she's an open slather up there. Not a demon in the burg.'
1941 Kylie Tennant *The Battlers* 118: Adelaide had been triumphantly certain that the shearers were 'demons', or plain-clothes detectives.
1959 Dorothy Hewett *Bobbin Up* 124: Queueing up for your dole tickets and then out again at the crack of dawn, before the demons got on your tail.
1961 Tom Ronan *Only a Short Walk* 19: Some smart demon . . . would start getting ideas. And those plain-clothes men knew how to stick to a track once they got on to it.

Demons The Melbourne V.F.L. team (previously the Red Demons, and the Redlegs) [f. team colours]
1973 Rev. Alan Walker, in Keith Dun-stan *Sports* 230: 'Ladies and Gentlemen gathered here on this great occasion, whichever team we may support – the Saints or the Demons – we can surely agree that we are joined together as brothers in Jesus Christ.'
1975 *Sunday Telegraph* 13 Apr. 38: Demons Slam the Roos.

Derby, Benghazi see **Benghazi**

dermo Dermatitis, in World War II army slang [abbr.]
1948 Sumner Locke Elliott *Rusty Bugles* in *Khaki, Bush and Bigotry* ed. Eunice Hanger (1968) 52: 'They send you south if you get dermo more than three times bad enough to put you in hospital.'
1972 'Darwin Interlude' *Comic Australian Verse* ed. Geoffrey Lehmann 165: My men are down with dermo and with every tropic curse.

dero A derelict, i.e. someone unemployed and destitute [abbr.]
1973 *Sun-Herald* 8 Apr. 9: 'And you bump into a lot of very strange people – druggies and deros.'
1975 Elizabeth Riley *All That False Instruction* 126: 'Dero came up to me in the city the other day, wanted twenty cents – and I knew why.'

derry An alarm, police search; in the expression 'to have a derry on', an attitude of hostility, a 'down', a grudge against [? f. the refrain 'derry, derry down']
1882 Rolf Boldrewood *Robbery Under Arms* (World's Classics 1949) 68: 'Said he knew a squatter in Queensland he could pass him [the stolen stallion] on to; that they'd keep him there for a year and get a crop of foals by him, and when the 'derry' was off, he'd take him over himself.' Ibid. 171: 'We could take a long job at droving till the derry's off a bit.'
1892 Henry Lawson 'A Derry on a Cove' *Verse* i 173: 'It's cruel when the p'leece has got a derry on a bloke.'
1893 J. A. Barry *Steve Brown's Bunyip* 199: 'Them's the coves as we've got a derry on.'

1908 E. S. Sorenson *Quinton's Rouse-about* 24: Murphy had a derry on those people, and was determined to make an example of them.

1915 C. J. Dennis *The Songs of a Sentimental Bloke* 49: I took a derry on this stror-'at coot / First time I seen 'im dodgin' round Doreen.

1926 K. S. Prichard *Working Bullocks* 51: 'Anybody got a derry on you?'

1937 Vance Palmer *Legend for Sanderson* 226: 'More interested in his job and in giving his men a fair spin than in raking off big profits. That was why the other contractors had such a derry on him.'

1958 Vince Kelly *The Greedy Ones* 214: 'She's got a derry on Porkreth, too, because he shot up her boy friend.'

Derwenter An ex-convict [f. the convict settlement on the Derwent river in Tasmania]

1853 John Rochfort *Adventures of a Surveyor* 51: The proprietor of our tent (an old Derwenter) stationed himself at the door to receive payment as we departed.

1865 J. F. Mortlock *Experiences of a Convict* (1965) 220: Among the officials were no less than three old 'Derwenters'.

1888 J. C. F. Johnson *An Austral Christmas* 49: In the bush in those days, when so many old 'Derwenters' and 'Cockatoo Islanders' were to be met with, Craig's past record would not have greatly militated against him.

1899 George Boxall *The Story of the Australian Bushrangers* 139: It was popularly supposed that these bushrangers were all convicts from 'Van Diemen's Land', hence they were known as 'Van Demonians', 'Derwenters' from the River Derwent, and 'Tothersiders.'

deuce, deucer To shear 200 sheep in a day; someone capable of this feat [f. *deuce* two]

1950 Jack Sorenson *Collected Poems* 32: I thought perhaps he may have chanced to hear / Of how I almost deuced them* at Murgoo. *'Deuce them' – To shear 200 sheep.

1953 Baker 69: *deucer*, a shearer who can shear 200 sheep or more a day.

devils on the coals As for 'beggars-on-the-coals' q.v.

1862 Arthur Polehampton *Kangaroo Land* 76: Instead of damper we occasionally made what are colonially known as 'devils on the coals', which I imagine are somewhat similar to Indian chupatties.

dice To reject, abandon [f. *dice* To lose or throw away by dicing OED 1618]

1944 Lawson Glassop *We Were the Rats* 50: 'I says, Mrs 'Aliburton, I haven't seen Snow since the day before yesterday. He hasn't diced me, has he?' 'Gee, Shirley,' she says, 'he musta got another girl friend.'

1953 T. A. G. Hungerford *Riverslake* 190: 'You want to make up your mind and dice whatever you don't want.'

1963 Frank Hardy *Legends from Benson's Valley* 213: 'No bastard puts my daughter in the family way then dices her . . . and gets away with it.'

dickon An exclamation of disbelief or rejection: *obs.* [? f. *Dickens*]

1894 *Bulletin* 5 Apr. 13: *Witness:* Then he biffed me. *Chief Justice:* And did you stouch him back? *Witness:* No. *Chief Justice:* Dicken. *Witness:* Swelp me.

1911 Louis Stone *Jonah* 68: 'Dickon ter you,' said Mrs Yabsley. 'Yer needn't think they're got up ter kill ter please yous.'

1915 J. P. Bourke *Off the Bluebush* 190: If Life's waitresses say 'Dicken!' / When you reach out for the chicken, / Cop the broth.

1929 Hal Eyre *Hilarities* 46: 'Those were the days when . . . we said 'No flies on you,' 'Dickon to that,' and similar things. So you see it was some time ago.

1936 William Hatfield *Australia through the Windscreen* 293: 'There's a catch in this Light Horse business. You've got to tie your horse up, feed and water him, and *groom* the bastard before you get near a bit of picking for yourself. Dickon to that. The infantry'll

do me.'
1949 Alan Marshall *How Beautiful Are Thy Feet* 91: He suddenly became playful and patted her leg above the knee. 'Some leg.' 'Don't paw like that.' 'Dicken you don't like being handled.'

didee Lavatory [*didy* diaper U.S. 1902 OED]
1965 Frank Hardy *The Yarns of Billy Borker* 56: 'Having the didee in the backyard isn't very convenient,' the wife says. 'How right you are,' he tells her, 'get the plumbers in and build the best toilet that money can buy, right inside the house.'

digger 1 An Australian gold-miner of the 1850s and later [? f. U.S.]
1852 Lord Robert Cecil *Goldfields Diary* (1935) 36: When the diggers address a policeman in uniform they always call him 'Sir', but they always address a fellow in a blue shirt with a carbine as 'Mate'.
1856 G. Willmer *The Draper in Australia* 67: We met with many diggers rambling from one gold-field to another.
1867 J. S. Borlase *The Night Fossickers* 2: I did not come, however, as a seeker of the yellow metal — I had no ambition to become a digger.
2 An Australian soldier of World War I or later; as a mode of address, abbr. to 'Dig'
1918 *Aussie* 18 Jan. 11: 'Digger' has taken the place of the time-honoured 'Cobber' in the parlance of the Australian soldier.
1926 J. Vance Marshall *Timely Tips for New Australians: Digger* A familiar term of address such as 'friend' or comrade. Originally it was only applied to soldiers but now its use is universal.
1932 Leonard Mann *Flesh in Armour* 83: One of the Mth, seated on the ground, cried to Charl, 'Give us a smoke, for Gawd's sake, dig.'
1953 T. A. G. Hungerford *Riverslake* 159: 'Hey, digger, you got any dough?' Ibid. 50: 'What about you, dig?' the big man demanded, pushing his face so close.
1965 Patrick White *Four Plays* 105: A

bit seedy, battered. Good features of the hatchet variety. The Digger type.
1971 *Australian* 25 Sep. 1: Diggers still being sent to Vietnam.

Digger, the Little William Morris Hughes (1864–1952) Australian Prime Minister in World War I, and diminutive in size
1919 *Daily Telegraph* 15 Sep. 6: The Little Digger [heading] ... There were wavings of hats and hands and handkerchiefs, and a wild burst of cheers for 'the Little Digger'.
1952 *Sydney Morning Herald* 29 Oct. 2: No title that he earned was so dear to Mr Hughes as that of 'The Little Digger', and today none will mourn his passing more deeply than the veterans of the first world war.
1956 J. T. Lang *I Remember* 242: It [the Country Party of 1922] didn't like Hughes and lost no opportunity to voice its opinions of the Little Digger.
1975 *Australian* 25 Jan. 16: The redoubtable Billy Hughes once observed that he trusted only two people – Jesus Christ and the Commonwealth Statistician (The 'Little Digger' incidentally added that he still wasn't too sure about the former).

dike (dyke) Urinal, lavatory, esp. for communal use, as in a school or army camp [f. *dike* ditch or trench OED 847]
1923 Manchon *Le Slang* 104: *Dike*, les cabinets. [OED]
1948 Sumner Locke Elliott *Rusty Bugles* in *Khaki, Bush and Bigotry* ed. Eunice Hanger (1968) 42: 'Make sure you do everything on the double ... run to mess ... run back ... run to the dike.'
1969 D'Arcy Niland *Dead Men Running* 47: Anyway, the dyke would be occupied. He knew that from experience, he had always been the last to get there.
1971 George Johnston *A Cartload of Clay* 138: 'I mean, be orright for a dike, I suppose [the name *Merde Alors*] but funny for a house.'
1974 David Williamson *Three Plays* 121: 'Get your hands off me. I'm going to the dyke.'

dill A simpleton, an incompetent [f. *dilly*]

1941 Baker 23: *Dil* A simpleton or fool (2) A trickster's victim.
1945 Gavin Casey *Downhill is Easier* 197: 'Them dills'll never find out who done him in.'
1957 Judah Waten *Shares in Murder* 50: 'You must think I'm a dill if you expect me to take any notice of it.'
1966 Patrick White *The Solid Mandala* 46: Waldo decided not to listen to any further dill's drivel.
1968 *The Barry Humphries Book of Innocent Austral Verse* 76: America is hard to gauge, / The way she backs and fills, / I often wonder, is she straight, / Or is she run by dills?
1975 *Bulletin* 28 Jun. 30: Queenslanders resent being looked on as a mob of dills.

dilly Foolish, silly, 'dopey-looking'; having lost one's presence of mind: *obs*. [*dilly* cranky, queer E. dial. OED 1873]

1906 Edward Dyson *Fact'ry 'Ands* 213–14: 'Who should come sprintin' upstairs but me nibs, pale's er blessed egg, hair on end – fair dilly.'
1912 R. S. Tait *Scotty Mac, Shearer* 71: 'I daresay you've seen a few puzzles in your time, and you have looked at them, and thought them over until you were likely to go dilly.'
1915 C. J. Dennis *The Songs of a Sentimental Bloke* 16: If this 'ere dilly feelin' doesn't stop / I'll lose me block an' stoush some flamin' cop!
1935 Kylie Tennant *Tiburon* 21: 'Bless you, lady, bless you,' he says, all dilly with joy, see, thinkin' he's on a good thing.
1970 Kenneth Slessor *Bread and Wine* 31: One translation which he [C. J. Brennan, d. 1932] has pencilled after the Latin words *ocules languidum tuens* – 'with a dilly look in her eyes'.

dillybag Aboriginal word for a small bag or basket, applied to similar small bags made and used by whites

1876 A. J. Boyd *Old Colonials* (1882) 283: 'What is there in the dillybag?' 'About enough beef and flour for a day's feed, and a pound of tea.'
1881 Mrs Campbell Praed *Policy and Passion* 179: Lord Dolph . . .armed with a dilly-bag and a trowel, clambered up the precipice to search for roots.
1953 *Sydney Morning Herald* 16 May 5: Mrs Eunice Woolcott Forbes said . . . that her bank account was a 'joint dilly bag' for the transactions of her bankrupt husband . . . and their children.
1959 Dorothy Hewett *Bobbin Up* 149: Jeanie was stuffing things into her dilly bag . . . Behind the long line of rovers the women were packing up tote bags and baskets.
1975 Hal Porter *The Extra* 213: Into their dilly-bags go sugar, pepper, salt, bread rolls.

ding *n*. 1 An Italian or Greek; a foreigner generally: *derogatory*

1941 Baker 23: *Ding* An Italian.
1948 K. S. Prichard *Golden Miles* 100: Serbs, Bulgarians, Italians and Greeks, who worked on the mines, were gathering in excited groups . . .over the latest news. The Dings, as the northern people were called, and the Dagoes, which included the southern European races, had never fraternised very much.
1957 Randolph Stow *The Bystander* 21: 'No speak-a too bad-a da English, eh?' 'She wouldn't talk like that, anyway,' Nakala said scornfully. 'She's not a Ding.' 'She says you're not a Greek,' Frank explained . . . 'Or is it an Italian. I never remember which is a Ding and which is a Dago.'
1962 Stuart Gore *Down the Golden Mile* 30: 'He's a Ding for mine. He was born in Italy, wasn't he?'
1971 Rena Briand *White Man in a Hole* 11: 'And them Greeks . . . if yer wanner leave them dirty dings they're gonna run yer outa town.'

2 (also *dinger*) Backside, anus

1948 Sumner Locke Elliott *Rusty Bugles* in *Khaki, Bush and Bigotry* ed. Eunice Hanger (1968) 96: 'In your great dinger, you rotten crawling choco.'
1953 T. A. G. Hungerford *Riverslake* 161: 'Why *my* mate, particularly?' 'Hell – he thinks the sun shines out of your dinger!'

1972 Geoff Morley *Jockey Rides Honest Race* 209: 'You can get fined or sent to gaol for kicking a cat in the ding, but it's okay if it's a three-month-old baby.'
1975 Les Ryan *The Shearers* 119: 'Ar, pigs to you!' 'In your dinger, too!'

3 A party, celebration [f. *wingding*]
1956 *Sydney Morning Herald* 18 Oct. 1: In New Guinea a party is called a 'ding' and a house is a 'donga'. So if they have a party at home it's a ding in their donga.
1967 Frank Hardy *Billy Borker Yarns Again* 40: It appears that he had drunk fifteen of them there drinking horns of beer at a Commemoration Day ding.
1972 Alexander MacDonald *The Ukelele Player under the Red Lamp* 205: Only there was no beer. Just trayfuls of battery-fluid and cochineal . . . that was the kind of ding it was, all very outer-space and quaint and inconceivably twee.
1974 *Australian* 20 Jun. 3: Seventy lonely women from all over Australia got together in Melbourne last night for a 'mid-winter ding' while several thousand miles away in the Antarctic their husbands and boyfriends prepared for a similar celebration.

ding *v.* To throw away, abandon, give up, esp. in the expression 'to ding it': *obsolescent* [f. thieves' slang: see quot. 1812]
1812 Vaux: *Ding* to throw, or throw away . . . To ding a person, is to drop his acquaintance totally, also to quit his company, or leave him for the time present.
1875 A. J. Boyd *Old Colonials* (1882) 68–9: 'If any man was to try and get along carryin' on the Northern road with only twelve horses, he'd very quickly find he'd have to ding it.'
1880 Rolf Boldrewood *The Miner's Right* (1890) 22: 'I say ding it this very night, and let's try for a show somewhere else.'
1896 Edward Dyson *Rhymes from the Mines* 74: Ding it? No. Where gold was getting I was on the job, and early.
1903 Joseph Furphy *Such is Life* (1944)

178: 'I'm as weak as a sanguinary cat. I must ding it.'

dingbat An Army batman: World War I slang: *obs.*
1919 W. H. Downing *Digger Dialects* 19: *Dingbat* See Batman. *Batman* An officer's servant.
1932 Leonard Mann *Flesh in Armour* 161: The lieutenant and his dingbat slid down into the trench.

dingbats, to be, have the To have delirium tremens; to be in an irrational state [N.Z. 1918 OED]
1924 *Truth* 27 Apr. 6: *Dingbats* To be annoyed; D.T.'s.
1925 Arthur Wright *The Boy from Bullarah* 66: 'It's enough to give a fellow the dingbats. I suppose you've been soaking up this damned stuff till it's sent you ratty, eh?'
1932 Leonard Mann *Flesh in Armour* 103: 'I think that corporal who came up's getting the dingbats. Cobber's head blown off, or something.'
1943 Margaret Trist *In the Sun* 29: 'May as well take another job soon,' he said, 'a man would only get dingbats hanging around here too long.'
1955 H. Drake-Brockman *Men Without Wives and other Plays* 90: 'Well, if you want my opinion, the poor dope musta been dingbats if he wasn't poking borak.'
1972 Richard Magoffin *Chops and Gravy* 106: *dings* ding-bats, dee-tees, delirium tremens, the horrors.

dinger see **ding**

dingo *n.* Aboriginal word for the native dog, a term of extreme contempt when applied to a man, because of the animal's reputation for cowardice and treachery
[1855 William Howitt *Land, Labour and Gold* ii 168: The coward dingo of the bush.]
1908 Henry Fletcher *Dads and Dan between Smokes* 116: 'Them townies must be a fair lot o' dingoes.'
1923 Con Drew *Rogues and Ruses* 133: 'You're not goin' to fight! . . . I always thought you were a flamin' dingo!'

1951 Eric Lambert *The Twenty Thousand Thieves* 26: They've got the equipment, these Ities, but they're dingoes ... as soon as it comes to the hand-to-hand stuff up go the hands and out they come yelling for mercy.'
1958 H. D. Williamson *The Sunlit Plain* 158: Any trick was good enough to put over that dingo.
1962 Tom Ronan *Deep of the Sky* 180: 'Jim Campbell was a different proposition. He was a bloody dingo.'
1973 *Australian* 21 Nov. 11: 'He has shown cowardly instincts by trying to restrain this action,' Mr Anthony said of Mr Whitlam. 'All I can say of him in the Australian language is that he is a dingo.'

dingo *v.* To behave like a dingo (also 'dingo out', 'turn dingo', 'act the dingo')
1935 *Bulletin* 29 May ii: In the second round he 'dingoed', letting us through repeatedly, much to his team-mates' disgust. [OED Suppl.]
1941 Baker 23: *Dingo* A term of contempt. Also, 'to dingo on', to betray, let down, 'rat on' a person.
1945 Margaret Trist *Now That We're Laughing* 133: 'That's the kind she is. Turn dingo on her own sister if it suited her.'
1952 Eric Lambert *The Twenty Thousand Thieves* 335: 'Where is Allison?' 'He dingoed at the last minute.'
1963 T. A. G. Hungerford *Shake the Golden Bough* 217: 'Now you've dingoed, and I wonder just what the hell mates are for.'

dingoes, did they forget to feed the Jocular greeting to an unexpected arrival
1968 Walter Gill *Petermann Journey* 13: He looked up, saw it was me, and barked, 'You again! Christ, ain't they fed the bloody dingoes lately?'

dinkum *n.* 1 Work, toil: *obs.* [E. dial. OED 1891]
1882 Rolf Boldrewood *Robbery Under Arms* (World's Classics 1949) 47: It took us an hour's hard dinkum to get near the peak. Sometimes it was awful rocky, as well as scrubby ... but there was no help for it.
2 An Australian soldier in World War I: *obs.*
1918 *Aussie* 18 Jan. 3: 'And how often do you get leave to Australia?' asked the inquisitive old lady. 'Once every war,' replied one of the dinkums, 'at the end of it.'
1919 W. H. Downing *Digger Dialects* 19: *Dinkums (The)* The 2nd Division. Also applied to the New Zealanders.

dinkum *a. & adv.* Authentic, genuine, esp. in the expression 'fair dinkum' ('on the level')
1894 *Bulletin* 5 May 13: *Chief Justice:* And did yer stouch him back? *Witness:* No. *Chief Justice:* Fair dinkum? *Witness:* Yes.
1906 Edward Dyson *Fact'ry 'Ands* 64: He pointed to the centre of his breasts and his eyes were round with inquiry. 'Fair dinkum', telegraphed Linda.
1911 Louis Stone *Jonah* 63: 'Garn, ye're only kiddin'!' she cried with an uneasy grin. 'Fair dinkum!' said Jonah.
1919 W. H. Downing *Digger Dialects* 19: *Dinkum* Genuine, reliable.
1922 Arthur Wright *A Colt from the Country* 78: 'It's like a story out of a book,' went on Bucks. 'But it's dinkum.'
1934 Vance Palmer *Sea and Spinifex* 285: 'Here we are, ladies and gentlemen: a dinkum love-offering.'
1945 Cecil Mann *The River* 19: 'It's a dinkum this time,' the Bombardier said.
1951 Ernestine Hill *The Territory* 433: If from the other side I can do anything for you, Paddy Murray or Bill Sheahan, I will, fair dinkum. Good luck, everybody. [from the will of a N.T. drover]
1965 William Dick *A Bunch of Ratbags* 237: 'I'm sorry, Cookie,' said Croker. 'I didn't know, fair dinkum I never.'
1973 *Australian* 15 Sep. 1: 'If we show we are dinkum [Mr Whitlam said], the trade union movement stands ready to show restraint in the interest of the whole people.'

dinkum oil see **oil**

dinky-di An intensive form of 'dinkum', usually with nationalistic overtones

1918 N. Campbell and L. Nelson *The Dinki-Di Soldier and other Jingles* [book title]
1924 *Truth* 27 Apr. 6: *Dinky-di* Integrity: reputable.
1939 Miles Franklin and Dymphna Cusack *Pioneers on Parade* 41: 'You raise my hopes that there are some real Australians.' 'Yes, we have some,' smiled Prim . . . 'My cousin is a dinki-di specimen.'
1973 *Australian* 19 Sep. 14: If one has the ability to drink oneself into an alcoholic stupor without falling flat on one's face in front of one's mates, one apparently has then achieved the true blue hallmark of excellence of today's dinky-di Aussie.

dinner, to be done like a To be completely worsted
1847 Alexander Harris *Settlers and Convicts* ed. C. M. H. Clark (1959) 88: 'If we don't give the rain time to wash out the horse-tracks we shall be done like a dinner.'
1892 Barcroft Boake 'Featherstonhaugh' *Bulletin* 11 Jun. 22 repr. in *Where the Dead Men Lie* (1897) 134: Already he heard a smothered roar –/ 'They're done like a dinner!' quoth Featherstonhaugh.
1901 *Grip* 5 Dec. [1]: The Southern Rivers 'Done like a Dinner' [headline]
1965 William Dick *A Bunch of Ratbags* 236: 'Chassa came out from behind the counter and done him like a dinner and threw him out the door.'
1975 *Australian* 10 Feb. 1: Senator Wriedt last night confirmed that he was seeking the Senate leadership. 'I am never hopeful in those sort of things,' he said. 'I was done like a dinner last time. I could be done like a dinner again.'

dinnyhayser A knockout blow; anything of exceptional size or force [f. the boxer Dinny Hayes]
1907 Nathan Spielvogel *The Cocky Farmer* 14: 'Then I gets a dennyaiser in the eye, and sits down suddenly.'

1925 E. S. Sorenson *Murty Brown* 106: 'Then Koponey slipped his anchor and made a dinnyaiser for his lake.' [a long and desperate trip]
1946 K. S. Prichard *The Roaring Nineties* 17: He . . . got him dancing mad and blowing like a grampus before he let him have a dinnyazer that knocked him.
1949 Ion L. Idriess *One Wet Season* 141: Here, too, the teamsters have their 'last drink'. A dinnyhayser, at times.

dip one's lid, to To raise one's hat to: (fig.) to salute
1915 C. J. Dennis *The Songs of a Sentimental Bloke* 21: 'This 'ere's Doreen,' 'e sez. 'This 'ere's the Kid.' / I dips me lid.
1975 Rodney Hall *A Place Among People* 238: 'I'm here to say I was wrong, I dip me lid to a fellow like you. You're a man.'

dip out (on) To withdraw, renege
1952 T. A. G. Hungerford *The Ridge and the River* 56: There wasn't a man in the section who would dip out on a patrol so long as he could drag one leg after the other.

Dirty Half Acre See quot.
1934 Thomas Wood *Cobbers* 107: There were seven hotels at the beginning of the Golden Mile, on a patch of ground called the Dirty Half Acre.

Dirty Half Mile See quot. 1970
1934 F. E. Baume *Burnt Sugar* 338: Mario could . . . mention Bondi and Coogee with detachment and grin knowingly when anyone spoke of the Dirty Half Mile.
1940 Arnold L. Haskell *Waltzing Matilda* 139: It [King's Cross] was once the centre of the red light district, 'the dirty half-mile'.
1951 Dymphna Cusack and Florence James *Come in Spinner* 189: 'Got above herself, she has. Stuck up in one of them flash joints round the Dirty Half Mile and for all I care, she can stay there and rot.'

1954 Peter Gladwin *The Long Beat Home* 11: The tram crawled up the last of the hill and swung into King's Cross and the conductor cried: 'All ashore for the Dirty Half-mile.'

1970 Kenneth Slessor *Bread and Wine* 18–19: Woolcott Street has become respectable and changed its name to King's Cross Road . . . William Street itself . . . has been transformed completely since the days when I walked its length coming back from the Stadium. Then it was less than half its present width, a narrow and somewhat sinister street lined on one side with frowsy terraces and dimly-lit shops. It was the original 'Dirty Half-Mile', a title afterwards transferred to Woolcott Street and now without a claimant.

Dirty Reds see Reds

dish, go for the big To plan a large bet, gamble for a large amount
1949 Lawson Glassop *Lucky Palmer* 74: 'A quid?' he asked scornfully. 'A quid? Only a quid! Cripes, you're playing with their dough now. Go for the big dish.'

dish up To defeat in a contest, worst completely [f. *dish* To 'do for', defeat completely OED 1798]
1916 *The Anzac Book* 101: He said to me: 'Corporal Wilson, / You've dished up the beggars in style.'
1919 J. Vance Marshall *The World of the Living Dead* 84: Me remish I lorst fer dishin' up a screw.

disperse Euphemism for destroying the natives: *obs*.
1887 E. M. Curr *The Australian Race* iii 20: To an observer of languages, it is interesting to note the new signification of the verb *to disperse*: that when a Black girl of fifteen is shot down she is said to be *dispersed*.
1890 J. A. Barry *Steve Brown's Bunyip* 182: Earliest dawn heralded the pitiless swoop of the native troopers on to the quiet camp. His tribe 'dispersed', baby Billy, the sole survivor, was brought to B—.

1918 C. Fetherstonhaugh *After Many Days* 232: One of the native police officers . . . told me that on one occasion when they were 'dispersing' (that was what it was called) some blacks, he saw Jerry, one of his boys, with a little picaninny boy in his hand. He was swinging the little chap round preparatory to knocking out his brains against a tree.

Dix(er), Dorothy A parliamentary question asked by a member of the Government party so that the Minister may make a prepared answer, to his own advantage [f. 'Dear Dorothy Dix' the newspaper feature consisting of answers to correspondents' problems]
1963 *Australian Financial Review* 31 Oct. 16: Queensland Senator Dame Annabelle Rankin may have been posing a 'Dorothy Dix' (political jargon for a planted question) to Senator Sir William Spooner.
1971 *Australian* 24 Apr. 5: Mr Barnard said Dr Forbes was reading from a prepared statement and obviously answering 'a question that is more commonly known in the House as a Dorothy Dixer'.

do To expend or consume completely; lose or forfeit
1859 Frank Fowler *Southern Lights and Shadows* 48: A wealthy tavern-keeper who came to England with us, used to boast of 'doing' his forty nobblers of brandy a day.
1908 E. G. Murphy *Jarrahland Jingles* 38: And it's all the same to me / How I gather in a crust / Doin' brass or goin' strong.
1921 *Aussie* 15 Mar. 54: 'Just done me last dollar up at the swi school.'
1928 Arthur Wright *A Good Recovery* 87: 'Got on th' shikker, done me money.'
1932 Leonard Mann *Flesh in Armour* 247: 'By Gawd,' said Darky softly, 'thirty-two good francs I've done.'
1948 Sumner Locke Elliott *Rusty Bugles* in *Khaki Bush and Bigotry* ed. Eunice Hanger (1968) 34: 'Done the lot . . . Done the flamin' lot. Yeah,

done me thirty quid. How's a bloke's luck.'

1959 Dorothy Hewett *Bobbin Up* 117: 'What do you want me to do, do me job cold?'

1960 Donald McLean *The Roaring Days* 199: 'I want a few quid for th' school tonight . . .' 'You'll get down there and do th' lot as usual.'

1974 David Ireland *Burn* 52: 'Don't bet on it, son. You might do your dough.'

do a Melba see **Melba**

do a perish see **perish**

do a walk see **walk**

do over 1 To bash up, equivalent to U.S. 'work over'; attack and destroy (military)

1944 Lawson Glassop *We Were the Rats* 76: 'Do this galah over,' he whispered in my ear. 'He's a king-hit merchant.'

1952 T. A. G. Hungerford *The Ridge and the River* 98: They could spend the night there and do the Jap camp over in the morning.

1965 William Dick *A Bunch of Ratbags* 177: Sometimes they'd eject some of the more rowdy ones of our mob and take them to the station and do them over.

1965 John Beede *They Hosed Them Out* 101–2: We had gone into France to do over some secret installations that the underground had pin-pointed.

1975 Les Ryan *The Shearers* 103: 'Get goin' before the mob does you over too.'

2 Applied to the male role in intercourse [f. *do with* have intercourse with OED 1175]

1952 T. A. G. Hungerford *The Ridge and the River* 172–3: 'Wait till you see a few of the girls in the villages in the hills, where they haven't been done over.'

1961 Mena Calthorpe *The Dyehouse* 101: 'You're not the first dame that's been done over, not by a long shot.'

1975 Richard Beilby *The Brown Land Crying* 110: 'Anyrate, 'e never done 'er over, if that's what ya worryin' about.'

do the lolly see **lolly**

dob in 1 To inform against, implicate, betray

1957 Judah Waten *Shares in Murder* 173: 'You said you'd go to the police and dob him in unless he coughed up . . . That's the story isn't it?'

1966 H. F. Brinsmead *Beat of the City* 144: 'But you feel such a rat to tell on her. To dob her in.'

1975 Rodney Hall *A Place Among People* 240–1: 'He came back to squeeze more money from his mother and she dobbed him in.'

dobber

1958 *Coast to Coast 1957–1958* 201: 'How's his flipping form? Dobber-in Number One?'

1974 John Powers *The Last of the Knucklemen* 95: 'Don't look at me, you bastards! I'm no bloody dobber!'

1975 Nancy Keesing *Garden Island People* 66: Henderson was known as a relentless 'dobber-in' of anyone who drank on the job.

2 To contribute (probably confused with 'dub in', as in 'dub up')

1954 Tom Ronan *Vision Splendid* 179: 'Very pleased to subscribe. Pity more of the staff aren't home. I'm sure they all dub in.'

1965 William Dick *A Bunch of Ratbags* 225: It was his birthday and we all dobbed in and bought him the latest black-and-white Italian-style bodgie jumper.

1968 Geoffrey Dutton *Andy* 197: 'The ground crew are dobbing in too,' said Rogerson, 'and there should be some other donations.'

1971 David Ireland *The Unknown Industrial Prisoner* 86: 'For the price of few cents a week, we can all have a ticket . . . Dob in, men!'

doctor A bush cook, esp. for a number of men [a ship's cook U.S. 1821 OED]

1868 C. Wade Brown *Overlanding in Australia* 71: Grumbling is contagious in its nature, so for this reason alone a good cook, or 'doctor', as he is called, is a necessary individual in a camp.

1888 'Overlander' *Australian Sketcher*

1: 'Well, if some of you fellows will just take a look round the cattle, and the doctor (all bush cooks are called the doctor) will put another bucket of tea and a log on the fire.'
1900–10 O'Brien and Stephens: *Doctor* A nickname for the station cook.
1908 Giles Seagram *Bushmen All* 192: 'By the way, we've no Doctor. All hands take it in turns to cook.'
1933 Acland: *Doctor* Slang for cook.

doctor, Albany, Fremantle see Albany, Fremantle

doctor, go for the To make an all out effort, esp. in horse-racing; bet all one's money
1949 Lawson Glassop *Lucky Palmer* 250: 'Passing the seven, Gelignite is only half a length in front of Laughing Water – Jim Minburry seems to be going for the doctor – closely followed by Harristine, Pirate Gold.' Ibid. 74: 'Go for the doctor. Slap a tenner on it.'
1951 Dal Stivens *Jimmy Brockett* 86: There were three of the bastards and they went for the doctor. But I had time to get on my guard.
1966 Tom Ronan *Strangers on the Ophir* 80–1: But a jackeroo ... whose horsemanship was of no standard at all suddenly sat down and started to go for the doctor. With his whip going like a flail and his spurs like pistons he drove his cuddy to the lead.
1976 *Sydney Morning Herald* 20 Apr. 13: 'I decided to go for the doctor rather than let Taras Bulba fight for his head.'

dodge 1 Used jocularly as 'to work', in the sense of being occupied in avoiding such work as comes along: thus a shepherd would be occupied in 'monkey-dodging' q.v. or keeping out of the way of sheep [cf. *to dodge Pompey* to evade work (Naval slang) OED 1929]
1936 Archer Russell *Gone Nomad* 27: My cattle-camp and sheep-dodging* days. *Sheep mustering and droving.
2 To acquire dishonestly, as in 'poddy-dodging' q.v. [? f. *dodge* a dishonest stratagem]

1965 Tom Ronan *Moleskin Midas* 149: 'For every poddy that's up in the Coronet breakaways there's a dozen blokes trying to dodge it off.'

dodger Bread, esp. in army, boarding school, etc.: *obsolescent* [cf. *dodge* a large irregular piece, a lump OED 1562]
1919 W. H. Downing *Digger Dialects* 19: *Dodger* Bread.
1924 *Truth* 27 Apr. 6: *Dodger* Bread.
1950 *Australian Police Journal* Apr. 112: *Dodger* Gaolbread.
1964 Thomas Keneally *The Place at Whitton* 91: 'A couple of rounds of mouldy dodger and you'll be right.'

doer A 'character', an incorrigible, an eccentric. Often 'a hard doer' q.v.
1919 W. H. Downing *Digger Dialects* 19: *Doer* A person unusually humorous, reckless, undisciplined, immoral or eccentric.
1924 *Truth* 27 Apr. 6: *Doer* Humorist.
1930 L. W. Lower *Here's Luck* 161: 'My crikeys!' he added. 'That young Stanley must be a bit of a doer!'
1958 Hal Porter *A Handful of Pennies* 95: 'A real doer ... oh, a dag when you got to know him.'

dog 1 An informer; one who betrays his associates, often in the expression 'turn dog' [U.S. 1846 OED]
1864 J. F. Mortlock *Experiences of a Convict* (1965) 78–9: Men betraying their companions or accepting authority over them are often called 'dogs', and sometimes have their nose bitten off – the morsel being termed 'a mouthful of dog's nose'.
1882 Rolf Boldrewood *Robbery Under Arms* (World's Classics 1949) 56: 'Are you going to turn dog, now you know the way in?'
1895 Cornelius Crowe *The Australian Slang Dictionary* 24: *dog* 'to turn dog', to turn Queen's evidence.
1903 Joseph Furphy *Such is Life* (1944) 252: 'I'd be turnin' dog on the station if I took advantage o' your message, to go round warnin' the chaps that was workin' on the paddick.'
1911 Edward Dyson *Benno, and Some*

of the Push 1: 'There isn't a bit o' common in treatin' women decent. If y' do, they'll dog on yer for a cert.'
1922 Arthur Wright *A Colt from the Country* 166: 'Never mind, Missus, I won't turn dog on the old boy. I'll see him through this.'
1937 *Best Australian One-Act Plays* 205: 'You don't expect me to turn dog on the union.'
1941 Kylie Tennant *The Battlers* 350: 'Old Sharkey turned dog on us, didn't he, Bet? Said he'd get me for abduction.'
1950 W. M. Hughes *Policies and Potentates* 226: It had been a neck and neck contest, and but for California's turning dog on the Chief Justice, President Wilson would have been defeated.
1962 Tom Ronan *Deep of the Sky* 30: Always someone would turn up who knew him as the man who had sent his mates to the gallows. No one, free immigrant, currency lad, or old lag, would eat, work or travel with Tully the Dog.
1973 Max Williams *Poems from Prison* 22: *Dog* informer.
2 A horse or sheep difficult to manage
1945 Baker 175: A *dog* is a horse difficult to handle.
1965 Leslie Haylen *Big Red* 117: The Ape tried giving him 'dogs' to shear. That is, old, rough, wrinkled wethers, knobbly, burry, dusty, hard to shear.

dogbox A compartment on a long-distance train, in a carriage with no corridor
1905 Nathan Spielvogel *A Gumsucker on the Tramp* 43–4: I found at last railway cars worse than the worst Australia possesses. The one I came down here in was a dog box. Under the seat was a collection of old wine bottles and broken lunch baskets, etc.
1941 Baker 24: *Dog-boxes* A contemptuous but adequately descriptive term for many passenger carriages on country railway services.
1958 E. O. Schlunke *The Village Hampden* 115: 'We had to get out of our sleepers into dog-boxes and found we still had over a hundred miles to go.'
1963 Bruce Beaver *The Hot Summer*

128: They found a dog-box all to themselves which meant an uninterrupted half hour between Mundulla and the first stop.

Dog Collar Act The Transport Workers' Act (1928) and the Transport Workers' (Seamen) Regulations (providing for the licensing of seamen), so styled by the Seamen's Union in challenges of 1935–6 and later
1939 *The Seamen's Journal* 1 Sep.: Vicious Acts that we are now shackled with such as the *Crimes Act*, the *Transport Workers' Act* (Dog Collar).
1941 Baker 24: *Dog Collar Act* The Aust. Transport Workers' Act.
1953 Dymphna Cusack *Southern Steel* 255: 'The Government put the Dog-Collar Act on the wharfies when they refused to load shipments of pig-iron.'
1957 Tom Nelson *The Hungry Mile* 74: This decision was helped by threats of the Lyons Government to impose the 'Dog Collar Act'.

dog's disease Influenza
1919 W. H. Downing *Digger Dialects* 19: *Dog Fever* A mild form of influenza.
1932 Leonard Mann *Flesh in Armour* 218: Half the platoon had had dog's disease.
1953 Baker 166: *dog's disease* Malaria. [as World War II slang]

dog tied up See quots
1906 A. B. Paterson *An Outback Marriage* 178: 'Paddy's 'ad a dorg tied hup 'ere (ie. an account outstanding) this two years.'
1900–10 O'Brien and Stephens: *Mad dog* An unpaid score at a public house.
1944 Lawson Glassop *We Were the Rats* 83: 'He's left so many dogs tied up all over Australia it's a wonder there're enough of 'em left to hold tin-hare meetings.'
1962 John O'Grady *Gone Fishin'* 124: 'I says what about me three pound six, I haven't got a dog tied up here, have I?'

dog, tinned Canned meat
1901 F. J. Gillen *Diary* (1968) 275:

I'm afraid it will take us some days to settle down to damper and tinned dog.
1901 Henry Lawson 'Jimmy Grimshaw's Wooing' *Prose* i 449: The Half-Way House at Tinned Dog (out back in Australia) kept Daniel Myers – licensed to retail spirituous and fermented liquors – in drink and the horrors for upward of five years.
1922 Edward Meryon *At Holland's Tank* 28: The jam stood on the table in its original tin, and the 'tinned dog' or tinned meat, was served likewise.
1950 Gavin Casey *City of Men* 326: 'We'll be living in a tent and eating tinned dog. It's no place for a woman.'

dogger A hunter of dingoes (native dogs)
1910 C. E. W. Bean *On the Wool Track* 55: He asked to be taken on as a dogger.
1934 Archer Russell *A Tramp-Royal in Wild Australia* 113: It is along the fences, most often, that the 'wild dogger' sets his traps, into which, more often than the wily dingo, steps the unsuspecting bustard.
1955 Douglas Stewart 'The Dogger' *Collected Poems* (1967) 137: Who'd be a dogger / Following where the dingoes follow / Sly shadows of water?
1967 Len Beadell *Blast the Bush* 109: Although the old bush professional government doggers had many tricks up their sleeves to catch their quarry, I'm sure this would have been something new to them.
1971 Colin Simpson *The New Australia* 489: As a dogger (dingo destroyer) Charlie had shot or trapped as many as 275 dingoes in one year, earning $60 a week plus $4 a 'scalp' (ears and tail).

dogging Dingo-hunting
1910 C. E. W. Bean *On the Wool Track* 55: A man is generally kept dogging, and the boundary rider gets a few pounds out of occasional scalps.
1919 W. R. Harris *Outback in Australia* 88: The German had been doing casual station work but was then 'dogging'.
1932 William Hatfield *Ginger Murdoch* 167: 'Yes, dogging – dingo-stiffening, you know.'
1937 Ernestine Hill *The Great Australian Loneliness* 96: Men that have 'gone dogging' over the ranges.
1965 *Australian* 15 Feb. 8: Peter . . . has been dogging for forty years. In ten years around the Alice they killed nearly 40,000 dogs.

dogleg fence See quots
1863 Rachel Henning *Letters* ed. David Adams (1963) 136: It is what is called a 'dog's-leg' fence, made of unbarked saplings, but crossways, and it looks quite pretty as it goes up and down the gullies.
1875 R. and F. Hill *What We Saw in Australia* 61: We made acquaintance with the 'dog's leg' fence. This is formed of bare branches of the gum-tree laid obliquely, several side by side, and the ends overlapping, so that they have somewhat the appearance that might be presented by the stretched-out legs of a crowd of dogs running at full speed. An upright stick at intervals, with a fork at the top, on which some of the cross-branches rest, adds strength to the structure. [Morris]
1901 Henry Lawson 'Water Them Geraniums' *Prose* i 577: The clearing was fenced in by a light 'dog-legged' fence (a fence of sapling poles resting on forks and x-shaped uprights).
1911 E. S. Sorenson *Life in the Australian Backblocks* 25: Dog-leg fences were [among] the leading features of the old bush home, and still are in many places; but in settled districts . . . two-rail and wire fences succeed the dog-leg.
1934 Steele Rudd *Green Grey Homestead* 75: Crossing your legs to steady yourself, and looking like a section in a dog-leg fence, your eyes will meet Josie's by accident.
1955 Alan Marshall *I Can Jump Puddles* 171: A decayed dog-leg fence, erected from trees felled along its line, encircled the paddock, in which saplings and scrub marked the return of the bush.

dogman A man who rides on the hook

of a crane, and directs operations by signals [f. *dog* sb. 7a OED]

1962 Robert Clark *The Dogman and other Poems* 2: The dogman dangles from the clouds, / Astride a beam of swinging air, / Unrealized hero of the crowds, / Whose upturned faces dimly stare.
1965 *The Tracks We Travel* ed. L. Haylen 42: The shrill whistle of the dogman 150 feet above warns us that he is signalling the winding driver to lower away.
1966 Jan Smith *An Ornament of Grace* 123: The smell of concrete new-mixed, the sight of swaying dogmen.
1974 Geoffrey Lehmann *A Spring Day in Autumn* 171: 'I'm a dogman,' he replied. 'I work high up on office buildings.'

dole-bludger Someone drawing unemployment benefits even though work is available

1977 *Bulletin* 22 Jan. 14: The last three Labor Ministers have all talked a lot about cracking down on 'dole bludgers' but there is little anyone at the top can do.

doley Someone on the dole, in the Depression of the 1930s

1943 Baker 27: *Doleys* Soldiers in employment platoons (Digger slang).
1953 *Caddie A Sydney Barmaid* 209: 'You needn't worry about 'im Caddie. 'E's a friend to all us doleys.'
1966 Elwyn Wallace *Sydney and the Bush* 108: 'You track dolies are more trouble than you're worth. Better bloody fed than I am.'

Doll, the Ray Lawler's play *Summer of the Seventeenth Doll*, first performed in 1955, and taken as marking a renaissance in Australian drama

1963 *Sydney Morning Herald* 16 Mar. 12: 'The Doll' Hits Iceland!
1974 *Southerly* 215: Since *The Doll* naturalism has retained its force in Australian drama.

doll, knock over a To incur the consequences entailed in any activity [? f. the contest of throwing at dolls at a sideshow]

1954 T. A. G. Hungerford *Sowers of the Wind* 142: 'Surely to God he knows that if he throws the ball he's got a chance of knocking over the dolly!' [i.e. contracting venereal disease]
1959 Gerard Hamilton *Summer Glare* 95: 'Knocking a doll' was an old belief among us youths. We had never believed the story of the stork or of the cabbage patch either. Years ago the big boys had told us a much better story. It was that inside all women there was a number of small babies sitting in a row, and when a man, or a boy big enough, knocked one over, it was born after nine months. Thus our saying 'to knock a doll'.

dollar The sum of five shillings (until the introduction of decimal currency in 1966) [f. equivalence of value with the U.S. dollar]

1911 Louis Stone *Jonah* 65: As she was rather suspicious of a wedding that cost nothing, she decided to give the parson a dollar to seal the bargain.
1924 *Truth* 27 Apr. 6: *Dollar* Five shillings.
1942 Gavin Casey *It's Harder for Girls* 55: 'I can get half a dollar from dad.'
1964 Tom Ronan *Packhorse and Pearling Boat* 119: With tobacco at twelve shillings per pound he found it hard to send more than a dollar a week up in smoke.

dollar, holey The 'ring' dollar authorized in 1813 by the striking of a circular piece (a 'dump' q.v.) from the centre of a Spanish dollar.

1849 J. P. Townshend *Rambles and Observations in New South Wales* 10–11: This place [Ulladulla] . . . is commonly called 'Holy Dollar'. The origin of the corruption of this native name is this; it used to be the practice to cut the centre out of a dollar, and the middle piece was called 'a dump' and the remainder of the original coin 'a holey dollar'.

dollar, not the full As for 'not the

full quid' q.v.

1976 Robert Drewe *The Savage Crows* 8: Was he the full dollar these days?

don 1 Doyen [f. *don* a leader, first class man, an adept OED 1634–1853]

1898 W. H. Ogilvie *Fair Girls and Gray Horses* 55: He's the don at every muster and the king of every camp.

1901 Henry Lawson *Verse* ii 2: He's a don at peeling spuds.

2 *The Don* Sir Donald Bradman, the cricketer

1949 J. Fingleton *Brightly Fades the Don* [book title]

1965 Wally Grout *My Country's Keeper* 12: 'The Don' looked ageless behind the sticks, and his cover drive was still the most exciting thing in cricket.

dona, donah (ō) Sweetheart, esp. in larrikin argot: *obs.* except for the saying 'Don't introduce your donah to a pal'. [f. Sp. *dona*, It. *donna* woman]

[**1859** Hotten: *Donna* and *Feeles* A woman and children.]

1874 *Melbourne Punch* 9 Jul. 276: [legend to a cartoon] *Cad* (yells to friend) 'Yar-icks – Nobby 'ere's Nixon with a new dona!' (Which being interpreted, meaneth that Nixon is paying his addresses to a fresh sweetheart).

1896 Nat Gould *Town and Bush* 103: When they dare not smash windows, they perform upon the faces and bodies of their female acquaintances, familiarly called 'donahs'.

1906 A. B. Paterson *An Outback Marriage* 23: To be discussed in this contemptuous way by a larrikin and his 'donah'.

1923 Jack Moses *Beyond the City Gates* 136: But at this moment Bill's donah became hysterical and fainted.

1945 Tom Ronan *Strangers on the Ophir* 123: 'This'll teach your donah who's the right bloke to go with,' jeered Luke.

dong *v.* To strike, punch

1916 Let. in Bill Gammage *The Broken Years* (1974) 233: I feel that the Corporal would have failed his manhood had he not 'donged' him.

1939 A. W. Upfield *The Mystery of Swordfish Reef* 228: 'Stop that, Bob, or I'll dong you one.'

1946 Margaret Trist *What Else is There?* 90: 'Don't you reckon it's funny when them girls go off in a car with a fellow and then dong him for kissing them?'

1956 Kylie Tennant *The Honey Flow* 159: 'I kept after him down the road ... donging him with rocks every chance I got.'

1963 John Cantwell *No Stranger to the Flame* 19: 'Some murdering bastard of a kid must have donged it with this gibber and then shot through.'

1970 Patrick White *The Vivisector* 10: She came up and donged him one with her skinny hand.

dong *n.* A blow

1932 L. W. Lower *Here's Another* 14: How would they like a dong in the gills with a golf ball?

donga A natural depression or gully; a makeshift shelter; a house (in New Guinea after World War II) [f. S. African *donga* A channel or gully formed by the action of water OED 1874]

1937 Ernestine Hill *The Great Australian Loneliness* 330: *Donga* Depression in sandy country.

1956 *Sydney Morning Herald* 18 Oct. 1: In New Guinea a party is called a 'ding' and a house a 'donga'. So if they have a party at home it's a ding in their donga.

1972 Turner 22: *Donga* 'a gully' was current among soldiers in the Second World War, expanding its meaning to include any kind of shelter, until now among the Europeans in New Guinea it is a local word for 'house'. Only *donga* among all these words seems likely to be traceable to the battlefields of the Boer War.

1975 *Overland 62* 7: Like many of the older houses [in Darwin] Bill's little donga has survived in some form, though the roof's gone, and a wall.

donkey-lick To defeat easily, esp. in horse-racing

1907 Arthur Wright *Keane of Kalgoorlie* 50: 'What's more, he can donkey-lick a stable full of crocks like Yalgoo.'

1944 *Truth* 13 Feb. 4: Breasley saw Kintore donkey-lick a field of youngsters in the Federal Stakes.
1958 Frank Hardy *The Four-Legged Lottery* 42: 'Who won the footie?' 'Ah, Richmond got donkey-licked.'
1971 *Sunday Sun* (Brisbane) 17 Oct. 14: Only last week I donkey licked the local kindy kids at drop the hankie.

donkey vote A vote recorded by simply numbering preferences down the ballot paper according to the alphabetical order of the candidates' names
1963 *Sydney Morning Herald* 23 Mar. 2: The 'Donkey Vote' in Australia.

Dons, the The Essendon V.F.L. team (also the Bombers) [abbr.]
1975 *Sunday Telegraph* 29 Jun. 38: Dons' Rally Pays Off.

don't argue The straight-arm warding off movement in Rugby football [f. illustration in the trademark of J. C. Hutton Pty Ltd: see quot. 1977]
1977 *Australian* 14 Apr. 18: Rugby football fans around the world know the straight-arm fend-off as a 'Don't argue', and its origins go back to the turn of the century. The creator of the symbol was Mel. B. Spurr, a pianist, singer, dancer, vaudevillian, monologist, cartoonist and story-teller. Mel Spurr starred in Melbourne's Tivoli, the Athenaeum Hall and the Town Hall in the golden days of vaudeville. Spurr invented the two man symbol and took it to Hutton's Melbourne manager. The 'Don't argue' slogan was quickly evolved, and in a short time became one of Australia's best-known trademarks.

Dooley, give someone Larry To administer punishment, give a hiding [unexplained, although a connection has been claimed with the pugilist Larry Foley]
1946 Alan Marshall *Tell Us About the Turkey, Jo* 104: I had driven him [the bull] back a week before and that morning I gave him Larry Dooley.
1962 Stuart Gore *Down the Golden Mile* 52: 'Gives that Buick of his flamin' Larry Dooley, don't he?' observed Horrigan as they watched the car go lurching and bucketing through the saltbush.
1969 Patsy Adam Smith *The Folklore of the Australian Railwaymen* 118: I nodded towards the Governor's train. 'They'll [the mosquitoes] give his nibs larry-dooley tonight.'
1973 Chester Eagle *Who could love the Nightingale?* 3: 'How're the kids treating you? They'd give you a bit of larry dooley, wouldn't they?'

double-bank 1 To yoke on a second team of bullocks to pull a load out of a bog, or to overcome some similar difficulty
1863 Rachel Henning *Letters* ed. David Adams (1963) 128: I should rather like to see them at the river or some of the bad creeks, where they 'double-bank the bullocks' as it is called: that is, put the whole team, thirty yokes perhaps, on to each dray to drag it over.
1877 Rolf Boldrewood *A Colonial Reformer* (1890) 323: 'But if you lose your team, and break your pole, and spoil your loading when you're on a long overland trip, how are you to help your mates or any other chap that's bogged, when they want you to double-bank? ... You've got to stand and look on, just like a broke loafer.'
1911 E. S. Sorenson *Life in the Australian Backblocks* 158: When he had burst it [the log] along the top he double-banked the middle wedge, which caused another to drop into the crack.
1913 John Sadleir *Recollections of a Victorian Police Officer* 168: The teamsters did not travel alone, for there were many places where double-banking was a necessity, and six or more horses in single file might often be seen hauling one load over some bad pinch.
2 (also *double-dink*) To double a load; carry an extra person on a horse or bicycle
1876 A. J. Boyd *Old Colonials* (1882) 77: 'By-and-by, down goes the mare,

dead beat . . . so we unpacked her, and double-banked my other mail-horse, and the inspector got along on the first one.'

1882 Rolf Boldrewood *Robbery Under Arms* (World's Classics 1949) 221: 'We must double-bank my horse,' whispers Jim . . . He jumped up, and I mounted behind him.

1898 George T. Bell *Tales of Australian Adventure* 30: 'Jump up in the saddle and carry your luggage in front of you, and I'll get up behind. Old Balley's used to double-banking.'

1933 R. B. Plowman *The Man from Oodnadatta* 233: 'I have only one spare riding camel . . . They could double-bank on him if they liked.'

1943 Charles Shaw *Outback Occupations* 120: It was back in the days when the boys were little fellows, still going to school, double-dink on the old brown mare.

1959 Gerard Hamilton *Summer Glare* 105: Once or twice I had double-dinked her home from school on my bike.

double dink see **double bank**

double drummer A variety of cicada [f. sound]

1951 Dymphna Cusack and Florence James *Come in Spinner* 105: There came the piercing crackle of a cicada. 'He's a double drummer.'

1974 Ronald McKie *The Mango Tree* 18: He had talked to her about his first puppy, the Black Prince and the Double-drummer he had caught in the garden.

doughboy Name given to the colonial versions of the doughboy ('A boiled flour dumpling' OED 1865), most often cooked in fat

1834 Let. in Edward Shann *Cattle Chosen* (1926) 58: Dawson fried some pork, and Phoebe cooked some dough-boys for dinner.

1846 G. F. Angas *Savage Life and Scenes in Australia and New Zealand* i 161: Our cook had not been idle: there were 'dampers', 'dough-boys', 'leatherjackets', 'johnny-cakes', and 'beggars-in-the-pan.'

1855 William Howitt *Land, Labour and Gold* i 117–8: A suet pudding, called a dough-boy . . . put into the fat, and when ready, beef steaks or mutton chops are fried.

1881 A. C. Grant *Bush-Life in Queensland* ii 142: The cook has with difficulty boiled doughboys, which, although tough and indigestible, are nevertheless hot, and are washed down with pannikins of steaming tea.

1904 Tom Petrie *Reminiscences of Early Queensland* 235: The prisoner made round things which passed as doughboys.

doughnut (golden) The vulva

1972 David Williamson *The Removalists* 53: 'We'll be in like Flynn there tomorrow night. We'll thread the eye of the old golden doughnut – no worries.'

1974 Barry Humphries *Barry McKenzie Holds His Own* 33: [Barry is watching an attractive girl] Ohh, I could hit that on the golden doughnut like a plate of porridge.

dover A bush knife, esp. in the expression 'flash your dover' as an invitation to eat; also food [f. brand name]

1870 Marcus Clarke *His Natural Life* ed. S. Murray Smith (1970) 616: 'Hang up your moke, my young Ducrow, sit down, and flash your Dover.'[1] 1 *Flash your Dover* is essentially *Colonial* slang. The majority of clasp knives imported in to the Australian colonies twenty years ago were made by one 'Dover'. Hence 'flashing your Dover' is equivalent to 'drawing your Toledo'.

1873 J. C. F. Johnson *Christmas on Carringa* 16: Ses he there's mutton and damper / And on the fire there's tea / So flash your Dover* hearty / For there's heaps for you and me. *Flash your Dover, draw out your knife, so called from the maker's name, 'Dover', on the orthodox bush knife of 25 to 30 years ago.

1881 G. H. Gibson 'A Ballad of Queensland' *Bulletin* 26 Mar. 8 in *Australian Bush Ballads* ed. Stewart and Keesing

(1955) 313: You were 'flashin' your dover' six short months ago / In a lambin' camp on the Paroo.

1885 *The Australasian Printers' Keepsake* 75: He ... returned with half a loaf of bread, part of a shoulder of mutton, and some cold potatoes. He roared exultingly – 'Here's the sanguinary dover for yer – now let us have a blooming pint!'

1908 Giles Seagram *Bushmen All* 164: 'He was a loud, red-faced man who used his blooming dover like a shovel.'

down, have a ~ on To have a grudge or prejudice against, to be hostile to [f. thieves' slang: see quot. 1812]

[1812 Vaux: *A down* is a suspicion, alarm or discovery, which taking place, obliges yourself and *palls* to give up or desist from the business or depredation you were engaged in; to *put a down upon a man*, is to give information of any robbery or fraud he is about to perpetrate, so as to cause his failure or detection.]

1835 *Colonist* 10 Sep. 289: To use the colonial slang, Up comes Mr Cory himself ... to Sydney, to have a *down* upon us, poor *misfortunate* Editor, for a libel!

1848 J. C. Byrne *Twelve Years' Wanderings in the British Colonies* i 266: His master had what is called a down upon him.

1849 Alexander Harris *The Emigrant Family* (1967) 90: Biddy, too, had 'a down' upon him, because it was well known that he had a 'down' on John Thomas.

1855 Raffaello Carboni *The Eureka Stockade* ed. G. Serle (1969) 14: I, a living witness, do assert that, from that day, there was a 'down' on the name of [Commissioner] Rede.

1863 R. Therry *Reminiscences of Thirty Years' Residence in New South Wales* 122: 'I am very sorry to tell your Grace that there's a great down upon the Romans in this country.'

1881 G. C. Evans *Stories told round the Campfire* 83: 'Now I know why he had such a down on me; he did not like to see us in possession of your father's property.'

1896 Henry Lawson 'Stiffner and Jim' *Prose* i 127: 'I had a down on Stiffner, and meant to pay him out.'

1907 Ambrose Pratt *The Remittance Man* 185: 'I can't see why you should have such 'a down' on him. How has he offended you?'

1917 A. B. Paterson *Three Elephant Power* 25: He ... had a desperate 'down' on canvassers generally.

Down Under Australia: rarely used by Australians themselves

1886 J. A. Froude *Oceana* 92: We were to bid adieu to the 'Australasian' ... She had carried us safely *down under*.

1916 *The Anzac Book* 145: He sat down to think, little dreaming that he was fulfilling Macaulay's prophecy concerning the man from 'down under' sitting on the ruins of London Bridge.

1951 Simon Hickey *Travelled Roads* 121: Because I came from 'Down Under', they gave me imposing statistics on petroleum, helium, sulphur, mercury, beef cattle.

1975 Ray Robinson *On Top Down Under: Australia's Cricket Captains* [book title]

drac(k) Unattractive, esp. as applied to women, in phrases like 'a drack sort' [?f. *Dracula's Daughter*]

1945 Baker 127: *Sope* is an old larrikin word ... the direct antithesis of *bonzer* ... *Drack* and *bodger* are modern equivalents.

1949 Ruth Park *Poor Man's Orange* 180: He was always stuck with drack types like Dolour Darcy.

1953 *A Sunburnt Country* ed. Ian Bevan 130: *Drack* (again especially of the female gender, in which case the ungallant phrase is 'a drack sack') means poor or unattractive. [Army slang]

1953 T. A. G. Hungerford *Riverslake* 94: 'Anyway, it's a football dance, not just one of those drac turns they slap on for the locals.'

1968 Geoffrey Dutton *Andy* 265: 'You blokes get on to some bloody drack subjects.'

1972 *Sydney Morning Herald* 26 Sep. 9:

Mr Hardy said he would put aside his memories ... of meeting Raquel Welch ('A drac sort – not nearly as good looking in the flesh as you would expect').

drag A prison term of three months (thieves' slang: see quot. 1812]
    1812 Vaux *Drag:* a cart. The *drag*, is the game of robbing carts, waggons, or carriages ... *Done* for a *drag*, signifies convicted for a robbery of the before-mentioned nature.
    1877 T. E. Argles *The Pilgrim* i 6: He expected to receive at the hands of the magistrates a term of imprisonment which he designated as a 'drag' (three months).
    1919 J. Vance Marshall *The World of the Living Dead* 87: *Drag* Sentence of three months.
    1939 Kylie Tennant *Foveaux* 311: 'I got a drag,' he said not too regretfully. Three months was a good deal less than he had expected.
    1950 *Australian Police Journal* Apr. 112: *Drag* 3 months' imprisonment.

drag the chain see **chain**

dragged screaming from the tart shop see **tart shop**

Dragons, the The St George (N.S.W.) Rugby League Team (also the 'Saints') [f. club emblem]
    1974 *Australian* 8 Aug. 20: Dragons will draw extra fire to beat Easts.

draw the crabs see **crabs**

draw the crow see **crow**

drink a horse see **horse**

drink with the flies see **flies**

drongo Someone who is stupid, clumsy, worthless [see quots 1946, 1958, 1977]
    1941 *Salt* 22 Dec. 36: An airforce recruit is a drongo, and this word, it is suggested, is taken from the name of a large clumsy flying bird found in the Cape York Peninsula.

1946 *Salt* 8 Apr. 22: Drongo a horse foaled in 1921 and retired in 1925 who failed to win a race, and after that anybody or anything slow or clumsy became a Drongo.
1948 Sumner Locke Elliott *Rusty Bugles* in *Khaki, Bush and Bigotry* ed. Eunice Hanger (1968) 33: 'Yeah ... a bloke 'ud have to go troppo in a hut full of drongoes like youse.'
1949 Ruth Park *Poor Man's Orange* 181: It wasn't his fault he was a drongo ... He didn't want to have pimples, or a thin neck, or that hair all snowflaked with dandruff.
1951 Dymphna Cusack *Southern Steel* 4: Free of the army for twenty-eight days at least! Rid of the drongos who got in your hair in the irritating friction of everyday contact over a long period.
1958 Tom Ronan *The Pearling Master* 181–2: His continued run of second placings, both in and out of the classroom, brought from a senior of some standing the comment that ... 'Weyland was another Drongo' ... They all knew about Drongo: the colt had been a popular fancy for the previous Derby at Flemington. After a careful preparation ... he had run second. Throughout Oliver's first year at school the horse continued running seconds. He dropped out of the quality races and competed in moderate class handicaps, but he never managed to have his number hoisted first by the judge ... Drongo, first synonymous with a capacity for always being narrowly beaten, gradually changed to be an epithet flung at anything or anybody too cow-hearted to try to win.
1963 Randolph Stow *Tourmaline* 63: 'Put your head back, drongo,' Kestrel said to Byrne.
1975 *Sydney Morning Herald* 5 Jul. 9: There's no doubt that Australia fields a very poor political team, that our orating drongoes pose a more serious threat to democracy than the falling dominoes of Asia.
1977 *Sun-Herald* 13 Feb. 120: The 1600 m Drongo Handicap – for apprentice jockeys and horses without a win

for more than a year – is raced in memory of a horse who gave his name to the language . . . running second in a VRC Derby and St Leger, third in an AJC St Leger and fifth in the 1924 Melbourne Cup. The trouble was he couldn't win in 37 starts.

droob A 'sad sack', hopeless-looking person [? f. *droopy*]
1945 Baker 156: *drube* A term of contempt for a person. [Army slang]
1948 Ruth Park *Poor Man's Orange* 181: A sick feeling entered Dolour's heart when she saw Harry standing there, his hands thrust into his pockets like packages and a little, saliva-stained fag stuck on his lower lip. Of all the nice boys going to Luna Park . . . she had to draw this droob.
1972 James Searle *The Lucky Streak* 50: 'You'll 'ave to wear something a bit decent . . . you look pretty drooby in them.'

drop A fall of wicket in cricket
1977 *Sunday Telegraph* 9 Jan. 62: A wicket-keeper who bats first drop, Tony is also skipper of the Nepean . . . side.

drop one's bundle see **bundle**

drum *v*. To impart necessary and reliable information; to set someone straight [see *drum n.*[1]]
1919 J. Vance Marshall *The World of the Living Dead* 30: Hurriedly he impressed upon me the exact location . . . and proceeded to 'drum me up' with the message.
1948 Sumner Locke Elliott *Rusty Bugles* in *Khaki, Bush and Bigotry* ed. Eunice Hanger (1968) 32: 'You never get out of here, mate – I'm drumming you.'
1957 Ray Lawler *Summer of the Seventeenth Doll* 98: 'And I'm drummin' yer, you don't pull your socks up pretty quick, you're gunna find next season that our mob have got a new ganger for keeps.'
1960 Anthony Kimmins *Lugs O'Leary* 76: 'I'm drummin' you,' pleaded the little man, 'he's a moral.'

drum *n*. 1 Information requisite to some particular situation; reliable information generally, esp. in the expression to 'give someone the drum'
[1812 Vaux: *Drummond*: any scheme or project considered to be infallible, or any event which is deemed inevitably certain, is declared to be *a Drummond*; meaning, it is as sure as the credit of that respectable banking-house, Drummond and Co.]
1937 K. S. Prichard *Intimate Strangers* 262: 'If I give my punter the drum from the field, you can't blame me, can you?'
1944 Lawson Glassop *We Were the Rats* 36: 'That was before I got the drum, as Spike would say, that Margaret might be going.'
1955 John Morrison *Black Cargo* 82: 'Why didn't you give us the drum then?'
1969 Thomas Keneally *The Survivor* 167: 'I was hoping for the drum on Antarctica, I was thinking you might cough up some Antarctic quintessence, something that can't be learnt from the journals.'
1971 George Johnston *A Cartload of Clay* 70: 'Listen, I'll give you the drum,' the big man was saying.
2 A swag, esp. in the expression 'hump one's drum' [? f. cylindrical shape]
1861 *Penguin Book of Australian Ballads* (1964) 87: No more through the bush we'll go humping the drum.
1868 T. Wade Brown *Overlanding in Australia* 64: He is 'humping his drum' (i.e. travelling) looking up a job.
1887 *All the Year Round* 30 Jul. 66: In Australia, the 'swag', also sometimes called a 'drum', is the bundle, generally consisting of a large blanket rolled up which contains the personal luggage of the man who carries, or 'humps' it.
1891 Henry Lawson 'On the Wallaby' *Verse* i 134: I am out on the wallaby humping my drum.
1905 'The Sheep-Workers' Lament' *The Old Bush Songs* ed. A. B. Paterson 55: But lonely now I hump my drum / In sunshine and in rain.
3 A brothel [f. thieves' slang: *Drum* a house, a lodging . . . *Flash drum*, a house

of ill-fame Hotten 1865]

c. **1882** *The Sydney Slang Dictionary* 3: *Drum, or Crib* House of ill repute.

1894 *Bulletin* 18 Aug. 14: Grog scarce, 'drums' shut.

1900–10 O'Brien and Stephens: *Drum* A brothel.

1924 *Truth* 27 Apr. 6: *Drum* A brothel.

1944 Lawson Glassop *We Were the Rats* 103: 'There's another drum down here,' said Eddie.

1951 Dymphna Cusack and Florence James *Come In Spinner* 254: 'This place has the rep. for being one of the safest drums in the town.'

1963 T. A. G. Hungerford *Shake the Golden Bough* 91: 'A drum?' Leroy said, his forehead wrinkled. Charlie thought for a moment, and then said: 'A cathouse.'

1975 Hal Porter *The Extra* 50: 'What's a nice boy like you doing in a drum like this?'

drum, run a To perform as tipped (turf slang)

1942 *Truth* 31 May 2: Ridden by McMenamin, Vanity Fair was always at an unprofitable quotation, more especially when she subsequently failed to 'run a drum'.

1945 Baker 174: A horse that *runs a drum* performs and wins as tipped.

1962 Stuart Gore *Down the Golden Mile* 261: 'Backed Sweet Friday for a spin . . . But it never run a drum.'

drummer 1 A commercial traveller [U.S. 1827 OED]

1886 P. Clarke *The New Chum in Australia* 124: A 'drummer' – that is, a commercial traveller.

1907 Charles MacAlister *Old Pioneering Days in the Sunny South* 146: I witnessed a fierce brawl between an aggressive bagman and a tipsy shearer . . . The 'drummer' got the worst of the fistic argument.

2 The slowest shearer, the one with the lowest tally in the shed

1898 *Bulletin* 1 Oct. 14: 'To carry the drum' is to be last man in the shed.

1911 E. S. Sorenson *Life in the Australian Backblocks* 240: The drummer, or slowest shearer, is about the only man who doesn't seem to care when supper-time comes.

1933 Acland: *Drummer* The slowest shearer in a shed.

1964 H. P. Tritton *Time Means Tucker* 92: In his previous sheds he had been drummer all the time.

3 See 'double drummer'

drunk as Chloe see **Chloe**

Dry, the The dry season of the year, the months without rain

1908 Mrs Aeneas Gunn *We of the Never-Never* 219: It was August, well on in the dry.

1938 Xavier Herbert *Capricornia* 115: People scoffed at O'Cannon's cotton, saying at first that it would never see the Wet through, then that it would never live through the Dry.

1943 Charles Barrett *Up North* 8: The black soil plains, impassable in the wet season, are 'Bay of Biscay' country in the '**dry**', when millions of ruts and cattle footprints have hardened into troughs and miniature craters.

1965 *The Tracks We Travel* ed. L. Haylen 78: On many such holdings, water has to be drawn from very great depths in the 'dry' in order to keep the cattle alive.

dry-blow, dry-blower, dry-blowing Goldmining terms for the process of separating out the gold when water is unavailable for 'washing'; hence any monotonous and unproductive activity

1894 *The Argus* 28 Mar. 5: When water is not available, as unfortunately is the case at Coolgardie, 'dry blowing' is resorted to. This is done by placing the pounded stuff in one dish, and pouring it slowly at a certain height into the other. If there is any wind blowing it will carry away the pounded stuff. [Morris]

1915 J. P. Bourke *Off the Bluebush* 103: 'Do you have any luck at the diggings,' I said / To a dryblower grizzled and grey.

1950 K. S. Prichard *Winged Seeds* 18: Dinny started dry-blowing his reminiscences as if Young Bill ... had never heard them before.

1967 Kylie Tennant *Tell Morning This* 50: Miss Montrose, who realised that she had struck pay-dirt at last after so much dry blowing at Grandma's conversation, clicked her tongue to express sympathy and interest.

duchess To treat anyone 'as a duchess', esp. applied to the courtesies extended by overseas governments to visiting Australian politicians, as though imposing on their naivety

1969 Leslie Haylen *Twenty Years' Hard Labour* 134: Cables from Londen, telling us about the Labor delegation flashing through London in Rolls Royces, of being 'duchessed' in the Commons or on the lawns at the Palace, didn't exactly send the Labor benches into transports of delight.

1973 *Sydney Morning Herald* 30 Apr. 20: 'Did Mr Heath give you any encouragement? Did he, to use a word of Mr Chifley, duchess you?'

1976 *Sun-Herald* 27 Jun. 38: It cannot be said that Malcolm Fraser was 'duchessed' during his memorable stay in Peking. But the flattering, seductive treatment he received did resemble the softening up process thus named to which Australian political leaders visiting London used to be exposed.

duck, blue see **blue duck**

duck, Burdekin, Hawkesbury see **Burdekin, Hawkesbury**

duck, wet enough to bog a Extremely wet

1879–80 Ned Kelly 'The Jerilderie Letter' in Max Brown *Australian Son* (1956) 272: The ground was that rotten it would bog a duck in places.

1920 *Bulletin Book of Humorous Verses* 9: And the ground was soft enough to bog a duck.

1934 Thomas Wood *Cobbers* 89: What about them tracks? ... Six inches of rain in three days would bog a duck.

1975 Ted Egan *Australian Voices* ed. Rosemary Dobson 89: The Six Mile is

a blacksoil plain, where you'd bog a duck after an inch of rain.

duckhouse, one up against your A point scored in some way against an adversary: *obs.*

1933 Norman Lindsay *Saturdee* 7: 'You think you hid me cap, so that's one up agen your duckhouse.'

1941 Baker 26: *Duck-house, up against one's* A phrase used to describe some setback to a person's plans: e.g., 'that's one up against your duck house', that baffles you, that makes you think.

duck-shoving Jockeying for position; manipulative action generally

1870 *Notes & Queries* 6 Aug. 111: Duck-shoving is the term used by our Melbourne cabmen to express the unprofessional trick of breaking the rank, in order to push past the cabman on the stand for the purpose of picking up a stray passenger or so. [Morris]

1944 Keith Attiwill *Cut-Lunch Commandos* 115: The moral ... is that he who would trip abroad must learn to conjugate the verb 'to wangle' – I wangle; thou wanglest; he duckshoves; and so on.

1972 Don Crick *A Different Drummer* 13: After a lot of duck-shoving, he finally got going.

1977 *Sun-Herald* 3 Apr. 15: The sensitive report has been shuffled off to a variety of Public Service committees for more study and evaluation, but all the Public Service duck-shoving will not change the basic arguments.

duff To steal cattle, esp. by branding unbranded calves ('poddy-dodging' q.v.) or by altering brands; to poach grass [f. *duffer* swindler, cheat OED 1756]

1869 E. C. Booth *Another England* 138–9: There was a 'duffing paddock' somewhere on the Broken River, into which nobody but the owner had ever found an entrance, and out of which no cattle had ever found their way ... The man who owned the 'duffing paddock' was said to have a knack of altering cattle brands. [Morris]

1875 Rolf Boldrewood *The Squatter's*

Dream repr. as *Ups and Downs* (1878) 162: 'I knew Redcap when he'd think more of duffing a red heifer than all the money in the country.'
1903 Joseph Furphy *Such is Life* (1944) 47: Such a sound at such a time is ominous to duffing bullock drivers.
1915 K. S. Prichard *The Pioneers* 222: 'Oh, why have you got yourself mixed up with duffing and crooked ways?'
1960 *Sydney Morning Herald* 2 Feb. 9: Spokesmen for graziers in N.S.W. and Queensland yesterday called for urgent Government action to combat cattle-duffing ... The police had formed a special 'duffing' squad.

duff, up the Pregnant [listed as Australian by Partridge, although used in England ?f. *the pudding club*]
1941 Baker 26: *Duff, up the* (of a woman) Pregnant.
1962 Gavin Casey *Amid the Plenty* 132: Good enough for the bastard, getting poor Freda up the duff, and taking her away.
1970 Alexander Buzo *The Front Room Boys* in Penguin *Plays* 49: 'They reckon she was up the duff not long ago, and blamed it on Donnie Dixon.'
1975 Xavier Herbert *Poor Fellow My Country* 57: 'Anyway, next thing she's up the duff. But to whom?'

duffer A mine that proves unproductive, esp. in expressions like 'sink a duffer', 'bottom a duffer' [see *duff v.*]
1861 T. McCombie *Australian Sketches* 193: 'It was a terrible duffer anyhow, every ounce of gold got from it cost £20 I swear.' [Morris]
1880 Rolf Boldrewood *The Miner's Right* (1890) 55: 'Bottomed a duffer, by gum, not the colour itself, no mor'n on the palm o' my hand.'
1889 Henry Lawson 'The Sleeping Beauty' *Verse* i 58: He sunk a duffer on the Flat.
1905 Randolph Bedford *The Snare of Strength* 8: 'Then two or three duffer rushes; they put the Central country out of court.'
1944 Brian James *First Furrow* 44: The last shaft he'd sunk ... A rank duffer.
1960 Donald McLean *The Roaring Days* 58: In the drought of '92 he'd sunk a shaft that turned out a duffer as far as silver was concerned.

dummy *n.* One who acts under his own name on behalf of someone else, to gain an illegal advantage: orig. applied to those employed by the squatters, when their runs were opened to 'free selection', to take up the best areas and so forestall genuine selectors
1865 *Australasian* 23 Jun. 5: There were twenty-two *bona fide* applicants, no dummies, and no certificate holders.
1886 Frank Cowan *Australia: A Charcoal Sketch* 32: *The Dummy* man of straw in buying land.
1901 Henry Lawson 'Water Them Geraniums' *Prose* i 578: I had an idea that he wasn't a selector at all, only a 'dummy' for the squatter of the Cobborah run. You see, selectors were allowed to take up land on runs, or pastoral leases. The squatters kept them off as much as possible, by all manner of dodges and paltry persecution. The squatter would get as much freehold as he could afford, 'select' as much land as the law would allow him to take up, and then employ 'dummies' (dummy selectors) to take up bits of land that he fancied about his run, and hold them for him.
1953 *Caddie A Sydney Barmaid* 178: 'This pub's a goldmine and they own three others in the country as well.' ... 'But how do they get round the licences?' 'Aw, they get over that hurdle by putting in a dummy.'

dummy *v.* **dummying** To act as a 'dummy'; the system so developed
1873 Anthony Trollope *Australia* ed. Edwards and Joyce (1967) 134: The ... system is generally called 'dummying' – putting up a non-existent free-selector – and is illegal.
1884 A. W. Stirling *The Never Never Land* 147: This 'dummying' consists of getting 'your sisters, your cousins and your aunts', indeed even your very shepherds, to 'select' for you in their own names, with the implied intention of handing over the land to you as soon as the title is complete, you, meanwhile,

paying all the charges.

1892 Gilbert Parker *Round the Compass in Australia* 75: He [the squatter] paid men to 'dummy' for him.

1903 Joseph Furphy *Such is Life* (1944) 35: 'Bob and Bat were dummying on the station at the time, and looking after the Skeleton paddock.'

1936 H. Drake-Brockman *Sheba Lane* 251: Begging the Government to take steps to suppress the dummying of luggers – the practice whereby a white man lent his name (at a price) to a coloured man, who was not allowed by law, to hold a pearling licence.

dump *n.* 1 Coin struck from the centre of a Spanish dollar in 1813, valued at 1s. 3d. [f. *dump* A term familiarly applied to various objects of 'dumpy' shape OED 1770; *Dumps* are also small pieces of lead, cast by schoolboys in the shape of money Grose 1811. (The term seems most often to be applied to the residue of some industrial process)]

1821 *Sydney Gazette* 5 May 2: A Number of BAD DOLLARS and DUMPS having been lately offered in Payment at the Bank of New South Wales, the Public, for their Information and Protection, are hereby apprised that the following Description of illegal Coin is much in circulation: – Dollars and Dumps that are not silver . . .

1826 *Hobart Town Gazette* 29 Apr. 1: The Spanish Dollar will be received at Four Shillings and Four-pence, the Colonial Dollar at Three Shillings and Threepence, and the Dump at One Shilling and One Penny.

1826 James Atkinson *An Account of the State of Agriculture and Grazing in New South Wales* 132: A piece was struck out of the centre of each [dollar]; this centre piece was called a dump, and was put into circulation at fifteen-pence sterling value.

2 Small coins, contemptuously referred to; any trivial amount

1826 *Sydney Gazette* 22 Apr. 2: The offender, who had money in both pockets, very cheerfully paid the fine, observing, 'that was the way to spend dumps'.

1905 Randolph Bedford *The Snare of Strength* 294: 'I'm that thirsty I'd drink with Nosey Bob the hangman. It doesn't matter a dump who pays.'

1915 J. P. Bourke *Off the Bluebush* 125: She hasn't been out for a flutter since then / And she don't care a dump for a dance.

3 A marble

1959 Gerard Hamilton *Summer Glare* 76–7: 'If you an' me were playing dumps' . . . 'I see,' he said. 'Dumps are marbles.'

dump *v.* 1 To press bales of wool

1872 C. H. Eden *My Wife and I in Queensland* 98: The great object of packing so close is to save carriage through the country, for however well you may do it, it is always repressed, or 'dumped' . . . by hydraulic pressure on its arrival in port, the force being so great as to crush two bales into one. [Morris]

1884 A. W. Stirling *The Never Never Land* 155: Other men pick up the fleeces, fold them and put them in bales, when they are pressed and sometimes 'dumped' i.e. subjected to hydraulic pressure to make carriage easier.

1910 C. E. W. Bean *On the Wool Track* 265: To squash each bale into about two-thirds of its original size by 'dumping' (which means binding it round so tightly that what was formerly its length is squeezed into about the same dimension as its breadth).

2 (of a wave) To break and hurl a surfer down

1938 Jack Moses *Nine Miles from Gundagai* 88: W'en de breakers dumped / Me at Curl Curl.

dumper A large wave that breaks suddenly and hurls the surfer down, instead of carrying him in to shore

1920 A. H. Adams *The Australians* 185: A dumper is a badly behaved breaker, easily recognisable by the expert, that instead of carrying you on its crest gloriously right up to the beach till you ground on the sand; ignominiously breaks as it strikes the shallow water and deposits you, smack! in a flurry of sand and water, any side up. Dangerous, too; you might break your arm.

1924 *Truth* 27 Apr. 6: *Dumper* A curling breaker.

1942 Gavin Casey *It's Harder for Girls* 153: Most of our mob didn't know what to do when they got in front of a 'dumper', but I could still manage them.

1954 Peter Gladwin *The Long Beat Home* 193: 'Not that one,' he yelled. 'It's a dumper'... He saw the wave's crest, instead of sliding, arch enormously and hang, and hurl her down and crash on her.

1965 Thomas Keneally *The Fear* 165: A dumper of a wave slammed down a confirmatory fist on the beach.

Duncan The rolled swag: *rare* [unexplained]

1905 Arthur Bayldon *The Western Track* 56: With tucker-bags and billy-cans and Duncan on their back / They trust to luck to pull them through, and face the Western Track.

1906 H. J. Tompkins *With Swag and Billy* 8: Choice may be said to lie between the knapsack, rucksack, and swag – good old Duncan or Matilda.

dungaree settler See quot. 1826

1826 James Atkinson *An Account of the State of Agriculture and Grazing in New South Wales* 29: I beg here to be understood as only alluding to the early Settlers, and the lower order of the present – what are technically termed in the Colony *Dungaree Settlers*, from a coarse cotton manufacture of India which forms their usual clothing; a more improvident, worthless race of people, cannot well be imagined.

1840 *Sydney Gazette* 8 Feb. 3 repr. in *Old Bush Songs* ed. Stewart and Keesing (1957) 29: I'll tell them about delegates, cooks mates and victuallers, / And give them a letter on Dungaree settlers.

1847 Alexander Harris *Settlers and Convicts* ed. C. M. H. Clark (1954) 4: It is a common assertion, that the poor Australian settler (or, according to colonial phraseology, the Dungaree settler; so called from their frequently clothing themselves, their wives and children in that blue Indian manufac-

ture of cotton known as Dungaree) sells his wheat crop from pure love of rum.

1880 Henry Kendall 'Christmas in the Splitters' Camp' *Poetical Works* ed. T. T. Reed (1966) 440: Byron's 'Address to the Ocean' / Would fall rather flat on these 'dungaree' chaps.

dunny A privy, esp. outside, and therefore used in figurative expressions of loneliness and isolation [f. *dunnakin* a necessary OED 1790; *dunegan* A privy A water closet Grose 1811]

1952 T. A. G. Hungerford *The Ridge and the River* 18: Right now there might be a Shinto under every bush, and me stuck out like a dunny in a desert.

1953 Baker 268: *Loneliness*: all by himself like a country dunny.

1959 Dorothy Hewett *Bobbin Up* 178: 'The only place you can read in peace in this joint is on the dunny seat.'

1974 *Sunday Telegraph* 8 Sep. 9: Someone once said he [Paul Hogan] was as Australian as a slab off a dunny door.

1976 *Australian* 22 Mar. 26: The influence is there, but it doesn't stick out like the proverbial Australian country dunny.

see **shouse**

dust Flour, in bush parlance

1878 G. H. Gibson *Southerly Busters* 25: 'A pint o'dust' – that was his low / Expression meaning flour.

1903 Joseph Furphy *Such is Life* (1944) 256: The storekeeper measured me out a pannikin of dust into a newspaper.

1919 W. R. Harris *Outback in Australia* 146: The proverbial free pannikin of 'dust' (flour).

1924 *Truth* 27 Apr. 6: *Dust* Flour.

dust, bull-, heifer- see **bull, heifer**

dyke see **dike**

E

Eagles 1 The Manly-Warringah Rugby League team (N.S.W.): also the Sea Eagles [f. club emblem, and Manly as a

seaside suburb]
2 The Southern District Australian Rules team (N.S.W.)

earbash To talk unremittingly, harangue [World War II slang]
1944 Lawson Glassop *We Were the Rats* 205: 'Are you going to sit there ear bashing all night?'
1953 Kylie Tennant *The Joyful Condemned* 22: 'She was ear-bashing me all over tea how you came lairizing round at our place like you owned it.'
1960 *Sydney Morning Herald* 7 Sep. 1: You are in a pub knocking back a few after work and being earbashed by a mate.
1975 *Bulletin* 8 Nov. 33: A Canberra dentist whose wife ear-bashed him unmercifully about her good score – her best ever in her golfing career.

earbasher A persistent talker, a bore
1946 Rohan Rivett *Behind Bamboo* 396: *Ear basher*, one who talks too much.
1954 *Coast to Coast 1953–1954* 85: He was an ear-basher and a known liar.
1965 William Dick *A Bunch of Ratbags* 155: Ape was dumb . . . and on top of this he was an ear-basher.
1975 *Sydney Morning Herald* 6 Sep. 12: Xavier Herbert is a cantankerous, outrageous old earbasher.

earbashing
1953 Dymphna Cusack *Southern Steel* 260: 'I think we might as well shut up now and give Pop and Mum a chance. They must be just about sick to death of this ear-bashing.'
1964 Gavin Casey and Ted Mayman *The Mile that Midas Touched* 23: He didn't need a lot of ear-bashing from Bill.
1975 *Sunday Telegraph* 17 Aug. 69: The latest in earbashing. Pop music blaring from two loudspeakers has suddenly arrived at the Opera House Harbourside restaurant.

earlies, the The early years of settlement in any region: N.T. and W.A.
1933 Charles Fenner *Bunyips and Billabongs* 65: However, the interesting story of the wild adventurers who lived on this remote island in the 'earlies' is not our subject.
1936 Archer Russell *Gone Nomad* 8: In the space of a few hours I had accomplished what it would have cost me five days to do in the pre-train, stage-coach days of 'the Earlies'.
1941 Charles Barrett *Coast of Adventure* 140: 'He loved to talk about his wonderful life up here in the Earlies'.
1951 Ernestine Hill *The Territory* 428: 'In those trails of yours, especially in the earlies, I suppose you've often travelled where no white man has ever been before you?'

easy Having no preference for one course of action over another, usually in the expression 'I'm easy' [listed by Partridge as 'R.A.F. coll.: since ca. 1938']
1942 Gavin Casey *It's Harder for Girls* 229: 'We might as well all stop here now,' said Clara. 'We'd just have to go down and come almost straight back.' 'I'm easy,' said Tom.
1955 John Morrison *Black Cargo* 90: Clarrie looks at me and Bob Grainger. 'What about it?' 'I'm easy,' I tell him, 'but a seven o'clock finish would do me.'
1966 Tom Ronan *Once There Was a Bagman* 191: Ned now wanted me to go to the Depot instead of to Hall's Creek. I was easy.

Echuca, no lucre at see **Tallarook**

Eels, the The Parramatta Rugby League team (N.S.W.) [one of the Ab. meanings of 'Parramatta' is 'place where the eels lie down']
1974 *Australian* 22 Jul. 18: Souths' drought against Eels ends.

Emma Chisit The Strine equivalent of 'How much is it?'
1964 *Sydney Morning Herald* 30 Nov. 1: Monica Dickens, busily autographing her books in a city store, signed one handed her by a woman shopper. Miss Dickens THOUGHT that the lady then said 'Emma Chisit'. 'Oh,' said Miss Dickens brightly. 'You'd like me to write your name in it?' And she

scrawled, 'To Emma Chisit'. 'I asked,' the lady said crossly, 'HOW MUCH IS IT?'

emu-bobber Someone employed to pick up after clearing or burning-off in the bush (emu-bobbing) [see quot. 1964]

1920 *Bulletin Book of Humorous Verses* 187: A score of 'emu-bobbers' came a tramping from the Bland.

1959 C. V. Lawlor *All This Humbug* 16: 'Emu bobbing' consisted of gathering up small timber and twigs.

1964 H. P. Tritton *Time Means Tucker* 87: We . . . went to Wingadee to work for a contractor at burning-off. This work is also known as 'stick-picking' or 'emu-bobbing'. A group of men bending to pick up the fallen timber, with heads down and tails up, look very much like a flock of emus.

1973 Roland Robinson *The Drift of Things* 79: I was on 'emu-bobbin'' with him. Tom would axe, cut and stack the big logs . . . I picked up the smaller timber and sticks and threw them on the stacks.

emu parade In the army, a parade to clean up an area by 'emu-bobbing'

1941 T. Inglis Moore *Emu Parade* [book title]

1951 Eric Lambert *The Twenty Thousand Thieves* 315: 'Round up some men for an emu parade and parties to tidy up slit trenches and fix guy ropes.'

end, to get one's ~ in To succeed in having intercourse with a woman

1969 William Dick *Naked Prodigal* 243: 'Look, you go and get your end in. I'll be O.K. You take your bird home, orright?'

1973 *Australian* 12 Apr. 8: Professor Clark says Barry McKenzie probably represents more Australian men than we realise. 'He's the smart aleck, crude chap with a great gift of the gab but not the slightest bit of interest in romantic love. His only interest is in how to get it in.'

1974 John Powers *The Last of the Knucklemen* 34: 'Well, twice a year, if you're lucky, you can put your end into a whore down in the town.'

Enzed, Enzedder A New Zealander [f. N.Z.]

1915 Ion L. Idriess *The Desert Column* (1965) 11: The Australians and En Zeds waited until the Turkish charge was within fifty yards and then every man blazed away.

1941 Baker 27: *Enzedder*, a New Zealander.

1943 *Khaki and Green* 28: There were a lot of prisoners there: Tommies, Enzeds, and . . . South Africans.

1949 Lawson Glassop *Lucky Palmer* 83: Approaching the home turn, Reed let the Enzedder go and he shot away with a winning break before you could say 'Phar Lap'.

1952 *Bulletin* 31 Dec. 10: Two Enzedders, E. P. Hillary and G. Lowe, will be included in Colonel Hunt's British Everest expedition, which will have its shot at the hill in the new year.

1970 Richard Beilby *No Medals for Aphrodite* 166: 'The Aussies and Enzeders are into it again.'

see **Kiwi**

esky Portable cooler for drinks, etc. [? f. *eskimo*]

1971 Craig McGregor *Don't Talk to Me about Love* 152: George and Sonia with a transistor and an Esky beside them in the wilderness.

1976 *Sunday Telegraph* 25 Jan. 26: 'Look, mate, I don't mind a tidal wave as long as it doesn't knock over my Esky.'

ethno A migrant [f. *ethnic*]

1976 *Sydney Morning Herald* 18 Aug. 1: There's been a backlash against the widespread use of the word 'ethnic'. A social worker with the Department of Social Security tells us that school pupils are now calling migrants 'ethnos'.

euchred Exhausted, destitute, at the end of one's resources [f. *euchre* outwit U.S. 1855 Mathews]

1946 K. S. Prichard *The Roaring Nineties* 34: 'I've got to get water for me

horses at the next tank, or we're euchred.'
1952 T. A. G. Hungerford *The Ridge and the River* 143: 'We can't do much more of that.' He pointed down the slope. 'We'd be euchred.'
1973 John Morrison *Australian by Choice* 83: This man has worked hard in Australia for forty years, but he's euchred now.

euchre To ruin, wreck
1974 *Australian* 12 Oct. 19: He sits in the mayoral car ('So many dials and buttons! I hope I don't euchre this thing').

Eulo Queen, the Isabel Robinson, later Gray (d. 1929), mistress of the Royal Mail Hotel at Eulo in south-western Queensland in the 1890s
1892 Barcroft Boake 'Skeeta' *Bulletin* 17 Dec. repr. in *Where the Dead Men Lie* (1897) 90: 'On the Paroo I saw him; he'd been / In Eulo a fortnight then, drinking, and driving about with 'The Queen'.
1902 Harry Morant 'For Southern Markets' in F. M. Cutlack *'Breaker' Morant* (1962) 145: We came through Eulo township and camped to see 'the Queen' / (As every drover has done who has through Eulo been!).
1964 H. P. Tritton *Time Means Tucker* 113: Of all the pub-keepers concerned in the many stories told of 'lambing-down', two women were running equal for pride of place, Mrs Brown of Grawin, and Isobel Gray, 'The Eulo Queen'.

expert, the In a shearing-shed, the man in charge of the machinery; anyone qualified to deal with farm machinery
1910 C. E. W. Bean *On the Wool Track* 195: The expert (the man in the engine-room).
1912 R. S. Tait *Scotty Mac, Shearer* 55: The expert was a fidgety German, and the alterations he had to make in his work gave rise to the suspicion that he was not as experienced in shearing machinery as he ought to have been.
1923 Steele Rudd *On Emu Creek* (1972) 168: Much time and 'language' would be wasted trying to locate the trouble and fix it [the reaper and binder] up, or waiting for an 'expert' to arrive to do it.
1964 H. P. Tritton *Time Means Tucker* 40: 'The expert' is another important man in the shed. He is responsible for the smooth running of the machinery and has to have a thorough knowledge of everything mechanical in the shed.

eyes, pick the ~ out To occupy the choice portions of a run, in order to make the rest of the territory unusable by another (a technique used in the conflict between squatter and selectors)
1865 *Australian* 23 Jun. 11: As the day advanced [at the land office], and sections were taken up, and the 'eye picked from the area'.
1881 *Adelaide Observer* 22 Oct. 44: His expression about the selectors being free to pick out Mr Gray's eyes was not really so savage as it sounded – only referring to what are called the 'eyes of the run', the watering places and choice blocks.
1892 Gilbert Parker *Round the Compass in Australia* 75: He [the squatter] paid men to 'dummy' for him, and ... he made it pretty hot for the beggars who did pick the eyes out of his country.
1975 Xavier Herbert *Poor Fellow My Country* 786: 'The general idea is they'll pick the eyes out of the land, and that you're helpin' 'em.'
see **peacock**

F

f.a.q. Fair average quality
1929 Sir Hal Colebatch *A Story of a Hundred Years* 249: There is considerable competition for the bagged wheat amongst the agents of the wheat merchants. It is purchased at bushel rates on what is known as the f.a.q. (fair average quality) basis.
1963 Hal Porter *The Watcher on the Cast-Iron Balcony* 155: Mother has questioned me about his scholarship ... and has heard me answer that it is

f.a.q. to mediocrity.

faceless men Term applied (esp. in the 1963 election campaign) to the non-parliamentary members of the Labor Federal Executive, who held power over the parliamentary representatives
1963 *Sydney Morning Herald* 3 Sep. 2: They will lay themselves open to the same charges they laid against the Opposition Leader, Mr Calwell, in accepting policy directions on North-West Cape from the 36 'faceless men' constituting the special A.L.P. Federal Conference.
1967 R. G. Menzies *Afternoon Light* 291: One of our great criticisms of the Labour Party was that every Labour Member of Parliament, from the leader down, was bound to accept the directions of the non-Parliamentary Federal Executive of the Labour Party; the 'thirty-six faceless men', as we were later to describe them with devastating effect.
1972 Don Whitington *Twelfth Man* 175: He [Mr Whitlam] destroyed the 'faceless men' myth that had dogged Labor like an albatross for years, and was used against every Labor leader whenever other ammunition was lacking.

factory (female) Place of detention for women convicts
1826 *Sydney Gazette* 18 Mar. 1: Wanted for the Use of the Female Factory at Parramatta, One Ton of Colonial Flax, scutched.
1827 P. Cunningham *Two Years in New South Wales* i 98: You come [in Parramatta] to the Female Factory, surrounded by a twelve-feet high wall, which, however, some of its liberty-loving inmates occasionally find no great difficulty in clambering over.
1832 'Australian Courtship' *Sydney Gazette* 14 Jul. 4 repr. in *Old Bush Songs* ed. Stewart and Keesing (1957) 20: But the lass I adore, the lass for me, / Is a lass in the Female Factory.
1844 Louisa Meredith *Notes and Sketches of New South Wales* 84: The second division of the township [of Bathurst] contains the gaol, police-office, female factory, barracks.
1855 John Lang *The Forger's Wife* 67: She was a convict who had absconded from the factory at Paramatta, some six years previously, and it was supposed she had perished in the bush.

fair crack of the whip see **whip**

fair go 1 The call in a two-up game indicating that all the rules have been satisfied and that the coins may be spun, and at the same time enjoining that there be no hindrance to the spinning
1911 Louis Stone *Jonah* 216–17: The seventh man threw down the kip, and Chook, as if obeying a signal, rose from his seat and walked into the centre of the ring. He handed five shillings to the boxer, and placed the pennies tail up on the kip. His stake was covered with another dollar, the betting being even money. 'Fair go!' cried the boxer. Chook jerked the coins upward with the skill of an old gaffer; they flew into the dome, and then dropped spinning. As they touched the canvas floor, a hundred voices cried 'Two heads!'
1925 Arthur Wright *The Boy from Bullarah* 17–18: For a few moments the spinner stood waiting, while the players noisily made their wagers, and then again the voice of the ring-keeper ran out. 'Fair go! Set a quid.' All eyes followed the spinning pennies as they rose in the air.
1949 Lawson Glassop *Lucky Palmer* 167: He handed the kip to the spinner . . . placed two pennies, tails up, on it with infinite care and said 'Fair go'. He heard a rustling in a corner, strode over, picked up two ten shilling notes off the canvas, crushed them in his hand, threw them out of the ring over his head, and growled, 'Yous knows the rules. No bets after I say "Fair go". I'm runnin' this game and I'm runnin' it proper.'
2 Any situation or arrangement which meets the basic requirements of fairness, with neither favour nor prejudice being shown; the elementary fair treatment to which anyone must be entitled

1907 James Green *The Selector* 37: 'I'll buy her first, then ride her,' replied Woolham. 'It's a fair go,' Patrickson exclaimed.
1919 W. H. Downing *Digger Dialects* 22: *Fair Go* Equitable treatment, a fair field and no favour.
1924 *Truth* 27 Apr. 6: *Fair-go* Just treatment.
1932 L. W. Lower *Here's Another* 84: All we ask is a fair go.
1945 Gavin Casey *Downhill is Easier* 146: 'He's given me a fair go, so far,' I stated.
1951 J. B. Chifley *The Light on the Hill* 56: I do not think the miners gave the Labor Government a fair go while it was in office.
1964 Donald Horne *The Lucky Country* 24: There is a whole set of Australian characteristics summed up in the phrase 'Fair go, mate'. This is what happened in Australia to the ideals of Liberty, Equality and Fraternity . . . The general Australian belief is that it is the government's job to see that everyone gets a fair go – from old age pensioners to manufacturers.
1973 Dr J. Cairns *Sunday Telegraph* 7 Oct. 30: Australia is no longer the country of 'a fair go'; it is a country of 'get what you can'.
3 'Fair go!' as an exclamation may be a protest, a plea, a humorous disclaimer: always as though appealing to basic principles
1938 *Smith's Weekly* 31 Dec. 4: When the laugh had gone on long enough, he would silence it by his opening words, 'Fair go, mob'.
1957 Randolph Stow *The Bystander* 187: 'You didn't happen to give her a bit of cheek, I suppose!' 'Fair go, boss,' Fred begged. 'I wouldn't cheek *your* missus. You know me better than that.'
1958 H. D. Williamson *The Sunlit Plain* 192: 'Struth, fair go, mate! I'm not a bloody magician. I can't pull money out of the air.'
1962 Alan Seymour *The One Day of the Year* 32: *Alf.* Wack and me are old mates. At the war together. *Jan.* Which one? *Alf.* Fair go. Second.
1970 Jessica Anderson *The Last Man's*

Head 133: 'I still think that was him, all right. No – fair go – I think it *could* have been him.'

fangs, put the ~ in To 'bite' q.v.
1919 W. H. Downing *Digger Dialects* 22: Fangs 'To put in the fangs' – to demand money, etc.
1932 Leonard Mann *Flesh in Armour* 250: They were all short of cash . . . 'I'll stick the fangs in him all right,' Tich averred.
1952 T. A. G. Hungerford *The Ridge and the River* 218: 'Give me a smoke,' Wallace suggested. 'If there's one thing I like, it's to sink the fangs into an officer.'
fang *v.*
1975 *Daily Telegraph* 10 Jul. 2: 'What if they'd fanged us for $8000 million?'

Farm, the 1 Australia, usually in the expression 'buying back the farm' (from overseas investors)
1973 *Australian* 10 Apr. 9: According to Mr Baume, 'buying back the farm' is partly government public relations.
1975 *Sun-Herald* 3 Aug. 7: The Minister for Minerals and Energy, Mr Connor, revealed this week his plans to 'buy back the farm' in less than three years.
2 Monash University, Victoria, as distinct from 'the shop' (University of Melbourne)
1964 *Sydney Morning Herald* 28 Aug. 2: Third University for Melbourne. La Trobe joins 'the Shop' and 'the Farm'.
3 Warwick Farm racecourse, N.S.W.
1975 *Sydney Morning Herald* 7 Nov. 14: Two likely 'stars' on trial at Farm.

farmer, Collins St, Pitt St see Collins St, Pitt St

fat, crack a Achieve an erection
1941 Encountered in conversation.
1968 Barry Humphries *The Wonderful World of Barry McKenzie* [56]: 'Pommy Sheilas? Aw, they're apples I s'pose – but the way I feel now I don't reckon [I] could crack a fat!'
1970 Jack Hibberd *White With Wire Wheels* in Penguin *Plays* 224: 'By

Christ, if he races her off, it'll be the last fat he ever cracks.'

1976 Robert Drewe *The Savage Crows* 88: When he'd cracked a fat against her ... 'Hey Stiffy,' she'd whispered in his ear, and giggled.

fat cake A variety of damper, fried in fat

1844 Louisa Meredith *Notes and Sketches of New South Wales* 163: His bread is 'damper', baked in the ashes, and varied occasionally by a 'fat cake' done in the fryingpan.

1847 Alexander Harris *Settlers and Convicts* ed. C. M. H. Clark (1954) 240: Whilst I put down at the wood-fire a couple of quart-pots for tea, my wife made some fat-cakes in the frying-pan.

1855 William Howitt *Land, Labour and Gold* i 117: A fat-cake is the same thing as a leather-jacket, only fried in fat, and is not only much sooner done, but is really excellent.

1900–10 O'Brien and Stephens: *fat-cake* bread or cake made with the addition of fat in some form.

Father's Day, happy as a bastard on see **bastard**

Faugh-a-ballagh (Fog-a-bolla) As an imperative, 'Be off!'; also used as a place-name: *obs.* [f. *Fag an Bealac* ('Clear the way') the regimental march of the 87th Foot, in late C19–20 the Royal Irish Fusiliers (Partridge)]

1885 *The Australasian Printers' Keepsake* 124: 'Be off wid yees at wanst, for Ould Fusty's on the prowl. *Faugh-a-ballagh!*' I cleared, for I knew he referred to the overseer.

1903 Joseph Furphy *Such is Life* (1944) 294: He would fetch food and water at the Faugh-a-ballagh Tank. Ibid. 293: 'Which Jack? Old Jack, or Young Jack, or Jack the Shellback, or Fog-a-bolla Jack?'

feather duster, a rooster one day and a ~ the next Catchphrase for the uncertainty of (political) success [? f. U.S. See quot. 1972]

1972 A. A. Calwell *Be Just and Fear Not*

266: Years ago I told the House of Representatives a basic truth that I had read in a United States publication. The writer said that a politician is 'a rooster one day and a feather duster the next.'

1973 Jim McNeil *The Old Familiar Juice* 83: 'To-day's rooster . . . is to-morrow's feather-duster.'

1976 *Sun-Herald* 25 Apr. 34: After last Sunday's Balmain-Eastern Suburbs League match, Senator Jim McClelland was quoted as applying to an off-form Easts' star 'Fred Daly's dictum' on parliamentarians: 'Today a rooster, to-morrow a feather duster' . . . Its author was the late Arthur Calwell.

feature with To achieve sexual intercourse with [given currency by the Barry McKenzie comic strip]

1965 Barry Humphries *Times Literary Supplement* 16 Sep. 812: Barry's amorous aspirations are expressed in a desire to 'feature with a lass'.

feeding time at the zoo see **zoo**

Fella, Big see **Big**

female factory see **factory**

fence, over the Unconscionable, unreasonable [also U.S.]

1930 K. S. Prichard *Haxby's Circus* 79: 'Bruiser's over the fence. He *makes* trouble.'

1941 Baker 28: *Fence, over the* Unreasonable, beyond the pale of commonsense or justice.

1943 Charles Shaw *Outback Occupations* 25: To fraternize with lolloping hares was a bit over the fence.

1964 *Sydney Morning Herald* 18 Sep. 11: Some publications which unduly emphasize sex were 'entirely over the fence', the Chief Secretary, Mr C. A. Kelly, said yesterday.

fiddley A one pound note [f. rhyming slang *fiddley did = quid*]

1941 Baker 28: *Fiddley* A £1 note.

1949 Lawson Glassop *Lucky Palmer* 175: 'Here's yer dough. Ninety fiddlies.'

1957 Ray Lawler *Summer of the Seventeenth Doll* 29: 'Two quid – two lousy fiddlies – a fortune!'
1963 *Sydney Morning Herald* 17 Aug. 11: I bet a thousand fiddlies to nothing old Dark is back again with us next year.
1975 Xavier Herbert *Poor Fellow My Country* 102: 'If I could only lay me hands on two hundred and fifty fiddleys.'

field, to bring (come) back to the To disturb someone's pretensions or delusions, to restore a sense of reality to a situation [f. the distinction between 'the favourite' and 'the field' in horseracing]
1944 Lawson Glassop *We Were the Rats* 82: 'Don't worry,' said Bert . . . 'The poor bastard's hopeless. He'll come back to the field.'
1977 *Sydney Morning Herald* 21 May 29: Hookes and the steady Craig Serjeant brought a tearaway Somerset back to the field at the delightful recreation ground here.

fifty 1 A 50 lb. bag of flour (or other commodity)
1914 Henry Lawson 'The Flour Bin' *Verse* iii 103: Though bakers' carts run out –/Still keeps a 'fifty' in it/Against a time of drought.
1959 Donald Stuart *Yandy* 98: 'D'you bring any flour? We're right out this last three days.' 'Yeah, we got two fifties for you.'
2 A glass of half 'old' and half 'new' beer (N.S.W.)
1971 Frank Hardy *The Outcasts of Foolgarah* 76: 'Five schooners of fifty, thanks love.'
1974 *Festival* ed. B. Buckley and J. Hamilton 55: He said he would have his usual middy of fifty.

Fiji uncle An imaginary rich uncle overseas, backing some venture in which the unwary may be persuaded to invest: *obs.*
1906 T. E. Spencer *How McDougal Topped the Score* 50: 'Coves with uncles in Fiji/Are frauds who are deceiving you.'

1908 Henry Fletcher *Dads and Dan between Smokes* 75: Of all ther mug games, this took ther bun. Ther three cards or the Fiji uncle wos nothin' to it.
1914 Henry Lawson 'Mitchell on the Situation' *Prose* i 716: They were both spielers . . . Their game was anything weaker or stupider than themselves that had cash or property, and when they were in Sydney their uncles lived in Fiji.
1928 Arthur Wright *A Good Recovery* 9: 'I'm beginning to think that rich uncle is like the one from Fiji, eh, Lance?'

fine day for travelling see **travelling**

fire In sport, to play to one's full capacity [f. an engine firing]
1977 *Australian* 19 Jan. 22: With three fine quick bowlers you can rest assured one will be firing at any given stage of a Test.

fire low, and lay them out The instruction relayed by Lieut.-Col. Tom Price to the Mounted Rifles on 31 Aug. 1890, the day of a mass meeting of unionists in Melbourne during the maritime strike
1890 *Truth* 19 Oct. 1: This is what Col. Price said to the Melbourne Mounted Rifles: ' . . . fire low and lay them out, lay the disturbers of law and order out, so that the duty will have to be again performed.'
1892 Henry Lawson *Verse* i 184: 'The Lay-'em-out Brigade' [poem title]
1971 Frank Hardy *The Outcasts of Foolgarah* 229: Lt. Colonel Gravel, receiving the order to fire low and lay them out, took a rifle . . . and fired the bullet shattering Moss's good leg.

firm To shorten in odds, the opposite of 'blow' (horse-racing)
1977 *Sun-Herald* 9 Jan. 43: Cool Look opened second favourite at 5-4 yesterday, but under consistent support firmed to start a solid even-money favourite.

Firm, the J. C. Williamson Ltd, theatrical entrepreneurs

1938 *Life Digest* Oct. 97: In the early 'eighties the famous firm known as 'The Triumvirate' came into being. Its components were J. C. Williamson, Arthur Garner and George Musgrove. Later they were invariably termed 'The Firm' and finally, after Musgrove separated from Williamson and Garner dropped out, the firm was J. C. Williamson, as it is today.

1945 *Salt* 16 Jul. 25: As acknowledged rulers of the Australian professional stage, J. C. Williamson Ltd. – known as 'The Firm' and consisting of the four brothers Tait – has frequently been attacked on these grounds.

1965 Hal Porter *Stars of Australian Stage and Screen* 279: The Firm's lukewarm, carbon-copy commercial successes which catch the social sheep, and the night-out-at-the-theatre-on-mum's-birthday celebrants.

1975 Robert Macklin *The Queenslanders* 291: Not to the Playhouse group this time but to 'The Firm', the biggest Australia had to offer.

first cab off the rank see **cab**

First Fleeter One who arrived in Australia with the First Fleet in 1788, usually a convict; a modern descendant of the arrivals on the First Fleet

1830 *HRA* xv 371: Of these, 5 came in the first Fleet. One of these first Fleeters died a few Years ago at the advanced Age of 104 Years without having lost a Tooth.

1848 H. W. Haygarth *Recollections of Bush Life in Australia* 93: A man who by his own account, is of so long standing in the neighbourhood as to have been what is called in the colony a 'first fleeter'.

1849 Alexander Harris *The Emigrant Family* (1967) 339: Principles of penal discipline . . . such as are now to be heard of only rarely and in the legends of 'first or second Fleeters'.

1870 Marcus Clarke *His Natural Life* ed. S. Murray-Smith (1970) 623: Mooney was one of the 'First Fleeters'.

1934 Mary Gilmore *Old Days – Old Ways* 267: In the days of the first fleeters . . . the hills and shores of Sydney Cove were sheets of flowers.

1940 Arnold H. Haskell *Waltzing Matilda* 93: The original rabbit was a 'First Fleeter'.

1977 *Australian* 24 Jan. 2: The Fellowship of First Fleeters will hold its annual dinner to celebrate Australia Day in Sydney on Saturday night.

fit as a mallee bull see **mallee**

fix someone up To attend to his wants, pay him what is due [cf. *fix* 8b OED 1889]

1939 Kylie Tennant *Foveaux* 121: 'Linnie will fix you up.'

1945 Cecil Mann *The River* 54: 'He must have his own sword, of course. I'm sure we'll be able to fix him up.'

1949 Lawson Glassop *Lucky Palmer* 117: 'If you can fix me up now I'll be able to get started' . . . 'Here's the dough, Sam,' said 'Lucky', 'and here's a couple of quid for yourself.'

1962 Gavin Casey *Amid the Plenty* 151: 'You could get him fixed up [with a job], sooner or later, couldn't you?'

1970 Alexander Buzo *The Front Room Boys* in Penguin *Plays* 29: 'You'd better go and see him and he'll fix you up. Through that doorway and first to your left.'

fiz-gig A police informer

1895 Cornelius Crowe *The Australian Slang Dictionary* 29: *Fizgig* a spy for a detective.

1924 *Truth* 27 Apr. 6: *Fizgig* Police informer.

1950 *Australian Police Journal* Apr. 112: *Fizz-gig, or Fizzer* A Police informant.

1957 Judah Waten *Shares in Murder* 14: He was known as the king of the fiz-gigs: no detective had more informers serving him.

flash one's dover see **dover**

flash jack Someone swaggering in behaviour and possibly ostentatious in dress [f. *flash* dashing, ostentatious, swaggering, 'swell' OED 1785]

1901 Henry Lawson 'The Golden Graveyard' *Prose* i 343: Dave Regan – lanky, easy-going Bush native; Jim Bently – a bit of a 'Flash Jack'.
1905 *The Old Bush Songs* ed. A. B. Paterson 26: 'Flash Jack from Gundagai'. [poem title]
1934 Archer Russell *A Tramp-Royal in Wild Australia* 41: 'Leave that kind of talk to flash Jacks.'

flat out like a lizard drinking see lizard

flax-stick A New Zealander: *obs*. [f. New Zealand flaxbush]
1896 Henry Lawson 'His Country – After All' *Prose* i 201: 'I always thought Australia was a good country,' mused the driver – a flax-stick.

flea, so bare you could flog a ~ across it Applied to land bare of vegetation
1866 Rolf Boldrewood 'A Kangaroo Drive' *Cornhill Magazine* xiv 740–1: The vast natural meadow was, as one of the stockmen feelingly observed, 'as bare of grass as the palm of your hand', while another gravely professed his belief 'that you could hunt a flea across it with a stock-whip.'
1903 Joseph Furphy *Such is Life* (1944) 207: The famine was sore in the land. To use the expression of men deeply interested in the matter, you could flog a flea from the Murrumbidgee to the Darling.
1964 Bill Wannan *Fair Go Spinner* 79: 'You could flog a flea across the paddocks, go home to dinner, and come back and *still* find him.'
1972 *Sydney Morning Herald* 10 Apr. 6: I first heard the expression 50 years ago. It was used to describe land so denuded of grass and herbage by drought as to be quite bare and devoid of possible cover, even for a flea . . . 'So bare that you could flog a flea across it'.

flies, drink with the To drink by oneself in a pub, indicating an unsociable attitude, or the aversion of others
1925 Arthur Wright *The Boy from Bullarah* 114: 'A few days ago a common

swaggie, drinking with the flies.'
1941 Baker 25: *Drink with the flies* A drink consumed without the company of others. Also, to drink alone.
1944 A. W. Upfield *No Footprints in the Bush* 90: He says he doesn't like drinking with the flies.
1957 R. S. Porteous *Brigalow* 212: 'I've got a bottle of O. P. rum with only two nips taken out of it. Didn't enjoy drinking with the flies.'

flies, no ~ on Applied to someone who is alert and astute [? f. habit of flies to settle on a sluggish beast: also U.S.]
1845 C. Griffith *The Present State of Port Phillip* 78: The person who excites their [the old hands'] greatest respect is the man who is alive to their attempts (or, as they express it themselves, *who drops down to their moves*) and the highest encomium they can pass on such a one is, *that there are no flies about him*.
1848 H. W. Haygarth *Recollections of Bush Life in Australia* 101: 'It's lucky we got them,' said Amos; 'there were "no flies" about that black bull.'
1932 Leonard Mann *Flesh in Armour* 305: They admitted, though, there were few flies on him.
1959 Eric Lambert *Glory Thrown In* 118: 'I bet Sophie knew what he was up to. There's no flies on *her*.'

flip oneself off To masturbate (of a man)

flipwreck Someone presumed to have been debilitated by the practice

floater 1 A meat pie in a plate of peas or gravy: esp. S.A. [listed by Partridge as dumpling in gravy or sausages in mash]
1959 *Australian Letters* Dec. 13: She bought me a floater, meat pie in a plate of peas.
1974 *Australian Women's Weekly* 11 Sep. 67: A floater consists of a meat pie submerged in a sea of pea soup, with a flavoring of tomato sauce or vinegar, depending on taste . . . Floaters were first sold in Adelaide by James Gibbs, a pastrycook who migrated from the English county of Devonshire before

the turn of the century. He set up a handcart at the corner of the two busiest streets, Rundle and King William.

2 Loose opal-bearing or gold-bearing rock of low value [f. *float* loose rock brought down by the action of water U.S. 1814 OED]

1937 Ernestine Hill *The Great Australian Loneliness* 232: It was a 'floater,' quite worthless, but an indication of the jewel in the country.

1962 Stuart Gore *Down the Golden Mile* 103: A detailed account of the finding of 'floaters' – little bits of gold-bearing rock that had broken away from the main body and worked – or 'floated' – downhill with the action of centuries of wind and weather.

flog the cat see cat

flogging parson see parson

floury baker A variety of cicada [f. colouring]

1951 Dymphna Cusack and Florence James *Come in Spinner* 106: 'Mine's a Floury Baker ... and mine's a Black Prince!' Young Jack and Andrew hold up their fists for her to peep at frosted fawn body and tan-and-black.

flow on *n.* & *v.* The process by which a wage increase granted to workers in one union by the Arbitration Commission results in a similar increase for workers in a related union; a wage increase so gained

1974 *Australian* 12 Oct. 4: $9 metal award flow-on for building workers ... A Deputy President of the Commission ... decided that last month's $9 increase in the Metal Trades Award should flow on to the Carpenters and Joiners Award. The hearing for flow-ons to this award is regarded as a test-case for the whole building industry.

flute, have the To talk incessantly: *obs.*
1896 T. W. Henry *The Girl at Birrell's* 23: 'You've got the flute properly to-night, Graham,' returned the other. 'You can gas for all hands.'

1908 E. S. Sorenson *Quinton's Rouse-about* 84: 'He never had much to say, though he'd chip in at times when Joe had the flute.'

fluter An incessant talker
1898 *Bulletin* 17 Dec. Red Page: An incessant talker is a *skiter* or a *fluter*, and a request to him to *pass the flute* or the *kip* is to allow someone else to 'do a pitch'.

1959 D'Arcy Niland *The Big Smoke* 178: 'Where's Phil the Fluter now?'

fly In Australian Rules football, to leap high to take a mark
1969 Alan Hopgood *And the Big Men Fly* [play title]

fly, give it a To chance it, make a trial of, have a go
1919 W. H. Downing *Digger Dialects* 24: *Fly (to give it a)* To make an attempt.
1928 Arthur Wright *A Good Recovery* 119: 'I'm willing to give it a fly, but –.'
1934 Thomas Wood *Cobbers* 19: 'We're proud of the Trots in Perth ... They come in for miles, some of 'em, to give it a fly.'
1949 Lawson Glassop *Lucky Palmer* 75: 'We're playing with their dough ... Might as well give it a fly.'
1976 *Sydney Morning Herald* 14 Sep. 2: 2SM's general manager, Mr G. Rutherford, said yesterday that the station was 'just having a fly at something.'
see **burl, go, lash**

flyblown Penniless, destitute: *obsolescent* [? f. the condition of flyblown meat]
1853 C. R. Read *What I Heard, Saw and Did at the Australian Gold Fields* 51: His friend rushes into the billiard room to relate poor Newchum's misery to his fraternity, who deeply regret that it did not fall to their lot 'flyblowing him'.* *Being 'fly-blown' is a Colonial term for being 'done up'.
1873 J. C. F. Johnson *Christmas at Carringa* 21: Just before we comes to a grog shanty on the road, he pulls up and ses – 'Look here, mate, you might as well do me a good turn, for I'm regular fly blowed.* *A rather unpleasant term used by the old school

of bushmen to signify that they are penniless, usually after 'knocking down' their cheque at some bush public house.

c.1882 *The Sydney Slang Dictionary* 4: *Fly-blown* To be thoroughly hard up.

1883 E. M. Curr *Recollections of Squatting in Victoria* 348: 'Six or eight of them, knocking down their cheques at Young's... as I heard, close up fly-blown (i.e., nearly penniless) the day before yesterday.'

1903 Joseph Furphy *Such is Life* (1944) 20: 'So he was flyblowed as usual in regard o' cash.' Ibid. 116: 'Well, after bin had like this, we went out on the Lachlan, clean fly-blowed.'

1931 William Hatfield *Sheepmates* 161: 'Sit in, some o' yous that aint flyblown – some o' yous that's got a month or two in, an' their IOU's is good, if there's no real Oscar about the joint.'

1966 Tom Ronan *Once There Was a Bagman* 25: 'They'd been on that Katherine railway job, living from pay to pay, and when it shut down they were flyblown.'

flybog Jam: World War I slang, in World War II often shortened to 'bog'

1920 *Aussie* Apr. Glossary: *Flybog* Jam.

1941 Baker 29: *Flybog* Jam.

1944 Jean Devanny *By Tropic, Sea and Jungle* 214: Sometimes you take a tin of flybog (treacle) with you as a luxury.

flyer A swiftly moving kangaroo, usually female; a half-grown kangaroo

1826 James Atkinson *An Account of the State of Agriculture and Grazing in New South Wales* 24: The animals of this kind that are not quite full grown are termed flyers; they are exceedingly swift.

1834 George Bennett *Wanderings in New South Wales* i 287: The males of this species [kangaroo] are called by the colonists 'foresters', the females 'flyers.'

1838 Thomas Walker *A Month in the Bush of Australia* 33: Who has not experienced a feeling of repugnance to the sport of kangaroo hunting on observing the young female (termed flyers).

1844 *Georgiana's Journal* ed. Hugh McCrae (1966) 129: On our way back, Dr Barker and Mr McCrae put up a kangaroo-doe, or 'flier', as it is called, and soon had the dogs in full chase.

1861 H. W. Wheelright *Bush Wanderings of a Naturalist* 4: In bush parlance, the old male kangaroo is called an 'old man'; the young female a 'flying doe'.

1927 Steele Rudd *The Romance of Runnibede* 199: While the halfgrowns, or 'flyers', were swifter than greyhounds, many of the 'old men' were in difficulties.

flying biscuit-tin The RAAF Beaufighter in World War II [f. square appearance]

1943 George Johnston *New Guinea Diary* 251: 'The flying biscuit-tin' is his [Wing Commander Bruce Walker's] name for the Beaufighter.

flying fox An overhead cableway from which buckets etc. are suspended, often as part of an elaborate system; an improvised cableway for conveying things across a gorge or river [f. the bat (*Pteropus*) so called]

1901 May Vivienne *Travels in Western Australia* 210: To convey the stone along the open cut to the mill there is a wonderful aerial tramway composed of wire cables, on which the trucks run high up in the air; it is a marvellous way of conveyance, but more peculiar still is what is here called the 'Flying Fox', which has an iron bucket on a single rope of twisted wire. Machinery on the top of the shaft and above the crushing mill conveys it to its destination; then the bucket empties as if by magic, and flies back to the bottom of the open cut, a quarter of a mile journey, to be again replenished.

1916 Henry Lawson 'The Passing Stranger at Burrinjuck' *Verse* iii 360: The 'flying foxes',/From the cable tower on the rocky height,/Seem to swerve with their swinging boxes,/Like damaged 'gents' who've been out all night.

1935 F. D. Davison and B. Nicholls *Blue Coast Caravan* 131: Then there was the 'flying fox', a contrivance of pulleys and wires that enabled the banana bunches to be drawn up from hill-side plantations where the incline was too steep for them to be carried.

1945 Elisabeth George *Two at Daly Waters* 82: A flying-fox was erected, and when the creek was running a banker, I packed sandwiches and cookies in boxes and Jerry and Stumpy took them across on the flying-fox.

1953 Archer Russell *Murray Walkabout* 41: On the river bank I passed beneath an immense wooden tower, somewhat like the pit-head of a mine. On the opposite bank of the river arose a similar construction; and stretching between the two towers ran a long steel cable. This was the overhead cableway, or 'flying-fox' as it is perhaps more often termed, for the transmission of material from the bank to the point of construction.

flying peanut Nickname of Joh Bjelke-Petersen, Premier of Queensland [because he is a peanut-farmer and flies his own plane]
1975 *Australian* 3 Dec. 6: Ignoring the 'go home Joh' and 'flying peanut' calls the Queensland Premier appealed to 'that great silent majority'.

Flying Pieman William Francis King (d. 1874), noted for such feats as walking from Sydney to Parramatta and back (thirty-two miles) in six hours, for a wager
1847 *Heads of the People* 31 Jul. 124: Francis King, better known as the flying pieman, undertook last week, without any consideration, except as he states the pleasure of gratifying the ladies, to walk 50 miles in twelve hours, for six successive days.
1859 Henry Kingsley *Recollections of Geoffry Hamlyn* ii 95–6: A rather small, wiry, active man ... in running superb, a pupil and *protégé* of the immortal 'flying pieman'.* *A great Australian pedestrian; now, I believe, gathered to his fathers.

Flynn, in like Seizing an opportunity

offered, esp. sexual [see quot. 1973]
1963 T. A. G. Hungerford *Shake the Golden Bough* 219: 'You're in like Flynn, and there's no turning back.'
1972 David Williamson *The Removalists* 53: 'We'll be in like Flynn there to-morrow night. We'll thread the eye of the old golden doughnut – no worries.'
1973 Alexander Buzo *Rooted* 137: *Flynn, in like* (also *in like Errol*), refers to the athletic and sexual prowess of the late Australian-born Hollywood actor.

forester Name given rather indiscriminately to the larger types of kangaroo, but sometimes restricted to *Macropus giganteus*
1804 R. Knopwood *Journal* in *Historical Records of Port Phillip* ed. J. J. Shillinglaw (1972) 184: Killd a very large kangaroo – a forester.
1826 James Atkinson *An Account of the State of Agriculture and Grazing in New South Wales* 24: The forester is the largest of the common kinds [of kangaroo], frequently weighing 150 lbs. It is seldom found in an open country, delighting in forests that have occasional thickets of brush.
1832 J. Bischoff *Sketch of the History of Van Diemen's Land* ii 27: There are three or four varieties of kangaroos; those most common ... are denominated the forester and brush kangaroo.
1843 Charles Rowcroft *Tales of the Colonies* iii 191: We saw five kangaroos – foresters – in the middle, and one prodigious fellow, whom the natives greeted with the title of boomah! boomah!
1859 John Lang *Botany Bay* 209: His kangaroo dogs ... had killed a forrester (a large species of kangaroo).
1864 J. F. Mortlock *Experiences of a Convict* (1965) 85: Three or four species of kangaroo – of sizes from the 'Forrester', as heavy as a man, down to the Wallaby, not bigger than a large hare, are found in the 'bush' [of Tasmania].

fork, write with a See quot.: *rare*
1951 Ernestine Hill *The Territory* 446:

Write account with a fork, to To charge three times as much.

form Expected mode of behaviour. To 'know someone's form' is to have summed him up, unfavourably; 'How's your rotten form?' is a jeering reproach, given currency in World War II slang [f. racing form]
1955 D'Arcy Niland *The Shiralee* 129: 'I know your form. I just wanted you to know that I know it.'
1957 Ray Lawler *Summer of the Seventeenth Doll* 47: *Bubba* Come in and see us if you've got the time, Roo. I'm on the perfumes. *Roo* Yeh. That's about my form, ain't it?
1961 Russell Braddon *Naked Island* 13: 'How's his rotten form! Steals anything.'
1975 Les Ryan *The Shearers* 104: 'That's just like your dirty rotten form,' Fetlock said. 'Go on. Get the cops.'

forties Thieves, swindlers: *obsolescent* [f. 'Ali Baba and the Forty Thieves']
1879 T. E. Argles *The Pilgrim* i 12: A collection of shock-haired ruffians – the dregs of the 'forties' – i.e. forty thieves – of the city.
c. 1882 *The Sydney Slang Dictionary* 8: *The Forties* The worst types of 'the talent', who get up rows in a mob, often after midnight and sometimes assault and rob, either in bar-rooms or the streets. Name originated with a gang in Sydney under 'Dixon the dog hanger', 'King of the Forties'.
1893 J. A. Barry *Steve Brown's Bunyip* 21: 'You want to get away amongst the spielers and forties of the big smoke?'
1894 G. N. Boothby *On the Wallaby* 254: The racing code is lax, and over and over again, we met men who made it their sole business, from year's end to year's end, to tramp the bush with a likely animal, practically living on what he earned them, either by winning, or what's technically termed 'running stiff'. These men are called Forties, otherwise Spielers or Blacklegs.
1910 C. E. W. Bean *On the Wool Track* 226: A few sharpers with a slight knowledge of shearing often get into a

big shed, and get a 'school' going – a nightly gamble. They are regularly called 'forties' – the forty thieves – and they sometimes make a pile out of young shearers.
1927 M. M. Bennett *Christison of Lammermoor* 194: Rowdies and 'forties' – gambling sharpers who travelled from shed to shed making five pounds by cheating for every five shillings they earned.
1966 Tom Ronan *Strangers on the Ophir* 76: The usual percentage of spielers and forties, rogues and vagabonds.

forty-foot pole see **pole**

fossick To search out small quantities of gold, esp. in abandoned diggings; to search, rummage for something [f. *fossick* to 'ferret out' EDD]
1852 James Bonwick *Notes of a Gold-Digger* 8: Though most of these may be wrought out, a good living may be got ... by the newcomer, in a little tin-dish fossicking in deserted holes.
1853 C. R. Read *What I Heard, Saw and Did at the Australian Goldfields* 119: People used to be perfectly satisfied at 'fossicking'* or 'nuggetting'. *Picking the gold out of the crevices of rocks, &c.
1867 John Morrison *Australia As It Is* 151: 'Fosacking' is the term given to the employment of those who go about searching for gold thus exposed on the surface of the ground, and the tools of those persons consist merely of a pocket-knife and hammer.
1896 Henry Lawson 'The Man Who Forgot' *Prose* i 158: The swag had been prospected and fossicked for a clue, but yielded none.
1901 May Vivienne *Travels in Western Australia* 187: There are always a lot of men fossicking (looking for gold at the surface) about Bayley's.
1923 Jack Moses *Beyond the City Gates* 119: He started early ... in order to give himself full time to fossick among likely-looking country.
1934 Tom Clarke *Marriage at 6 a.m.* 46: *Fossick* – to dig or search, e.g. for gold.

fossicker

1867 J. S. Borlase *The Night Fossickers* 94: The 'night fossickers' – miscreants who watched for the richest holes during the day, marked them, and plundered them at night.

1923 Jack Moses *Beyond City Gates* 119: Luck was with the fossicker and they hit it thick and heavy.

1962 Alan Marshall *This is the Grass* 60: An old fossicker clumped into the bar with his heavy, hob-nail boots.

Four bob Robbo see **Robbo**

fox 1 To pursue stealthily, to 'shadow'

1892 Henry Lawson 'Billy's "Square Affair"' *Verse* i 226: The 'gory' push had foxed the Streak, they foxed her to the park.

1899 Henry Lawson 'Jack Cornstalk' *Prose* ii 47: I cannot say for certain that Jack has his own way of making love – never having been guilty of what he would call 'foxin'' him – a very dangerous proceeding, by the way.

1900–10 O'Brien and Stephens: *Fox* To stalk anyone without being observed (thieves).

1918 Bernard Cronin *The Coastlanders* 174: 'You've been foxing me and Red all the morning ... I think it's about time you came out into the open.'

2 To chase and retrieve a cricket ball, etc. [juvenile]

1942 Leonard Mann *The Go-Getter* 3: The batsman said, 'You bowled it, you fox it!'

1943 Margaret Trist *In the Sun* 87: Then a ball came down near her and rolled away beyond her. 'Fox it, Eleanor', called someone, and Eleanor ran swiftly after it.

fox, flying see **flying fox**

foxie A fox-terrier [abbr.]

frame An emaciated animal, esp. horse or bullock [U.S. 1880 OED]

1903 Joseph Furphy *Such is Life* (1944) 249: 'By-the-way, there's four of your frames left – out near those coolibahs.'

1946 A. J. Holt *Wheat Farms of Victoria*

327: 'You raise and kill a decent beast yourself and divide it with your neighbour. When it comes for his turn he picks out some rangy old frame with only hair on it.'

see **carrion**

Fred The ordinary, unimaginative Australian; the average consumer [? a coinage of Max Harris]

1973 Max Harris *The Angry Eye* 21: Even down where the Freds are browsing in their nocturnal pastures, the herd heroes are largely wasted. The John Laws and Brian Hendersons of Fredsville could well be their own men, real individuals down in the jungle of the sub-culture. Ibid. 139: I'm not sure whether they switch over from Homicide out in Fredland or not.

1975 *Sunday Telegraph* 20 Apr. 90: The Centura is aimed at what is loosely known as the average Fred market – the ordinary family motorist who wants basic transport for a price and who is not an imported car buff.

see **Alf, Ocker**

Freddie, blind An imaginary figure representing the highest degree of disability or incompetence, and so used as a standard of comparison [derived by Baker (1953: 53n) from a blind hawker in Sydney in the 1920s]

1944 Dal Stivens *The Courtship of Uncle Henry* 188: 'He doesn't want to go on with tonight. Blind Freddy could see that.'

1959 Anne von Bertouch *February Dark* 203: 'Blind Freddy could've seen there would be prawns that night.'

1966 Betty Collins *The Copper Crucible* 56: 'I know there's a principle involved – blind Freddie could see that.'

1970 Richard Beilby *No Medals for Aphrodite* 49: 'Christ, Harry, Blind Freddie could have beaten the Ities with one hand tied behind his back!'

1975 Hal Porter *The Extra* 218: All the characters who've been around since Julius Caesar was a pup, and wouldn't fool blind Freddy.

Fremantle doctor See quots

1941 Baker 30: *Fremantle doctor* A refreshing sea-breeze that blows into Fremantle and Perth after hot weather, esp. in the evening.
1972 G. C. Bolton *A Fine Country to Starve In* 2: The 'Fremantle doctor', the afternoon sea-breeze which so often tempered the more than Mediterranean heat of the city in January and February.
1974 *Sunday Telegraph* 22 Dec. 27: Just as the Fremantle 'doctor' (a sea breeze) arrived as a lifesaver to weary cricketers, so the season of Christmas comes like a breath of fresh air.
see **Albany doctor**

frenchy A condom [f. *French letter*]
1970 Patrick White *The Vivisector* 188: 'And never found nothun – but a used Frenchie!'
1975 Robert Macklin *The Queenslander* 33: He hadn't used a frenchy either.

frog A condom [f. *French letter*]
1970 Alexander Buzo *The Front Room Boys* in Penguin *Plays* 40: ' "Jees I forgot the frog", he said . . . I was disgusted. I put my pants back on and told him to take me home immediately.'

front To appear before, 'front up'
1945 Kylie Tennant *Ride on Stranger* 67: Mr Litchin was . . . making frantic signs to Beryl who fronted him much in the manner of a ruffled kitten.
1950 *Australian Police Journal* Apr. 112: *Front, To* To appear before. 'Front' the court.
1961 *Sydney Morning Herald* 20 May 2: So the delo fronted him and said 'If we don't get gloves we'll walk off!'
1969 Alan O'Toole *The Racing Game* 154: 'I say straight up into the Murray with this bloke the next time he fronts.'
1974 John Powers *The Last of the Knucklemen* 29: 'They reckon it's strange you don't front down there any more – not since that night.'

front, more ~ than Myers, Foy and Gibson's An excessive 'hide', 'cheek', effrontery [f. facade of large departmental stores in Melbourne and Adelaide]

1958 Frank Hardy *The Four-Legged Lottery* 87: 'Must get back to the game. Some of these bastards have more front than Myers; might get their hand caught in the tin.'
1966 Baker 347: *more front than Foy and Gibson's,* said of a person who is extremely daring in his or her demands, or of a girl with large breasts.

frontage 'Land which abuts on a river or piece of water, or on a road' (OED 1622–1875). Not an Australian term, but much used in land settlement.
1840 HRA xxi 114: The principal (though of course not the sole) circumstance, which gives to some pastoral lands a much higher value than to others, is the command of Water or 'Water frontage' as it is usually called in the Colony.
1863 R. Therry *Reminiscences of Thirty Years' Residence in New South Wales* 261–2: I took up a tract of country with thirty miles of frontage to the Murrumbidgee river.
1875 Rolf Boldrewood *The Squatter's Dream* repr. as *Ups and Downs* (1878) 22: The herd had spread by degrees over the wide plains of 'the back', as well as over the broad river flats and green reed-beds of 'the frontage'.
1908 Giles Seagram *Bushmen All* 262: Leaving the creek frontage to their kinsfolk, they contented themselves with the back country.
1942 Tip Kelaher *The Digger Hat* 22: The 'hoppers' who have lately found the need / To come in from the scrub to flog the 'frontage' of its feed.

fruit for the sideboard An access of good fortune, esp. extra income for minor luxuries
1966 Baker 157: *fruit for the sideboard,* easy money. [as underworld cant]

frying pan 1 Applied to one brand superimposed dishonestly on another [f. appearance]
1857 F. Cooper *Wild Adventures in Australia* 104: 'This person was an "old hand" and had got into some trouble . . . by using a "frying pan

brand''. He was stock-keeping in that quarter, and was rather given to "gulley raking". One fine day it appears he ran in three bullocks belonging to a neighbouring squatter, and clapt his brand on the top of the other so as to efface it.'

1941 Baker 30: *Frying pan brand:* A large brand used by cattle thieves to cover the rightful owner's brand.

1951 Ernestine Hill *The Territory* 444: *Frying-pan* A botched cattle brand.

2 Equivalent to 'small time' (cf. 'tea and sugar' burglar)

1864 J. F. Mortlock *Experiences of a Convict* (1965) 93: Some, unarmed, prowl about, watch the inmates of a dwelling away, and then pilfer. These are called 'frying-pan' bushrangers, being looked upon with much contempt.

1966 Tom Ronan *Strangers on the Ophir* 46: 'Oh, just a frying-pan fighting man who blew in from Coronet with a silver cheque.'

full Used in various comparisons to indicate drunkenness

1911 Louis Stone *Jonah* 226: ' 'Ard luck, to grudge a man a pint, with 'is own missis inside there gittin' as full as a tick.'

1941 Baker 30: *Full as an egg (goog, tick)* Completely drunk.

1951 Dymphna Cusack and Florence James *Come in Spinner* 367: 'She's been as full as a goog ever since 'er boy friend went back.'

1955 D'Arcy Niland *The Shiralee* 86: 'The same old Lucky. Full as a boot and happy as Larry.'

1959 Hal Porter *A Bachelor's Children* 285: 'I'm going to get full as a State School . . . blind sleeping drunk!

1961 Patrick White *Riders in the Chariot* 448: 'I bet that nephew of yours will be full as a piss-ant by eleven!'

1964 Lawson Glassop *The Rats in New Guinea* 151: 'We'll get as full as the family po.'

furphy 1 A water-cart made by Furphy of Shepparton, Victoria

1916 *The Anzac Book* 56n: Furphy was the name of the contractor which was written large upon the rubbish carts that he supplied to the Melbourne camps. The name was transferred to a certain class of news item, very common since the war, which flourished greatly upon all the beaches.

1955 E. O. Schlunke *The Man in the Silo* 208: The wood-and-water-Joey came trudging along with a load of water slopping out of the Furphy.

1959 C. V. Lawlor *All This Humbug* 95: Walter drove his old mare, Polly, in his 'Furphy' water cart. This was a nickname given to this particular type of water cart which was considered to be the best type of all, and was patented by a Mr Furphy, of Shepparton, in Victoria. [referring to the 1930s]

1969 Patsy Adam Smith *The Folklore of the Australian Railwaymen* 25: Lying there in my bed [in the 1920s] I'd hear the rattle of kerosine tins, buckets, tin dishes, even the rumble of a horse-drawn furphy, the little iron tank on wheels.

2 A rumour thought to have arisen in gossip around the water-cart in World War I (a latrine rumour); any false report

1916 C. J. Dennis *The Moods of Ginger Mick* 122: I know wot I wus born fer now, an' soljerin's me game, / That's no furphy.

1918 *Aussie The Australian Soldier's Magazine* 18 Jan. 3: A Tassie indignantly urges us to deny the Furphy that Tasmania is seeking a separate peace.

1919 W. J. Denny *The Diggers* 67: We were not quite certain of our destination and 'Furphies'* became rife. *This word is used by Australian soldiers to signify rumours without foundation. It originated in a Victorian camp from the name of the proprietor of the sanitary carts – Furphy.

1924 *Truth* 27 Apr. 6: *Furphy* Wild rumour.

1932 Leonard Mann *Flesh in Armour* 269: All this could portend only one thing. Each day lent truth to the furphies.

1946 Rohan Rivett *Behind Bamboo* 371: We sat around all the morning yarning, drawing rations, and hearing optimistic furphies which I was in no mood to believe.

1953 T. A. G. Hungerford *Riverslake* 147: 'Had you heard this furphy about Radinski?'

1963 Hal Porter *The Watcher on the Cast-Iron Balcony* 78: Anyway, we do not attempt to disbelieve the furphy.

fuzzy-wuzzy Term applied in World War II to natives of Papua New Guinea working as stretcher-bearers, etc. [Applied to Soudanese in 1892, from appearance of hair OED]

1952 T. A. G. Hungerford *The Ridge and the River* 205: They had already had their reward – a slushy poem written from the gratitude of a soldier's heart and dedicated to them, the fuzzy-wuzzy angels, the Christs with black faces.

1972 John Bailey *The Wire Classroom* 31: These are the Fuzzy-Wuzzy Angels, now known as coons, and of course refused membership or even entry to the club, except as servants.

G

Gabba, the The Queensland Cricket Association ground at Woollongabba, a suburb of Brisbane [abbr.]

1976 *Sydney Morning Herald* 26 Nov. 13: Test hopes on line at the Gabba.

galah An ass, nincompoop, sometimes in the expression 'mad as a gumtree full of galahs' [? f. the cockatoo so named]

1944 Lawson Glassop *We Were the Rats* 142: 'When will these galahs wake up? It's a wonder there aren't no gum-trees around fer'em ter nest in.'

1948 Sumner Locke Eliott *Rusty Bugles* in *Khaki, Bush and Bigotry* ed. Eunice Hanger (1968) 30: 'Bit of a galah yourself, aren't you?'

1957 D'Arcy Niland *Call Me When the Cross Turns Over* 39–40: Poor old Dummy, lying in a hospital bed in Port Augusta, pinching the nurses' bottoms and telling the doctors what a lot of galahs they were.

1962 Dymphna Cusack *Picnic Races* 97: 'Mad as a gum tree full of galahs,' McGarrity stormed. 'Why don't they pay cash?'

1969 Leslie Haylen *Twenty Years' Hard Labor* 201: One has only to listen to the speeches on Grievance Day to realize that the private member has been reduced to the status of a political galah.

1971 David Ireland *The Unknown Industrial Prisoner* 255: 'I hope when we ask for something we need in the way of safe working ... we won't be out-voted by office galahs that don't know what we're talking about.'

1975 Les Ryan *The Shearers* 45: 'Hey!' Sandy shouted. 'Some galah has hooked me mug!'

galah session An interval on the Flying Doctor radio network when anyone may come on to the air, to exchange gossip [see quot. 1961]

1959 Jon Cleary *Back of Sunset* 111: 'You're just in time for the galah session. I never take that meself. Can't stand a bar of a lotta women magging their heads off.'

1961 Barbara Jefferis *Solo for Several Players* 30: 'They [galahs] make a noise like a bunch of women nattering. That's why they call it the galah session. There's this time every morning when they can get on their radios and have a good mag to each other.'

1967 John Yeomans *The Scarce Australians* 58: In the evenings, before short wave reception deteriorates too much, the air is thrown open for what is called the 'Galah Session', during which anybody can come on the air and call anybody else for a gossip, provided he or she can get a word into the hubbub of scores of other voices talking at once.

1971 Robin Miller *Flying Nurse* 103: During the gossip or 'galah' sessions, people can hear the cheerful voices of their 'next door neighbours' – who may be more than 100 miles away.

Galloping Greens see **Greens**

gallows A frame from which the carcass of a slaughtered beast could be suspended

1847 Alexander Harris *Settlers and Convicts* ed. C. M. H. Clark (1954) 159: Another convenience it [the stockyard] must contain is what is called 'the gallows' for hauling up a beast that has been slaughtered, to take the hide off.

1900 Henry Lawson 'The Selector's Daughter' *Prose* i 62: Her father finished skinning, and drew the carcase up to a make-shift 'gallows'.

1877 Rolf Boldrewood *A Colonial Reformer* (1890) 350: Close to the side of the house was a stockyard, comprising the 'gallows' of the colonists, a rough, rude contrivance consisting of two uprights and a crosspiece for elevating slaughtered cattle.

1906 A. B. Paterson *An Outback Marriage* 68: At the back were the stockyards and the killing pen, where a contrivance for raising dead cattle – called a gallows – waved its arms to the sky.

1955 Mary Durack *Keep Him My Country* 95: The butcher's gallows stood out eerily against the rising yellow moon.

galoot An awkward and stupid fellow [U.S. 1869 OED]

1903 Joseph Furphy *Such is Life* (1944) 9: 'And that strapping red-headed galoot, riding the bag of bones beside him.'

1912 Henry Lawson 'Grandfather's Courtship' *Prose* i 879: 'You'd best see that big galoot safe out the gate, Harriet, or he'll forget to shut it.'

1924 C. J. Dennis *Rose of Spadgers* 112: That pie-faced galoot.

1930 *Bulletin* 16 Jul. 21: The big galoot spends 'arf 'is time a-'anging round my place.

1948 K. S. Prichard *Golden Miles* 325: O'Reilly accused him of being a silly old galoot to be acting soft about Frisco.

1960 Donald McLean *The Roaring Days* 215: 'I've just thought of something that will interest Ian. What a galoot I am not to think of it sooner.'

galvo Galvanized iron [abbr.]

1977 *Sydney Morning Herald* 5 Mar. 11: Risk drowning yourselves in canoes made from sheets of galvo.

game as Ned Kelly, a pebble, a pissant see **Ned Kelly, pebble, pissant**

Gap, the Cliff near South Head (Sydney) which has been the scene of suicide attempts: the offer of 'a one-way ticket to the Gap' is a sign of disfavour

1867 J. R. Houlding *Australian Capers* 223: They stood for a short time, and gazed into the Gap – that fatal chasm.

1925 Seymour Hicks *Hullo Australians* 251: The Gap is a jumping off place for all those who don't believe in the allotted span.

1945 Baker 196: *Over the Gap, to go* To commit suicide.

1959 Dorothy Hewett *Bobbin Up* 18: 'Reckon she'll throw 'erself over the Gap?'

1975 *Quadrant* Jul. 34: Do you want to be an editor? Yeah, like I want a one-way ticket to the Gap.

garbo A garbage-collector, dustman [abbr.]

1953 Baker 105: *garbo* a garbage man.

1973 *Sun-Herald* 8 Apr. 9: Being a 'garbo' has compensations, according to Joe.

Garden, Cabbage see **Cabbage**

Gazette, Bagman's, Hominy see **Bagman's, Hominy**

gazob A 'mug', fool: *obs.* [? f. *gazabo* a fellow, 'guy' U.S. 1896 OED]

1906 Edward Dyson *Fact'ry 'Ands* 162: 'But I thought barrer-pushin' was er game fer gazobs?'

1915 C. J. Dennis *The Songs of a Sentimental Bloke* 42: Ar! but 'e makes me sick! A fair gazob!

1924 *Truth* 27 Apr. 6: *Gazob* A foolish person.

geebung Derisive term for an uncultivated native-born Australian (cf. *stringy bark*); place-name for any remote and primitive locality [f. *geebung* the native plum (*Persoonia*) a small and tasteless fruit]

1859 D. H. Deniehy *Southern Cross* 12 Nov. 2: Born and bred (the Geebung is

always a native) where pecuniary success is with the majority . . . the Geebung's first business is to make money. [The term is used idiosyncratically by Deniehy to denote the Australian equivalent of Arnold's 'philistine'.]
1874 Charles de Boos *The Congewoi Correspondence* 109: You know morer these things than I do, seein' as I'm only a poor old geebung, as ain't up to the ins and outser politics.
1895 A. B. Paterson 'The Geebung Polo Club' *The Man from Snowy River* 43: It was somewhere up the country, in a land of rock and scrub, / That they formed an institution called the Geebung Polo Club.
1900 Henry Lawson *Prose* i 21: 'Bogg of Geebung' [story title] Ibid. 295: 'He drank again, and no wonder – you don't know what it is to run a *Geebung Advocate* or *Mudgee Budgee Chronicle*, and live there.'

geek *v.* & *n.* Look [? f. *geck* to toss the head OED 1724]
1919 W. H. Downing *Digger Dialects* 25: *Geek* (vb. or n.) Look.
1954 T. A. G. Hungerford *Sowers of the Wind* 190: 'There's a circus down by the dance-hall, a Jap show,' Waller volunteered. 'What about having a geek at that?'
1970 Jack Hibberd *White With Wire Wheels* in Penguin *Plays* 204: 'It's just a good solid reliable car. Just have a geek at the figures. It doesn't compare with the Valiant.'
1974 Robert Adamson *Zimmer's Essay* 20: 'Aw – give us a geek.'
see **gink**

General, the The imaginary presiding genius of General Motor-Holden's
1974 *Sunday Telegraph* 21 Apr. 74: The General knows the selling game and with his back to the wall in the Australian market he's not going to pull any punches.
1977 *National Times* 9 May 54: Why estimates of the General's profits can be so different. [heading]

geri See quot.

1977 *Sydney Morning Herald* 5 Apr. 7: Geris (short for geriatrics) is applied by the young to anyone over 40, and has replaced 'oldies' in the Ocker vocabulary.

get a bag, off one's bike, on like a bushfire see **bag, bike, bushfire**

get one's end in, a guernsey, a load of see **end, guernsey, load**

get on one's quince see **quince**

get the spear see **spear**

get up To win (of a horse; sometimes a sporting team)
1949 Lawson Glassop *Lucky Palmer* 48: 'The way you bet you're up for a bundle if the favourite gets up.'
1958 Frank Hardy *The Four-Legged Lottery* 176: Snozzle Purtell timing his run, getting up in a punishing photo finish.
1974 *Australian* 6 Nov. 22: Rival owner sorry Leilani didn't get up.

getting any? sc. sex: current in Services slang in World War II, with stock replies
1945 Baker 124: The jocular greeting between man and man, *gettin' any?*
1951 Dal Stivens *Jimmy Brockett* 125: 'Getting any, Jimmy?' he'd asked a couple of nights ago. 'You bet,' I told him. 'I have to put an extra man on.' Ibid. 174: 'Getting any, smacker?' I'd ask him. More often than not he'd come back at me, 'I've got to climb trees to get away from it.'
1973 Alexander Buzo *The Roy Murphy Show* in *Three Plays* 103: 'Morning, Col. Getting any? That's the stuff.'

getting off at Redfern see **Redfern**

Ghan, the See quot. 1969
1933 F. E. Baume *Tragedy Track* 21: This train, once known as the Ghan, because it was largely patronised by Afghans going to the then railhead of Oodnadatta, to-day is making history.
1957 A. W. Upfield *Bony Buys a*

Woman 31–2: I came down the Birdsville Track on the mail truck to Marree, caught 'The Ghan' to Coward Springs, where I contacted Constable Pierce.

1961 George Farwell *Vanishing Australians* 164: In the pre-diesel days, there were two 'Ghans'. In popular parlance there was the 'Flash Ghan', the passenger train that had sleeping berths and served meals on board; and the 'Dirty Ghan', a mixed train that had cattle trucks as well as carriages. On the Dirty Ghan you carried your own tucker, and at whistle-stops climbed down to boil your billy in the saltbush and spinifex.

1969 Patsy Adam Smith *Folklore of the Australian Railwaymen* 250: The Ghan, that now runs from Port Augusta to Alice Springs but was named back when the line ran only as far as Oodnadatta. Railway literature gives two explanations for the name, one that it was named Ghan because of the many Afghan camel men using it, the other that it was because of the number of Afghans and their families living at Oodnadatta, the railhead.

1976 *Australian* 11 Feb. 1: Copter rescue for Ghan. Two RAAF helicopters and a light plane last night airlifted all 79 passengers and crew of the Ghan train, which is stranded by floods near Oodnadatta.

ghost, grey see **grey ghost**

gibber 1 A boulder: *obs.* [Ab. word for 'stone': Morris 1834]

1847 Alexander Harris *Settlers and Convicts* ed. C. M. H. Clark (1954) 87: He did not object to stow himself . . . under the 'gibbers' (overhanging rocks) of the river.

1882 Rolf Boldrewood *Robbery Under Arms* (World's Classics 1949) 62: A kind of gully . . . something like the one we came in by, but rougher, and full of gibbers (boulders).

2 A stone of the size thrown by children

1893 Dan Healey *The Cornstalk* 66: 'Now boys, get your gibbers, here's a man beating seventeen of us.'

1908 E. S. Sorenson *Quinton's Rouse-*

about 146: They could all bowl, having practised in spare time with gibbers, using the hut for wicket.

1949 *Coast to Coast 1948* 34–5: He could also hurl goolies, gibbers, and plain bluemetal with devastating accuracy.

1963 John Cantwell *No Stranger to the Flame* 19: 'Some murdering bastard of a kid must have donged it with this gibber and then shot through.'

3 A wind-polished stone, esp. in the phrase 'gibber plain' [almost a technical term in geology, rather than a colloquialism]

1906 J. W. Gregory *The Dead Heart of Australia* 51: Our journey lay mainly over sand plains and 'gibber' plains; these last have a hard brown soil, littered with rough fragments of schist and quartzite.

1933 R. B. Plowman *The Man from Oodnadatta* 17: From the unfenced buildings of Blood's Creek Store, the gibber tablelands spread far and wide.

1938 Francis Ratcliffe *Flying Fox and Drifting Sand* 231: 'Gibbers' are the iron-stained, wind-polished stones that are strewn on the surface of so much of the arid Australian inland.

1959 David Forrest *The Last Blue Sea* 23: His eyes were not cheerful, but hard, hard as a gibber plain under a summer sun.

1971 Rena Briand *White Man in a Hole* 11: Where it passes through gibber* country it would be corrugated again within a month, he predicted. *Rock-strewn.

gibber gunyah A rock cave

1847 Alexander Harris *Settlers and Convicts* ed. C. M. H. Clark (1954) 117: I coincided in his opinion that it would be best for us to camp for the night in one of the ghibber-gunyahs. These are the hollows under overhanging rocks, and afford a most welcome shelter where they are met with in wet weather.

1878 Rolf Boldrewood *An Australian Squire* repr. as *Babes in the Bush* (1900) 260: The 'gibber gunyahs', or rock caves, which the aboriginals and their canine friends had inhabited apparently from the most remote ages.

gig *v.* 1 To look at [see *gig n.*²]
1953 Ruth Park *A Power of Roses* 164:
'A girl don't want people giggin' her
when she's just starting to branch out.'
1959 Baker 112: *To gig (at)* To stare.
1965 Kylie Tennant *Tell Morning This*
393: 'Let's have some light on it,' his
host muttered. 'Can't waste our whole
bloody life gigging out of windows.'
2 '? To befool, hoax' (OED 1795); to
make fun of
1953 Baker 103: *gig* To tease.
1969 Wilda Moxham *The Apprentice*
149: He scowled. He didn't ever like
being gigged.

gig *n.* 1 'A queer-looking figure, an
oddity; *dial.* a fool' (OED 1777–1856)
1945 *Salt* 13 Aug. 11: 'I'm not going
to look like a gig for the sake of a few
principles.'
1953 T. A. G. Hungerford *Riverslake*
19: He knew that, behind their bland
glances, they were saying to themselves, 'Who's this gig?'
1960 Ron Tullipan *Follow the Sun* 97:
'Man's a gig to take that kind of risk!'
1971 Johnny Famechon *Fammo* 72:
They were terrible, those early inter-
views, and my friends used to rubbish
me when I made such a gig of myself.
2 A look, glance [? variant of *geek*, *gink*]
1924 C. J. Dennis *Rose of Spadgers* 65:
'Is this 'ere coot,' I arsts, 'well knowed
to you?' / The parson takes another gig.
'Why, yes.'
1949 John Morrison *The Creeping City*
8: 'You pay sixpence to go in and have
a gig at his fern-gully and fishponds.'
1973 Frank Huelin *Keep Moving* 145:
'I scarpered like a scalded cat – didn't
even get a good gig at her.'

giggle-house A mental asylum
1919 W. H. Downing *Digger Dialects*
26: *Giggle-house* Lunatic asylum.
1957 D'Arcy Niland *Call Me When the
Cross Turns Over* 116: 'Your own
brother is half in the rats with worry
and anxiety. Unless something's done
he'll end up in the giggle-house.'
1973 Frank Huelin *Keep Moving* 169:

The 'Giggle-house', a large, barrack-
like building once used as a mental
home.

gilgai, gilgie 1 'A saucer-shaped depression in the ground which forms a
natural reservoir for rain-water. *Ghilgais*
vary from 20 to 100 yards in diameter,
and are from five to ten feet deep.'
(Morris) [Ab.]
1903 Joseph Furphy *Such is Life* (1944)
68: Verifying the tracks of the thirsty
bullocks so near the gilgie that it seemed
a wonder they hadn't walked into it.
1931 Vance Palmer *Separate Lives* 231:
Their horses feeding on Denison's grass
and drinking from his gilgais.
1938 Eric Lowe *Salute to Freedom* 301:
She was almost running . . . sometimes
disappearing altogether as she stumbled
into the dip of a gilgi hole.
2 A freshwater crayfish found in such
holes
1944 *Coast to Coast 1943* 174: Watching a gilgie hole he saw after a time
the waving antennae and the cautious
claws, then the black head and part of
the body come out. He threw a bit of
bark at the water and the gilgie jerked
back into the hole.
1965 Colin Johnson *Wild Cat Falling*
12: 'What say we catch gilgies?'

gin at a christening, like a see christening

gin burglar A white man who has
casual sexual relations with Aboriginal
women
1947 W. E. Harney *North of 23°* 77:
We had the eternal clash of 'gin burglar'
versus 'gin shepherd'.
1971 Keith Willey *Boss Drover* 46: The
manager would refer to 'combos' and
'gin burglars' as though they were
social outcasts. But let his wife go away
for a while . . . and he would be down
to the blacks' camp in no time.
gin burglary
1965 *Australian* 5 Feb. 10: In Hall's
Creek gin burglary is the local hobby.
What chance could she have, however
advanced, in an area where the station
ringers divide girls into three classes,

'albinos' (white), 'creamies' (half-castes) and 'studs' (black) — and treat them accordingly.

gin jockey As for 'gin burglar'
1955 D'Arcy Niland *The Shiralee* 121: He hated the ignominy of capitulating to a harlot, and a black one at that. Macauley, the gin-jockey, they could say. The black velvet for Macauley.
1963 Randolph Stow *Tourmaline* 84: 'Anything out of the camp'd do for Kes' . . . 'Ah, he's a gin-jockey too, is he?'
1968 Frank Hardy *The Unlucky Australians* 13: 'The only whites who drink in the Bull Ring are nigger-lovers and gin jockeys.'
1975 Xavier Herbert *Poor Fellow My Country* 54: 'They only have to see you treating an Aboriginal woman like a human being to raise the cry *Gin Jockey*.'

gin shepherd 1 A white man who co-habits with Aboriginal women: *rare*
1929 K. S. Prichard *Coonardoo* 54: Sam Geary had been known as 'a gin shepherder' for some time and a family of half-castes swarmed about his verandas.
2 Someone seeking to protect Aboriginal women from white men: *derogatory*
1947 W. E. Harney *North of 23°* 75: The age old instinct to protect his herd was strong in Joe. 'A gin shepherd' the bagmen called him, but Joe only smiled when they called him that, as he knew that here was one who had been unsuccessful in the hunt.
1954 Tom Ronan *Vision Splendid* 58: She had a self-imposed, utterly sincere mission to save the lubras from the lust of the white men. She failed in her endeavour, earned herself the name of the 'greatest gin shepherd in the country', and was eventually responsible for her husband losing his job because he couldn't keep men.
1971 Keith Willey *Boss Drover* 46: The practice of separating the women from the combos was known as 'gin shepherding'.

ging A catapult (juvenile)

1933 Norman Lindsay *Saturdee* 152: Peter took out his ging to make a show of catapulting a stone at a non-existent bird.
1965 Colin Johnson *Wild Cat Falling* 13: I put a stone in the ging and let fly.
1968 Geoffrey Dutton *Andy* 93: A ging, you know, a dirty great catapult, a real beaut.

ginger See quot. 1945
1945 Baker 139: A prostitute who robs a man by taking money from his clothes is known as a *gingerer*. She usually works with an accomplice. To *ginger* and *gingering* are associated terms.
1953 Kylie Tennant *The Joyful Condemned* 5: 'I've just gingered the copper. Give him his pants back when he gets too noisy'. . . . 'Gingering', or robbing prospective clients, was considered low taste, but after all the man was a copper.
1961 Xavier Herbert *Soldiers' Women* 306: 'Call the cops and prove it for yourself. They'd like to do business with the gal who gingered Plug for his roll.'

gink 1 A fellow, 'guy', interchangeable with *gig*: *derogatory* [U.S. 1910 OED ? f. *geck, geke* a fool, simpleton 1515]
1924 *Truth* 27 Apr. 6: *Gink* A peculiar fellow.
1939 Miles Franklin and Dymphna Cusack *Pioneers on Parade* 35: 'Quick! Look at that gink over there. Isn't he a cut!'
1946 Rohan Rivett *Behind Bamboo* 396: *Gink* term of abuse.
1954 Bant Singer *Have Patience Delaney* 16: Up front the gink in the blue suit . . . stands up and peers after the ambulance.
1966 H. F. Brinsmead *Beat of the City* 18: 'They're bossed around by an old gink who's some crazy sort of parson.'
1971 Barbara Vernon *A Big Day at Bellbird* 185: He understood that long gink with her was her fiancé.
2 A look (? variant of *geck*)
1961 Robert S. Close *Hooves of Brass* 121: 'And get a gink at that chin, mates!'

1962 Stuart Gore *Down the Golden Mile* 205: 'Come up to my camp on the way home in the morning and have a gink at it then.'

give away Abandon, give up, cease operations [? f. *give it best*]
[1892 Henry Lawson 'Cross the Border' *Verse* i 179: Workmen struggle, and are beaten, and they give it best and go.]
1948 Sumner Locke Elliott *Rusty Bugles* in *Khaki, Bush and Bigotry* ed. Eunice Hanger (1968) 98: *Andy:* How's the garden going, Ot? *Ot:* Give it away.
1949 Lawson Glassop *Lucky Palmer* 195: 'I don't mind ordinary competition, but if I've got to compete with a horse I think it's about time I gave the game away.'
1955 John Morrison *Black Cargo* 14: 'If it was me I'd give it away,' I say to Tiny. 'He's got Buckley's chance.'
1961 Patrick White *Riders in the Chariot* 408: 'What's wrong with your job, Alf? You haven't given it away?'
1971 Colin Simpson *The New Australia* 157: 'Well, I gave the city away. Best thing I ever did, and my wife agrees.'

glad, gladdie A gladiolus

Glad, Our Miss Gladys Moncrieff (1892–1976), singer who took leading roles in *Maid of the Mountains* (1921, 1942), *Rio Rita* (1926) and in Gilbert and Sullivan productions
1939 *Life Digest* Mar. 99: A very vital and kindhearted woman is Gladys; everyone's friend, she is known to countless Australians simply as 'Our Gladys'.
1974 *Australian* 20 Nov. 3: Our Glad ill. Gladys Moncrieff has been admitted to a Gold Coast private hospital suffering from a virus complaint.

glassy, just the Superlative; the one who excels, is most admired: *obsolescent* [f. the 'glassy' as the most prized marble]
1906 Edward Dyson *Fact'ry 'Ands* 166: 'They're all right, ain't they?' asked the man, and he dusted them [the trousers] carefully. 'Oh, they're jist ther glassy.'
1911 Steele Rudd *The Dashwoods* 25:

'I said it would be just the glassy marble – the sort of thing I'd like to be at.'
1915 C. J. Dennis *The Songs of a Sentmental Bloke* 42: 'E's jist the glarsey on the soulful sob, / 'E'll sigh and spruik, an' 'owl a love-sick vow.
1920 *Aussie* 15 May 34: 'Old Bill was the oil – the glassy – oh Hell!'
1951 Dymphna Cusack and Florence James *Come in Spinner* 300: 'Low profits and quick turnover, and this is the glassy marble.'

Gloria Soame The 'Strine' formulation of 'a glorious home'
1965 *Sydney Morning Herald* 6 Jan. 1: The first advertisement in pure Strine reached our 'classified' department yesterday. It advertised a 'gloria soame' of 14 squares, with amenities.
1971 Frank Hardy *The Outcasts of Foolgarah* 11: But Gloria Soames all and dominating the scene atop the hill.

glory box A box kept by young women for storing clothes etc. in preparation for marriage: *obsolescent* (U.S. *hope chest*)
1915 Louis Stone *Betty Wayside* 244: It was her glory box, containing all her treasures that she had gathered together against such a day as this.
1934 F. S. Hibble *Karangi* 110: They came to gossip and rave over the glory-box, being frank in their envy.
1947 H. Drake-Brockman *The Fatal Days* 299: 'Remember that glory-chest you admired down the furniture store?'
1959 Dorothy Hewett *Bobbin Up* 167: Johnny had . . . broken all her glory-box utility set.
1966 Bruce Beaver *You Can't Come Back* 118: 'That's my glory-box . . . I'm saving up things so I can get married and get away from here.'
1975 Rodney Hall *A Place Among People* 149–50: 'She has been buying quite good quality things for her glory box.'

gluepot A depression in which a cart or wagon becomes bogged
1885 *The Australasian Printers' Keepsake* 84: Bullocks to make one more effort to extricate the dray from a 'glue-

pot'.

1903 Joseph Furphy *Such is Life* (1944) 55: 'Hello! where's Damper?' 'Stuck in a gluepot, jist in front o' the (adj.) hut,' replied Mosey.

1906 Mrs Harrison Lee *One of Australia's Daughters* 145: 'What about riding . . . over roads that have earnt the names of glue-pots?'

1949 George Farwell *Traveller's Tracks* 74: It was only just under water, but underneath was red mud – a real gluepot.

gnamma see **namma**

go bung see **bung**

go for the century see **century**

go for the doctor see **doctor**

go for one's quoits see **quoits**

go, give it a As for 'give it a burl' q.v.

1924 *Truth* 27 Apr. 6: *Give it a go* To make an attempt.

1934 Thomas Wood *Cobbers* 10: 'Besides, we want people from the other side to see our State. Give it a go!'

1946 Kylie Tennant *Lost Haven* 114: 'Going to give it a go tomorrow?'

1950 Gavin Casey *City of Men* 288: With Joe he would be giving himself a chance – the only chance he would ever be likely to get. 'I'll give it a go,' he announced suddenly.

1964 Donald Horne *The Lucky Country* 39: Impelled to action, Australians 'give it a go'. They try something to see if it works, pretty sure that it will.

1971 Robin Miller *Flying Nurse* 172: Damascus airport was closed by fog, but . . . I was prepared to give it a go.

go nap on see **nap**

go over the hill see **hill**

go the knuckle see **knuckle**

go through To abscond, make a swift departure, esp. to avoid some obligation (interchangeable with 'shoot through')

1943 Baker 34: *Go through* To desert from a northern base to the south. War slang.

1949 Lawson Glassop *Lucky Palmer* 79: 'When will you fellows wake to it? Here it is twenty to twelve and you blokes are still believing he'll be here. Can't you see he's gone through?'

1951 Eric Lambert *The Twenty Thousand Thieves* 222: He shrugged. 'I'll probably have to go through meself again.' He said it as though going A.W.L. was as casual a thing as shaving.

1973 Frank Huelin *Keep Moving* 179: *Gone through* Left town.

go to the pack see **pack**

goat, a hairy A racehorse which performs badly

1941 Baker 34: *Hairy goat, run like a* (used esp. of horses) To perform badly in a race.

1951 Dymphna Cusack and Florence James *Come In Spinner* 40: 'The last one you gave me [as a racing tip] ran like a hairy goat.'

1956 J. T. Lang *I Remember* 150: They told him it was a 'hairy goat', but Smithy decided it would be better to ride the 'hairy goat' than not have a mount. [recalling 1904]

1965 John Beede *They Hosed Them Out* 192: Our skipper, from the time we got near the enemy coast, flew like a hairy goat.

1969 Osmar White *Under the Iron Rainbow* 110–11: If there'd been a few hairy goats galloping around and a couple of bookies standing on whisky cases it'd have looked like the bloody Roebourne races.

Godzone Australia [f. the use of this heading (for 'God's own country') in a series of articles in *Meanjin Quarterly*]

1966 *Meanjin Quarterly* 133: Godzone (1) The Retreat from Reason [Note:] This is the first of a new series of commentaries on the reality of present-day life and living in God's Own Country.

1976 *Australian* 15 May 21: Godzone's richest acres. A fine-focus on the best addresses in Australia.

goer A project, proposal likely to be put into effect or to succeed
1977 *Bulletin* 29 Jan. 29: The film is now finally a goer. Hellwig's money is in and the rest will come from private investment . . . and film commissions.

golden doughnut see **doughnut**

golden girl An Australian woman athlete who has won an Olympic gold medal; any outstanding Australian sportswoman [f. the 1956 Olympics, when Australia won the women's relay, and Betty Cuthbert three gold medals]
1956 *Sunday Telegraph* 2 Dec. 3: Golden Girls Triumph in Relay. Ibid. 9 Dec. 1: Australia's four 'golden girls' led the parade of athletes in a moving closing ceremony at the main Olympic stadium today.
1973 *Sydney Morning Herald* 11 Jan. 15: Golden girls set new swim times.
1974 *Australian* 7 Aug. 21: Whatever happened to Evonne Goolagong – our golden girl who won this year's Australian tennis title.

golden hole A very rich mining claim
1855 Raffaello Carboni *The Eureka Stockade* ed. Geoffrey Serle (1969) 176: Below at a depth of 140 feet in a . . . hundred pounds weight Golden Hole.
1861 Horace Earle *Ups and Downs* 290: 'Here's luck, Tom!' . . . 'A golden hole to you, Tom!' sounded from every quarter.
1880 Rolf Boldrewood *The Miner's Right* (1890) 32: The adjacent lot to the highly satisfactory 'golden-hole claim', as the miners phrased it, was to be had for the pegging-out first.
1896 Henry Lawson 'An Old Mate of Your Father's' *Prose* i 67: Poor Martin Ratcliffe – who was killed in his golden hole.
1950 K. S. Prichard *Winged Seeds* 22: 'Everywhere they tapped the reef, she was lousy with gold. They thought they'd struck a golden hole.'

Golden Mile, the See quot. 1971

1901 May Vivienne *Travels in Western Australia* 210: From this place one has a glorious view of the other great mines on the Golden Mile, so-called on account of the marvellous quantity of gold that has been and still is being extracted from its depths – Lake View, Great Boulder, Ivanhoe, Boulder Perseverance, and Golden Horseshoe.
1908 E. G. Murphy *Jarrahland Jingles* 120: He has toiled along the Golden Mile among the cyanide.
1971 Colin Simpson *The New Australia* 557: The Golden Mile lies between Kalgoorlie and Boulder and is an extraordinarily rich auriferous reef area that is actually about two miles long and a third of a mile wide and has been mined to thousands of feet.

Goldfields scavenger As for 'willy-willy': *rare*
1929 Jules Raeside *Golden Days* 341: Goldfields residents also knew of the 'Willy-willy', or, as it was sometimes called 'the Goldfields Scavenger'.

golly *v. & n.* To spit (juvenile)
1938 Encountered in conversation.
1941 Baker 32: *Gollion* A gob of phlegm.
1975 Les Ryan *The Shearers* 153: *Gobber* Ejaculation of saliva; a golly.

gonce Money: *obsolescent* [? Yiddish]
1899 W. T. Goodge *Hits! Skits! and Jingles!* 159; 'The nearest guess will get the gonce as sure as you are there!'
1901 *Bulletin Reciter* 183: Yes, I'm doin' pretty middlin', / And I'm layin' up de gonce. Ibid. 194: And the nearest guess will get the gonce.
1916 Joseph Furphy *Poems* 17: Gonce to men of enterprise.
1918 Bernard Cronin *The Coastlanders* 114: 'They know how to treat a gent in them places, provided he has the gonze.'
1941 Baker 32: *Gons* Money.

gone a million see **million**

gone to Moscow see **Moscow**

good iron see **iron**

good-oh Expression of agreement or approval; a state of well-being

1924 *Truth* 27 Apr. 6: *Goodo* All right.

1925 Seymour Hicks *Hullo Australians* 225: I never say 'Thank you' now – I simply says 'Good-oh!'

1940 Arnold Haskell *Waltzing Matilda* 36: If your companion says 'good oh' you know that he understands and approves.

1948 *Coast to Coast 1948* 122: 'Gee, you look good-o.'

1958 Frank Hardy *The Four-Legged Lottery* 36: 'Gee it must be good-oh at the races, Dad.' 'It's good-oh, all right.'

1963 Arthur Upfield *The Body at Madman's Bend* 69: 'Happen to see a tall bloke?' 'Yes, he just passed me.' ... 'Goodoh!'

good on you Expression of approval, congratulation, goodwill

1908 Giles Seagram *Bushmen All* 84: One man said, 'Good on yer, Mac.'

1922 Arthur Wright *The Colt from the Country* 171: 'Good on you, mate,' he said. 'We'll have a go.'

1935 Kylie Tennant *Tiburon* 273: 'Good on her,' Polly said cheerfully. 'May be the best thing she's ever done.'

1942 Gavin Casey *It's Harder for Girls* 166: 'Good on you, dad,' said Williams over the side. 'Aw, go t' hell!' chattered the old man.

1954 *Sydney Morning Herald* 10 Feb. 4: More than 10,000 people at Newcastle Sportsground today clapped and shouted, 'Good on you, Philip', when the Duke of Edinburgh quickly opened up an umbrella to shield the Queen from the rain. Ibid. 19 Feb. 6: Shouts of 'Good on you, Liz' and 'Good on you, Phil'.

1964 William Dick *A Bunch of Ratbags* 242: 'Good on yuh, Charlie. Good on yuh, Terry,' they said as they patted us on the back.

1974 L. Oakes and D. Solomon *Grab for Power* 486: 'We want Gough! We want Gough!' chanted the crowd. When he entered the Picador they sang 'Advance Australia Fair'. 'Good on yer, Gough baby!' they shouted. 'Good on yer, mate!'

gooley A stone of a suitable size for throwing (juvenile) [? f. Hindustani *goli* a bullet, ball]

1924 *Truth* 27 Apr. 6: *Gooley* A stone.

1941 Baker 32: *Gooly* A stone or pebble.

1949 Ruth Park *The Harp in the South* 47: 'Someone's been bunging goolies through her window.'

1963 John Cantwell *No Stranger to the Flame* 20: 'I lobbed it with a gooley and knocked it cold.'

1974 David Ireland *Burn* 18: 'Garn, get out of it,' Gunner says, 'before I let fly with a goolie.'

Gordon, in more trouble than Speed Beset with extraordinary difficulties [f. the character in the comic strip]

1971 Alan Reid *The Gorton Experiment* 381: Scott, a pathetic figure in some ways, who had been in more trouble than Speed Gordon while Customs Minister, went quietly.

1974 John Powers *The Last of the Knucklemen* 14: We might just find ourselves in more trouble than Flash Gordon.

Gordon, went through like Speed Jocular reply to request for someone's whereabouts

1948 Sumner Locke Elliott *Rusty Bugles* in *Khaki, Bush and Bigotry* ed. Eunice Hanger (1968) 31: 'Andy Edwards ... Andy Edwards there?' 'Went mad and they shot him.' 'Went through like Speed Gordon.'

see **shot through on the padre's bike, went for a crap and the sniper got him**

Government house The residence of the owner or the manager on a sheep or cattle station, as distinct from the 'barracks' and the 'hut' qq.v., more often just 'the house'

1887 Simpson Newland *The Far North Country* 12: The 'Government House', as the operator's residence is called [at Charlotte Waters Telegraph Station], is the principal building, chiefly remarkable for ugliness and heat.

1896 Henry Lawson 'Stragglers' *Prose* i 91: 'Government House' is a mile away [from the wool shed], and is nothing better than a bush hut: this station belongs to a company.

1919 W. R. Harris *Outback in Australia* 2: 'Government House' (the owner's or manager's residence) on a big sheep-station.

1936 A. W. Upfield *Wings Above the Diamantina* 77: Heading this class trilogy on the average station is the owner or manager, and his family. They reside in what is termed 'government house', the main residence on the property and centre from which it is directed.

1951 Ernestine Hill *The Territory* 444: *Government House* The homestead of a head station.

Government man A convict

1820 *The Evidence of the Bigge Reports* ed. J. Ritchie (1971) i 85: Mr. Cox has allowed me to have a Government man in consequence of my marriage.

1835 *Colonist* 30 Apr. 140: He there meets with . . . somebody's government man or convict-servant, who is desirous, of course, to treat him to some rum.

1843 Charles Rowcroft *Tales of the Colonies* ii 235: 'I must warn you, that we never speak of the convicts in this country by that term; we always call them "government men", or on some occasions, prisoners; but we never use the word "convict", which is considered by them as an insulting term.'

1854 W. Shaw *The Land of Promise* 49: The asperity of the word *convict* shocks their ears, so the more mollifying term of 'government man' has been substituted.

1864 James Armour *The Diggings, the Bush, and Melbourne* 16: From the talk that followed I learnt that nearly all the company had been 'Government men', as convicts style themselves.

1874 Charles de Boos *The Congewoi Correspondence* 148: As to bandicoots, they're like Government men, they never turn out in wet weather, but keep theirselves snug at home.

Government stroke The indolent working style of a government employee, originally on road work

1855 C. R. Thatcher 'The Bond Street Swell' cit. R. Ward *The Australian Legend* (1958) 117: And then he went upon the roads, / As many a young swell must . . . / You may see him do the Gov'ment stroke / At eight bob every day.

1873 A. Trollope *Australia* ed. Edwards and Joyce (1967) 190: In colonial parlance the government stroke is that light and easy mode of labour – perhaps that semblance of labour – which no other master will endure, though government is forced to put up with it.

1876 Rolf Boldrewood *A Colonial Reformer* (1890) 236: 'As long as they have their grub and their wages they'll hang it out . . . regular Government stroke, as we say in this country.'

1903 Ada Cambridge *Thirty Years in Australia* 216: The labourer naturally prefers the Government stroke, and can be tempted away from that easy and pleasant way of passing his time only by an increased rate of wages.

1916 Macmillan's *Modern Dictionary of the English Language* 781: *government stroke* a half-hearted way of doing work, supposed to be characteristic of some government employees.

1933 Leslie Haylen *The Game Darrells* 172: The awful exhibition of the government stroke in the building of this line.

1949 George Farwell *Traveller's Tracks* 93: Why should the white fellow have a monopoly of the government stroke?

1969 Osmar White *Under the Iron Rainbow* 108: 'Once them New Australians get the idea of the Government stroke and union rules they leave the Aussies for dead when it comes to bludging.'

graft *n.* Work, esp. manual labour [? f. *grave* to dig c. 1000 OED; *graft* work of any description EDD 1891]

1853 John Rochfort *Adventures of a Surveyor* 47: Afterwards I could have obtained an engagement in my own profession at 300 l. a year, but, finding that I could make more money by 'hard graft', as they call labour in the colonies, I would not take it.

1892 William Lane *The Workingman's Paradise* 104: 'I've been out of graft for months and haven't got any money.'

1896 Edward Dyson *Rhymes from the Mines* 23: Not a man of us is weary, though the graft is pretty rough.

1935 Kylie Tennant *Tiburon* 199: He was tired of being an agrarian organiser in this west that regarded hard graft and bad food and hard times as just as inevitable as a dust storm.

1957 Sydney Hart *Pommie Migrant* 81: 'What a mug ya are to come 12,000 miles to do this kind of graft for a living.'

graft *v.* To work; to work hard
[1859 Hotten: *Graft* to go to work]

1892 Harry Morant 'Paddy Magee' *Bulletin* 20 Feb. 14: What are you doing now, Paddy Magee?/Grafting, or spelling now, Paddy Magee?

1900 Henry Lawson 'Drought-stricken' *Prose* ii 96: They were very poor – often lived and grafted on damper, tea, and sugar.

1910 C. E. W. Bean *On the Wool Track* 129: 'He can't ride. He can graft a bit; but he's not much intelligence, oh no. He's an Englishman.'

c. 1919 Herbert Scanlon *Much in Little* 29: He informed me that he was grafting in the quarries.

1941 Kylie Tennant *The Battlers* 7: 'He grafted like a team of bullocks, and . . . had me out ploughing and clearing and fencing.'

grafter A hard worker

1901 F. J. Gillen *Diary* (1968) 277: Stephen like his brother John is an old friend of mine and a great grafter.

1918 C. J. Dennis *Backblock Ballads* 29: And though still a steady grafter, he grew restless ever after.

1953 *Caddie A Sydney Barmaid* 12: He was a grafter* and worked out in the bush six days a week. *In Australia a grafter is a very hard worker.

grandfather's pudding An improvised bush delicacy: see quot.

1951 Ernestine Hill *The Territory* 426: 'grandfather's puddin' – stale damper

soaked in black tea and sprinkled with sugar.

Grannies Variant of 'apples' q.v. [f. the Granny Smith apple]

1963 Bruce Beaver *The Hot Summer* 115: 'She'll be Grannies', cackled the ragged informant.

Granny *The Sydney Morning Herald* (founded 1831 as *The Sydney Herald*) [see quot. 1931]

1851 *The Press* 23 Apr. 189: In the same number of 'My Grannie O', (which we beg to submit as a very good cognomen for the *Herald* and its antiquated and obsolete notions on the subject of government), there is a letter from the honorable member for Northumberland.

1901 Henry Lawson *Prose* ii 125: Even some London Conservative dailies come wonderfully refreshing to me after the *Sydney Morning Herald* ('Grannie').

1931 *A Century of Journalism* 239: The *Herald* has long been affectionately – and sometimes contemptuously – known as 'Granny'. The nickname being supposed to refer to its age, its allegedly conservative methods and the untiring energy with which it has always dealt out advice, comment, and criticism.

1940 Arnold L. Haskell *Waltzing Matilda* 176: The dean of papers is the *Sydney Morning Herald*, 'Grannie', an organ of conservative views and amazing respectability.

1950 Jon Cleary *Just Let Me Be* 241: 'You're beginning to talk like some old spinster,' Harry said. 'You'll be writing letters to Granny Herald next.'

grape on the business, a Someone whose presence spoils things for others; an odd man out [? variant of *gooseberry*]

1941 Baker 32: *Grape on the business, A* (of a person) One who is a blue stocking, a wallflower or a drag on cheery company.

1944 Lawson Glassop *We Were the Rats* 9: 'I've got nobody to go with. All the girls'll be going with their boy friends and I don't want to be a grape on the

business.'
1946 Alan Marshall *Tell us about the Turkey, Jo* 62: She hasn't got a bloke. She is a grape on the business.

grasshopper, knee-high to a Used to express diminutive size, or extreme youth [listed by Partridge as Canadian]
1941 Kylie Tennant *The Battlers* 7: 'When I wasn't knee-high to a grasshopper he had me out ploughing and clearing and fencing.'
1951 Dal Stivens *Jimmy Brockett* 161: Ever since I'd been knee-high to a grasshopper I'd loved the fight game.
1961 Tom Ronan *Only a Short Walk* 135: Only a little thing – knee-high to a grasshopper, you could say.

grasshoppers Visitors to Canberra, esp. in tourist groups, as distinct from the permanent residents
1965 *Sydney Morning Herald* 3 Jul. 5: A full bus-load of 'grass-hoppers' (the Canberra term for tourists – 'they eat everything in sight and never have a drink').
1969 Leslie Haylen *Twenty Year's Hard Labor* 204: The private member has, however, his visitors from the electorate. Now ... they arrive in such numbers that they have come to be called 'the grasshoppers'. They come in a cloud, eat everything about the place.
1972 *Sydney Morning Herald* 3 Nov. 6: At last the politicians are gone from Parliament and have dispersed to their electorates ... King's Hall ... has been taken over by 'grasshoppers' – an old Canberra nickname for tourists.

greasy 1 An outback cook; any cook for a collection of men [f. grease on clothes]
1873 J. C. F. Johnson *Christmas on Carringa* 1: Bill, who himself was our *chef d' cuisine* ... in the vernacular, cook or 'greasy', had on this occasion quite excelled his usual excellence.
1919 W. H. Downing *Digger Dialects* 27: *Greasy* A cook.
1938 *Smith's Weekly* 19 Nov. 22: 'Greasy' was the officers' mess cook, but sad to relate, he was not an expert.

1953 T. A. G. Hungerford *Riverslake* 148: 'God, cooks aren't people!' Carmichael retorted ... 'I'm going to write a book about greasies one day!'
2 A shearer
1956 F. B. Vickers *First Place to the Stranger* 134: 'When those five greasies get moving they'll shear a lot of sheep.'
1963 *Sydney Morning Herald* 17 Aug. 11: A lot of greasies (shearers) get hen trouble. Some shearers' wives reckon we shearer blokes are either too tired, too drunk or too far away.
1975 Les Ryan *The Shearers* 123: 'The greasies have hung up. Why can't we?'

greasy pig, a In two-up, a throw of tails after a succession of heads
1949 Lawson Glassop *Lucky Palmer* 174: 'Come on, gents, he's done 'em four times. Here's a chance for a greasy pig!'

great Australian adjective, novel see **Australian**

Greek's, the The local milk bar, café, etc. (often run by Greeks)
1977 Ted Roberts *Lindsay's Boy* in *Five Plays* ed. Alrene Sykes 234: 'Should be out celebrating. What about a feed at the Greeks?'

green cart The van supposed to take people to the mental asylum
1959 Dorothy Hewett *Bobbin Up* 109–10: 'You're mad, that what's up with you. They'll come for you in the green cart one of these days me lady and not before time.'
1975 *Overland 62* 27: The green cart will come for me, and I'll disappear into Callan Park, and that will be some kind of solution.

greengrocer A variety of cicada [f. colouring]
1951 Dymphna Cusack and Florence James *Come in Spinner* 106: 'Mine's a Greengrocer – look!' Durras opened his hand carefully, showing a cicada with iridescent wings folded back on a body of delicate green.
1959 Anne von Bertouch *February*

Dark 124: Through the shimmer of heat and the drilling song Helen saw the beautiful cicadas of childhood, the Black Prince, the Greengrocer, the Yellow Monday, held on a child's small hand.

greenie A supporter of the 'green bans' imposed by the Builders Labourers Federation in 1973 on demolition and development projects considered contrary to principles of 'conservation'; a trendy conservationist
1973 *Nation Review* 28 Sep. 1572: The local greenies have despaired of stopping the dreaded post office tower by indirect means, and have started on a little direct action.
1973 *Australian* 1 Oct. 7: The middle class 'greenies' have an unusual stake in the elections.

Greens, the Galloping The Randwick (N.S.W.) Rugby Union team (also the Wicks) [f. team colours]
1974 *Australian* 26 Sep. 20: Eels to knock gloss off the Greens.

grey In two-up, a double-headed penny, or a penny with two tails [f. English thieves' slang OED 1812–68]
[1812 Vaux: *Gray:* a half-penny, or other coin, having two heads or two tails, and fabricated for the use of gamblers, who, by such a deception, frequently win large sums.]
1898 *Bulletin* 3 Sep. 32: He'd simply smashed the two-up school / (Assisted by a 'grey'!)
1943 Baker 35: *Gray* A double-tailed penny.
1946 K. S. Prichard *The Roaring Nineties* 387: A spieler had been caught ringing in the grey, a two-headed penny, and the boys were giving him a rough time. Ibid. 125: 'The grey', a penny with two tails.
1975 Les Ryan *The Shearers* 153: *Greys* Double tail pennies.

grey ghost A N.S.W. parking policeman, successor to the 'brown bomber' q.v. [f. colour of uniform]
1976 *Sydney Morning Herald* 10 Jul. 1:

Don't think you can park just anywhere in the City during the national strike – the police will get the Grey Ghosts on the job.

grey meanie A parking policeman in Victoria [f. colour of uniform]
1971 *Sunday Australian* 1 Aug. 3: Mr McMahon walked into the hotel's lounge and took tea. Meanwhile one of Melbourne's famous 'grey meanies' slapped the ticket on the Prime Minister's car.

grid (iron) A bicycle: *obsolescent*
1941 Baker 32: *Grid (iron)* A bicycle.
1942 Gavin Casey *It's Harder for Girls* 125: 'Here, you go on, on my grid, an' I'll do the walking.'
1962 Stuart Gore *Down the Golden Mile* 128: Riding his father's ramshackle old grid; wobbling, with a leg thrust under the top bar to reach the offside pedal.

grog General term for alcoholic drink, usually beer [f. *grog* as rum (and water) OED 1770]
1938 Xavier Herbert *Capricornia* 256: 'Sorry – I've knocked your grog over. Let's buy another ... What are you drinking?' 'Double whiskey.'
1949 Lawson Glassop *Lucky Palmer* 8: 'Likes his beer, does Darky.' Clarrie groaned. 'The grog,' he said. 'He can't beat the grog.'
1953 *The Sunburnt Country* ed. Ian Bevan 126: Grog is beer: and beer, to the A.I.F. is sacred. The first sound heard from any Australian convoy arriving in any foreign port will always be the cry 'How's the beer?'
1964 George Johnston *My Brother Jack* 379: 'We could go up to the Royal Empire and have a grog.'
1973 Alexander Buzo *Rooted* 44: 'Hammo had been on the grog and he didn't give way to his right and this bloke smashed into him.'
grog on To continue steady drinking
1965 John Beede *They Hosed Them Out* 185: We grogged on till closing time; it was evident we all had one thing in common – a liking for the amber liquid.
grog-up As for 'beer-up'

1962 Alan Seymour *The One Day of the Year* 77: 'We're sick of all the muck that's talked about this day . . . It's just one long grog-up.'
see **sly-grog**

Groper As for 'Sandgroper' q.v.
1908 E. G. Murphy *Jarrahland Jingles* 29: 'Give me the goblet of good ruddy wine!'/Cried a Groperland Poet who gropes.
1926 J. Vance Marshall *Timely Tips for New Australians*: Groper A West Australian.
1929 Jules Raeside *Golden Days* 125: Many of the 'Gropers' (early settlers) of the West.

Grouper A member of one of the 'Industrial Groups' set up in the Labor Party in 1945–6 to counter Communist influence in the trade unions
1955 *Sydney Morning Herald* 27 Apr. 1: Last year the groupers altered the rules to give two delegates for every 250 members from a State electoral council.
1956 *Daily Telegraph* 11 Apr. 3: Supporters of the industrial groups have laid charges against non-groupers.
1959 Dorothy Hewett *Bobbin Up* 128: 'That Grouper Short stopped my Frank sellin' 'is *Tribs* outside the Trade Union Club.'
1964 *Australian* 22 Jul. 8: They tend to see themselves as upholders of the pure faith of anti-Grouperism.

groupie A participant in the Group Settlement scheme in Western Australia in the 1920s, under which hundred-acre allotments were made to English emigrants in the backward south-west
1972 M. L. Skinner *The Fifth Sparrow* 119: Few of the 'groupies' knew anything about farming at all and the raw land daunted and frustrated them.

grouse Excellent, outstanding: *obsolescent* [origin unknown]
1924 *Truth* 27 Apr. 6: Grouse something good.
1944 Lawson Glassop *We Were the Rats* 5: 'You know them two grouse sheilas we've got the meet on with tomorrer

night?'
1953 T. A. G. Hungerford *Riverslake* 74: 'Seven o'clock, O.K.?' 'Yeah, that'll be grouse.'
1959 Eric Lambert *Glory Thrown In* 72: 'That was grouse!' he said . . . 'You should have been in it.'
1963 John Cantwell *No Stranger to the Flame* 81: 'Same when we were kids – always getting between me and the grouse things.'
1974 Jim McNeil *How Does Your Garden Grow* 111: 'And then there's the advertising in the papers . . . usually with a grouse sheila in the picture all ready to get her gear off if yer use whatever stuff they're trying to sell yer.'

grouter, come in on the To seek benefit from a situation not of one's own making, esp. in two-up by withholding any bet until a run of heads or tails indicates that a change must soon occur (hence a 'grouter bet')
1919 W. H. Downing *Digger Dialects* 27: *Grouter* An unfair advantage. 'Come on the grouter' – gain an unfair advantage.
1941 Baker 36: *Grouter* One who takes advantage of others. (2) An unfair advantage. Whence 'on the grouter', on the lookout for something for nothing.
1944 Lawson Glassop *We Were the Rats* 113: 'I reckon you Seventh Div. jokers have come in on the grouter.' I felt ashamed. 'Our turn'll come,' I said. 'We've got to do some more training yet.' Ibid. 129: 'Looks as if you blokes are going to come in on the grouter.'
1946 K. S. Prichard *The Roaring Nineties* 125: Sometimes a successful bettor twisted, after backing heads, and backed tails: 'Catching the grouter,' that was called. But a grouter bettor could only have one or two bets a night.
1949 Lawson Glassop *Lucky Palmer* 174: 'A real grouter bet, gents,' he said. 'Any tailie who missed out on that run of heads can come in on the grouter now.'
1965 Wally Grout *My Country's 'Keeper* 90: I saw a cove who had been watching

me play the machine step up to it, whip in a few coins, and crack the jackpot. A nice easy way to earn a living. We call that 'coming in on the grouter.'

1970 Richard Beilby *No Medals for Aphrodite* 239: Turk was an inveterate tail-better while Squeaker liked to 'come in on the grouter', when the odds against the spinner had considerably lengthened.

grubber Hospital [listed by Partridge as 'A casual ward: tramps' c. (−1932)']

1973 Frank Huelin *Keep Moving* 90: 'How'd 'ya feel, mate?' he asked. 'Ya'll have ter go ta th' grubber.'

grunter A promiscuous woman [f. *pig* prostitute]

1973 Alexander Buzo *Rooted* 70: 'I'll line up a bird for you, too. I know a couple of grunters.'

gub, gubbah Aboriginal term for a white

1972 *Sydney Morning Herald* 2 Nov. 12: Mr Gub is . . . the white man. The word is the diminutive of garbage.

1973 *Australian* 12 Dec. 14: He [Kevin Gilbert] sat in a coffee shop in Redfern with his present European wife Cora (his 'favourite gubbah').

guernsey, get a To gain recognition or approval; succeed [f. selection in a sporting team]

1918 Let. in Bill Gammage *The Broken Years* (1974) 218: In 1918 troops chosen for an attack 'got their guernseys.'

1964 George Johnston *My Brother Jack* 298: 'As long as you're going to get a guernsey, that's the main thing.'

1974 Senator J. McClelland *Australian Humanist* No. 31 7: This extra channel . . . will give us . . . programmes for ethnic groups, art, technology, all the things that are never going to get a guernsey in the present setup.

1976 *Sydney Morning Herald* 30 Apr. 1: Sydney gets a guernsey in the book, *The 300 Best Hotels in the World*, just published by Thomas Cook.

guiver, gyver Flattering pretence; loquacity; general 'carry-on': *obsolescent* [? Yiddish]

1864 *Thatcher's Colonial Ministrel* 13: 'I'll give you the sack pretty quick, / If my wife you offend with your guiver.'

1889 Barrère and Leland 436: *Guiver* (theatrical) flattery, artfulness.

1899 W. T. Goodge *Hits! Skits! and Jingles!* 18: I ain't got the style and guiver / Of them bank clerks and students and sich.

1901 *The Bulletin Reciter* 16: And you should have seen his guiver when he scalped the bullock-driver.

1902 Henry Fletcher *The Waybacks in Town and at Home* 22: 'But yous a bloke as knows ther inside runnin' o' things; tell me, straight, what's this Federation guiver all amount ter?'

1915 C. J. Dennis *The Songs of a Sentimental Bloke* 79: I s'pose the wimmin git some sorter fun / Wiv all this guyver.

1924 *Truth* 27 Apr. 6: *Guyver* Pretence.

1951 Dal Stivens *Jimmy Brockett* 102: Helen didn't put on as much guiver as the others.

1962 Dymphna Cusack *Picnic Races* 19: 'Lotta jumped-up blow-ins putting on more guyver than the Governor's wife.'

Gulf country The country near the Gulf of Carpentaria in Queensland

1872 *Punch Staff Papers* 62: Talk of the Gulf country, and the Great Australian Bight − they are fertile paradises compared to the district between Albany and Perth.

1892 Barcroft Boake 'Skeeta' *Bulletin* 17 Dec. 14 repr. in *Where the Dead Men Lie* (1897) 87: And gave Harry Parker the order to go to 'the Gulf' for the mob.

1901 Henry Lawson 'Telling Mrs Baker' *Prose* i 416: He was going North to new country round by the Gulf of Carpentaria . . . I and my mate Andy M'Culloch, engaged to go with him. We wanted to have a look at the Gulf Country.

1906 A. B. Paterson *An Outback Marriage* 4: He was out in the Gulf-country in the early days.

1911 C. E. W. Bean *The Dreadnought of the Darling* 96: You find the cattle to this day farther out − in the country which is still unfenced up by 'the Gulf'.

n. The Gulf of Carpentaria is known by Australians as 'the Gulf'.

1938 Eric Lowe *Salute to Freedom* 570: 'Up in the Gulf country some of the boys used to send stories to Brisbane and Sydney papers. They got a few bob out of it.'

1957 R. S. Porteous *Brigalow* 10–11: 'I put in two years jackerooing in the Gulf Country.'

gully-raker 1 One of those engaged in 'gully-raking' q.v.

1869 E. C. Booth *Another England* 138: The old fellow had lost his team, and had been seeking them ever since. Hearing that the 'gully-rakers' about were not very particular, he had travelled down the river as far as Shepperton.

2 A long whip

1881 A. C. Grant *Bush-Life in Queensland* i 40: Following up his admonition by a sweeping cut of his 'gully-raker', and a report like a musket-shot.

1919 W. K. Harris *Outback in Australia* 85: Long whips with short handles, and short whips with long handles, eight strands and upwards, from the redoubtable old 'gully-rakers' to the exaggerated thong affixed to a hunting crop.

gully-raking The rounding up of un-branded cattle by searching the gullies and other places where they may have been overlooked; illegally appropriating cattle by this practice [*gully* in Australian usage is not limited to a channel made by a watercourse]

[**1855** William Howitt *Land, Labour and Gold* ii 225: Our way from Bendigo was through a rather fine country, with ever-succeeding swells and glades, or gullies, as they call them here; though a gully, to my mind, is a deep, narrow ravine torn out by a watercourse. But here the broadest and smoothest valleys, or any dimple amongst the hills, is a gully.]

1847 Alexander Harris *Settlers and Convicts* ed. C. M. H. Clark (1954) 140: If he could find an unbranded beast in the bush, had no qualms about making it his own by clapping his brand on it.

In this way, by a process technically called 'gully-raking', he had quad-rupled the little herd his father gave him.

1857 F. Cooper *Wild Adventures in Australia* 104: 'He was stock-keeping in that quarter, and was rather given to "gulley raking". One fine day it appears he ran in three bullocks belonging to a neighbouring squatter, and clapt his brand on top of the other so as to efface it.'

1875 Rolf Boldrewood *The Squatter's Dream* repr. as *Ups and Downs* (1878) 236: A long-legged, brown-faced, long-haired son of the soil, of the worst type of pound-haunting, gully-raking bush native, returned without the horses.

gumsucker A native of Victoria; a native-born Australian [? f. *gumtree*: see quot. 1885]

1855 William Howitt *Land, Labour and Gold* i 24: Bitten twice by the over 'cute 'gum-suckers' as the native Victorians are called.

1859 Frank Fowler *Southern Lights and Shadows* 24: Your thorough-bred gum-sucker never speaks, without apostrophising his 'oath', and interlarding his diction with the crimsonest of adjectives.

1865 J. F. Mortlock *Experiences of a Convict* (1965) 230: Both Sydney and Melbourne boast of establishments dignified by the term University; being on a par with English public schools. The attempt to educate, as at Cambridge or Oxford, young 'gumsuckers' savours of the absurd.

1885 *The Australasian Printers' Keepsake* 20: Our Colonial lads showed their right to the appellation of 'Gumsucker', by chewing transparent lumps that appended from the silver-wattle.

1903 Joseph Furphy *Such is Life* (1944) 44: 'When anybody calls him a Port Philliper, or a Vic., or a 'Sucker, he comes out straight . . . 'I'm a Cornstalk, born in New South Wales.'

1914 Nathan Spielvogel *The Gumsucker at Home* 9: I hoped to wander all around Victoria, spending a few weeks in each place, and so in the course of four or five years to know all about the land of the Gumsucker.

gumtree, up a In great difficulties, in a state of confusion (like an animal which has been treed) [? U.S. song 'possum up a gumtree' Mathews 1831]
[1888 W. S. S. Tyrwhitt *The New Chum in the Queensland Bush* 150: The opossum, more generally known as the possum, as a rule occupies his proverbial position in a gum tree.]
1941 Baker 33: *Gumtree, up a* In trouble, in a quandary.
1945 Gavin Casey *Downhill is Easier* 87: They wanted to know whether or not we'd been kidded up a gum-tree, and they shouted and roared a lot about it.
1958 Douglas Stewart *Four Plays* 163: 'He's up a gum-tree. Bushed, I tell you, near Greta./He's running round in circles.'
1973 *Sun-Herald* 25 Mar. 108: Up a gumtree [heading] During the Yugoslav Premier's visit, energetic policemen went along the shores of Lake Burley Griffin shaking young gum trees. Security cars in the motorcade were marked with special markings on the roofs, so they could spotted by police sharpshooters overhead.

gun *n. & a.* A shearer with a high tally; anyone pre-eminent in some activity [f. *big gun, great gun* OED 1815]
1898 'Whaler's Rhyme' *Bulletin* 9 Jul. Red Page repr. in *Old Bush Songs* ed. Stewart and Keesing (1957) 250: There's brand-new-chums and cockies' sons,/ They fancy that they are great guns.
1933 Acland: *Gun, big gun* A really fast shearer, one who could ring most sheds.
1940 Ion L. Idriess *Lightning Ridge* 152: The 'gun shearer' there was a two hundred-a-day man, the tally of the lowest was over a hundred a day.
1957 D'Arcy Niland *Call Me When the Cross Turns Over* 131: He was a champion at other things too. He was a gun potato-digger and pea-picker.
1961 George Farwell *Vanishing Australians* 51: You heard tales of 'gun' drovers still in the saddle, of famous

ones now passed away.
1971 *Sydney Morning Herald* 29 Oct. 14: He [John Benaud] was N.S.W.'s gun batsman last summer with 782 runs with an average of 55.86.

Gundy, no good to Applied to something adverse: *obsolescent* [origin unknown]
1919 W. H. Downing *Digger Dialects* 35: *No good to gundy* Of no advantage.
1922 E. O'Ferrall *Bodger and the Boarders* 46: One of them scrawled 'I don't want none of youre dam sympathy. Out 'ere it's 107 in shade and all that there talk about comin and settin be fires made me sweat like an orse. No good to Gundy.'
1923 Jack Moses *Beyond the City Gates* 128: 'Taint no good to Gundy to see the fluid go,/When you're cockyin' and battlin' and live on what you grow.
1937 *Best Australian One-Act Plays* 204: 'That's not the point. Privately's no good to Gundy. The shilling's neither here nor there.'

gunyah An Aboriginal hut (Morris, 1798), but applied colloquially to shelters improvised by whites
1853 S. Mossman and T. Banister *Australia Visited and Revisited* 53: He [the gold-digger] would be as much at home lying down in his dirty clothes for weeks together, in a tent or bark gunya, as he was at home on his straw pallet in his mud cabin.
1859 Let. in M. H. Walker *Come Wind, Come Weather* (1971) 96: Our gunyah was between two young trees being placed from one to the other about four feet from the ground. Against this sheets of bark were reared overlapping one another, on these heavy branches were laid to keep them in place and at each end boughs were put to keep out the wind.
1903 William Craig *My Adventures on the Australian Goldfields* 113: Other shelter and accommodation had, however, to be obtained, and the following day we procured from Spring Creek the necessary calico for a 'gunyah'.
1919 E. S. Sorenson *Chips and Splinters*

12: The sawyers, whose home was a bark gunyah nearby, were tradesmen whose work was important to them.

guts, come (give) one's To inform to the police, or other authority
[c. **1882** *The Sydney Slang Dictionary* 2: *Come it* To inform.]
1953 Kylie Tennant *The Joyful Condemned* 295: The sullen, big oaf, baited and jeered at by everyone, a man who had 'come his guts to the coppers', was almost driven desperate.
1959 Dorothy Hewett *Bobbin Up* 135: 'She's in the manager's office half the day, with her legs crossed so you can see everythin' she's got, givin' him all our guts.'
1966 Elwyn Wallace *Sydney and the Bush* 141: 'Me? Come me guts? A top-off?'

guts, the good Reliable information (mainly Services slang)
1919 W. H. Downing *Digger Dialects* 27: *Guts* The substance or essential part of a matter, information.
1946 Rohan Rivett *Behind Bamboo* 396: *Good guts* news, information, secret radio news.
1948 Sumner Locke Elliott *Rusty Bugles* in *Khaki, Bush and Bigotry* ed. Eunice Hanger (1968) 33: 'Got any good guts on replacements?' Ibid. 57: 'Heard the late good guts on the leave?'
1952 Jon Cleary *The Sundowners* 154: 'Wireless is going to be a bloody big thing one of these days, and I'm studying to get the good guts on it.'
1965 William Dick *A Bunch of Ratbags* 196: 'What about Sharon?' asked Joey. 'How much does she charge, Elaine? Give us the good guts on her.'
1975 Les Ryan *The Shearers* 83: 'We'll get the good guts soon.'

guts, in the In two-up, referring to bets placed 'in the ring' as distinct from 'on the side'
1948 Sumner Locke Elliott *Rusty Bugles* in *Khaki, Bush and Bigotry* ed. Eunice Hanger (1968) 30: 'I'll spin 'em for a quid . . . Get set in the guts . . . Another two bob for the guts.'

1951 Eric Lambert *The Twenty Thousand Thieves* 235: 'Heads it is! I want two quid in the guts! Gentlemen, I require two fiddleys in the old comic cuts!'
1975 Les Ryan *The Shearers* 96: 'Money up or shut up!' Lofty called out. 'Four quid wanted in the guts.'

guts, rough as Extremely rough or uncouth
1966 Bruce Beaver *You Can't Come Back* 118: 'I'm shy all right, but I'm not smooth . . . I'm rough as guts.'
1968 Frank Hardy *Unlucky Australians* 11: 'The old Territorian is a good bloke, rough as guts but his heart's in the right place.'

gutser, come a To 'come a cropper' (used both literally and figuratively)
1918 *Aussie* 18 Jan. 3: 'It's stoo,' said the pugnacious looking cook, emphatically, 'and if anyone says it aint stoo he can come outside.' 'I say it aint stoo,' said Private Kummagutzer.
1919 W. H. Downing *Digger Dialects* 27: *Gutzer* A disappointment; a misfortune. 'To come a gutzer' – suffer a reverse of fortune.
1933 Norman Lindsay *Saturdee* 215: Snowey . . . stood upright on the top rail of the fence, and saying scornfully to Peter, 'Bet yer can't do this', threw himself recklessly off it and landed such a gutser that he knocked all the wind out of himself and lay there crowing and gasping.
1936 Miles Franklin *All That Swagger* 381: 'The banks will fetch old Robert a gutser one of these days.'
1945 Gavin Casey *Downhill is Easier* 127: 'They've come a gutzer once, an' they won't try again for a while.'
1953 Dymphna Cusack *Southern Steel* 385: He'd come a terrible gutser if anything ever went wrong; but nothing would ever go wrong with Anne.
1963 Jon Cleary *A Flight of Chariots* 179: 'They thought we'd knuckle under, but they came a gutser.' 'A gutser?' 'Came a thud. Made a mistake.'
1973 Patrick White *The Eye of the Storm* 493: He stumbled into a pothole:

could have come a gutser.

gutter In goldmining, the channel of an old watercourse, now auriferous

1855 William Howitt *Land, Labour and Gold* ii 275: The gold here runs in veins, or gutters as they call them, – that is, it appears to lie in the channels of the ancient watercourses, which now are buried from 80 to 160 feet in clay.

1857 *Thatcher's Colonial Songster* 8: The gutter at home, and the gutter out here, / Are things widely different, to all is quite clear.

1880 Rolf Boldrewood *The Miner's Right* (1890) 81: If we happened to drop right down on the 'gutter', or main course of the lead, we were all right.

1899 W. T. Goodge *Hits! Skits! and Jingles!* 49: The chaps that struck the gutter and the boys that whipped the cat; / We were like a band of brothers, there was no mistaking that.

1903 Joseph Furphy *Such is Life* (1944) 64: I shall pick out of each consecutive month the 9th day for amplification and comment . . . This will prospect the gutter of Life (gutter is good) at different points.

gutter-gripper A motorist who drives with one arm out of the car window gripping the 'gutter' on the roof

guzinter A schoolteacher: *obsolescent* [see quot. 1945]

1945 Baker 133: A schoolteacher is called variously a *chalk-and-talker*, *guzinter* (i.e. one 'guzinter' two, two 'guzinter' four, etc.)

1951 Dal Stivens *Jimmy Brockett* 52: I wanted to ask the old guzinter where all his bright boys were today, but I let it pass.

gym Small quantities of gold, esp. if pilfered from the mines [see quot.]

1941 K. S. Prichard *The Roaring Nineties* 209: The miners used him to get rid of a bit of gym, which was what they called the gold they got out of a mine with the Gympie hammer. It was easy to get away with in their crib bags or billies. Ibid. 379: 'It's no use objectin'

to the boys gettin' away with a bit of gym.'

gyver see **guiver**

H

hairy goat see **goat**

hall, bachelors' see **bachelors' hall**

hammer, to be on someone's To pursue, to maintain pressure upon [explained by Baker (1945:286n) as rhyming slang: *hammer and tack = track*]

1942 *Truth* 31 May 12: Someone 'drums' me there's two 'Jacks' on me 'hammer'.

1944 Lawson Glassop *We Were the Rats* 140: 'We can't stop. The Jerries might be right on our hammers for all we know.'

1955 D'Arcy Niland *The Shiralee* 37: The child was on his hammer from the moment he woke. She pestered him impatiently.

1956 Kylie Tennant *The Honey Flow* 157: 'The only way to get the best out of a dope like Mongo is to keep on his hammer all the time.'

1962 Ron Tullipan *March into Morning* 96: 'We have such a small force and the Japs are right on our hammer.'

1975 Les Ryan *The Shearers* 5: 'The shearing committee will be on your hammer later on.'

Handicap, Benghazi see **Benghazi**

hang up 1 To tether (a horse) [U.S. 1835 OED]

1859 Henry Kingsley *Recollections of Geoffry Hamlyn* i 124: 'Come down off the bridge, my love, and let us talk together while I hang up the horse.'

1887 W. S. S. Tyrwhitt *The New Chum in the Queensland Bush* 128: The three quiet horses are led out of the yard and hung up by the bridle outside.

1900 Henry Lawson 'Bill, the Ventriloquial Rooster' *Prose* i 143: The fellows from round about began to ride in and

hang up their horses round the place.
1930 Vance Palmer *The Passage* 281:
He hung up his mare at the fence and
stumbled over the uncropped grass.
1962 Alan Marshall *This is the Grass*
60: 'Why didn't you hang up your
horse outside?'
2 To hang up the shears i.e. stop work
1962 *Sydney Morning Herald* 24
Nov. 12: A shearer putting in a wet
ticket, after a majority dry vote, can
'hang up' and go to the huts without
dismissal.
1974 Les Ryan *The Shearers* 123: 'The
greasies have hung up. Why can't we?'

hanging state, the Victoria, before the
abolition of capital punishment in 1975

happy as a bastard on Father's Day see
bastard

happy as Larry see **Larry**

Harbour, our Sydney Harbour, as referred to by the local residents
1883 R. E. N. Twopeny *Town Life in
Australia* 19: I suppose that nearly
everyone has heard of the beauties of
Sydney Harbour – 'our harbour', as the
Sydneyites fondly call it.
1892 Francis Adams *Australian Life*
194: When he got to Sydney . . . he set
to taking stock of 'their harbour', their
town, and their people.
1914 Nathan Spielvogel *The Gumsucker
at Home* 111: Sydney folk ask your
opinion about 'our 'Arbour', Ballarat
folk about 'our lake', and Warrnambool
folk about 'our breakwater'.
1925 Seymour Hicks *Hullo Australians*
242: 'Our 'arbour' as its owners humorously and lovingly call it is indeed a
veritable marvel.
1933 Leslie Haylen *The Game Darrells*
186: If a resident . . . asked her what she
thought of 'our 'arbour', even then she
did not give herself away.
1940 Arnold L. Haskell *Waltzing Matilda* 136: Sydney . . . is dominated by the
Harbour, 'our harbour' as it is so
proudly called.
1965 Graham McInnes *The Road to
Gundagai* 71: 'Our 'Arbour, Our Bridge

and Our Bradman' was the Melbourne
jibe at Sydney.

hard doer A stronger version of a
'doer' q.v.
1926 K. S. Prichard *Working Bullocks*
168: Terrible Tommy's patter and jokes
. . . had been on the road as long as he
had, but never failed to make the
country people laugh – if it was only
good humouredly – to see such old
hard-doers again.
1932 Leonard Mann *Flesh in Armour*
242: He tried to reassure himself that,
after all, it had been merely a youth's
brag, the commonest sort – the brag of
being a hard-doer with the girls.
1934 Thomas Wood *Cobbers* 19: 'They
come in for miles, some of 'em, to give
it a fly. Real hard do-ers, y' know.'
1947 Gavin Casey *The Wits are Out* 55:
Everybody looked at him with amusement and admiration, and laughed.
'He's a hard doer,' someone said,
chuckling.

hard word, put the ~ on Used most
often of a man seeking sex (outside
marriage) and as the expression for
bringing matters to a point, but applied
also to other requests that approach an
ultimatum (cf. *put the acid on*)
1919 W. H. Downing *Digger Dialects*
28: *Hard word* An outrageous demand.
(Put the hard word on)
1926 J. Vance Marshall *Timely Tips for
New Australians*: To 'put the hard word
on' To make a request.
1936 H. Drake-Brockman *Sheba Lane*
192: 'I loved him, and I found out I
wasn't any better than the others when
he started to put the hard word on me.'
1939 Kylie Tennant *Foveaux* 359: The
landlord tried to make love to her, or,
as she termed it, 'put the hard word on
her.'
1945 Gavin Casey *Downhill is Easier*
16: 'We should have put the hard
word on that office bloke for a few
bob.'
1951 Dal Stivens *Jimmy Brockett* 117:
If I'd slung a diamond bracelet her way
before I'd put the hard word on her,
it'd have been a very different story.

1963 Jon Cleary *A Flight of Chariots* 178: 'I like my bit of fun, but I'm not a bastard. I don't go around putting the hard word on lonely wives.'
1972 *Sydney Morning Herald* 9 Mar. 'Look' 2: She [Lady Hasluck] deplored the absence of a museum devoted exclusively to historic Australian costumes, and added 'Is it one we should put the hard word on the Government for?'

hat, black see **black**

hat, to throw one's ~ in first To test the likely reception beforehand
1953 *Caddie A Sydney Barmaid* 248: As he walked in through the back door I said: 'Hadn't you better throw your hat in first?'
1960 Ron Tullipan *Follow the Sun* 53: 'There is, I suppose, a need to throw my hat in where you're concerned, Julie?'
1975 Xavier Herbert *Poor Fellow My Country* 343: It was Fay McFee again, declaring in her brassy contralto that she supposed she ought to throw her hat in first, but didn't have one.

hatter A bushworker who lives and works alone; a bush eccentric [? f. *mad as a hatter* OED 1849]
1853 John Rochfort *Adventures of a Surveyor* 66: The Bendigo diggings are suitable for persons working singly . . . Such persons are humorously called 'hatters'. They live alone, in a tent often not more than six feet long, three feet high, and three feet wide.
1865 *The Australian Journal* 9 Dec. 226–7: Nobody cared about him for a mate, and, indeed, he never looked after one himself, but went and worked as a hatter at some surfacing which had just been struck on the side of Ironbark Gully.
1873 Rolf Boldrewood 'The Fencing of Wanderowna' *A Romance of Canvas Town* (1898) 36: I always hated the 'hatter' or solitary shepherd system.
1883 George Darrell *The Sunny South* (1975) 34: 'Grump is a digger who fossicks and digs along without mates,

and that's what we call a hatter.'
1900 Henry Lawson 'No Place for a Woman' *Prose* i 398: I was surprised to hear of a wife, for I thought he was a hatter.
1911 C. E. W. Bean *The Dreadnought of the Darling* 99: The life [of the boundary rider] was the most solitary in Australia, and men were apt to turn into 'hatters', as they call them, strange silent fellows who from sheer disuse of human society have almost become unable to endure living amongst other men.
1928 Vance Palmer *The Man Hamilton* 196: 'I know what's the matter with you, Conlon: you're getting bush-shy, like some of these old hatters.'
1946 K. S. Prichard *The Roaring Nineties* 27: Ford was a regular hatter . . . surly and uncommunicative.
hatting
1902 Henry Lawson 'That Pretty Girl in the Army' *Prose* i 488: When a man drops mateship altogether and takes to 'hatting' in the Bush, it's a step towards a convenient tree and a couple of saddle-straps buckled together.

Hawkesbury duck See quot.: *obs.*
1845 James Tucker *The Adventures of Ralph Rashleigh* (1952) 96: He had been roasting a *Hawkesbury duck* – which was the colonial phrase for a cob of parched maize.

Hawkesbury rivers The shivers [rhyming slang]
1941 Baker 35: *Hawkesbury rivers* The shivers (rhyming slang).
1951 Dal Stivens *Jimmy Brockett* 72: I had the Hawkesbury Rivers every time I thought of what could happen if the press boys got on to it.

Hawks, the The Hawthorn V.F.L. team
1950 *Melbourne Sun* 8 Apr. 3: It was Cazaly who changed Hawthorne's nickname from the 'Mayblooms' to the 'Hawks'.
1975 *Sun-Herald* 27 Jul. 60: Hawks battle home by four points.

head over turkey see **turkey**

head, pull your ~ in Equivalent to 'shut up' or 'come off it' (in schoolboy parlance in the 1940s, 'Pull your head in, they'll think it's a cattle truck', addressed to a passing train, etc.)
1944 Lawson Glassop *We Were the Rats* 111: 'It's no use sayin', "Put ya head in, they'll think it's a cattle truck". It bloody well is a cattle truck!'
1953 T. A. G. Hungerford *Riverslake* 20: 'Pull your head in,' Charlesworth advised him, 'or get it knocked off.'
1963 John Cantwell *No Stranger to the Flame* 20: 'I know you, Max Sinclair. So pull your silly skull in.'
1974 *Australian* 4 Jan. 1: When reporters continued questions, the Minister for Minerals, Mr Connor became angry and said: 'Give us a bloody chance to work it out. Come off this, pull your bloody head in.'

heading them Playing two-up [f. throwing 'heads']
1890 A. G. Hales *Wanderings of a Simple Child* 10: I saw a large crowd of the genus digger, engaged in the refined pastime known to the elite of the back blocks as 'heading 'em'.
1897 Henry Lawson 'The Boss's Boots' *Verse* i 320: Just keep away from 'headin' 'em', and keep away from pubs.
1915 C. J. Dennis *The Songs of a Sentimental Bloke* 15: Jist 'eadin' 'em, an' doin' in me gilt.
1930 Frank Hives *The Journal of a Jackaroo* 8: On Sunday mornings there would be a 'school' in the backyard of the hotel, when the game of 'heading them' would be indulged in for high stakes.
1959 Anne von Bertouch *February Dark* 69: 'We might just as well take up heading 'em for a living,' said Peter. 'Heading 'em?' said Helen. 'Two-up,' said Max.
1964 *Sydney Morning Herald* 25 Apr. 11: A mob of ringers (station hands) in for a sublimating grog-up and full of beer and nostalgia start 'heading 'em' in the bar.

Heart, Dead see **Dead**

heifer dust A variant of bulldust [OED 1927]
1941 Baker 35: *Heifer dust* Nonsense, 'bullsh'.
1951 Dal Stivens *Jimmy Brockett* 52: If Jimmy Brockett had any say, kids would not have to clutter up their brains with a lot of the heifer dust that is pushed up to them.
1955 D'Arcy Niland *The Shiralee* 96: 'All they could do was take his money and string him a line of heifer dust as long as your arm.'

heifer paddock A girls' boarding school: *obs.*
1885 Mrs Campbell Praed *Australian Life* 50: 'Next year I shall look over a heifer-paddock in Sydney and take my pick.' N.B. Heifer-paddock in Australian slang means a ladies' school.
1897 Mark Twain *Following the Equator* 221: 'heifer-paddock' – young ladies' seminary.

hen's teeth, scarce as Very scarce [listed by Partridge as 'mostly Australian']
1965 John Beede *They Hosed Them Out* 203: 'You'll find they're as scarce as hen's teeth on this squadron.'
1966 Elwyn Wallace *Sydney and the Bush* 133: Work was scarcer than hens' teeth.
1976 *Bulletin* 16 Oct. 53: 'I'd really like to be in PR or travel, but those jobs are scarce as hen's teeth.'

herbs, give it the To give extra power (esp. applied to accelerating a car) [? f. extra taste given by the addition of herbs]
1957 Randolph Stow *The Bystander* 116: 'Go on, give him the herbs. Bet he doesn't even notice you're there.'
1961 *Age* 20 May Lit. Suppl. 17: One teaser I want explained . . . is 'herbs' for a car's horse power.
1975 Don Townshend *Gland Time* 140: 'Them glands have given him more herbs than a tractor.'

Hexham greys Mosquitoes of exceptional size [f. place-name in N.S.W.]
1895 A. B. Paterson *The Man from Snowy River* 170: They breed 'em at

Hexham, it's risky to vex 'em, / They suck a man dry at a sitting, no doubt.

1964 H. P. Tritton *Time Means Tucker* 12: The Hexham swamps are the home of the famous 'Hexham Greys', the biggest and hungriest mosquitoes in Australia, or maybe in the world. And it is no exaggeration to say there were millions of them.

Highlanders, the The Gordon (N.S.W.) Rugby Union team [f. the regiment so named]

hill, go over the ~ Abscond, clear out (Army slang)

1966 Don Crick *Period of Adjustment* 35: 'If you don't want to be in it, get out,' Jim said. 'Go over the hill.'

Hill, the The uncovered area in front of the scoreboard at Sydney Cricket Ground

1925 Seymour Hicks *Hullo Australians* 246: A place they call the Hill is occupied by thousands of barrackers . . . who are sure they understand cricket better than the umpires.

hill, the light on the see **light**

Hills, the Surry Hills, a suburb of Sydney, N.S.W.

1966 Elwyn Wallace *Sydney and the Bush* 2: Molly was one of the few who always had plenty of money and to the Hillites she was a good sport with a heart as big as The Hills itself.

holey dollar see **dollar**

holding In funds

1924 *Truth* 27 Apr. 6: *Holdin'* Possessing money.

1932 William Hatfield *Ginger Murdoch* 29: 'If you want a few bob, I'm holdin' sweet.'

1949 Ion L. Idriess *One Wet Season* 189: Sir Perceval was holding and insisted on doing the lordly.

1959 Tom Ronan *Moleskin Midas* 165: 'Well, it's like this, matey. We ain't holding too well just now.'

1963 Alan Marshall *In Mine Own Heart* 166: 'How're ya holding?' Darkie asked

me, looking intently at me with hard, suspicious eyes. 'I've got thirty bob,' I said.

holts, in At grips with; in dispute, quarrelling or fighting [f. *holt* U.S. 1823 OED]

1935 R. B. Plowman *The Boundary Rider* 123: 'Hefty looking brute. Wouldn't like to get into holts with him.'

1947 Norman Lindsay *Halfway to Anywhere* 215: 'You'll mull the part properly unless you get to holts with her like you was really doing a bear-up.'

1952 T. A. G. Hungerford *The Ridge and the River* 83: 'I noticed you and him in holts a couple of times today!'

1966 D. H. Crick *Period of Adjustment* 162: Had I come to holts with him over it, I might have said that I couldn't think of Jim Campion as being part of Furnley's machinery.

home Great Britain, from a colonial standpoint: *obsolescent*

1864 'The Rising Generation' *Thatcher's Colonial Songster* 102: At home of course you're well aware / A child is sent to school / To learn to cipher, read, and write, / That he mayn't grow up a fool: / . . . But out here those horn contrivances / Don't trouble the kids at all.

home and dried, home and hosed, home with a rug on Used of successfully completing some enterprise with a margin to spare [f. horseracing]

[**1919** W. H. Downing *Digger Dialects* 28: *Home-and-fried* Safe, correct.]

1922 Arthur Wright *A Colt from the Country* 37: 'If my prayers can help him,' laughed Sadie, 'he's home and dried, as Tommy would say.'

1934 Thomas Wood *Cobbers* 96: Charles would make a book . . . and he would lay two to one port-wine jelly, five to two apple pie. Nine times out of ten he was, in his own phrase, home in the stall with a rug on.

1951 Dal Stivens *Jimmy Brockett* 219: I was home and dried.

1959 Eric Lambert *Glory Thrown In* 219: 'Look!' he yelled to Christy. 'A

and C Companies home and hosed!'
1967 Frank Hardy *Billy Borker Yarns Again* 18: 'Don't tell a soul: number six, Hairy Legs, is home and hosed.'
1972 *Bulletin* 26 Aug. 11: The government is home and hosed and can thank the budget.

homestead Used in a special sense like 'house' q.v. for the residence of the owner or manager on a station, significantly set apart from the barracks and the men's hut [N.Z. 1849 OED]
1903 Joseph Furphy *Such is Life* (1944) 66: I had drawn up to Goolumbulla homestead with six tons of wire. The manager, Mr Spanker ...
1952 Jon Cleary *The Sundowners* 221: Halstead was a good bloke, better than most bosses; but the homestead was an enemy camp and no worker worth his salt ever stepped across the boundary.
1965 Graham McInnes *The Road to Gundagai* 248: Everyone knew that J. M. Molesworth was the boss, that he lived in an enormous homestead and that he was worth a hundred pounds or so.

hominy Prison food, used in expressions like 'hominy bus', 'hominy gazette' (gaol rumours)
1895 Cornelius Crowe *Australian Slang Dictionary* 36: *Hominey* prison fare.
1953 Baker 129: The jail tram that runs between Darlinghurst Police Station and Long Bay Gaol is called the *hominy bus*.
1919 J. Vance Marshall *The World of the Living Dead* 85: O, no more I'll quiz The Hominy Gazette for shearin' news / Or'll use the Holy Bible fer me fags.

honey bag As for 'sugar bag' q.v.
1931 Vance Palmer *Separate Lives* 65: He imitated the old king cutting out a honey-bag with the bees around him.

honkoe Vague term of abuse: *rare* [cf. U.S. *honkie* abusive term directed towards whites by blacks]
1953 Baker 106: *honk*, a bad smell.
1965 William Dick *A Bunch of Ratbags* 42: 'I don't care about them honkoes

over at the Mont, they're only wackers.'

hooer Possibly a variant of 'whore', but applied to men in a generally derogatory way, like 'bastard'
1952 T. A. G. Hungerford *The Ridge and the River* 31: Cranky old hooer! White thought, with a wry smile. Always on the bloody job.
1962 Stuart Gore *Down the Golden Mile* 152: 'What the hell's those two silly hooers tryin' to *do* – kill their bloody selves!'
1975 Les Ryan *The Shearers* 63: 'Ar, go to blazes, you drunken hooer.'

hook up To 'pull' a racehorse, deliberately prevent it from winning
1949 Lawson Glassop *Lucky Palmer* 245: 'Owners always want favourites hooked up. I know it all.'

hooks, put the hooks into As for 'put the nips into'

hoon A procurer of prostitutes; general term of insult
1938 Xavier Herbert *Capricornia* 338: 'You flash hoon,' he went on.
1953 Baker 124: *hoon* or (by rhyme) *silver spoon*, a procurer of prostitutes.
1973 Jim McNeil *The Chocolate Frog* 48: 'A hoon! A weak mug that bludges beer money off weak molls!'
1976 *Cleo* Aug. 33: Hoon is a nebulous sort of word. It means someone living off the girls. He is not a pimp for them, he can be a standover man. It is an insult to be called a hoon ... something worse then a bludger.

hoop A jockey [origin obscure]
1941 Baker 36: *Hoop* A jockey.
1949 Lawson Glassop *Lucky Palmer* 245: 'It'll be a soda for a hoop like you. It won't be hard to get her beaten.'
1951 Dal Stivens *Jimmy Brockett* 100: We dropped hints to various hoops, owners and trainers we'd done favours for that we didn't want their horses to win.
1969 Alan O'Toole *The Racing Game* 79: 'We'll see if this hoop of yours has turned up.'

1975 *Bulletin* 28 Jun. 66: He was very fast at writing large-type headlines for the page one – like . . . Star Weds Top Hoop.

Hooray, Hooroo Equivalent to 'Cheerio' as a farewell
1931 William Hatfield *Sheepmates* 238: 'Well, hooroo!' And he was gone in the direction where the fire glowed like a dropped cigarette butt.
1939 Kylie Tennant *Foveaux* 278: 'Well, hoo-ray, I'll be seeing you.'
1942 Leonard Mann *The Go-Getter* 221: 'So long, Chris.' 'Hooray, boy.'
1951 Dymphna Cusack and Florence James *Come in Spinner* 396: Lofty thrust his head through the window and waved. 'Hoorroo!'
1959 Anne von Bertouch *February Dark* 193: 'We'll see you later. Hooray.'
1969 Patsy Adam Smith *Folklore of the Australian Railwaymen* 175: Then he said 'Hooroo' and I left to take the seven camels back the 350 miles by myself.

hoot Money [N.Z. 1879: see quot. 1896]
1881 G. C. Evans *Stories Told Round the Campfire* 265: Why the very stuff you are now drinking has been bought with 'hoot' obtained from stolen goods.
1896 *Truth* 12 Jan. 4: There are several specimens of bush language transplanted from the Maori language. 'Hoot' is a very frequent synonym for money or wage . . . The Maori equivalent for money is *utu* pronounced . . . with the last syllable clipped.
1898 Joshua Lake *Australasian Supplement* to *Webster's International Dictionary* 2024: *Hoot* (Maori *utu* vengeance) Payment; reward; recompense; rate of wages (Slang, N.Z.)
1937 Xavier Herbert *Capricornia* 301: 'On the construction you could make a pot of hoot in no time.'
1942 Sarah Campion *Bonanza* 154: 'Carn't raise the hoot, ole Mick carn't!' they said.
1962 Hal Porter *A Bachelor's Children* 185: 'He's got plenty of hoot; has shares in everything from here to Perth.'
1977 *Sun-Herald* 24 Jul. 111: 'It's about

a Q.C. and his wife, who live in Point Piper and obviously have lots of hoot'.

horse, jump a ~ over the bar, eat or drink a ~ To sell a horse for liquor or supplies
1900–10 O'Brien and Stephens: *Jumping your horse over the bar* to sell his horse or mortgage it to the publican so as to prolong his spree.
1904 Laura M. Palmer-Archer *A Bush Honeymoon* 349: *Jumped over the bar* Paid away for liquor.
1919 E. S. Sorenson *Chips and Splinters* 34: It had been . . . given to a rabbit-poisoner known as 'Billy-the Rooster' for a skewbald packhorse which Billy had 'jumped over the bar'.
1957 'The Poor Bushman' in *Old Bush Songs* ed. Stewart and Keesing 229: My horses all sold – they'd jumped over the bar –/ And I got the dirty kick-out.
1962 Tom Ronan *Deep of the Sky* 101: When his rations were exhausted he 'ate a horse' – that is, sold one for what he could get and converted the proceeds into supplies.

horse, to sell a See quots
1964 Tom Ronan *Packhorse and Pearling Boat* 234: 'Selling a horse' . . . a very simple substitute for the cards and dice and, when there are fourteen in the party, much quicker. The barman collects the two bobs and, on a scrap of paper, writes down a number between fifty and a hundred. Then the party forms up in a group, someone starts counting at any number between one and ten, and whoever calls the figure the barman has written down scoops the pool.
1939 R. H. Croll *I Recall* 54: You 'sell a horse' by putting in a shilling apiece, one member writes a number down privately, then all count as in a kiddies' game. The person who calls the hidden number scoops the pool and buys the drinks.

horse, working off a dead see **dead horse**

hosed, home and see **home**

hostie An air hostess [abbr.]
1975 *Australian* 26 Mar. 10: For poor
old Western Australia, already isolated
by flooded railway lines and impassable
roads, the final separation caused by
the hosties' strike is the last straw.

hottie A hotwater bottle [abbr.]

house, the On a station, the residence
of the owner or manager, and so distinct
from the accommodation for the station
hands (the men's hut), for the jackeroos
(the barracks) and others
1869 Marcus Clarke *The Peripatetic
Philosopher* 41: At the station where I
worked for some time . . . three cooks
were kept during the 'wallaby' season
– one of the house, one for the men,
and one for the travellers.
1876 A. J. Boyd *Old Colonials* (1882)
81: 'The squatters know well enough
when a man is fit for the house or the
kitchen, and they consider a gentleman's a gentleman, no matter what he's
employed at.'
1893 J. A. Barry *Steve Brown's Bunyip*
202: The dealer, having pretty well
cleaned out 'the hut', determined to
try his luck at 'the House'.
1901 Rolf Boldrewood *In Bad Company*
285: After the changes which turned
the homesteads of the larger stations
into small villages, the 'big house', as
it came to be called, was no longer
expected to accommodate the proprietor, the overseer, and the young gentlemen learning Colonial experience, in
addition to every wanderer that turned
up. The overseer generally had a com-
modious if, perhaps, plainly-furnished
cottage allotted to him. This came to be
known as the 'barracks', and to be used
as a convenient abode for strangers and
pilgrims, as well as for the storekeeper,
the working overseers, and the young
gentlemen.
1921 M. E. Fullerton *Bark House Days*
117: I was a favourite with the men,
being even then a reader of the newspapers. I constituted myself the medium
by which the huts were supplied with
the weeklies as soon as the house was
finished with them.

1936 William Hatfield *Australia
Through the Windscreen* 64: It is pitiful
to see the perturbation on the face of a
manager when a presentably dressed
traveller pulls up at a station where he
must be given accommodation, trying
to guess correctly whether the stranger
is a 'house' or a 'hut' man.
1973 John Morrison *Australian by
Choice* 116: Across the garden I had
got a glimpse of the long verandah of
the House; coloured lights, moving
figures: the Boss and his wife, the
Overseer, one of the jackeroos, guests
from a neighbouring station.

Howe, Jacky Sleeveless flannel shirt [f.
shearer (1855–1922) so named]
1930 *Bulletin* 9 Apr. 19: Long Jim was
telling us how . . . it took nine bars of
soap to wash his 'Jacky Howe' flannel.
1933 Acland: *Jacky Howe* Sleeveless
singlet, cut nearly to the waist under
the arms.
1940 Ion L. Idriess *Lightning Ridge* 97:
He was clad only in loose pants and a
Jacky Howe flannel.
1949 Ruth Park *Poor Man's Orange*
122: He had finished his tea and was
sitting in his Jackie Howe, which is a
singlet with the sleeves out of it, and
called after a famous shearer, of the
blade days.

hoy Bingo or housie: Queensland [? f.
shout]
1975 Bruce Dawe *Just a Dugong at
Twilight* 30: The State Crown Law
Office, Queensland, was called upon to
decide whether the game known as
'Hoy' was illegal or not.

Hoyt's, the man outside The commissionaire outside Hoyt's Theatre in Melbourne in the 1930s, so elaborately
dressed as to seem a person of consequence, and jocularly referred to as the
authority for various reports
1953 Baker 133: *Hoyts, the man outside*
A mythical person who starts all false
rumours; the source of stolen property
which an innocent(!) receiver is found
to have in his possession.
1961 Frank Hardy *The Hard Way* 85:

'Struth, it's funny enough for a fat bludger dressed up like the man outside Hoyt's[1] to come into a prison cell in the middle of the night.' [1]Uniformed announcer outside Hoyt's Theatre in Melbourne who wears a most elaborate uniform.

1966 Hal Porter *The Paper Chase* 64: The Regent, the State, the Capitol, the Plaza, Hoyt's de Luxe (where the commissionaire, hoarsely and non-stop, brays himself into fame and the Australian vernacular as The Man Outside Hoyt's) — are, at the height of the Depression, at the height of their magnificence.

1975 *Sydney Morning Herald* 5 Jul. 9: We might be better off to abandon pre-selections and elections, and choose our politicians by having the Governor (or the man outside Hoyts) stick pins into the telephone book.

Hughie Name given to God in the outback, esp. in the expression 'Send 'er down, Hughie' used when it is raining hard [Partridge lists 'Send her down, David']

1918 L. J. Villiers *The Changing Year* 12: Down Hughie* pours *Hughie = the rain.

[1919 W. H. Downing *Digger Dialects* 44: *Send her down, Steve! Let it rain on.*]

1922 *Bulletin* 26 Jan. 22: The missionary tackled him [the aboriginal boy] with 'Who made this country, Peter?' 'Dunno' — says Peter — 'was here when I came.' 'Well,' says Parson, 'who is it makes the rain?' Peter knew that all right. 'Ole Hughie,' he answered promptly.

1946 K. S. Prichard *The Roaring Nineties* 30: Miners and prospectors would turn out and yell to a dull, dirty sky clouded with red dust: 'Send her down! Send her down, Hughie!'

1951 Seaforth Mackenzie *Dead Men Rising* 210: 'All you want to do is get married and have kids,' he said. 'Don't worry about the money. Hughie looks after that, my boy.' The Corporal was diverted. 'Who's this Hughie?' he said ... 'Ah,' Gell said, affecting a gravity which was not altogether false. 'You don't say "God", you see, because

nobody believes in God but everybody believes in Hughie. I dunno — it's just a thing you hear the boys say.' Ibid. 207: 'Hughie's throwing it down all right.'

1964 H. P. Tritton *Time Means Tucker* 92: With only a couple of thousand to go 'Hughie' answered the prayers of the loppies with a fairly heavy shower. Ibid. 42: To the best of my belief, it was at Charlton [in 1905] that 'Hughie' as the chief deity in the job of controlling the weather came into being.

1969 Osmar White *Under the Iron Rainbow* 163: The clouds burst. 'Send her down, Huey!' cried the man in the wheelchair, raising clenched fists and flinging back his head.

1975 Robert Macklin *The Queenslander* 30: He threw his head back and laughed as the rain splashed on his face. 'Send her down, Hughie.'

hum *n.* A cadger, sponger: *derogatory*

1915 J. P. Bourke *Off the Bluebush* 190: If you cannot be a spendthrift, be a hum.

1919 J. Vance Marshall *The World of the Living Dead* 70: Almost beneath the bottom rung of the social ladder there is ... the 'hum', the unskilled derelict or derelict-to-be who stands upon the 'pub' corner kerb, 'bites' all and sundry, and, at regular intervals succeeds in getting lumbered for 'vag'.

1937 *Best Australian One-Act Plays* 163: 'Generally winds up with ... one of 'em nipping you for a couple of bob ... Perfect hums some of 'em.'

1953 *Caddie A Sydney Barmaid* 183: In a class of his own is the hum. Some of these are casuals, temporarily out of cash, but with an unquenchable thirst. But it's the professional who merits recognition, for he has developed the technique of the bite until it is almost one of arts.

1957 D'Arcy Niland *Call Me When the Cross Turns Over* 136: 'Rigby's a twister. He's a hum and a liar.'

hum *v.* To borrow, scrounge (not used in such a pejorative sense as the noun)

1915 J. P. Bourke *Off the Bluebush* 77: Got no coin to treat a pal! Got no face to hum!

1919 W. H. Downing *Digger Dialects* 29: *Humm* To cadge.

1919 W. R. Harris *Outback in Australia* 47: 'What'll happen to *us* if you townies start on the 'humming' game?'

1937 Xavier Herbert *Capricornia* 257: 'You're only humming for a drink. Nick off home.'

humbug Used not only to imply sham and deception, but also to suggest nuisance, fuss and bother, trouble: *rare* [? Pidgin]

1937 Xavier Herbert *Capricornia* 275: 'Do you like the job?' 'No-more!' she cried, wrinkling a pretty nose. 'All dem sister proper humbug.' 'How's that?' 'All time roustin'. All time tink we go out wid boys.'

1946 W. E. Harney *North of 23°* 158–9: The greatest problem on station, mission or government compound is the dogs ... Should you become desperate and destroy a number of these dogs, the natives might be annoyed at first, but afterwards they would tell you that 'it more better, as dog too much humbug'.

1959 C. V. Lawlor *All This Humbug* 21: 'How came it [Humbug Creek] by that name?' 'Well, they tell me that a man named John Regan discovered it, and because it was such a nuisance when it was in flood, and hard to find in his exploring trips from the Bland, he called it a Humbug.'

hump bluey, the drum, the swag To follow the life of the swagman, carrying one's belongings on one's back

1855 William Howitt *Land, Labour and Gold* i 226: He 'humped his swag', in diggers' phrase that is, shouldered his pack, and disappeared in the woods.

1861 *Penguin Book of Australian Ballads* (1964) 87: No more through the bush we'll go humping the drum.

1883 R. E. N. Twopeny *Town Life in Australia* 244–5: He 'humps his drum', or 'swag', and 'starts on the wallaby track', i.e. shoulders the bundle containing his worldly belongings, and goes out pleasuring.

1892 Henry Lawson 'Jack Dunn of Nevertire', *Verse* i 222: He humped his bluey by the name of 'Dunn of Nevertire'.

1895 A. B. Paterson *The Man from Snowy River* 84: The lonely swagman through the dark / Must hump his swag past Chandos Park.

1898 David W. Carnegie *Spinifex and Sand* 156: He had saved enough money to pay his passage to Perth; and from there he 'humped his bluey' to Coolgardie, and took a job as a miner.

1911 E. M. Clowes *On the Wallaby Through Victoria* 278: An expression used for what in England we call 'tramping' is 'humping the swag' or 'the bluey'.

1934 Tom Clarke *Marriage at 6 a.m.* 46: *Hump your bluey* pack up, move on.

1943 Maurice Clough *We of the A.I.F.* 45: Men who have lived on billy tea / And damper, humping their 'bluey'.

1961 George Farwell *Vanishing Australians* 44: 'When I first set eyes on him, he was humping his drum, hoofing it down the road from Tilpa.'

humpy An Aboriginal bark hut (Morris, 1846), but also applied to any rude shelter or hut constructed by a white

1881 A. C. Grant *Bush Life in Queensland* i 133: To dwell in the familiar old bark 'humpy', so full of happy memories. The roof was covered with sheets of bark held down by large wooden riders pegged in the form of a square to one another. [Morris]

1896 Henry Lawson 'In A Dry Season' *Prose* i 79–80: The only town I saw that differed much from the above consisted of a box-bark humpy with a clay chimney, and a woman standing at the door throwing out the wash-up water.

1919 Edward Dyson *The Escapades of Ann* 91: Ryan was an unmitigated nuisance, his old humpy was an eyesore in a neighbourhood that was beginning rather to fancy itself.

1924 *Truth* 27 Apr. 6: *Humpy* bush hut.

1931 Vance Palmer *Separate Lives* 12: His humpy was on the edge of the settlement, a ragged lean-to made of slabs and old iron that he had built in his spare time out of such scraps as his neighbours discarded.

1949 Ion L. Idriess *One Wet Season* 83: A fair-sized bush humpy, built of cypress-pine, cool and roomy, roofed with paperbark, walled by corrugated iron, hobstone floor.

1959 Dorothy Hewett *Bobbin Up* 19: Looking round the three-roomed humpy, sunken sideways with damp and age.

hungry Grasping, stingy, often as part of a nickname: *derogatory*

1855 William Howitt *Land, Labour and Gold* ii 294: At one station I asked two men who were resting with their cart by the road-side whose station that was? 'Hungry Scott's' was the reply.

1891 Rolf Boldrewood *A Sydney Side Saxon* 166: 'I was never to say stingy about a trifle of rations like 'hungry Jackson'.

1895 A. B. Paterson 'Saltbush Bill' *Collected Poems* 27: And he knew where the hungry owners were that hurried his sheep ahead.

1902 Henry Lawson 'Two Sundowners' *Prose* i 99: They came to a notoriously 'hungry' station, where there was a Scottish manager and storekeeper.

1936 Miles Franklin *All That Swagger* 320–1: If Danny had been known as Hungry Delacy instead of Honest Danny he might have transmitted a strain to make his sons financial nabobs.

1948 K. S. Prichard *Golden Miles* 74: 'There's some hungry bastards,' the men said, 'making big money on their ore, and never give the poor bugger boggin' for 'em a sling back.'

1959 Dorothy Hewett *Bobbin Up* 198: 'She works two jobs in two mills and she's hungry . . . She's real bonus-happy.'

1962 J. Marshall and R. Drysdale *Journey Among Men* 153: The old story of the 'hungry' sheepfarmer who . . . runs as many sheep as possible on unimproved pastures.

1975 Les Ryan *The Shearers* 51: 'There are some hungry bastards in the game.'

Hungry Mile, the The part of Sussex Street, Sydney, fringing the waterfront, with the office of the Waterside Workers

Federation

1930 Ernest Antony *The Hungry Mile* 5: To see Sydney wharfies tramping down the hungry mile.

1957 Tom Nelson *The Hungry Mile* 75: The stretch along Sussex Street was called the 'Hungry Mile' by the wharfies . . . a very apt title indeed.

1960 Ron Tullipan *Follow the Sun* 173: 'I'm going to the Hungry Mile to be a wharfie.'

1973 *Sydney Morning Herald* 2 Aug. 7: When I was much younger the 'Hungry Mile' of Sydney waterfront was an area of glamour.

hunt To drive away, dismiss

1870 Rolf Boldrewood 'Shearing in Riverina' *In Bad Company* (1901) He . . . makes a calculation as to who are unreasonably bad, and who, therefore, will have to be 'hunted'.

1928 Arthur Wright *A Good Recovery* 69: 'Walk!' she repeated. 'My horse – ' 'I've hunted Boora. You're coming with me, or walking home.'

1941 Kylie Tennant *The Battlers* 235: 'Thanks for looking after the kid.' 'I couldn't do no less,' the woman answered loudly. 'I'm not one to hunt kids.'

1953 T. A. G. Hungerford *Riverslake* 24: 'The grog's got him. He'll get hunted soon.'

1975 Xavier Herbert *Poor Fellow My Country* 1132: 'What'll I do . . . hunt him?'

hunt up a cow see **cow**

hut, the (men's) On a station, the accommodation provided for the station-hands, usually a large structure, but distinct from 'the house' and 'the barracks' qq.v.

1843 Charles Rowcroft *Tales of the Colonies* ii 258: 'Mr Clover came into the hut, the men's hut . . . John Buttress did not go on being ordered out: Mr Clover then took him by the collar, and shoved him out of the hut.'

1869 Marcus Clarke *The Peripatetic Philosopher* 41: I have seen as many as twenty able bodied hungry men come up to a home-station with the stereo-

typed inquiry, 'Want any hands, sir?'
and receiving a reply in the negative
. . . go merrily down to the 'men's hut'
and, having smoked, eat some two
pounds of 'fat wether' per man.

1873 A. Trollope *Australia* ed. Edwards
and Joyce (1967) 138: The labouring
man . . . is sent to the 'hut'. There is a
hut at every station, fitted up with
bunks, in which the workmen sleep.
Here the wanderer is allowed to stretch
his blanket for the night – and on all
such occasions two meals are allowed
him.

1893 J. A. Barry *Steve Brown's Bunyip*
202: The dealer, having pretty well
cleared out 'the Hut', determined to try
his luck at 'the House'.

1901 Rolf Boldrewood *In Bad Company*
11: The 'men's hut' came first into
view – a substantial dwelling, with hor-
izontal sawn slabs and shingled roof, a
stone chimney and a dining-room.

1911 E. M. Clowes *On the Wallaby
Through Victoria* 103: The shearers live
– that is, sleep and eat – in what is
known as 'the hut', a long narrow
structure with bunks at either side, in
two tiers, each bunk just long enough
to hold a man.

1931 William Hatfield *Sheepmates* 76:
'Rough diamond, you know, used to be
in the Hut – stockman, horse-breaker
and all that you know, though I say
you can't hold it against a man because
he came from the Hut.'

hut, upside-down see **upside-down**

hydraulic (jack) Nickname for anyone
with the habit of 'lifting' things, i.e. a
thief, esp. on the waterfront

1977 *Sunday Telegraph* 24 Apr. 136:
'They call him Hydraulic – he'll lift
anything that isn't nailed down'.

I

iceberg Someone who regularly takes
an early morning swim throughout the
winter, esp. as a member of a club;
anyone who braves the water on a cold
morning

1932 L. W. Lower *Here's Another* 12:
'One of the toughest surfs I've experienced this winter. All the Icebergs
agreed.'

1952 A. G. Mitchell Suppl. to Chambers' *Shorter English Dictionary* 796:
Iceberg one who surfs regularly
throughout the winter.

1964 Tom Ronan *Packhorse and Pearling Boat* 79–80: I admit that I did not
join the icebergs who favoured cold
showers even on the bitterest winter
mornings.

1974 Geoffrey Lehmann *A Spring Day
in Autumn* 174: 'I'm a regular swimmer
myself, right in the middle of winter.
They reckon I'm the oldest iceberg in
Sydney.'

identity (old) A resident of long standing in a particular place [N.Z.: see quot.
1874]

1862 *Thatcher's Dunedin Songster* 2:
'The Old Identity' [song title]

1874 Alexander Bathgate *Colonial Experiences* 26: The term 'old identities'
took its origin from an expression in a
speech made by one of the members of
the Provincial Council, Mr E. B. Cargill,
who in speaking of the new arrivals,
said that the early settlers should endeavour to preserve their old identity.
The strangers, who were inclined to
laugh at the aboriginals as a set of old
stagers, caught up the phrase, and
dubbed them 'old identities'. A comic
singer helped to perpetuate the name
by writing a song.

1880 Rolf Boldrewood *The Miner's
Right* (1890) 213: Some of the old
identities still survived.

1885 *The Australasian Printers' Keepsake* 15: The 'old identities' of Stawell
become quite garrulous concerning this
most famous street of tents.

1896 Edward Dyson *Rhymes from the
Mines* 42: 'Twas old Flynn, the identity,
told us / That the creek always ran
pretty high.

1901 F. J. Gillen *Diary* (1968) 11: Met
Harry Pannell an old identity of the
interior who has been a teamster on
three inhospitable roads since the days
of the construction of the line.

1915 J. P. Bourke *Off the Bluebush* 94:

'Dan the Hatter An Old North Country Identity' [poem title]
1929 Jules Raeside *Golden Days* 42: Volumes could be written about many of the identities of those days.
1937 A. W. Upfield *Mr Jelly's Business* 77: 'Several of the old identities swear that he must be nearer ninety than eighty.'
1973 Alexander Buzo *Rooted* 77: 'I was in the pub having a quiet beer with a few Werris Creek identities, when this bloke came up and started picking a blue with Simmo.'

ignore, to treat with To deliberately ignore someone's presence or request
1938 *Bulletin* 6 Jul. 26: The habit of 'treating with ignore' our own industrial experience is quite wrong.
1943 Baker 83: *Treat with ignore, to* To overrule (Digger slang).
1946 Alan Marshall *Tell us about the Turkey, Jo* 202: At first he treats me with ignore, then he answers me back, then he just looks at me.
1963 John O'Grady *The Things They Do to You* 110: I saw her a couple of times, and attempted to discuss the work and the weather . . . But, as we used to say in those days [in the war], she 'treated me with ignore'.
1975 *Sydney Morning Herald* 1 Jul. 7: With gathering speed downhill, the train treated Wollstonecraft with ignore.

illywhacker A professional trickster, esp. operating at country shows [derived by Baker (1945:138) from *spieler*]
1941 Kylie Tennant *The Battlers* 183–4: An illy-wacker is someone who is putting a confidence trick over, selling imitation diamond tie-pins, new-style patent razors or infallible 'tonics' . . . 'living on the cockies' by such devices, and following the shows because money always flows freest at show time. A man who 'wacks the illy' can be almost anything, but two of these particular illy-wackers were equipped with a dart game.
1943 Baker 40: *Illywhacker* A trickster or spieler.

1975 Hal Porter *The Extra* 15: Social climber, moron, peter-tickler, eeler-spee, illy-wacker.

imbo An imbecile; a criminal's victim [prison slang]
1953 Baker 125: Australia's underworldsters have commemorated the services of their victims by calling them any of these assorted terms: . . . *imbo*.
1974 Jim McNeil *How Does Your Garden Grow* 141: *Imbo* (colloquial abbreviation) imbecile.

in it, to be To participate, join in a planned action (in the imperative, usually an appeal to group loyalty)
1928 Arthur Wright *A Good Recovery* 37: 'It's a queer business,' ventured Trilet, 'and if I'm to be in it, I want to know the strength of it.'
1945 Gavin Casey *Downhill is Easier* 149: 'We're goin' for a couple o' days shootin' in the mornin',' South said to me. 'You'd better be in it.'
1951 Frank Hardy *Power Without Glory* 520: Just then an enthusiastic marcher called out. 'Be in it, mate', and the man dragged the woman after him. 'Come on, Liz. We gotta march with 'em.'
1957 John O'Grady *They're a Weird Mob* 88: 'Are you on?' 'Am I on?' 'Yeah, will yer be in ut?' 'Thank you, Joe. I will be in it'. 'Good-o. Bring yer gear out Saturday.'
1962 Alan Seymour *The One Day of the Year* 68: 'It's too sweet, that stuff. I won't have any.' 'Go on, be in it.'
1965 William Dick *A Bunch of Ratbags* 198: Elaine continued to try to coax me to come into her place to sleep with her, but I wouldn't be in it.

inked Drunk, incapacitated
1898 *Bulletin* 1 Oct. 14: To get drunk is to get 'inked'.
1919 W. H. Downing *Digger Dialects* 29: *Inked* Drunk.
1924 *Truth* 27 Apr. 6: *Inked* To be drunk.
1951 A. W. Upfield *The New Shoe* 94: 'What is he like when properly inked?' 'Quiet as Mary's lamb,' was the surprising answer. 'Ten beers and he goes

to sleep.'
1969 Patsy Adam Smith *Folklore of the Australian Railwaymen* 85: Driver found well and truly inked and lying down to it.

Innisfail, in jail at see **Tallarook**

I.P. 1 Intending purchaser
1876 Rolf Boldrewood *A Colonial Reformer* (1890) 187: I hope the I.P. (intending purchaser) is a good plucked one.
2 Irate parent (visiting a school)

iron, good Expression of approval or agreement: *obsolescent* [see quot. 1908: Partridge lists *bad iron* a failure, a mishap, bad luck]
1895 *Bulletin* 9 Feb. 15: Oh, she's a good iron, is my little clinah.
1898 *Bulletin* 17 Dec. Red Page: Good-iron, synonymous with 'Bravo!'
1908 *Australian Magazine* 1 Nov. 1250: 'Good iron', a very Australian approbatory ejaculation, comes from quoits, the players in the old days being wont to call the phrase after the manner of 'good ball' of the cricketers.
1936 Miles Franklin *All That Swagger* 100: 'Good iron! I don't rob little boys.'
1941 Baker 32: *Good iron* (something) good, pleasant, desired.

iron *v.* To 'flatten'
1953 Baker 104: *To iron*, to attack or fight (a person) i.e. *to flatten* him.
1965 William Dick *A Bunch of Ratbags* 228: Argles was ready behind the big bloke to king-hit him and iron him out.
1970 Barry Oakley *A Salute to the Great McCarthy* 37: 'You see their bruiser over there? Leave him to me. First, I iron him out, that's the signal. Then we run all over them.'
1974 Jim McNeil *How Does Your Garden Grow* 126: 'How many [pills] yer take?' 'Told yer. Half a dozen.' 'Oh well, that'll iron yer right out.'

Island, the Cockatoo Island Gaol (until 1919)
1910 Henry Lawson 'The Rising of the Court' *Prose* i 664: The Sergeant seems anxious to let Mrs Johnson off lightly. It means anything from twenty-four hours or five shillings to three months on the Island for her.

Isle, the Apple see **Apple**

issue, that's the Equivalent to 'That's the lot' [Services slang]
1919 W. H. Downing *Digger Dialects* 29: *Issue* (1) A portion; (2) 'to get one's issue' – to be killed.
1930 Frederic Manning *Her Privates We* 351: 'What are you talkin' about?' ...'The whole bloody issue,' said Bourne, comprehensively. 'Officers, and other ranks.'
1941 Baker 38: *Issue* All, everything, the lot.
1962 Alan Seymour *The One Day of the Year* 73: 'Y' got no family, a room in a boardin' 'ouse – and us. And that's the issue.'

J

jack 1 The anus, backside
[1896 J. S. Farmer and W. E. Henley *Slang and its Analogues* iv 33: *Jacksy-pardy*, the posteriors]
1951 Seaforth Mackenzie *Dead Men Rising* 196: 'He thinks the feller had it [the concealed cord] up his jack ... It's so thin it'd easily go into the rectum.'
2 *The jack* Venereal disease
1954 T. A. G. Hungerford *Sowers of the Wind* 3: 'Pencillin'll take care of that. They reckon they just pump you full of it, and bingo! No more jack!'
1958 Hal Porter *A Handful of Pennies* 23: 'Jack is the euphemism,' said the Major, 'for venereal disease.'
1962 Alan Marshall *This is the Grass* 164: 'I tell you I was crook. I wanted to get to town. It's no good, a man with jack on the job.'
1971 David Ireland *The Unknown Industrial Prisoner* 37: 'You bastards tell me if he pisses in there with us. I don't want the jack.'
jacked up Infected
1962 Alan Marshall *This is the Grass*

164: 'I got a dose from a sheila I went out with . . . she was jacked up and I was the mug.'

jack of, to be To be fed up with something, to the point of rejecting or abandoning it
1896 Edward Dyson *Rhymes from the Mines* 98: No, you can't count me in, boys; I'm off it – /I'm jack of them practical jokes.
1908 E. G. Murphy *Jarrahland Jingles* 58: And Brim's in London on his 'ace', /Of Andrew Barr a trifle 'jack'.
1944 Jean Devanny *By Tropic, Sea and Jungle* 155: I used to like to get out on my pat for a week – prospecting you know – but not for more than a week. Too much of it makes you jack of it quick.
1965 William Dick *A Bunch of Ratbags* 69: 'There ain't nothin' much to do, is there? I'm getting jack of these holidays.'
1970 Jessica Anderson *The Last Man's Head* 201: 'You know my feelings about it, I made them clear the other day. I'm jack of it.'

jack up *v*. 1 To give in, collapse [*To jack up* To give up suddenly or promptly OED 1873]
1903 Joseph Furphy *Such is Life* (1944) 178: 'I ain't a man to jack-up while I got a sanguinary leg to stan' on; but I'm gone on the inside, some road.'
2 To reject, abandon [*To jack up* to throw up, give up, abandon OED 1873]
1880 Henry Kendall 'Jim the Splitter' *Poetical Works* ed. T. T. Reed (1966) 159: The nymph in green valleys of Thessaly dim / Would never 'jack up' her old lover for him.
1880 Rolf Boldrewood *The Miner's Right* (1890) 35: Having that morning decided to 'jack up' or thoroughly abandon work at our present claim.
1895 Cornelius Crowe *The Australian Slang Dictionary* 39: Jacked Up (or chucked up), suddenly leaving off doing work.
3 To refuse orders, esp. as a collective action (Services slang); to refuse or abandon a task assigned, as though going

on a protest strike
1898 Rolf Boldrewood *A Romance of Canvas Town* 253: The half-used plates and dishes were to me as things loathsome. They operated prejudicially upon my dinners in prospect even, as well as upon those which had 'gone before'. So, as a man, a gentleman, and a squatter, I 'jacked up' at the cookery.
1936 Miles Franklin *All That Swagger* 470: 'Grandfather always took Grandma with him everywhere until she jacked up.'
1951 Eric Lambert *The Twenty Thousand Thieves* 277: The night parade was fixed for seven. When the time arrived, only the N.C.O.s remained in the company lines . . . B Company had 'jacked-up'!
1959 David Forrest *The Last Blue Sea* 38: 'They'll jack-up like they did on the Townsville wharf.'

jack up *n*. The action of refusing orders, esp. if collective
1948 Sumner Locke Elliott *Rusty Bugles* in *Khaki, Bush and Bigotry* ed. Eunice Hanger (1968) 94: 'By gee, if I'm not on the next draft I'm telling you there's going to be the biggest jack-up you ever saw.'
1953 *The Sunburnt Country* ed. Ian Bevan 125: This jacking up is a procedure which no army but the Australian could tolerate. It is not mutiny . . . It consists simply of selecting some minor regimental parade or order and boycotting it, to a man, as a public expression of a legitimate grievance.
1959 *Daily Telegraph* 16 Sep. 19: Askin backs 'Jack-Up' of Bus Drivers.

jackaroo (jackeroo) A young man of good connections working on a station as a cadet to gain experience of station management
1873 Rolf Boldrewood 'The Fencing of Wanderowna' *A Romance of Canvas Town* (1898) 70: 'It's very hard on the poor man . . . You won't want no hands from shearing except two or three Jackaroos.'
1878 G. H. Gibson *Southerly Busters* 19n: Young gentlemen getting their

'colonial experience' in the bush are called 'jackeroos' by the station-hands.

1877 *Tibb's Popular Songbook:* With crawlers two and a Jackeroo / You make a noble start.

1896 Henry Lawson 'She Wouldn't Speak' *Prose* i 114: There was a lot of jackeroo swells [in the pub dining-room], that had been on a visit to the squatter, or something, and they were sitting down at dinner; and they seemed to think by their looks that we ought to have stayed outside and waited till they was done – we was only two rough shearers, you know.

1917 A. B. Paterson *Three Elephant Power* 49: For assistants, he [the manager] had half a dozen of us – jackeroos and colonial experiencers – who got nothing a year, and earned it. We had, in most instances, paid premiums to learn the noble art of squatting.

1934 Tom Clarke *Marriage at 6 a.m.* 46: *Jackeroo* an apprentice on a station.

1973 Patrick White *Southerly* 136: While I was a jackeroo I used to shut myself up at night with a kerosine lamp and write.

jackerooing Working as a jackeroo
1875 Rolf Boldrewood *The Squatter's Dream* repr. as *Ups and Downs* (1878) 239: 'A year or two more of Jackerooing would only mean the consumption of so many more figs of negrohead, in my case.'

1957 R. S. Porteous *Brigalow* 10–11: 'I put in two years jackerooing in the Gulf Country and finally tossed it in to do the overland trip.'

jackass, laughing the The kookaburra, *Dacelo gigas* (Morris 1798)

1827 P. Cunningham *Two Years in New South Wales* i 232: The loud and discordant noise of the *laughing jackass.*

1834 George Bennett *Wanderings in New South Wales* i 138: The peculiar noise of the laughing or feathered jackass (*Dacelo gigantea*), which increases from a low to a loud thrilling gurgling laugh, was often heard.

1847 Alexander Harris *Settlers and Convicts* ed. C. M. H. Clark (1954) 67: Every night when the 'laughing jack-

ass', the settler's clock, a common bush bird, calls him home from the field.

1859 Henry Kingsley *Recollections of Geoffry Hamlyn* ii 4: Below us, in the valley, a mob of jackasses were shouting and laughing uproariously.

1902 Henry Lawson 'Lord Douglas' *Prose* i 494: Barcoo-Rot, who took Mitchell seriously (and would have taken a laughing jackass seriously).

Jack the Painter A coarse green tea used in the bush, apt to colour the utensil or the mouth: *obs.*

1852 G. C. Mundy *Our Antipodes* i 329: Another notorious ration tea of the bush is called 'Jack the painter'. This is a *very* green tea indeed, its viridity evidently produced by a discreet use of the copper drying pans in its manufacture.

1855 William Howitt *Land, Labour and Gold* i 240: Till I saw and tasted them, I had no idea that commodities so vile could be procured in any part of the world . . . Jack-the-painter tea, that is, a green preparation of leaves of some kind, which taste like a mixture of copperas and verdigris, and leave a green scum on the infusion.

1877 Rolf Boldrewood *A Colonial Reformer* (1890) 413: He drank his 'Jack the Painter' tea milkless, most probably, and flavoured with blackest sugar.

1918 C. Fetherstonhaugh *After Many Days* 30: The Colonial tea had two names, 'Jack the Painter', that was the green tea, and it had a whiff of paint.

1924 *Truth* 27 Apr. 6: *Jack the Painter* strong bush tea.

Jackey, Jackie Generic name for the Australian Aboriginal

1885 *The Australasian Printers' Keepsake* 26: All the valleys where . . . Jacky Jacky hurled his boomerang.

1898 D. W. Carnegie *Spinifex and Sand* 154: Handed him a plate of scraps for his dinner, calling out, 'Hi, Jacky-Jacky, this one your tucker', to which Jim replied with stern dignity, 'Who the h– are you calling Jacky-Jacky? Do you think I'm a – blackfellow?'

1916 Joseph Furphy *Poems* 12: And

Jacky in his native scrub, / On bandi-coot and yam.

1930 *Bulletin* 6 Aug. 20: Jacky lets him-self be caught because he regards the calaboose as a convenient camping-place, where he can enjoy plenty white-pfeller tucker.

1944 *Salt* 31 Jan. 6: 'Here's the Good Oil about Jackie' [title of review of W. E. Harney's *Taboo*]

1954 Tom Ronan *Vision Splendid* 216: 'Now a Jacky with new clothes every two months and five sticks of tobacco a week can look down on us and he's going to keep doing so.'

1965 Frank Hardy *The Yarns of Billy Borker* 113: 'Just like calling an Ameri-can negro Sambo, or an Australian aboriginal Jacky. The white man who says it means well, but it's patronising, if you get what I mean.'

1972 Basil Fuller *West of the Bight* 152: 'We'll fetch a Jackie and let him try.' When the native came more time passed while he combed the country afresh.

Jackey, to sit up like To sit up straight, 'as large as life', almost cheekily

1941 Baker 38: *Jacky, sit up like* To behave, sit up straight.

1948 H. Drake-Brockman *Sydney or the Bush* 176: Cripes, the way they sat there, stiff as Jacky, not saying a word.

1958 Peter Cowan *The Unploughed Land* 182: 'Arriving in state today,' he said. 'Sitting up here in the front like Jacky.'

1969 Patsy Adam Smith *Folklore of the Australian Railwaymen* 180: As we were rattling along north to Darwin I happened to look back out of the guard's van and there they [the hoboes] were – sitting up like Jacky in the com-missioner's car behind us.

1975 Hal Porter *The Extra* 139: He's telling Edinburgh, and those writers sitting up like jacky in tiers behind him, about the construction of his next book.

Jacko Generic name for the Turkish soldier in the Gallipoli and Palestine campaigns in World War I

1918 Let. in Bill Gammage *The Broken Years* (1974) 136: Our position is serious as Jacko is giving us chaps a bad time

further back & we are pretty well cut off & cant get rations.

1935 H. R. Williams *Comrades of the Great Adventure* 23–4: The impet-uousity of the Anzacs was too much for 'Jacko', who steadily gave ground before the vehemence of the onslaught.

jackshay, jackshea A quart-pot

1881 A. C. Grant *Bush-Life in Queens-land* i 209: The party, therefore, carry with them a light blanket apiece, stowed away in the folds of which is each man's supper and breakfast. Hobbles and Jack Shays[1] hang from the saddle-dees. 1 A tin quart-pot, used for boiling water for tea, and contrived so as to hold within it a tin pint-pot.

1885 'The Broken-hearted Shearer' *Old Bush Songs* ed. Stewart and Keesing (1957) 267: I've some tea, and some tobacco, and a half a bar of soap, / Some flour and some matches, a billy, and jackshay.

1892 Barcroft Boake 'Down the River' *Bulletin* 6 Feb. 15 repr. in *Where the Dead Men Lie* (1897) 114: The sunlight glances, / Silver-gilding the bright 'Jack Shay'.

1911 E. S. Sorenson *Life in the Austra-lian Backblocks* 276: Empty boulli-cans were used for the same purposes as are now the specially made 'billy cans'. Quart pots, jackshays, pannikins, and other relatives followed as a matter of course.

1932 Ion L. Idriess *The Desert Column* 119: Before daylight, we warily re-turned to the oasis and boiled our jackshays.

Jacky Howe see **Howe**

jake All right, in good order, 'apples' [U.S. 1921 Mathews]

1919 W. H. Downing *Digger Dialects* 29: *Jake* Correct.

1924 *Truth* 27 Apr. 6: *Jake* All right, in order.

1932 Leonard Mann *Flesh in Armour* 266: 'I think she was jake.'

1944 *Coast to Coast 1943* 192: Every-thing was O.K. he told himself. Every-thing jake.

1957 Vance Palmer *Seedtime* 184: 'Easy to believe the ship's come home to port at last and everything's jake.'
1965 William Dick *A Bunch of Ratbags* 242: 'We're all right mate; she's jake.'

jakerloo
1938 Xavier Herbert *Capricornia* 189: 'Not wounded, are you?' . . . 'I'm jakerloo.'

jam, to put on To adopt an affected speech or manner
   c. **1882** *The Sydney Slang Dictionary* 5: *Jam (Putting on)* Assuming false airs of importance.
1888 E. Finn *Chronicles of Early Melbourne* ii 780: 'Putting on jam', a phrase of modern slang, and increasing in popularity.
1901 Miles Franklin *My Brilliant Career* 219: People who knew how to conduct themselves properly, and who paid one every attention without a bit of fear of being twitted with 'laying the jam on'.
1951 Dal Stivens *Jimmy Brockett* 30: Sadie put on a bit of jam when she talked, but not too much.

jammy
1911 Alfred Searcy *By Flood and Field* 291: A new chum fellow with notions of city decorum, and not a little 'jammy', ran over from the store.

Jaycee Member of a Jaycee club (of the Junior Chamber of Commerce) [U.S. 1946 OED]
1976 *Sydney Morning Herald* 12 Jun. 23: Jaycees work to relieve the sufferings of others. Members of Jaycee clubs in NSW have raised more than $6,000 . . . to improve public awareness of cystic fibrosis.

jerran Afraid [Ab.]
1847 Alexander Harris *Settlers and Convicts* ed. C. M. H. Clark (1954) 122: I began to feel rather 'jerran', as the blacks say (*i.e.* timorous).

jerry to, to To become 'wise' to [U.S. 1908 Mathews]
1911 Arthur Wright *Gamblers' Gold* 111: 'I always thought I'd seen yer somewhere, but I on'y jerried ter yer when yer was dealin' it out.'
1919 W. H. Downing *Digger Dialects* 30: *Jerry* To understand suddenly.
1938 Xavier Herbert *Capricornia* 232: 'Use y' bit o' brains,' he says, 'an take a jerry to y' self.'
1945 Cecil Mann *The River* 26: 'I've just taken a jerry to y'. Never struck me before. You got your woman here.'
1950 *Australian Police Journal* Apr. 116: *Jerry* To be awake to.
1975 *Bulletin* 26 Apr. 44: I should've jerried when the guy gave me a tug.

jersey, get a As for 'get a guernsey' q.v.

Jessie, more hide (arse, cheek) than An excess of effrontery [f. the elephant at Taronga Park Zoo, d. 1939 *aet.* 67]
1951 Dal Stivens *Jimmy Brockett* 130: 'You've got more cheek than Jessie the elephant!' I said.
1962 Stuart Gore *Down the Golden Mile* 21: 'More arse than Jessie,' the barman gloomily informed the bar at large, as the swing door flipped shut behind them.
1965 Eric Lambert *The Long White Night* 81: 'You've got more arse than Jessie,' I told him.
1968 Rodney Milgate *A Refined Look at Existence* 59: 'I knew that was coming. More hide than Jessie the . . . '
1975 Les Ryan *The Shearers* 143: 'The bastard's got more hide than Jessie,' he said.

Jets, the Newtown (N.S.W.) Rugby League team (also the 'Blues')
1974 *Sydney Morning Herald* 15 Jul. 13: Manly ground Jets.

jeweller's shop In mining, a pocket or patch glistening with gold; a rich claim
1855 Raffaello Carboni *The Eureka Stockade* ed. G. Serle (1969) 10: The jewellers shops, which threatened to exhaust themselves in Canadian Gully were as much the talk of the day.
1861 Horace Earle *Ups and Downs* 328: The produce was so vast that the holes there . . . were known throughout the entire field as jewellers' shops.

1870 Marcus Clarke *His Natural Life* ed. S. Murray-Smith (1970) 801: 'Bottomed a jeweller's shop, eh?'

1880 Rolf Boldrewood *The Miner's Right* (1890) 133–4: This was the famous 'jeweller's shop', where the very earth seemed composed of gold dust, with gold gravel for a variety.

1903 William Craig *My Adventures on the Australian Goldfields* 218: They sank over a 'pocket' at the foot of the reef . . . and dropped upon a veritable 'jeweller's shop'.

1950 Gavin Casey *City of Men* 57: 'We're on leaders now that are going to take us right into the jeweller's shop.'

1960 Donald McLean *The Roaring Days* 62: 'A jeweller's shop might be under your feet, or it might be a duffer.'

jim The sum of £1: *obs.* [see quot. 1945]

1906 Edward Dyson *Fact'ry 'Ands* 214: He was tearin' ratty t' raise another jim . . . 'Twas only fer a day, he said, cause he was goin' under er operation yes'day ter recover ther lost goblin.

1911 Arthur Wright *Gambler's Gold* 76: It was the loud-voiced winner speaking with a mouthful of saveloy and peas. 'Here's 'arf a jim for y'.'

1915 J. P. Bourke *Off the Bluebush* 61: For many, many years ago / You cost a modest 'jim'.

1936 H. Drake-Brockman *Sheba Lane* 158: 'But we've got a choice little mob, three hundred-odd at twenty jims a head.'

1945 Baker 109: £1 – *jim* (from the old English slang *jimmy o' goblin*, a sovereign).

Jimmies, Jimmy Brits A fit of nerves; a state of anger [rhyming slang for 'shits', f. the boxer Jimmy Britt, who toured Australia in World War I]

1941 Baker 13: *Brits up, have the* To be afraid, alarmed.

1952 T. A. G. Hungerford *The Ridge and the River* 116: 'I'm sorry, Clem,' he said . . . 'Must be a touch of the Jim-brits.'

1957 D'Arcy Niland *Call Me When the Cross Turns Over* 48: 'Thirsty weather, this. Give you the jimmy brits.'

1972 Don Crick *A Different Drummer* 37: He gave me a touch of the Jimmy Brits.

1975 Les Ryan *The Shearers* 120: 'Gees!' Sandy exclaimed in awe. 'Has he got the jimmy brits!' 'We're for it,' Lofty said.

see **Britt, Edgar**

Jimmies, Jimmy Grants Immigrants: *obs.* [rhyming slang]

1845 E. J. Wakefield *Adventure in New Zealand* ii 180: Knots of whalers, who had come on a cruise to the new settlement, were loitering about . . . curiously divided between contempt for the inexperience of the 'jimmy-grants,' as they call the emigrants, and surprise at the general industry and bustle prevailing.

1859 Henry Kingsley *Recollections of Geoffry Hamlyn* ii 154: 'What are these men that we are going to see?' 'Why, one,' said Lee, 'is a young Jimmy (I beg your pardon, sir, an emigrant), the other two are old prisoners.'

1878 Rolf Boldrewood *An Australian Squire* repr. as *Babes in the Bush* (1900) 270: 'The country was worth living in, not like it is now, overstocked with 'jimmies' – a lot of useless trash.'

1895 James Kirby *Old Times in the Bush of Australia* 144: As soon as he got to camp, he unyokes, and we found out from him that he was a 'Jimmy-grant' (emigrant), and was loaded with stuff for a station.

1924 *Truth* 27 Apr. 6: *Jimmy* An immigrant. Word now obsolete.

1963 Xavier Herbert *Disturbing Element* 91: When we kids saw people on the street dressed like that we would yell at them: 'Jimmygrants, Pommygranates, Pommies!'

Jimmy Woodser see **Woodser**

job To punch, clout [f. *job* to peck, dab, stab, prod, punch; in pugilistic language, to strike with a sharp or cutting stroke OED 1537]

1900 Henry Lawson 'Andy Page's Rival' *Prose* i 362: 'I'll find out for you, Andy. And, what's more, I'll job him for you if I catch him!'

1915 C. J. Dennis *The Songs of a Senti-mental Bloke* 121: *Job, to* To smite.
1924 *Truth* 27 Apr. 6: *Job, to* To attack: to strike.
1950 Brian James *The Advancement of Spencer Button* 123: 'I'll job you, Saw-kins, if you say I boned two bags of lollies.'
1961 Mena Calthorpe *The Dyehouse* 77: 'He jobbed him,' Larcombe said ... 'Laid him out cold.'
1974 David Williamson *Three Plays* 57: 'If you lay a hand on me, I'll fucking well job you. Right?'

jockey Someone travelling with the driver of a taxi who can claim to have already hired it if the destination of an intending passenger would mean an unprofitable trip; anyone riding with the driver by arrangement
[1900–10 O'Brien and Stephens: *Bre-wer's jockey* Melbourne – a man who rides about with the driver of a brewer's waggon helping him load and unload on the chance of a share of the drinks which fall to the lot of a brewer's man.]
1945 Baker 140: A *jockey* is a taxi-driver's accomplice who pretends to be a passenger in order to encourage legiti-mate travellers to pay extortionate fares to secure the taxi.
1974 John Powers *The Last of the Knucklemen* 58: 'One of the cattle stations used a helicopter for spottin' stray cattle. I jockeyed for the pilot.'

jockey, gin see **gin jockey**

Joe On the Victorian goldfields, a trooper enforcing the regulations of Governor C. Joseph La Trobe; a warning cry of the approach of a trooper
1854 Raffaello Carboni *The Eureka Stockade* ed. G. Serle (1969) 48: From my tent, I soon heard the distant cries of 'Joe!' increasing in vehemence at each second. The poor soldiers were pelted with mud, stones, old stumps, and broken bottles.
1855 William Howitt *Land, Labour and Gold* i 400: Hermsprong rode away followed by his men, and by the ex-ecrations of the whole diggings in that

quarter, expressed in the well-known cry of 'Joe! Joe!' – a cry which means one of the myrmidons of Charley Joe, as they familiarly style Mr La Trobe, – a cry which on all the diggings resounds on all sides on the appearance of any of the hated officials.
1864 *Thatcher's Colonial Minstrel* 22: The crowd were very peaceable, / The traps rode to and fro, / The license-hunting days are past, / So no one sang out 'Joe'.
1870 Marcus Clarke *His Natural Life* ed. S. Murray-Smith (1970) 722: The flat instantly bristled with waving arms. 'Run, mate, run! Joe! Joe! Joe!' and at the sound of the dreaded watchword, a dozen un-licensed ones abandon tub and cradle, making, like rabbits, for the deeper burrows.
1919 W. H. Downing *Digger Dialects* 30: *Joey* A military policeman.
c. 1926 'Alpha' *Reminiscences of the Goldfields* 75: The signal adopted an-nouncing the arrival of the police was, 'Joe, Joe, Joe'.
1953 *Caddie A Sydney Barmaid* 140: A whistled Joey from a barmaid was the danger signal [of the proprietor's ap-proach].
joeing, being joed
1854 Raffaello Carboni *The Eureka Stockade* ed. G. Serle (1969) 21: A mob soon collected round the hole; we were respectful, and there was no 'joeing'.
1857 *Thatcher's Colonial Songster* 7: But if he were to ride down the Ballarat – road, / I rather think he would be jolly well 'joed'.
1882 A. J. Boyd *Old Colonials* 160: No one wears a coat – if a bank manager even wore a coat he would be 'joed'.* *'Joed', *i.e.* hooted.
1903 William Craig *My Adventures on the Australian Goldfields* 255: No more amusing sight could be witnessed than the retreat of the miners up the preci-pitous sides of the ranges, where in security they 'Joe'd' and jeered the police to their hearts' content.

Joe Blake 1 A snake [rhyming slang]
1941 Baker 39: *Joe Blake* A snake.
1951 Ernestine Hill *The Territory* 446:

There is little rhyming slang in the Territory. A snake is always 'Joe Blake'.
1958 Peter Cowan *The Unploughed Land* 40: It should make a nice camp. Might be a few Joe Blakes; still, they're anywhere.
1964 H. P. Tritton *Time Means Tucker* 88: A snake can look remarkably like a slender branch and several times a day you would see men jump back with a string of curses after almost picking up a 'Joe Blake'.
2 *the Joe Blakes*: see quot. 1969
1944 Alan Marshall *These Are My People* 155: 'You feel nothin' when you're on a bender . . . You get the Joe Blakes bad after a few weeks.'
1969 Osmar White *Under the Iron Rainbow* 153: It's the electricity in the air that gives a man the joe-blakes* just before the Wet. *Rhyming slang: Delirium – Seeing Snakes – Joe Blakes.

Joe Blow A nondescript; the average man; the man in the street [also U.S.]
1966 Peter Mathers *Trap* 73: You couldn't tell him from Joe Blow.
1974 *Sydney Morning Herald* 1 Oct. 11: The union hoped that this did not mean the introduction of direction of labour. It asked: 'Is the "dole" to be withheld if Joe Blow will not leave home, wife and children at Albury, to live in a labour camp for eleven months of the year?'

joes, the A fit of depression
1915 C. J. Dennis *The Songs of a Sentimental Bloke* 41: It gimme Joes to sit an' watch them two!
1937 *Best Australian One-Act Plays* 181: 'This place gives me the joes.'
1942 Leonard Mann *The Go-Getter* 97: The weather's bad enough to give a man the joes.
1955 Mary Durack *Keep Him My Country* 182: 'Soothing!' Millington exclaimed. 'It fair give me the joes.'

joey 1 A baby kangaroo, carried in the mother's pouch [Morris 1839]
2 A baby, an infant
1887 *All the Year Round* 30 Jul. 67:

'Joey' is a familiar name for anything young or small, and is applied indifferently to a puppy, or a kitten, or a child.
1898 Morris: *Joey*, n. (2) Also slang used for a baby or little child, or even a young animal.
1948 K. S. Prichard *Golden Miles* 75: 'A girl never knows when she'll be bringin' home a joey if she goes with you.'
1955 D'Arcy Niland *The Shiralee* 27: 'Got a joey with yer, have yer? And what's your name, young 'un?'

joey, wood and water see **wood and water**

John, John Hop A cop [? f. *gendarme* and rhyming slang]
1909 Edward Dyson *Fact'ry 'Ands* 99: 'He had er John in tow . . . ther policeman was fer me.'
1915 C. J. Dennis *The Songs of a Sentimental Bloke* 15: Me, that 'as done me stretch fer stoushin' Johns.
1918 Harley Matthews *Saints and Soldiers* 73: The Nipper had an idea they were policemen – 'John Hops'.
1923 D. H. Lawrence *Kangaroo* 356: 'Police!' snarled Jack. 'Bloody John Hops!'
1935 Kylie Tennant *Tiburon* 278: 'No Johns ain't goin' to the bother of shiftin' us,' Stainer Rod declared.
1946 Dal Stivens *The Courtship of Uncle Henry* 76: Next Morning when I turn up at the shop there are two John Hops there.
1958 H. D. Williamson *The Sunlit Plain* 25: 'I hope she hasn't got that dirty, greasy john hop with her.'
1966 Bruce Beaver *You Can't Come Back* 63: 'No brothers or sisters?' I asked her, just like a john, getting the drum on her.
1975 Xavier Herbert *Poor Fellow My Country* 1151: Brumby Toohey . . . had the Provosts after him now, instead of the Johns as of old.

Johnny Bliss see **Bliss**

Johnny-cake Similar to damper, but

190

closer in size to a scone: made basically of flour and water, and cooked in the ashes or in a pan [f. the name of a flat cake of corn bread U.S. 1739 Mathews]

1846 G. F. Angas *Savage Life and Scenes in Australia and New Zealand* i 161: Our cook had not been idle: there were 'dampers', 'dough-boys', 'leather-jackets', 'johnny cakes', and 'beggars-in-the-pan.'

1862 Rachel Henning *Letters* ed. D. Adams (1963) 102: Tom lit a great fire and made some beautiful 'johnny cakes' – thin soda cakes which are baked in about ten minutes and are the best bread you ever ate.

1893 Henry Lawson *Letters* 53: No work and very little to eat: we lived mostly on Johnny cakes and cadged a bit of meat here and there.

1905 'The Old Bullock Dray' *Old Bush Songs* ed. A. B. Paterson 6: We'll have leather jacks, johnny cakes, / And fritters in the pan.

1962 J. Marshall and R. Drysdale *Journey Among Men* 165–6: Take some flour and water and mix them together into a paste. This is worked into a thin, stiff, saucer-shaped wafer which must be dropped flat on the glowing embers of a raked over or dying fire. When the dough is cooked crisp you have a johnny-cake. (Some bush cooks mix a bit of fat with the flour.)

1964 H. P. Tritton *Time Means Tucker* 121: 'Yair,' he said, 'I'd be flatter than a Johnny cake.'

Johnny Raw A new chum, novice, new recruit [colonial application of *Johnny Raw* nickname for an inexperienced youngster OED 1813]

1845 Thomas McCombie *Arabin* 248: 'I think,' said Arabin, 'you have managed to get very cleverly out of a scrape.' 'Yes, I am no Johnny Raw,' replied the other.

c. 1845 *Ralph Rashleigh* (1952) 30: These . . . were a sort of *pariahs* among the prisoners, chiefly *Johnny Raws*, or country chaps, apprentices, or others, who had no acquaintances to assist them while in gaol.

1888 E. Finn *Chronicles of Early Melbourne* ii 905: The 'Expirees' regarded the others with a feeling of pitying contempt, a species of simpletons who should have stayed at home. They called them 'Johnny Raws' and 'New Chums'.

1908 *Australian Magazine* 1 Nov. 1251: A 'jackeroo' (a new chum on a station out for colonial experience) is supposed to be 'Jacky Raw' with a kangaroo's tail as it were.

1941 Baker 39: *Johnny Raw* A 'new chum'.

Johnny Warder see **Warder**

joker A fellow, chap [N.Z. 1868 OED]

1900 Henry Lawson 'Meeting Old Mates' *Prose* i 165: 'I haven't seen him for more than three years. Where's the old joker hanging out at all?'

1908 E. S. Sorenson *Quinton's Rouseabout* 205: 'So yer didn't get that joker?' said Tracey.

1929 Herbert Scanlon *Old Memories* 13: 'If it wasn't for me, you two jokers would never have got a spot.'

1942 Gavin Casey *It's Harder for Girls* 218: 'What're you jokers doing tonight?' asked Winch. 'Like to come to a party?'

1951 Dal Stivens *Jimmy Brockett* 84: 'I heard a couple of jokers are out to get you.'

1965 Eric Lambert *The Long White Night* 88: 'Don't you recognize this joker?' 'Why should I? Who is he?'

jonic, jonnick Genuine, fair, reliable: *obsolescent* [E. dial. *jannock* fair, straightforward OED 1828]

1874 Charles de Boos *The Congewoi Correspondence* 173: 'I don't think as he acted jonick.'

1923 Jack Moses *Beyond the City Gates* 112: I'm camping down in Logan's, at the old pub in the Glen, / Where the fluid's always jonick.

1935 H. R. Williams *Comrades of the Great Adventure* 163: 'You don't say so!' said Elliott feigning surprise. 'Yes, it's jonick,' continued Peter.

1953 T. A. G. Hungerford *Riverslake* 166: 'Got the knife right into him.' 'Jonic?' 'Jonic!'

journo A journalist [abbr.]
1971 *Southerly* 271: Many who met Slessor in his more formal and conservative moments would have regarded him as the most journo of journos.
1974 David Williamson *Three Plays* 157: 'Didn't I hear you were living with someone? . . . A young journo or something.'

joy, bullocky's see **bullocky's joy**

joy, cocky's see **cocky's joy**

jug handle see **monkey**[2]

Julia Creek, things are weak at see **Tallarook**

July fog See quots
1893 Francis Adams *The Australians* 167: The shearer . . . crawling up to the shed with his 'mate' after the dispersal of the 'July fog' (the dead season when no shearing is done).
1945 Baker 90: *the July fog*, the dead season when no shearing is done.

jumbuck A sheep [? Ab. or pidgin for *jump up*]
1824 Let. cit. Ramson 107: To two Brothers of mine, these monsters exposed several pieces of human flesh, exclaiming as they smacked their lips and stroked their breasts, 'boodjerry patta! murry boodjerry! – fat as jimbuck!!' i.e. good food, very good, fat as mutton.
1843 John Hood *Australia and the East* 197: These useful blacks were put upon the foot of the 'jimbucks', and with equal success.
1851 John Henderson *Excursions and Adventures in New South Wales* i 207: He thought proper to leave his flock of jimbucks (as they call the sheep).
1867 R. J. Houlding *Australian Capers* 230: Your 'jumbucks'* will gambol, and nibble their feed. *Jumbuck is the

native name for a sheep.
1900 Henry Lawson 'A Rough Shed' *Prose* i 464: Unthinkable adjectives and adverbs, addressed to jumbucks, jackeroos, and mates indiscriminately.
1919 W. K. Harris *Outback in Australia* 11: This collie rounds up all the 'jumbucks'* *Sheep.

jump a horse over the bar see **horse**

jump, take a running ~ at yourself Equivalent to 'get lost', 'go to blazes'
1941 Baker 75: *Take a run at yourself* Run away! Go to the devil!
1977 *Sunday Telegraph* 22 May 59: We can only hope that when this unlikely Pommie lot get here they manage to take a series of running jumps at themselves.

jump up A sudden steep rise in a road: mainly N.T. and W.A.
[1844 Louisa Meredith *Notes and Sketches of New South Wales* 70: The main portion of the road is *bad* beyond an English comprehension; sometimes it consists of natural step-like rocks protruding from the dust or sand one, two, or three feet above each other, in huge slabs the width of the track, and over these 'jumpers', as they are pleasantly termed, we had to jolt and bump along.]
1894 G. N. Boothby *On the Wallaby* 189: A little later the line crossed the Burdekin River, by means of what seemed to us a most dangerous bridge, technically termed a 'jump up' . . . The descent on one side and the ascent on the other are very steep.
1948 H. Drake-Brockman *Sydney or the Bush* 230: Buncker turned the wheel sharply to avoid a jump-up in the track.
1964 Tom Ronan *Packhorse and Pearling Boat* 151: On the first stage out from Hodgson we climbed a jump-up: not a cliff, nor an escarpment, nor a bluff, but in the magnificently adequate basic English of the cattle country, a jump-up.

jump up whitefellow An expression

reflecting an Aboriginal belief that those with white skins are reincarnations of dead blacks

1830 Robert Dawson *The Present State of Australia* 158: 'When he makes blackfellow die,' I said, 'what becomes of him afterward?' 'Go away Englat (England),' he answered, 'den come back white pellow.' This idea is so strongly impressed upon their minds, that when they discover any likeness between a white man and any one of their deceased friends, they exclaim immediately, 'Dat black pellow good while ago jump up white pellow, den came back again.'

1860 Mrs Alan MacPherson *My Experiences of Australia* 227: Their notions regarding a future state appear to be very vague and unformed ... but some enunciate the somewhat startling theory 'Me jump up whitefellow'. I have heard an anecdote of some poor creature who was to expiate on the gallows a murder he had committed, and his last words previous to execution were 'Very good, me jump up white-fellow; plenty sixpence then.'

1882 A. J. Boyd *Old Colonials* 198: The trooper had a suspicion that if shot, his deceased relative would not 'jump up whitefellow'.

1927 M. M. Bennett *Christison of Lammermoor* 109: One old gin wanted to claim Munggra [Christison] as a defunct brother who had 'jumped up white fellow'.

jungle juice See quot. 1945

1945 Baker 157: *jungle juice* Any alcoholic beverage concocted by servicemen in the tropics.

1948 Sumner Locke Elliott *Rusty Bugles* in *Khaki, Bush and Bigotry* ed. Eunice Hanger (1968) 75: 'He hasn't half been on the jungle juice.'

1958 Randolph Stow *To the Islands* 19: 'In the war, the cartoons I could never understand about going troppo and drinking jungle juice.'

1968 Geoffrey Dutton *Andy* 268: The Americans had two bottles of bourbon and one of jungle juice made from fermented coconut milk and surgical alcohol.
see **snake juice**

just quietly see **quietly**

K

kadoova, off one's Deranged, off one's head: *rare* [? f. *cady, kadi* hat]

1941 Baker 50: *Off one's kadoova* To be silly, cranky, stupid.

1946 Dal Stivens *The Courtship of Uncle Henry* 72: I reckoned then Thompson was a bit off his kadoova.

kanga 1 Money [? f. rhyming slang *kangaroo = screw*]

1969 Alan O'Toole *The Racing Game* 6: 'On account of you being a mighty bloke, and sending Ape that kanga without asking any questions, we're all agreed on one thing. You're getting the biggest share.'

2 A jackhammer [? f. 'hopping' motion, also brand name]

1975 *Sun-Herald* 20 Jul. 13: A bone-shaking ride on a 'kanga' – a jackhammer, to the uninitiated.

kangaroo To move jerkily (used of a car when the engine is warming up)

1964 *Sydney Morning Herald* 14 Sep. 1: Be on the lookout for a grey car kangarooing through the Manly area. Mrs – has just received her driver's licence.

1971 Craig McGregor *Don't Talk to Me about Love* 187: The car ... jerked and kangarooed off into the night.

Kangaroos, the 1 The Rugby League team representing Australia internationally

1933 *Sydney Morning Herald* 14 Sep. 12: The Australian Rugby team, the 'Kangaroos' beat Yorkshire today by 13 points to nil.

1949 *Sydney Morning Herald* 25 Sep. 17: Kangaroos had it easy.

2 The North Melbourne V.F.L. team

1975 *Sunday Telegraph* 10 Aug. 55: Roos catch the Tigers in hectic scramble.

kangaroos in one's top paddock, to have See quots
1908 *Australian Magazine* 1 Nov. 1250: If you show signs of mental weakness you are either balmy, dotty, ratty or cracked, or you may even have white ants in your attic or kangaroos in your top paddock.
1941 Baker 40: *Kangaroos in one's top paddock, to have* To be silly, crazy.
1946 Dal Stivens *The Courtship of Uncle Henry* 70: Talked like a toff himself, he did, but he had kangaroos in the top paddock, as you'll see.

Kanowana chutney An improvised bush delicacy: N.T. [f. place-name]
1951 Ernestine Hill *The Territory* 425: 'Kanowana chutney' – which is a bottle of Worcestershire sauce stirred into a tin of plum jam.

Kath, Kathleen Mavourneen An indefinite period (from the refrain of the song 'It may be for years, it may be forever'): applied to a gaol sentence, and by transfer to an habitual criminal [listed by Partridge as 'An indefinitely long term of imprisonment' (N.Z. 1914), and 'The hire purchase system' (Anglo-Irish 1932)]
1941 Baker 40: *Kath* An indeterminate gaol sentence. *Kathleen Mavourneen* . . . An habitual criminal.
1950 *Australian Police Journal* Apr. 116: *Kathleen Mavourneen* Declared an habitual criminal. ('It may be for years . . .')
1951 Simon Hickey *Travelled Roads* 38: One hawker owed £75 to his supplier . . . and called to tell him that he was on a Kathleen Mavourneen (it may be for years, it may be forever) trip to Beirut.

keep nit see **nit**

Kelly, Ned see **Ned Kelly**

Kenso 1 Kensington, a suburb of Sydney, N.S.W.

2 The University of New South Wales (at Kensington)

kero Kerosine (paraffin) [abbr.]
1938 Xavier Herbert *Capricornia* 148: 'Take it and buy some tucker and kero.
1965 *The Tracks We Travel* ed. L. Haylen 43: I could hear the old clock ticking away behind the kero tin where I had thrown it.
1969 Osmar White *Under the Iron Rainbow* 76: These times with kero refrigerators and bottled gas it was different.
1973 Frank Huelin *Keep Moving* 171: A shallow wash dish made from another cut-down kero-tin.

kick on To carry on, with just enough funds for the purpose
1949 Lawson Glassop *Lucky Palmer* 153: 'I knew him when I used to slip ten bob out of the till . . . so he could kick on with it.' 'You can often kick on with ten bob,' said Lucky judicially.
1957 Ray Lawler *Summer of the Seventeenth Doll* 50: 'What about all those times when you've carried me – every year when I've run dry down here you've kicked me on?'

kick the tin To make a contribution [? f. rattling of collection box]
1966 Baker 230: Such suggestions as *kick the tin* . . . to the person who is due to buy drinks.
1969 Leslie Haylen *Twenty Years' Hard Labor* 36–7: He [Mr Chifley] gave me £50 for my campaign funds out of his own pocket and said, rather unnecessarily I thought, 'I'm kicking the tin for a few others as well so you needn't mention this.'
1976 *Sunday Telegraph* 30 May 34: When A.L.P. president Bob Hawke was appealing for money to help pay the Federal election campaign debt of $300,000, the NSW Labor Party was claiming it could not afford to 'kick the tin'.

Kidman's delight Golden syrup or 'cocky's joy' q.v. [f. Sir Sidney Kidman (1857–1935), a famous cattleman]
1935 R. B. Plowman *The Boundary*

Rider 187: The better class employer added [to the station rations] a tin of jam per week, or its equivalent in 'Bullocky's Joy' (treacle) or what was later known as 'Kidman's Delight' (golden syrup).
1943 Baker 44: *Kidman's blood mixture* Treacle.

kidstakes Pretence, nonsense; as an exclamation, equivalent to 'Fiddlesticks': *obs.* [f. *kid* to hoax, humbug OED 1811]
1916 C. J. Dennis *The Moods of Ginger Mick* 88: Mick reads the boys them ringin' words o' praise;/But they jist grins a bit an' sez 'Kid stakes!'
1919 W. H. Downing *Digger Dialects* 30: *Kid-stakes* Insincere flattery; inveiglement; a wheedling or deceitful speech or action.
1922 Arthur Wright *A Colt from the Country* 201: 'It was no kid stakes,' declared Bucks. 'The old man had the roll ready.'
1938 Xavier Herbert *Capricornia* 567: 'I didn't see him, I tell you.' 'You told his Ma you did.' 'That was only kidstakes.'
1945 Gavin Casey *Downhill is Easier* 138: All his kidstakes during the afternoon had probably been caused by his jealousy of Peter South.

killer A bullock or sheep to be killed for meat
1897 I. Scott *How I Stole over 10,000 Sheep in Australia and N.Z.* 9: 'You know the killers, don't you?' . . . i.e. the sheep the boss used for his own mutton at the house. [OED]
1929 K. S. Prichard *Coonardoo* 112: Warieda had gone out after a killer, cut up the beast and given everybody in the uloo his or her share.
1931 Vance Palmer *Separate Lives* 124: He had put it [the bullock] among the herd of killers in the home paddock in the hope that the new overseer might use it for beef in mistake.
1949 *Coast to Coast 1948* 149: 'The killers are in the paddock behind the pen. You can leave the meat hanging.'
1957 R. S. Porteous *Brigalow* 232: 'We'll have to get a killer in tomorrow.

We're just about out of meat.'
1966 Tom Ronan *Once There Was a Bagman* 36: Most of my time seemed to be spent chasing killers . . . In between meat-chasing trips I was supposed just to find myself something to do.

Kimberley mutton, oyster, walkabout See quots [place-name in N.W. Australia]
1945 Tom Ronan *Strangers on the Ophir* 39: A meat fritter known in the Kimberleys as a 'Burdekin Duck', and on the Burdekin as a 'Kimberley Oyster'.
1959 Jon Cleary *Back of Sunset* 167: The roast goat, Kimberley mutton, as it was called.
1971 Keith Willey *Boss Drover* 72: Horses . . . would die in hundreds from what we called the Kimberley walkabout. This was a disease which set a horse walking, round and round and up and down, knocking into trees and rocks and never stopping to eat, until in a few hours or days he would literally have walked himself to death.

Kinchela, putting ~ on them See quots: *obs.*
1897 *Bulletin* 25 Sep. Red Page: 'Putting Kinchela on 'em' is evidently inspired by the fact that one Kinchela, some years ago, wrote and published a pamphlet on the art of sharpening and 'keeping' shears. The expression was at first confined exclusively to shear-sharpening but in time came to have a wider application.
1911 E. S. Sorenson *Life in the Australian Backblocks* 233: The blades are pulled back and the knockers filed down, so the shears will take a bigger blow. This is called 'putting kinchler on them', from the fact that it was first adopted by John Kinsella, who died in Armidale about August 1902.

king In combinations like 'cattle king', 'shepherd king', 'squatter king', 'wool king'
1908 W. H. Ogilvie *My Life in the Open* 25: Tyson, the Queensland cattle king, who died a few years ago.
1936 Ion L. Idriess *The Cattle King: The Story of Sir Sidney Kidman* [book

title]
1951 Ernestine Hill *The Territory* 306:
Then he had been a cattle king. Now,
with a swag for home, he made up his
mind for a last camp.
1962 Tom Ronan *Deep of the Sky* 30:
The only survivor of those who had
worked for the two great Australian
Cattle Kings, Tyson and Kidman.
1875 Rolf Boldrewood *The Squatter's
Dream* repr. as *Ups and Downs* (1878)
277: Entering the parlour in a suit of
rough tweed, he felt much more like a
shepherd king of the future than the
death-doomed pioneer ... of the preceding few days.
1921 William Baylebridge *An Anzac
Muster* 26: 'I am settling portions of my
holding with embryonic sheep-kings
– those ambitious trouble-hunters I
spoke of.'
1945 Elizabeth George *Two at Daly
Waters* 15: Bill had been working for
Sir Samuel McCaughey, the sheep king
of New South Wales, on his Riverina
stations.
1891 Francis Adams *Fortnightly Review*
Oct. 542: All the old profuse hospitality,
the hunts and dances and four-in-hands
of the squatter kings, live now but as a
dim tradition.
1869 *Australian Journal* Jul. 685: *Wool
King* A squatter.
1900 Henry Lawson 'Middleton's Peter' *Prose* i 257: The Australian squatter
is not always the mighty wool king that
English and American authors and
other uninformed people imagine him
to be!
1911 E. J. Brady *River Rovers* 46: This
splendid territory, embracing millions
of acres of irrigable land ... cannot
remain forever in the possession of a
few dozen wool kings and foreign
investors.
1947 Vance Palmer *Hail Tomorrow* 18:
'The man who ... found this country
grovelling at the feet of a few fat-bellied
wool-kings and gave it a backbone and
a soul.'

king *v.* Abbr. of 'king-hit' q.v.
1959 Gerard Hamilton *Summer Glare*
97: 'Ken kinged him.'

1962 Alan Marshall *This is the Grass*
144: 'If a bloke comes at you buttoning
up his coat you always king him when
he's on the last button. It's just common
sense.'
1975 *Bulletin* 26 Apr. 45: 'He kinged
a floorwalker.'

King Billy The imaginary patriarch of
the Aboriginal race; nickname for any
Aboriginal singled out from the rest
1898 D.W. Carnegie *Spinifex and Sand*
190: Finding the water that King Billy
(for so had we named the Buck) eventually took us to.
1902 Henry Lawson 'A Bush Publican's
Lament' *Prose* i 467: An' supposin' Ole
King Billy an' his ole black gin comes
round at holiday time and squats on the
verander.
1921 M. E. Fullerton *Bark House Days*
52: It was a great blessing that the old
creek had cut its course through that
valley. Even before King Billy's traditions began it had wormed itself there
between the hills.
1975 Richard Beilby *The Brown Land
Crying* 35: 'You'll see Captain Cook
coming ashore from the South Perth
ferry ... And I suppose there'll be a
few Aborigines, King Billy with his
nulla-nullas and spears.'

king-hit *n.* A knockout punch; a surprise punch, probably unfair
1924 *Truth* 27 Apr. 6: *King-hit* The
winning blow in a fight.
1935 H. R. Williams *Comrades of the
Great Adventure* 192: Swung with ter-
rific force, the unusual weapon scored
a 'king hit' which spreadeagled the
second 'Jack'.
1944 Lawson Glassop *We Were the Rats*
76: 'Do this galah over,' he whispered
in my ear. 'He's a king-hit merchant.'
1960 Ron Tullipan *Follow the Sun* 128:
'He's a king-hit merchant, always has
been, and when he misses the surprise
shot, he doesn't get a second free one
with a bloke like me.'
1969 Don Whitington *The House Will
Divide* xiii: Where Menzies might have
used subtle ju-jitsu pressure on a nerve
and Holt would have favoured a cun-

ning ankle trap, Gorton employed a king hit that everyone, including the umpire, could see and deplore.
1975 *Sydney Morning Herald* 9 Aug. 3: Judge censures 'cowardly king hit' by policeman.

king-hit *v.* To deliver a knockout punch, or a surprise punch, probably unfair
1962 Stuart Gore *Down the Golden Mile* 277: 'King-hit me, the bastard,' he muttered. 'With me own gun!'
1965 William Dick *A Bunch of Ratbags* 88: I was learning the art of streetfighting: how to king-hit and how to rabbit-chop, how to gouge their eyes.
1972 John Bailey *The Wire Classroom* 140: The previous cop at Wendi who had been known to king-hit a native who had spat on the pavement near his wife.

king-pin The leading figure, most important person [U.S. 1867 OED ? f. *king-bolt* a main or large bolt in a mechanical structure OED 1825]
1915 C. J. Dennis *The Songs of a Sentimental Bloke* 102: But 'struth! 'E is king-pin! The 'ead serang!
1926 K. S. Prichard *Working Bullocks* 258: 'My!' Mary Ann gasped incredulously, 'and you was the king pin last week, Mark.'
1938 H. Drake-Brockman *Men Without Wives* 78: 'Andy, where is old man Lovatt?' 'Out on the run. For the moment I'm king-pin.'
1957 Judah Waten *Shares in Murder* 99: 'Then he must be the biggest fence of the lot. The kingpin. The daddy of all fences.'

kip The small flat piece of board from which the coins are tossed in two-up [cf. *kep* to catch EDD 1781; *keper* a flat piece of wood secured in the mouth of a horse to prevent his eating the corn EDD 1897]
1898 *Bulletin* 17 Dec. Red Page: The kip is the piece of wood used in 'two-up'.
1904 Henry Fletcher *Dads Wayback: His Work* 12: An' most everyone, high an' low, rich an' poor, plays up ther coin, an' heads 'em off the kip.

1911 Louis Stone *Jonah* 215: The spinner placed the two pennies face down on the kip, and then, with a turn of the wrist, the coins flew twenty feet into the air.
1916 C. J. Dennis *The Moods of Ginger Mick* 108: 'It's like two-up: I'm 'eadin' 'em this trip;/But lookin', day be day, to pass the kip.'
1949 Lawson Glassop *Lucky Palmer* 167: He handed the kip to the spinner ... placed two pennies, tails up, on it with infinite care and said 'Fair go.'

kipper An Englishman (Services slang in World War II) [f. the prominence of kippers in English diet. See also quots 1946, 1962]
1946 *Daily Telegraph* 22 Jan. 11: Hansen told Mr Goldie, S. M. that the girls called them 'Pommies' and 'kippers'. 'I understand that in Australia "kipper" means two-faced and gutless,' Hansen added.
1954 T. A. G. Hungerford *Sowers of the Wind* 204: 'The kippers have got orders not to go about alone now.'
1962 J. Marshall and R. Drysdale *Journey Among Men* 190: This unlovable trait has led to the application of the expression *kipper* to a certain type of Englishman. A kipper, by virtue of its processing, has become two-faced with no guts.
1975 *Bulletin* 30 Aug. 63: The Australian naval slang term for a Pommy matelot is – or was – 'bloody kipper'. Retrospective lower-deck etymology gives the derivation as 'A two-faced bastard with no guts.'

kiss-and-ride See quot.
1975 *Sydney Morning Herald* 16 Jan. 6: The kiss-and-ride system – the wife drops her husband off at the station or terminal, keeps the car for her own use during the day, and picks him up at night.

kitchen tea A pre-wedding party to which the guests bring some item of kitchen equipment as a gift
1934 Tom Clarke *Marriage at 6 a.m.* 17: Tom Rawlings led me off to see the bride

at a 'kitchen tea' . . . it was so called because each guest brought a kitchen utensil as a wedding-gift.
1943 Kylie Tennant *Time Enough Later* 200: 'I beg of you, restrain them from any idea of visitings and junketings and gruesomeness in the form of kitchen teas.'

Kiwi *n*. & *a*. A New Zealander [f. the bird unique to New Zealand OED 1918]
1935 H. R. Williams *Comrades of the Great Adventure* 210: 'We're darned lucky we are not all beaten up like your Kiwi friend.'
1965 *Daily Telegraph* 13 Apr. 64: We never had less than 150 Aussie and Kiwi girls on our own temporary staff.
1976 *Australian* 11 Feb. 19: Testing time looms for promising Kiwi colt.

kleiner As for 'clinah' q.v.
1899 W. T. Goodge *Hits! Skits! and Jingles!* 17: Well, spare me days, kleiner, I love yer!

knock *n*. An act of intercourse; a promiscuous woman [f. *knock v*.[1]]
1965 William Dick *A Bunch of Ratbags* 199: I had caused him to miss out on a knock many weeks ago with Elaine, and he had never forgiven me. Ibid. 158: To tell your best mate that one of his family was a knock was unethical and uncalled for.

knock *v*. 1 To copulate with [OED 1598], in Australia more common in expressions like 'knock off', or 'do a knock with' (to strike up an acquaintance, seeking favours)
1933 Norman Lindsay *Saturdee* 138: 'Supposin' I was to do a knock with girls, what 'ud I say to them?'
1969 William Dick *Naked Prodigal* 112: 'She all right? Does she look like she knocks?'
1971 Frank Hardy *The Outcasts of Foolgarah* 15: 'Well, he's not knocking orf my sister-in-law and that's for sure.'
2 To disparage, criticize, find fault with [U.S. 1896 Mathews]
1892 William Lane *The Workingman's Paradise* 85: 'Admit it's a business con-

cern and that everybody growls at it, it's the only paper that dares knock things.'
1903 Joseph Furphy *Such is Life* (1944) 32: 'Hold on, hold on,' interrupted Mosey. 'Don't go no furder, for Gossake. Yer knockin' yerself bad, an' you don't know it.'
1936 H. Drake-Brockman *Sheba Lane* 128: 'I hate "knocking" you – why the hell you and dad didn't get into partnership beats me.'
1958 E. O. Schlunke *The Village Hampden* 233: 'She seemed to be so nice and friendly, I wasn't going to knock my good luck.'
1975 *Sun-Herald* 15 Jun. 4: Mr Whitlam last night lashed out at critics within the Labor movement who were 'knocking' his Government's efforts.

knocked, knocked out Killed or wounded in action (Services slang)
1918 Let. in Bill Gammage *The Broken Years* (1974) 220: Am leaving now to go over to the attack. If you receive this, I shall have been knocked out.
1918 Harley Matthews *Saints and Soldiers* 73: Then the machine-gun corporal got knocked out.
1932 Leonard Mann *Flesh in Armour* 312: 'Corporal Jeffreys knocked, sir,' he said.
1944 Lawson Glassop *We Were the Rats* 128: 'If a section leader got knocked, somebody . . . would just take over and the rest would follow without question.'
1951 Eric Lambert *The Twenty Thousand Thieves* 230: 'It's a pity he couldn't have been knocked!'

knock back *v*. 1 To reject
1930 *Bulletin* 19 Feb. 51: 'Not the sort of man we want from all I've heard of him. I knocked him back.' [OED]
1935 Kylie Tennant *Tiburon* 271: A number . . . failed to make any application on the grounds that they weren't 'going to give old Ma Claufield the satisfaction of knocking them back'.
1938 Eric Lowe *Salute to Freedom* 267: 'It's just that I don't want you to feel disappointed if you get knocked back.'

1944 Lawson Glassop *We Were the Rats* 104: 'Ya still goin' ter be true to Margaret? Still goin' to keep knockin' back the sheilas?'
1966 Tom Ronan *Strangers on the Ophir* 46: 'I knocked him back for credit and put him to sleep with a special drink.'
2 To drink, consume [OED 1931]
1962 J. Marshall and R. Drysdale *Journey Among Men* 164: He took the top off one [bottle] and poured himself a glassful. He knocked this back in one hit.
1973 H. Williams *My Love Had a Black Speed Stripe* 140: He kept knocking back the whisky I kept slipping into his glass.
1975 Don Townshend *Gland Time* 231: He was knocking back the grogs at an alarming rate.

knock bandy see **bandy**

knock down *v.* To spend (esp. a cheque) until funds are exhausted, generally on liquor
1853 C. R. Read *What I Heard, Saw and Did on the Australian Goldfields* 98: A volume might almost be written on the ridiculous manner in which this class of people squander away their money; many, I have heard boasting at the diggings, as to the shortness of time in which they could 'knock down' a thousand or two pounds, and return to the diggings, without sufficient to buy a pickaxe.
1867 J. R. Houlding *Australian Capers* 386: A jolly shepherd 'knocking down' a year's wages.
1873 A. Trollope *Australia* ed. Edwards and Joyce (1967) 203: The labourer who can live and save his money, who can refrain from knocking down his cheque, may no doubt in Queensland become the real lord of all around him and dwell on his own land in actual independence.
1883 E. M. Curr *Recollections of Squatting in Victoria* 348: 'All I've heard of was a Devil's River lot, six or eight of them, knocking down their cheques at Young's.'
1891 Henry Lawson *Verse* i 135: For the bushman gets bushed in the streets

of a town, / Where he loses his friends when his cheque is knocked down.
1905 'On the Road to Gundagai' *The Old Bush Songs* ed. A. B. Paterson 25: In a week the spree was over and the cheque was all knocked down, / So we shouldered our 'Matildas', and we turned our backs on town.
1919 W. K. Harris *Outback in Australia* 74: 'Knocking down a cheque' is not a common occurrence in the Bush nowadays, but there are still some Outback townships which look forward to the periodical visit of hands from some of the 'further out' stations.
1946 Ion L. Idriess *In Crocodile Land* 209: 'A bushie had blown in that day and started to knock down his cheque.'

knock out To earn [N.Z. 1871 OED]
1881 A. C. Grant *Bush-Life in Queensland* i 31: These were part of the Ipswich tribe, and knocked out a precarious living by hunting in the bush and begging in the town.
1896 Edward Dyson *Rhymes from the Mines* 93: Yet Jo contrived to knock out bread and butter, / And something for a dead-broke mate.
1941 Baker 42: *Knock out, to* To earn (a certain sum of money).
1975 *Bulletin* 30 Aug. 16: What about the school-teacher, the young computer programmer or plumber knocking out about $200 a week.

knock over a doll see **doll**

knockabout man A station-hand doing odd jobs; a rouseabout
1868 Marcus Clarke 'Swagmen' repr. in *The Peripatetic Philosopher* (1869) 41: At the station where I worked for some time (as 'knock-about man').
1880 Rolf Boldrewood *The Miner's Right* (1890) 60: 'If we don't make a rise before that time, we shall have become wages men, bush-rangers, or knock-about-men on a station – farm-labourers.'
1916 Macmillan's *Modern Dictionary of the English Language* 785: *knockabout man* (bush term) a general labourer, employed about a squatter's homestead,

or on a sheep- or cattle-run; a man who makes himself generally useful in the shearing-sheds, etc.

knockback n. A refusal; rejection of an overture, often sexual [E. dial. 1902 OED]
1919 W. H. Downing *Digger Dialects* 31: *Knock-back* A refusal.
1933 Frank Clune *Try Anything Once* 25: There was no need for any further hands about the place. This was rather a blow, but already I was getting used to knock-backs and I felt that something or other would turn up.
1941 Kylie Tennant *The Battlers* 181: The busker, always ready to save money, and realising from several 'knock-backs' that he had little hope of lodging in the town, immediately pre-empted the vacant sleeping-place.
1957 Ray Lawler *Summer of the Seventeenth Doll* 101: 'Yeh – you, the great lover that's never had a knock back.'
1963 Frank Hardy *Legends from Benson's Valley* 11: 'I get a lot of knock backs but I get a lot of naughties.'
1975 Les Ryan *The Shearers* 76: 'Please yourself,' he said, looking like Humphrey Bogart after a knock-back. 'I'll be around.'

knockdown, the An introduction [U.S. 1865 OED]
1916 C. J. Dennis *The Moods of Ginger Mick* 149: *Knock-down* A ceremony insisted upon by ladies who decline to be 'picked up'; a formal introduction.
1924 *Truth* 27 Apr. 6: *Knock down* An introduction.
1938 *Bulletin* 6 Jul. 48: 'Another bloke gave me a knockdown to 'im.'
1950 Jon Cleary *Just Let Me Be* 9: 'She'll never give you a knock-down while you're just a milkman. You'll have to go up in the world.'
1969 Osmar White *Under the Iron Rainbow* 75: There'd be a lot of fellers who knew Don. One of them might give me a knockdown to him.

knocker 1 Common sense: *obs.*
1900 Henry Lawson 'Two Larrikins' *Prose* i 231: 'The old woman might

have had the knocker to keep away from the lush while I was in quod.'
2 Someone addicted to fault-finding, disparagement of what others praise [f. *knock v.²*]
1923 Jack Moses *Beyond the City Gates* 154: The 'knocker' of his home town is, on this line of deduction, a 'knocker' of his Empire; a destroyer of thought, labour, and enterprise.
1961 *Meanjin* 399: 'For one terrible moment I thought you were going to be a knocker. In Merulga there's no place for knockers.'
1962 Max Harris *Australian Civilization* ed. P. Coleman 57: It is said that Australians are 'knockers'; that is, they gain pleasure from seeing superiority in talent, intellect or energy reduced to the scale of average mediocrity.
1972 Keith Dunstan *Knockers* [book title]

knocker, on the Promptly, on demand, esp. in the expression 'cash on the knocker' [listed by Partridge as English slang for 'on credit']
1962 Jon Cleary *The Country of Marriage* 297: Sid was a man who wanted cash on the knocker.
1967 Frank Hardy *Billy Borker Yarns Again* 71: 'Settle our monthly bills dead on the knocker.'
1972 Richard Magoffin *Chops and Gravy* 106: *Cash on the knocker* immediate cash payment.
1975 *Australian* 12 Aug. 9: 'He has to pay cash on the knocker for everything he buys, but he has to wait two or three months for payment from the big firms.'

knot in bluey, put a To prepare to travel, prepare for action
1945 Tom Ronan *Strangers on the Ophir* 144: 'And put a knot in your bluey yourself, Joe, I've got a job for you.'
1966 Baker 108: The expression *to put* (or *tie*) *a knot in* (a swag strap) means to quit a job.

know more than one's prayers see **prayers**

knuckle, go the To punch, fight
1944 John Devanny *By Tropic, Sea and Jungle* 160: I always got on well with the blacks, because I never went the knuckle on them, and never interfered with their women.
1959 D'Arcy Niland *The Big Smoke* 15: 'He reckoned you could go the knuckle a bit.'
1962 Stuart Gore *Down the Golden Mile* 26: Then he said: 'Want to watch out for them quiet snoozers. Sometimes they can go the knuckle a bit themselves.'
1975 Richard Beilby *The Brown Land Crying* 156: 'Old Sam goin' the knuckle. Well, whaddya know.'

knuckle sandwich A punch in the mouth
1973 Alexander Buzo *Norm and Ahmed* 12: 'He tried to hang one on me at Leichhardt Oval once, so I administered a knuckle sandwich to him.'

L

lady, white see **white lady**

lady's waist A 5 or 7 oz glass of beer [f. shape]
1941 Baker 42: *Lady's waist* A gracefully shaped glass in which beer is served (2) Whence, the drink served.
1954 *Sydney Morning Herald* 8 Nov. 2: Calling for an appropriately named Sydney 'lady's waist' in Adelaide would probably result in being hauled off to gaol.

lair A showoff; a flashily dressed person; a term of general contempt (esp. 'mug lair') [see *lairy*]
1935 Kylie Tennant *Tiburon* 106: He was also considered something of a lare among the girls.
1944 *Coast to Coast 1943* 51: He saw a mug-lare with a yellow tie ogle the girl.
1958 Gavin Casey *Snowball* 208: He didn't want to dress like a lair, and he rejected the brilliant blazer and the too-pale grey slacks he'd bought . . . three months earlier.
1962 Ron Tullipan *March into Morning* 28: 'A lot of young lairs get flash on motor-bikes.'
1974 John Powers *The Last of the Knucklemen* 30: 'I don't get hustled into punch-ups with two-bob lairs.'

lair around, lair up To behave like a lair, dress like a lair
1952 T. A. G. Hungerford *The Ridge and the River* 23: Having a bath and a shave, getting into clean clothes . . . to lare up at the dance.
1955 H. Drake-Brockman *Men Without Wives and Other Plays* 83: 'He's a trimmer. Always laring around. No good to girls.'
1962 Stuart Gore *Down the Golden Mile* 64: 'He climbs out of the cockpit, all laired up in this red rig-out and whiskers.'
1975 Xavier Herbert *Poor Fellow My Country* 397: 'Better go and wash yo'-self.' 'Sure,' said Nobby. 'Think I'm goin' leave the lairin' up all to you?'

lairize To behave like a lair
1953 Kylie Tennant *The Joyful Condemned* 22: 'She was ear-bashing me all over tea how you came lairizing round at our place like you owned it.'
1965 Wally Grout *My Country's 'Keeper* 139: Most people thought I did it 'lairising' – being a show-off, as we say at home. It seemed to them I had caught the ball and spilled it only when throwing it in the air, a favourite flourish of 'keepers.
1970 Jessica Anderson *The Last Man's Head* 116–17: 'I pretty soon lost my taste for that part of it, the lairising part.' Ibid. 171: Alec tended to mistrust and stigmatise as lairising all such devised gaiety and charm.

lairy Flashily dressed; (of colours) bright and showy: *obsolescent* [? f. *leery* wide-awake, knowing, 'fly' OED 1796]
1906 Edward Dyson *Fact'ry 'Ands* 160: Minnie piped something to the effect that she would disdain to be 'found drownded with a bloke what done-up

'is 'air dead leary', next morning the elaborate festoons had disappeared from Chiller's brow, and his hair was parted with the oily precision characteristic of Sunday-school superintendents and reputable young barbers.

1915 C. J. Dennis *The Songs of a Sentimental Bloke* 35: Fer 'er sweet sake I've gone and chucked it clean: / The pubs and schools an' all that leery game. Ibid. 122: *Leery* Vulgar; low.

1932 Leonard Mann *Flesh in Armour* 291: 'Who've we got?' 'Lairey Ridley.' They laughed . . . Captain Ridley had been a recognized hard-doer. His helmut was tilted rakishly over his left ear and his tunic and light coat were of the ultra fashionable style.

1949 Lawson Glassop *Lucky Palmer* 142: 'You ought to see the rug I got for Bunny. All done in my colours, red, green and gold. Classy, eh? Some of the boys reckon it's too lairy, but I reckon it's a beaut.'

1964 David Ireland *Image in the Clay* 47: 'There was the travelling rodeo at the next town. All the boys lairy in big hats and check shirts.'

1975 Rodney Hall *A Place Among People* 13: Chick nodded in the direction of a newcomer heading for the bar, 'That's a lairy rig-out isn't it?'

lamb down To defraud a 'chequed up' bushman by keeping him drunk until his funds are supposedly exhausted [f. helping a ewe to give birth]

1869 Marcus Clarke *A Colonial City* ed. L. T. Hergenhan (1972) 162: *To lamb-down* – that is, to make drunk and incapable – of course originated with some shepherd.

1878 G. H. Gibson *Southerly Busters* 24: He got upon the spree, / And publicans was awful cheats / For soon lamm'd down was he.

1888 E. Finn *Chronicles of Early Melbourne* ii 546: The publican's harvest consisted chiefly in fleecing (or 'lambing down', as it was technically termed) the stockmen, bullock-drivers, shepherds and shearers who made periodical trips to Melbourne for a 'spree' or to 'knock down their money'.

1902 Henry Lawson 'A Bush Publican's Lament' *Prose* i 469: 'Someone's sure to say he was lambed down an' cleaned out an' poisoned with bad Bush liquor at my place.'

lambing down The process or experience of being 'lambed down'

1873 J. B. Stephens *Black Gin* 51: It is the Bushman come to town . . . / Come to spend his cheque in town, / Come to do his 'lambing down'.

1885 'The Broken-hearted Shearer' *Bulletin* 31 Oct. 5 in *Old Bush Songs* ed. Stewart and Keesing (1957) 267: But it's nothing when you're used to it to do a lambing down.

1903 Joseph Furphy *Such is Life* (1944) 328: The lambing down of two stalwart fencers by a pimply old shanty-keeper.

1910 C. E. W. Bean *On the Wool Track* 215: When sheep are lambing men are sent into the paddocks to see that everything goes smoothly. The process is called 'lambing down'. By a gentle metaphor the words have been transferred to the assistance which in the old days it was customary for publicans to give to men who came in to get rid of a cheque.

larrikin 1 A young street rowdy [*larrikin* a mischievous or frolicsome youth EDD Suppl.]

1870 Marcus Clarke *A Colonial City* ed. L. T. Hergenhan (1972) 78–9: The larrikin has been a little noisy lately. The daily press records his doings with unction. For instance, on Sunday morning last, at about 3 o'clock, a respectable young man, who was a carpenter, 'strolls' into that pleasant lounge, Wright's Gin Palace, and in a jovial manner 'shouts' for some dozen . . . Feeling a strange hand in his pocket, he remonstrates, whereupon he is mobbed, kicked, struck and hustled into the street. The constables, after a protracted search and a severe struggle, arrested three of the gang.

1877 T. E. Argles *The Pilgrim* I viii 5: Here, packed like sardines, are a motley crew of that hideous excrescence of blind-alleys and right-of-ways – the

Sydney Larrikin – and the female companion he so much affects.
1883 R. E. N. Twopeny *Town Life in Australia* 98: The 'larrikins', as they are called . . . roughs of the worst description, insulting and often robbing people in Melbourne itself, and moving about in gangs with whose united force the police is powerless to cope . . . In a younger stage they content themselves with frightening helpless women, and kicking every Chinaman they meet.
1888 J. A. Froude *Oceana* 138: There is an idle set at the lower end of the scale: noisy, riotous scamps, who are impertinent to peaceful passengers, and make rows at theatres, a coarse-type version of the old Mohawks – they call them *Larrikins.*
1896 Henry Lawson 'A Visit of Condolence' *Prose* i 32: 'How dare you talk to me like that, you young larrikin? Be off! or I'll send for a policeman.'
1911 Louis Stone *Jonah* 67–8: They were dressed in the height of larrikin fashion – tight-fitting suits of dark cloth, soft black felt hats, and soft white shirts with new black mufflers round their neck in place of collars – for the larrikin taste in dress runs to a surprising neatness. But their boots were remarkable, fitting like a glove, with high heels and a wonderful ornament of perforated toe-caps and brass eyelet-holes in the uppers.
1924 *Truth* 27 Apr. 6: *Larrikin* A rowdy, ill-mannered youth.
larrikiness, larrikinism
1892 William Lane *The Workingman's Paradise* 43: As they stood in George-street, waiting for their bus, a high-heeled, tightly-corsetted, gaily-hatted larrikiness flounced out of the side door of a hotel near by.
1870 *The Australian* 10 Sep. 3: A slight attempt at 'larrikinism' was manifested. [Morris]
1875 A. J. Boyd *Old Colonials* (1882) 52: Let the state take cognizance of 'larrikinism' as an offence against the law.
2 In a more favourable sense, as though referring to authentically 'Australian' characteristics of non-conformism, irrev-

erence, impudence (projected on to the larrikin as romanticized by Lawson and C. J. Dennis)
1973 Donald Horne *Australian* 12 Apr. 8: The Australian style swings back and forth between the larrikin and the suburbanite . . . Evatt was the larrikin type, Hasluck the suburbanite. The way Connor is handling the Minerals and Energy ministry, announcing things without any inquiry, I'd describe him as the larrikin type.
1974 *Sydney Morning Herald* 29 Jun. 11: The heroine with a larrikin streak [article on Joan Sutherland]

Larry Dooley see **Dooley**

Larry, happy as Completely happy [origin obscure]
.**1905** Joseph Furphy *Rigby's Romance* ed. R. G. Howarth (1946) 62: 'But now that the adventure was drawing to an end, I found a peace of mind that all the old fogies on the river couldn't disturb. I was as happy as Larry.'
1910 Henry Lawson *Prose* ii 216: And Frank Myers – 'As happy as Larry in Castlebarry.'
1915 Louis Stone *Betty Wayside* 254: 'If it hadn't been for that busybody we'd have been happy as Larry, and nobody any the wiser.'
1922 Arthur Wright *A Colt from the Country* 88: 'The old boy is as happy as Larry.'
1934 Thomas Wood *Cobbers* 25: He said he was as happy as Larry to see a fresh face.
1946 K. S. Prichard *The Roaring Nineties* 369: 'I'm as happy as Larry to be on the job again,' Alf exclaimed eagerly.
1957 Ray Lawler *Summer of the Seventeenth Doll* 15: She wanted a doll on a walking-stick too, she said . . . and in the end that's what they had to bring her back. Well, she was as happy as Larry; off she went to bed, one in each hand.
1966 Hal Porter *The Paper Chase* 125: Here I am solitary, happy as Larry, singing to myself, and busy as a weaver.

lash, have a To take part in something,

make an attempt at

1941 Baker 42: *Lash at, have a* To make an attempt at (something).

1948 Ruth Park *Poor Man's Orange* 222: The blithe pipings of old men who safe [from the fight] up on their balconies, leaned over rails and exhorted everyone to 'ave a lash.

1952 T. A. G. Hungerford *The Ridge and the River* 16: 'Don't buy any trouble unless you're forced into it – we don't want to stir the bastards up until we're better settled in here, just in case they decide to have a lash.'

1965 Eric Lambert *The Long White Night* 151: 'Let someone also have a lash at Rommel and his bloody Nazi Youth.'

1970 Jack Hibberd *Who?* in Penguin *Plays* 146: 'We might even have a lash at some juicies ourselves.'

last shower, didn't come down in see **shower**

later, see you An expression of farewell (not a proposal for a later meeting)

1942 Gavin Casey *It's Harder for Girls* 75: 'Well,' I said, 'I'd better get along.' 'Yes,' said Phil. 'I gotter pick up some packages. See you later.'

1948 William Beard *'Neath Austral Skies* 177: ''Ooray,' returned the drover, shaking Ralph's hand. 'See you later!'

1965 Patrick White *Four Plays* 346: (*Hikers move off*). *First Hiker* See you later then!

laughing jackass see **jackass**

Laura Norda Strine equivalent of 'law and order'

lay-by *n.* & *v.* To secure an item for sale by making a deposit and paying instalments until the full price is paid, without interest charges, the goods being taken only when payment is complete

1930 *Sydney Morning Herald* 16 Oct. 4: Avail yourself of our Lay-by service. [Hordern's advertisement]

1932 *Sydney Morning Herald* 5 Dec. 1: A New Service! / 'Lay-By' at Farmer's / Lay-Away-a-Gift Plan! / Farmer's now assist with a practical, worryless 'Lay-By'.

Begin tomorrow and lay a gift away each day until your list is completed. Farmer's grant you ample time in which to pay the balance without any hardship on your purse. When your thoughts, in future, turn to 'Lay-By', think of Farmer's quality stocks now easily within your reach.

Leaping Lena Nickname of the train running from Birdum to Darwin

1940 Ernestine Hill *The Great Australian Loneliness* 124: There is a train a week in the Territory . . . They call it Leaping Lena. One terminus is Birdum, three shacks in the bush, and the other the first breaker of the Indian Ocean . . . The Sentinel – Leaping Lena's official name – is a string of scarcely glorified cattle trucks.

1945 G. H. Johnston *Pacific Partner* 149: When Australia declared war, Leaping Lena had to be entrusted overnight with vital military movements. In fact, she became the only troop train in the Northern Territory.

1962 J. Marshall and R. Drysdale *Journey Among Men* 44: Jouncing from side to side in this machine, which he informed us was known as Leaping Lena or the Abortion Express.

leatherjacket A kind of pancake, made from dough and fried in fat

1846 G. H. Haydon *Five Years in Australia Felix* 151: A plentiful supply of 'leatherjackets' (dough fried in a pan).

1853 S. Mossman and T. Banister *Australia Visited and Revisited* 126: 'Leatherjackets' – An Australian bush term for a thin cake made of dough, and put into a pan to bake with some fat. The term is a very appropriate one, for tougher things cannot well be eaten.

1855 William Howitt *Land, Labour and Gold* i 117: The leather-jacket is a cake of mere flour and water, raised with tartaric acid and carbonate of soda instead of yeast, and baked in the frying-pan; and is equal to any muffin you can buy in the London shops.

1894 Henry Lawson *Prose* i 52: 'I wish

I had just enough fat to make the pan siss; I'd treat myself to a leather-jacket; but it took three weeks' skimmin' to get enough for them theer dough-boys.'

leatherneck A rouseabout in a shearing shed, etc.: *obsolescent*
1898 *Bulletin* 1 Oct. 14: The rouse-abouts [are] 'leathernecks'.
1941 Baker 43: *Leather-neck* A station 'rouseabout'.

leghorn, white see **white leghorn**

leg-opener Alcohol, esp. wine or spirits, thought of as making women more vulnerable sexually
1959 Dorothy Hewett *Bobbin Up* 93: 'Gotta bit of leg opener in the back seat of the heap.'
1965 Leslie Haylen *Big Red* 133: There was a bottle of wine or two there for a birthday party or for the women at Christmas time. Shearers had been known to buy a bottle of Charlie's 'leg opener' to knock off a sheila.
1968 Geoffrey Dutton *Andy* 154: The bottle of sparkling burgundy (a dis-gusting drink, apart from its legendary powers as leg-opener).
1975 Les Ryan *The Shearers* 108: 'Leg opener?' Sandy asked. Baldo said 'A bottle of each mate. Gin, and lemon.'

lemons, to go in To do something with a will: *obs.*
1903 Joseph Furphy *Such is Life* (1944) 17: 'Grass up over yer boots, an' the carrion goin' into it lemons.'
1904 Laura M. Palmer-Archer *A Bush Honeymoon* 350: *Going in lemons* Enthus-iastically.

lemony Annoyed, peeved [? f. sour-ness]
1941 Baker 31: *Go lemony at* To become angry, express anger towards someone.
1944 Dal Stivens *The Courtship of Uncle Henry* 75: He's as lemony as hell when he opens the door and doesn't say a word to me.

leso A lesbian [abbr.]

1976 Dorothy Hewett *The Tatty Hol-low Story* 118: 'What's up with you? Are you a leso or something?'

lid, to dip one's see **dip**

life, go for your An expression of en-couragement, as though guaranteeing no interference
1928 Arthur Wright *A Good Recovery* 128: 'I'll get plenty of witnesses from the west as soon as ever they're wanted. Go for your life, cobber; I'll be ready.'
1939 Kylie Tennant *Foveaux* 362: 'He'd go for his life, if we asked him.'
1947 Gavin Casey *The Wits are Out* 27: 'I'd just as soon have sherry,' Myra said. 'Then get a bottle and go for your life,' Bill said.
1949 John Morrison *The Creeping City* 63: 'Then go for your bloody life!' Bob got up and waved his hand as if the whole matter were already disposed of. 'I ain't standing in your way.'
1959 Anne von Bertouch *February Dark* 248: 'D' you mind if I take your hurricane lamp and run up to the house?' 'No. Go for your life.'

life wasn't meant to be easy A saying associated since 1976 with Malcolm Fraser, Australian Prime Minister (1975-), in commending government policies [cf. the proverb 'Life is not all beer and skittles'; Longfellow, 'Life is real! Life is earnest' ('A Psalm of Life'); G. B. Shaw *Back to Methuselah* (World's Classics 1945) 263: 'Life is not meant to be easy, my child; but take courage: it can be delightful']
1977 *Australian* 3 May 3: The Prime Minister, in an address to the A.C.T. Liberal Party last night, lamented that he should have taken out a copyright on his now famous statement 'Life wasn't meant to be easy' . . . 'It occurred to me [when the Consumer Price Index fell] that there are times when life is a little easier than it's meant to be.'

light on Sparsely supplied, of short weight
1944 Lawson Glassop *We Were the Rats* 122: 'You're a bit light on too, aren't

you?' 'Purely a temporary state of poverty, Reynolds old boy.'
1973 Frank Huelin *Keep Moving* 133: 'Yous blokes waitin' f'r a feed?' the cook asked, thrusting his head out of the galley. 'Might be a bit light on.'
1975 *Overland* 62 25: The heroines were a bit light on the ground, but there was always La Passionara.

light on the hill, the The symbol of the socialist objective of the Australian Labor Party
1949 J. B. Chifley policy speech *Sydney Morning Herald* 15 Nov. 4: We do say that it is the duty and responsibility of the community, and particularly those more fortunately placed, to see that our less fortunate fellow citizens are protected from those shafts of fate which leave them helpless and without hope. This is the objective for which we are striving. It is, as I have said before, the beacon, the light on the hill, to which our eyes are always turned, and to which our efforts are always directed.
1967 R. G. Menzies *Afternoon Light* 129: The Socialist objective, his 'light on the hill', must not be blotted out or obscured in this way.
1974 *Australian* 26 Apr. 8: In 1971 and 1972 the left wing became quiescent . . . Where there had existed a wild passion to get to the socialist 'light on the hill', quieter, more disingenuous instincts were mobilized. The changes proved profitable.

line 1 A line of patter, a 'technique', esp. in such expressions as 'doing a line', 'selling a line' for a male approach to women [also U.S.]
1941 Kylie Tennant *The Battlers* 101: 'A man might do a line with her, dippy or not.'
1946 Dal Stivens *The Courtship of Uncle Henry* 71: I ambled over to her and started selling her a line.
1951 Dymphna Cusack and Florence James *Come in Spinner* 364: 'My dear, he's a wow. And what a line! He calls me his little dream-dust and kisses me as though I was made of glass.'
1961 Nene Gare *The Fringe Dwellers* 286: 'I'm gunna do a line with the little gel that wants to go to Perth with me.'
1966 Roger Carr *Surfie* 51: Femmies are pretty good at handing out a line of rubbish when they want.
2 A girl or woman, as an amorous prospect
1944 Lawson Glassop *We Were the Rats* 5: 'You seen that new blonde barmaid at the Royal? A real good line.'
1954 T. A. G. Hungerford *Sowers of the Wind* 74: 'You looking for a sheila, sarge? . . . I can put you on to some, only it'll cost you yen. They're good lines, though.'

Line, Brisbane see **Brisbane**

Lions, the The Fitzroy V.F.L. team
1976 *Sunday Telegraph* 18 Apr. 55: The Lions led by eight points by half-time.

Lithgow flash, the Miss Marjorie Jackson (b. 1932), of Lithgow N.S.W., winner of Gold Medals for the 100 and 200 metres sprint at the Olympic Games in 1952
1952 *Sydney Morning Herald* 10 Aug. 1: A pennant with the words 'Lithgow Flash' flew from the bonnet. At the rear was a banner with the words 'Hail, Marjorie Jackson'.

Little Digger, the see **Digger**

lizard A shepherd; a man maintaining boundary fences (and so crawling along or stretching out in the sun)
1908 Giles Seagram *Bushmen All* 127: The term 'lizard' was one rather contemptuously applied to the shepherds by the horsemen. Ibid. 240: 'This blessed lizarding is bad enough, but wood and water joey is worse.'
1931 W. Hatfield *Sheepmates* 120–1: 'You're goin' in the camp, aren't you? – Not goin' lizardin'?' . . . 'Yes,' said Hallett, 'you'd be better out in the camp with me than crawlin' around a fence like a fly-catcher lizard.'
1937 Arthur Upfield *Winds of Evil* 174 –5: 'What bloke wouldn't be depressed at coming down to a fence lizard! . . .

Come down to fencin' and you want to know why a bloke's depressed.'

lizard, flat out as a ~ drinking Working 'flat out', without a moment to spare
1944 Jean Devanny *By Tropic, Sea and Jungle* 227: The mother [kangaroo-rat] went one way and the young one another . . . It ran straight, as flat out as a lizard drinking.
1951 Dal Stivens *Jimmy Brockett* 70: The Wednesday of that week I was flat out like a lizard drinking when the phone rang.
1952 Jon Cleary *The Sundowners* 183: 'You've been flat out like a lizard drinking, but this cove is right with you all the time.'
1970 Max Harris *Australian* 10 Jan. 14: Have you ever copped the way those girls serve the community at the Sydney Telephone Exchange? Flat out like lizards drinking, all day long.

lizards, stiffen (starve) the An exclamation of astonishment, protest, disbelief: sometimes 'Stone the crows and stiffen the lizards' (comic strip Australian)
1944 Lawson Glassop *We Were the Rats* 204: 'God starve the lizards,' said Eddie, 'another dud. Reckon half their bloody shells are duds.'
1965 Eric Lambert *The Long White Night* 89: 'Starve the bloody lizards!' breathed Clancy. 'Now I've seen the lot!'

load of, get a Take notice of, get an 'eyeful' of [U.S. 1929 OED]
1941 Baker 44: *Load of, get a* To take notice of, understand.
1952 Jon Cleary *The Sundowners* 133: Bluey looked at Sean and jerked a thumb at Venneker. 'Get a load of who's talking?'
1959 Dorothy Hewett *Bobbin Up* 178: 'Get a load of that, when she bends over!'
1965 Frank Hardy *The Yarns of Billy Borker* 147: 'Get a load of this outfit. Look at me flamin' hat.'
1975 Les Ryan *The Shearers* 14: 'Hey, Lofty! Get a load of that!' he said, as a

blonde salesgirl in a white uniform entered.

lob (in) To arrive, turn up
1915 C. J. Dennis *The Songs of a Sentimental Bloke* 56: 'Twas at a beano where I lobs along / To drown them memories o' fancied wrong.
1924 E. J. Brady *Land of the Sun* 89: A man who would insist on telling things lobbed in.
1931 Vance Palmer *Separate Lives* 220-1: 'When I lob home,' said Chook, 'd'you know the first thing I'll do?'
1950 K. S. Prichard *Winged Seeds* 24: 'You never knew who'd lob into the camp.'
1973 John Morrison *Australian by Choice* 187-8: She was the first woman Sam spoke to when he lobbed in the town.

Lochinvar An abductor of lubras: N.T. [f. the poem by Sir Walter Scott]
1951 Ernestine Hill *The Territory* 311: Lochinvars sold the women to the drovers and the stations at £10 a head, but they didn't have it all their own way. A good many were speared.

lock on with, to To fight (juvenile)
1959 Gerard Hamilton *Summer Glare* 107: When I looked around they were fighting – 'locked on' as we called it. Ibid. 108: 'Why did you lock on with Nancy this arvo?' I said.

logs, the Gaol: *obs.* [f. timber used in construction]
1870 Marcus Clarke *His Natural Life* ed. S. Murray-Smith (1970) 784: 'Tomorrow morning – Mac, we'll have all these fellows comfortably in the logs.'
1873 Rolf Boldrewood 'The Fencing of Wanderowna' *A Romance of Canvas Town* (1898) 119: The aforesaid lock-up, popularly known as 'The Logs' from the preponderating quantity of these massive timbers displayed in the floor, the wall, and indeed the ceiling of the edifice.
1903 Joseph Furphy *Such is Life* (1944) 369: 'It seems sort a' hard lines when a man's shoved in the logs for the best

three months in the year for a thing he never done.'

lolly A sweet, esp. coloured [abbr. of *lollipop*]
1854 Catherine Spence *Clara Morison* (1971) 278: Fanny ran away to the nearest lolly shop, and all her brothers and sisters followed her.
1859 Oliné Keese *The Broad Arrow* i 324: 'She wouldn't give me any more lollies.'
1883 R. E. N. Twopeny *Town Life in Australia* 54: You will see babies without number left in the blazing sun, some hanging half-way out of their perambulators, others sucking large painted 'lollies' or green apples.
1900 Henry Lawson 'The Songs They Used to Sing' *Prose* i 37: We got lollies (those hard old red-and-white 'fish lollies' that grocers sent home with parcels of groceries).
1911 Louis Stone *Jonah* 93: The trays heaped with sweets coloured like the rainbow, pleased his eye, and, remembering Ada's childish taste for lollies . . .
1931 Vance Palmer *Separate Lives* 64: Coloured lollies in bottles that made the mouth water.

lollyboy The vendor of a tray of sweets and ice cream at the cinema
1971 G. Johnston *A Cartload of Clay* 45: The lights came on for interval and the lolly boys were shuffling raucous with their trays.

lolly, do the To lose one's temper, presence of mind
1959 Dorothy Hewett *Bobbin Up* 178: 'Keep an eye on me machine will you Jeanie. S'pose we'll haveta keep it goin' now Dick's doin' his lolly.'
1962 Criena Rohan *The Delinquents* 132: 'Don't start talking to me as though you were a plain-clothes cop,' said Lola, 'or I'm liable to do the lolly.'
1964 Thomas Keneally *The Place at Whitton* 18: 'I didn't want to antagonize them, and the first one I meet, I do my lolly with him.'
1971 Frank Hardy *The Outcasts of Fool-*

garah 116: A strong debater even if prone to do the lolly on the Red issue.

lollywater Soft drink, esp. if coloured
1945 Baker 231: *lolly-water* soft drink. [as an example of derivation from pidgin]
1948 Sumner Locke Elliott *Rusty Bugles* in *Khaki, Bush and Bigotry* ed. Eunice Hanger (1968) 56: 'Only one bottle of lolly water per man.'
1953 *The Sunburnt Country* ed. Ian Bevan 127: The greatest indignity that ever befell the hapless defenders of Darwin was not the Japanese air-raids . . . [but] that its garrison was issued not with beer, but with bottled cordial. This they christened, contemptuously, 'lolly water': and weed killer could not have been more detested.
1966 Hal Porter *The Paper Chase* 300: 'Soda-water please. And you can ask the bar-boy for a bottle of lolly-water for yourself.'
1968 Thomas Keneally *Three Cheers for the Paraclete* 5: Under Brendan's sporadic directions, the car left the lolly-water ambience of the big streets and found its way among terraces.

London to a brick A statement of betting odds (a brick = £10) popularized by the racing commentator Ken Howard (1914–76)
1965 Frank Hardy *The Yarns of Billy Borker* 108: 'Close: but Magger by a head,' the course announcer Ken Howard says, 'London to a brick on Magger.'
1974 *Sydney Morning Herald* 1 Jan. 2: A Howard trademark was his confident prediction of the winner in a tight finish – 'It's London to a brick on.' . . . Where did the expression 'London to a brick on' come from? 'I don't know, but I probably picked it up in the billiards halls when I was younger,' he said. 'I used to meet a lot of Damon Runyon characters, listen to their talk and pick up some of their expressions.'

long oats see **oats**

long colonial, a see **colonial**

long sleever A tall glass of beer: *obsolescent* [f. *sleever* measure of 13 fluid ounces OED 1896]

1877 T. E. Argles *The Pilgrim* viii 18: I should blow the froth from off the festive 'long sleever'.

1887 *All the Year Round* 30 Jul. 67: A frequent invitation is to take a 'long sleeved 'un', that is, a drink from a long pint glass.

1890 A. G. Hales *Wanderings of a Simple Child* 98: 'If you like to stand another long sleever, I'll give you some more.'

1905 Joseph Furphy *Rigby's Romance* ed. R. G. Howarth (1946) 26: The old gentleman, of course, took a long sleever, looking with ostentatious pity at the Doctor's sarsaparilla.

1908 Henry Fletcher *Dads and Dan between Smokes* 126: Yous can get a bloke with a long sleever hat, frock coat, an' made ter order pants.

1931 *Henry Lawson by his Mates* 126: Forty years ago there were many hospitable places between Hay Street and the Town Hall where one could procure 'long sleevers' of colonial beer for three-pence.

1975 Xavier Herbert *Poor Fellow My Country* 1144: Sims had a long-sleever.

Loo, the Woolloomooloo, a Sydney suburb

1893 Daniel Healey *The Cornstalk* 39: Tim Bunyip was of Austral birth, / Born at the classic 'Loo.

1908 *Evening News* 7 Jul. 7: The camphor trees ... will in a day or so become the centre of attraction to the rising generation of the 'Loo' on the warpath for cheap firewood.

1924 *Truth* 27 Apr. 6: 'Loo Woolloomooloo, suburb of Sydney.

1930 *Bulletin* 24 Dec. 42: 'I'm off back home to me job and the 'Loo.'

1959 Dorothy Hewett *Bobbin Up* 15: The shabby, genteel poverty of bed sits and bed and breakfast, running downhill into the slummy rabbit warrens of Paddo and the Loo.

look, take a ~ at A wry injunction intended to draw attention to the realities of a situation

1943 Dymphna Cusack *Morning Sacrifice* 27: 'Take a look at me, cherub, and remember that nothing comes to the woman who waits.'

1957 Ray Lawler *Summer of the Seventeenth Doll* 78: 'Glamorous nights! I mean – look at us.'

1959 Eleanor Dark *Lantana Lane* 21: 'By golly!' they will snort bitterly. 'Just take a look at us, and then take a look at the graziers! They have it all taped.'

loppy A rouseabout

1898 *Bulletin* 1 Oct. 14: The rouseabouts [are] 'leathernecks', 'spoonbills', 'loppies', or 'Jacks'.

1911 L. St Clare Grondona *Collar and Cuffs* 85: 'Loppy' as the rouseabout is called.

1964 H. P. Tritton *Time Means Tucker* 92: With only a couple of thousand to go 'Hughie' answered the prayers of the loppies with a fairly heavy shower.

lower than a snake's belly see **snake**

luck of Eric Connolly see **Connolly**

Lucky Country, the The Australia of the 1960s, from a book of that title (1964) by Donald Horne

1969 *Australian* 13 Sep. 11 C: Illegitimacy in the Lucky Country.

1970 Donald Horne *The Next Australia* 19: When I invented the phrase 'The Lucky Country' it was quickly misunderstood as it quickly caught on ... So a phrase that was intended as an ironic rebuke became a phrase of self-congratulation.

1970 Jon Cleary *Helga's Web* 140: Suddenly she hated all Australians, the whole lucky country as they called themselves.

1974 *Sun-Herald* 29 Dec. 15: In two years of power, the Whitlam Government has turned 'the lucky country' upside down and achieved none of its aims.

lucky, strike me A catch-phrase of the comedian Roy Rene ('Mo') and the title of a film in which he starred in 1935

[1859 Hotten *Strike me lucky!* a simple form of an oath common amongst the lower orders when making a bargain, and appealing to their honour.]

lurk 1 A dodge, a scheme, stratagem
1951 Dal Stivens *Jimmy Brockett* 113: It might be a good lurk to float it into a company and get out while the going was good.
1961 George Farwell *Vanishing Australians* 76: It [lambing down] denoted a lurk used by some publicans.
1972 Basil Fuller *West of the Bight* 31: 'He knew all the lurks, o' course.'
1975 *Australian* 15 Sep. 7: 'There are a lot of lurks down in Canberra,' he said ... 'They pay senators $37 a day while in Canberra – that's too much. And you can take a relative down four times a year.'
2 A job, occupation (close in implication to 1)
1915 C. J. Dennis *The Songs of a Sentimental Bloke* 20: I found 'er lurk / Was pastin' labels in a pickle joint.
1953 T. A. G. Hungerford *Riverslake* 189: 'I dunno why you don't take up teaching again. That's your lurk.'
1962 Alan Marshall *This is the Grass* 159: 'What's your lurk, anyway?' 'I just knock around,' I said ... I added, 'I'm a clerk.'

M

mad as a cut snake, as a meat-axe Out of one's mind; extremely annoyed
1932 William Hatfield *Ginger Murdoch* 30: 'But you're mad!' said Mick, 'mad as a cut snake!'
1946 Dal Stivens *The Courtship of Uncle Henry* 75: He was mad as a cut snake about everything and wanting to put the boot in.
1951 Seaforth Mackenzie *Dead Men Rising* 203: 'Mad as a cut snake,' Johnson said admiringly, 'and there's not a better feller in the whole camp.'
1964 Dan Reidy *The Road to Tabuggeree* (1967) 33: 'That's Noisy Joyner's; he's as mad as a snake on a chain.'
1975 Don Townshend *Gland Time* 148: 'Never seen anythin' like it. Mad as a cut snake she was.'
1946 *Coast to Coast 1945* 252: 'The cow's mad – mad as a meat-axe!' Jack said with conviction.
1974 David Ireland *Burn* 97: 'Struth, love, you're mad as a meat-axe.'
see **silly as a two-bob watch**

mad, he went ~ and they shot him Jocular reply to a request for anyone's whereabouts (World War II slang)
1944 Lawson Glassop *We Were the Rats* 47: 'I just came in for a yarn with Happy. Where is he?' 'If ya referrin' ter Mr Simpson he went mad and they shot him.'
1948 Sumner Locke Elliott *Rusty Bugles* in *Khaki, Bush and Bigotry* ed. Eunice Hanger (1968) 31: 'Andy Edwards ... Andy Edwards there?' 'Went mad and they shot him.'
1953 *The Sunburnt Country* ed. Ian Bevan 129: 'He went mad and they shot him' is the routine answer to any superior seeking the whereabouts of a subordinate.
1975 *Woman's World* 8 Oct. 71: Father was unusually late home, having been held up in a traffic jam. Five-year-old son, tired of waiting for Dad, announced, 'Perhaps he went mad and they shot him.'
see **went through like Speed Gordon, gone for a ride on the padre's bike, went for a crap and the sniper got him**

mad mick see **mick**

madwoman's custard (knitting, lunch-box), all over the place like a In complete disarray
1953 T. A. G. Hungerford *Riverslake* 18: 'What a joint! All over the place like a mad woman's knitting.'
1957 D'Arcy Niland *Call Me When the Cross Turns Over* 199: 'In the end he was blood from head to hocks and all over the place like a mad woman's custard.'
1973 Alexander Buzo *Norm and Ahmed* 10: 'I floored this bloody Kraut. Really laid him out. He was all over the place

like a mad woman's lunch box.'

maginnis, a crooked A hold (as in wrestling) that puts an opponent at a complete disadvantage: *obs.* [derived by Baker (1966: 126) from a wrestler called McGinnis]
1900–10 O'Brien and Stephens: *putting the McGinnis on* To put an opponent or combatant hors-de-combat. A grip or hold that cannot be unlocked or resisted.
1903 Joseph Furphy *Such is Life* (1944) 15: 'You see, Tom,' he remarked to me, 'this fixter'll put the crooked maginnis on any fence from 'ere to 'ell.'
1905 Joseph Furphy *Rigby's Romance* ed. R. G. Howarth (1946) 66–7: 'I could see my way to Agnes in a more manly, off-hand way than depending on the sort of crooked maginnis I had on her.'

maggoty Angry, bad-tempered [*maggoty* freakish, whimsical OED 1678–1864]
1919 W. H. Downing *Digger Dialects* 33: *Maggotty* Angry.
1941 Baker 45: *Maggoty* Angry, irritable, 'snooty'.
1951 Dal Stivens *Jimmy Brockett* 31: I didn't need to, but I shaved every day and my old man made me maggotty by asking me one day, 'Do you shave up or down?'
1959 David Forrest *The Last Blue Sea* 74: 'He's down there in the R.A.P. going maggotty about doctors and Japs and boongs.'

Magpies, the 1 In N.S.W., the Western Suburbs Rugby League team [f. black and white colours]
1976 *Sunday Telegraph* 11 Apr. 58: Magpies breakfast on the Berries.
2 In Victoria, the Collingwood V.F.L. team
1974 *Sunday Telegraph* 8 Sep. 84: Magpies get home easily.

Mainland, the Australia, from a Tasmanian standpoint
1934 Thomas Wood *Cobbers* 164: They are tied to Australia – 'the mainland', they call it ... 'the mainland' is an object of suspicion, envy, and dislike.
1958 Christopher Koch *The Boys in the Island* 15: He lived in an island. At six years old he knew about that. He heard it at school, and knew about it from Uncle Charlie's talk about the Mainland, Australia.
1968 Geoffrey Dutton *Andy* 200: 'Soon as I blew from the book, I headed down for the Old Tassy ... I'll get over on the Mainland soon, or up the islands.'
1975 Don Townshend *Gland Time* 33: The mainland was foreign to him and always would be foreign. On Monday morning he flew back to Tasmania.

Maitland, Dean A silent person [f. the film *The Silence of Dean Maitland*, 1914 and 1934, based on the novel by Maxwell Grey]
1948 Sumner Locke Elliott *Rusty Bugles* in *Khaki, Bush and Bigotry* ed. Eunice Hanger (1968) 88: *Ot:* Poor old Dean Maitland ... *Vic.* There must have been a lot on his mind. I never saw him speak the whole time he was here.
1969 R. S. Whitington *The Quiet Australian* 98: The twenty-two players were far too tense to talk during the twenty-minute break. Twenty-two 'Dean Maitlands' sipped their tea in silence.

Major's line, the The route followed by Major Thomas Mitchell in his expedition of 1836, opening up Victoria for pastoral settlement
1853 *Letters from Victorian Pioneers* ed. T. F. Bride (1898) 52: We followed the track of those before us ... and in a short distance came on the Major's line, which was easily recognized at this time.
1855 William Howitt *Land, Labour and Gold* ii 99: Well might Sir Thomas Mitchell, in his route across this colony at this season of the year, describe it as a splendidly grassed country. We crossed his track, still called the Major's Line, a short time ago.
1883 E. M. Curr *Recollections of Squatting in Victoria* 22: Being again in Melbourne in January 1841, he purchased a sheep station which was situated on

the Major's line*, about seventy miles from Melbourne, and five miles southwest from where the town of Heathcote now stands. *The 'Major's line' is a term signifying the track, or line of road, formed by the drays of Major (afterwards Sir Thomas) Mitchell in his explorations. In some localities the track or road which his drays left behind is called 'the Major' to this day.

Mal, Big Mr Malcolm Fraser, Australian Prime Minister 1975– [f. height]
1976 *Sydney Morning Herald* 30 Aug. 1: Big Mal has urged us to spend up, and his latest support comes from the Champagne Information Centre.

mallee, the Equivalent to 'the scrub' in expressions like 'take to the mallee' [f. the mallee scrub in Victoria]
1958 E. O. Schlunke *The Village Hampden* 127: 'They're going to lynch you, Rogerson,' Harry told him, grinning. 'You'd better take to the mallee before they come for you.'

Mallee bull, fit as a Extremely fit: Victorian [see quot. 1974]
1962 John Morrison *Twenty-three* 163: 'How's Bubby?' 'Fit as a Mallee bull! Got another tooth . . . '
1969 William Dick *Naked Prodigal* 257: 'You're orright, are yuh?' 'Fit as a mallee bull and twice as dangerous.'
1974 Jim McNeil *How Does Your Garden Grow* 45: *Mick:* Ha! (*Posing*) Fit as a mallee bull! Ibid. 141: *A mallee bull* is thus a beast toughened by spartan living conditions.
1976 *Australian* 31 May 8: 'There's a fairly high degree of male homosexuality among male [ballet] dancers but they seem to range from one extreme to the other, where some guys can do absolutely astonishing things – the proverbial Mallee Bulls, if you like. Their bodies are so finely tuned and dance is such a physical thing.'

Mallee gate See quot.
1966 *Coast to Coast 1965–1966* 150: 'D' you know what a Mallee gate is, Bob?' 'Yes, it's a short loose panel, just droppers and wires.'

mallee root A prostitute [rhyming slang]
1941 Baker 45: *Mallee root* A prostitute.

Malley's cow See quot.: N.T.
1951 Ernestine Hill *The Territory* 441: 'By the look o' the sun I better get a move on, missus. I'm Malley's Cow. I'm a goner!' Ibid. 445: *Malley's Cow** A person gone away. *Back in Monaro folklore one Malley in a mustering-camp was told to hold a particular cow. When the boss came back and asked for it, Malley grinned. 'She's a goner,' he said.

Maluka, the The chief, the boss [Ab.]
1908 Mrs Aeneas Gunn *We of the Never-Never* 11: The Maluka – better known at that time as the new Boss for the Elsey.
1928 Martin Boyd *The Montforts* 238: 'You'd better come and see the Maluka.' 'What's that?' ventured Raoul. 'It's aboriginal for headmaster.'
1971 Keith Willey *Boss Drover* 140: An aboriginal with me said: 'Pickum grass, Maluka.'

mangle A bicycle (juvenile) *obs.* [? f. humorous resemblance]
1941 Baker 45: *Mangle* A bicycle.
1965 Graham McInnes *The Road to Gundagai* 122: 'Where's the grid?' 'My bike!' 'Yeah, the old mangle; isn't this where we left it?' [recalling the 1920s]

Maoriland New Zealand [f. Maoris as the original inhabitants]
1884 *Maoriland An Illustrated Handbook to New Zealand* [book title] (Morris)
1896 Henry Lawson *Prose* i 209: They battled round together in the North Island of Maoriland for a couple of years.
1905 *Bulletin* 12 Jan. Red Page: A certain poet went down from Tasmania to Maoriland, and fell among words, which stripped him of his simplicity and stunned him, and never departed leaving him half dead.

1930 *Bulletin* 2 Jul. 11: Everyone had contributed at least one good lie except the man from Maoriland.

Maorilander

1942 Eve Langley *The Pea Pickers* 411: In the corner of his paddock, on the site of the Maorilander's tent, stood another's.

marble, to make one's ~ good To make the grade, confirm or improve one's status or prospects (cf. *alley*) [N.Z. 1926 OED]

1950 Brian James *The Advancement of Spencer Button* 162: 'He's trying to make his marble good, all right.'

1963 Don Crick *Martin Place* 223: 'Take my tip, if you wanter make your marble good: say nothing.'

marble, to pass in one's To give up, die (cf. *alley*)

1908 *Australian Magazine* 1 Nov. 1250: Instead of dying you can 'chuck a seven', 'pass in your marble', or 'peg out'.

1918 Arthur Wright *Over the Odds* 102: 'I suppose the old pot knew y' old man before he passed in his marble,' ventured Dick.

1924 *Truth* 27 Apr. 6: *Throw in the marble* To relinquish.

1951 Dal Stivens *Jimmy Brockett* 304: 'I'm not going to pass in my marble just yet.'

1961 George Farwell *Vanishing Australians* 77: He . . . went into a coma, and it was some time before the coves he was shouting woke up that he'd really passed in his marble.

Marble Bar, till it rains in Indefinitely [f. N.S.W. town of low rainfall]

1943 Douglas Stewart *Ned Kelly* in *Four Plays* (1956) 172: 'And we'd have held this country against the troopers / Till it rains in Marble Bar!'

March, the The march of ex-servicemen on Anzac Day

1945 Cecil Mann *The River* 136: Clarkey is not in the March this year.

1962 Alan Seymour *The One Day of the Year* 79: 'We started at a pub in King Street straight after the march.'

Mardi Gras A carnival held at any time of the year [f. *Mardi Gras* (Shrove Tuesday) as a festival]

1977 *Sunday Telegraph* 16 Jan. 76: A closing highlight of the Festival of Sydney will be a huge Mardi Gras at the Haymarket on the night of Saturday, January 29.

mark, marking Abbr. of 'earmark', generalized to cover the whole process of ear-marking, docking and castrating lambs; also a euphemism for 'castrate'

1898 Alfred Joyce *A Homestead History* ed. G. F. James (1969) 82–3: It was usual . . . to give them a bonus of a shilling a head for all lambs marked over a certain percentage, generally eighty-five per cent . . . A few weeks after the completion of the lambing, the work of emasculation, tail-docking and ear-marking would be gone through.

1905 *The Old Bush Songs* ed. A. B. Paterson 49: Then at the lamb-marking a boss they'll make of you. / Now that's the way to get on, Jimmy Sago, Jackaroo.

1911 E. S. Sorenson *Life in the Australian Backblocks* 143: When the pens are full there is a blessed respite while the lambs are marked . . . The markers are ranged on the outside of the pen, and operate on the lambs as they are dumped on the rail by the catchers, who hold a foreleg and a hindleg in each hand. Knives and teeth are used alternately by the operators.

1933 Acland: *Mark* To ear-mark. Now a frequent euphemism for *cut and tail*. *Cutting and tailing* was the old name for earmarking, castrating and taking the tails off lambs, all of which operations are performed together. *C. and t.* is the general name mostly used by shepherds, but (owing to more ladies living up country, I suppose) is being replaced by *tailing* or *marking*.

1946 Dal Stivens *The Courtship of Uncle Henry* 140: 'There are a few lambs want marking, but I was thinking of – ' said the boss, and before he could finish the bloke was running to the paddock and

213

pulling out his Jno. Baker knife.

market, go to To behave in a violent or angry way (superseded by 'go to town')

1898 *Bulletin* 17 Dec. Red Page: To *get narked* is to lose your temper; also expressed by *getting dead wet* or *going to market*.

1908 W. H. Ogilvie *My Life in the Open* 83: Playful or vicious, according to their breeding and temperament, almost all of them [the horses] 'prop' or 'go to market' in some form or other.

1941 Baker 46: *Market, go to* To become angry, complain bitterly (about something).

1948 K. S. Prichard *Golden Miles* 29: 'She goes to market when I get shickered,' Bill admitted.

marines, dead see **dead marines**

Maroons, the A sporting team representing the state of Queensland, esp. in Rugby League football [f. team colours]

1973 *Sydney Morning Herald* 12 Jul. 13: A Blue Day for the Maroons.

mary A girl or woman [Pidgin]

1876 A. J. Boyd *Old Colonials* (1882) 234: They [the natives] fail to comprehend how it is that a Chinaman who is 'baal white fellow' can get a white woman for a wife. They say, 'Chinaman got'im white Mary; blackfellow get'im white Mary.'

1885 Mrs Campbell Praed *Australian Life* 74: He asked what the Blacks wanted, and Boney replied, 'Altogether numkull; altogether marra white Maries.' ['To kill every one; and to take away the white women.']

1919 W. H. Downing *Digger Dialects* 56: *Mary* Woman [under heading Papua (Pidgin English)]

1931 Vance Palmer *Separate Lives* 68: 'White mary no walk about all day. She belonga one boss, sit down longa one house.'

1956 Tom Ronan *Moleskin Midas* 326: 'Harness up the buggy and take this Mary back to town.'

Mary Lou, on the On credit: *rare*

[rhyming slang *Mary Lou = blue* (credit, while 'red' is debit)]

1949 Lawson Glassop *Lucky Palmer* 248: He was betting on credit – 'Lucky' called it betting 'on the blue', 'on the Mary Lou', or 'on the nod'.

mate 1 A working partner; an habitual companion; a fellow-participant in some corporate activity (always a man)

1845 C. Griffith *The Present State ... of Port Phillip* 79: Two [bushworkers] generally travel together, who are called mates; they are partners, and divide all their earnings.

1847 Alexander Harris *Settlers and Convicts* ed. C. M. H. Clark (1954) 176: It is quite surprising what exertions bushmen of new countries, especially mates, will make for one another, beyond people of the old countries. I suppose ... difficulties prevailing make them more social and mutually helpful.

1864 James Armour *The Diggings, the Bush and Melbourne* 23: After much talk about the perfidy of former mates, he said that ... he would take me for a partner.

1880 Rolf Boldrewood *The Miner's Right* (1890) 136: 'We have been firm friends and true mates all this time.'

1899 Henry Lawson 'Crime in the Bush' *Prose* ii 35: Then there is the unprovoked, unpremeditated, passionless, and almost inexplicable bush murder, when two mates have lived together in the bush for years, until they can pass days and weeks without exchanging a word.

1915 Let. in Bill Gammage *The Broken Years* (1974) 59: Where are the rest of my 13 mates? ... myself I consider lucky getting away from the acres of dead men.

1947 John Morrison *Sailors Belong Ships* 20: Poor old Joe! Too much courage and too little brain ... A grand mate, though.

1953 *The Sunburnt Country* ed. Ian Bevan 126: No cry rings louder in the A.I.F. than this ... 'Don't bludge on your mates.'

1960 Donald McLean *The Roaring Days* 1: 'My mate' is always a man. A female may be my sheila, my bird, my charley, my good sort, my hot-drop, my judy or my wife, but she is never 'my mate'.

2 As a mode of address, indicating equality and friendliness

1852 Lord Robert Cecil *Goldfields Diary* (1935) 36: When the diggers address a policeman in uniform they always call him 'Sir', but they always address a fellow in a blue shirt with a carbine as 'Mate'. 'Mate' is the ordinary popular form of allocution in these colonies.

1862 Arthur Polehampton *Kangaroo Land* 99: A man, who greeted me after the fashion of the Bush, with a 'Good day, mate'.

3 As a neutral or hostile mode of address, to someone not an acquaintance

1944 Lawson Glassop *We Were the Rats* 75: 'I'm not looking for trouble.' 'Yer may not be bloody well lookin' fer it, mate, but yer'll bloody well get it.'

1953 T. A. G. Hungerford *Riverslake* 50: 'I'll remember you, mate. You'll keep!'

1974 *Sydney Morning Herald* 14 Feb. 7: At 8.26 that evening a train arrived at Gosford. The destination sign on the platform was not shown. I asked a station attendant (attired in a dirty open-necked shirt and trousers, recognizable only by a dirty cap) if the train was the North-West Mail. 'I wouldn't have a clue, mate,' was the reply.

mateship The fellowship implied in *mate*[1], and given currency by Henry Lawson: not really a colloquialism [OED 1593]

1894 Henry Lawson 'The Cant and Dirt of Labor Literature' *Prose* ii 27: When our ideal of 'mateship' is realised, the monopolists will not be able to hold the land from us.

1910 *Australian Magazine* Aug. 610: With such eloquence did he preach the gospel of communistic 'mateship' that he soon had even hundreds of men selling all they had, and following him to the social El Dorado in far-off Paraguay.

1959 Dorothy Hewett *Bobbin Up* 124: There was mateship, sharing a billy of bitter-black tea, a smoke and a yarn.

1973 Max Harris *The Angry Eye* 77: Historians have come to accept fairly calmly the notion that the Australian national philosophy of 'mateship' emerged from what was perhaps the world's only homosexual social ordering of things.

Matilda A swag [f. woman's name: origin otherwise obscure. See Richard Magoffin *Fair Dinkum Matilda* (1973)]

1893 Henry Lawson 'Some Popular Australian Mistakes' *Prose* ii 24: A swag is not generally referred to as a 'bluey' or 'Matilda' – it is *called* a 'swag'.

1899 W. T. Goodge *Hits! Skits! and Jingles!* 159: In the morning came a swaggie with 'Matilda' across the flat.

1910 John X. Cameron *The Spell of the Bush* 55: 'I sling Matilda on my back and steer whichever way she slews me.' 'Matilda!' repeated O'Carroll. 'Bluey.'

1915 J. P. Bourke *Off the Bluebush* 62: But, ah! a wintry wind / Awakes Matilda's charms: / I calmly spread the old girl out / And snuggle in her arms.

1924 *Truth* 27 Apr. 6: *Matilda* Aussie term for swag.

1939 R. H. Croll *I Recall* 81: Mostly to me that has meant tramping the bush; often it has implied carrying Matilda, the swag.

1962 J. Marshall and R. Drysdale *Journey Among Men* 116: It was good to stretch out in the arms of Matilda at the end of the day, and slowly smoke a cigarette. Ibid. 146: We unrolled our Matildas between the dunes.

Matilda, waltzing Carrying the swag, an expression given currency by A. B. Paterson's poem with this title, composed in 1895 and published in *Saltbush Bill J.P.* (1917), since achieving the status of an unofficial national anthem

1893 Henry Lawson 'Some Popular Australian Mistakes' *Prose* ii 24: No bushman thinks of 'going on the wallaby' or 'walking Matilda', or 'padding the hoof'; he goes on the track – when forced to it.

1902 Henry Lawson 'The Romance of the Swag' *Prose* i 501: Travelling with the swag in Australia is variously and picturesquely described as 'humping bluey', 'walking Matilda', 'humping Matilda', 'humping your drum', 'being on the wallaby'.

1917 A. B. Paterson *Saltbush Bill* 23: Who'll come a-waltzing Matilda with me?

1944 M. J. O'Reilly *Bowyangs and Boomerangs* 45: There was a vast difference between those swaggies of the early goldfields and the professionals found 'Waltzing Matilda' along the banks of the Darling, Murray or Murrumbidgee.

meanie, grey see grey meanie

meat-axe, mad as a see mad

meat pie, as Australian as a Unmistakably Australian [f. prominence of meat pie in Australian diet]

1972 *Bulletin* 13 May 41: I am drawn back to 'Lane End' each week to see Meillon, his face as genuinely Australian as a meat pie, give his performance.

1972 *Sunday Australian* 16 Apr. 4: Apart from his name and his forebears, Barassi with his wide grin and fierce desire to win is as Australian as a meat pie.

Melba, to do a To make a habit of returning from retirement, in a number of 'farewell' performances [f. Dame Nellie Melba 1861–1931]

1971 *Australian* 20 Feb. 22: The later years were marked by a seemingly endless round of farewell performances. 'Doing a Melba', they call it.

1976 *Sydney Morning Herald* 28 Apr. 23: 'There will be no Nellie Melbas for me . . . I have retired and I will not play again,' a sad Langlands told me.

merchant Used similarly to 'artist', in combinations like 'stand over merchant', 'king-hit merchant', usually with some derogatory suggestion

1944 Lawson Glassop *We Were the Rats* 133: 'Just a top-off merchant, that's all he is.'

1951 Dymphna Cusack and Florence James *Come in Spinner* 253: 'He was nothing but a bloody stoush merchant any way.'

1954 T. A. G. Hungerford *Sowers of the Wind* 9: 'I'm no lurk merchant, Mark,' Craigie said placidly.

1965 *The Tracks We Travel* ed. L. Haylen 122: 'If these panic-merchants only knew when to leave alone!'

merino, pure An early colonist priding himself on his freedom from the convict taint; a member of the most affluent and socially prominent class [f. breed of sheep]

1827 *Monitor* 13 Jan. 2: A round-about story has come to us . . . which, as it operates greatly to the credit of the pure Merino Bank, for which we have such an ardent regard . . . we shall here detail for the amusement of our readers.

1827 P. Cunningham *Two Years in New South Wales* ii 116: Next, we have . . . such as have legal reasons for visiting this colony; and . . . such as are free from that stigma. The *pure Merinos* are a variety of the latter species, who pride themselves on being of the *purest blood* in the colony.

1863 R. Therry *Reminiscences of Thirty Years' Residence in New South Wales* 58: The term *pure merino*, a designation given to sheep where there is no crossblood in the flocks, was applied to mark a class who were not only free and unconvicted, but who could boast of having no collateral relationship or distant affinity with those in whose escutcheon there was a blot. These *pure merinos* formed the topmost round in the social ladder.

1893 Francis Adams *The Australians* 56–7: It was in the interests of this narrow-minded and insignificant horde, reinforced by their allies, the 'pure merinos' (the big squatters), that a university was built up on the played-out model of the old Oxford. Ibid. 63: His early manhood found him [Henry Parkes] a counter-jumper in a Sydney toy-shop, eager to show his parts by impassioned and turbid 'sprouting' against 'the pure merinos' – the squattocracy and officialism of the hour.

1936 Miles Franklin *All That Swagger*

262: Norah was consulted, being married and of the pure merino squattocracy.
1954 Tom Ronan *Vision Splendid* 113: 'Old Mentmore . . . is one of your pure merino sportsmen: member of all the big racing clubs down south.'

mermaid A weighbridge inspector (road hauliers' slang)
1976 *The Sun* 28 May 7: Department of Main Roads weighbridge inspectors . . . are called 'mermaids' . . . because they have scales.

metho Methylated spirits [abbr.]
1935 Kylie Tennant *Tiburon* 23: The two metho-drinkers were escorted out firmly.
1949 Judith Wright *Woman to Man* 35: 'Metho Drinker' [poem title]
1950 Brian James *The Advancement of Spencer Button* 168: A drinking party . . . had taken a supply of spirits – mostly 'metho' – to a cave on the foreshores.
1955 Alan Marshall *I Can Jump Puddles* 159: 'He'd been on the metho for a couple of days, they say. He rolled into the fire in the night.'
1973 Alexander Buzo *Rooted* 96: 'He died of alcoholism . . . Went on the metho, slept in the park, fell apart at the seams.'

mick A Roman Catholic: *derogatory* [f. 'Mick' for an Irishman]
1934 'Leslie Parker' *Trooper to the Southern Cross* (1966) 89: We used to have a song at school:
Catholic dogs
Jump like frogs
which we always yelled at the Micks.
1939 Patrick White *Happy Valley* 25: Protestants called him a Micky, but he didn't mind.
1951 Dal Stivens *Jimmy Brockett* 231: Only a few revolutionaries, dingoes, loafers and a mob of Micks don't want to get into the war.
1964 George Johnston *My Brother Jack* 159: 'I don't care whether she's a mick or a Protestant or a holy roller.'
1972 David Williamson *The Removal-ists* 26: 'Five kids in seven years. Bastard's a mick.'
1975 Nancy Keesing *Garden Island People* 62: He maintained with supporting evidence which was plainly true at least for Garden Island, that the public service was 'given over to the micks', but did not hold this against Roman Catholics.

Mick, Crooked A mythical figure of N.T. and N. Queensland credited with prodigious feats
1945 Tom Ronan *Strangers on the Ophir* 234: Chris Christian, reared on the legends of his ancestors, agreed . . . that Thor, god of the thunders, rode high. The irreverent votaries of a newer and more humorous folklore commented 'Crooked Mick was kicking the billy-cans about.'
1966 Bill Wannan *Crooked Mick of the Speewah* [book title]

mick, mad A pick [rhyming slang]
1924 *Truth* 27 Apr. 6: *Mad mick* a pick.
1941 Baker 45: *Mad mick* A pick.
1946 Rohan Rivett *Behind Bamboo* 397: *Mad mick* pick
1953 T. A. G. Hungerford *Riverslake* 224: 'I swung a mad-mick there for eighteen months during the depression.'
1973 Frank Huelin *Keep Moving* 78: 'Well, I won't buy drinks for any bloody gangers, just for a chance to swing a mad mick.'

micks, a pair of The call of 'tails' in two-up. At first erroneously explained as 'heads' (see quots 1919, 1941), an explanation as yet unsupported by any evidence. Quot. 1938 is to be interpreted in the light of the tradition that the spinner backs heads. [Origin obscure: the 'tail' of the pennies used in two-up represents Britannia and her trident]
1919 W. H. Downing *Digger Dialects* 33: *Mick* (1) The Queen's head on a coin (e.g. 'Micks are right', when two heads have turned up in a game of 'two-up'); (2) a queen in a pack of cards
1938 John Robertson *With the Cameliers in Palestine* 198: The New

Zealanders are very religious men. Their priests lead them out to a quiet spot where they can pray. The priest spreads out a holy mat with marks on it which means something they have great faith in. He kneels down beside the mat, then a row of worshippers kneel all round him, with another row bending over them, and another row standing behind them. The worshippers throw their offerings on to the holy mat, and the priest places two coins on a short piece of polished wood which he calls a kip, and raising his eyes to the sky, he throws up the coins as an offering to Allah. All the worshippers raise their eyes also to the sky, and then bow solemnly over the mat, and say together, 'God Almighty', and the priest answers, 'A pair of Micks', which means that the offerings are not accepted, or he may say, 'Oh Lord, he has done 'em again,' and the joyful cries of some of the worshippers show that Allah is pleased, and so they, too, are glad.
1941 Baker 46: *Mick* The 'head' of a penny.
1953 T. A. G. Hungerford *Riverslake* 126: 'I got ten bob to say he tails 'em – ten bob the micks!'
1966 Baker 242: If a spinner throws two 'tails' he is said to *mick them* or throw *two micks*.

micky A bull calf, usually unbranded
1876 Rolf Boldrewood *A Colonial Reformer* in *A Town and Country Journal* 9 Dec. 942: The wary and still more dangerously sudden 'Michie', a two-year-old-bull (so called after an eminent Australian barrister famous for bringing his 'charges' to a successful issue). [1890 edition, ii 98, reads 'micky' and omits the derivation]
1881 A. C. Grant *Bush-Life in Queensland* i 227–8: Straining, roaring, jumping, dashing violently against the rails, a yellow brindled Micky is dragged up . . . Red-hot brands are now brought from the fire.
1893 Harry Morant 'Since the Country Carried Sheep' *Bulletin* 4 Mar. 19: The 'mickies' that we've branded there! The colts we used to ride!

1924 *Truth* 27 Apr. 6: *Micky* An un-branded, uncastrated calf approximating a year in age.
1933 R. B. Plowman *The Man from Oodnadatta* 63: Taking up the head-rope the boss lassoed a big micky (bull calf).
1945 Tom Ronan *Strangers on the Ophir* 82: Some battler earmarks a mangy mickey.
1951 Ernestine Hill *The Territory* 445: *Mickey* A half-grown bull calf, un-branded.
1961 George Farwell *Vanishing Australians* 68: Bill is also enthusiastic about the cod of a mickey (young bull) roasted over the coals at branding time.

mickey, chuck a To throw a fit, panic
1952 T. A. G. Hungerford *The Ridge and the River* 22: 'And he don't chuck a micky every time something goes off behind him!'

middy A measure of beer: in N.S.W., 10 oz.; in W.A., 7 oz.
1945 Baker 169: The *middy*, a beer glass containing nine ounces, is a measure used only in N.S.W. hotels.
1953 Baker 138: The nearest approximation to the Queensland *pot* is the N.S.W. *middy*, which holds 10 oz. of beer. At the time of writing my previous book, the size of the *middy* was fixed at nine ounces.
1972 John O'Grady *It's Your Shout, Mate!* 15: 'A glass is five ounces [in Western Australia], a middy is seven ounces, an' a pot's ten. Got it?' Ibid. 67: 'Now I've been down in Sydney [from Queensland], see. Why do they call a pot a middy?' . . . . 'Because it's midway between nothing and a pint.'
1976 David Ireland *The Glass Canoe* 150: Poor Liz . . . She didn't have the same old bounce, and she went down from schooners to middies.

mike A cup of tea: *rare*
1949 Ruth Park *Poor Man's Orange* 101: ''Ere's yer mike,' said his host, shoving over a pannikin of stewed and boiling tea.

Mile, the Golden see Golden

Mile, the Hungry see Hungry

milfissed the balfastards see balfastards

milko A milkman [abbr. or from cry]
[1865 J. F. Mortlock *Experiences of a Convict* (1965) 120: He proposed that I should carry his pails round the town and shout out 'Milk O!' at the customers' doors.]
1969 Mena Calthorpe *The Defectors* 180: The milko hesitated, then he ran along the street rattling the crates and bottles.
1976 *Australian* 14 Feb. 40: One loyal disciple rings up each week from Melbourne, just for the milko's tips.

million, gone a In a hopeless state; utterly disadvantaged or defeated [see quot. 1969]
1916 C. J. Dennis 'The Battle of the Wazzir' in A. H. Chisholm *The Making of a Sentimental Bloke* (1946) 131: Fer young Bill wus gone a million, an' 'e never guessed the game.
1919 J. Vance Marshall *The World of the Living Dead* 128: 'Times are mighty hard too. You've gotter keeep up appearances or else you're gonner million.'
1922 Arthur Wright *A Colt from the Country* 142: 'What hope would you have when that came out? You'd be gone a million.'
1924 Steele Rudd *Me an' th' Son* 129: 'Let him ... reckon th' horse is going to buck to the right when ud bucks to th' left, an' he's gone a million.'
1930 K. S. Prichard *Haxby's Circus* 187: 'If it weren't for you, I'd be gone a million on the minx.'
1942 Gavin Casey *It's Harder for Girls* 212: 'If they drop their bundles they're gone a million.'
1951 Dal Stivens *Jimmy Brockett* 232: 'If Pat Regan gets hold of her before we do, we're gone a million.'
1969 Sir Paul Hasluck *Sun-Herald* 24 Aug. 48: When I was a boy in Western Australia ... there was a Premier, John Scaddan (1911–16) who was usually

referred to among our friends as 'Gone a Million, Jack' ... Scaddan increased spending from loan funds, which in those days meant State public borrowing, to a level with which the State was quite unfamiliar and, in answering criticism, made some such remark as 'What's a million?' and gained a nickname that was intended to brand him as a careless person.
1973 Frank Huelin *Keep Moving* 107: 'What evidence would we have to prove it wasn't us? We'd be gone a million!'
1976 *Australian* 1 Mar. 1: 'Gough's gone a million' It's the end for Whitlam. We have the votes, say party rivals.

Ming Nickname of R. G. Menzies (1894–), Australian Prime Minister 1939–41, 1949–66 [f. pronunciation of Menzies as 'Mingis', and Ming the Mercilesss in the Speed Gordon comic strip]
c. 1954 Communist Party of Australia *'Our Bob': Further Misadventures of Ming (the Merciless) Menzies* [pamphlet title]
1975 *Australian* 4 Jul. 8: The swinging vote, which ended the Ming Dynasty after 23 years, has swung back to whence it came.

miserable Close-fisted, stingy, mean [OED 1484; E. dial. 1816–59]
1903 Joseph Furphy *Such is Life* (1944) 17: 'The more swellisher a man is, the more miserable he is about a bite o' grass for a team, or a feed for a traveller.'
1941 Baker 46: *Miserable* Mean-spirited, miserly.
1958 Frank Hardy *The Four-Legged Lottery* 183: 'Not all bookies are miserable; some of them are happy-go-lucky, generous blokes. They make money easily and spend it easily, give to charity and so forth. Pittson is miserable.'
1976 *Australian* 20 May 6: A 'lousy dollar a day!' Could any government be more miserable?

Mo The comedian Roy Rene, b. Harry van der Sluice (1892–1954)

mob 'A large number, the Australian

noun of multitude, and not implying anything low or noisy' (Morris): used almost as a technical term of cattle, etc., but more colloquially of people, as of a group with common interests

1838 Thomas Walker *A Month in the Bush of Australia* 8: I beheld a level plain, as even as a bowling green, not a rise nor a tree nor an object of any kind to interrupt the view, with the exception of 'mobs' of cattle scattered over the surface.

1852 G. C. Mundy *Our Antipodes* i 53: There are to be found round the doors of the Sydney theatre a sort of 'loafers', known as the Cabbage-tree mob . . . an unruly set of young fellows, native-born generally.

1853 S. Mossman and T. Banister *Australia Visited and Revisited* 82: This was a mixed herd of cattle, or as the squatters call them, a 'mob' of two hundred head.

1857 *Thatcher's Colonial Songster* 22: She said in return she'd just landed, as one / Of Missis Chisholm's mob.

1878 Rolf Boldrewood *An Australian Squire* repr. as *Babes in the Bush* (1900) 248: Ardmillan, Forbes and Neil Barrington, with all the 'Benmohr mob', as they were somewhat disrespectfully [1900 familiarly] called, were in the vanguard.

1918 Harley Matthews *Saints and Soldiers* 148: Big Snowy and his mob were back in camp behind the line.

1959 Anne von Bertouch *February Dark* 66: 'You can't get out of line with this mob, they don't miss a trick.'

1962 Alan Seymour *The One Day of the Year* 16–17: 'I'm sick of elegant young men talking of tapered shoes and Jags and MGs, in fact I'm sick of everybody in our mob, everybody.'

1973 H. Williams *My Love Had a Black Speed Stripe* 27: It's bad enough having McMahon and Whitlam and that lot without worrying about Tito and his mob.

mock (mockers), to put the ~ on To frustrate someone's plans; to place a hoo-doo on someone, destroy his luck [see *moz*]

1911 Edward Dyson *Benno, and Some of the Push* 33: 'All toms is 'erlike t'me,' he said . . . 'but, all the same, it's up t'me t'put a mock on that tripester.'

1923 Con Drew *Rogues and Ruses* 115: 'They'll have to race without me to-morrow. I've got a mocker hung on me.'

1938 Xavier Herbert *Capricornia* 473: 'Comin' here to put the mocks on us,' said Kit. 'Might be there's a reward.'

1941 Lawson Glassop *Lucky Palmer* 62: 'It's that sheila,' he said. 'She's put the mocker on us . . . We'll never have a good trot until you get rid of her.'

1965 Wally Grout *My Country's 'Keeper* 206: I hope I am not 'putting the mock' on Norm because my feelings are the same as the rest of the Australian Test players: when O'Neill is a doubtful Test starter the job always looks grimmer.

1974 David Ireland *Burn* 21: 'You tryin' to put the mockers on me?'

mocker Clothes [Partridge lists *mockered up* dressed in one's best: low: late C.19–20]

1953 Baker 106: *mocker*, clothes in general.

1961 Frank Hardy *The Hard Way* 77: 'They're fulla new mocker, see. Good clothes I got from mugs in Pentridge.'

1976 David Ireland *The Glass Canoe* 55: 'Now who's got good mocha on?' he says, looking round . . . Danny's gone mad for the occasion and has his grey suit on that he wears to weddings, funerals and smokos.

mockered up

1953 *Caddie A Sydney Barmaid* 223: 'I won't be likely ter be gettin' mokkered up before Saturday, so I'll pop me clobber termorrer ter raise the wind.'

moll at a christening see **christening**

molly-dooked, molly-dooker Left-handed; a left-handed person [? f. *mauly* fist OED 1780]

[**1926** J. Vance Marshall *Timely Tips for New Australians*: *Mauldy* Left-handed.]

1941 Baker 47: *Mollydooker* A left-handed person. Whence, 'molly dook' (adj.) left-handed.

1969 Hal Porter *Southerly* 8: Someone molly-duked, atheist, over-educated, young, leftist, Queensland-nurtured.

1975 *Sydney Morning Herald* 30 Aug. 11: A word of good cheer to all molly-dookers.

monarch, monaych Aboriginal term for the police: W.A. [see quot. 1975]

1961 Nene Gare *The Fringe Dwellers* 35: 'Skippy gets off. An ya know the first thing e says ta them monarch? E turns round on em an yelps, "An now ya can just gimme back that bottle."'

1975 Richard Beilby *The Brown Land Crying* 10: Myra was terrified. The coppers! Monaych! The native word contained a history of oppression: the Men with Chains!

Monday, yellow see yellow Monday

mong A mongrel [abbr.]

1923 Jack Moses *Beyond the City Gates* 152: 'What does it matter? He was only a mong!'

1933 *Bulletin* 16 Aug. 39: 'Most likely he just felt faint, same as you get on *any* job, and went out to it for a minute. And the mong fired him!'

1944 Jean Devanny *By Tropic, Sea and Jungle* 227: It takes a good mong dog to catch a rat-kangaroo in the bush.

1957 R. S. Porteous *Brigalow* 16: An irritable voice called, 'Go and lie down, you rotten mong.'

1967 *Southerly* 199: The bludging, dirty mong to whom she had . . . entrusted heart and hand.

monkey 1 A sheep

1881 A. C. Grant *Bush-Life in Queensland* i 88: Sheep lost on Saturday imperatively constrained every one on the head-station to look for them . . . and no one felt better pleased than he did to see the last lot of 'monkeys', as the shearers usually denominated sheep, leave the head-station.

1893 Francis Adams *The Australians* 137: A 'mob' of the wild, timid, yet inquisitive 'monkeys' (sheep).

1905 'The Wallaby Brigade' in *The Old Bush Songs* ed. A. B. Paterson 126 and note: You've only to sport your dover and knock a monkey over – / There's cheap mutton for the Wallaby Brigade. To knock a monkey over is to kill a sheep, monkey being slang for sheep in many parts of the bush.

1924 *Truth* 27 Apr. 6: *Monkies* A bush term for sheep.

1934 Brian Penton *Landtakers* 414: 'You'd have the stock, you say. Thirty or forty thousand monkeys all told, not reckoning cattle and horses.'

1942 Sarah Campion *Bonanza* 161: 'If only a man could breed sheep with fifty ribs apiece instead of – well, however many ribs the bleeding monkeys *do* have – he'd make his fortune!'

monkey-dodger A shepherd

1912 R. S. Tait *Scotty Mac, Shearer* 138: 'Behold in me chief serang, head monkey dodger to the high and holy Hungry Harris.'

2 See quot. 1959 [cf. *monkey-rope* U.S. 1851 OED]

1911 E. S. Sorenson *Life in the Australian Backblocks* 207: Novices and others who lack proficiency use . . . a monkey (a strap looped between the D's for the right hand to grip).

1959 Desmond Martin *Australia Astride* 194: *Monkey.* Also known as a Wagga grip or jug handle. It is used by weak riders to mount, or to try and ride buckjumpers.

3 The vulva

1970 Patrick White *The Vivisector* 111: 'Too much dirty water. That's what's wrong with Spargo. 'E'd carry 'is bed any time a woman up an' showed 'im 'er monkey.'

monte, monty A certainty, 'a sure thing' [f. card game U.S. 1841 Mathews]

1894 Henry Lawson *Verse* i 269: 'I've got a vote for Hughie – but it ain't no monte yet.'

1901 *The Bulletin Reciter* 182: 'It's the biggest bloomin' monte / Dat 'as ever come our way.'

1908 E. S. Sorenson *The Squatter's Ward* 122: 'It's a monty the little squib would let out a yell jest as I was gettin' clear.'

1930 K. S. Prichard *Haxby's Circus* 41:
'She's the chance of a life-time,' he
yelled. 'The biggest bloomin' monty
ever started on a racecourse.'

1945 Cecil Mann *The River* 52: As
they're rushing up the straight, old
toothless Past: He's a monty? We
always were lucky.

moosh Gaol porridge [variant of *mush*]

1945 Baker 141: Jail food is *moosh*.

1950 *The Australian Police Journal*
Apr. 116: *Moosh* Gaol porridge.

1967 B. K. Burton *Teach Them No More*
17: Moline took his plate back to his
cell, where he pushed his unwilling
spoon into glutinous material. The food
resisted the spoon's assault. 'What's
this muck?' 'That's mush,' Ted explained. 'I knew an old lagger once. He
was quite famous. He made little statues
out of his mush.'

1973 Jim McNeil *The Chocolate Frog*
117: Mush prounounced to rhyme with
push, prison porridge.

mopoke A dreary or stupid fellow [see
quot. 1845]

1845 Richard Howitt *Impressions of
Australia Felix* 233: 'A more-pork kind
of fellow' is a man of cut-and-dry
phrases; a person remarkable for
nothing new in common conversation.
This, by some, is thought very expressive; the more-pork being a kind
of Australian owl, notorious for its
wearying nightly iteration, 'More pork,
more pork.'

c. 1905 Joseph Furphy *The Buln-Buln
and the Brolga* ed. R. G. Howarth (1948)
124: 'Plop them in the tub, an' let
them soak a minit, you morepoke,' I
replied.

1910 H. H. Richardson *The Getting of
Wisdom* 205: At the idea of shutting
herself up wholly with such mopokes,
of cutting herself off from her present
vital interests, Laura hastily recon-
sidered her decision.

moral A 'moral certainty' (OED 1646)
i.e. certain to win, esp. in horseracing
[**1847** Alexander Harris *The Emigrant

Family ed. W. S. Ramson (1966) 279:
It was a moral certainty that the three
white cattle were from the same stock.]

1878 Rolf Boldrewood *An Australian
Squire* repr. as *Babes in the Bush* (1900)
175: It was understood that he was
entered on the chance of the two cracks
destroying each others chances, in one
of the numerous accidents to which
such races are liable, in which case
Bargo would be a 'moral'.

1889 *The Arrow* 20 Jul. 1: A school-
teacher recently asked his class 'What
is a moral?' And with one accord came
the answer 'A dead bird, sir.'

1916 C. J. Dennis *The Moods of Ginger
Mick* 40: 'E 'as struck it fer a moral.
Ginger's found 'is game at last.

1944 Lawson Glassop *We Were the Rats*
16: 'Think Tiger will win?' he asked.
'He's a moral,' I said. 'A lay-down
misere. I might have two quid on him.'

1952 T. A. G. Hungerford *The Ridge
and the River* 14: 'They're a moral to
lamp your footprints where you came
into the road from the track.'

1965 John Beede *They Hosed Them Out*
121: Clarkey, given enough grog, we
felt, was a moral to talk.

1970 Richard Beilby *No Medals for
Aphrodite* 253: 'They're a moral to be
after those guns. We'd better get out!'

1975 Les Ryan *The Shearers* 79: 'Andy
Burns rang last night . . . reckons Dallas
is a moral in the first.'

Moreton Bay rot See quot. [place-
name]

1918 C. Fetherstonhaugh *After Many
Days* 207: All the ills that flesh is heir
to in a new and tropical country, to
harass us, such as fever and ague,
Moreton Bay rot (skin scurvy), Belyando
Spue (pyrosis or water brash), sandy
blight.

Moscow, gone to, in In pawn
[c. **1882** *Sydney Slang Dictionary* 6:
Moskeener To pawn with a view to
obtaining more than the actual value
of an article.]

1941 Baker 47: *Moscow* A pawnshop.
'To moscow something': to pawn it.

1953 *Caddie A Sydney Barmaid* 217:

222

'Me clobber's already in Moscow, an'
so is me tan shoes.'

mossie (z) A mosquito [abbr.]
1941 Baker 47: *Mossie, mozzie* A mosquito.
1959 Dorothy Hewett *Bobbin Up* 76–7:
They sat in the cool on the back verandah, slapping at the mozzies.
1966 Elwyn Wallace *Sydney and the Bush* 60: 'A cowdung fire does the trick, you know. The mossies can't stand it.'

mote To move rapidly: *obsolescent*
1937 *Bulletin of the Australian English Association* Jul. 2: For many years now Australian schoolboys have been using it [mote] in the more general sense of 'move quickly', so that often they say in praise of an athlete 'There is no doubt he can mote.'
1941 Baker 47: *Mote* To move quickly (used of a vehicle or athlete).

motherless Used as an intensive, esp. in the phrase 'motherless broke'
1898 *Bulletin* 17 Dec. Red Page: To these are prefixed the adjectives *motherless* and *dead*, thus *dead motherless broke*.
1916 Arthur Wright *Under a Cloud* 35:
'I'm stone motherless meself an' I could do with that hundred Booth is offerin'.'
1925 E. S. Sorenson *Murty Brown* 135:
'That leaves me stony, motherless broke again.'
1945 Gavin Casey *Downhill is Easier* 20: I'd only known Reg when we were both stone motherless broke.
1961 George Farwell *Vanishing Australians* 67: The fact that he would be stone motherless broke was hardly worth mentioning.
1972 Alexander Macdonald *The Ukelele Player under the Red Lamp* 247: Happy, full as a boot, and stone motherless broke.

motser, motza A large gambling win; a 'certainty' that would ensure such a win: *rare* [unexplained]
1943 Baker 51: *Motser, motza* A large sum of money.

1950 *Australian Police Journal* Apr. 116: *Motza* A lot of money.
1970 Richard Beilby *No Medals for Aphrodite* 214: 'The Stuka'll be a motsa to have a go at him.'

Movement, the The Catholic Social Study Movement established in 1945 as 'a loose national alliance of Catholic actionists, particularly unionists, with the object of fighting communism in the union movement' (Patrick O'Farrell *The Catholic Church in Australia* (1968) 264)
1951 Frank Hardy *Power Without Glory* 634: 'I have here the most recent report of 'The Movement' which, as you know, is the arm of Catholic Action in the Trade Unions'.... 'In each diocese or suburb we have set about establishing cells of The Movement and in many factories and Trade Unions we have similar groups.'
see **grouper**

moves, if it ~ , shoot it; if it doesn't, chop it down Reputedly an Australian national motto
1963 Alan Ross *Australia 63* 202: The country had still to be conquered. The general attitude was: 'If it moves, shoot it. If it stands still, chop it down.'
1964 *Sydney Morning Herald* 4 May 2:
'If it moves, shoot it; if it doesn't, chop it down.' So goes the old Australian saying, and according to our foresters it has been the motto of this country for too long.
1971 George Johnston *A Cartload of Clay* 77: 'Remember the old rule we had about coming to grips with this country, when we were trying to settle it? If it grows chop it down, if it moves, shoot it.'
1971 Bill Hornadge *A Squint Down Under* 24: If it moves, shoot it. / If it doesn't, chop it down. Australian Motto.

mozz, to put the ~ on To prejudice someone's chances, place a 'jinx' on something [f. *mozzle*]
1924 C. J. Dennis *Rose of Spadgers* 75:
'Too much soul-ferritin' might put the moz / On this 'ere expedition.'
1941 Baker 47: *Put the moz on someone*

To inconvenience a person.
1956 Alan Marshall *How's Andy Going?*
200: 'Looking ahead like that never
does any bloody good to any man,'
observed Pat. 'It puts the moz on him.'
1963 Hal Porter *The Watcher on the
Cast-Iron Balcony* 81: Mother is wishing
Miss Brewer some female ill, is putting
the mozz on her.
1974 Keith Stackpole *Not Just for
Openers* 32: She felt she put the moz on
him . . . She couldn't bear to go in case
she was a jinx.

mozz As for 'put the mozz on'
1941 Baker 47: *Moz* To interrupt, hind-
er.
1965 Frank Hardy *The Yarns of Billy
Borker* 107: 'Don't mozz a man,' I tells
him. 'You're well named, I'll say that
for you, Calamity.'
1974 John Powers *The Last of the
Knucklemen* 49: 'Don't let him mozz
you, Monk.'

mozzle Luck, bad luck [f. Heb. *mazzal*
luck]
1898 *Bulletin* 17 Dec. Red Page: *Mozzle*
is luck . . . *Good mozzle* = good luck;
Kronk mozzle = bad luck.
1903 Joseph Furphy *Such is Life* (1944)
280: 'And how much do you stand to
lose, if your mozzle is out?' I asked.
1919 Edward Dyson *Hello, Soldier!* 32:
'Twas rotten mozzle, Neddo. We had
blown out every clip.

muck, Sing 'em Supposed advice of
Nellie Melba to Clara Butt on undertaking
a tour of Australia
1928 W. H. Ponder *Clara Butt: Her
Life Story* 138: 'So you're going to
Australia!' she [Melba] said. 'Well, I
made twenty thousand pounds on my
tour there, but of course *that* will never
be done again. Still, it's a wonderful
country, and you'll have a good time.
What are you going to sing? All I can
say is – sing 'em muck! It's all they can
understand!'
1934 Vance Palmer *The Swayne Family*
170: 'Show you're higher organism by
adapting yourself. Appeal to sense of
fun. Turn dark cloud inside out. Sing

'em muck.'
1949 *Sydney Morning Herald* 1 Oct. 8:
We can imagine the scene at the pub-
lishing house when the unprofitable
author calls in for his royalty cheque.
'No, sir,' says Mr Chapman, shaking a
forlorn head and pointing to the shelves
of unsold copies . . . 'If you were only
to do something like 'Sun and Shade'
by the author of 'Ursula's Wooing', we
might strike a winner, and everyone
would be happy. Give 'em muck, sir!
Give 'em muck!'

muddie A Queensland mudcrab
1977 *Australian* 8 Jan. 1: Each year
the people of N.S.W. eat 200,000 of the
prize Queensland muddies, which is all
right except that they are eating mud
crabs that Queenslanders are not allowed to eat.

Muddy, Little The river Yarra, Victoria
[f. colour of water. *Big Muddy* is the
Missouri]
1965 *Nation* 3 Apr. 10: Few people
could draw the breath of conscience
and describe the Yarra as a proud river
sweeping southward to the sea, Little
Muddy nevertheless commands great
local affection, whatever is said about
it in another place.

mudlark See quot. 1941 [variant of
mudrunner]
1941 Baker 47: *Mudlark* A racehorse
that runs well on a muddy course. Also
footballers who play on a sodden field.
1951 Dymphna Cusack and Florence
James *Come in Spinner* 40: 'Could yer
blame 'im?' Elvira asked reproachfully.
'Raining like it was last Saturdee? 'E's
no mudlark.'
1975 *Sunday Telegraph* 6 Apr. 48: Born
Star a Mudlark. Born Star, a two-year-
old, yesterday outclassed the field at
Sandown in his first start on a rain-
affected track.

mud map A sketch drawn by a bushman
on the ground, to give directions
1919 E. S. Sorenson *Chips and Splinters*
14: The mud maps that Phineas draws
on the road with a stick when directing

some unfortunate wanderer.

1936 Ion L. Idriess *The Cattle King* 102: He built up the fire, then sat back on his heels, and with a stick scraped the ground clear. 'I'll make you a mud map.'
1956 Tom Ronan *Moleskin Midas* 171: 'I want a fresh horse and some tucker and a mud map for getting to town without hitting too many roads.'
1962 J. Marshall and R. Drysdale *Journey Among Men* 37: 'I'll draw yer a mud map the way they went.'

mulga A species of acacia: colloquially 'the mulga' may refer to uninhabited or inhospitable regions generally
1928 Vance Palmer *The Man Hamilton* 26: Manager of this isolated place in the mulga, a hundred miles away from anywhere.
1934 Jean Devanny *Out of Such Fires* 277: 'Why don't you come with us? You belong in the mulga.'
1946 Rohan Rivett *Behind Bamboo* 397: *Mulga*, the surrounding jungle.
1952 Jon Cleary *The Sundowners* 198: 'You've heard what they call 'em down in the city. Bushwackers. The mugs from the mulga.'
1973 Alexander Buzo *Rooted* 87: 'Gary's gone away for the weekend, cavorting in the mulga with the Werris Creek push.'

mulga wire As for *bush telegraph*[2]
1899 T. Quinn *The Well Sinkers* 100: 'How do you hear it, Micky?' 'Mulga wires, missus, mulga wires.'
1908 E. S. Sorenson *Quinton's Rouseabout* 186: 'They'll be that delighted to find it was only a mulga that they'd toast you as "a jolly good fellow".'
1913 Henry Lawson 'Triangles of Life' *Prose* i 658: Tom had been out early, or had got what we call a bush telegraphy or mulga wire.
1933 R. B. Plowman *The Man from Oodnadatta* 21: The padre was not surprised to find that Stan was aware of his coming. Throughout the Inland news travels far and fast by means of the 'mulga wire'.
1937 Ernestine Hill *The Great Australian Loneliness* 207: Warned by mulga

wires of the approach of a white woman . . . there were some of them who 'went bush' rather than meet me.
1950 K. S. Prichard *Winged Seeds* 297: 'The troops 've had it all by mulga.'

mullet, like a stunned Dazed, so unaware as to be almost unconscious
1953 Baker 267: *Dullness* (looking) like a stunned mullet.
1963 John O'Grady *The things they do to you* 147: I returned and lay on the bed like a stunned mullet.
1974 Jack Hibberd *Dimboola* 46: 'Just look at him! Just look at him. Looks like a stunned mullet.'
1977 *Australian* 16 May 1: Mr Hawke said yesterday the Federal Government had responded like a stunned mullet to his acceptance of the proposed Industrial Relations Bureau.

mullock, to poke To mock, ridicule [f. *mullock* the rubbish heaped at the top of a mineshaft]
1916 C. J. Dennis *The Moods of Ginger Mick* 74: I own me eyes git brighter / When I see 'em pokin' mullock at the everlastin' sea.
1924 *Truth* 27 Apr. 6: *Mullock, to poke* To deride.
1931 Vance Palmer *Separate Lives* 210: 'D'you think I'm going to sit in that galley with Curran and the other blokes all poking mullock at me?'
1942 Gavin Casey *It's Harder for Girls* 153: The chaps poked mullock at me, but it wasn't that that hurt.
1957 Ray Lawler *Summer of the Seventeenth Doll* 71: 'Oh, so that's what you got me in for, is it – to poke mullock?
1962 John Morrison *Twenty-Three* 86: 'I heard what you said when you grabbed that rope. Poking mullock at us because we won't go out over an empty hatch.'
see **borak**

munga Food (Army slang) [origin uncertain: see quots 1919, 1970]
1919 W. H. Downing *Digger Dialects* 34: *Mungaree* (Arab.) – Bread. *Mungy* (Fr., Manger) – Food; a meal.
1944 Lawson Glassop *We Were the Rats*

114: 'They're lining up for mess,' said Harry. 'Any starters for the Mungareer[1] Stakes?' [1]Food.

1945 Baker 157: *munga* Food. Whence, *hard munga*, iron rations, *soft munga*, normal rations or civilian food. [World War II slang]

1963 Lawson Glassop *The Rats in New Guinea* 149: 'Sit down and have some *munga*, John,' I said.

1965 Patrick White *Four Plays* 123: 'Okay, Nola! Shan't keep anyone waiting when the *mungareer's* on the table!'

1970 Richard Beilby *No Medals for Aphrodite* 37: 'It tastes better when it's fried, but it's not bad munga' ... 'What does that word mean, please?' 'Food.' Turk explained the soldier-Arabic 'mungaree', shortened Australian-wise to 'munga'.

murder, to cry bloody To make a hullabaloo, like The Man from Ironbark when the city barber, for a joke, slashed the back of a red hot razor across his throat [cf. the English 'cry blue murder']

1895 A. B. Paterson *The Man from Snowy River* 67: And all the while his throat he held to save his vital spark, / And 'Murder! Bloody Murder!' yelled the man from Ironbark.

Murray cod, on the On the nod, i.e. on credit [rhyming slang]

1977 *Weekend Australian* 23 Jul. Magazine 1: A punter, well known in Sydney, who bets on 'the murray cod' (the nod) walked into City Tattersalls on Monday settling day carrying $240,000 cash.

Murrumbidgee whaler A swagman camping in the bends of the Murrumbidgee or any other river, and a byword for indolence [see *whaler*]

1873 J. C. F. Johnson *Christmas on Carringa* 16: Men when on the tramp through the Riverina country often carry a piece of twine and a hook to catch cod or blackfish. This is termed Murrumbidgee Whaling.

1878 G. H. Gibson *Southerly Busters* 177: Murrumbidgee whalers are a class of loafers who work for about six months in the year – i.e., during shearing and harvest, and camp the rest of the time in bends of rivers, and live by fishing and begging.

1885 *The Australasian Printers' Keepsake* 72: [He] eyed Bob very suspiciously, muttering 'spieler' and 'Murrumbidgee whaler'.

1906 H. J. Tompkins *With Swag and Billy* ix: Such a proceeding is common enough in the country where it is considered undignified to walk, since it savours too much of the Murrumbidgee whaler. To have admitted having walked from daylight until dark is to give yourself away as a downright vagrant sundowner.

1953 Archer Russell *Murray Walkabout* 147: He was a 'Murrumbidgee whaler', the river prototype of the tramping sundowner.

mush see **moosh**

muscle, a ball of see **ball**

mushie A mushroom [abbr.]

muster, bangtail, Tambaroora, tarpaulin see **bangtail, Tambaroora, tarpaulin**

Muswellbrook, things are crook at see **Tallarook**

mutton, underground see **underground mutton**

Myers, more front than see **front**

my troubles, worries see **troubles, worries**

myxo Myxomatosis, disease used to exterminate rabbits [abbr.]

1953 *Daily Telegraph* 22 Jan. 6: Trappers said tonight that the incidence of 'myxo' was waning, and the rabbit population was increasing.

1966 *Coast to Coast 1965–1966* 135: 'The myxo'll look after the rabbits ... Them C.S.I.R.O. blokes did a good job there.'

1971 David Ireland *The Unknown In-*

dustrial Prisoner 294: 'There's a poor devil of a rabbit out there in the mangroves. Got a dose of myxo?'

N

nailrod A coarse dark tobacco: *obs.*
1890 A. J. Vogan *The Black Police* 200: He hands our black friend a piece of 'nailrod' with which to charge his evening pipe.
1891 C. J. Brennan *Southerly* (1963) 171: Pleasant incense of Long Cut and Nailrod commingled.
1896 Henry Lawson 'Drifted Back' *Prose* i 235: 'You can give me half-a-pound of nailrod,' he said.

namma hole See quots [Ab.]
1842 G. F. Moore *A Descriptive Vocabulary of . . . the Aborigines of Western Australia* 2: Amar, subst. A hole or pool of water in a rock. Ibid. 167: Water, standing in a rock – Gnamar.
1893 *Australasian* 5 Aug. 252: The route all the way from York to Coolgardie is amply watered, either 'namma holes' (native wells) or Government wells being plentiful on the road. [Morris]
1901 May Vivienne *Travels in Western Australia* 339: Native wells as 'nammaholes' have saved many a prospector from death by thirst.
1916 Macmillan's *Modern Dictionary of the English Language* 790: *namma hole* serving as a natural well, or storage-place for rainwater.
1929 K. S. Prichard *Coonardoo* 52: His eyes, namma holes in viscid orbits, glittered at her, as he swung his naked feet.

nan nan A straw hat; a young man affecting this as part of a mode of dress; a 'lair': *obs.* [origin obscure: cf. *nana*]
1899 Henry Lawson 'If I Could Paint' *Prose* ii 38: A boarding-house keeper, with two or three grown-up white-shirted, stand-up-and-turn-down collared (mother does all their linen herself), straw-hatted, cigarette-smok-ing sons . . . I'd like to paint her and the children – and the 'nan-nan' sons.
1899 W. T. Goodge *Hits! Skits! and Jingles!* 39: One little maid with a bashful smile / Given for a salutation; / Two little dudes of the nan-nan style / Bent on captivation.
1900–10 O'Brien and Stephens: *Nan-nan* A straw hat for men's wear.

nana (ah) 1 The head, in such expressions as 'off one's nana', 'do one's nana' [? f. *banana*]
1894 A. B. Paterson 'Hughey's Dog' in *The World of Banjo Paterson* ed. C. Semmler (1967) 29: 'Off his nanny again,' thought the boss, 'the sooner he goes the better.'
1968 *Coast to Coast 1967–1968* 9: 'Arright, Mister Mighty Boss. Don't do your narna.'
1975 *Australian* 8 Feb. 13: 'We've all learned to laugh at ourselves and our predicament,' Trevor England said. 'If we hadn't we'd all be off our nanas.'
2 A fool, an ass [listed by Partridge as English, a *softy* f. soft fruit]
1965 Graham McInnes *The Road to Gundagai* 148: Although he was obviously a gent, he was not a 'tonk' or a 'nana' . . . he was all right.
3 Applied to haircut [? f. resemblance to banana shape]
1941 Baker 48: *Nana* (*hair*) *cut:* A utilitarian haircut in which the back of the head is closely shaved.
1966 *Coast to Coast 1965–1966* 35: If you used a brush-back, wore the hair long, or horror of horrors, had a *nana* haircut.

nanto A horse: *obsolescent* [? Ab. see quot. 1957]
1889 *The Arrow* 20 Jul. 2: And then the cove looks at our / 'Nantos' and says he, 'Well, I'm your man.'
1907 Alfred Searcy *The Australian Tropics* 116: While at the 'Bar' we saw a Myall nigger who, if he had never seen nanto (horse) before, at any rate had never mounted one.
1911 Sydney Partrige *Rocky Section* 12: 'Take old Vagabond and run him on the section, and you'll always have a

second nanto if anything happens to the other.'

1935 H. H. Finlayson *The Red Centre* 98: The house boys knew 'nantos' from A to Z and were good trackers, keen on the job.

1957 W. E. Harney *Life Among the Aborigines* 12: They saw many . . . with their strange 'nantus' (a word in reference to the distended nose of a horse after it has been ridden hard).

nap Blankets, bedding etc. [f. *nap* the pile on a fabric OED c. 1440]

1892 Barcroft Boake 'A Song from a Sandhill' *Bulletin* 2 Apr. 13 repr. in *Where the Dead Men Lie* (1897) 59: Drip, drip, drip! and one's 'nap' is far from dry.

1918 C. Fetherstonhaugh *After Many Days* 279: That night he could not catch the donkey, and he had to camp without any 'nap' (blankets).

1926 L. C. E. Gee *Bushtracks and Goldfields* 41: The quarts were boiled and an after-dinner supply of coffee made, the 'nap' spread out on soft sandy spots, the two travellers reclined with pipes.

1933 R. B. Plowman *The Man from Oodnadatta* 2: The blackboy's nap (blankets, waterproof sheet, etc) filled in the rear compartment.

1968 Walter Gill *Petermann Journey* 24: I knew where to put my 'nap', the Territory word for a 'swag'.

nap, go ~ on In Australia, most often used negatively, meaning 'not to be keen on', 'not to favour, not to care for [f. card game: *to go nap* to stake all one can, to speculate heavily OED 1884]

1932 William Hatfield *Christmastown* 43: Didn't go nap on wine himself. A drop of whisky, now –.

1939 Miles Franklin and Dymphna Cusack *Pioneers on Parade* 105: 'She knows I don't go nap on him, and I have to be careful not to seem prejudiced.'

1955 Patrick White *The Tree of Man* 80: 'I never went nap on the priests meself.'

1957 D'Arcy Niland *Call Me When the Cross Turns Over* 184: But he never went nap on the city, he said, and now he had done with it for good.

1961 A. W. Upfield *Bony and the White Savage* 59: 'The woman who runs the bookshop knows we don't go nap on the sexy stuff.'

narangy Joseph Furphy's term for those whose status on stations entitled them to be quartered in the barracks q.v.; hence a subaltern on a station, someone with authority lower than that of the manager [Ab.]

[**1793** J. Hunter *Historical Journal* ed. J. Bach (1968) 273: *Narrong*, Any thing small.

1855 John Lang *The Forger's Wife* 121: He had mixed a good deal with the blacks . . . when he used the word 'narang' (small) but 'bidgee' (good), the groom did not quite comprehend the gentleman's praise of his horse.]

1903 Joseph Furphy *Such is Life* (1944) 254: Being a little too exalted for the men's hut, and a great deal too vile for the boss's house, I was quartered in the narangies' barracks. Ibid. 65: Jack Ward, the senior narangy, made some remark . . . the two junior narangies supported Ward. Ibid. 270: The four narangies . . . went to the veranda of the boss's house for their day's orders.

1941 Baker 48: *Narangy* As for 'silvertail'.

nark *n.* A spoilsport [f. *nark* a police informer OED 1865]

1898 *Bulletin* 17 Dec. Red Page: An informer or mar-plot is a *nark* or a *Jonah*.

1908 *Australian Magazine* 1 Nov. 1251: *nark*, a spoil-sport.

1919 W. H. Downing *Digger Dialects* 35: *Nark* A malevolent or bad-tempered person; a spoil-sport.

1928 Vance Palmer *The Man Hamilton* 94: 'Oh, don't be a nark, Miss Byrne,' he coaxed her.

1933 Frank Clune *Try Anything Once* 81: Lieutenant Hennessy fulfilled the most exacting requirements of what a 'nark' should be.

1946 Kylie Tennant *Lost Haven* 369: Here he was spoiling things for two

kids, like a crabby old nark.
1959 Dorothy Hewett *Bobbin Up* 33:
'You're turnin' into a real nark,' Hazel
said sulkily.
1961 Patrick White *Riders in the
Chariot* 347: Others still, suspected him
of being some kind of nark or perv, and
cursed him as he lifted them out of
their own vomit.
nark *v.* To annoy, thwart [f. *nark* to
annoy, vex, irritate, exasperate EDD
1888]
1975 Richard Beilby *The Brown Land
Crying* 200: 'Ya'd do anything to nark
me, anything to put me down, wouldn't
ya?'

narked Peeved, angry
1896 Henry Lawson 'The Shearing of
Cook's Dog' *Prose* i 96: The cook
usually forgot all about it in an hour . . .
But this time he didn't; he was 'narked'
for three days.
1898 *Bulletin* 17 Dec. Red Page: To *get
narked* is to lose your temper.
1903 Joseph Furphy *Such is Life* (1944)
21: 'I notice the other feller was a bit
narked when he seen me on the horse
to-day.'
1911 Louis Stone *Jonah* 9: 'Orl right,
wot are yer narked about?'
1946 Margaret Trist *What Else is
There?* 135: 'Gee, Mum's going to be
narked,' said Billy. 'You'll have to
stick up for me, Ruby.'
1958 *Coast to Coast 1957–1958* 104:
'Most of 'em are after wives for their
boys. They're real narked now.'
1963 A. W. Upfield *The Body at Madman's Bend* 180: 'She raised it to half
the wages this morning. Then looked
narked 'cos we went slow.'

Nasho Compulsory military training
(abolished in 1972); a youth undergoing
such training [abbr. of *National Service*]
1962 Criena Rohan *The Delinquents*
52: 'I'm not keen on Nashos,' she said.
'I prefer bodgies.'
1966 Bruce Beaver *You Can't Come
Back* 5: Sam, the new one, was just
eighteen and due for his Nasho training.
1975 David Malouf *Johnno* 70: Now
the Grand Central was the drinking
place of 'Nashos'.

national game, Australia's Two-up
1930 L. W. Lower *Here's Luck* 70:
He had a small piece of wood in his
hand, on which were balanced two
pennies. The national game was in
progress.
1963 Frank Hardy *Legends from Benson's Valley* 108: The demise of the
bookmakers increased attendance at the
Sunday sessions of Australia's national
game. The two-up school operated on
the plateau above the valley.
1976 *Bulletin* 10 Jan. 45: There's no
greater humiliation than being a failure
at the national game.

naughty Sexual intercourse [f. *go
naughty, do the naughty* OED 1869]
1959 Eric Lambert *Glory Thrown In*
106: 'Until I met Thelma, I always
thought that sheilas had to be talked
into a bit of a naughty.'
1963 Frank Hardy *Legends from Benson's Valley* 11: He put his arm around
her, patting her buttock. I smiled,
remembering his oft-repeated remark:
'I get a lot of knock backs but I get a
lot of naughties.'
1972 Geoff Morley *Jockey Rides Honest
Race* 71: 'These sheilas fascinate me . . .
I want them to invite me in for a good
old-fashioned naughty.'
1975 Xavier Herbert *Poor Fellow My
Country* 439: 'I'll give you a new dress
. . . and we'll 'ave a bit of a party, and
then another naughty, eh?'

neck, go under someone's To forestall
an action contemplated by another, usurp
someone else's prerogative [? f. horse
racing]
1953 T. A. G. Hungerford *Riverslake*
61: 'I wouldn't want to go under your
neck,' Randolph said sarcastically. Ibid.
220: 'Why jack up? . . . You just race
in the mob from the office and go under
our necks.'
1961 Mena Calthorpe *The Dyehouse*
120: 'She knew she was going under
Patty What's-her-name's neck. We
can't shed tears of blood over these
dames.'

1977 *Sunday Telegraph* 6 Feb. 128: Is Queensland Premier Joh Bjelke-Petersen getting under Neville Wran's neck? Joh is touring the north-west of Western Australia with mining magnate Lang Hancock.

neck-to-knees An old-fashioned bathing costume
1910 *Daily Telegraph* 20 Jun. 17: Neck to knee costumes have been for some time past insisted on at all popular resorts.

Ned Kelly 1 A name applied to anyone with 'bushranging' attributes [f. the famous bushranger (more strictly, bank-robber) hanged in 1880]
1941 Baker 41: *Kelly, Ned* Any person of buccaneering business habits.
1953 *The Sunburnt Country* ed. Ian Bevan 129: Phrases such as 'do a Ned Kelly' ... lend so much verve and colour to the Australian serviceman's vocabulary.
2 The belly: *rare* [rhyming slang]

Ned Kelly, game as Extremely plucky and insouciant
1945 Roy Rene *Mo's Memoirs* 24: He was game as Ned Kelly, and he'd ride anything.
1953 Dymphna Cusack *Southern Steel* 41: 'Is that kid game? Game as Ned Kelly.'
1958 H. D. Williamson *The Sunlit Plain* 90: In fact, to pay him his due compliment, he was as game as Ned Kelly.
1966 Don Crick *Period of Adjustment* 66: 'Are you game?' 'As Ned Kelly.'

neddy A horse; in plural, usually race horses [f. *neddy* a donkey OED 1790]
1887 *Tibb's Popular Songbook* 9: So they saddled up their Neddys / And like loafers sneaked away.
1895 Cornelius Crowe *The Australian Slang Dictionary* 52: *Neddy* a horse.
1901 Rolf Boldrewood *In Bad Company* 217: 'Just as we was a-saddlin' up – some of us had one neddy, some two – a mob of horses comes by.'
1918 Bernard Cronin *The Coastlanders* 74: A hot cinder lit on my neddie's

rump.
1965 William Dick *A Bunch of Ratbags* 40: My old man was backing the neddies as usual.
1975 Les Ryan *The Shearers* 69: 'Joe Clement's neddy – Wingay. Station hands reckon he's home and hosed.'

neg driving The offence of driving negligently [abbr.]
1973 Alexander Buzo *Rooted* 44: 'Remember the time ... when Hammo had a prang in his B and got dobbed in for neg driving?'

Never-Never, the The regions remote from civilization, and as yet unsettled or unexplored, at first referring to north-western Queensland or northern Australia generally. The term was given currency by Mrs Aeneas Gunn's classic *We of the Never-Never* (1908) [see quot. 1857]
1857 F. Cooper *Wild Adventures in Australia* 68: I had the cattle mustered, and the draft destined for the Nievah vahs* ready for the road. *Nievah vahs, sometimes incorrectly pronounced never nevers, a Cameleroi term signifying unoccupied land.
1875 Rolf Boldrewood *A Colonial Reformer* (1890) 174: 'But here is seems to be the Never-Never country, and no mistake.'
1882 A. J. Boyd *Old Colonials* 202: My soliloquy ends with the inquiry, 'What on earth is to be done in this wretched Never-never* country?' *Never-never is the far outside country beyond the centres of civilization.
1893 Francis Adams *The Australians* 11: Beyond this [the pastoral land west of the Dividing Range] lie vast realms of 'scrub' – more or less occupied for another four or five hundred miles westward, till the outskirts of the great central desert are reached, and we pass into no man's land, or 'the never-never.'
1899 W. T. Goodge *Hits! Skits! and Jingles!* 89: It was on the Never-Never where the Jackeroos endeavour / To be very, very, clever with the strangers imbecile.
1901 Henry Lawson 'Shall We Gather

at the River' *Prose* i 509: He was known from Riverina down South in New South Wales to away up through the Never-Never Country in Western Queensland.
1906 Joseph Furphy *Rigby's Romance* ed. R. G. Howarth (1946) 228–9: My undercurrent of thought was persistently dwelling upon that glimpse into the Never-never of my companion's soul.
1917 A. B. Paterson *Three Elephant Power* 41: The typical Australian bullock ... is bred away out in Queensland, on remote stations in the Never Never land, where men live on damper and beef, and occasionally eat a whole bottle of hot pickles at a sitting.
1959 Dorothy Hewett *Bobbin Up* 21: 'I can remember when Bondi was just a heapa sand hills and scrub, goin' dirt-cheap. Nobody'd buy it then. We thought it was out in the never-never. An look at it now.'

new chum 1 A newly arrived prisoner in a gaol or hulk [English thieves' slang]
1812 Vaux: *Chum*: a fellow prisoner in a jail, hulk, & c; so there are *new chums* and *old chums*, as they happen to have been a short or a long time in confinement.
1830–1 Henry Savery *Quintus Servinton* (1962) 287: 'There's near a thousand chaps here [in the hulk] ... 'twont do to draw no distinctions like, with new chums.'
c. **1845** James Tucker *Ralph Rashleigh* (1952) 51: As Ralph and his associates in punishment marched past these dens [in the hulk], they were saluted by obstreperous shouts of 'New chums! New chums!' from both sides.
2 Any new arrival, inexperienced in the conditions into which he has come
1838 T. L. Mitchell *Three Expeditions* i 99: He was also what they termed a 'new chum', or one newly arrived.
1849 Alexander Harris *The Emigrant Family* (1967) 141: Indeed, no one but a 'new chum' could have missed the course from the feeding ground to the hut.
1859 Frank Fowler *Southern Lights and Shadows* 26: I have already said that the young Australian is systematically insolent to the new-chum ... A new-chum is fair game for anyone.
1869 Marcus Clarke *The Peripatetic Philosopher* 3: 'New Chums' [essay title]
1873 A. Trollope *Australia* ed. Edwards and Joyce (1967) 413: The idea that Englishmen, – that is, newchums, or Englishmen just come from home, – are made of paste, whereas the Australian, native or thoroughly acclimatized, is steel all through, I found to be universal.
1886 Percy Clarke *The New Chum in Australia* [book title]
1901 Henry Lawson 'Send Round the Hat' *Prose* i 474: A new-chum parson, who wanted a subscription to build or enlarge a chapel, or something, sought the assistance of the Giraffe's influence with his mates.
1929 Jules Raeside *Golden Days* 50: We were all new chums, and very indifferent bushmen, but our enthusiasm over-ruled our ignorance.
1935 F. D. Davison and B. Nicholls *Blue Coast Caravan* 21: He was taking his craft through channels marked only in his memory. 'This is no place for a new chum to fool about,' he remarked as we came to the narrows.
1957 Sydney Hart *Pommie Migrant* 159: 'You a new chum?' he asked. It was the first time I'd heard the expression.
1971 Rena Briand *White Man in a Hole* 132: Newchums at opal mining, they were soon involved talking 'shop' with Johnny while I set the billy on the fire.

New South, sunny An affectionate or jocular way of referring to New South Wales: *obsolescent*
1905 *The Old Bush Songs* ed. A. B. Paterson 61: Sunny New South Wales [ballad title]
1922 Arthur Wright *A Colt from the Country* 83: 'With that finished ... we can kiss good-bye to sunny New South for a spell.'

nick To move smartly, to decamp [cf. E. dial. *nip* to move rapidly or nimbly OED 1825; *nit* to depart hurriedly]

1896 Ethel Turner *The Little Larrikin* 274: He had been . . . trying to induce the driver . . . to promise at the end of the journey to 'nick away and come too.'
1901 Miles Franklin *My Brilliant Career* (1965) 189: If you go to a picnic, just when the fun commences you have to nick off home and milk.
1938 Xavier Herbert *Capricornia* 257: 'You're only humming for a drink. Nick off home.'
1939 Kylie Tennant *Foveaux* 177: 'If Curly hadn't nicked round that screen . . .'
1946 K. S. Prichard *The Roaring Nineties* 94: 'Guess you're dying for a cup of tea . . . I'll nick over to the camp and put on the billy.'
1957 Ray Lawler *Summer of the Seventeenth Doll* 124: 'Is it the boys he's nicking off with on Monday?'

Nifty Nev Mr Neville Wran, N.S.W. Premier 1976– (from his style in politics)
1977 *Bulletin* 20 Aug. 35: Nifty Nev gave a farewell party for Diamond Jim at the Wrans' Woollahra pad.

night's a pup see pup

ning nong see nong

nips, to put in the As for 'bite' q.v.
1919 W. H. Downing *Digger Dialects* 35: *Nip* To cadge (or 'Put in the nips').
1937 *Best Australian One-Act Plays* 398: 'He came along to put the nips in, so I gave him a couple of bob.'
1949 Lawson Glassop *Lucky Palmer* 230: 'You can't put the nips into old Alf. He's got death adders in his pockets.'
1955 D'Arcy Niland *The Shiralee* 41: 'He was here yesterday, too. Put the nips into me for tea and sugar and tobacco in his usual style. The biggest bludger in the country.'
1973 Frank Huelin *Keep Moving* 48: Parsons, priests, doctors, lawyers and professional people generally were legitimate prey, and we had no scuples about 'putting the nips' into them.

nit A cry to warn of the approach of some authority; (as a verb) to decamp hurriedly
[**1864** Hotten: *Nix!* The signal word of schoolboys to each other that the master, or other person in authority, is approaching]
1882 *The Sydney Slang Dictionary* 10: *Nit* Get away (usually from a foe), make tracks.
1899 Henry Lawson 'If I Could Paint' *Prose* ii 38: I'd call it 'Nit! There's Mother'.
1911 Louis Stone *Jonah* 8: Suddenly there was a cry of 'Nit! 'Ere's a cop!' and the Push bolted like rabbits.

nit, to keep To act as sentinel (or 'cockatoo' q.v.) esp. for someone engaged in some illegal activity
1940 Ion L. Idriess *Lightning Ridge* 20: Bill kept nit for his elder brother who was courting a girl, and earned a shilling.
1952 T. A. G. Hungerford *The Ridge and the River* 10: 'Send two men a couple of hundred yards up and down the track to keep nit.'
1957 Ray Lawler *Summer of the Seventeenth Doll* 44: 'Keepin' nit for the S.P. bookies, eh.'
1963 Gunther Bahnemann *Hoodlum* 79: Jerry, the lookout man stayed there, to keep nit.
1971 David Ireland *The Unknown Industrial Prisoner* 77: They had transgressed the unwritten law that you didn't let yourself go to sleep while you were keeping nit for your mates.

nitkeeper One who 'keeps nit'
1935 *Bulletin* 22 May 21: That outlaw the sulphur-crested cockatoo is not the only bird to post a 'nit-keeper' when transgressing against society.
1943 *Khaki and Green* 101: Outside a window an abo was acting in a mysterious manner, reminiscent of a nitkeeper in the days of S.P. bookies.
1963 Frank Hardy *Legends from Benson's Valley* 108: An elaborate network of nitkeepers on all sides frustrated the new policeman for three weeks.

1971 David Ireland *The Unknown Industrial Prisoner* 77: The Great White Father called in at the wharf at six one morning, just the time the nit-keeper should have wakened those who were down.

nobbler A glass of liquor, usually spirits and water [origin obscure]
1851 *Illustrated Australian Magazine* Nov. 248: The public houses are crowded with friends taking their last nobbler.
1853 John Sherer *The Gold-Finder of Australia* 177: I have only had two noblers* (as they are called) since I came to the place, and paid 1s. 6d. per nobler. *Noblers are tumblers of spirits and water, which, with the gambling propensities of the colonists, threaten to swamp the prosperity of the country.
1854 C. H. Spence *Clara Morison* 171: 'A nobbler is half a glass of spirits, generally brandy, and when it is taken neat, it means that is is undiluted.'
1867 J. R. Holding *Australian Capers* 132: 'Regular bars . . . where any men can go and call for a 'nobbler'.
1873 A. Trollope *Australia* ed. Edwards and Joyce (1967) 660: A nobbler is the proper colonial phrase for a drink at a public-house.
1885 Mrs Campbell Praed *Australian Life* 103: Having accepted at my hands the customary 'nobbler', he would sit down for half-an-hour, talking.
1905 'The Shepherd' *The Old Bush Songs* ed. A. B. Paterson 116: He was going a pace, / Shouting nobbler after nobbler, with a smile upon his face.
nobblerize
1857 *Thatcher's Colonial Songster* 23: And she'd sit in the tent, while to work he went, / And all day nobblerise.
1883 R. E. N. Twopeny *Town Life in Australia* 70: But there are two other liquids – whisky and brandy – which play an important part in nobblerising.

no-hoper A horse with no prospect of winning; a man of whom nothing can be expected; a general term of contempt
1943 Baker 53: *No-hoper* An outsider

(Racing slang).
1945 Tom Ronan *Strangers on the Ophir* 121: There were actually eight runners in it: the three favourites; three no hopers hardly up to hack-race standard.
1957 Ray Lawler *Summer of the Seventeenth Doll* 53: 'There's no excuse for that sort of thing, you're just a no-hoper.'
1966 Patrick White *The Solid Mandala* 18: 'A couple of no-hopers with ideas about 'emselves', he would grumble, and then regurgitate: 'The Brothers Bloody Brown!'
1970 Jon Cleary *Helga's Web* 8: His mother had prayed that he might become a priest, but God in his wisdom had recognised a religious no-hoper when he saw one.

nong Someone stupid or ineffectual: derogatory [? f. E. dial. *nigmenog* a very silly fellow OED 1700: see also quot. 1865]
[1865 Hotten: *Ning-nang* horse-coupers' term for a worthless thorough-bred.]
1953 Baker 171: *nong* A simpleton or fool. [as World War II slang from New Guinea and the islands]
1958 Hal Porter *A Handful of Pennies* 30: 'Old or not old, he's one of them: he's only a nong'. [i.e. one of the Japanese during the Occupation]
1959 Dorothy Hewett *Bobbin Up* 127: Stan had never carried a bunch of flowers in his life before, and said he felt like a nong-nong.
1962 J. Marshall and R. Drysdale *Journey Among Men* 143: The traveller who . . . has mislaid his letter of credit, is not necessarily a crook but merely a bit of a *nong* who should be put in funds and told gently to try not to do it again.
1969 Leslie Haylen *Twenty Years Hard Labour* 210–11: The continuance of compulsory voting means that the 'nongs', the indifferent and the plain bloody stupid, will continue to dominate the voting in the Commonwealth and the States for years to come.
1974 Sir Charles Cutler *Sydney Morning Herald* 26 Sep. 8: Personally, I think the people of Australia have been

betrayed by the most divided, disorganized group of academic nongs that have ever been in charge of this country.

noodle, noodling To prospect for opal in mullock heaps; to work carefully on a selection of opal-bearing rock
1902 *Queensland Department of Mines Geological Survey* No. 177 cit. J. S. Gunn *An Opal Terminology* (1971) 30: Some splendid opal is found . . . by turning over and searching the old heaps and mullock – 'noodling'.
1921 K. S. Prichard *Black Opal* 73: They went noodling together, or gathering wild flowers. Ibid. 157: Potch gave him some scraps of sun-flash, and colour and potch to noodle, and he sat and snipped them contentedly.
1948 E. F. Murphy *They Struck Opal* 128–9: New industries began cropping up – such as that called 'lousing the dumps'. This was carried out by a small army of women and children, who picked over the opal dirt on the dumps, looking for any loose opals that the miners may have missed. . . . The Queensland and Lightning Ridge name for this practice – noodling – seems a more logical one. It originated from the discovery of small egg-shaped opals. . . . A visiting geologist tabbed these 'nodules' . . . The miners soon altered the name to 'noodles'.
1971 Rena Briand *White Man in a Hole* 27: 'Why don't you have a go at noodling*?' he suggested. *Local term for scraping the rubble heaps in search of opal.
1976 Morris West *Bulletin* 20 Mar. 40: 'It takes two months for a novel to germinate with me. One fiddles with it, noodles it and then the day comes when I'm ready to go.'

norks A woman's breasts [origin uncertain: the wrapping on Norco butter shows a cow's udder]
1962 Criena Rohan *The Delinquents* 157: 'Hello, honey, that sweater – one deep breath and your norks will be in my soup.'
1966 Baker 215: *nork*, a female breast,

usually in plural. (Ex Norco Co-operative Ltd., a butter manufacturer in N.S.W.)
1970 Barry Oakley *Let's Hear it for Prendergast* 71: 'Wow, she's peeled right off. What norks!'
1973 Patrick White *The Eye of the Storm* 593: Hits herself in the eye with an independent nork it isn't any laughing matter.

Normanton cocktail See quot. [f. place-name]
1963 John Cantwell *No Stranger to the Flame* 38: 'Give us a Normanton cocktail, darl – a gin and two blankets,' one of the cutters said.

North, the Deep Queensland: *derogatory* [f. the 'Deep South' and its associations of intolerance in U.S.A.]
1974 Peter Porter *Australian* 5 Oct. 13: I learned that things have changed but not enough to placate the southerners, for whom Queensland in general and Brisbane in particular are sources of scorn and contempt. 'The Deep North' is the phrase used in Sydney.

northern myth, the The belief in north Australia as having vast potentialities awaiting exploitation, attacked by B. R. Davidson in *The Northern Myth* (1965)
1969 Osmar White *Under the Iron Rainbow* 50: Kununurra . . . is the focal point of hope for all those whose faith in the northern myth remains unshaken by the repeated failure of large agricultural projects in the Australian tropics.

Northern Territory champagne See quot.
1973 *Sunday Telegraph* 26 Aug. 112: Evidence was given that many Aboriginals drink 'Northern Territory champagne' – methylated spirits mixed with health salts.

nose, on the Ill-smelling; offensive, viewed with disfavour (popularized as World War II slang)
1941 Baker 49: *Nose, on the* (Said of things) disliked, offensive.

1944 Lawson Glassop *We Were the Rats* 273: 'One of them base wallopers . . . He's on the nose.'
1946 Rohan Rivett *Behind Bamboo* 398: *On the nose*, ill-smelling, unsavoury, suggestive of dishonesty.
1953 Dymphna Cusack *Southern Steel* 138: 'The beer's on the nose and the plonk'd make a willy-wagtail fight an emu.'
1959 Dorothy Hewett *Bobbin Up* 42: 'It's on the nose alright. Stinks of bugs.' Ibid. 29: 'Gawd your language is on the nose Dawnie.'
1960 Nancy Cato *Green Grows the Vine* 46: 'You know, pongs. It means something's on the nose.'
1973 Frank Huelin *Keep Moving* 20: He removed his boots and the narrow strips of rag wrapped round his feet. 'By cripes! They're a bit on the nose,' said my mate, wrinkling his nose.
1974 *Australian* 12 Dec. 13: Australian singer Helen Reddy has become a naturalised U. S. citizen. In a small ceremony in a Los Angeles Federal court building this week, she renounced her Australian citizenship and swore everlasting loyalty to the Stars and Stripes. A bit on the nose, we think.

nose, have a ~ on To hold in disfavour [cf. *snout*]
1903 Joseph Furphy *Such is Life* (1944) 17: 'I don't blame ole Martin to have a bit of a nose on me,' continued Mosey laughingly.

note A £1 note
1867 J. R. Houlding *Australian Capers* 131: 'Mr Buckles had not half a dozen notes (pounds) when he landed here three years ago.'
1885 *The Australasian Printers' Keepsake* 95: 'You'll easily pick up five notes a week.'
1899 George Boxall *The Story of the Australian Bushrangers* 191: Then the traveller would say that he was willing to pay 'a note' for their recovery.
1934 F. E. Baume *Burnt Sugar* 353: He took one look at the cheque and dashed for the 'phone. 'A hundred notes, Maise. A hundred notes.'

1942 Gavin Casey *It's Harder for Girls* 18: I gave mum a score of notes, and she bought a new outfit and went down for the wedding.

novel, the great Australian see Australian

nuddy, in the In the nude
1953 Baker 104: *nuddy*, nude, especially in the phrase *in the nuddy*.
1959 Dorothy Hewett *Bobbin Up* 42: 'Take your bloody clothes and quit standin' there half in the nuddy.'
1963 John Cantwell *No Stranger to the Flame* 15: 'Been swimming – in the nuddy and on me pat.'
1975 Xavier Herbert *Poor Fellow My Country* 116: 'You're not shocked by my bathing in the nuddy, are you?'

nugget *n*. 1 A lump of gold [f. *nug* a lump, a block; *nugget* a lump of anything EDD 1853]
1852 G. C. Mundy *Our Antipodes* iii 322: Gold was not so plentiful as was anticipated, – not to be picked up on the hill-sides in an afternoon's stroll; nor were nuggets* to be dug up, like potatoes, by the bushel. *The word nugget among farmers signifies a small compact beast – a runt; among goldminers a lump, in contradistinction to the scale or dust gold.
2 An unbranded calf
1882 Rolf Boldrewood *Robbery Under Arms* (World's Classics 1949) 21: So, as Jim had lighted the fire, we branded the little red heifer calf first – a fine fat six-months-old nugget she was – and then three bull calves.

nugget *v*. 1 To pick out nuggets of gold
1852 Lord Robert Cecil *Goldfields Diary* (1935) 31: He himself was snugly 'nuggeting' (picking out nuggets with a pen-knife or oyster knife) on his own behalf.
1857 F. Cooper *Wild Adventures in Australia* 103: The speaker . . . had been there, nuggetted from the surface-rocks three ounces of the pure metal in two days.
2 To appropriate unbranded calves

1881 Mrs Campbell Praed *Policy and Passion* 25: 'It is said that she has an eye to business, and does not disdain nuggeting*.' *To *nugget*: in Australian slang, to appropriate your neighbours' unbranded calves. Ibid. 182: 'If he does steal a calf now and then, I know several squatters who are given to "nuggeting".'

nuggety Stocky, thickset
1874 Charles de Boos *The Congewoi Correspondence* 141: He's just oner them short, square-built, nuggetty kinder fellers.
1887 *All the Year Round* 30 Jul. 67: A native of New South Wales is known as a 'cornstalk', because the men generally grow tall and thin. The opposite kind of build, short and thickset, is called 'nuggetty'.
1901 Henry Lawson 'Poisonous Jimmy Gets Left' *Prose* i 354: He was a short, nuggety man, and could use his hands, they said.
1924 Gavin Casey *It's Harder for Girls* 16: Molly was tall and dark . . . The chap she got hold of was just the opposite, a nuggety, fair little bloke.
1969 Osmar White *Under the Iron Rainbow* 107: He was a nuggety little bloke and moved as if he could handle himself in a blue.

Nullarbor nymph A semi-naked woman reported near Eucla in 1972
1972 *Sun-Herald* 2 Jan. 7: An Adelaide railway worker said today he thought the elusive 'Nullarbor Nymph' reported to have been seen hand-feeding giant kangaroos near Eucla, was his missing 27-year-old daughter . . . She matched the description of the half-naked blonde reported to have been seen several times.
1973 *Australian* 31 Jan. 1: 'If,' he [Prince Charles] said at an Australia Day dinner, 'I've put my foot in it, I should probably be given a compulsory exit visa to the Antipodes and there find my name linked romantically (in the best traditions) with the naughty Nullarbor Nymph.'

O

oats, long See quots
1964 H. P. Tritton *Time Means Tucker* 111: 'Long oats', as part of the bush vernacular, went out with the horse. If you went to a pub or a dance and left your horse tied to a fence all night, you were said to be feeding him on long oats. Ibid. 110: 'I never let a mate's horse chew long oats, so I put 'em in the stable and feed 'em.'

Ocean Hell, the Norfolk Island, as a place of secondary punishment in the convict system
1855 William Howitt *Land, Labour and Gold* ii 8: They are the vilest of the vile, the incorrigible, the refuse of the mass of convict scoundrelism, who are sent thither from Sydney or Van Diemen's Land to work in chains, whence Norfolk Island is styled the Ocean Hell.
1864 J. F. Mortlock *Experiences of a Convict* (1965) 67: The commandants preceding him [Maconochie] . . . ruled with such injudicious severity, as to make the place well deserving its Australian name, 'The Ocean Hell'.

ocker The uncultivated Australian, a term superseding 'Alf' q.v.; the nickname of anyone called Stevens [A colloquial form of names like Oscar, made a generic term by a character called Ocker played in a series of T.V. sketches by Ron Frazer (see quot. 1975)]
1927 *Sunday Sun* 1 May 'Us Fellers' [comic strip in 'Sunbeams'] 1: 'And you know what I did to 'Ocker' Stevens at school on Wednesday don't you?'
1939 Kylie Tennant *Foveaux* 122: 'Will you get out of this, Okker,' Miss Montague requested irritably . . . Oscar responded in brotherly fashion.
1959 D'Arcy Niland *The Big Smoke* 185: 'Ocker White lost more than I did. Ocker White, he's got a lot to remember and a lot to forget.'
1971 George Johnston *A Cartload of Clay* 71: The big man would be a good player, a vigorous clubman, a hearty participant in the companionship of the

club bar. He was a type Julian had sometimes talked to him about, what the boy called an 'Ocker'.

1974 *Sydney Morning Herald* 24 Apr. 6: That image, of the RSL itself as a sabre-rattling élitist organisation with an over-privileged influence on governments, and of RSL members themselves as beer-swilling, 'pokey-playing' Ockers, has, executives believe, faded if not totally evaporated.

1975 Ron Frazer *Sun* 20 Aug. 37: 'Back in the Ocker days, guys would come up to me in their thongs and shorts and with a can in their hand and say, 'Y'know, mate, I know a guy just like that Ocker character.'

ockerdom, ockerina, ockerism

1975 Max Harris *Australian* 18 Jan. 18: The resurgence of an aggressive Australian ockerdom was coincident with the first election of the Whitlam Government and the discovery of a 'new nationalism'.

1975 *Sunday Telegraph* 27 Jul. 96: Ockerina of the week was surely the woman on the Eastern Suburbs bus, studying a race guide while slurping down a meat pie.

1974 Peter Porter *Australian* 5 Oct. 13: The new Australian boorishness is known as Ockerism, from a slob-like character called Ocker in a television series – the embodiment of oafish, blinkered self-satisfaction.

off like a bride's nightie see **bride**

off one's kadoova, pannikin see **kadoova, pannikin**

offside To act as an 'offsider'
1883 Let. in Mary Durack *Kings in Grass Castles* (1959) 272: I have put up a yard on Galway since Uncle Jerry left. Pumpkin and Kangaroo offsiding.
1917 R. D. Barton *Reminiscences of an Australian Pioneer* 93: I met a blackfellow who was offsiding for the horse-driver, and was called Archie.
1960 A. W. Upfield *Bony and the Kelly Gang* 167: Bony was asked to offside for Joe Flanagan, the settlement's electrician.

offsider The assistant to a bullock-driver, walking on the offside of the team; a helper of any kind, in a subordinate position; an understudy
1880 Henry Kendall 'Jim the Splitter' *Poetical Works* ed. T. T. Reed (1966) 159: And, as to a team, over gully and hill, / He can travel with twelve on the breadth of a quill, / And boss the unlucky 'offsider'.
1903 Joseph Furphy *Such is Life* (1944) 229: 'That's jist the sort o' thing would put a hump on me. Sort o' off-sider for a gang o' Chinks! My word!'
1905 'The Old Bullock Dray' *The Old Bush Songs* ed. A. B. Paterson 6 and 8 note: They say there's no delay / To get an off-sider / For the old bullock dray. An offsider is a bullock-driver's assistant – one who walks on the offside of the team and flogs the bullocks on that side when occasion arises. The word afterwards came to mean an assistant of any kind.
1910 C. E. W. Bean *On the Wool Track* 168: An 'offsider' ... is a gentleman who is learning bullock-driving, and who is allowed to try his apprentice tongue on the offside of the bullock team. The term is transferred to the assistant whom the cook must engage at a big shed.
1919 E. S. Sorenson *Chips and Splinters* 14: He was able to ride after bullocks and act as offsider at pinches for his father.
1930 Vance Palmer *The Passage* 262: 'My little spree's come to an end, Mick, so you'll have to pick up another offsider.'
1953 *Caddie A Sydney Barmaid* 211: ''I'll get me offsider. He's outside in the cart.' He trotted outside, returning with a lad of about fourteen.
1962 Gavin Casey *Amid the Plenty* 196: 'They want a storeman ... Not a boss storeman to run it, just an offsider.'

oil Reliable information, esp. in expressions like 'the dinkum oil', 'the good oil'
1916 C. J. Dennis *The Moods of Ginger Mick* 87: Now that's the dinkum oil from Ginger Mick.

1919 W. H. Downing *Digger Dialects* 36: *Oil* News; information.

1922 Arthur Wright *A Colt from the Country* 126: 'That's Dreamy Dan's owner,' remarked Knocker; 'we'll get the oil in a minute.'

1934 F. E. Baume *Burnt Sugar* 346: 'You're O.K. That's why I'm giving you the right oil.'

1937 A. W. Upfield *Mr Jelly's Business* 145: 'You oughta 'ave come with me acrost to the pub when I gave you the oil.'

1946 *Coast to Coast 1945* 33: 'You better play a hand or two,' he said shortly, 'and get the oil about the place.'

1953 *Caddie A Sydney Barmaid* 179: Ivy gave me the oil about him. 'Better look out for the old ram, he walks in his sleep.'

1970 Richard Beilby *No Medals for Aphrodite* 279: 'I told ya, son. We're goin' to Crete. I got the good oil.'

oil-rag, to live on the smell of an Metaphor for the ability to survive on minimum food or income [listed as a characteristic Irish expression in P. W. Joyce *English as We Speak it in Ireland* (1910) 129]

[**1893** Simpson Newland *Paving the Way* 228: 'I'd rather live on the smell of a greasy rag here than make millions in a climate like that.']

1903 Joseph Furphy *Such is Life* (1944) 39: It is easier. . .to recognise the various costly vintages than to live contentedly on the smell of an oil rag.

1911 E. S. Sorenson *Life in the Australian Backblocks* 267: 'There was Bill Brown . . . livin' on the smell of an oil rag for years.'

1951 Dymphna Cusack and Florence James *Come in Spinner* 149: 'Oh, Bridie always could live on the smell of an oil rag.'

1963 O. Bonutto *A Migrant's Story* 13: An argument against the admission of Italians into Australia, was that they would undermine the Australian standard of living because of their frugality and ability to live on 'the smell of an oil rag.'

Old Barn, the see **barn**

Old Bus, the Sir Charles Kingsford-Smith's name for his aircraft *The Southern Cross*

old chum The converse of 'new chum' q.v. (quot. 1812)

1846 C. P. Hodgson *Reminiscences of Australia* 22: Remember it may soon be your turn to act the same part, and give an asylum and 'Bush' education to the 'New Chum'*. *'New Chum' in opposition to 'Old Chum'. The former 'cognomen' peculiarizing the newly arrived emigrant, the latter as a mark of respect attached to the more experienced Colonist.

1855 Raffaello Carboni *The Eureka Stockade* ed. G. Serle (1969) 13: I frequently saw horrid scenes of blood; but I was now an old chum and therefore knew what was what in colonial life.

1905 'The Squatter of the Olden Time' *The Old Bush Songs* ed. A. B. Paterson 108: And quaffs his cup of hysonskin, the beverage old chums choose.

1924 *Truth* 27 Apr. 6: *Old chum* Experienced person.

Old Dart, the England [origin obscure]

1832 Pierce Egan *Book of Sports* cit. G. C. Ingleton *True Patriots All* (1952) 119: News has been received from London, of this extraordinary match, which excited exceeding interest amongst the sporting fraternity in the *Old Dart*.

1908 E. S. Sorenson *Quinton's Rouseabout* 206: Murty unexpectedly came in for something like £800 by the death of a distant and almost forgotten relative in the old dart.

1923 Jack Moses *Beyond the City Gates* 170: Bring it to the notice of those chaps with a bit of cash in the 'Old Dart'.

1941 Sarah Campion *Mo Burdekin* 89: 'Still as green,' interjected Dad, 'as a pommy straight from th' "Old Dart"!'

1953 *Caddie A Sydney Barmaid* 26: When he came out to Australia he decided to forget his relatives in the

'Old Dart'*, so he changed his name by deed-poll. *Slang term for England.
1962 Stuart Gore *Down the Golden Mile* 261: 'Gettin' too much of the good Aussie beer into you, instead of that warmed-up bilge water they sell in the Old Dart.'
1975 Xavier Herbert *Poor Fellow My Country* 1234: 'Even those you know have some degree of radicalism are identifying themselves with the Old Dart.'

old hand 1 An ex-convict
1845 C. Griffith *The Present State . . . of Port Phillip* 76: The old hands are men, who, having been formerly convicts (or lags as they are generally termed) have become free by the expiration of their sentences.
1852 G. C. Mundy *Our Antipodes* i 93: A convict, *eo nomine*, is seldom mentioned in N.S.W. He is 'a prisoner of the Crown', an 'old hand', a 'government man'.
1865 Henry Kingsley *The Hillyars and the Burtons* 57: Now and then you will find a jail-bird who will, in appearance, pass muster among honest men; but in this case the word 'Old hand' was too plainly written on the face to be mistaken.
1901 Henry Lawson 'The Golden Graveyard' *Prose* i 342: Mother Middleton was an awful woman, an 'old hand' (transported convict) some said.
2 Someone long established in a particular place or mode of living; a person of particular experience (quots 1843, 1848 could include ex-convicts, but would not be confined to them)
1843 John Hood *Australia and the East* 215: The *amor patriae* is strong among the 'old hands', as the fathers of the colony are called; but then it shows itself merely in the wish to sell their share of it for an enormous price!
1846 C. P. Hodgson *Reminiscences of Australia* 25: Having allowed your friend as the older 'hand', and therefore better skilled in bush eccentricities. n. 'Hand' synonymous with Chum; not elegant appellations, but very significant.

1848 H. W. Haygarth *Recollections of Bush Life in Australia* 26: Upon hearing a party of what are called 'old hands' in the country talking together . . . a stranger might not unreasonably suppose that he was listening to a race of people who had forgotten their mother tongue, and adopted that of the devil in its stead.
1862 Arthur Polehampton *Kangaroo Land* 60: It was and is a constant source of ambition among 'new chums', especially the younger ones, to be taken for 'old hands' in the colony.
1916 Let. in Bill Gammage *The Broken Years* (1974) 116: My new men are all frightfully keen and anxious to get into a scrap – and I will admit that many of us 'old hands' are beginning to hanker after powder again.
1937 Ernestine Hill *Ports of Sunset* 41: Who will tell stories like that when the old hands are gone? Not the neat bank-clerks and motor salesmen of to-day, I fancy.
1959 Dorothy Hewett *Bobbin Up* 149: Alice and Lil, both old hands, were all tidied up, waiting for the signal to switch off.
1963 Gunther Bahnemann *Hoodlum* 11: Warder Frankston was an old hand in houses of detention, reformatories, and jails.

old handism
1859 Frank Fowler *Southern Lights and Shadows* 15: The battle of 'old-handism' against 'new chumism' is not ever-lastingly waging in Victoria as it is in New South Wales.

oldie A member of the older generation [OED 1874]
1960 A. W. Upfield *Bony and the Kelly Gang* 168: 'The oldees can natter and gossip and tell tales.'
1972 Geoff Morley *Jockey Rides Honest Race* 210: 'Things are getting better, but it's a slow process. You've got to give us oldies a chance.'
1971 David Ireland *The Unknown Industrial Prisoner* 196: It was no joke to be forty-five with fifty not far away and them looking to get rid of the oldies.

old man Of exceptional size (from the term applied to the fully grown kangaroo)

1834 George Bennett *Wanderings in New South Wales* i 286: Many persons when alone are afraid to face a large 'old man' kangaroo.

1845 R. Howitt *Impressions of Australia Felix* 233: I stared at a man one day for saying that a certain allotment of land was 'an old-man allotment': he meant a large allotment – the old-man kangaroo being the largest kangaroo.

1861 H. W. Wheelwright *Bush Wanderings of a Naturalist* 4: In bush parlance, the old male kangaroo is called 'an old man'.

1903 Joseph Furphy *Such is Life* (1944) 122: A picaninny alternative, that, you say? I tell you, it proved an old-man alternative before it ran itself out.

1934 Archer Russell *A Tramp-Royal in Wild Australia* 190: Central Australia was experiencing . . . its usual climatic respite from days of blistering heat in an 'Old Man' sand storm.

Old Tin Shed, the see **Tin Shed**

Old Viceroy, the see **Viceroy**

on In agreement, willing to take part, often in the expression 'Are you on? 'You're on' denotes the acceptance of a bet [cf. *on* adv. 13c OED 1812: having a wager on something]

1880 Rolf Boldrewood *The Miner's Right* (1890) 136: 'I'm on,' answered Joe, a ray of humour irradiating his honest countenance.

1883 George Darrell *The Sunny South* (1975) 29: 'What do you say if we throw them into the fish pond?' 'I'm on!' 'So am I!'

1903 Joseph Furphy *Such is Life* (1944) 128: 'If each of you gives me a kiss, of her own good will, I'll promise not to tell. Are you on?' Ibid. 281: 'Failing the fulfilment of either double, the wager is off?' 'That's it. Are you on?'

1900–10 O'Brien and Stephens: *On* I am on, I am willing, I am game.

1916 Let. in Bill Gammage *The Broken Years* (1974) 160: We heard a wounded chap crying out, he was in 'No Man's

Land' . . . I said 'Who's coming over' another chap said 'I'm on' so over the parapet we crawled.

1939 Kylie Tennant *Foveaux* 350: 'Are you on?' Herb asked impatiently as he began to remove his coat. 'I'll give it a go.'

1949 Lawson Glassop *Lucky Palmer* 89: 'I'll have a pony on it.' 'You're on,' said Lucky, turning to him with a beaming smile.

on, it was ~ (for young and old) An expression for an outbreak of disorder, any general absence of restraint

1951 Eric Lambert *The Twenty Thousand Thieves* 258: Peter Dimmock bounded between the tents leaping into the air at every few paces and whooping: 'It's on! It's on for young and old!'

1955 John Morrison *Black Cargo* 77: 'A day come when some of our blokes in Sydney just put their coats on and walked off the job. It was on then for young and old.'

1969 William Dick *Naked Prodigal* 49–50: Just before closing time a brawl started when some bloke walking by spilt beer on Ackie so Ackie's young brother king hit him and the bloke's mate stepped in so Archie hit *him* – and then it was on.

1971 David Martin *Hughie* 106: He almost forgot about it until the evening of Sunday when the party was due and when, in Harry's words, it was on for young and old.

1975 *Australian* 12 Aug. 3: Because of the rain and peak-hour traffic, he sought a police escort. 'It was on for young and old. The police had the way clear all the way down to York St . . . but at North Sydney we realised we were not going to make it.'

on it sc. the liquor

1938 Eric Lowe *Salute to Freedom* 38: He knew how drink affected Brand, and he muttered to his wife, 'He's on it proper to day, mother.'

1945 H. M. Moran *Beyond the Hill Lies China* 105: For days, while he was 'on it' he did everything horrible except beat his wife.

1956 Patrick White *The Tree of Man* 141: 'It is him,' she said finally. 'It is that bastard. He is on it again.'

1968 *Coast to Coast 1967–1968* 157: 'You've got the shakes,' he said. 'Been on it, have you?'

on the grass See quot. 1941

1941 Baker 51: *On the grass* Free, at large. A criminal is 'on the grass again' after being released from gaol.

1962 Alan Marshall *This is the Grass* [book title]

on the grouter see **grouter**

on your pat see **pat**

on thirds see **thirds**

on the track see **wallaby track**

oncer See quot.

1976 *Sun-Herald* 12 Dec. 15: A 'oncer' is the term coined by politicians for those elected in a landslide and can only expect to serve one term in Parliament.

one day of the year, the Anzac Day (25 April) commemorated as a public holiday

1945 Cecil Mann *The River* 149: 'As you all heard the Padre and Premier both say at the service, it is the one day in the year which we, with very great pride, can call our *own* Day.'

1962 Alan Seymour *The One Day of the Year* [play title]

1971 Frank Hardy *The Outcasts of Foolgarah* 211: A retired officer of high rank . . . out late celebrating the One Day of the Year.

1974 David Ireland *Burn* 115: I never went to a march on Anzac Day. I can always remember the kids that died up there in the slush . . . I don't have to wait for one day of the year.

one them, to In two-up, to throw a head and a tail

1949 Lawson Glassop *Lucky Palmer* 168: The pennies hit the canvas. One

jumped in the air, landed and lay flat. It was a tail. 'And he's – ' began the fat man. The other penny ran a few feet and stopped. It was a head. ' – one'd 'em!' finished the fat man.

ones, two The cry in two-up when the spinner throws a head and a tail

1911 Louis Stone *Jonah* 217: He set two pounds of his winnings, and tossed the coins. 'Two ones!' cried the gamblers, with a roar.

1925 Arthur Wright *The Boy from Bullarah* 17: Ronter possessed himself of the kip, and, placing the pennies upon it, spun them high into the air. 'Two ones.'

onka Finger: *rare* [rhyming slang *Onkaparinga* (place-name) = *finger*]

onkus Disordered, out of action, gone wrong

1924 *Truth* 27 Apr. 6: *Onkus* Unpleasant; absurd.

1941 Baker 51: *Onkus* All wrong, incorrect; (of machinery) out of order.

1947 Norman Lindsay *Halfway to Anywhere* 84: He took a pull at it, adding: 'A bit onkus, but drinkable. Have a swig.'

open slather see **slather**

open, they were sc. the pubs (when times of business are prescribed by law)

1942 Sarah Campion *Bonanza* 19: It was eleven – 'they' were open.

Orchid, Blue see **Blue**

oscar Cash: *obsolescent* [rhyming slang from Oscar Asche (1871–1936) the Australian actor]

1919 W. H. Downing *Digger Dialects* 36: *Oscar* Money.

1931 William Hatfield *Sheepmates* 161: 'Sit in, some o' yous that aint flyblown . . . an' their I.O.U.'s is good, if there's no real Oscar about the joint.'

1942 Leonard Mann *The Go-Getter* 16: 'Get the oscar off Tom soon's I see him. He's honest.'

1959 D'Arcy Niland *The Big Smoke* 21:

'If you'd been fighting all those blokes in the ring you'd have more oscar in your kick now than the Prime Minister himself.'

O.T., the The Overland Telegraph line from Adelaide to Darwin
1933 F. E. Baume *Tragedy Track* 36: A telephone system as far north as Ryan's Well, 78 miles along the O.T.
1942 Charles Barrett *From a Bush Hut* 38: I followed the O.T. (overland Telegraph) down to the Alice, where I hopped the rattler.

Our Glad, Harbour see **Glad, Harbour**

out of the box see **box**

outback *n. & a.* The regions remote from the settled districts
1875 Rolf Boldrewood *The Squatter's Dream* repr. as *Ups and Downs* (1878) 31: The whole party . . . rode silently along the indistinct trail which led 'out back'.
1893 Henry Lawson 'Some Popular Australian Mistakes' *Prose* ii 24–5: Australian poetical writers invariably get the coastal scenery mixed up with that of 'Out Back' . . . We wish to Heaven that Australian writers would leave off trying to make a paradise out of the Out Back Hell.
1898 W. H. Ogilvie *Fair Girls and Gray Horses* 125: I was travelling, weak and footsore, on a river road Out Back.
1930 Edward Shann *An Economic History of Australia* 125: They fenced paddocks which grew larger and larger as the carrying capacity grew lighter 'out-back' – where paddocks of 20 or 40 thousand acres are not rare.
1966 Craig McGregor *Profile of Australia* 160: In the outback Australians have had to wrestle with some of the harshest physical conditions in the world.

outbackery The conscious cultivation of 'outback' values
1966 Tom Ronan *Once There Was a Bagman* 124: The phase of life, now sneered at by our pharisaical, suburban, scholarship-nurtured intelligentsia – 'Outbackery' they call it – has its intervals of excellence.
1971 *Bulletin* 14 Aug. 49: 'No violence, no sex, no self-conscious outbackery; the only complaint, the book is too short. [book review]

outer, on the Not favoured to win, not given a chance; disliked, ostracized [? f. the outside track in racing]
1924 *Truth* 27 Apr. 6: *Outer, on the* to be poor; to be outside.
1926 J. Vance Marshall *Timely Tips for New Australians*: To be 'on the outer' To be penniless.
1928 Arthur Wright *A Good Recovery* 157: 'You told me yourself that you were the cause of my being on the outer.'
1944 Jean Devanny *By Tropic, Sea and Jungle* 97: He had been thrown on the 'outer' at the completion of a job for Cinesound Studios, Sydney, and with his few remaining pounds he had made his way north.
1953 T. A. G. Hungerford *Riverslake* 174: 'And you're on the outer for sticking up for him?'
1958 Thea Astley *Girl with a Monkey* 44: 'I'm already on the outer with this bunch. I can't afford to make a mistake.'
1966 Don Crick *Period of Adjustment* 77: 'Harold was engaged to another girl and I think his father took a dim view of him breaking it off. Puts me a bit on the outer at the moment.'
1970 Ivan Southall *Bread and Honey* 54: Warren had always been on the outer, like a stray dog, always getting pushed.

over the fence see **fence**

overland *v.* **overlanding** *n.* To drove cattle long distances
1871 Marcus Clarke *Old Tales of a Young Country* 163: 'Overlanding' was a profitable and, withal, romantic occupation. Young men of spirit, wearied of the capital, and prompted by love of gain and adventure, purchased cattle and sheep in New South Wales, and drove them 'overland' to the 'New Orleans' of Colonel Torrens.

1923 Jack Moses *Beyond the City Gates* 119: When I met him first he was in charge of a mob, overlanding from the Gulf to Vic.
1971 Keith Willey *Boss Drover* 48: The big road trains have taken the work away from the drover nowadays but at one time overlanding cattle paid big money, provided you knew your job.

overlander A man droving cattle over long distances, and so one of the more dashing of the bushworkers
1841 George Grey *Journals of Two Expeditions of Discovery* ii 183: The Overlanders are nearly all men in the pride of youth, whose occupation is to convey large herds of stock from market to market and from colony to colony.
1848 H. W. Haygarth *Recollections of Bush Life in Australia* 120n: An overlander is one who makes long expeditions from one colony to another with stock, either for the purpose of finding new pasture land on which to establish himself, or to take advantage of a favourable market.
1857 F. Cooper *Wild Adventures in Australia* 66: The overlanders are the pioneers ... in taking large herds of cattle beyond the boundaries far into the bush, and finding a 'run' or tract of land, sufficiently well grassed and watered for their purpose ... and protect the cattle from the aggressions of the natives until other 'squatters', following in their tracks muster in sufficient numbers ... when the overlanders relinquish their charge, and with another herd repeat the process.
1863 Rachel Henning *Letters* ed. D. Adams (1962) 136: Two atrocious young 'overlanders', first-rate specimens of the free-and-easy Australia. They ... came up and shook hands patronizingly with Biddulph, who had never seen them before in his life, and ... turned out their horses ... so that they might make themselves comfortable here for some days.
1865 'The Overlander' in *The Queenslanders' New Colonial Camp Fire Song Book* 11: We steer up to the girls, that

rig themselves with grandeur, / And while they sweat our cheques – they swear, they love the Overlander.
1907 Alfred Searcy *In Australian Tropics* 125: If a crowd of overlanders and backblockers happened to be present, things would be made lively.
1915 Vance Palmer *The World of Men* 39: An overlander who was travelling to some far river in the South to take charge of a mob of cattle.
1933 F. E. Baume *Tragedy Track* 85: The grave ... stands mutely to remind the overlander of the tragedy.

oyster, Kimberley see **Kimberley**

P

pack, go to the To lapse into a lower state; deteriorate, fall into disrepute [listed by Partridge as a New Zealandism]
1915 C. J. Dennis *The Songs of a Sentimental Bloke* 94: I've sent the leery bloke that bore me name / Clean to the pack wivout one pearly tear. [? in error for 'sent packing']
1919 W. H. Downing *Digger Dialects* 26: *Go to the pack* Deteriorate.
1924 *Truth* 27 Apr. 6: *Pack, go to the* To fall away; to collapse.
1938 Francis Ratcliffe *Flying Fox and Drifting Sand* 245: I learned of areas which had gone completely to the pack, where man had given nature best, and the holdings had been abandoned one by one.
1948 Patrick White *The Aunt's Story* 267: 'I was devoted to 'is kids, Lilian and little 'Enry, though 'Enry went to the pack.'
1958 Gavin Casey *Snowball* 118: 'You wait till he gets a bit older. Them abos always go t' the pack.'
1963 Don Crick *Martin Place* 196: 'Things are goin' to the pack. If they get any shorter of work, they'll close down.'

packing them, packing death Scared, i.e. holding back nervous diarrhoea (Services slang in World War II)

1951 Eric Lambert *The Twenty Thousand Thieves* 132: 'He's packing them badly. He's quite useless.'

1959 David Forrest *The Last Blue Sea* 69: You know something, thought Ron Fisher, you're no good. You're packing them.

1961 Russell Braddon *Naked Island* 44: 'Who's panicking?' 'You are, son. Fair packing 'em, y' are.'

1971 David Ireland *The Unknown Industrial Prisoner* 132: 'They were packing the shits when he went off his head in the control room last time.'

1975 Les Ryan *The Shearers* 6: 'That bloke will be packing 'em all the way to the border.'

Paddo Paddington, the Sydney suburb
1945 *Coast to Coast 1944* 163: 'Just down the road a piece I live, down in Paddo.'

1959 Dorothy Hewett *Bobbin Up* 15: Running downhill into the slummy rabbit warrens of Paddo and the Loo.

1964 Arthur Staples *Paddo* [book title]

1974 *Australian* 14 Aug. 3: Paddo gets a National Trust rating.

paddock, heifer see **heifer**

paddock, saddling see **saddling paddock**

paddock, wouldn't be seen (dead) with someone in a (forty-acre) An expression of extreme dislike [Australian version of 'not being seen dead in a ten-acre field']
1900 Henry Lawson 'Andy Page's Rival' *Prose* i 362: 'You needn't think you're goin' to cotton on with me any more after this! I wouldn't be seen in a paddock with yer.'

padre's bike, gone for a ride on the Jocular reply to any request for someone's whereabouts (World War II slang)
1953 *The Sunburnt Country* ed. Ian Bevan 129: '*He went mad and they shot him*' is the routine answer to any superior seeking the whereabouts of a subordinate. An alternative version is that he has '*gone for a ride on the padre's bike.*'

see **went through like Speed Gordon, went for a crap and the sniper got him**

Painter, Jack the see **Jack the Painter**

pakapoo ticket, like a Untidy, disordered: *obsolescent* [f. the difficulty in deciphering a Chinese betting slip]
[**1911** Louis Stone *Jonah* 92: He had come down early to mark a pak-ah-pu ticket at the Chinaman's in Hay Street.]

1951 Eric Lambert *The Twenty Thousand Thieves* 144: Henry opened Dooley's pay-book, the pages of which showed liberal sprinklings of the red ink in which fines and convictions were entered. 'What a pay-book!' he sighed. Dooley grinned. 'Like a pak-a-poo ticket,' he agreed.

1972 Alexander Macdonald *The Ukelele Player under the Red Lamp* 227: His bi-weekly betting lists made an average pakapoo ticket look like a model of stark simplicity.

1975 *Bulletin* 29 Nov. 17: Senate elections, because of the complexity of the system . . . are more in the nature of a pack-a-poo ticket.

pan out To 'turn out', yield results [f. the pan used in washing alluvial gold U.S. 1868 Mathews]
1898 D. W. Carnegie *Spinifex and Sand* 70: Plans so simple on paper do not always 'pan out' as confidently expected.

1908 *Australian Magazine* 1 Nov. 1250: 'Pan out' obviously comes from the old alluvial worker.

1911 Alfred Searcy *By Flood and Field* 78: The sun was low in the west as we wended our way back to the camp, all hands being satisfied that the crabbing expedition had 'panned out' in rare style.

1928 Vance Palmer *The Man Hamilton* 146: 'If you don't worry about it, it's got a knack of panning out right.'

1959 D'Arcy Niland *The Big Smoke* 11: It doesn't pan out the way you've built it up for yourself.

pannikin, off one's Out of one's mind [variant of 'off his head', the pannikin being a familiar utensil to the bush-worker]
1895 Cornelius Crowe *Australian Slang Dictionary* 56: *Off his pannikin*, silly.
1899 Steele Rudd *On Our Selection* 107: 'I seen 'im just now up in your paddick, an' he's clean off he's pannikin.'
1904 Henry Fletcher *Dads Wayback: His Work* 13: 'Gamblin' takes 'em clean off their pannikins.'
1916 C. J. Dennis *The Moods of Ginger Mick* 126: 'Per'aps I'm orf me pannikin wiv' sittin' in the sun.
see kadoova

pannikin boss Someone with minor authority over his fellow-workers: *derogatory*
1898 Morris: *Pannikin-boss*, or *Pannikin-overseer*, n. The term is applied colloquially to a man on a station, whose position is above that of the ordinary station-hand, but who has no definite position of authority, or is only a 'boss' or overseer in a small way.
1907 Charles MacAlister *Old Pioneering Days in the Sunny South* 27: The cause of that rib-cracking journey was my sister's marriage to Sergeant Doyle, before mentioned, and I went along as a kind of country page, or 'pannikin overseer', on the journey.
1928 J. Vance Marshall *Timely Tips for New Australians: Pannikin boss* A shift boss. A man in charge of a small gang of workmen.
1950 Gavin Casey *City of Men* 170: What a hell of a life, anyway, with a pannican boss standing over you all day.
1959 Dorothy Hewett *Bobbin Up* 72: All their unshakable distrust of the pannikin boss, the boss's man . . . the lowest of the low in a world where dog ate dog.
1969 D'Arcy Niland *Dead Men Running* 121: Father Vaughan seemed to project himself as no more than the mouthpiece of a pannikin boss of a God who sounded like a brutal and violent pirate.

pannikin snob
1953 *Caddie A Sydney Barmaid* 41: My mother-in-law was a pannikin snob as my father would have said.

panno Abbr. for 'pannikin boss': *derogatory*
1957 Tom Nelson *The Hungry Mile* 50: So we decided to follow the 'panno' and tracked her to the Australian Stevedoring Industry Board Office.
1960 Ron Tullipan *Follow the Sun* 31: 'I thought he might have been a panno. Perhaps it's only the panno blood makes him choose his drinking mates with such care.'
1965 Frank Hardy *The Yarns of Billy Borker* 24: Within a week [of having won the lottery], he jobbed the panno, snatched his time and bought an air ticket to gay Paree.

Panthers, the The Penrith, N.S.W., Rugby League team [f. club emblem]
1976 *Sun-Herald* 9 May 68: Manly try blitz tames the Panthers.

paper bag, couldn't fight one's way out of a To lack strength, fighting skill [also U.S.]
1918 N. Campbell and L. Nelson *The Dinky-di Soldier* 5: W'y, you can't fight yer way thro' a brown paper bag!
1941 Baker 28: *Fight one's way out of a paper bag, couldn't* To be a weakling.
1955 Alan Marshall *I Can Jump Puddles* 136: 'Skeeter couldn't fight his way out of a paper bag,' Joe asserted.
1963 A. W. Upfield *The Body at Madman's Bend* 62: 'Feller named Grogan wants to fight and he can't fight his way out of a paper bag, and everyone knows it.'
1974 David Ireland *Burn* 44: 'Billy, you're not worth a bumper,' Joy says. 'You couldn't fight your way out of a paper bag.'

paper yabber see yabber

paradise, the working man's see working man's

parcel post Epithet applied to the newly

arrived and inexperienced, esp. N.T. [see quot. 1946]

1931 William Hatfield *Sheepmates* 118 : Hallett took charge of the three 'parcel post' men and showed them a bunk where they could deposit their belongings.

1946 W. E. Harney *North of 23°* 23 : Young lads bursting with romance and itching to be out in the wide open spaces, would sign on in the cities to work on far inland stations. 'Parcel post men' they called them; that is, they were labelled and addressed to a certain place, and travelled as a parcel does in the mail.

1951 Ernestine Hill *The Territory* 431 : 'Parcel post' was influence – a station manager, or a jackeroo from the cities, who might be the boss's nephew, or going to marry his daughter . . . 'He come up by parcel post', they still say. 'He don't know nothin'.'

1974 *Australian* 28 Dec. 14 : 'In the old days, no fences at all. You just went from one place to another, mustering. But everyone got lazy. All parcel post boys, new chums from the city.'

Parramatta 1 A cloth originally manufactured in the gaol factory at Parramatta, N.S.W.

1826 James Atkinson *An Account of the State of Agriculture and Grazing in New South Wales* 131 : The coarse woollens are known in the Colony by the appellation of Parramatta cloth, having been first made there.

1827 P. Cunningham *Two Years in New South Wales* i 46 : The government gangs of convicts . . . and the solitary ones straggling here and there, with their white woollen Paramatta frocks and trowsers.

1840 J. Pitts Johnson *Plain Truths* 54 : There is at Botany Bay a very coarse cloth manufactory; it is termed Parramatta cloth, and is solely used for convicts' clothing, it is manufactured by Mr Simeon Lord, and is very cheap.

1843 John Hood *Australia and the East* 345 : A fabric, called Paramatta cloth, much used in the clothing of convicts, is also made.

1846 C. P. Hodgson *Reminiscences of Australia* 30 : Not in shirt and trowsers, but in polished boots and 'paramatta' *coat. *'Paramatta' a peculiar tweed, made in the colony and chiefly at Paramatta.

2 Parramatta gaol

1941 Kylie Tennant *The Battlers* 7 : 'I went to Parramatta. I was in an' out up to the time I was eighteen.'

1951 Dymphna Cusack and Florence James *Come in Spinner* 269 : 'Whether you done it for love or for cash, you'll end up in Parramatta just the same.' . . . 'If they stick me back in Parra, I swear I'll beat it again.'

1973 Jim McNeil *The Chocolate Frog* 10 : In the midst of life we are in Parramatta. That is to say, in prison.

parson, the flogging Rev. Samuel Marsden (1764–1838), noted for his severity as a magistrate

pass in one's marble see **marble**

pat, on one's Alone [rhyming slang for 'Pat Malone']

1908 *The Australian Magazine* 1 Nov. 1251 : 'On my own' (by myself) became 'on my Pat Malone' and subsequently 'on my Pat' a very general expression nowadays.

1908 Mrs Aeneas Gunn *We of the Never-Never* 146 : He travels day after day and month after month, practically alone – 'on me Pat Malone', as he calls it.

1916 C. J. Dennis *The Moods of Ginger Mick* 110 : But torkin' straight, the Janes 'av done their bit. / I'd like to 'ug the lot, orl on me pat!

1938 Xavier Herbert *Capricornia* 132 : 'Who's paying?' asked Oscar. 'Abo Department?' 'Oh no,' said Lace lightly. 'I'm doing it on my pat.'

1959 D'Arcy Niland *The Big Smoke* 146 : 'On the way he's got to make a bit of a call, so he leaves you on your pat in the car.'

1966 Don Crick *Period of Adjustment* 68 : I asked him what was he doing now? 'Out on the Pat Malone. Second hand cars and spares.'

Patch, Cabbage see cabbage

patriotic six, the The six independent members of the Legislative Council of Van Diemen's Land (Charles Swanston, Michael Fenton, John Kerr, William Kermode, Thomas Gregson, Richard Dry) who in 1845 resigned their seats in protest against the Appropriation Bill, and were in 1848 reinstated by the Queen

1852 John West *The History of Tasmania* i 252: The cause of 'the patriotic six', as they were called, was eagerly espoused by the colony.

pay dirt, to strike (bottom on) To reach the object of one's search, achieve success [f. goldmining U.S. 1856 Mathews]

1892 Henry Lawson 'The Bush Undertaker' *Prose* i 53: He set to work to dig it [the grave] up, and sure enough, in about half-an-hour he bottomed on payable dirt.

1946 Kylie Tennant *Lost Haven* 331: Mr Cassell's party was the only one that approached anything like payable dirt.

1965 David Martin *The Hero of Too* 73: Neither . . . [was] in a position to further his research. It was a pity, but not unexpected; a man did not strike pay-dirt at the first attempt.

1975 *Sydney Morning Herald* 15 Nov. 55: West Indies batsmen struck pay dirt aplenty at the SCG yesterday.

pea, the The one likely to emerge as the winner in a competition; the person in a favoured position; the person in a position of authority [Partridge lists *pea* The favourite; one's choice: low: 1888]

1911 Edward Dyson *Benno, and Some of the Push* 206: Mr Dickson . . . ran his eye down the card and chanced it. 'Dandy's the P,' he said. 'Put yer whole week's wash on Dandy, 'n' hold me responsible if the goods ain't delivered.'

1953 Baker 118: Other expressions used by racing fans include *pea*, a horse that is being ridden to win, especially when there is doubt about the genuineness of other runners.

1958 Frank Hardy *The Four-Legged*

Lottery 190: 'I've got the tip about it. Old Dapper Dan earwigged at the track. Swordsman is the pea.'

1969 Mena Calthorpe *The Defectors* 17: 'For the time being, I'm satisfied.' 'You're the pea,' Mick said.

1973 Alexander Buzo *Rooted* 92: 'He's had his eye on her for some time, you know, but I'm the pea, she said.'

1974 *Sun-Herald* 1 Sep. 15: The usual assumption has been that the Social Security Minister, Mr Hayden, 41, would move into the Treasury . . . Recent events have cast some doubts on that. The Deputy Prime Minister and Overseas Trade Minister, Dr Cairns, now seems the 'pea' for any change at the Treasury.

pea, on the Deranged (like cattle driven mad by eating the Darling pea q.v.)

[**1864** Rachel Henning *Letters* ed. David Adams (1963) 180: Biddulph showed him the poison plant that grows in the desert between here and the Flinders and which killed so many of our sheep . . . . The sheep went quite mad after eating it. It is a pretty shrub with whitish leaves and a crimson pea-shaped blossom.]

1903 Joseph Furphy *Such is Life* (1944) 288: 'Ill-natured, cranky beggar, Alf is – been on the pea – but there's no end of grass in his paddock.'

1908 Giles Seagram *Bushmen All* 224: 'He's got the Darling Pea right enough. Mad as a hatter.'

1932 'Bushman's Farewell to Queensland' *Old Bush Songs* ed. Stewart and Keesing (1957) 200: There's poison grass and Darling peas / Which drive the cattle raving mad.

peacock 'To peacock a piece of country means to pick out the *eyes* of the land by selecting or buying up the choice pieces and water frontages, so that the adjoining territory is practically useless to anyone else.' (Morris, 1898)

1916 Macmillan's *Modern Dictionary of the English Language* 793: *peacocking* The selection and purchase of the best and most conveniently situated lands in a district, *esp.* those which give access to a stream, the object of this land-grabbing process being to render the other areas of little or no value.

peanut, the flying see flying

pebble An indomitable or incorrigible man or beast: *obsolescent*
1870 Marcus Clarke *His Natural Life* ed. S. Murray-Smith (1970) 627: 'You're not such a pebble as folks seem to think,' grinned Frere.
1876 Rolf Boldrewood *A Colonial Reformer* (1890) 49: We had an old blue half-bred buffalo cow and her son, a four-year-old black bullock . . . He was a regular pebble.
1916 C. J. Dennis *The Moods of Ginger Mick* 114: They wus pebs, they wus narks, they wus real naughty boys.
1941 Baker 53: *Pebble* A person (occasionally an animal) hard to control. (2) A larrikin, a street tough.

pebble, game as a Courageous, with staying-power (often of horses): *obsolescent*
1893 K. Mackay *Outback* 188: Cabbage Tree Ned is as game as a pebble, and may try to dash through in spite of us.
1895 A. B. Paterson 'The Open Steeplechase' *The Man from Snowy River* 72: But they both were game as pebbles – neither one would show the feather.
1906 K. S. Prichard *The New Idea* 6 Jul. 45: He's firm and upright on his old grey nag, and game as a pebble.
1918 C. Fetherstonhaugh *After Many Days* 223: Traveller was game as a pebble, and he just passed Quadrant on the post and no more.

pee in the same pot, to Feminine equivalent of 'to piss in each other's pockets' q.v.: to be on terms of great familiarity

perish (perisher), to do a To come near to death, esp. from lack of water or food; to suffer any kind of deprivation or ordeal
[1882 Rolf Boldrewood *Robbery Under Arms* (World's Classics 1949) 499: He was as sober as a judge between one

burst and another . . . Then he most times went in an awful perisher – took a mouth to it, and was never sober day or night the whole time.]
1894 *The Argus* 28 Mar. 5: When a man or party has nearly died through want of water, he is said to have 'done a perish.' [Morris]
1899 Henry Lawson 'Pursuing Literature' in Australia' *Prose* ii 113: Did a three-months' unemployed 'perish', and then went with a mate to a sawmill in the Hutt Valley.
1910 Henry Lawson 'A Tale with Horns' *Prose* i 714: 'It was cold 'n' I did a perish because I'd come without me big coat.'
1929 K. S. Prichard *Coonardoo* 60: 'We near done a perish for water.'
1934 Archer Russell *A Tramp-Royal in Wild Australia* 223: 'You'd a done a perisher . . . but for him.'
1955 Mary Durack *Keep Him My Country* 281: 'A man could do a perish before anyone would know. I'd like a quid for all the blokes I buried on that track.'
1961 George Farwell *Vanishing Australians* 160: Wells lost consciousness and had to be nursed along to camp. On a second sortie, Bejah, in his turn, nearly did a perish.

permanents, the The Permanent Building Societies
1972 *Sydney Morning Herald* 11 Aug. 12: An analysis of the record of the permanents' shows that in June 1971, already one in every 14 people in NSW had an account with a society.

perv *n.* 1 A pervert [abbr.]
1949 Ruth Park *Poor Man's Orange* 38: 'That dirty old cow, always making up to kids . . . Merv, Merv, the rotten old perv.'
1959 Eric Lambert *Glory Thrown In* 18: 'He was a perv. Special attention given to small boys.'
1961 Patrick White *Riders in the Chariot* 399: 'Hannah . . . took an intelligent interest in the private life of any perv. The old whore would nearly pee herself watching a drag act in some of her own

clothes.

1967 B. K. Burton *Teach Them No More* 139: 'Stand up, you two bloody pervs,' he was saying, pointing at Terry and his friend.

1976 Gwen Kelly *The Middle-Aged Maidens* 48: 'Such lovely masculine Arab-type men. I'm a real perv. about Arab-type men.'

2 Someone given to 'perving'; the act of 'perving'

1963 John Cantwell *No Stranger to the Flame* 15: 'Never even saw him. Might have been a spook.' She did up the top button on the green blouse. 'Even spooks like a bit of a perv.'

1974 Keith Stackpole *Not Just for Openers* 38: After the next ball had been bowled, the blokes' heads would turn around unobtrusively so they could have a 'perv' at a bird in a mini-skirt walking down the aisle.

perve *v.* To act as voyeur; to observe and relish the female form or the intimacies of others

1944 Lawson Glassop *We Were the Rats* 183: 'Doing a bit of perving again?' I asked, looking at the gallery of nudes he had gathered from all sorts of magazines.

1962 David Forrest *The Hollow Woodheap* 153: He had ... sunglasses on, through which he was making a careful inventory of every bikini-clad female ... 'Well,' said Paddy reasonably, 'if you're going to perve, you might as well be honest about it.'

1970 Patrick White *The Vivisector* 233: 'You're a kind of perv – perving on people – even on bloody rocks!'

peter 1 A till, cash register (thieves' slang) [f. *peter* a portmanteau or trunk OED 1668]

[**1812** Vaux: *Peter* a parcel or bundle, whether large or small; but most properly it signifies a trunk or box.]

1895 Cornelius Crowe *The Australian Slang Dictionary* 57: *Peter* a till.

1924 *Truth* 27 Apr. 6: *Peter* Cash box.

1950 *Australian Police Journal* Apr. 119: *Tickle the peter* To embezzle or steal funds, usually by the servant of an employer.

1957 Judah Waten *Shares in Murder* 100: He simply did not like investigating rich men, respectable citizens ... even bank clerks who had obviously 'tickled the peter' as the saying went.

2 The witness box

1895 Cornelius Crowe *The Australian Slang Dictionary* 56: *Peater* the witness box.

1958 Vince Kelly *The Greedy Ones* 14: 'Mounting the peter. Going into the witness box.'

Phar Lap An improvised bush delicacy: N.T. [name of race horse]

1951 Ernestine Hill *The Territory* 426: They specialized in 'Phar Laps', wild dog with the hair burnt off, trussed and cooked in the ashes.

piano player in a brothel Someone implicated in an activity, but accepting no moral responsibility for it

1972 *Hansard* 21 Sep. 1741: Mr Bury: Have the trade union leaders paid any more than lip service to decrying violence? Have they taken any effective action, or have they adopted the general, traditional attitude of the man playing the piano on the ground floor of the brothel and affecting neither to know nor care what goes on upstairs?

Piccadilly bushman See quots

1941 Baker 53: *Piccadilly bushman* A wealthy Australian who lives (or lived) in the West End of London.

1961 Ray Lawler *The Piccadilly Bushman* [play title]

piccaninny Tiny, little [a West Indian term for a child (OED 1657) applied to Australian Aboriginals]

1870 W. M. Finn *Glimpses of North-Eastern Victoria* 29: If any of the Coburglars or Merrivillains from Pentridge Stockade ever escape to Rutherglen, I would not give much for the safety of this 'Piccaninny Bank.'

c. **1905** Joseph Furphy *The Buln-Buln and the Brolga* ed. R. G. Howarth (1948) 107: 'Blackfellers mostly goes in for a piccaninny fire – jist three sticks, with the ends kep' together.'

1975 *Sydney Morning Herald* 15 Sep. 1: 'Nambawan pikinini b'long Misis Kwin' is the pidgin English term for his [Prince Charles'] position as first son of the Queen and heir apparent to the throne.

piccaninny dawn (light) The approach of dawn, first light

1848 W. Westgarth *Australia Felix* 104: Great numbers were mustering from the surrounding country, and . . . the hut would be attacked before 'piccininni sun'.* *About daylight in the morning.

1903 Randolph Bedford *True Eyes and the Whirlwind* 321: By pickaninny daylight, the mounted men were in motion, and Quinn and his camel went with them.

1933 R. B. Plowman *The Man From Oodnadatta* 9: 'Picaninny daylight, Dick!' . . . While the stars paled before the approaching dawn, the white man lit the fire and prepared breakfast.

1945 Tom Ronan *Strangers on the Ophir* 12: That first pale flush of dawn which the bushman calls 'Piccaninny daylight' showed in the eastern sky.

1958 Gavin Casey *Snowball* 125: He was up before the piccaninny dawn, and in the first gentle glow of it he slid out of the house on his bare feet.

1970 Richard Beilby *No Medals for Aphrodite* 219: It was almost dawn, the 'piccaninny daylight' of the Big Country back home.

picker-up A shed-hand, lower in the hierarchy than the shearer, who gathers the fleece after it has been shorn

1892 G. L. James *Shall I Try Australia?* 99: The 'picker-up' stands over the filmy looking rug which lies in a heap on the floor, gathers it up deftly, and bearing it to the table, flings it neatly out full length, with the cut side downwards.

1901 Rolf Boldrewood *In Bad Company* 454: The shearers proper are all white men. The pickers-up and sorters of the fleece are a trifle mixed, the former

being chiefly aboriginal blacks, some of the latter Chinamen.

1910 C. E. W. Bean *On the Wool Track* 166: The rouseabouts, the pickers-up, and sweepers, and tarboys, and the rest are paid by the day . . . the shearers . . . are not being paid when not shearing.

1964 H. P. Tritton *Time Means Tucker* 40: Pickers-up took the fleece as it fell on the 'board' (shearing floor) and spread it skin-side down on the wool table.

picnic A troublesome experience [f. *picnic* used ironically]

1898 Morris *Picnic, n.* Besides the ordinary meaning of this word, there is a slang Australian use denoting an awkward adventure, an unpleasant experience, a troublesome job.

1906 A. J. Tompkins *With Swag and Billy* 69: Decent grassland is scarce where this sort of country is pressed into service, and what a picnic it must be to muster.

1945 Baker 263: We call a wild confusion or a particularly difficult task a *picnic.*

1952 A. G. Mitchell Supplement to Chambers' *Shorter English Dictionary* 801: *picnic* an awkward situation: a troublesome happening or accident: a to-do, hullabaloo, mess-up.

1955 D'Arcy Niland *The Shiralee* 38: 'All I know is I'm going to have one helluva picnic if she doesn't find it.'

picnic races Race meetings held in country areas, and regarded as a social occasion

1896 Nat Gould *Town and Bush* 224–5: Picnic race-meetings are got up in various parts of the country. These meetings are for amateur riders only . . . The owners of the horses running at picnic races are generally men of means.

1911 C. E. W. Bean *The Dreadnought of the Darling* 294: Up country they seem to judge their towns by two infallible criteria. If a town has picnic races or a polo week, it is 'alive'. If it has not, it is 'dead'. The population for many miles around spends these weeks in town –

generally there are several dances as well.

1939 Miles Franklin *All That Swagger* 470: She was ... familiar to the public through the pictures of her ... leading-in her father's winners at picnic races.

1941 Kylie Tennant *The Battlers* 149: The hotel was crowded with the *élite* who had come into town for the week of the picnic races.

1962 Dymphna Cusack *Picnic Races* [novel title]

1972 *Sunday Telegraph* 15 Oct. 132: And what is the big event? Why everyone, but everyone, is getting ready for the Bong Bong Picnic Races next Saturday. Mr Richmond assures us it's 'a very, very toney' event. 'We get our young socialities stalking around with woolly terriers,' he said.

pie-eater (biter) Someone who is 'small-time', of little account (? living on meat pies instead of proper meals): *derogatory*

1911 Edward Dyson *Benno, and Some of the Push* 144: 'Little Benny's frenzy when the game got goin' would freeze yer blood. He was that angry with the South pie-biters, he didn't care what 'appened to 'em, 'n' the way he screamed at the doomed wretches ...'

[**1922** Arthur Wright *A Colt from the Country* 122: 'They're meat-pie bookies, all right.' he exclaimed displaying a bunch of tickets. 'Had to make four bets of it.']

1949 Lawson Glassop *Lucky Palmer* 96: 'The trouble is, Mr Hughes, you're too good for the pie-eating bookmakers round these parts. You bet too well for them, Mr Hughes.'

1953 Baker 134: *pie-eater* (or *cruncher*) A small-time crook. [in prison slang]

1953 Kylie Tennant *The Joyful Condemned* 166: 'He's one of those big he-men that go sneaking around the park waiting to switch some chromo's hand bag. Just a pie-eater.'

1958 Frank Hardy *The Four-legged Lottery* 176: 'Look at 'em. Here, out on the Flat, on the Hill, even in the members' enclosure. Pie and tomato sauce. Gravy running down one side of the sleeve, sauce down the other. Leaning

forward away from the wind ... A nation of bloody pie-eaters.'

1975 Keith Miller *Sun* 10 Jan. 52: A bunch of pie-eaters. Excuse me if I find an expression from my old mate, the late Siddie Barnes, but that's what the English team has turned out to be.

pig-iron Bob Nickname given to Mr R. G. Menzies, Attorney-General in the Lyons Government, after he invoked the Transport Workers Act in 1935 when watersiders refused to load the *Dalfram* with iron for Japan

1965 Thomas Keneally *The Fear* 127: The Japanese and Pig-Iron Bob Menzies ('Thank God he's finished with politics for good,' said the priest. 'I'd prayed for that.')

1975 *Australian* 1 Nov. 21: Remember the days when 'Pig Iron Bob' decorated every railway siding?

pigs Expression of disagreement or derision [abbr. of 'in a pig's eye (arse)', listed by Partridge as U.S.]

1919 W. H. Downing *Digger Dialects* 38: *Pig's ear* A contemptuous ejaculation.

1933 Norman Lindsay *Saturdee* 124: 'Pigs to you, yer old man's got the stringholt.' Ibid. 165: Peter had to cover his confusion by saying 'Pigs to you' as he went out kicking the door.

1951 Eric Lambert *The Twenty Thousand Thieves* 322: 'Pig's arse to that!' another voice cried. 'A jack-up – that's the shot.' [In 1963 edn, 198, 'Pig's to that!']

1957 Ray Lawler *Summer of the Seventeenth Doll* 76: 'Get yourself a job somewhere.' 'Like in a paint factory? Pigs I will!'

1965 John Beede *They Hosed Them Out* 192: I said defensively, 'The wheel slipped off the runway.' 'Pig's bum,' he replied.

1969 George Johnston *Clean Straw for Nothing* 307: 'That's because she won't face realities.' 'Pig's arse. And anyway who are you to talk?'

1975 Les Ryan *The Shearers* 119: 'Ar, pigs to you!' 'In your dinger, too!'

piker A wild bullock [? f. *piker* a vagrant OED 1838]
1887 *All the Year Round* 30 Jul. 67: 'Pikers' are wild cattle.
1898 W. H. Ogilvie *Fair Girls and Gray Horses* 55: He's the lad to stop the pikers when they take you on the rush.
1904 Laura M. Palmer-Archer *A Bush Honeymoon* 347: *Piker* Wild bullock.
1936 Ion L. Idriess *The Cattle King* 62: The boy bought a teamster's cast-off bullock for two pounds. It was an old piker, worked to the very bone.
1955 Mary Durack *Keep Him My Country* 352: *Piker* A troublesome beast to muster.

pimp *n.* A sneak, tell-tale (mainly juvenile); an informer to the police or other authority: *derogatory* [f. *pimp* pander OED 1607]
1938 Xavier Herbert *Capricornia* 567: 'I'm not a pimp'. 'What you mean pimp?' 'I'm not a police-informer.'
1939 Kylie Tennant *Foveaux* 399: 'A very nice, beautiful, lovely day', Mrs. Metting answered sourly, 'for any landlord's pimps that can go sneakin' about'.
1942 Gavin Casey *It's Harder for Girls* 51: 'I just say I'm not a pimp', Brownie insisted, beginning to blubber.
1958 Frank Hardy *The Four-Legged Lottery* 182: 'Don't worry, I've drummed him. We have ways of dealing with pimps and squealers.'
1963 Alan Marshall *In Mine Own Heart* 205: 'I'm a wake-up to pimps.'

pimp *v.* To act as a pimp
1945 Gavin Casey *Downhill is Easier* 109: 'This dago bastard pimped on him to Hayes, an' lost him his job'.
1948 K. S. Prichard *Golden Miles* 28: 'There was a man pimping for the boss, a while ago. Fell down a winze on the two hundred foot level. Nasty accident it was.'
1957 Judah Waten *Shares in Murder* 155: 'You made up to me so you could get me to pimp on Charlie for you.'

pineapple, the rough end of the Hostile or unfair treatment

1961 Ray Lawler *The Piccadilly Bushman* 37: 'He'll know what I mean when I talk of getting the wrong end of the pineapple.'
1976 *Sydney Morning Herald* 23 Oct. 9: Waffling witnesses, even those of lofty social standing, were given short shift, if not the rough end of the pineapple.

ping pong, aerial see **aerial**

pink To shear closely so that the colour of the skin shows through
1899 W. T. Goodge *Hits! Skits! and Jingles!* 113: The leathery necks he pinked 'em too,/Did Gentleman Jack of Jamberoo.
1905 'Flash Jack from Gundagai' *The Old Bush Songs* ed. A. B. Paterson 27 and note: I've pinked 'em with the Wolseleys and I've rushed with B-bows, too. 'Pinking' means that he had shorn the sheep so closely that the pink skin showed through.

pink-hi, pinkeye A 'walkabout': holiday celebration [Pidgin]
1929 K. S. Prichard *Coonardoo* 34: Every year at midsummer, for as long as Coonardoo could remember, the tribes for a hundred miles about had gathered for pink-eye on Wytaliba.
1936 H. Drake-Brockman *Sheba Lane* 131: He found his natives in good tucker and clothes and gave the faithful Jimmy – most wonderful gift – a horse and cart for the yearly pink hi, when he visited his tribe.
1937 Ernestine Hill *The Great Australian Loneliness* 329: *Pink-hi* Holiday, walkabout.
1962 J. Marshall and R. Drysdale *Journey Among Men* 89: We talked with a party of aborigines camped in the river bed. They had quit their station jobs, as they are prone to do, and had gone on a hunting walkabout and a 'pink-eye'.
1969 Osmar White *Under the Iron Rainbow* 139: This year Nolan's Ford Picnic Races and Rodeo – One Thousand Dollars in prizes, Bar-B-Que, Grand Ball, Red Donovan and his Combo –

was obviously going to be a successful pink-eye.

pinkie Cheap wine [? f. colour]
1935 Kylie Tennant *Tiburon* 93: Staines, nodding his fat, puffy face into his cup of pinkie ... hadn't a very good head for the cheap raw wine he was drinking.
1941 *Coast to Coast* 23: 'Better put that bottle away ... If the trooper comes round somebody'll be getting into trouble for selling Charley pinkeye again.'
1959 Dorothy Hewett *Bobbin Up* 69: He'd drink anything they reckoned, plonk, pinkie, straight metho.
1966 Elwyn Wallace *Sydney and the Bush* 125: 'Only a bullocky's hut and a "pinkie bar" right out there alone in the wilds.'

pipe In the early years of the Australian colonies, a lampoon on someone in authority, rolled into a cylinder and left in public places
1816 Wentworth Papers (Mitchell Library): 'Lampoon or pipe, directed against George Molle, March 1816' [heading to set of verses]
1852 John West *History of Tasmania* i 107: Malice, or humour, in the early days, expressed itself in what were called *pipes* – a ditty, either taught by repetition or circulated on scraps of paper: the offences of official men were thus hitched into rhymes.

piss in someone's pocket, to To ingratiate oneself, be on very familiar terms with [*Pissing down anyone's back* Flattering him Grose 1811]
1967 Kylie Tennant *Tell Morning This* 283: 'Soon's they knew you was in with Numismata, they all want to piss in your pocket.'
1969 Christopher Bray *Blossom Like a Rose* 165: 'I don't mean to piss in yer pockets, but youse blokes are all right.'
1971 Frank Hardy *The Outcasts of Foolgarah* 77–8: 'I appeared before him many a time when I worked for the Union. If we piss in his pocket, he's just as apt to come our way.'

1975 Xavier Herbert *Poor Fellow My Country* 90: 'Not only do you let him piss in your pocket, but import the stuff for him to piss with.'
see **pee in the same pot**

pissant around To mess about
1945 Baker 87: Someone is *pissanting around* when he is messing about.
1951 Dymphna Cusack and Florence James *Come in Spinner* 307: 'I been pissantin' round the Northern Territory most of the time.'
1959 Gerard Hamilton *Summer Glare* 138: 'Struth, you pissant around like a rooster that's too old.'

pissant, game as a Very brave or angry [**1934** Archer Russell *A Tramp-Royal in Wild Australia* 115: 'Must be nearly eighty ... Straight as a gun-barrel an' game as an ant.']
1945 Baker 87: *game as a piss ant*.
1962 Ron Tullipan *March into Morning* 59: 'The old white lady [q.v.] makes you as game as a pissant.'
1975 Richard Beilby *The Brown Land Crying* 82: 'Ho! Real piss-ant, ain't 'e,' Bamma jeered. 'I like ya, boy. Ya got guts.'

Pitt Street or Christmas (Palm Sunday), not to know whether it's To be in a state of confusion
1951 Dymphna Cusack and Florence James *Come in Spinner* 330: 'She's that pie-eyed, she don't know whether it's Pitt Street or Christmas.'
see **Tuesday or Bourke Street**

Pitt Street farmer See quots [f. Pitt St as one of the main streets of Sydney's business life]
1945 Baker 198: In Sydney a business man with minor farming interests is called a *Pitt Street farmer*.
1971 *Sunday Australian* 6 Jun. 8: Australia's 9000 Pitt Street farmers – the businessmen, stockbrokers, doctors, barristers and solicitors who make a tidy profit on the side by owning or sharing a farm. Most earn at least $16,000 a year from the venture, although few visit their properties.

1974 *Australian* 16 Jan. 10: Pitt and Collins Streets farmers are costing Australia between $10 and $15 million a year in lost tax, according to the Bureau of Agricultural Economics. What a surprise.
see **Collins Street farmers**

plant *n.* 1 'A hoard of stolen goods; also the place where they are hidden' (OED 1796)
[1812 Vaux: The place of concealment is sometimes called *the plant* . . . To *spring a plant*, is to find any thing that has been concealed by another.]
1853 John Sherer *The Gold-Finder of Australia* 166: He informed me that he had a 'plant', which he would make over to me, as it might be 'sprung' whilst he was in gaol.
1882 Rolf Boldrewood *Robbery Under Arms* (World's Classics 1949) 55: 'So take care and don't act foolishly, or you'll lose a plant that may save your life, as well as keep you in cash for many a year to come.'
2 The portable equipment of a drover, bullock-driver or other bushworker [f. *plant* The fixtures, implements, machinery and apparatus used in carrying on any industrial process OED *sb.* 6, 1789]
1903 Joseph Furphy *Such is Life* (1944) 311: 'Stewart has bought his plant, and engaged him permanently.'
1917 R. D. Barton *Reminiscences of an Australian Pioneer* 179: I had to buy a plant-dray and three horses.
1945 Tom Ronan *Strangers on the Ophir* (1966) 16: At sundown he drove a plant of horses to the soak.
1951 Ernestine Hill *The Territory* 445: *Plant* A station or drover's outfit – horses, drays, cars, saddles.
1969 Osmar White *Under the Iron Rainbow* 126: 'Bring her over to the plant,' he [the dogger] said. 'I'll boil up a billy.'

plant *v.* To conceal, secrete, usually with illegal intent [f. English thieves' slang OED 1610]
[1812 Vaux: *Plant* To hide, or conceal any person or thing, is termed *planting* him, or it.]

1827 P. Cunningham *Two Years in New South Wales* ii 59–60: An acquaintance in Van Dieman's land, who had ordered his eldest boy to give up a plaything to a younger . . . was puzzled to make out the meaning of the latter, on its afterwards running in to him and calling out, 'Pa! Bill has *planted* it' (hid it).
1838 Thomas Walker *A Month in the Bush of Australia* 15: I doubt not the fellows have had our horses planted.
1848 Charles Cozens *Adventures of a Guardsman* 142: The practice . . . of *planting* the bullocks of the various teams on the road and so keeping them until their owners are induced to offer a reward for finding them.
1882 A. J. Boyd *Old Colonials* 74: 'He loads up a keg of rum, and to make sure it wouldn't be touched he plants* it in a barrel of sugar. *To *plant* in bush parlance is *to hide*.
1936 Dal Stivens *The Tramp and other stories* 143: 'Of course she'll hang around you . . . she knows you've got that money planted . . . don't be a bloody fool.'
1958 H. D. Williamson *The Sunlit Plain* 234: 'That's why I planted these bottles in this here tent – so I'd have somewhere for a quiet gargle.'
1959 Dorothy Hewett *Bobbin Up* 20: He waddled out . . . to fumble and curse under the stairs, where he planted his home brew.
1973 Frank Huelin *Keep Moving* 15: 'We'll plant our swags and have a look at this other joint.'

plaster As for 'poultice' q.v.
1932 Leonard Mann *Flesh in Armour* 248: 'The books must have got a plaster.'

plate A plate of sandwiches etc. brought by each person attending a social gathering as a way of catering for it
1962 Stuart Gore *Down the Golden Mile* 110: 'We might start by having some sort of social. Nothing elaborate, you know. Just perhaps all the ladies could bring a plate.'

pleuro Pleuropneumonia (as a disease of cattle)

1874 Rolf Boldrewood *My Run Home* (1897) 176: 'Do you ever have any pleuro among your cattle?' said I, 'I heard something about it in England.'
1885 Mrs Campbell Praed *Australian Life* 244: 'Pleuro is very bad our way. I don't believe much in inoculation – do you?'
1892 Henry Lawson 'The City Bushman' *Verse* i 214: Did you fight the drought and pleuro when the 'seasons' were asleep?
1917 A. B. Paterson *Three Elephant Power* 42: Providence sends the pleuro, and big strong beasts slink away by themselves, and stand under trees glaring savagely till death comes.

plod *n.* 1 The piece of ground on which a miner is working; the work card relating to this: W.A.

1941 Baker 55: *Pitching the plod* 'The exchange of words' between miners 'on the state of the ground when coming on or going off shifts.'
1948 K. S. Prichard *Golden Miles* 72: He had to go to the office for his plod – the card on which he filled in particulars of the work he was doing, its position in the mine, and the hours he was working. Ibid. 74: He held an 'unofficial' plod, because he was bogging for a machine man.

2 A yarn, a 'spiel' (see quot. 1941 above) [f. *plod* a short or dull story; a lying tale EDD]

1945 Gavin Casey *Downhill is Easier* 136: 'I suppose he told you the whole plod?' I sneered. Ibid. 162: He bought pots for the three of us, and started off on his plod.
1954 T. A. G. Hungerford *Sowers of the Wind* 241: 'That's the plod he put up, anyway.'
1975 Xavier Herbert *Poor Fellow My Country* 1126: 'Put in a plod for me, mate.'

plonk Cheap wine, or any improvised alcoholic drink; wine, from the standpoint of the beer drinker [Franklyn records *plink plonk* = *vin blanc*]

1941 Kylie Tennant *The Battlers* 128: 'Keep off the plonk,' Thirty-Bob said in an undertone to the Stray. 'They just spilt some on my boot and it burnt a hole.'
1946 Dal Stivens *The Courtship of Uncle Henry* 72: 'Jessie's been on the plonk again . . . Goes round the wine bars at the Cross.'
1952 Jon Cleary *The Sundowners* 228: 'I'd finish up in the gutter, a plonk fiend, maybe even drinking metho.'
1960 John O'Grady *Cop This Lot* 210: 'Wot's better than beer?' Pat asked. 'Vino rosso. Vin rouge. Rotwein. The civilised and incomparable juice of the grapes.' 'Gees,' Pat said. 'Yer don' mean bloody plonk, do yer?'
1962 Alan Marshall *This is the Grass* 130: 'Round-the-world-for thruppence' they called the plonk that brought them their shielding stupor.
1975 Don Townshend *Gland Time* 15: When Butch looked into his red-flushed face and his rose-coloured murky eyes he knew he had been on the plonk again.

plonko A plonk-addict

1963 Alan Marshall *In Mine Own Heart* 187: 'You end up a plonko with bells ringing in your head.'
1965 William Dick *A Bunch of Ratbags* 69: 'We could go and see if there's any plonkos under Martin's Bridge and chuck rocks at 'em.'
see **pinkie**

poddy-dodger (dodging) A cattleduffer who appropriates unbranded calves [f. *poddy* a hand-fed calf]

1945 Tom Ronan *Strangers on the Ophir* 9: 'He'll be a doctor or a lawyer or a banker with no need to go poddydodging for a living like his old jail-bird of a Dad.'
1946 W. E. Harney *North of 23°* 93: Some of the small struggling 'poddy dodgers' would now and then bring in a few bullocks and sell them to the butcher, who would give them a credit at the store.
1951 Ernestine Hill *The Territory* 445: *Poddy-dodgers* Cattle duffers who adopt weanable calves.

1957 R. S. Porteous *Brigalow* 61: Mick did a bit of poddy-dodging when things were slack . . . He might lift a few head of cleanskins now and then.

point the bone see **bone**

poisoner A cook, esp. for a collection of men
1905 E. C. Buley *Australian Life in Town and Country* 23: The shearers' cook is always a competent man and supplies his clients with the best fare obtainable, utterly 'belying' the name of 'poisoner', usually bestowed upon him.
1936 Archer Russell *Gone Nomad* 14: I had to take my turn at butchering the ration sheep and as 'slushy' to 'Dough-boy' Terry, the cook – 'camp poisoner', as we affectionately called him.
1969 Lyndall Hadow *Full Cycle* 208: 'I'm not much good at cooking but I'll try.' 'Never you mind about that. Up north we've got the best poisoners in the country.'
see **doctor**

poke borak, mullock see **borak, mullock**

poke in the eye with a burnt stick, better than a An expression of qualified pleasure, usually a retort
1974 *Bulletin* 6 Jul. 44: An Australian way of expressing ecstasy is to say: 'It's better than a poke in the eye with a burnt stick.'

pokies, the Poker-machines [abbr.]
1967 Donald Horne *Southern Exposure* 44: In the clubs of Sydney the poker machines ('the pokies') stand up in dozens and more beer flows than in a hotel.
1975 *Bulletin* 9 Aug. 23: Bingo is rapidly assuming the place in the Queensland lifestyle that is held by the pokies in New South Wales.

polar bear's behind, as cold as Very cold
1944 Lawson Glassop *We Were the Rats* 5: 'I . . . sneaks in just in time to see Jerry knock Binghi as cold as a Polar bear's backside.'
1951 Dal Stivens *Jimmy Brockett* 227: I'd only seen her about three times in the last four or five years. Mostly, she was cold as a polar bear's behind.
1971 John O'Grady *Aussie Etiket* 85: In the words of an anonymous poet of genius, 'Cold as an iceberg, gloomy and glum, / Cold as the hair on a polar bear's bum.'

pole on To impose, sponge on someone [? f. *poll* practise extortion OED 1521–1613]
1906 Edward Dyson *Fact'ry 'Ands* 66: 'What rot, girls, why don't yer get a shift on?' cried Feathers virtuously . . . 'polin' on the firm like this.'
1919 W. H. Downing *Digger Dialects* 38: *Poll* To take advantage of another's good nature.
1938 Xavier Herbert *Capricornia* 529: 'Call me a wastrel, would ya? You – why you're poling on Jesus Christ!'
1947 Vance Palmer *Hail Tomorrow* 10: 'I asked him why he should come up north and pole on men who were trying to win decent conditions for themselves, but he said he wanted a holiday.'
1953 *Caddie A Sydney Barmaid* 220: 'And while there's anything in the Sutton cupboard, Caddie,' he assured me when I said I couldn't stay and pole on them, 'it's yours.'

pole, up the In error, in disorder, confused [cf. *up the pole* in the wrong, tipsy OED 1896, 1904]
1906 Edward Dyson *Fact'ry 'Ands* 188: Then, as a bright afterthought, she added, 'Yer fair up the pole!'
1915 C. J. Dennis *The Songs of a Sentimental Bloke* 47: The dreams I dreamed, the dilly thorts I thunk / Is up the pole, an' joy 'as done a bunk.
1950 Jon Cleary *Just Let Me Be* 108: 'If I go and see 'em now, tell 'em what I done and why I done it, I'd be well and truly up the pole.'
1965 William Dick *A Bunch of Ratbags* 92: 'Right,' said Curly, agreeing with Ronnie's logic for once. He generally

thought Ronnie was all up the pole when giving advice to someone.
1970 Richard Beilby *No Medals for Aphrodite* 244: 'We'd a' been up the pole without him, that's why we didn't send him on his way.'

pole, wouldn't touch it with a forty-foot An expression of extreme aversion or complete rejection [? variant of the English 'wouldn't touch it with a barge pole']
1903 Joseph Furphy *Such is Life* (1944) 27: 'The young feller he used to come sometimes an' just shake hands with her, but otherways he wouldn't touch her with a forty-foot pole.'
1937 *Best Australian One-Act Plays* 248: 'I wouldn't have touched those girls, myself, with a forty-foot pole!'
1941 *Coast to Coast* 167: 'Me take the harness off him!' my mother said, surprised. 'Why, I wouldn't touch that mad thing with a forty-foot pole.'
1958 E. O. Schlunke *The Village Hampden* 26: Business of the more or less shady sort that our reputable men wouldn't touch with a forty-foot pole.
1965 Graham McInnes *The Road to Gundagai* 180: 'I wouldn't touch it with a forty foot pole!' he gulped.

poler 1 The horse or bullock harnessed alongside the pole of the wagon
1863 Samuel Butler *A First Year in Canterbury Settlement* ed. R. A. Streatfield (1914) 95: The leaders ... slewed sharply round, and tied themselves into an inextricable knot with the polars, while the body bullocks ... slipped the yoke.
1870 Marcus Clarke *His Natural Life* ed. S. Murray-Smith (1970) 617: The huge waggons, the white body of a camping 'poler', and the three ragged figures round the glowing logs.
1919 W. K. Harris *Outback in Australia* 18: We had to blindfold that poler before we could put him in the 'body-lead'.
2 Someone given to 'poling on' others
1938 Xavier Herbert *Capricornia* 528: 'You long-jawed poler,' Norman roared. 'Living on the fat of the land, while your poor damn flock feeds on soup and coconuts and what they can root out of the bush.'
1952 A. G. Mitchell Supplement to Chambers' *Shorter English Dictionary* 801: *poler* one who sponges on another, or avoids his fair share of work.

pollies Politicians [abbr.]
1973 H. Williams *My Love Had a Black Speed Stripe* 28: I reckon they should keep argument out of politics altogether, but the pollies would never wear it.
1974 *Bulletin* 12 Oct. 12: Pollies peel off the tax perks.

Pom, Pommy An English immigrant; an English national: *derogatory* [see quot. 1920]
1915 Let. in Bill Gammage *The Broken Years* (1974) 86: We call the Regulars – Indians and Australians – 'British' – and Pommies are nondescript. Ibid. 240 (1916): They're only a b– lot of Pommie Jackeroos and just as hopeless. All they think of is their dress and their mess.
1916 *The Anzac Book* 31: 'A Pommy* can't go wrong out there if he isn't too lazy to work.' *Pommy – short for pomegranate, and used as a nickname for immigrants.
1920 H. J. Rumsey *The Pommies, or New Chums in Australia* (Introduction): Few people seem to know the origin of the word, but I can well remember its introduction in the early seventies ... Thousands of immigrants were arriving by the old clipper ships, and the colonial boys and girls, like all schoolchildren, ready to find a nickname, were fond of rhyming 'Immigrant', 'Jimmygrant', 'Pommegrant' and called it after the new chum children. The name stuck and became abbreviated to 'pommy' later on.
1922 Henry Lawson 'Gentlemen All' *Prose* i 920: There was the good and grateful pommy who had a fair start in life; the pommy rotter, known on every immigrant ship, with such slings off as 'Just like the Australians', etc.
1926 K. S. Prichard *Working. Bullocks*

76: 'Kitty married Gaze's brother . . . the pommy cocky who's got Drakes' old place.'

1931 William Hatfield *Sheepmates* 271: 'Not a bad sort of a poor coot, either, for a Pommy.' (The odious word had just drifted out [c. 1912] from the wharves and the railway construction camps.)

1952 Jon Cleary *The Sundowners* 49: 'A stuck-up bastard, ain't he? . . . Must be a mate of your Pommy cobber.'

1963 Xavier Herbert *Disturbing Element* 90–1: He still wore the heavy clumsy British type of clothing of the day. When we kids saw people on the street dressed like that [before 1914] we would yell at them: 'Jimmygrants, Pommygranates, Pommies!'

1973 Prince Charles [at an Australia Day dinner in London] *Sydney Morning Herald* 3 Feb. 2: All the faces here this evening seem to be bloody Poms.

1974 *Bulletin* 15 Jun. 38: Then there's the joke about the board that's supposed to be outside every Australian lion park: 'Cars $1; cars with senior citizens, 50 cents; Poms on bicycles, free.' Then the story goes on. A Pom did ride his bike into one of the lion parks. The lions rejected the Pom but ate the bicycle.

Pommy bastard, pommyland, whingeing pommy

1951 Dal Stivens *Jimmy Brockett* 214: Like most of these pommy bastards, he had funny ways but he wasn't a bad old bloke at heart.

1968 George Mikes *Boomerang* 66: It is always the Pommy Bastards who, instead of being grateful, keep on complaining.

1975 *Sunday Telegraph* 9 Feb. 96: A Sydney man will appear before the Royal Commission into Human Relationships later this month and allege that the fashionable T-shirts emblazoned with the words Pommie Bastards are libellous and discriminatory.

1957 Randolph Stow *The Bystander* 21: 'I'm a Pommy. And going back to Pommy-land, after twenty-four years.'

1967 Frank Hardy *Billy Borker Yarns Again* 61: Sir Robert himself wanted to be a whiskey-taster at the Melbourne Show, but ended up as some kind of wharfie over in Pommy Land.

1962 J. Marshall and R. Drysdale *Journey Among Men* 189: The British national pastime of 'grousing' . . . has given rise in Australia to the derisive expression *wingeing pommy*.

1972 Thomas Keneally *The Chant of Jimmie Blacksmith* 17: 'Pass a law to give every single wingeing bloody Pommie his fare home to England. Back to the smoke and the sun shining ten days a year and shit in the streets. Yer can have it.'

1975 *Sunday Telegraph* 3 Aug. 110: His derogatory remark about whingeing Poms and the decline of the British Empire.

Pompey, to dodge To steal grass; to work on a sheep station [cf. *to dodge Pompey* to avoid work (Naval slang f. *Pompey* as the establishment at Portsmouth)]

1868 C. Wade Brown *Overlanding in Australia* 53: As for grass he must get what he can. He is necessitated to do a little trespassing on the quiet, which he calls 'dodging Pompey' thereby getting his sheep better fed.

1908 Giles Seagram *Bushmen All* 234: 'Yer don't s'pose that Dick the Devil an' Black Jim are just dodgin' Pompey at Bulla-bullina waiting for the traps to come and fetch 'em.'

see **dodge, monkey-dodger, poddy-dodger**

Pong A Chinese: *rare* [f. frequency of Chinese names like Wong]

1938 Xavier Herbert *Capricornia* 339: 'Your grandmother was a lubra and your grandfather was a Pong.'

1941 Baker 56: *Pong* A Chinese.

1957 Dal Stivens *The Scholarly Mouse* 65: We saw he was too tall to be a Pong or an Eyetoe, though there was something about him that made us think of both.

pongo An infantryman in World War I; an Englishman [? f. *pong* smell]

1919 W. H. Downing *Digger Dialects*

38: *Pongo* A soldier; one of the rank and file.

1920 *Aussie* Glossary: *Pongo* Infantryman.

1945 Baker 160: *pongo* An Englishman [as Air Force slang in World War II].

1972 Turner 109: Like Australians, New Zealanders call the English *pommies*, but also have a variant *pongo* which seems rather less tolerant in its tone.

pony 1 The sum of £25 [OED 1797]

1895 Cornelius Crowe *The Australian Slang Dictionary* 60: *Pony* £25.

1922 Arthur Wright *A Colt from the Country* 121–2. 'Are you prepared to go a pony with me?' 'Let me see,' hesitated Yalty. 'Er – pony – er –.' 'Twenty-five quid,' said Knocker.

1950 *Australian Police Journal* Apr. 117: *Pony* £25.

1975 Les Ryan *The Shearers* 69: 'I have a pony to say he can win.'

2 A small glass of beer: in N.S.W., 7 oz; in Victoria and W.A., 4 oz. [U.S. 1849 Mathews]

1895 Cornelius Crowe *The Australian Slang Dictionary* 60: *Pony* a small glass of beer.

1953 *Caddie A Sydney Barmaid* 87: He . . . leaned on the counter, and ordered a pony of lager.

1959 Gerard Hamilton *Summer Glare* 155: Os pulled a beer each for me and Tommy and a pony for himself. He always drank small beers.

1965 Graham McInnes *The Road to Gundagai* 222: Mr Watson . . . poured himself a tiny glass of beer. 'Just a pony,' he said.

poofter The commonest term for a male homosexual, or man of effeminate appearance: *derogatory* [Partridge lists *puff* a sodomist c. 1870]

1900–10 O'Brien and Stephens: *Pouf or poufter* a sodomite or effeminate man.

1941 Baker 56: *Poofter* A homosexual.

1953 T. A. G. Hungerford *Riverslake* 49: He hawked disgustingly and spat on the floor between his feet. 'They want men in the unions, not poofters.'

1965 Hal Porter *Stars of Australian Stage and Screen* 280: During the last ten years or more, there have been imported a coterie of *untalented* English homosexuals, English tonks unheard of outside their home country, to dominate sections of the Australian theatrical scene. If one cannot protest against the employment of the Pommy poofter instead of the Aussie poofter, one can record dismay at the employment of fifth raters who got nowhere near even spear-holding in Drury Lane.

1969 William Dick *Naked Prodigal* 12: I turned and exploded. 'You poofter bastard!' I yelled . . . 'I'll kill him. The bastard's a poofter. He touched me up.'

1973 Keith Dunstan *Sports* 232: The Tigers were five goals down but pulling up fast. Professor Turner heard a thirtyish, beer-gutted supporter scream: 'You bloody Commo, poofter, mongrel bastard.' This, he said, brilliantly released racial, political, sexual and male chauvinist prejudices.

poofteroo

1966 Patrick White *The Solid Mandala* 18: 'You ought to move in with that pair of poofteroos across the road.'

pooh, in the Euphemism for 'in the shit'

1961 Jack Danvers *The Living Come First* 177: 'I guess it's my fault if you're rather in the pooh with the Adelaide police.'

1970 Richard Beilby *No Medals for Aphrodite* 229: 'If they catch you with her, then you're really in the pooh.'

1975 Xavier Herbert *Poor Fellow My Country* 873: 'She'll put you in the poo if she writes anything 'bout you.'

pool To inform upon, incriminate; to involve someone against his will [cf. *put in*]

1919 W. H. Downing *Digger Dialects* 39: *Pool* To involve; cast blame or a burden on.

1928 Arthur Wright *A Good Recovery* 117: 'Leave the sheilas alone; they're sure to pool a man sooner or later.'

1932 William Hatfield *Ginger Murdoch* 282: To rig that evidence against him –

pool him.

1942 Leonard Mann *The Go-Getter* 313:
'I got pooled into it,' he explained.
1967 Kylie Tennant *Tell Morning This*
85: 'A man thought he'd do the decent
thing and tide a girl over a patch of
trouble, and she pools him every time.
You can't prove it isn't your kid.'

poon Equivalent to 'nong', but less
commonly used [? f. *poind* (*poon*) a silly,
useless, inactive person; one easily imposed on EDD]

1941 Baker 56: *Poon* A lonely, somewhat crazy dweller in the Outer Beyond
(2) A simpleton or fool.
1972 Geoff Morley *Jockey Rides Honest
Race* 73: 'They don't look for the guts
of a lecture; just the mistakes. Then
they can get up and shoot their mouths
off and everybody else nods wisely
and tries to pick up the mistakes of
the poon that's just said his piece.'
1974 David Williamson *Jugglers Three*
69: 'What possessed Keren to shack
up with a poon like you?'

pooned up Flashily dressed
1943 Baker 60: *Poon up* To dress up,
especially in flashy fashion.
1951 Dal Stivens *Jimmy Brockett* 48:
Some of 'em were young lairs, all
pooned up to kill.
1972 Arthur Chipper *The Aussie
Swearer's Guide* 48: *Pooned up* Dressed
to impress, often with sexual success
in view.

popping up, how are you How are you
getting on?: *obs.*
1894 Henry Lawson 'The Mystery of
Dave Regan' *Prose* i 328: 'How are yer?'
'Oh! I'm all right!' he says. 'How are
yer poppin' up?'
1900–10 O'Brien and Stephens: *Popping up* getting on.
1907 Nathan Spielvogel *The Cocky
Farmer* 16: 'Whatto, Joe. How are you
popping up?'
1933 Norman Lindsay *Saturdee* 10:
'What-oh, Stinker, how you poppin'
up?'
1942 Sarah Campion *Bonanza* 207:
'Howya poppin', cobber?'

poppy, tall 1 A person with a high
income: given currency by J. T. Lang
in N.S.W. in the 1930s by his policy
of 'taxing the tall poppies' (see quot.
1970) [? f. Tarquin's decapitation of the
tallest poppies at Gabii]

1931 *N.S.W. Parliamentary Debates* 30
Jul. 4840: The Premier cannot truth-
fully say that a measure which deals
with a certain section of the community
which he refers to as the privileged
class and as 'tall poppies' is in accord
with the Melbourne agreement.
1931 *Sydney Morning Herald* 6 Aug. 8:
'I'll put it on the shoulders of those
able to bear it,' he [Mr Lang] shouted
when it was pointed out to him by
the Opposition that 'lopping the tall
poppies' meant in some cases 80 or
90 per cent.
1961 Mena Calthorpe *The Dyehouse*
143: 'We've got more useless ornaments
on the payroll than we can carry as it
is. Too many tall poppies waiting to
be cut down.'
1970 J. T. Lang *The Turbulent Years*
147: The next [step] was the introduction of the bill to reduce all government salaries to a maximum of £10 a
week. I referred to those being paid
more than that amount [in 1931] as the
'tall poppies'.
1973 *Sydney Morning Herald* 7 Aug. 1:
Mr Cameron said the Public Service
Board had developed a 'compulsive
urge' to lavish public funds on the
'tall poppies' of the Public Service.
1975 J. G. Gorton *Sydney Morning
Herald* 8 Apr. 6: Labor is obsessed with
the 'tall poppies', and seems determined to pull them down. But tall
poppies, more and more tall poppies,
are what this country needs. The
chance to grow to a height is the
chance for many to express themselves.
2 Anyone eminent in any way
1967 John Yeomans *The Scarce Australians* 85: The average city Australian
is a complete conformist. If there is one
place where the genuine eccentric is
crushed, the tall poppy lopped and
the penetrating discussion stifled, it is
Australia.

1973 Patrick White *The Eye of the Storm* 465: Things were what they used to be, the tall poppies bowing mock apologies to those who held them guilty of the worst.

1976 *Bulletin* 28 Feb. 25: In local slang he [Mr Whitlam] is a 'tall poppy', someone egregious in stature and therefore vulnerable to the scythe.

1976 *Sydney Morning Herald* 26 Apr. 17: Auburn, playing a man short for most of the second half, lopped their second tall Soccer poppy in a week yesterday. Auburn ... held Western Suburbs to a scoreless draw.

port Portmanteau [abbr.]

1908 E. G. Murphy *Jarrahland Jingles* 82: Silently they packed their 'ports' and flitted to the West.

1915 J. P. Bourke *Off the Bluebush* 122: They see a young chap with a 'port' on his back.

1944 Dal Stivens *The Courtship of Uncle Henry* 53: 'You take your port up and come back to the car.'

1954 Tom Ronan *Vision Splendid* 262: He dragged his ports up to the tram stop and took them to the railway cloakroom.

1972 Richard Magoffin *Chops and Gravy* 46: Roly grabbed his port ... charged towards the bus.

possie (pozzy) A chosen position (given currency by the Gallipoli campaign) [abbr.]

1915 Tom Skeyhill *Soldier Songs from Anzac* 16: But 'e [the sniper] never shows 'is pozzy.

1916 *The Anzac Book* 10: The new sniper's pozzy down at the creek. *Pozzy or possie – Australian warrior's short for 'position', or lair.

1925 Arthur Wright *The Boy from Bullarah* 99: 'Quick, get a pozzy with the machine.'

1942 Gavin Casey *It's Harder for Girls* 217: We started on a short course of heavy drinking, hanging on to our possies at the bar and letting the mob push about and roar for drinks behind us.

1959 D'Arcy Niland *The Big Smoke*

213: They've all got their drinking places, and even their drinking possies, their special barmaids, their individual codes.

1970 Patrick White *The Vivisector* 620: 'Should have got here early – got us a good pozzy. Never be in the picture now.'

possum, stir the To liven things up, create a disturbance; raise issues that others wish left dormant [? f. *playing possum* U.S. 1822 Mathews and song *Possum up a Gumtree* 1831]

1907 Charles MacAlister *Old Pioneering Days in the Sunny South* 51: Sometimes a strong sailorman, just off a six months' cruise, would favour us with 'Nancy Lee' or other jolly sea-songs, or an ambitious carrier or drover would 'rouse the 'possum' by giving some long-winded ditty of the time.

1908 E. S. Sorenson *The Squatter's Ward* 144: 'I mean to stir the 'possum in Sultan Susman from this out. I'm a different woman now.'

1949 Ruth Park *Poor Man's Orange* 9: A mission was like a tonic. It stirred the 'possum in the people, and for months afterwards they could still feel the enthusiasm.

1972 *Sydney Morning Herald* 31 Oct. 3: Senate seat offer to stop 'stirring'. 'I could be sitting in Parliament now without any great cost provided I forgot this idea of stirring the possum,' he [Mr Gordon Barton] said.

post-and-rail tea A bush tea in which the floating particles resemble a post-and-rail fence

1851 *The Australasian* 298: Hyson-skin and *post-and-rail* tea have been superseded by Mocha, claret, and cognac.

1852 G. C. Mundy *Our Antipodes* i 329: A hot beverage in a tin pot which richly deserved the epithet of 'post and rails' tea; it might well have been a decoction of 'split stuff' or 'iron bark shingles'.

1887 *All the Year Round* 30 Jul. 66: The tea so made [in a billy] is naturally of rather a rough and ready description, and when the stalks and coarse particles of the fragrant leaf float thickly thereon, it is sometimes graphically styled 'post-and-rails' tea.

1899 W. T. Goodge *Hits! Skits! and Jingles!* 75: There is 'post and rails' and 'brownie'/For yer breakfast now, yer know.

1904 Tom Petrie *Reminiscences of Early Queensland* 243: The tea then was all green tea, and very coarse, like bits of stick – indeed it was christened 'posts and rails'.

1936 Archer Russell *Gone Nomad* 24: Flour, 'post and rail' tea (the cheapest kind), black sugar, salt and meat, were the only rations provided.

postholes, a load of An unloaded truck (in road hauliers' slang)

1976 *Sun* 28 May 7: Postholes (*a load of*) An empty load.

postie A postman [abbr.]

1957 D'Arcy Niland *Call Me When the Cross Turns Over* 99: 'Don't forget to watch for the postie,' she called.

1970 Patrick White *The Vivisector* 202: 'He was a postie. The kind that turns scraggy later ... always hurryin' ter reach the next box.'

pot A measure of beer: in Victoria and Queensland 10 oz.; in W.A. various sizes

1918 N. Campbell and L. Nelson *The Dinky-Di Soldier* 12: I'd buy them a pot or a shandy,/(An' they'd always allow me to pay.)

1946 Dal Stivens *The Courtship of Uncle Henry* 76: Three pots had never made me see things before. It got me worried.

1974 S. H. Courtier *Listen to the Mocking Bird* 76: Across from the Flinders Street entrance to the station, I entered the bar of a pub and ordered a pot of beer.

pot, put someone's ~ on To inform upon; destroy someone's prospects [? f. *pot* to outdo, outwit, deceive OED 1562]

[**1868** 'The Song of the Sundowner' *Sydney Punch* 14 Nov. 195 repr. in *Old Bush Songs* ed. Stewart and Keesing

(1957) 231: To refuse us tucker, our game they'll kill,/And no doubt at last will 'pot us'.]

1911 Arthur Wright *Gamblers' Gold* 138: 'Why should I pot the bloke? He done me a good turn, an' th' police is no good to me.'

1919 W. H. Downing *Digger Dialects* 40: *Put his pot on* Report him.

1935 F. D. Davison and B. Nicholls *Blue Coast Caravan* 178: He saw some blacks with whom he was familiar standing on the platform under guard of a policeman. 'Hullo, what's up?' One of them replied, 'Aw, somebody's been putting our pot on.'

1949 Ruth Park *Poor Man's Orange* 190: 'If she opens her big mouth I'll tell the world she was right in there with the rest of them. I'll put her pot on, the bitch, thinking she's so holy.'

1957 Vance Palmer *Seedtime* 119: 'There's an election coming on, and there's a chance I'll be dumped ... This afternoon's work has probably put my pot on.'

potato, not the clean Of bad repute (sometimes with reference to a convict background) [? negative of the English expression *the potato* the (very, real or proper) thing, what is correct or excellent OED 1822–80]

1877 Rolf Boldrewood *A Colonial Reformer* (1890) 38: 'Well,' said Mr Cottonbush, smiling and wincing slightly, 'it ain't quite the clean potato, of course [to travel one's sheep and steal a neighbour's grass]; but if your sheep's dying at home, what can you do?'

1881 G. H. Gibson 'A Ballad of Queensland' *Bulletin* 26 Mar. 8 repr. in *Australian Bush Ballads* ed. Stewart and Keesing (1962) 313: You weren't quite the cleanly potato, Sam Holt,/And you hadn't the cleanest of fins.

1908 Giles Seagram *Bushmen All* 318: 'He's an awful fool, and – and not exactly the clean potato.'

1921 K. S. Prichard *The Black Opal* 148: 'I ain't always been what you might call the clean potato.'

1931 Miles Franklin *Back to Bool Bool* 233: She was only the great-grand-

daughter of old Larry Healey of Little River, none so clean a potato, if rumour was correct.
1962 Tom Ronan *Deep of the Sky* 42: Some of the grand old pioneers and land-takers of history were not quite the clean potato.

poultice 1 A mortgage
1932 K. S. Prichard *Kiss on the Lips* 184: Mick Mallane ... sayin' if the bank wanted his farm, poultice or no poultice, it'd have to go out and take it from him, and he'd be waitin' for 'm with his gun loaded.
1934 Thomas Wood *Cobbers* 134: Men talked about their blister, or their poultice, which means a mortgage, with complacency.
1958 *Coast to Coast 1957–1958* 137: When the farm was free of its 'poultice', her father had promised to hand over to Sam ... But droughts and a fall in the price of wheat kept him battling to pay even interest on the mortgage.
2 A large sum of money
1951 Eric Lambert *The Twenty Thousand Thieves* 235: 'It's only two days to pay day and I've got a poultice in that pay-book of mine.'
1957 D'Arcy Niland *Call Me When the Cross Turns Over* 33: Like another time I got paid off, and it was a whacking big poultice, and I went into Pirie.
see **plaster**

Poverty Point Corner of Park and George Streets, Sydney, as the meeting-place of out-of-work theatricals
1889 *Bulletin* 15 Jun. 7: At Poverty Point [heading to theatrical column]
1974 *Sydney Morning Herald* 5 Jun. 1: The north-east corner of Park and George Streets was the gathering place of out-of-work theatricals who met to gossip and discuss local productions at the turn of the century. The memory of 'Poverty Point', as it was known, is to be perpetuated. On Monday night, Sydney City Council will set aside $120 for a bronze footpath plaque to mark the site.

pox doctor's clerk, dressed up like a Dressed nattily, but in bad taste
[**1954** T. A. G. Hungerford *Sowers of the Wind* 263: 'What were you before you joined up? A pox-doctor's clerk?']
1965 Eric Lambert *The Long White Night* 136: 'They was all dressed like they was at Buckingham Palace and Foran was done up like a pox doctor's clerk.'
1971 Frank Hardy *The Outcasts of Foolgarah* 191: The Tiger of Bengal himself, dressed up like a pox doctor's clerk, wearing more medals than an American general.
1973 *Nation Review* 8–14 Jun. 1064: Good money was laid among the better class workingmen that he [Mr Don Dunstan] would, on this auspicious occasion, come up with an outfit to be the envy of every poxdoctor's clerk in the land.
1974 Barry Humphries [as Barry McKenzie] *Bulletin* 19 Jan. 13: If Al Grassby wants to convert me or any other clean-living Australians into getting dressed up like Lord Muck and getting round kitted up like a flamin' pox doctor's clerk, old Grazza's going to have his time cut out.

prawn, come the raw To try to impose on someone (Services slang in World War II)
1942 *Salt* 25 May 8: *Don't come the raw prawn* Don't try to put one over me.
1946 Rohan Rivett *Behind Bamboo* 398: *Raw prawn* something far-fetched, difficult to swallow, absurd.
1948 Sumner Locke Elliott *Rusty Bugles* in *Khaki, Bush and Bigotry* ed. Eunice Hanger (1968) 36: 'The filthy rotten Crab, he'd better not come the raw prawn on us.'
1959 Eric Lambert *Glory Thrown In* 41–2: 'Don't ever come the raw prawn with Doc, mate. He knows all the lurks.'
1968 Rodney Milgate *A Refined Look at Existence* 28: 'Don't come the raw prawn ... you know there's no such thing. Things don't happen just like that.'
1975 Les Ryan *The Shearers* 85: 'What do you think I am, a drongo? I take hundreds of bets, and we get blokes

here who try to come the raw prawn.'

prayers, to know more than one's Not
to be as innocent as one may seem
1934 F. S. Hibble *Karangi* 167: 'Claudie
knows more than her prayers.'
1951 Frank Hardy *Power Without Glory*
512: Poor kid had been isolated from
life; she was innocent and emotional,
and young fellows to-day knew more
than their prayers.
1957 Ray Lawler *Summer of the Seventeenth Doll* 12: 'She's a good kid, that.'
'Yeh. I'd say she knows more than her
prayers, just the same.'

prego Pregnant [abbr.]
1951 Dymphna Cusack and Florence
James *Come in Spinner* 226: Guinea's
face lighted with unholy glee. 'A
Parker prego? Did I hear right?'
1965 Patrick White *Four Plays* 94:
'Can't resist the bananas.' 'Yeah. They
say you go for them like one thing when
you're preggo.'

prezzie A present [abbr.]
1961 Jon Rose *At the Cross* 141: 'I
bought you quite a lot of prezzies.'
1975 *Australian* 24 Apr. 13: From . . .
endeavours yesterday to discover what
presents the Whitlams were taking
overseas with them, we can inform you
of the following piece of government
policy: From this day forth no public
announcements will be made about
the nature of prime ministerial pressies.

pricker, to have the To be in an angry
state: *rare* [variant of *get the needle*]
1945 Baker 121: A man in a temper is
said . . . *to have* . . . *the pricker*.
1955 D'Arcy Niland *The Shiralee* 102:
'You've got the pricker properly, eh?
You'll knock him into next week, will
ya?'

Prince Albert, Alfred see **Albert,
Alfred**

prop To pull up unexpectedly (originally of a horse)
1844 *Georgiana's Journal* ed. Hugh
McCrae (1966) 127: Suddenly my pony

propped, and I just had time to disen-
gage my limb from the pommel before
he started to roll himself on the beach.
1876 Rolf Boldrewood *A Colonial Reformer* (1890) 8: The colt . . . stopped
with death like suddenness; his rider
was shot on to the crown of his head
with startling force . . . 'My word, sir,'
was his single remark, 'I didn't think
he'd ha' propped like that.'
1908 W. H. Ogilvie *My Life in the Open*
83: Playful or vicious . . . almost all
of them 'prop' or 'go to market' in
some form or other.
1929 K. S. Prichard *Coonardoo* 67:
'The horse shied, propped and shot
Ted fair over his head.'
1959 Dorothy Hewett *Bobbin Up* 121:
They stuck out their jaws, and propped,
and fought.
1969 Thomas Keneally *The Survivor*
70: Seconds later a university sedan,
driven by George the university guard,
wheeled fast in through the gate and
propped at the front of the house.
1970 Patrick White *The Vivisector* 602:
The present mob might have trampled
Rhoda underfoot if it hadn't suddenly
realized she was something beyond
its experience, so it propped, and
divided.

prop *n.* The action of propping
1881 A. C. Grant *Bush-Life in Queensland* i 201: A sudden fierce prop, and
Roaney has shot behind Sam's horse.

public A public (i.e. government)
school, as distinct from a Catholic one;
a child attending such a school
1959 Dorothy Hewett *Bobbin Up* 56:
Frank was a Forbes boy, youngest son
of a local cockie. He and Beryl had
gone to the 'public' together, partnered
each other at the local 'hop'.
1972 Philip Hickie introduction to
Peter Kenna *The Slaughter of St. Teresa's
Day* 7: They [the Irish and Italians of
Paddington in the 1950s] were even
further isolated by the Roman Catholi-
cism into which they were born. The
world was divided into Catholics and
'Publics'.

pufterlooner A kind of scone made of

dough and fried in fat [f. the way it rises during cooking]

1853 S. Mossman and T. Banister *Australia, Visited and Revisited* 126: 'Leatherjackets' – an Australian bush term for a thin cake made of dough, and put into a pan to bake with some fat ... The Americans indulge in this kind of bread, giving them the name of 'Puff ballooners', the only difference being that they place the cake upon the bare coals.

1870 Marcus Clarke *His Natural Life* ed. S. Murray-Smith (1970) 577: 'Have a puffterlooner, Master Dick,' suggests Derwent Jack, 'or a bit o' sweetcake.'

1906 A. B. Paterson *An Outback Marriage* 149: A tin plate of light, delicately-browned cakes of the sort known as 'puftalooners'.

1935 F. D. Davison and B. Nicholls *Blue Coast Caravan* 186: There was bush honey and a great platter of puff-de-loonies, all warm and crisp and golden brown.

1940 Ion L. Idriesss *Lightning Ridge* 82: Puftaloons are tasty though; fry them in fat, then smother them with treacle and swallow 'em while greasy.

1964 Tom Ronan *Packhorse and Pearling Boat* 140: A camp oven full of 'puff de loons' (fried scones to the uninitiated).

1970 Patrick White *The Vivisector* 10: Mumma started telling all she had heard next door, with the kids stuffing on Mrs Burt's cold puftaloons.

1975 *The Commonsense Cookery Book* 181: Puftaloons (Fried Scones) [recipe]

pull your head in see **head**

punched, bored or see **bored or punched**

pup, the night's a It's early yet

1915 Henry Lawson 'A Foggy Night in Antwerp' *Prose* i 913: The night was not even a pup yet – it was broad daylight, being Northern summer.

1921 K. S. Prichard *The Black Opal* 103–4: 'You're not taking her away yet, Michael? The night's a pup!'

1934 Vance Palmer *Sea and Spinifex*

165: 'What about coming out on the water for awhile? Night's still a pup.'

1949 Lawson Glassop *Lucky Palmer* 73: 'We'll get him in. The day's only a pup yet.'

1957 Judah Waten *Shares in Murder* 171: 'You still have time to take the young lady out ... The night's a pup.'

1968 Geoffrey Dutton *Andy* 198: 'Are you thinking of driving out to Hanging-stone to-night?' 'It's only forty miles and the night is a pup.'

1975 Hal Porter *The Extra* 99: The night's the sort of pup we don't usually abandon, but abandon it abruptly we do.

pure merino see **merino**

push A crowd; a band of larrikins; an intellectual and cultural clique or others with some bond of association (see quot. 1896) [f. English thieves' slang]

1812 Vaux: *Push* a crowd or concourse of people, either in the streets, or at any public place of amusement &c., when any particular scene of crowding is alluded to, they say, *the push*, as *the push*, at the *spell* doors; *the push* at the *stooping-match*, &c.

1890 *The Argus* 26 Jul. 4: 'Doolan's push' were a party of larrikins working ... in a potato paddock nearby. [Morris]

1892 Henry Lawson 'The Captain of the Push' *Verse* i 186: As the night was falling slowly down on city, town and bush,/From a slum in Jones's Alley sloped the Captain of the Push.

1896 Henry Lawson 'For Auld Lang Syne' *Prose* i 267: He was the first of the old push to go – we use the word push in its general sense, and we called ourselves the Mountain Push because we had worked in the tourist towns a good deal ... We were plasterers, bricklayers, painters, a carpenter, a labourer and a plumber.

1911 Edward Dyson *Benno, and Some of the Push* [book title]

1924 *Truth* 27 Apr. 6: *Push* A crowd of larrikins.

1939 Kylie Tennant *Foveaux* 263: 'If I did join anything, it wouldn't be your push.'

1942 Tip Kelaher *The Digger Hat* 25:
I've spent it on the beaches with all
the surf-club 'push'.
1963 John Cantwell *No Stranger to the
Flame* 74: 'My mother and uncle and
brother are well up in the holy Roman
circles of this town. You one of their
push?'
1963 *Sunday Telegraph* 20 Jan. 2: The
Royal George Hotel, at the corner of
King and Sussex Streets ... has for
some years been the headquarters of
members and ex-members of the
Sydney University Libertarian Society
known simply as 'The Push'.
1973 Alexander Buzo *Rooted* 87:
'Gary's gone away for the weekend,
cavorting in the mulga with the Werris
Creek Push.'

put someone in To inform against,
implicate [not recorded in the OED,
although it occurs in Jonson's *Bartho-
lomew Fair* II ii 71]
1922 Arthur Wright *A Colt from the
Country* 153: 'I might have a chance
with the girl again.' 'After what you
did to put her in?' laughed the detective. 'I like your hide.'
1951 Seaforth Mackenzie *Dead Men
Rising* 52: 'Nothing would give me
greater pleasure than to put you in,
only that's about the one thing I've
never done in my life.'
1959 Dorothy Hewett *Bobbin Up* 71:
'Why doncha put her in to the foreman?'
1966 Peter Cowan *Seed* 106: 'I suppose
when they make you a prefect you'll
put us in.'
1975 *Sydney Morning Herald* 3 Jul. 11:
A lagger is someone who puts people
in to the police.
see **dob in, pool, pot**

putty, up to Worthless, useless (sometimes abbr. to 'upter' q.v.)
1919 W. H. Downing *Digger Dialects*
52: *Up to putty* Bad; useless; ineffectual.
1924 C. J. Dennis *Rose of Spadgers*
119: Once let 'em tangle, an' you take
the blame / You're up to putty, an'
yeh've lost the game.
1941 Baker 58: *Putty, up to* Worthless,
of no importance.

Q

quack A doctor, without the implication that he is unqualified
1919 W. H. Downing *Digger Dialects*
40: *Quack* A medical officer.
1938 Xavier Herbert *Capricornia* 144:
'That noo quack says he's got a crook
heart.'
1946 Dal Stivens *The Courtship of Uncle
Henry* 150: 'The nearest quack was in
Myralie, twenty miles away.'
1953 *Caddie A Sydney Barmaid* 223:
'Well,' said Bill, 'wot did the quack 'ave
ter say?'
1960 John Iggulden *The Storms of
Summer* 169: 'I'll get the quack at the
Bush Hospital to have a look at it in
the morning.'
1976 David Ireland *The Glass Canoe*
136: 'I go along to this quack and he
says Get back to the surf and get some
green vegetables into you.'

quandong Someone disreputable, living
by his or her wits [unexplained: the
quandong is the native peach, or its red,
berry-like fruit. Cf. *geebung*]
1939 Kylie Tennant *Foveaux* 311: In
this crowd of low heels, quandongs and
ripperty men, she looked at her ease
and yet not of them.
1973 Frank Huelin *Keep Moving* 178:
Quandong Hobo who bludges or imposes on another.
1977 Jim Ramsay *Cop it Sweet* 75:
Quandong Female who makes a practice
of remaining virtuous after being wined
and dined.

quanger A quince (juvenile)
1977 *Sydney Morning Herald* 5 Mar. 11:
We had an abandoned quince orchard
where we used to wage the most
fantastic quanger wars.

Queensland sores See quot.
1892 G. L. James *Shall I Try Australia?* 242: 'Queensland Sores', or
'Barcoo rot' are, I believe, generally
attributed to excessive thinness and
poverty of the blood, caused by the
great heat and absence of vegetable
diet.

question, if it's a fair An apparent apology for curiosity [also English, in Joyce's *A Portrait of the Artist as a Young Man* ch. 4]

1903 Joseph Furphy *Such is Life* (1944) 30: 'Who's this Mother Bodysark – if it's a fair question?' asked Cooper.

1955 D'Arcy Niland *The Shiralee* 86: 'I don't want to be quizzy, Mac, but, if it's a fair question what's the drum?'

quid, not the full Not 'all there', deficient [f. *quid* pound]

1953 Baker 132: *full quid* In full possession of one's faculties; a person who is said to be *ten bob* or *ten deaners* or even *tuppence* in the *quid,* is held to be a few shingles short.

1968 Geoffrey Dutton *Andy* 93: 'Yer mad. I don't think yer got a full quid,' commented the sailor.

1972 Ian Mofitt *The U-Jack Society* 227: We avoid individuality as firmly as we suspect joy ('You're not the full quid!').

1975 *Sydney Morning Herald* 5 Jul. 9: It's perfectly clear that not all members of our community are the full quid.

quietly, just Confidentially, between ourselves

1941 Baker 40: *Just quietly* Between you and I.

1951 Eric Lambert *The Twenty Thousand Thieves* 161: 'Just quietly, he's up for a decoration.'

1972 Turner 109: *Just quietly* in Australia means 'between you and me' but tends to become a frequent and meaningless tag in New Zealand, just quietly.

quilt To clout with the fist [E. dial. 'to beat, thrash, flog' OED 1832]

1945 Baker 120: *quilt* and *stoush* a person. [as fighting terms]

1973 Donald Stuart *Morning Star Evening Star* 111: More than one bloke I've seen Joe quilt good and proper for trying to make a joke of it.

quince, get on one's To irritate, exasperate [unexplained]

1941 Baker 58: *Quince, get on one's* To annoy or aggravate deeply.

1959 Gerard Hamilton *Summer Glare* 45: 'That kid gets on my quince.'

1974 Desmond O'Grady *Deschooling Kevin Carew* 95: In an unguarded moment, he told Bull Moynihan 'This joint is getting on my quince.'

quit it up Stop it (juvenile)

quoit Buttocks [Partridge: 'ex roundness']

1941 Baker 58: *Quoit* The buttocks.

1951 Eric Lambert *The Twenty Thousand Thieves* 165: 'See those jokers sitting on their quoits over there?'

1954 T. A. G. Hungerford *Sowers of the Wind* 176: 'He blew the tripes outa me for nothing at all, and then he kicks a Nip in the coit.'

1972 John Bailey *The Wire Classroom* 82: 'I think he needs a good kick up the coit,' says Cromwell.

quoits, go for one's See quots [unexplained]

1941 Baker 58: *Quoits, go for one's* To travel quickly, go for one's life.

1952 Jon Cleary *The Sundowners* 34: 'Going for the lick of his coit up the street.'

R

rabbit-killer A blow to the back of the neck, like a karate chop [f. *rabbit punch* from the way a game-keeper puts a rabbit out of pain OED 1915]

1942 Gavin Casey *It's Harder for Girls* 23: I took a rush and gave him a rabbit-killer that must have nearly broken his neck.

1963 Criena Rohan *Down by the Dockside* 255: He ... had accounted for a couple more before he collected the rabbit killer that finally put him out of action.

rabbit-oh A hawker of rabbits for eating [f. the cry]

[1910 Thomas E. Spencer *Why Doherty Died* 84: When I ought to think of bizness, I can only think of you, / And instead of 'rabbit-oh' I sings out 'Liza'.]

1911 Arthur Wright *Gambler's Gold* 75: Engaged in the hopeless task of

trying to win the Rabbit-O man's money.
1943 Kylie Tennant *Time Enough Later* 181: Mrs Drew knew all about her neighbours from the butcher and the grocer and the rabbito.
1953 *Caddie A Sydney Barmaid* 199: I turned the corner of my street to see the rabbito's* horse and cart standing outside my gate. *An itinerant street seller of rabbits.
1975 *Sydney Morning Herald* 9 Apr. 1: Now 65, he is probably the last rabbit-oh in Sydney. 'I started helping my dad when I was just a boy,' he recalled. 'There were more rabbit-ohs then, but they've all died, or got old and given it away. Same as I'm going to do.' And he went on his way, shouting 'Rabbit-ohs!'

Rabbit-ohs, the The South Sydney Rugby League team ['The nickname has its origins in the 1930's Depression when club officials raised money for the players by raffling and hawking rabbits' *National Times* 4 Aug. 1975 36]
1975 *Australian* 21 Jul. 16: Rabbitohs hit rock bottom.

rabbit-proof fence A fence marking the borders between certain Australian states, therefore used as a point of reference
1957 Randolph Stow *The Bystander* 29: God! he thought. That's the coldest little bitch this side of the rabbit-proof fence.
1962 John O'Grady *Gone Fishin'* 24: 'You wouldn't find a politer bloke this side of the rabbit-proof fence.'
1965 *The Tracks We Travel* ed. L. Haylen 75: A little, bow-legged, gappy-toothed ex-shearer from the other side of the rabbit-proof fence, chipped in.
1976 Dorothy Hewett *Bon-bons and Roses for Dolly* 28: 'Best little ticket takers this side of the rabbit-proof. Oh! We were a great team.'

race, not in the Given no chance at all
1945 Margaret Trist *Now That We're Laughing* 73: 'With you and Daffy dressed up, none of us others will be in the race,' said Maureen.
1953 T. A. G. Hungerford *Riverslake* 227: 'See that bloke?' He pointed down the road after the vanished car. 'A few years ago he wouldn't have been in the race to own a car like that.'
1956 J. T. Lang *I Remember* 34: The trade unions realised that if the Chinese could get away with long hours and low pay they would not be in the race to get better conditions.

race off To seduce; whisk away with a view to seduction
1965 William Dick *A Bunch of Ratbags* 185: Three of Knuckles's boys had raced Sharon off to the park to see if they could do any good for themselves.
1969 Wilda Moxham *The Apprentice* 87: 'That's one bird you won't race off,' Rufe said. 'I know her, and the bloke she's with.'
1970 Jack Hibberd *White with Wire Wheels* in Penguin *Plays* 224: 'By Christ, if he races her off, it'll be the last fat he ever cracks.'
1971 Rena Briand *White Man in a Hole* 30: 'If I don't race a sheila orf at night, I start thinkin' and can't sleep.'

races, picnic see **picnic races**

rack off To go missing; as an imperative, 'Get lost' [? variant of *nick off, fuck off*]
1975 *Sun-Herald* 29 Jun. 83: 'Rak Off Normie' [title in list of pop records]
1976 *Australian* 3 Sep. 4: Rack orf Jack – we ain't allowed to serve minors no more. [cartoon caption]

Rafferty (Rafferty's) rules No rules at all [? *reffatory* refractory EDD]
1928 *Bulletin* 5 Jan. 37: M.Q. (and Rafferty) Rules [title of paragraph on a boxing match]
1935 *Sydney Morning Herald* 28 Dec. 11: Rafferty rules may suit Mr Keenan and the Communist party, but they are repugnant to the trade union movement.
1941 Baker 58: *Rafferty rules* No rules at all, applied to any system, organization or contest run in slipshod fashion.
1956 Miles Franklin *Laughter, Not for a*

Cage 34: Dr Mulhaus... being no English gentleman, follows Rafferty's rules with exhilarating results.
1964 H. P. Tritton *Time Means Tucker* 34: The Show adjourned at noon for the races. They seemed to be run on the 'Rafferty Rules' principle, but I heard no complaints.
1974 *Bulletin* 18 May 63: Rafferty's rules predominate.

rager 'An old and fierce bullock or cow, that always begins to rage in the stock-yard' (Morris)
1876 Rolf Boldrewood *A Colonial Reformer* (1890) 225: The 'ragers' observing this movement [into the receiving yard] keep wildly and excitedly 'ringing'.

rainbow See quots
1919 W. H. Downing *Digger Dialects* 40: *Rainbow* A reinforcement, or member of non-combatant corps, who joined a fighting unit after the Armistice. (Rainbow after the storm).
1935 H. R. Williams *Comrades of the Great Adventure* 174: 'Rainbow' was the nickname given to fellows who came to France after the 'storm' was over.
1944 Lawson Glassop *We Were the Rats* 153: We remembered, too, how, when we had passed them [the Sixth Division] on the way up, they had called us the 'long thinkers' and 'rainbows'. 'Rainbows?' we had asked. 'Yeah,' they replied, 'you're rainbows all right. You always see a rainbow after a storm.'

raining, if it was ~ pea soup, I'd get hit on the head by a fork An expression (with many variants) of habitual ill luck
1950 K. S. Prichard *Winged Seeds* 29: 'Unluckiest man I ever knew. If it was raining pea soup, he'd only have a fork.'
1954 T. A. G. Hungerford *Sowers of the Wind* 69: 'If it was rainin' palaces I'd get hit on the head with the handle of the dunny door.'
1967 Frank Hardy *Billy Borker Yarns Again* 88: He was so unlucky that when it was raining Paris night clubs he got hit on the head with a Woolloomooloo

plonk shop.
1970 Richard Beilby *No Medals for Aphrodite* 169: 'Gawd, we're an unlucky battalion, we are. If it was rainin' virgins we'd be washed away with a poofta, dinkum!'

ram *n. & v.* A trickster employed to 'set up' victims for another [*ramp* to rob or swindle OED 1812]
[1812 Vaux: *Ramp* to rob any person or place by open violence or suddenly snatching at something and running off with it.]
1941 Baker 59: *Ram* A trickster's confederate.
1952 *Coast to Coast 1951–1952* 199: Siddy might have been ramming for you, but what you didn't know, my lad, was that he was helping me to hook you. You were a goner from the start.
1964 H. P. Tritton *Time Means Tucker* 33: A gentleman with an umbrella, three thimbles and a pea was demonstrating how 'the quickness of the hand deceives the eye' and was raking in the money at a great rate. When business slackened, another gentleman would pick up the pea with surprising regularity. This would bring the crowd back to try their luck again. No one seemed to wake up to the fact that the second gentleman was 'ramming' for the first gentleman.
see **amster**

rammies Trousers: *rare* [? f. Malay *rami* a fibre or garment woven from it]
1919 W. H. Downing *Digger Dialects* 41: *Rammies* Breeches.
1943 Baker 63: *Rammies* Trousers.
1953 T. A. G. Hungerford *Riverslake* 42: 'Elastic for the old girl's rammies.'

rap A 'boost', a commendation (interchangeable with *wrap* q.v.)
1939 Kylie Tennant *Foveaux* 176: 'Everyone wants to be seen with a high-up feller. When I pass the time of day to a cove he feels that's a rap for him, see?'
1959 D'Arcy Niland *The Big Smoke* 12: 'His old man give him a rap, and that's

all I know.'

1963 Football coach reported in Keith Dunstan *Sports* (1973) 229: 'And if someone does something good, takes a good mark, give him a rap. Tell him.'
1974 *Sun* 19 Feb. 12: A few raps in the right places and I was chosen for City first against Country and then for NSW against Queensland.

rap up To speak highly of, 'boost' (interchangeable with *wrap up* q.v.)
1957 D'Arcy Niland *Call Me When the Cross Turns Over* 138: 'You dream and feel hopeless, I don't.' 'Rapping yourself up a bit, aren't you?' Ibid. 174: 'They couldn't rap him up enough then.'

rapt Overjoyed, carried away (interchangeable with *wrapped* q.v.)
1974 Keith Stackpole *Not Just for Openers* 114: Poor O'Keefe wasn't so rapt; he took none for 121. Ibid. 122: Travelling in the bus back to the Waldorf that evening, everyone was rapt.
1976 *Australian* 21 Jan. 1: Thommo tops the PM with $63,000 a year. 'All I can say is I'm rapt.'

ratbag An eccentric or stupid person [see *rats*]
1937 William Hatfield *I Find Australia* 138: 'You brought one rat-bag *in*,' said Ewens to me, 'so now do me a favour by taking one off my hands.'
1945 Roy Rene *Mo's Memoirs* 102: I don't want to give you the idea that we were nothing but a lot of ratbags, because we weren't.
1959 Gerard Hamilton *Summer Glare* 129: I told myself I had been a bloody ratbag for letting myself get worked up over Dookie.
1962 R. D. FitzGerald *Southmost Twelve* 31: I will go out and hear the strain / of rat-bag orators at large.
1965 Patrick White *Four Plays* 185: 'It's that Miss Docker.' 'That old rat-bag!'
1975 Don Townshend *Gland Time* 134: 'She's a bloody ratbag.'

rathouse The lunatic asylum [see *rats*]

1922 Arthur Wright *A Colt from the Country* 83: 'He'll be the long-lost boy, instead of the guy that's missed and landed in the rat-house.'
1943 Margaret Trist *In the Sun* 44: 'Livin' so much alone's no good to anyone. It'll drive you to the rat house.'
1953 T. A. G. Hungerford *Riverslake* 190: 'You'll end up in the rat-house.'

rats, to have (be); ratty To be odd, eccentric, irresponsible [? f. *ratty*, wretched, mean, miserable OED 1885]
1894 Henry Lawson *Prose* i 57: 'Rats' [story title]
1902 Henry Lawson 'Gettin' Back on Dave Regan' *Prose* i 367: 'I can't make it out at all. I believe she's gone ratty.'
1908 Henry Fletcher *Dads and Dan between Smokes* 65: In a town a whole population gets rats together, an' though they's all clean daft at times, yet, 'cause they all thinks alike, they don't doubt they's sane.
1922 Arthur Wright *A Colt from the Country* 86: 'There was a rough-up in a pub; he got a knock, had a fit, and went real ratty, and that was the end of him.'
1942 Sarah Campion *Bonanza* 17: Mo had watched all this . . . imagining what it must be like to be mad. Not raving, dangerous, mad but simple rats, like Bogy.

rattle the pan To 'kick the bucket', die
1948 A. W. Upfield *An Author Bites the Dust* 140: 'The last time he forgot was just before he rattled the pan.'

raw prawn, come the see **prawn**

razoo, not a (brass) No money at all. The expression is always negative (no one is ever mentioned as *having* a razoo, and no coin of the name exists) [? f. *not a soul*]
1931 William Hatfield *Sheepmates* 268: 'Richards never has a rahzoo.'
1939 Leonard Mann *Mountain Flat* 120: 'I wouldn't give you a razoo.'
1947 John Morrison *Sailors Belong Ships* 187: 'I wouldn't give you a razhoo for anything between there and

Charmian Road.'
1957 Ray Lawler *Summer of the Seventeenth Doll* 35: 'I picked him up in Brisbane a week ago. By then he hardly had a razoo.'
1964 Jon Cleary *A Flight of Chariots* 361: 'Poor bastard,' he heard one of the men nearby say. 'I wouldn't give a brass razoo for his chances out there.'
1975 Jessica Anderson *The Commandant* 155: The pile had been stolen. Every penny. Every last brass razoo.

read, you wouldn't~about it Expression of mingled incredulity and disgust
1950 Jon Cleary *Just Let Me Be* 135: 'Everything I backed ran like a no-hoper. Four certs I had, and the bludgers were so far back the ambulance nearly had to bring 'em home. You wouldn't read about it.'
1962 Dymphna Cusack *Picnic Races* 249: He drew a deep breath. 'You wouldn't read about it.'
1973 H. Williams *My Love Had a Black Speed Stripe* 69: You wouldn't read about it. A bloke his missus reckoned was a doctor of philosophy, whatever that was, and just about the biggest dill you could meet.

red blanket See quot.
1926 Alfred Giles *Exploring in the Seventies* 127: Tinned meat in 6 lb tins ('red blanket' we called it). The tins were painted red without labels or description of contents.

Redfern, getting off at *Coitus interruptus* [f. Redfern as the station immediately before Sydney Central; see quot. 1970]
1956 Heard in conversation.
1970 *Times Literary Supplement* 4 Dec. 1422: To get off at Redfern ... is dull and unoriginal. Since the nineteenth century, natives of Newcastle upon Tyne have described the procedure alliteratively as *getting out at Gateshead*. [A correspondent commenting on a review of Partridge]

red hot Extreme, unreasonable, 'over the odds'

1896 Henry Lawson 'Jones's Alley' *Prose* i 38: When ... she paused for breath, he drew a long one, gave a short whistle, and said: 'Well, it's red-hot!'
1907 Arthur Wright *Keane of Kalgoorlie* 107: 'It's red hot,' put in Dave, 'th' way these owners makes 'er pore man give 'em a lump in th' sweep.'
1924 *Truth* 27 Apr. 6: *Red 'ot* Unfair; extreme.
1941 Baker 59: *Red Hot* Unreasonable, unfair. e.g. 'a red hot price'.

Redlegs, the The Melbourne V.F.L. team, in 1930; since the Red Demons, then the Demons [f. team colours]

Reds, the (Dirty) The Drummoyne, N.S.W., Rugby Union team [f. team colours]
1974 *Sunday Telegraph* 8 Sep. 87: The complete lack of flair in the whole Drummoyne outfit raises doubts that the Dirty Reds could have done anything if given more chances.

red steer (bull), the A bushfire
1930 *Bulletin* 21 May 20: There had been a number of grass fires in the district, and suspicion falling on 'Monkey' Brown ... he was accused of loosing the 'red bull' on the community.
1941 Baker 59: *Red Steer, the* Fire, esp. a bush-fire. (Bush slang.)
1963 John Cantwell *No Stranger to the Flame* 12: The cane-cutter, made negro by sun and by soot from fires (Red Steers, they called them).
1971 Frank Hardy *The Outcasts of Foolgarah* 118: Like the bushfires: hadn't he patented the special extinguisher to end the blight of the red steer for all time?

reffo A European refugee: *derogatory* [abbr.]
1941 Baker 59: *Reffo* A refugee from Europe.
1951 Dymphna Cusack and Florence James *Come in Spinner* 278: 'The woman's a Viennese.' 'Oh, a reffo?'
1961 Patrick White *Riders in the Chariot* 221: He was, in any case, a blasted foreigner, and bloody reffo,

and should have been glad he was allowed to exist at all.

1968 Geoffrey Dutton *Andy* 98 : 'Those bloody reffos always pitch that yarn.'

1970 Jon Cleary *Helga's Web* 33–4: Reffo was a term that had been out of date for years; he wondered where the Italian had picked it up.

rego Motor vehicle registration [abbr.]

1975 *Sydney Morning Herald* 15 Nov. 67: Austin 1800, 8 mths rego. Gd tyres, radio. Heater. Goes well. $450 o.n.o.

remittance man Someone sent out to the colonies by his family, and sustained there by funds remitted at regular intervals; 'one who derives the means of an inglorious and frequently dissolute existence from the periodical receipt of money sent out to him from Europe' (Morris)

1897 Mark Twain *Following the Equator* 33: He was a 'remittance man', the first one I had ever seen or heard of . . . dissipated ne'er-do-weels belonging to important families in England and Canada were not cast off by their people while there was any hope of reforming them, but when that last hope perished at last, the ne'er-do-weel was sent abroad to get him out of the way . . . When he reached his destined port he would find a remittance awaiting him there. Not a large one, but just enough to keep him a month. A similar remittance would come monthly thereafter.

1901 Henry Lawson 'The Story of "Gentleman-Once"' *Prose* i 533: 'The remittance system is an insult to any manhood that may be left in the black sheep, and an insult to the land he is sent to. The cursed quarterly allowance is a stone round his neck which will drag him down deeper in a new land than he would have fallen at home. You know that remittance men are regarded with such contempt in the Bush that a man seldom admits he is one, save when he's drunk and reckless and wants money or credit.'

1905 Joseph Furphy *Rigby's Romance* ed. R. G. Howarth (1946) 81: 'You uncivilized animal; you're just about

fit to associate with remittance men.'

1907 Ambrose Pratt *The Remittance Man* 27: 'A remittance man. He hasn't sixpence in the world, beyond a pittance he receives quarterly, through my father's bank from England – about £10 I think. His relatives allow him that to keep him away from home.'

1937 *Best Australian One-Act Plays* 61: 'These fellows are all the same – a ne'er-do-well – a remittance man.'

1946 Judith Wright *The Moving Image* 17: 'Remittance Man' [poem title]

retread 1 A World War I soldier re-enlisting in World War II

1941 *Salt* 22 Dec. 36: *retread* a 1914–18 soldier enlisted a second time.

2 A retired schoolteacher returning to a temporary appointment

1950 Brian James *The Advancement of Spencer Button* 267: There were three 'retreads' among the men.

1953 Baker 142: *retread,* a schoolteachers' word for a teacher who has been recalled to duty from retirement.

ribuck see **ryebuck**

Rice, a roll Jack ~ couldn't jump over See quot. 1945

1945 Baker 107: A man well supplied with cash . . . may even be fortunate enough to have *a roll Jack Rice couldn't jump over.* Jack Rice was a racehorse noted for his performances over hurdles.

1954 Tom Ronan *Vision Splendid* 119: 'I've got a roll Jack Rice couldn't jump over.' Marty produced one of those wads of currency Mr Toppingham had seen only in the cruder American films and started peeling off ten-pound notes.

1960 John O'Grady *Cop This Lot* 82: 'Man walks around with a roll in 'is kick Jack Rice couldn't jump over, an' 'e's not worth a zac.'

1970 Jon Cleary *Helga's Web* 267: 'I never seen twenty thousand in cash before. Somehow you'd think it'd amount to a pile Jack Rice couldn't jump over.' Helidon wondered who Jack Rice was, then remembered it was a famous hurdle horse with a prodigious leap.

ridge (ridgie-didge) Genuine, 'on the level' [f. *ridge* gold OED 1665 (thieves' slang)]

[1812 Vaux: *Ridge* gold, whether in coin or any other shape]

1945 Baker 126: We also describe something especially good as . . . *ridge*.

1950 *Australian Police Journal* Apr. 117: *Ridge (or reet)* Right; or O.K.

1953 *The Sunburnt Country* ed. Ian Bevan 130: *Ridgy Didge* (derived from 'rigid digger', in its turn meaning a straight-up soldier, and hence implying integrity) means 'the truth'. The phrase is used invariably either as a simple question 'Ridgy Didge?' or as an unequivocal assurance: 'Ridgy Didge!'

1953 Kylie Tennant *The Joyful Condemned* 294: 'He'll tell you himself I'm ridgey-dite. I worked for him.'

1963 Lawson Glassop *The Rats in New Guinea* 153: 'It's ridgie-didge,' said Eddie. 'Spit me death.'

1971 David Ireland *The Unknown Industrial Prisoner* 130: 'I convinced her the whole thing was ridge! She went away thinking up recipes, how to get some variety into roast sparrow.'

right, she'll be An expression of general reassurance

1958 H. D. Williamson *The Sunlit Plain* 77: Eddie West smiled faintly at Deborah Tindall and whispered, 'She'll be right.'

1968 *Coast to Coast 1967–1968* 125: 'She'll be right, mate,' the man consoled him.

1971 Henry Williams *Australia – What is it?* 114: If the madmen triumph and the button is pressed and this earth is reduced to a smouldering radio-active cinder, maybe, out on the old Barcoo or somewhere out west, there will be a survivor, a lone battler to emerge from his timber-and-corrugated shack, look out across the ruined planet, roll up his sleeves and roll himself a smoke, and say, 'She'll be right, mate.'

1974 *Sunday Telegraph* 6 Oct. 63: Mundine's confidence of success is expressed with a 'She'll be right, mate' –

and he has most of the Spanish-speaking hotel staff using the Strine phrase. Each time they see him the porters, bell boys and desk clerks greet Mundine with 'She'll be right, mate.'

1975 *Australian* 15 Nov. 20: Ten years ago all was beer and sport, good on yer, mate and she'll be right. Any sort of intellectual achievement was knocked and if you wanted to do your own thing the only place to do it was abroad.

ring *n*. The buttocks, anus [f. shape]

1952 T. A. G. Hungerford *The Ridge and the River* 130: 'I'd get shot in the ring, that's what I'd get,' said Wallace.

1965 Randolph Stow *The Merry-go-Round in the Sea* 174: 'I bet I would have booted him in the ring if he hadn't run.'

1968 Thomas Keneally *Three Cheers for the Paraclete* 152: He said softly, 'It is your *episcopal* ring that I am supposed to kiss, My Lord.'

1974 Jack Hibberd *Dimboola* 9: 'Where do I sit?' 'On your ring.'

ring *v*. 1 Used of cattle forming themselves into a mass, with those on the outside circling the herd; used of horsemen riding about such a herd

1868 C. Wade Brown *Overlanding in Australia* 77: After an hour's amusement of this sort, they stop of their own accord. This evolution is termed 'ringing'. It is a food sign rather than otherwise.

1876 Rolf Boldrewood *A Colonial Reformer* (1890) 225: A desultory entry into the receiving yard then takes place . . . The 'ragers' observing this movement keep wildly and excitedly 'ringing', like a first-class Maelstrom.

1906 A. B. Paterson *An Outback Marriage* 169: By degrees, as the horses went round them, the cattle began to 'ring', forming themselves into a compact mass, those on the outside running round and round.

2 To prove oneself the fastest shearer in the shed [f. *ringer*[1]]

1895 A. B. Paterson *The Man from Snowy River* 88: They had rung the sheds of the east and west, / Had beaten the cracks of the Walgett side.

1905 'Flash Jack from Gundagai' in *The Old Bush Songs* ed. A. B. Paterson 27: And once I rung Cudjungie shed, and blued it in a week. [note] i.e. he was the ringer or fastest shearer of the shed, and he dissipated the earnings in a single week's drunkenness.

1923 Jack Moses *Beyond the City Gates* 47: In his third year of shearing, Gray 'rung' Wetherina, out west.

3 To ringbark q.v.

1853 S. Mossman and T. Banister *Australia, Visited and Revisited* 197: He destroyed the trees by 'ringing' them; that is, cutting off a strip of bark round the butt of the tree, which prevents the sap ascending, and thereby kills them.

1860 Mrs Alan MacPherson *My Experiences of Australia* 121: Formerly it was well wooded, but from the grass becoming valuable for pasture, all the trees have been ringed, that is a ring of bark a foot or so in depth has been cut out all round the trunks, and the trees have in consequence perished.

1885 Mrs Campbell Praed *Australian Life* 34–5: [Blacks] were only pressed into service when shepherds were scarce, or 'rung' trees (that is, gums which had been barked and allowed to wither) required felling.

ringbark To kill a tree by cutting off a strip of bark around the trunk

1877 Rolf Boldrewood *An Australian Squire* repr. as *Babes in the Bush* (1900) 50: 'Dead – every one of 'em, Miss,' explained their ruthless conductor. 'They've been ringbarked, more's the pity.'

1887 W. S. S. Tyrwhitt *The New Chum in the Queensland Bush* 29: The quality of the grass of course is much injured by the existence of so many trees, and especially by trees that suck the moisture out of the ground as gums do, it is therefore the practice to have all freehold land ... 'ringbarked'. On some runs large numbers of men are employed for months together in nothing else but killing all the trees by cutting a ring round them with an axe.

1890 Henry Lawson 'Skeleton Flat' *Verse* i 64: When the squatter's men came with the death-dealing axe, / And ringbark'd the Skeleton Flat.

1930 *Bulletin* 8 Jan. 20: Two new hands ... were ringbarking on Blade's selection.

1957 R. S. Porteous *Brigalow* 150–1: 'The bullock paddock is nearly all ringbarked and there's still a bit of nourishment in the grass.'

1970 Germaine Greer *The Female Eunuch* 287: Mother went out the next day and ringbarked it, so it definitely died, and had to be felled after all.

ringer 1 The fastest shearer in a shed; the outstanding man in any activity [f. *ringer* anything superlatively good EDD 1896]

1870 Rolf Boldrewood 'Shearing in Riverina' *In Bad Company* (1901) 313: The 'Ringer', or fastest shearer of the whole shed ['assembly' in 1901].

1886 John Farrell 'My Sundowner' *How He Died* (1913) 77: Flash Dick, the Ringer / From Wilson's shed, where they had just cut out.

1892 Henry Lawson 'At the Tug-of-War' *Verse* i 114: 'Twas in a tug-of-war where I – the guvnor's hope and pride – Stepped proudly on the platform as the ringer of my side.

1901 Rolf Boldrewood *In Bad Company* 432: I also hear that the 'ringer' in the pick and shovel brigade is a Hawkesbury man.

1910 C. E. W. Bean *On the Wool Track* 196: The man who shears most sheep is the 'ringer'.

2 A stockman, drover, general station hand [f. *ring v.*[1]]

1910 John X. Cameron *The Spell of the Bush* 48: Dam-sinkers, fencers, scrub-cutters, ringers, and other men doing contract work in the vicinity.

1937 Ernestine Hill *The Great Australian Loneliness* 330: *Ringers* Drovers' men, wheeling round the cattle day and night on the road.

1964 *Sydney Morning Herald* 25 Apr. 11: If a mob of ringers (station hands) ... start 'heading 'em' in the bar.

ringie The ringkeeper in two-up [abbr.]

1941 Baker 60: *Ringie* The keeper of a

two-up school.
1951 Frank Hardy *Power Without Glory* 323: Red Ted was 'Ringie.' He supervised the game in the ring itself, seeing that the pennies were spun fairly, and calling the results.

ring the tin See quot.
1972 *Sydney Morning Herald* 24 Feb. 12: A foreman at the mine is the subject of a 'ring the tin' ruling by members of the Workers' Industrial Union of Australia, the city's [Broken Hill] largest union with 2,500 members. . . . According to union officials, 'ring the tin' ruling means that the foreman will not be spoken to by WIU men who work under him. The ban will apply 24 hours a day on and off the mine lease.

rip you, wouldn't it see **wouldn't it**

ripper As for 'beaut' [OED 1851]
1951 Eric Lambert *The Twenty Thousand Thieves* 182: 'Good letter, Chips?' A gurgle. 'It's a ripper!'
1969 Alan O'Toole *The Racing Game* 200: 'Not a bad run,' I observed . . . 'A ripper,' Badger agreed.
1973 *Australian* 7 Jul. 16: I love this ripper country / Of funnel webs and sharks / With blowies big as eagles / Where your car gets booked by narks.
1975 *Bulletin* 15 Feb. (cover): Ripper party at Terrigal. Back to the slog in Canberra this week.

rise, make a To achieve some kind of prosperity: *obs.*
1876 Rolf Boldrewood *A Colonial Reformer* (1890) 183: 'I haven't seen my poor old mother for five years good, and I must go, if I was never to make a rise again.'
1902 Henry Lawson 'The Bulletin Hotel' *Verse* ii 7: But he'll pack up in a hurry and he'll seek a cooler clime, / If I make a rise in England and I get out there in time.
1903 Joseph Furphy *Such is Life* (1944) 114–15: 'Not much chance of a man makin' a rise the way things is now.'
1916 C. J. Dennis *The Moods of Ginger*

Mick 18: Ginger Mick's bin at the races, an' 'e'd made a little rise.
1940 Ion L. Idriess *Lightning Ridge* 99: Andy sank five hundred shafts, toiled for years and years, and never made a rise.

rivers, Hawkesbury see **Hawkesbury**

roaring days, the The period of the gold discoveries, romantically viewed
1897 Henry Lawson 'The Lights of Cobb and Co.' *Verse* i 339: But these seem dull and slow to me compared with Roaring Days.
1921 M. E. Fullerton *Bark House Days* 116: We loved the stories of the 'roaring fifties'.
1936 William Hatfield *Australia Through the Windscreen* 53: In its roaring days 'The Duchess' was better than many a goldmine.

roar up To rebuke, upbraid
1919 W. H. Downing *Digger Dialects* 42: *Roar up* Upbraid; abuse.
1920 *Aussie* Apr. (glossary): *Roar us up* Loudly abuse.
1947 Norman Lindsay *Halfway to Anywhere* 69: Bill was able to roar him up, anyway, for having the blinkin' cheek to come shoving his nose into Bill's affairs.

Robbo, four bob See quots
1897 *Bulletin* 23 Jan. 11: 'Four Bob Robbo' – four shillings Robinson, who lived in the classic suburb of Waterloo, Sydney . . . came into a bit of money and bought a horse and trap. The money was spent, and Robinson tired of the horse, which got poor; so he then sometimes let out the horse and trap (both somewhat worse of wear) for 4s. per half-day. There was a run on the cheap hire, and Rob. bought two other horses and traps, which he let out at same price. A neighbouring livery-stable keeper and his employés resented Rob's cutting-down prices and, when any of the rival's equipages passed, used to cry out, in derision, 'Four Bob Robbo!' The cry was taken up by the kids, and has now become a Waterloo classic. It

has already cost one person £2 and costs, the magistrate ruling that 'Four Bob Robbo!' shouted after the original in the street, constituted insulting language calculated to create a breach of the peace.
1900–10 O'Brien and Stephens: Robinson, familiarly known as 'Robbo' – a Sydney dealer, i.e. costermonger, having accumulated money, set up as a dealer's liveryman in '94. Previous to his going into the business the usual rate per day for a dealer's horse and cart was six shillings, but Robbo cut the rates and let out a horse and cart at four shillings per day. These turnouts were called by the opposition livery men and hirers 'Robbos, / four bobs / shillings'. Robbo extended his livery business and let out buggies and hansom cabs at four shillings per day all of which came to be known as 'four bob robbos' and then by abbreviation 'robbos' ... The term spread, and any horse and trap was called by street boys a robbo ... Robbo has come to be applied to anything inferior, or a take-down or swindle.
1906 A. J. Tompkins *With Swag and Billy* 51: Right out of the haunts of the motor, the bike and the Robbo.
1939 Kylie Tennant *Foveaux* 430: 'Ever 'eard of Bert Robinson? ... 'E kept a livery stable down at the Foot. I s'pose you've 'eard of the Four-bob Robbos, then? The chaps used to go an' hire a cart for four bob and take it round loaded with vegetables. The kids used to call after 'em, "Four Bob Robbo, Four Bob Robbo".'

Rocket The tennis player Rod Laver (b. Rockhampton, Queensland)
1976 *Australian* 21 Apr. 21: Rodney George Laver, alias the Rockhampton Rocket, has been the most prolific winner of major tournaments in the history of tennis.

rocking-horse manure, as scarce as Very scarce
1954 Tom Ronan *Vision Splendid* 41: 'Tailor-made smokes are as rare as rocking-horse manure around here.'

roll up A mass meeting of workers to deal with some issue of common concern; any assembly of people
1870 Rolf Boldrewood 'Shearing in Riverina' *Town and Country Journal* 12 Nov. 13: The bell sounded, but instead of the usual cheerful dash at the sheep, each man stood silent and unmoved in his place. Someone uttered the words 'roll up!' and slowly, but with one impulse, the sixty men converged and began to walk towards the end of the shed.
1880 Rolf Boldrewood *The Miner's Right* (1890) 308: 'Can't we have a few words without your ... making as much noise as if you'd hired the bellman for a roll-up?'
1898 D. W. Carnegie *Spinifex and Sand* 120: A 'roll up' would be called, and those who cared to put themselves forward, would form judge, jury, police and all. The general verdict was notice to quit within so many hours – an order that few would dare to neglect.
1929 Jules Raeside *Golden Days* 139: In cases of any misdemeanour on the part of a digger, the usual course adopted was to sound the tocsin of the tin dish, and summon a 'roll-up', which consisted of a congregation of all miners, who constituted themselves for the nonce into a court of justice.
1937 Miles Franklin *Back to Bool Bool* 248: 'We are all making for the grand roll-up at Bool Bool.'
1962 Alan Seymour *The One Day of the Year* 65: 'They still get a good rollup.'

Roos see **Kangaroos**

Rooshians see **Russians**

rooster one day and a feather duster the next see **feather duster**

Roosters, the The Eastern Suburbs (N.S.W.) Rugby League team (also the Tricolours) [club emblem]
1974 *Sunday Telegraph* 15 Sep. 96: Roosters flying high.

root *n.* 1 An act of intercourse, esp. from the male point of view [? f. *rut*. Not

included in the OED, although implied in the word-play in *The Merry Wives of Windsor* IV i 42–6 cf. *root* male member]
1938 Encountered in conversation.
1958 Sir Roderic Chamberlain *The Stuart Affair* (1973) 111: He heard Moir ask Stuart, 'Did you have a root?' and Stuart reply, 'I had a tight one.'
1961 Frank Hardy *The Hard Way* 77: One shabby criminal struck a match revealing . . . a sign scrawled on the wall: 'Best American root – ring such and such a number.'
1973 Alexander Buzo *Rooted* 43: 'Hey, do you remember the time he got pissed out of his mind and fronted up to this old duck and asked her for a root?'
1974 Peter Kenna *A Hard God* 33: 'Have you ever gone all the way with a girl? . . . You know what I mean. Have you ever had a real root?'
2 A partner in intercourse
1971 Frank Hardy *The Outcasts of Foolgarah* 196: 'You're not only the best root in Foolgarah but good-natured as well.'
1973 Alexander Buzo *Rooted* 139: *weekend root* a casual partner.
1974 Barry Humphries *Barry Mckenzie Holds his Own* 4: 'Going back to Oz, mate? What route are you taking?' 'No one, sport. I'm travelling with me Aunty Edna.'
1976 David Ireland *The Glass Canoe* 147: Johnny Bickel . . . thought she'd be an easy root and began to take notice of her.

root *v.* 1 To copulate with, esp. from the male standpoint [see *root n.*]
1958 Sir Roderic Chamberlain *The Stuart Affair* (1973) 12: I took her bathers off. Then I raped her. She was hard to root.
1966 Patrick White *The Solid Mandala* 185: 'We'll root together so good you'll shoot out the other side of Christmas.'
1969 William Dick *Naked Prodigal* 118: 'The fat one, Leslie, roots like a rattle-snake.'
1974 David Williamson *Three Plays* 14: 'Country tarts would root a wombat if they thought he was going to be a doctor one day.' Ibid. 15: 'Bloody

stunning. Almost too beautiful to root. Worries me a bit.'
1976 Dorothy Hewett *The Tatty Hollow Story* 108: 'I'm going to root the arse off you, and give you a bun in the oven.'
get rooted Insulting advice, like 'get stuffed'
1961 Mena Calthorpe *The Dyehouse* 186: 'He can get rooted, for all I care,' Collins said bitterly.
1974 David Ireland *Burn* 29: 'I can tell anyone in the world to go and get rooted.'
2 To cause an upheaval, consternation esp. in the expression 'Wouldn't it root you!' (World War II slang) abbr. to 'Wouldn't it!' q.v.
1945 Baker 152n: The authentic digger form is *Wouldn't it root you!* A regimental paper 'Wiry' (1941) took its name from the first letters of the words in this phrase.
1964 George Johnston *My Brother Jack* 306: 'You know, and how they always wanted me to join 'em? Well – this'll root you – 1 bloody *have*, sport.'
3 To worst, disable, put out of commission esp. in the p.pl. 'rooted'
1951 Dal Stivens *Jimmy Brockett* 244: 'It looks as though we're rooted, smacker,' I told Herb.
1973 *Sydney Morning Herald* 16 Nov. 17: Mr Snedden said to Mr Whitlam across the house table; 'You are gutless'. Mr Whitlam replied; 'It is what he (Dr Forbes) puts in his guts that has rooted him!' Dr Forbes . . . said: 'I want these words to go on record so the people will know what an arrogant, foul-mounthed individual this man is.'
1974 John Powers *The Last of the Knucklemen* 93: 'The Hun's rooted . . . Done like a dinner.'
1975 Xavier Herbert *Poor Fellow My Country* 970: 'They're all right chasin' burglars and molls, them blokes . . . but put 'em in the bush, they're rooted.'

root, mallee see **mallee**

ropeable Enraged (i.e. needing to be tied up, put under restraint)
[**1910** P. W. Joyce *English as We Speak it in Ireland* 125: 'I was fit to be tied.'

A common expression among us to express great indignation.]

1874 Charles de Boos *The Congewoi Correspondence* 195: I don't know a nastier smell than the smeller new togs just fresh from the tailor's goose, and the thoughter that amost made me ropeable.

1898 Rolf Boldrewood *A Romance of Canvas Town* 322: 'Your aunt would be ropeable?' 'I believe you,' anwered his companion. 'Blew me up sky high.'

1905 Joseph Furphy *Rigby's Romance* ed. R. G. Howarth (1946) 44: 'Up comes Moses, ropeable – and what d' you think he done?'

1919 Henry Lawson 'The Row at Ryan's Pub' *Verse* iii 385: 'Don't get ropable, or moony – and, above all, don't get spoony.'

1945 Kylie Tennant *Ride on Stranger* 122: 'When I think of that rat, it makes me just *ropeable*!'

1956 Patrick White *The Tree of Man* 278: 'I often remember how you broke that washstand at Yuruga. Mother was ropeable.'

1963 John Cantwell *No Stranger to the Flame* 125: 'She was going to have my kid, but she dropped it when another bloke put the acid on. I got ropeable and did her.'

rort 1 A rowdy party; a 'stunt' (World War II slang) [f. *rorty* fine, splendid, jolly OED 1864]

[1941 Baker 61: *Rort* (2) A crowd]

1952 T. A. G. Hungerford *The Ridge and the River* 81: 'Out we go on another bloody rort, so what's the use of saving a day?'

1963 John Cantwell *No Stranger to the Flame* 31: Life at the pub was one long post-operational rort, a perpetual celebration of imagined kills.

1969 George Johnston *Clean Straw for Nothing* 78: I am not, strictly, a true devotee of the wild Australian 'rort' and always remorseful in my hangovers.

1973 Alexander Buzo *Rooted* 93: 'We're holding a birthday party for Simmo . . . We'll need the whole house. It's going to be a real rort.'

2 A deception, racket, dodge

1936 Jean Devanny *Sugar Heaven* 20: 'The cockies are supposed to pay this retention money into the bank . . . but normally they don't pay it in. They keep the use of it through the season and we draw the bare amount at the end of the cut. It's the greatest rort ever.'

1941 Baker 61: *Rort* A dodge, scheme or racket.

1954 T. A. G. Hungerford *Sowers of the Wind* 141: 'He could take lessons from old Craigie – he's well in on all the rorts?'

1975 *Sun-Herald* 12 Oct. 15: It didn't matter about the VIP plane or car 'rorts'. These matters were 'sensationalised' by the press, they said.

rorter See quots

1941 Baker 61: *Rorter* A professional sharper: a hawker of worthless goods: one who practises sly dodges to obtain money.

1962 Alan Marshall *This is the Grass* 64: 'He's a small-time rorter. I know him.' Ibid. 159: Rorters like Flogger prepared to fleece any man who stood staring around him.

1973 Frank Huelin *Keep Moving* 178: *Rorter* Hobo who makes and sells articles such as clothes-pegs, toasting forks, and various pieces of wire work. [in the Depression]

1975 *Bulletin* 26 Apr. 44: *rorters* (petty con men).

rosella 1 A sheep losing its wool, and therefore easy to shear (The pink skin showing through could recall the plumage of the parakeet so called.)

1910 C. E. W. Bean *On the Wool Track* 193: If there is an old ewe in the pen, a 'rosella' as they call her, with most of the lower wool worn off, she goes the first.

1933 Acland: *Rosella* A sheep that has cast most of his wool before shearing, so is very easy to shear.

1964 H. P. Tritton *Time Means Tucker* 119: Among the sheep were three 'rosellas'. These are sheep with the wool falling off, and are very popular with shearers. In fact, a shearer's idea

of Paradise is a shed full of 'rosellas'.
2 See quot.
1898 Morris: 'In Northern Australia, it is a slang name for a European who works bared to the waist ... The scorching of the skin by the sun produces a colour which probably suggested a comparison with the bright scarlet of the parrakeet so named.'

rosiner A stiff drink; any enlivening influence [f. *rosin* to supply with liquor; to make drunk OED 1729 (from the resin applied to violin strings)]
[1865 Hotten: *Rosin* beer or other drink given to musicians at a dancing party.]
1945 Baker 170: *rozner* is a stiff pick-me-up.
1947 H. Drake-Brockman *The Fatal Days* 114: 'I've not had a solitary spot since four. I need a rosiner.'
1954 Tom Ronan *Vision Splendid* 345: Two nips that old Block had and the one I poured into Peter. They were rozeners I'll admit, but still the three I've had out of this second bottle haven't been exactly small.
1973 Donald Stuart *Morning Star Evening Star* 53: There's no harm in a bit of a rosiner after a hard day's travel, just once in a while.

rotate you, wouldn't it see **wouldn't it**

rotten Drunk [f. *rotten* as 'over-ripe', 'saturated with']
[1910 P. W. Joyce *English as We Speak it in Ireland* 126: A person considered very rich: – That man is rotten with money.]
1941 Baker 61: *Rotten, to get* To become exceedingly drunk.
1953 T. A. G. Hungerford *Riverslake* 135: 'Monday to-morrow – blasted work again. God, could I get rotten!'
1966 Roger Carr *Surfie* 128: All this because I'd got rotten.
1971 Johnny Famechon *Fammo* 145: A reporter from one of the Sydney papers – he was the last to leave, rotten.
1975 Xavier Herbert *Poor Fellow My Country* 1028: 'That's the actual cathar-

sis of drinking for me . . . not just getting rotten.'

rough as bags, guts see **bags, guts**

roughie 1 Something 'hard to take', unfair
[1907 Nathan Spielvogel *The Cocky Farmer* 51–2: 'Don't we have to stiffen the sinews when we are up to it with a roughie to shear?']
1939 Kylie Tennant *Foveaux* 122: 'Kelly put a roughie over Charlie to-day.'
1970 Richard Beilby *No Medals for Aphrodite* 269: 'I bluffed him, put a roughie over him.'
2 A horse at long odds, an outsider that wins
1934 Steele Rudd *Green Grey Homestead* 155: Those who had lost a wager or two will turn to Bell and say: 'You knew something about the roughie!'
1951 Dymphna Cusack and Florence James *Come in Spinner* 40: 'He's a roughie so 'e'll go out at long odds.'
1958 Frank Hardy *The Four-Legged Lottery* 14: 'I might just have a shilling on a roughie.'
1975 *Sun-Herald* 10 Aug. 57: Smith Roughie Upsets Crowd. Punters demonstrated after trainer Tom Smith won the Second Tennyson Graduation with 20–1 outsider Alterego at Rosehill yesterday.

rouse (roust) on, to To upbraid, berate [? *roust* to shout, roar OED 1513]
1900–10 O'Brien and Stephens: *Rouse* abuse or vilify.
1911 Louis Stone *Jonah* 126: ' 'E niver rouses on me. W'en 'e gits shirty, I just laugh, an' 'e can't keep it up.'
1915 C. J. Dennis *The Songs of a Sentimental Bloke* 88: If she 'ad only roused I might 'a smiled./She jist seems 'urt an' crushed; not even riled.
1924 *Truth* 27 Apr. 6: *Rouse* To upbraid.
1934 Vance Palmer *Sea and Spinifex* 182: 'Combo's one of those sulky devils that forget nothing . . . Can't take a bit of rousing as part of the day's work.'
1941 Sarah Campion *Mo Burdekin* 139: 'And 'avin 'im roust hell outa me for

it.'
1951 Dymphna Cusack *Say No to Death* 30: 'Auntie used to rouse on me frightfully because I spent so much time on the beach.'
1961 Ray Lawler *The Piccadilly Bushman* 31: 'Don't rouse at me, Alec.'
1970 Patrick White *The Vivisector* 10–11: He hung around Mumma, waiting for her to settle, and she didn't roust on him.

rouseabout (roustabout) An unskilled labourer in a shearing shed or on a station; any general employee of low status; a worker on an oilfield [*rouseabout* a restless creature never easy at home OED 1778; *roustabout* a wharf labourer or deckhand U.S. 1868 OED]
1881 *Chambers' Journal* 5 Mar. 157: During shearing . . . there are thirty-six hands employed on Greenwood, together with about the same number of 'Rouseabouts'; these being men and boys who pen the sheep, pick up the fleeces as they are shorn, and sort and pack the wool, &c.
1887 *All the Year Round* 30 Jul. 66–7: A man who does odd jobs about a station and who can be put to any kind of work, is called a 'roustabout'.
1892 G. L. James *Shall I Try Australia?* 97: The 'roustabout' or 'rouseabout' implies a general utility man or boy in a shearing shed, the term is used frequently to denote all hands besides the shearers.
1902 Henry Lawson 'Two Sundowners' *Prose* i 100: They struck West-o'-Sunday station, and the boss happened to want a rouseabout to pick up wool and sweep the floor for the shearers.
1919 E. S. Sorenson *Chips and Splinters* 73: The boss was soon down, and the spread at once caught his eye. Barwon purposely mistook him for a rouseabout.
1933 F. E. Baume *Tragedy Track* 40: She knows how to deal with the wildest men of the North, and woe betide any drover or rouseabout who presents her with a cheque that is doubtful.
1951 Dymphna Cusack and Florence James *Come in Spinner* 39: 'They'll

probably stick you in as rouseabouts in a lunatic asylum, seeing the experience you've 'ad 'ere.'
1971 Colin Simpson *The New Australia* 518: The average young oilfield workers, called a 'roustabout', needed to have more than muscles. Technical competence was also called for and most, I was told, had had five years of secondary education.
rouser [abbr.]
1896 Henry Lawson 'Stragglers' *Prose* i 92: They are all shearers, or at least they say they are. Some might be only 'rousers'.

Roy The 'trendy' Australian, opposite to 'Alf' q.v.
1960 Murray Sayle *Encounter* May 28: The Australian business-man or big land-owner, the button-down shirt, lightweight suit type of smoothie from the North Shore Line in Sydney or Toorak Road in Melbourne, with his spurious 'taste' and 'culture' . . . In current Australian terminology, this is the 'Roy' type.
1965 *Nation* 27 Nov. 21: Middle-class 'Roys' in sports cars and yachting jackets.
1971 Frank Hardy *The Outcasts of Foolgarah* 143: The young executives, the in-people, call them what you like, the Roys, the jet set, the status seekers from Perisher Valley to Palm Beach, and none of them worth a pinch of shit if it comes to doing an honest day's work.

Royal Alfred see **Alfred**

rubbish To disparage, dispose of contemptuously
1953 T. A. G. Hungerford *Riverslake* 20: 'If Verity was going to tramp you for burning the tucker . . . he would have rubbished you long before this.'
1969 Alan O'Toole *The Racing Game* 120: Andrew Killburn rubbished the very notion.
1971 David Ireland *The Unknown Industrial Prisoner* 352: They rubbished him every chance they got, why should he always go back for more?

rubbity A pub [rhyming slang *rubbity-dub*]

[1898 *Bulletin* 17 Dec. Red Page: *Drum* – derived from the kettle-drums (evening parties) of the days of the Georges – was a high-class word, but it fell. The cockney turned it into *rub-a-dum-dum*; the Australian now calls the same thing a *rubadey*.]
1941 Baker 62: *Rubberdy, Rubbity, Rubby:* A public house. Rhyming slang on 'rub-a-dub-dub' for 'pub'.
1957 D'Arcy Niland *Call Me When the Cross Turns Over* 101: 'How about a gargle? Down to the rubberdy, come on.'
1962 David Forrest *The Hollow Woodheap* 11: 'Where . . . is The Eagle on the Hill?' 'A rubbedy in South Australia.'
1973 Alexander Buzo *Rooted* 63: 'Been down the rubbity lately?' 'No, I haven't hit the hops for a couple of weeks.'

Rules As for 'Aussie Rules' q.v.
1946 Dal Stivens *The Courtship of Uncle Henry* 18: In those days . . . they played Rules in long pants that reached below the knee.
1976 *Sydney Morning Herald* 27 May 22: Rules penalty upsets Saints.

Rules, Rafferty's see **Rafferty's**

Rum Rebellion The deposition of Governor Bligh in 1809 by officers of the N.S.W. Corps, noted for their trafficking in rum
1855 William Howitt *Land, Labour and Gold* ii 118: From the date of this 'rum rebellion', and the forcible deposition of poor Bligh . . . the system of political grants went on swimmingly.
1871 Marcus Clarke *Old Tales of a Young Country* 38: The Rum-Puncheon Revolution [chapter title]
1938 H. V. Evatt *Rum Rebellion* [book title]

run over the bastards see **bastards**

rush The sudden migration of people to a gold discovery
1855 William Howitt *Land, Labour and Gold* i 174: Very little, if any, gold will be got out of the whole of this rush . . . Indeed, it seems to be a general opinion that the rush was planned by the people . . . who saw that they were watched, and resolved to mislead their watchers.
1861 T. McCombie *Australian Sketches* 2nd Series 78: An excellent opportunity presented itself to me of seeing the first great 'rushes' to the Australian goldfields.
1900 Henry Lawson 'The Story of the Oracle' *Prose* i 279: 'My Uncle Bob was mates with him on one of those 'rushes' along there – the 'Pipeclay', I think it was, or the 'Log Paddock'.
1915 K. S. Prichard *The Pioneers* 152: 'Hear Pat and Tom Kearney have cleared out to the new rush? Eaglehawk, isn't it?'

Russians (Rooshians) Wild cattle [? f. *rush*]
1845 D. Mackenzie *The Emigrant's Guide* 118: These wild Russians, as they are here called, will . . . clear at the first leap a stockyard six feet in height.
1849 Alexander Harris *The Emigrant Family* (1967) 53: 'Are there any "Rooshans" in the mountains?' he inquired.
1861 H. W. Wheelwright *Bush Wanderings of a Naturalist* 58: I always looked out on the plains, and whenever I saw a bullock standing sulking by itself, I always gave it a wide berth; such a one is generally a 'Roosian.'
1876 Rolf Boldrewood *A Colonial Reformer* (1890) 222: The head stockman there covenanting . . . to give the Rainbar folks a turn, and draft their 'Roosians' for them.

rustbucket A car in a dangerously rusted condition [f. application to ships]
1965 *Daily Telegraph* 23 Apr. 20: It was a rust-bucket. That means a very badly rusted car.
1972 Ian Moffitt *The U-Jack Society* 121: 'They look beautiful, but underneath they're rust-buckets.'

ryebuck (ribuck) Possessing some degree of excellence; genuine; as a retort, an expression of full agreement: *obs.*

1895 *Bulletin* 9 Feb. 15: I'm ryebuck and the girl's okay.

1898 *Bulletin* 17 Dec. Red Page: *Ryebuck* (all right) is no doubt an abbreviation of 'all right, my buck'.

1911 Louis Stone *Jonah* 11: 'Oh, I don't suppose you'll be missed,' replied Chook graciously. 'Rye buck!' cried Jonah.

1915 C. J. Dennis *The Songs of a Sentimental Bloke* 72: 'E'n in the days when she's no longer fair / She's still yer wife', 'e sez. 'Ribuck', sez I.

1916 C. J. Dennis *The Moods of Ginger Mick* 42: But the reel, ribuck Australia's 'ere, among the fightin' men.

1924 *Truth* 27 Apr. 6: *Ribuck* Expression of assent.

1943 Charles Shaw *Outback Occupations* 17: 'Ribuck, boss,' he says; 'but y're wastin' y'r time.'

1957 *Old Bush Songs* ed. Stewart and Keesing 267: 'The Ryebuck Shearer' [ballad title]

S

saddling paddock The bar in the Theatre Royal, Melbourne, known in the nineteenth century as a resort of prostitutes; any known place of rendezvous [f. *ride* for the male role in intercourse]

1868 Marcus Clarke 'Melbourne Streets at Midnight' *Argus* 28 Feb. repr. in *A Colonial City* ed. L. T. Hergenhan (1972) 102: That door leads to the 'ladies refreshment-room', but is known to its fast frequenters by another name.

1876 Julian Thomas 'The Theatre Vestibules' *Argus* 1 Jul. 4 repr. in *The Vagabond Papers* ed. Michael Cannon (1969) 232: The stranger, strolling out during an entr' acte [at the Royal], would be still more surprised at Melbourne manners and customs, as witnessed in the Vestibule. This is generally crowded with men and larrikins, smoking and chaffing the loose women who pass in and out ... The stranger sees that the women, possibly picking up a male companion, all enter the compartment which was previously closed,

and which is now guarded by swing doors. Curiosity will doubtless prompt him to enter, and he will find himself in the far-famed 'saddling paddock' of the Royal. It is a small bar, presided over by a man – the proceedings here are too unpleasant for a barmaid to witness. Here the most notorious women of Melbourne nightly throng, and run in the companions they have caught in the stalls or in the vestibules.

c. **1880** T. E. Argles *The Pilgrim* i 6: At the Royal, however, the machinery of pimping, of 'saddling' is carried on openly; and the entrance lobby of the theatre set apart as a haven for scores of flaunting members of the demimonde.

1955 D'Arcy Niland *The Shiralee* 66: The first ... screamed for help when the game got real. The second, they were so often in the saddling paddock it wasn't natural.

1958 Gavin Casey *Snowball* 29: The ribald, popular name of the enclosure round the Government Dam was 'the saddling paddock'.

1958 Jack Lindsay *Life Rarely Tells* 213: After a while he smoothed his hair ... 'Back to the good old saddling-paddock' – by which he meant Maisie's bedroom.

Saints, the 1 In N.S.W., the St George Rugby League team (also the Dragons)

1974 *Sydney Morning Herald* 3 Aug. 63: Exit of a great Saint.

2 In Victoria, the St Kilda V.F.L. team

1916 C. J. Dennis *The Moods of Ginger Mick* 33: Wot time the footer brings the clicks great joy, / An' Saints er Carlton roughs it up wiv 'Roy.

1976 *Sunday Telegraph* 30 May 54: Demons too good for the Saints.

salts, go through like a dose (packet) of To move very quickly, demolish opposition [f. Epsom salts as an aperient]

1941 Baker 25: *Dose of salts, go through (something, someone) like a* To accomplish a task very rapidly: to deal drastically with a person.

1968 Geoffrey Dutton *Andy* 92–3: 'In the Army you can go through the world

like a packet of salts.'
1971 R. F. Brissenden *Winter Matins*
26: Goes through the homestead like
a dose of salts, / Clears out the bludgers.
1974 David Ireland *Burn* 10: He'd go
through this town like a packet of salts.

Salute, Australian, Barcoo see **Australian, Barcoo**

Salvo (Sally) A member of the Salvation
Army
1896 *Bulletin* 31 Oct. 27: The Salvo's
Error [story title]
1908 C. H. S. Matthews *A Parson in
the Australian Bush* 256: 'Well, I was
rared a Carthlick, but I haven't followed
it up much. To tell ye the truth, I class
'em all alike – priests, parsons, "salvos",
and all the lot of 'em.'
1911 Louis Stone *Jonah* 271: 'I've 'eard
old women at the Salvos' meetings talk
like this, tellin' of the wonderful things
they found out w'en they got converted.'
1936 Ion L. Idriess *The Cattle King* 189:
The surest place to find Sid Kidman,
when in town on a Saturday night, was
among the crowd around the 'Sallies'.
1951 Dal Stivens *Jimmy Brockett* 249:
He gasped . . . like the Salvo bloke the
time I put a fiver in his collection plate
at Central Railway.
1959 Dorothy Hewett *Bobbin Up* 55:
She had already been saved by the
Salvoes, baptized into the Plymouth
Brethren . . . changed her Sabbath for
the Seventh Day Adventists.
1965 Graham McInnes *The Road to
Gundagai* 239: Those who suffered
most were the Salvation Army, or the
Salvoes as they were known to us.

sandgroper A native of Western Australia [see quot. 1963]
1896 Henry Lawson *Letters* (1970) 62:
W.A. is a fraud. The curse of the country is gold . . . The old Sand-gropers are
the best to work for or have dealings
with. The Tothersiders are cutting each
others' throats.
1926 J. Vance Marshall *Timely Tips for
New Australians*: Groper A West Australian.

1934 Thomas Wood *Cobbers* 14: If
there had been no sand in Western
Australia to goad people into reprisals,
everybody there might have been
tempted to lie on his back and bask
in the sunshine. As it is, inhabitants
of other States talk of 'Sand-gropers',
slightingly; but groping has paid. W.A.
can afford to smile.
1946 K. S. Prichard *The Roaring Nineties* 214: 'I'm a sand-groper,' she
snapped . . . 'Don't know anything
about London or Paris.'
1963 Xavier Herbert *Disturbing Element* 2: The name Sand Groper measured the contempt of the easterners
for the comparative infertility of the
West and the social backwardness of
its first settlers.
1974 *Sunday Telegraph* 30 Jun. 36:
Mining millionaire Lang Hancock has
a sizeable number of sandgropers prepared to support his view that Western
Australia should be detached from the
rest of the nation.

sandy blight Name given to trachoma
or any kind of conjunctivitis, when the
eyes smart as though filled with sand
[1834 George Bennett *Wanderings in
New South Wales* i 302–3: There is an
affection of the eye . . . called by the
colonists the 'blight' . . . The integu-
ments surrounding the orbit were
puffed up so much, as totally to close
the eye, which was found much in-
flamed, as in acute opthalmia, and attended with symptoms, in some degree
similar, with severe itching and prick-
ing pain, as if sand had been lodged in
it, with a profuse flow of tears.]
1846 *Georgiana's Journal* ed. Hugh
McCrae (1966) 228: Cuts, splinter
wounds, boils, and sand-blight, have
been successfully treated.
1853 C. R. Read *What I Heard, Saw,
and Did at the Australian Goldfields*
43: The most disagreeable and painful
complaint, was a kind of opthalmia,
called sandy blight . . . The pain is most
excruciating, being as if the eyes were
filled with broken glass and sand, caus-
ing a great discharge.
1870 W. M. Finn *Glimpses of North-*

Eastern Victoria (1971) 35: The day I called [at the school] the 'sandy blight' was so prevalent that many children were absent.
1892 G. L. James *Shall I Try Australia?* 242: One pest of the bush and plains is 'Sandy Blight' or inflammation of the eyes – it is, I believe, called 'sandy' owing to the pain being exactly similar to that which grains of sand upon the eyeball could cause.

sanger A sandwich
1974 Jim McNeil *How Does Your Garden Grow* 26: 'Nothing like the old cheese sanger for a man on the go.'

sav Saveloy [abbr.]
1970 Patrick White *The Vivisector* 216: 'I bought a few savs I thought we'd do for supper.'

save, have a saver See quot. 1882 [f. *To make saver:* to insure against or compensate for a loss OED 1613 *obs.*]
c. **1882** *The Sydney Slang Dictionary* 7: *Save* To give part of one bet for part of another. A and B have backed different horses, and they agree that in the event of either one winning he shall give the other, say 5. This is called 'saving a fiver', and generally is done when scratchings and knockings-out have left the field so that one of the two speculators must be a winner. Form of hedging.
1891 Nat Gould *The Double Event* 123: 'Wells says Perfection will win,' said Lady Mayfield to Jack Marston, 'but I've put a saver on Caloola.'
1917 A. B. Paterson *Three Elephant Power* 17: 'I had a quid on,' he says. 'And,' (here he nerves himself to smile) 'I had a saver on the second, too.'
1958 Gavin Casey *Snowball* 168: A lot of people who had bet on Benny – and made sure of a saver on the Negro – put on a few shillings more at the ringside.

scale To practise some kind of fraud, obtain something without paying: now used most often of travelling on public transport without paying a fare [? f. *scale* to split off scales or flakes from (coin)

for purposes of fraud OED 1576]
1916 Arthur Wright *Under a Cloud* 32: 'How'd that happen,' asks Bill Odzon. 'Didn't think anyone could scale you.'
1933 Colin Wills *Rhymes of Sydney* 13: See the shoppers, toppers, tabs / Scalers by the score / Hopping off / Dropping off / Darting into shore.
1941 Baker 63: *Scale, to* To ride on a train, tram or bus without paying a fare: esp. to ride a tram footboard in this way . . . (2) To steal: to rob someone (3) To swindle a person, to take him down: to deceive. Whence, 'Scale 'em Corner', a George Street corner, near Central Station, Sydney, 'where appointments are made when one had no intention of keeping them.'
1950 Brian James *The Advancement of Spencer Button* 64: Boys who lived mostly on the streets, scaling on trams . . . selling papers, running messages.
1953 Dymphna Cusack *Southern Steel* 3: Bumping in on the back of the old steam trams, too often scaling on the footboards because he hadn't the money to pay the penny fare.
1975 *Sydney Morning Herald* 18 Oct. 18: Excitements not mentioned at home were scaling on trams and fighting with rival gangs.
scaler
1924 *Truth* 27 Apr. 6: *Scaler* A fraud.

school A two-up school, or any company of gamblers; a group of drinkers
[**1812** Vaux: *School* a party of persons met together for the purpose of gambling.]
1890 A. G. Hales *Wanderings of a Simple Child* 10: As I pushed my way through the throng, I at once perceived that 'school' was in.
1910 C. E. W. Bean *On the Wool Track* 226: A few sharpers with a slight knowledge of shearing often get into a big shed, and get a 'school' going – a nightly gamble.
1915 C. J. Dennis *The Songs of a Sentimental Bloke* 87: 'Come 'round an' try yer luck at Steeny's school.'
1929 Jules Raeside *Golden Days* 145: Among such a variety of men the gambling spirit was of course strong,

and regularly organised 'schools' were arranged.

1944 Alan Marshall *These are My People* 82: 'If I got into a school with some of these mugs round here they'd be penniless in two hours.'

1960 Donald McLean *The Roaring Days* 199: 'I want a few quid for th' school tonight, so don't be a bastard.'

1965 John Beede *They Hosed Them Out* 91: Lesser schools contented themselves with minor games of slippery sam, pontoon or black jack.

schoolie A schoolteacher

1907 Nathan Spielvogel *The Cocky Farmer* 33: The prettiest of all the girls was the schoolie, and didn't she lead the lads a dance.

1958 Gavin Casey *Snowball* 17: 'Tough type for a schoolie, he is.'

1966 Hal Porter *The Paper Chase* 118: The Tretheways are the only ones poor enough ... to accept a boarder. The schoolie always stays with them.

1974 Thea Astley *A Kindness Cup* 5: His cutaway donned for the occasion – running the bejesus out of a back-town schoolie – stank in the heat.

schooner A 15 oz. glass of beer in N.S.W., a 9 oz. glass in S.A. [f. *schooner* a tall glass of beer U.S. 1877 Mathews]

1939 Kylie Tennant *Foveaux* 52: The cries of 'Two of half and half', 'Schooner of new', 'Pint of old'.

1954 *Sydney Morning Herald* 8 Nov. 2: 'In Adelaide we call that a schooner' ... I expressed sympathy at such extreme myopia. 'A schooner, my friends, is a large glass,' I told him.

1967 B. K. Burton *Teach Them No More* 107: 'Just think of it – schooners of beer again, with white froth on the top, and cold all the way down your throat.'

scone hot See quot. 1941

1938 Xavier Herbert *Capricornia* 530: Halfcaste Shillingsworth goes Copra Co scone-hot!

1941 Baker 63: *Scone-hot* An intensive to describe great vigour of attack, scolding or speed. e.g., 'Go for someone scone-hot', to reprimand severely. (2)

Exorbitant, unreasonable. (3) Expert, proficient. e.g. 'He's scone-hot at shearing.'

1944 *Coast to Coast 1943* 116: 'I don't want Reg going me scone hot because his wife's not capable of looking after herself.'

1957 R. S. Porteous *Brigalow* 223: 'Look out fer 'im,' Mick yelled. ''E'll go ya, scone 'ot.'

1967 Kylie Tennant *Tell Morning This* 139: 'When my big brother Jim come home from work, he went Dad scone hot.'

1974 David Ireland *Burn* 136: 'When he finds out he'll go me scone-hot.'

scoot, on the On a spree [? f. *scoot* to go away hurriedly]

1924 *Truth* 27 Apr. 6: *Scoot* To clear out; also continued bout of drunkenness.

1936 Ion L. Idriess *The Cattle King* 131: 'I'm sorry to hear Eureka is on the scoot.' 'He's not. They don't go on the scoot out there. Thcy drink dynamite and bust.'

1946 Dal Stivens *The Courtship of Uncle Henry* 74: 'Doesn't he like her getting on the scoot?'

1962 Stuart Gore *Down the Golden Mile* 120: 'Make mine a glass this time, seein' I have to go on the scoot with you booze artists to-night.'

1975 Xavier Herbert *Poor Fellow My Country* 1019: 'We could've ... gone on a proper scoot.'

score between the posts Have intercourse with a woman [f. football]

1973 Alexander Buzo *Rooted* 89: 'Oh I get it, you're setting up for a naughty to-night, are you? ... Gunna score between the posts, are you?'

scrammy Nickname for a man with a defective hand or arm [f. E. dial. *scram* (*skram*) awkward; stiff, as if benumbed OED 1825]

1822 *HRA* x 776: A Man, who goes by the name of Scrummy Jack. [described by another deponent p. 775: 'he was a little Man, and has a dun or withered Arm']

1902 Barbara Baynton *Bush Studies* 44: Scrammy 'And [story title]
1906 A. B. Paterson *An Outback Marriage* 33: Scrammy Doyle (meaning Doyle with the injured arm).
1912 'Goorianawa' *Lone Hand* 1 Oct. 30 repr. in *Old Bush Songs* ed. Stewart and Keesing (1957) 273: And the sprees I've had with Scrammy Jack are more than I can count.

scrape *n. & v.* To copulate with
1959 Donald Stuart *Yandy* 4: Like Jessie, Larrian was ready to scrape with the whitefellers.
1969 Osmar White *Under the Iron Rainbow* 64: She said she didn't mind lying down for white men at three dollars a time . . . All the girls got scraped by someone . . . She'd give the old sergeant a scrape for free and he'd make things easy for her while she was in the lockup.
1975 Robert Macklin *The Queenslander* 43: 'We rolled her over on the beach and started scraping.'

scratch, be scratching To be struggling, in difficulty
1930 Vance Palmer *The Passage* (1944) 65: He and Bob had to scratch for a living the best way they could. Ibid. 160: 'We'll have to scratch for another year or two to pay off the new boat.'
1939 Kylie Tennant *Foveaux* 235: A preliminary boxer for a time, but now, as he said, 'scratching for a living.'
1953 T. A. G. Hungerford *Riverslake* 202: 'If his mob gets in next election they'll whip up a nice old depression, just like they did the last time, and we'll all be scratching for jobs again. The only difference is that there'll be a million or so of these bludgers scratching with us.'
1962 Alan Marshall *This is the Grass* 202: 'Not that I read much. I've been too busy scratching for a crust.'

screamer, two-pot Someone very susceptible to alcohol
1959 Dorothy Hewett *Bobbin Up* 21: 'Look at Lou. She's a two-pot screamer, always 'as been.'
1972 John de Hoog *Skid Row Dossier* 95: 'It says experienced and sober, ya bloody two-pot screamer.'

scrub, the Anywhere remote from civilization, or in expressions like 'head for the scrub', 'out in the scrub', any place to which one might abscond, or avoid contact with one's fellows [f. scrub as a wooded but inhospitable region: see quot. 1834]
[1834 J. D. Lang *A Historical and Statistical Account of New South Wales* i 354: In sterile regions, however, on rocky mountain-tracts, or on sandy plains, the forest degenerates into a miserable scrub, as the colonists term it; the trees are stunted in their growth and of most forbidding aspect.]
1956 Kylie Tennant *The Honey Flow* 270: If Col had won the toss and proposed first, I don't think it would have made any difference, except that Elsie might have taken to the scrub.
1959 David Forrest *The Last Blue Sea* 31: 'You see that bloke with the blue-an'-white arm-band comin', you 'ead f'r the scrub.'
1962 John Morrison *Twenty-Three* 194: 'You just get up in the morning, pack whatever you can lay hands on, and head for the scrub.'
1972 Peter Kenna *The Slaughter of St. Teresa's Day* 48: 'I'd arranged to ride in from the scrub and join Marty and the girls there.'
1976 *Australian* 9 Oct. 25: I have just spent a few relaxing weeks in the scrub – no offence meant – and have to report that Queensland offers a couple of items we could well do with down here, which is NSW.
see **mallee, mulga, tall timber**

scrub aristocracy People with social pretensions in 'the scrub'
1900 Henry Lawson 'The Hero of Redclay' *Prose* i 296: 'The banker, the storekeeper, one of the publicans, the butcher . . . the postmaster, and his toady, the lightning squirter, were the scrub-aristocracy.'

scrub bull A 'loner' (see quot. 1967) [cf. *scrubber*]

1966 Baker 82: Another synonym for *hatter* is *scrub bull*.

1967 Barry Oakley *A Wild Ass of a Man* 68: 'I'm different from the herd, and at that school they don't like the wanderers, the scrub bulls who forage for their nourishment in their own way, alone.'

1975 Xavier Herbert *Poor Fellow My Country* 702: The Scrub Bull, of all people, getting interested in settling the country.

scrubber A term for cattle that have run wild, or never been branded [f. *scrub*]

1859 Henry Kingsley *Recollections of Geoffry Hamlyn* ii 125: 'It's lucky you've got them [the cattle] cheap, for the half of them are off the ranges.' 'Scrubbers, eh?' said the Major.

1878 Rolf Boldrewood *An Australian Squire* repr. as *Babes in the Bush* (1900) 268: 'May the devil take ye for a cross-grained contrary brindle-hided straggling bastard of a scrubber'. [addressed to a heifer]

1898 W. H. Ogilvie *Fair Girls and Gray Horses* 55: And he loves the merry rattle of the stockwhip and the tramp / Of the cockhorned mulga scrubbers when they're breaking in the brush.

1911 E. S. Sorenson *Life in the Australian Backblocks* 126: A few quiet cattle are pastured in the open, near where the scrubbers water, to act as decoys. The scrubbers come out at night.

1955 Mary Durack *Keep Him My Country* 167: As the younger stockmen closed in around the scrubbers Benjamin took his place.

1961 George Farwell *Vanishing Australians* 29: 'Remember those wild-looking scrubbers we moonlighted?'

scrum Threepence: *obs.*

1902 Henry Lawson 'Send Round the Hat' *Prose* i 472: The crown was worn as thin as paper by the quids, half-quids, casers, bobs and tanners or sprats – to say nothing of the scrums – that had been chucked into it.

1941 Baker 64: *Scrum* A 3d piece.

Sea Eagles, the As for 'Eagles' q.v.

1975 *Bulletin* 9 Aug. 21: 'What would you do,' asked the notice [on a Manly church], 'if Jesus Christ came to Manly?' To which some Sea Eagle-fancier had replied: 'Play him in the centre alongside Fulton and move Branighan out to the wing.'

seagull A casual wharf labourer [f. the bird's habit of waiting for and swooping on scraps]

1965 Frank Hardy *The Yarns of Billy Borker* 115: 'He was a casual wharfie at the time I'm telling you about . . . and they call casuals 'seagulls'.

secko A sex pervert [abbr.]

1949 Ruth Park *Poor Man's Orange* 38: 'Just look at that dirty ole secko, will you?' he said disgustedly.

1961 Peter Mathers *Australian Letters* Jun. 48: It'll be like the city next. Seckoes everywhere.

1961 Frank Hardy *The Hard Way* 75: 'A secco', the Bush Lawyer whispered. 'Been flashing it . . .'

1969 William Dick *Naked Prodigal* 13: 'You look like you'd be the sorta bloke who'd take little kids down a lane and give 'em two bob, yuh bloody secko.'

1974 *Bulletin* 6 Apr. 45; 'I noticed Australians use a lot of diminutives, like Chrissie, pressie and journo.' 'In jails sex offenders are called seckos,' I told him.

see you later see **later**

send her down, Hughie see **Hughie**

septic A Yank [f. rhyming slang *septic tank* = *Yank*]

1976 *Cleo* Aug. 33: Even before R and R, Americans [at King's Cross] were septics (septic tanks - yanks). Septic is now general usage.

serve An adverse criticism, reprimand [? f. tennis, or serving a summons]

[**1812** Vaux: To *serve* a man, also sometimes signifies to maim, wound, or do him some bodily hurt, and to *serve* him *out and out*, is to kill him.]

1977 *Australian* 1 Jun. 3: He [John

Osborne] did manage to convey that he had a fairly miserable time in Australia, but he was glad to be leaving and he would be giving the country a serve in an unnamed English newspaper if it was willing to pay enough for his views. 1977 *Bulletin* 25 Jun. 3: He gives the ockers a big serve on Page 50.

session A period of steady drinking, in a group
1949 Lawson Glassop *Lucky Palmer* 215: 'I'll join you in a beer later, but I don't want to get into a session.'
1955 D'Arcy Niland *The Shiralee* 51: 'I don't want to make a session of it. I had a helluva night.'
1969 Christopher Bray *Blossom Like a Rose* 8: 'The pub's bin open five minutes! The session's begun!'
1973 H. Williams *My Love Had a Black Speed Stripe* 47: Back to work for the mugs and back to the Trades Hall and another grog session for Walters.

settler's cake See quot.
1843 Charles Rowcroft *Tales of the Colonies* iii 93: 'There's a real settler's cake for you, gentlemen, made nice and light, like a pancake, only it wants eggs and milk.'

settler's clock The kookaburra, or laughing jackass [see quot. 1827]
1827 P. Cunningham *Two Years in New South Wales* i 232: The loud and discordant noise of the *laughing jackass* (or *settler's clock*, as he is called), as he takes up his roost on the withered bough of one of our tallest trees, acquaints us that the sun has just dipped behind the hills ... Again the loud laughter of the *jackass* summons us to *turn out*, and take a peep at the appearance of the morning.
1847 L. Leichhardt *Journal of an Overland Expedition* 234: I usually rise when I hear the merry laugh of the laughing-jackass *(Dacelo gigantea)*, which, from its regularity, has not been unaptly named the settler's clock.
1856 G. Willmer *The Draper in Australia* 224: The settlers prize this bird very much and do not destroy it, as it not

only kills snakes, but rouses the inmates of the huts at day-break, while at night it is heard just as it is getting dark. From these circumstances it is called the settler's clock.
1873 A. Trollope *Australia* ed. Edwards and Joyce (1967) 210: The laughing jack-ass ... is also called the settler's clock.
1919 E. S. Sorenson *Chips and Splinters* 82: 'The Settlers' Clock', as the settlers know, / Was only a kookaburra.
1943 *The Swagman's Note-book* ed. Charles Barrett 14: 'Settler's clock' may have been used in the early days, it has long been obsolete as a name for our laughing cavalier in feathers.

settler's friend Stringy bark and greenhide
1856 G. Willmer *The Draper in Australia* 216–17: The bark is fibrous, and being very tough, it was a few years ago looked upon as the settler's friend; even now it is much used for tying purposes, and in the absence of rope it certainly is still a capital substitute. It is no uncommon thing still to hear men in the bush speak of this bark and the green hide (the latter is used for halters) as the settler's friend.

settler's matches See quot.
1891 Henry Lawson 'The Shanty on the Rise' *Verse* i 156: And we walked so very silent – being lost in reverie –/ That we heard the 'settlers matches' gently rustle on the tree. *settlers matches. The thin loose bark hanging on the trunks of white box, ash, and other smooth barks.

seven, throw a To die; to faint; to have a vomiting attack [f. six as the maximum score marked on dice]
1894 Henry Lawson 'Martin Farrell' *Verse* i 269: 'I am pretty crook and shaky – too far gone for hell or heaven, / An' the chances are I'm goin' – to "do the seven".'
1898 *Bulletin* 17 Dec. Red Page: If anyone dies it is known as *throwing the seven.*
1908 *The Australian Magazine* 1 Nov.

1250: Instead of dying you can 'chuck a seven'.
1919 W. H. Downing *Digger Dialects* 49: *Throw a seven* Die. (Probably arose from dicing. It is impossible to throw a seven-spot.)
1926 L. C. E. Gee *Bushtracks and Goldfields* 32: They all reckoned that it was touch and go with me, that I was a 'goner', that I was bound to 'throw a seven'.
1932 A. W. Upfield *A Royal Abduction* 201: 'If she sees the thing she won't scream and throw a seven [faint]. She'll shoot.'
1958 Vince Kelly *The Greedy Ones* 104: 'Throwing a seven?' 'Collapsing – having a fit – fainting.'
1966 Tom Ronan *Once There Was a Bagman* 217: The partially digested fruit must have swollen inside me, for before long I was chucking sevens around the flat as I had done a few years before when I had that touch of ptomaine poisoning.

shag on a rock, like a Isolated, deserted, exposed [OED records *wet as a shag* 1835]
1845 R. Howitt *Impressions of Australia Felix* 233: 'Poor as a bandicoot', 'miserable as a shag on a rock' &c.; these and others I very frequently heard them make use of.
1929 Jules Raeside *Golden Days* 16: The flood waters did not subside, and we were there like three shags on a rock.
1942 Gavin Casey *It's Harder for Girls* 216: There are plenty of people in the street, but it's no good roosting in the gutter like a shag on a rock.
1952 T. A. G. Hungerford *The Ridge and the River* 53: 'I got no time to be standin' here like a flamin' shag on a rock!'
1960 John Iggulden *The Storm of Summer* 100: 'We're stuck here like a shag on a rock until we get the net up, aren't we?'
1971 David Ireland *The Unknown Industrial Prisoner* 275: 'It's easy enough to curse England. Leaving us out here like a shag on a rock, but I don't apologize for being British.'

shake To steal [f. *shake out* to rob OED c. 1412]
[1812 Vaux: *Shake* to steal, or rob.]
1854 W. Shaw *The Land of Promise* 33: There commenced a torrent of interrogation, mostly in slang, 'what's he shook?' 'has he sloped?' and other flash phrases.
1869 *The Australian Journal* Jul. 685: *To shake* To steal. *Shook* Stole.
1889 Rolf Boldrewood *Nevermore* (1892) 77: 'What the blazes has a chap like that any call to shake a horse for?'
1906 Joseph Furphy *Rigby's Romance* ed. R. G. Howarth (1946) 251: 'What's come o' them two black horses o' yours?' 'Gone.' 'Sold?' 'Shook.'
1924 *Truth* 27 Apr. 6: *Shook* Stolen.
1935 Kylie Tennant *Tiburon* 198: 'I shook a tin o' petrol from Pearson's garage last night,' he said under his breath.
1965 Patrick White *Four Plays* 105: 'You don't think I'd shake anything off Ern? 'E's my mate!'

shanghai A catapult [f. *shangan* (*shangie*) A stick cleft at one end for putting on a dog's tail EDD]
1863 *The Leader* 24 Oct. 17: Turn, turn thy shangay dread aside, / Nor touch that little bird. [Morris]
1900–10 O'Brien and Stephens: *Shanghai* boy's catapult.
1910 H. H. Richardson *The Getting of Wisdom* 205: Home was, alas! no longer the snug nest in which she was safe from the slings and shanghais of the world.
1934 Vance Palmer *Sea and Spinifex* 94: 'No you don't want to trouble about the likes of them. Unless it's to go after them with a shanghai.'
1941 Sarah Campion *Mo Burdekin* 292: *Shanghai* Catapult.
1957 R. S. Porteous *Brigalow* 204: He gave a guilty start rather like a small boy stretching his shanghai for a trial shot at the family cat!
1965 William Dick *A Bunch of Ratbags* 130: I went back to making my new shanghai.

shanty A public house, esp. unlicensed; a 'sly-grog shop' [OED] [f. the structure so called]

1864 J. Rogers *New Rush* 52: The Keepers of the stores and shanties grieve.

1875 A. J. Boyd *Old Colonials* (1882) 103: The Grog Shanty [chapter title]

1880 Rolf Boldrewood *The Miner's Right* (1890) 64: Any attempt to limit the licensing produced such a crop of 'shanties' or sly-grogshops.

1894 Henry Lawson 'The Spooks of Long Gully' *Prose* i 249: The son did die that night in the 'horrors' in a shanty.

sharkbait(er) Someone who swims further out than the other surfers, as though tempting the sharks

1912 Arthur Wright *Rung In* 34–5: It might be only some foolhardy 'shark baiter' as he heard the more venturesome of the bathers termed.

1920 A. H. Adams *The Australians* 177: Farther out in the deep water swam the venturous line of experts, technically known as 'shark-bait'.

1930 *Bulletin* 13 Aug. 45: By swimming past the first line of breakers Alma had declared herself to be that disquieting disturber of peace, a shark-baiter.

1941 Baker 65: *Sharkbait* A swimmer, esp. one who swims out beyond the breakers.

1951 Dymphna Cusack and Florence James *Come in Spinner* 221: 'Why didn't you come out with me?' 'Not me. I've given up shark-baiting. Mug's game.'

1967 K. S. Prichard *Subtle Flame* 99: 'I'm no good at shark baiting!'

Sharks, the The Cronulla-Sutherland Rugby League team, N.S.W. [f. club emblem, and proximity of Cronulla to the sea]

1975 *Sydney Morning Herald* 21 Jul. 13: Rogers kicks Sharks home.

sharp, so ~ as to cut oneself A reproof of over-cleverness

1903 Joseph Furphy *Such is Life* (1944) 278: 'Gosh! you've been on the turkey; you'll be cutting yourself some of these times.'

1910 H. H. Richardson *The Getting of Wisdom* 142: 'If you're so sharp you'll cut yourself!'

1957 Randolph Stow *The Bystander* 123: 'You'll cut yourself one day, you're so sharp.'

sharpie Member of a teenage cult with 'short back and sides' haircut, the counterpart of the English 'skinhead'

1965 William Dick *A Bunch of Ratbags* 202: The more a sharpie protested he was not a bodgie, the more they [the police] laughed and belted him.

1972 *Sydney Morning Herald* 20 Jan. 2: It was alleged in evidence that Still died during an incident involving 'sharpies' and 'long-hairs' outside Greystanes Progress Hall.

1975 *Sun-Herald* 13 Apr. 7: A sharpie is usually aged between 14 and 19 years. The boys wear their hair cropped short on the top and sides and longer at the back. The girls often wear 'dolly' makeup and have their ears pierced. Tattoos are often worn by both sexes. The sharpies wear blue jeans or high-waisted slacks supported by old-fashioned braces, matched with a tee shirt and sometimes a woollen cardigan . . . They usually keep well clear of the beachside suburbs, the home of their arch-enemies, the surfies.

she's apples, jake, sweet see **apples, jake, sweet**

shears, off (the) Used of sheep just shorn

1896 Thomas W. Heney *The Girl at Birrell's* 69: Now and again a buyer visited the stations to get cheap sheep 'off shears'.

1903 Joseph Furphy *Such is Life* (1944) 64: I camped with a party of six . . . bound for Deniliquin, with 3,000 Boolka wethers off the shears.

1964 Tom Ronan *Packhorse and Pearling Boat* 147: It [the shearing shed] had never been used. The sheep had arrived off-shears and had been promptly annihilated by the depredations of meat-hungry aboriginals.

shed A shearing shed

1857 F. Cooper *Wild Adventures in Australia* 105: 'He was bound for the shearing through New England. By this time, most likely, he has set in at some of the sheds on the Namoi.'

1902 Henry Lawson 'Two Sundowners' *Prose* i 96: The number of men employed is according to the size of the shed – from three to five men in the little bough-covered shed of the small 'cockatoo', up to a hundred and fifty or two hundred hands all told in the big corrugated iron machine shed of a pastoral company.

1908 E. S. Sorenson *Quinton's Rouseabout* 24: Towards the end of winter crowds of men passed through on their way to the early sheds.

1919 W. K. Harris *Outback in Australia* 153: Shearing has to be stopped for two or three days, and instructions must be promptly forwarded to the men in charge of the sheep on their way to the 'shed' to camp temporarily.

1934 F. E. Baume *Burnt Sugar* 249: 'You might be a shed hand or just a hobo.'

sheila A girl or woman. Not derogatory, although no woman would refer to herself as a 'sheila' [f. *Sheela* as generic name for an Irish girl, counterpart of *Paddy* for a man]

[1828 *Monitor* 22 Mar. 1053: Many a piteous Shela stood wiping the gory locks of her Paddy, until released from that duty by the officious interference of the knight of the *baton*.

1859 Hotten 90: *Shaler* a girl.

1910 P. W. Joyce *English as We Speak it in Ireland* 320: *Sheela* a female Christian name ... Used in the South as a reproachful name for a boy or man inclined to do work or interest himself in affairs properly belonging to women.]

1895 Cornelius Crowe *The Australian Slang Dictionary* 72: *Shaler* a girl.

1885–1914 'The Spider by the Gwydir' *Australian Ballads* ed. Russel Ward (1964) 122: And he bit that rookin' sheila on the stern./Then the sheila raced off squealin',/And her clothes she was un-peelin':/To hear her yells

would make you feel forlorn.

1919 W. H. Downing *Digger Dialects* 44: *Sheila* A girl.

1928 Arthur Wright *A Good Recovery* 117: 'Leave the sheilas alone, they're sure to pool a man sooner or later.'

1931 Vance Palmer *Separate Lives* 220: 'There was a sheelah back in Salisbury who did her block on me,' Chook was saying.

1949 Lawson Glassop *Lucky Palmer* 28: 'Not married yet, eh?' Lucky laughed. 'Do I look like a mug?' he asked ... 'Sheilas don't interest me. They're not worth a bumper.'

1958 Christopher Koch *The Boys in the Island* 69: 'Should get on to some sheilas out there too. You want to come?'

1965 Patrick White *Four Plays* 111: 'We used to lie and talk about what we was goin' ter eat. An' the sheilas we was goin' ter do.'

1973 H. Williams *My Love Had a Black Speed Stripe* 17: Beats me how any bloke can enjoy himself talking with women. Sheila talk has always driven me up the wall.

1975 *Australian* 22 Sep. 1: Fat, lazy and going to seed ... That's yer spoilt Ocker sheila.

shelf *n. & v.* An informer; to inform upon [? to put away on a shelf]

1926 J. Vance Marshall *Timely Tips for New Australians: Shelf* A slang word denoting an informer.

1953 T. A. G. Hungerford *Riverslake* 20: 'If you spoil this one I damn well will shelf you.'

1958 Vince Kelly *The Greedy Ones* 104: 'We were mates in this affair and you don't shelf your mates. And anyone who does shelf a mate has got to take what's coming to him.'

she-oak Colonial beer; *obs.* [? f. the native oak, a species of casuarina, and *oak* = cask]

1873 J. C. F. Johnson *Christmas on Carringa* 1: Able to put away at a sitting a larger quantity of colonial 'sheoak' than any man of his inches.

1881 G. C. Evans *Stories told round the Campfire* 17: 'Perhaps so,' he remarked,

'but when a man expects a drink of brandy, it is a great sell to find it is only sheoak.'
1893 J. A. Barry *Steve Brown's Bunyip* 282: Hastily finishing his pint of 'sheoak'.
1899 W. T. Goodge *Hits! Skits! and Jingles!* 125: We scorned the foreign yolk, / And much preferred she-oak, / And stuck to beer.

shepherd To hold a mining claim without working it, in order to deny others; (sporting) to ward off a player tackling a member of one's own team
1855 William Howitt *Land, Labour and Gold* i 172: It is common practice for them to mark out one or more claims in each new rush . . . But only one claim at a time is legal and tenable. This practice is called shepherding.
1965 Frank Hardy *The Yarns of Billy Borker* 21: 'Did the players in the other team run across and stop him?' 'No fear, his team mates shepherded them off.'

shepherd's companion The willy wagtail
1870 E. B. Kennedy *Four Years in Queensland* 117: The 'shepherd's companion' is a species of water wagtail exceedingly tame, and frequenting the most desolate parts of the bush.
1908 W. H. Ogilvie *My Life in the Open* 5: Round and round your horse's feet flutters the black wagtail, the 'shepherd's companion' of the Bush, flying on ahead, then waiting or fluttering back.

sherbet Beer: *jocular*
1917 Henry Lawson 'Romani' *Verse* iii 214: And beer that *we* called 'sherbet'.
1965 John Beede *They Hosed Them Out* 204: At mid-day I hit myself with a few sherbets.
1973 Fred Archer *The Treasure House* 18: He had a strident voice and with a few sherbets under his belt you knew he was about.

shicer A mining claim that proves unproductive; a swindler (shyster) [G.

scheisser and English (see quot. 1859) and U.S. slang (*shyster* 1846 Mathews)]
[**1859** Hotten *Shice*, nothing; 'to do anything for *shice*', to get no payment. The term was first used by the Jews in the last century . . . *Shicer*, a mean man, a humbug, a 'duffer', – a worthless person, one who will not work.]
1855 Raffaello Carboni *The Eureka Stockade* ed. G. Serle (1969) 8: The whole flat turned out an imperial shicer.
Ibid. 14: A hole was bottomed down the gully, and proved a scheisser.
1858 *Thatcher's Colonial Songster* 66: T'other day a German friend of ours, / His name is Mister Kaiser, / Blushed like a girl of sixteen, / When I mentioned the word '*shicer*'.
1867 J. R. Houlding *Australian Capers* 127: The hole was no good, or what they called a 'shicer'.
1885 *The Australasian Printers' Keepsake* 64: 'In the opening once or twice, sir, / You'll be reckon'd as a shycer.'
Ibid. 71: 'He was full up of such a shicin' practice.'
1898 Morris: *Shicer* (2) A man who does not pay his debts of honour.
1958 Jack Lindsay *Life Rarely Tells* 213: 'There's nothing I hate more'n a shicer.'

shick, shickered, shickery Drunk [Yiddish]
[**1859** Hotten: *Shickery*, shabby, badly]
1878 Rolf Boldrewood *An Australian Squire* repr. as *Babes in the Bush* (1900) 121: 'I'm always that fresh after a good night's sleep, when I've had a bit of a spree that I could begin again quite flippant. Old Tom had a goodish cheque this time, and was at it a week afore I came in. He was rayther shickerry.'
1898 *Bulletin* 17 Dec. Red Page: *shiker* drunk.
1911 Louis Stone *Jonah* 124: 'Whose cart is it?' inquired Pinkey. 'Jack Ryan's,' answered Chook, ''e's bin shickered since last We'n'sday, an' I'm takin' it round fer 'is missis 'an the kids.'
1915 C. J. Dennis *The Songs of a Sentimental Bloke* 81: 'E'd 'ad a couple, but 'e wasn't shick.

1922 Arthur Wright *A Colt from the Country* 44: 'He's half dead, anyhow,' declared Farvall, 'and he's shikkered as well.'
1945 Gavin Casey *Downhill is Easier* 9: They sat outside the pub in the sun every day, and most of them got a bit shickered on pension day.
1961 Patrick White *Riders in the Chariot* 261: 'I'm gunna get out of this!' he announced at last. 'I'm gunna get shickered stiff!'
1973 *Sydney Morning Herald* 25 Oct. 2: A backbench senator referred today to the Jackson Pollock painting, 'Blue Poles' bought by Australia for $1.3 million as 'shicker art' . . . Later outside the Senate he said that by 'shicker art' he meant paintings done by people who were shickered, or drunk.

shicker *n.* Liquor
1916 C. J. Dennis *The Moods of Ginger Mick* 154: *Shicker* Intoxicating liquor.
1928 Arthur Wright *A Good Recovery* 85: 'Yes, I've been on the shikker,' he answered huskily.
1945 Roy Rene *Mo's Memoirs* 49: One night the magician had been on the shicker, and with a fine disregard for life and limb he let the lion out.
1958 H. D. Williamson *The Sunlit Plain* 58: 'He was on the shicker when I was there last week.'

shicker *v.* To drink, get drunk
1913 Henry Lawson 'Benno and his Old 'Uns' *Prose* i 805: Her Old 'Un 'shickered' till he got 'mucked' every pay day.
1924 *Truth* 27 Apr. 6: *Shicker* To drink.
1951 Dymphna Cusack and Florence James *Come in Spinner* 33: 'He'd gamble his shirt off on any damn thing that's got a leg to run on, but he doesn't shicker.'

shilling in, a As for 'a bob in' q.v.
1942 Gavin Casey *It's Harder for Girls* 83: We had another shilling in, and bought some bottles to take to the restaurant.

shingle short, a Weak in the head

[variant of the English 'a tile loose']
1852 G. C. Mundy *Our Antipodes* iii 17: The climate is productive . . . of chronic diseases rather than acute ones. Let no man having, in colonial phrase, 'a shingle short' try this country. He will pass his days in Tarban Creek Asylum.
1869 *Australian Journal* Jul. 685: A *shingle short* The colonial rendering of the English phrase, 'A tile loose'.
1881 Mrs Campbell Praed *Policy and Passion* 173: 'I have heard Lady Dolph say that I have "a shingle loose".'
1895 Henry Lawson 'The Fate of the Fat Man's Son' *Verse* i 280: The Fat Man's son was an Anarchist, a couple of shingles short.
1908 Henry Fletcher *Dads and Dan between Smokes* 65: So ther balmy cove takes to solitude an' ther bush quite natural. That 'counts fer some o' them, ther extra special shingle-shorters.
1928 Miles Franklin *Up the Country* 9: 'The only time I ever saw her, she seemed a shingle short.'
1941 Charles Barrett *Coast of Adventure* 15: 'A shingle short? Not much.'
1966 Patrick White *The Solid Mandala* 82: He accepted Arthur his twin brother, who was, as they put it, a shingle short.

shinplaster A promissory note issued by bush storekeepers and others, and used as a kind of currency. The name 'shinplaster' was often associated with the brittleness of the paper, which meant that the notes would disintegrate before they were cashed [U.S. 1824 Mathews]
1952 G. C. Mundy *Our Antipodes* i 163: Paper, for the most trifling sums, is current in the provinces, like 'shin plasters' in America. A great many more of these flimsy representatives of bullion than are really requisite are issued. It is averred . . . that certain large proprietors make a practice of paying wages by orders, written purposely on small and thin scraps of paper, and that they pocket many hundreds a year by the loss or destruction of these frail liabilities in the hands of rough, careless and unsober

characters.

1888 E. Finn *Chronicles of Early Melbourne* ii 546: These orders came to be known as 'Sticking Plasters', but I never could see the applicability of the phrase ... The landlord no sooner clutched the 'plaster' than he had it changed for cash.

1919 E. S. Sorenson *Chips and Splinters* 33: In that part the common mediums of exchange were cheques and shinplasters. Bank notes were rare, and a sovereign was a novelty.

1929 Sir Hal Colebatch *A Story of a Hundred Years* 458: A practice very generally in vogue up to the early nineties, when an order on Monger of York or Throssell of Northam was accepted with greater alacrity than a sovereign; a practice that still maintains throughout the Kimberleys, where there is no bank north of Broome, land where the 'shin-plasters' of Connor, Doherty, and Durack, and of many hotel and storekeepers, form the regularly accepted currency.

1937 Ernestine Hill *The Great Australian Loneliness* 329: *Shin-plaster* Bush currency, credit chits issued by an outpost storekeeper.

1956 Tom Ronan *Moleskin Midas* 264: He baked all his shin-plasters in the oven so that half of them would fall to pieces before they were cashed.

1974 *Australian* 27 Dec. 7: He pulls out an old shinplaster he picked up on a trip through Hall's Creek. It was a sort of personal printed postal note storekeepers and the like used to give when there was a shortage of coins and notes of the realm. This one was dated November 1, 1936, and signed Robert R. Smith.

shiralee A swag: rare until used as a title of novel by D'Arcy Niland

1892 Gilbert Parker *Round the Compass in Australia* 49: 'Let him down easy and slow ... Drop in his shirallee and water-bag by him.'

1898 Morris: *Shirallee* slang term for a swag or bundle of blankets.

1941 Baker: *Shiralee* A bluey or swag.

1955 D'Arcy Niland *The Shiralee* [book title]

shirtlifter A male homosexual

1966 Baker 216: *shirt lifter* a sodomite.

1974 Barry Humphries *Bulletin* 19 Jan. 13: When I first seen them photos of him in his 'Riverina Rig' I took him for an out-of-work ballet dan₁ ᵔr some kind of shirtlifter.

shivoo A party, celebration, esp. if noisy [f. *shivoo (shebo)* a disturbance, 'row', shindy EDD]

1849 Alexander Harris *The Emigrant Family* (1967) 62: A 'Shiveau' at the Hut.

1889 John I. Hunt *Hunt's Book of Bonanzas* 82: 'Y'see, Jones had been to a lodge night shivoo, and he and the boys had a gay old time, you bet.'

1896 Thomas W. Heney *The Girl at Birrell's* 150: 'I wan' to know 'ow many's to be 'ere at the shivoo.'

1908 Henry Fletcher *Dads and Dan between Smokes* 56: A real tip-top Rookwood shivoo is worth a terrace o' houses to ther undertakers.

1919 W. H. Downing *Digger Dialects* 16: *Chivoo* A celebration.

1926 K. S. Prichard *Working Bullocks* 14: 'There's a shivoo at Marritown,' he cried teasingly. 'Me and Red's thinkin' of going on in.'

1939 Miles Franklin and Dymphna Cusack *Pioneers on Parade* 84: 'Do you think you'll be fit for another shivoo to-morrow?'

1959 Xavier Herbert *Seven Emus* 13: One of those bush shivoos where a great deal of energy is stamped out in bucolic frolic and as much poured back in the form of alcohol.

1970 Patrick White *The Vivisector* 625: On the morning after the big shivoo at the State Gallery.

shook on, to be To be enthusiastic about, infatuated with

1882 Rolf Boldrewood *Robbery Under Arms* (World's Classics 1949) 87: 'I am regular shook on this old moke.' Ibid. 602: When he saw how handy I was in the yard he got quite shook on me.

1901 Henry Lawson 'Joe Wilson's

Courtship' *Prose* i 546–7: He was supposed to be shook after Mary too.
1916 C. J. Dennis *The Moods of Ginger Mick* 154: *Shook on* Infatuated.
1926 K. S. Prichard *Working Bullocks* 301: 'What's took Deb?' Mrs Pennyfather exclaimed . . . 'Didn't know she was so shook on Mark Smith.'
1957 Ray Lawler *Summer of the Seventeenth Doll* 31: 'She's not too shook on the whole thing.'
1965 Patrick White *Four Plays* 117: 'She got shook on these vitamins they write about in the magazines.'
1975 *Sunday Telegraph* 29 Jun. 49: Like Chappell, I'm not all that shook on cocktail parties myself.

shoot it, if it moves see **moves**

shoot through As for 'go through' q.v.
1951 Seaforth Mackenzie *Dead Men Rising* 37: 'I'm shooting through – my woman's sick and I've waited longer than I should have.'
1957 Randolph Stow *The Bystander* 191: 'Just shoot through, son, and leave us to settle this.'
1962 John Morrison *Twenty-Three* 181: 'And – let us have it in plain Australian – while he was taking the call you shot through.'
1970 Richard Beilby *No Medals for Aphrodite* 233: 'You can shoot through on your own if you like, but I'm going to get her to Athens somehow.'
see **Bondi tram**

Shop, the The University of Melbourne
1889–90 *Centennial Magazine* ii 218: It related how 'a medical student came up to the Shop' as a freshman, and 'thought through his exams. he would speedily pop.'
1902 Louis Esson let. to A. G. Stephens (Mitchell Library MS A1926): In certain quarters, not so very far distant from the University Wilson Hall, you are decidedly unpopular. I have had many an argument at the 'Shop', regarding the R. Page.
1918 Geoffrey Wall *Letters of an Airman* 15: I would be quite glad to get the Shop exam. results. They are generally published in a big list in 'The Argus' about January.
1941 Baker 66: *Shop, the* Melbourne University. Student's slang.
1964 George Johnston *My Brother Jack* 260: 'The years at the Shop gave me nothing except a worthless B.A. and the privilege of being thrown into the University lake.'

short of a sheet of bark see **bark**

short, a shingle see **shingle**

shot At the end of one's tether [? f. shooting one's bolt]
1945 Gavin Casey *Downhill is Easier* 183: It was eight miles along the track to the Bordertown road, and late at night you could easily walk the twelve miles along that to Bordertown without seeing a vehicle. I realized I was shot.

shot, have a shot at To try to 'get at' or 'take a rise' out of someone [f. *shot* a remark aimed at someone, esp. in order to wound OED 1841]
1915 K. S. Prichard *The Pioneers* 150: He was working for a shot at Donald Cameron through Young Davey.
1945 John Morrison *Sailors Belong Ships* 38: Mick, standing in the square, can't resist a shot at Beck. 'You were a long time making up your mind about this!' he yells.
1952 T. A. G. Hungerford *The Ridge and the River* 31: He was a sour bastard at times, and closed like a clam if he suspected that a man was having a shot at him.
1969 William Dick *Naked Prodigal* 46: 'You should know, Kenny. Yuh ain't worked much this year,' said Raincoat, having a shot at me.
1971 Keith Willey *Boss Drover* 28: We all knew him as Alec. If you called him 'Sir Alexander' he would reckon you were having a shot at him.
1975 Xavier Herbert *Poor Fellow My Country* 1103: It was typical of Jeremy to have that shot at Finnucane. Still, it was done with a grin.

shot, that's the Expression of approval

1953 T. A. G. Hungerford *Riverslake* 143: 'That's the shot – buy a bit of land, and grow things.'
1963 Jon Cleary *A Flight of Chariots* 370: 'I think a good strong cuppa brew would be the shot.'
1970 Jessica Anderson *The Last Man's Head* 201: 'That's the shot,' said Stock with intimate approbation. 'You're doing a good job. Keep it up.'
1976 David Ireland *The Glass Canoe* 227: 'That's the shot,' said Mick. 'Stick around and guard the place.'

shouse A lavatory [abbr. of *shithouse*]
1941 Baker 66: *Shouse* A privy.
1951 Dal Stivens *Jimmy Brockett* 214: I seen that now as plain as a country shouse although I didn't like it when she told me so.
1963 Hal Porter *The Watcher on the Cast-Iron Balcony* 56: The weatherboard dunny for which the modish names of the period include such as Aunt Mary, Houses of Parliament, the Little House, Down-the-back, Lavvy and Shouse.
1968 Thomas Keneally *Three Cheers for the Paraclete* 84: 'I'd like some trees on it, pines, and gums, so you don't have to see your neighbour's shouse first thing each morning.'
1971 David Ireland *The Unknown Industrial Prisoner* 82: 'Anyone seen Terrazzo?' 'Probably in the shouse.'
1975 Les Ryan *The Shearers* 98: Dewlap, who had been standing at the back of the ring, all alone like a country s'house, now sidled up.

shout *v.* To buy drinks for others, or to stand any similar 'treat' [f. *to stand shot* to meet the expenses, pay the bill (for all) OED 1821; *shot* the charge, reckoning OED 1475]
1855 Raffaello Carboni *The Eureka Stockade* ed. G. Serle (1969) 92: 'You shouted nobblers round for all hands – that's all right; it's no more than fair and square now for the boys to shout for you.'
1864 *Thatcher's Colonial Minstrel* 104: At ten o'clock we'd then toss up to see who was to shout.

1876 A. J. Boyd *Old Colonials* (1882) 268–9: This 'shouting', as 'treating' is termed in the colonies, is the curse of the Northern goldfields. If you buy a horse you must shout, the vendor must shout, and the bystanders who have been shouted to must shout in their turn.
1899 Henry Lawson 'The Stranger's Friend' *Verse* i 369: For he'd shout the stranger a suit of clothes, and he'd pay for the stranger's board.
1917 A. B. Paterson ' "Shouting" for a Camel' *Saltbush Bill* 48: And there's plenty human camels who, before they'll see you waste it, / Will drink up all you pay for if you're fool enough to shout.
1924 *Truth* 27 Apr. 6: *Shout* To buy a drink.
1939 Kylie Tennant *Foveaux* 140: Any time Tommy tried to shout the family to the picture show there was a unanimous firm refusal.
1958 H. D. Williamson *The Sunlit Plain* 11: 'You'd better cash a cheque for me, Mick. I'd like to shout for the mob, too. This one's on me, you blokes.'
1969 William Dick *Naked Prodigal* 75: 'Like to come and have a beer with me? I'll shout.'

shout *n.* 1 A free drink, or free round of drinks
[1853] *Letters from Victorian Pioneers* ed. T. F. Bride (1898) 127: On regaining his senses . . . he applies to the landlord, who tells him that he is in debt; that the £60 is expended. On asking how – 'How?' repeats the host, 'do you forget the shout you stood – the shout for all hands?'
1860 Charles Thatcher *The Victorian Songster* Part 5 149: For they did me brown for half-a-crown, / The price of that 'ere shout.
1877 Rolf Boldrewood *A Colonial Reformer* (1890) 421: I threw my money about – must have a round of drinks for luck. I never saw a publican yet that could refuse to serve a 'shout'.
1890 Henry Lawson 'The Glass on the Bar' *Verse* i 69: 'We owe him a shout – leave the glass on the bar.'

2 One's turn to buy drinks; in the expression 'my shout', the acceptance of this or any similar expense

1902 Henry Lawson 'Send Round the Hat' *Prose* i 472: He was almost a teetotaller, but he stood his shout in reason.

1911 Louis Stone *Jonah* 101: Chook cried out, ''Ere, 'arf a mo' – this is my shout!' They were near the ice-cream stall, where trade was brisk.

1923 Jack Moses *Beyond the City Gates* 100: 'Have a drink?' 'No,' said Jones, 'it's my shout.'

1946 Dal Stivens *The Courtship of Uncle Henry* 197: We all drank together and ordered again. It was my shout.

1954 Seaforth Mackenzie *The Refuge* 16: 'Come up and have a cup of coffee – my shout.'

1974 John Powers *The Last of the Knucklemen* 22: 'I'll drink to that. Whose shout?'

show '(Now only U.S. and Austral.) An opportunity for displaying or exerting oneself; a chance, "opening". Phr. *to give* (a person) *a show*; *to have* or *stand a* (or *no*) *show*' (OED): obsolescent

1876 Rolf Boldrewood *A Colonial Reformer* (1890) 183: As he's a gentleman, he's bound to give you a show.

1893 Henry Lawson *Letters* 54: I could not get a show in Auckland, so I spent my last pound to come down here.

1901 *The Bulletin Reciter* 97: But he still thought they'd a kind of show if only the food would last.

1906 Joseph Furphy *Rigby's Romance* ed. R. G. Howarth (1946) 258: 'I stand a good show, if there's a vacancy.

shower A dust-storm, in such expressions as 'Bedourie shower', 'Darling shower', 'Wilcannia shower' [f. placenames]

1898 Morris: *Darling Shower* A local name in the interior of Australia, and especially on the River Darling, for a dust storm, caused by cyclonic winds.

1903 Joseph Furphy *Such is Life* (1944) 331: The steady intensity of the shower augmented as I went on . . . the air was thick with skipping crumbs of hard

dirt, which rattled on my skull like hail; in fact, everything not anchored to the ground was at racing speed, and all in the same direction. Ibid. 361: Here was the true key to the Wilcannia shower.

1924 *Truth* 27 Apr. 6: *Darling shower* – A dust-storm in Riverina.

1933 A. B. Paterson *The Animals Noah Forgot* (1970) 38: Nature visits the settlers' sins / With the Bogan shower, that is mostly dust.

1936 Ion L. Idriess *The Cattle King* 195: 'That Bedourie shower yesterday was a beauty. There must have been thousands of tons of dust flying through the air.'

1961 George Farwell *Vanishing Australians* 174: A Darling dust storm – a 'Wilcannia shower', as they used to be called.

shower (rain), I didn't come down in the last A claim to a larger share of experience and shrewdness than one is being credited with

1906 Joseph Furphy *Rigby's Romance* ed. R. G. Howarth (1946) 256: '*He* didn't come down with the las' rain. Pity that sort o' bloke ever dies.'

1944 Lawson Glassop *We Were the Rats* 51: 'Listen, Mr Wilkerson,' I says, 'I'm awake-up, I am. Ya doan need ter come that stuff with me. I didden come down in the last shower.'

1951 Frank Hardy *Power Without Glory* 259: 'It's no use lying to me, Arty,' John West said. 'I didn't come down in the last shower.'

1962 Alan Seymour *The One Day of the Year* 56: 'How did you know?' 'I didn't come down in the last shower.'

1971 Barbara Vernon *A Big Day at Bellbird* 135: 'I didn't come down in the last shower, and neither did you.'

shrewdie A shrewd person [abbr. of *shrewd head*]

[1915 C. J. Dennis *The Songs of a Sentimental Bloke* 43: Now, this 'ere gorspil bloke's a fair shrewd 'ead.]

1916 Arthur Wright *Under a Cloud* 35: 'Look here, Wilson, you're not such a shrewdie as you imagine.'

1919 W. H. Downing *Digger Dialects* 45: *Shrewdy* See *shrewd head. Shrewd head* A cunning person.
1945 *Coast to Coast 1944* 85: He nudged Sam. 'A shrewdie, this bloke, eh? You can tell by his dial.'
1958 Gavin Casey *Snowball* 19: The young shrewdies sometimes seemed to have an uncanny knack of summing certain things up.
1969 Sir Arthur Fadden *They Called Me Artie* 13: A syndicate of Mackay shrewdies figured in another picturesque incident.
1975 Xavier Herbert *Poor Fellow My Country* 365–6: Shrewdies, that they were, ... they joined forces after years of enmity.

shypoo Liquor of poor quality; a public house of low reputation [origin obscure]
1901 *The Bulletin Reciter* 30: Paddy Grady's 'Hessian Palace' was a scene of wild delight, / And we drank the shypoo deeply, till the lateness of the night.
1908 E. G. Murphy *Jarrahland Jingles* 108: ... and the swell exclusive club, / Have swept the shypoo shanty from its lair amid the scrub.
1936 H. Drake-Brockman *Sheba Lane* 237: 'How about managing that shipoo for me?'
1962 Tom Ronan *Deep of the Sky* 218: A hostelry ... restricted to the sale of beer and wine. Locally this was known as the 'Shypoo Shop'. I'm not sure of the derivation of 'Shypoo'. I think it is bastard Chinese for soft drink. To the sturdy second wave of pioneers of West Kimberley, beer and wine were soft drinks.

sickie A day's sick leave, taken whether one is sick or not
1953 T. A. G. Hungerford *Riverslake* 11: Now and then there would be one or more off on a sickie – they changed their jobs so frequently that they never let their sick leave accumulate.
1959 Dorothy Hewett *Bobbin Up* 81: She wished she could take a sickie tomorrow, but it was payday.
1969 Osmar White *Under the Iron Rainbow* 109: 'Put the bludger on a sickie, boss,' he says to me.
1972 *Sun-Herald* 16 Apr. 136: 'Sickies' last year cost Australian industry more than a million dollars in lost man-hours, according to the latest report on industrial absenteeism.

silent cop See quot. 1934
1934 Thomas Wood *Cobbers* 122: A circle in the middle of cross-roads ... round which all traffic changing direction must swing; a round yellow blob, known here as the Silent Cop, or the Poached Egg.
1959 Dorothy Hewett *Bobbin Up* 2: This was the corner, by the silent cop, where she and Roy had come to grief.

silly as a two-bob watch, as a wheel see *watch, wheel*

Silver City, the Broken Hill, N.S.W. [f. mining of silver]
1919 W. K. Harris *Outback in Australia* 16: Broken Hill (the famous silver-field in New South Wales) is a great centre for the camels, and ... on the north side of the Silver City the teams may be seen starting off.
1956 Ion L. Idriess *The Silver City* [book title]
1974 *Australian* 12 Oct. 19: Landslide in Seedy Silver City.

silvertail Someone affluent and socially prominent: *derogatory*
1890 A. J. Vogan *The Black Police* 116: A select circle of long-limbed members of those upper circles who belong to the genus termed in Australian parlance 'silver-tailed', in distinction to the 'copper-tailed' democratic classes.
1908 E. G. Murphy *Jarrahland Jingles* 116: And when they're playing billiards in their flannel tennis suits, / We feel like heaving something at these silvertail galoots.
1929 K. S. Prichard *Coonardoo* 63: 'Mrs Bessie knew what she was doin' when she asked that damned young silver-tail to spend a winter on Wytaliba.'
1939 Kylie Tennant *Foveaux* 430: 'Even now you got no idea the real bang-up

people who come from Foveaux, doctors and sirs and silvertails of all sorts.'
1947 Gavin Casey *The Wits are Out* 125: 'Mr Fleming doesn't build for basic-wage earners,' Bill said nastily. 'He hangs around waiting his chance to build for the silvertails.'
1951 Dal Stivens *Jimmy Brockett* 87: The Bascombes were silvertails. They were dirty with money.
1963 Frank Hardy *Legends from Benson's Valley* 71: Duncan he hated twice: impersonally as a silver tail and the biggest employer in the town; and personally as the man who had sacked him for insubordination.
1970 Patrick White *The Vivisector* 127: 'Come on down, fuckun little silvertail! We'll put a frill around yer!'

sing'em muck see **muck**

six-bob-a-day tourist An Australian soldier on active service in World War I: *jocular* [f. the daily rate of pay, the highest to a private in any army at the time]
1916 Tom Skeyhill *Soldier Songs from Anzac* 28: But 'e called me a chocolate soldier, / A six-bob-a-day tourist too.
1918 Let. in Bill Gammage *The Broken Years* (1974) 265–6: Its na poo war now barring a few minor little affairs . . . but I don't fancy us 6/- a day tourists will be required to do any of it.

six o'clock swill see **swill**

skerrick A fragment, esp. in negative expression (not a skerrick', etc.) [*skerrick* a particle, morsel, scrap, atom EDD 1863]
1931 Ion L. Idriess *Lasseter's Last Ride* 205: Half a goanna's tail, the long thin end with not a skerrick of meat on it.
1937 Vance Palmer *Legend for Sanderson* 72: 'He didn't leave you any money, eh?' 'Not a skerrick,' Neil told him.
1947 H. Drake-Brockman *The Fatal Days* 116: Eddie had rushed off without leaving a skerrick of kindling; he often did.
1961 Patrick White *Riders in the Chariot* 226: 'There ain't no 22-gauge, Harry,' the gentleman announced. 'Not

a bloody skerrick of it.'
1975 Hal Porter *The Extra* 215: There isn't a skerrick of liquid.

skillion (skilling) *n.* A lean-to attached to another building, esp. with a sloping roof [*skilling* a shed or outhouse, esp. a lean-to OED 1389]
[1799 Rev. Richard Johnson Let. 26 Aug. *Evangelical Magazine* (1800) 299: Making further search in the house, blood was discovered in different parts, particularly in a small skilling, where, as afterwards appeared, my friend was dragged.
1826 James Atkinson *An Account of the State of Agriculture and Grazing in New South Wales* 100: The barn may be built with lean-to's or skillings all round.]
1843 Charles Rowcroft *Tales of the Colonies* i 120: House . . . to be divided into one large room, twenty feet long; a passage ten feet wide; and on the other side of the passage four rooms . . . At the back of the long room of twenty feet, a skillion, to serve as a kitchen, &c.
1846 C. P. Hodgson *Reminiscences of Australia* 39: Skillions formed by a sloping verandah to receive the sheep in from the fold as required.
1877 Rolf Boldrewood *A Colonial Reformer* (1890) 351: At the back a skillion, a lower roofed portion of the building, contained several smaller rooms.
1893 Henry Lawson 'The Selector's Daughter' *Prose* i 62: She went to her bedroom – a small, low, slab skillion, built on to the end of the house.
1905 Randolph Bedford *The Snare of Strength* 25: Forby told them in a harsh voice to take the milk into the skillion.
1919 E. S. Sorenson *Chips and Splinters* 60: The fireplace was as wide as a skillion, and deep.
skillion *a.* In the phrase 'skillion roof' (as distinct from a 'gable' roof) referring to the sloping type of roof on a skillion
1911 James Nangle *Australian Building Practice* 171: *Lean-to Roof* This kind (sometimes called a Skillion Roof) . . . is generally used only in rear buildings, or verandahs where no ceilings are required.

1966 *Coast to Coast 1965–1966* 136: It was little more than a skillion-roofed shack.

skin beginning to crack A sign of extreme thirst: *jocular*
[1930 L. W. Lower *Here's Luck* 266: 'I'm so dry I'm beginning to break out in little cracks.']
1957 R. S. Porteous *Brigalow* 96: 'Come on . . . You know bloody well yer skin's crackin'.' We drank quite a few beers that afternoon.
1961 George Farwell *Vanishing Australians* 80: It took him some hours to yoke up his bullocks; then his skin began to crack – as the bush saying puts it – for want of a drink.
1964 H. P. Tritton *Time Means Tucker* 101: 'Right now my flaming skin is cracking I'm so dry.'

skinner A betting coup [f. English thieves' slang: see quot. 1812]
[1812 Vaux: *Skin* to strip a man of all his money at play, is termed *skinning* him.
1865 Hotten: *Skin-the-lamb* When a non-favourite wins a race, 'bookmakers' are said to 'skin the lamb', under the supposition that they win all their bets, no person having backed the winner.]
1895 Cornelius Crowe *The Australian Slang Dictionary* 74: *Skinner*, a term in racing, signifying that a horse not backed wins the race, thereby giving the book-makers a skinner.
1907 Arthur Wright *Keane of Kalgoorlie* 66: Although he had gone up in the weights considerably, his owner decreed that he should win the Rosehill handicap, and give the 'shop' another 'skinner'.
c. 1914 A. B. Paterson 'Racehorses and Racing in Australia' in *The World of 'Banjo' Paterson* ed. C. Semmler (1967) 323: No matter what wins the bookmaker cannot lose anything, while they will skin the lamb to some tune should an outsider get home. Ibid. 324: The bookmakers who bet while the race is being run offer ten to one but won't lay it to much money. They don't want to spoil a real good 'skinner', by laying

a lot of money in running.
1934 Thomas Wood *Cobbers* 97: Charles laid down his fork and said it was a skinner for the books.
1949 Lawson Glassop *Lucky Palmer* 88: 'Didn't you hear the bookies cheer? It was a skinner.'
1958 Frank Hardy *The Four-Legged Lottery* 175: This percentage varies from, say, 12½ per cent if a well-backed horse wins to 100 per cent if a rank outsider gives a 'skinner'.
1974 *Sydney Morning Herald* 8 Oct. 17: Skinner for bookmakers.

skite *v.* To boast or brag [f. Scottish *bletherskate* a noisy, talkative fellow OED c. 1650; U.S. 1848]
1857 *Thatcher's Colonial Songster* 18: If ever you get into a fight, / Of course you'll not forget to skite.
1881 A. C. Grant *Bush-Life in Queensland* ii 78: 'Bosh! – you're always skyting about what you'll do.'
1899 Henry Lawson 'The Stranger's Friend' *Verse* i 369: The worst of it was that he'd skite all night on the edge of the stranger's bunk.
1907 Nathan Spielvogel *The Cocky Farmer* 12: 'I says that you are always skiting about what you are going to do.'
1916 C. J. Dennis *The Moods of Ginger Mick* 43: We've slung the swank fer good an' all; it don't fit in our plan; / To skite of birth an' boodle is a crime.
1932 Leonard Mann *Flesh in Armour* 34: In such an atmosphere, it was not hard even for Frank Jeffreys to skite a bit, though he was outdone easily by Charles.
1945 Gavin Casey *Downhill is Easier* 69: I managed to do it without actually telling lies, or skiting too much.
1957 Ray Lawler *Summer of the Seventeenth Doll* 113: 'Lyin' comes as natural to him as skiting.'
1963 John Cantwell *No Stranger to the Flame* 75: 'And spoil my big moment? I feel like skiting – first time I had anything much to skite about.'

skite *n.* 1 Boastful talk; showing-off
1860 Charles Thatcher *The Victoria Songster* Part 5 160: You don't often see

a chap given to 'skite,/Can do very much when it comes to a fight.
1910 E. W. Hornung *The Boss of Taroomba* 180: 'Then none o' your skite, mate,' said Bill, knocking out a clay pipe against his heel.
1916 *The Anzac Book* 99: If there's one thing I hate, it is skiting.* *Skiting – Australian for 'swanking' in speech. 'Skite' – blatherskite.
1918 C. J. Dennis *Digger Smith* 53: P'r'aps we 'ave 'ad some skite knocked out, an p'r'aps we see more clear.
1918 Geoffrey Wall *Letters of an Airman* 85: This notepaper is a part of it, quite unnecessary skite. I thought you might like a sample of it, though.
1933 Norman Lindsay *Saturdee* 115: 'Ponk's the bloke to take the skite outer him.'
1947 H. Drake-Brockman *The Fatal Days* 295: 'We call that skiting.' 'What's that?' 'Boasting.'
2 (*skiter*) Someone given to skiting; a boaster
1898 *Bulletin* 17 Dec. Red Page: An incessant talker is a *skiter*.
1906 Joseph Furphy *Rigby's Romance* ed. R. G. Howarth (1946) 222: 'In spite of Rigby's very complimentary insinuation that I'm a skite and a liar, the wagon was gone.'
1916 C. J. Dennis *The Moods of Ginger Mick* 155: *Skiter* A boaster.
1933 Norman Lindsay *Saturdee* 181: Taunts began to hurtle... 'Who's a stinkin' skite?'
1962 Alan Marshall *This is the Grass* 47: 'He'd take a rise out of any skite he met.'
1969 *Australian* 23 Sep. 2: Australians should not see themselves as boastful, arrogant skites, the Governor-General, Sir Paul Hasluck, said yesterday.

slag To spit
1965 William Dick *A Bunch of Ratbags* 238: He cleared his throat and spat on the car grille. 'Hell,' muttered Ritchie, 'he's slaggin' on me car!'

slanter (schlanter, slinter) A trick: *rare* [? f. Du. *slenter*]
1915 C. J. Dennis *The Songs of a Senti-*

mental Bloke 55: The slanter game I'd played wiv my Doreen... I seen what made me feel fair rotten mean.
1919 W. H. Downing *Digger Dialects* 45: *Slanter* (*or Schlanter*) A trick. 'To run a schlanter' – to make no genuine effort to win a game.
1925 Arthur Wright *The Boy from Bullarah* 133: 'A shlanter ' he bellowed.
1965 Frank Hardy *The Yarns of Billy Borker* 70: The Greatest Slanter in the History of the Racing Game [story title]

slather, an open A situation in which there is no hindrance to what one wishes to do
1919 J. Vance Marshall *The World of the Living Dead* 71: 'Try the races up Dingo Creek way... They say she's an open slather up there. Not a demon in the burg.'
1949 John Morrison *The Creeping City* 227: 'You're asking to be allowed an open slather at an essential public service without being challenged.'
1955 D'Arcy Niland *The Shiralee* 209: 'You mean that would give her open slather?'
1975 Hal Porter *The Extra* 197: Let other writers gang up like metalworkers for an open slather.

sledging In cricket, the taunting of a batsman by members of the opposing team in order to undermine his confidence
1975 *Sun-Herald* 21 Dec. 49: But 'sledging'... or the gentle art of talking a player out... has no place in women's cricket.

sleever, long see **long sleever**

sling To pay a bribe or gratuity, esp. as a percentage of wages or winnings
1939 Kylie Tennant *Foveaux* 172: 'I'm slinging it to Hamp,' Bardy said sullenly.
1949 Lawson Glassop *Lucky Palmer* 5: 'Clarrie, he ain't gone off in six months. Must sling to the cops. Wonder how much he pays 'em.' Ibid. 21: 'Here's a fiver for you... Don't say I didn't sling.'
1953 T. A. G. Hungerford *Riverslake*

130: 'Sling, Stefan!' When the Pole looked at him uncomprehendingly Murdoch whipped a ten-pound note out of the bundle and handed it to the ring-keeper. 'He don't know,' he explained. 'It's the first time he's played.'
1971 Frank Hardy *The Outcasts of Foolgarah* 56: On first name terms with every shire President so long as they didn't forget to sling when back-handers came in.
1975 Les Ryan *The Shearers* 155: *Sling* Tip for services rendered.

sling (back) Any payment so made
1948 K. S. Prichard *Golden Miles* 74: 'There's some hungry bastards,' the men said, 'making big money on their ore, never give the poor bugger boggin' for 'em a sling back.' The sling back might be ten bob on pay-day, or no more than a few pots of beer, but was always appreciated. Ibid. 82 Sling backs to the shift boss got some men their jobs.
1971 Frank Hardy *The Outcasts of Foolgarah* 34: The Garbo's margin for skill was only two bucks above the basic, but you had to take bottles into account and the sling from cafes who wanted extra tins emptied.

sling off (at) To deride, ridicule, abuse [variant of 'throw off' q.v.]
1911 Steele Rudd *The Dashwoods* 24: 'I heard yer both slingin' off.'
1921 K. S. Prichard *Black Opal* 112: The rest of the men continued to 'sling off', as they said, at Bully and Roy O'Mara as they saw fit.
1942 Gavin Casey *It's Harder for Girls* 236: 'It was just some chaps'd been slinging off at him,' I said.
1951 Dal Stivens *Jimmy Brockett* 250: Until he came to work for me I'd always slung off at book learning.
1963 John Cantwell *No Stranger to the Flame* 86: 'Stop it,' Barry said, flushing. 'Stop slinging off.'
1975 Mary Rose Liverani *The Winter Sparrows* 232: She glowered at the driver suspiciously. Was he slinging off at her?

slip into To attack
1973 Jim McNeil *The Old Familiar Juice*

66: 'I'll slip inter you inner minute!'
1974 Keith Stackpole *Not Just for Openers* 83: He turned to the grandstand and expressed his feelings. The Press slipped into him over that.

Slippery Charlie see **Charlie**

slot See quots
1953 Baker 129: *slot* or *peter*, a prison cell.
1976 *Cleo* Aug. 33: Some of the old heads are in the slot, he says. The slot is jail.

slug *n. & v.* (To make) a heavy charge or demand [? analogous to *sock, sting*]
1941 Baker 68: *Slug* A heavy bill. Also, 'get slugged': to be charged excessively.
1946 K. S. Prichard *The Roaring Nineties* 326: Alf knew the mine-owners were slugging the prospectors and alluvial diggers.
1970 Alexander Buzo *The Front Room Boys* in Penguin *Plays* 39: 'Ar jees, another slug at the wallet.'
1977 *Sun-Herald* 9 Jan. 3: Gold Coast beats death tax slug.

slushy Unskilled assistant to a bush cook; any unskilled kitchen help [f. *slush* refuse fat or grease obtained from meat boiled on board ship OED 1756]
[1859 Hotten: *Slushy* a ship's cook.]
1899 Henry Lawson 'A Rough Shed' *Prose* i 465: 'We hate the boss-of-the-board as the shearers' "slushy" hates the shearers' cook.'
1901 A. Searcy *The Australian Tropics* 295: We shot two or three kangaroo and a few birds just for immediate use. I volunteered as 'slushy', so as soon as I had skinned and cleaned one of the kangaroos, I put some of the meat on the coals.
1919 W. H. Downing *Digger Dialects* 46: *Slushey* A mess orderly.
1924 *Truth* 27 Apr. 6: *Slushy* A kitchen hand.
1936 Archer Russell *Gone Nomad* 14: I had to take my turn at butchering the ration sheep and as 'slushy' to 'Dough-boy' Terry, the cook.
1946 K. S. Prichard *The Roaring Nine-*

ties 64: Cursing and sweating over the cooking, and rousing hell out of Bill to find a slushy to help in the kitchen.

1953 *Caddie A Sydney Barmaid* 25: Nellie, a wisp of a girl who was slushie at Mrs Murphy's boarding-house. Slushie was the name given to anyone who worked at a camp boarding-house.

sly grog (shop) Liquor sold without a licence; a place where it is sold

[1812 Vaux: *Sly* Any business transacted, or intimation given, privately, or under the rose, is said to be *done upon the sly.*]

1829 H. Widowson *The Present State of Van Diemen's Land* 24: There are . . . upwards of thirty licenced public houses in the town . . . to these . . . I may safely add a like number of 'sly grog shops', as they are called.

1840 T. P. MacQueen *Australia as she is and as she may be* 23: Increased powers ought to be given to the magistrates and police to prevent the nuisances usually termed sly grog shops.

1855 William Howitt *Land, Labour and Gold* i 339: She is well known as a sly grog-seller, and has been fined some dozen times or more.

1861 T. McCombie *Australian Sketches* 62: Before a start could be made in pursuit they were far beyond reach, most likely secure in some of the sly grog tents which everywhere abounded.

1880 Rolf Boldrewood *The Miner's Right* (1890) 64: Any attempt to limit the licensing produced such a crop of 'shanties' or sly-grogshops.

1901 Henry Lawson 'The Babies in the Bush' *Prose* i 415: I was beastly drunk in an out-of-the-way shanty in the Bush – a sly grog shop.

1957 Ray Lawler *Summer of the Seventeenth Doll* 44: 'Keepin' nit for the S.P. bookies, eh – drummin' up trade for the sly grogs.'

1969 William Dick *Naked Prodigal* 64: We were on our way to the sly grog joint to buy a dozen bottles.

smartarse An offensively clever person

1937 Heard in conversation.

1962 Alan Seymour *The One Day of the Year* 49: 'Going round with smart-arsed little sheilas from the North Shore. It's all wrong, son.'

1965 William Dick *A Bunch of Ratbags* 245: 'Anyhow, where else could we go, do you know, smartarse?'

1970 Barry Oakley *A Salute to the Great McCarthy* 28: 'That smart arse from the city.'

smell of an oil-rag, live on the see oil-rag

Smells, City of Melbourne: *obs.*

[1890 A. J. Vogan *The Black Police* 380: My trip to Melbourne, – Smel-bourne, as the *Bulletin* calls it rightly.]

1897 *Bulletin* 18 Dec. 11: What a pious howl went through the City of Smells quite recently when Mrs Sutherland hinted that some of the Melbourne goody goody owned 'bad' houses.

Smithy Sir Charles Kingsford Smith (1897–1935), the Australian aviator

1936 *Daily Telegraph* 14 Aug. 7: 'It would provide a real tribute to "Smithy" because he did not favor statues and would . . . have preferred something of a utilitarian character.'

1965 *Daily Telegraph* 13 Apr. 66: Jet flight on 'Smithy' route.

1975 *Sydney Morning Herald* 24 Apr. 3: 'Smithy's' relics coming home . . . The collection, which includes logbooks and maps from 'Smithy's' greatest flights, will be brought from America in June.

smoke To decamp hurriedly, 'vamoose' [cf. *like smoke* very quickly, rapidly OED 1833]

1893 *Sydney Morning Herald* 26 Jun. 8: 'Smoke' . . . is the slang for the 'push' to get away as fast as possible. [Morris]

1896 Henry Lawson 'Stiffner and Jim' *Prose* i 124: 'Smoke be damned,' I snarled, losing my temper. 'You know dashed well that our swags are in the bar, and we can't smoke without them.'

1941 Baker 68: *Smoke, to* To decamp, make oneself scarce.

1961 Patrick White *Riders in the*

303

Chariot 415: Dubbo had gone all right. Had taken his tin box, it seemed, and smoked off.

in smoke In hiding
1924 C. J. Dennis *Rose of Spadgers* 72: 'Jist now,' says Brannigan, 'Spike Wegg's in smoke. / Oh, jist concerns a cove 'e tried to croak.'
1928 A. W. Upfield *The House of Cain* 76: 'When the lady comes out of smoke . . . give it her with my compliments.'
1938 *Smith's Weekly* 31 Dec. 12: A cove beckoned me and said: 'Your mate's in smoke and can't show up.'
1945 Kylie Tennant *Ride on Stranger* 203: The New Zealand delegate returned anonymously, slipped ashore and 'went into smoke' like some famous criminal.
1951 Simon Hickey *Travelled Roads* 128: They are not sure whether you are the present President or the one before, come out of 'smoke' again.
1967 K. S. Prichard *Subtle Flame* 252: 'Meanwhile Tony's got to be kept in smoke?'

smoke, the big The city [f. *smoke* as the mark of a metropolis: applied to London (see quot. 1864) although the Australian use – almost invariably the 'big smoke' – is recorded earlier]
[**1864** Hotten: *Smoke* London. Country-people when going to the metropolis frequently say, they are on their way to the Smoke, and Londoners when leaving for the country say, they are going out of the Smoke.]
1848 H. W. Haygarth *Recollections of Bush Life in Australia* 6: At first he has some power of choice in fixing on a resting-place for the night; but, as he gradually leaves behind him the 'big smoke' (as the aborigines picturesquely call the town), the accommodations become more and more scanty.
1893 J. A. Barry *Steve Brown's Bunyip* 21: 'You want to get away amongst the spielers and forties of the big smoke?'
1901 Rolf Boldrewood *In Bad Company* 214: 'Goin' to the big smoke to blue our cheques.'
1918 Bernard Cronin *The Coastlanders* 114: 'I'd clear fer the big smoke,' he

says, 'and hit the high places.'
1946 *Coast to Coast 1945* 32: 'He says he's going to the big smoke to die.'
1959 D'Arcy Niland *The Big Smoke* [book title]
1964 David Ireland *Image in the Clay* 81: 'Fresh from the big smoke, too. Learn anything in the city?'
1970 Barry Oakley *A Salute to the Great McCarthy* 2: 'It kind of proves a point about them cities – keep away from the big smoke, see what happened to McCarthy?'

smoko 1 A break from work for smoking and refreshment; the food and drink then taken
[**1855** R. Caldwell *The Gold Era of Victoria* 129: A curious practice exists in the Colony of taking a 'smoking time' in the forenoon for a quarter of an hour, and again in the afternoon for a quarter of an hour. All the men leave off work and deliberately sit down and smoke.]
1881 *Adelaide Observer* 31 Dec. 46: 'I must go to "smoke O".'
1890 *The Worker* Mar. 14: Smoke Ho! [heading of column of miscellaneous news items]
1899 Henry Lawson 'A Rough Shed' *Prose* i 464: 'We go through the day of eight hours in runs of about an hour and twenty minutes between smoke-ho's. . . . I've worked from six to six with no smoke-ho's for half the wages.'
1919 W. K. Harris *Outback in Australia* 152: The men were having five minutes' 'Smoke-oh!' and were overhauling their machines preparatory to beginning on the final batch of ewes for the day.
1930 Vance Palmer *The Passage* 247: At smoko, when they took a spell in the middle of loading the boat.
1947 John Morrison *Sailors Belong Ships* 50: Half-past three. Smoko. We get thirty minutes . . . Many stevedores don't leave the hold during smoko; they just curl up on the softest bit of cargo they can find and go to sleep.
1954 Tom Ronan *Vision Splendid* 179: 'If you blokes aren't coming down for your smoko I'll throw it away.'
1959 D'Arcy Niland *The Big Smoke* 114:

'I'll make you a bit of smoko.'
1961 *Sydney Morning Herald* 22 May 2:
The job committee meets whenever
necessary during smoko.
1971 Frank Hardy *The Outcasts of
Foolgarah* 12: The camera crew better
take a smoko and come back after
lunch.
2 An informal social gathering, concert
etc.
1918 G. A. Taylor *Those Were the Days*
30: The State Governor was present,
and it was a rare incident for that distinguished party to grace an Art Society
'Smoko'.
1923 Jack Moses *Beyond the City Gates*
71: The 'Smoko' held annually in connection with the Wattle Flat Exhibition,
is invariably described, year in and
year out, as the great social gathering
of the season.
1976 *Australian* 24 Apr. 18: The Leader
of the Opposition, Mr Whitlam, worked
in his Sydney office and attended a
'smoko' at Wentworthville RSL club
last night.

smoodge (smooge) To ingratiate oneself, make a display of affection [? f.
smudge to kiss (cf. *smouch*); to covet,
long for; to sidle up to; to beg in a
sneaking way EDD 1839]
1908 E. G. Murphy *Jarrahland Jingles*
111: Amid the pop of the champagne
cork, / The smoodgeful speech and
cheers.
1910 C. E. W. Bean *On the Wool Track*
170: 'We reckon 'e smoogged [smoodg-
ed in later editions] for a bit after that.
But it wasn't any good.'
1915 C. J. Dennis *The Songs of a Sentimental Bloke* 39: 'Lady, be yonder
moon I swear!' sez 'e./An' then 'e
climbs up on the balkiney; / An' there
they smooge a treat.
1939 Kylie Tennant *Foveaux* 49: He
patiently disentangled himself from her
embrace and set about cutting the sandwiches. 'Don't smooge to me.'
1942 Gavin Casey *It's Harder for Girls*
9: A rug was reckoned to provide
privacy enough for a bit of smoodging.
1955 D'Arcy Niland *The Shiralee* 122:
'He'd go round to the kitchen for a

hand-out, and if there was no blokes
about, he'd come the smoodge to the
women for a bit of a love-up.'
1973 Patrick White *The Eye of the
Storm* 480: She came smoodging up at
her father and he answered, but gently
. . . and kissed her.
smoodger Someone given to 'smoodging'
1910 Edward Dyson *The Missing Link*
5: 'Kidder' a term that has gone out
recently in favour of 'smoodger', and
which implies a quality of suave and
ingratiating cunning backed by ulterior
motives.
1924 *Truth* 27 Apr. 6: *Smooger* One
who fawns.
1934 Vance Palmer *Sea and Spinifex*
229: 'Better hunt him home, Sid, home
to his mother . . . yes, show him how
we treat smoodgers.'

snack Something easy to accomplish, 'a
piece of cake'
1941 Baker 68: *Snack* A certainty.
1952 T. A. G. Hungerford *The Ridge
and the River* 138: There was nothing
to it . . . It was a snack.
1961 Mena Calthorpe *The Dyehouse*
150: 'In Hughie's day he'd make this a
snack.'
1970 Richard Beilby *No Medals for
Aphrodite* 274: 'How could I do that,
Harry?' 'Easy. It'll be a snack.'

snag A bush cook: *rare*
1911 E. S. Sorenson *Life in the Australian Backblocks* 91: Concerning fighting
cooks the tales are legion. I remember
one snag . . . who cooked abominably,
but rendered his position tenable by
punching the ringer.

snagger A rough shearer [see quot.
1969]
1887 *Tibb's Popular Songbook* 11: I
found a lot of snaggers / Not a shearer
in the mob, / At Mumba signed for
seventeen / With a bonus of three bob.
1885–1914 'Click Go the Shears' *Australian Ballads* ed. Russel Ward (1964)
120: The ringer looks round and is
beaten by a blow, / And curses the
snagger with the bare-bellied yeo.

1969 Bobbie Hardy *West of the Darling* 106: Since they were slow, inexpert, and rough in their performances, the poorest shearers in the shed were nicknamed 'snaggers'.

snags Sausages (rarely used in the singular)
1941 Baker 68: *Snags* Sausages.
1949 Ruth Park *Poor Man's Orange* 33: 'I know. Let's have sausages.' The tension in Mumma's housewifely heart disappeared. Good old snags. They were always there to be fallen back on.
1953 T. A. G. Hungerford *Riverslake* 199: 'Give him a hand to open up some more snaggers, Randy.'
1968 A. Clifford *Send her down, Hughie!* 169: Sausages are 'snags' (a highly important part of the Australian diet).
1975 *Australian* 13 Nov. 2: Snags and mash at Burton bash.

snake A sergeant, esp. in the term 'snake pit' for sergeants' mess
1943 Baker 73: *Snake pit* A sergeants' mess. (War slang)
1948 Sumner Locke Elliott *Rusty Bugles* in *Khaki, Bush and Bigotry* ed. Eunice Hanger (1968) 91: 'Andy Edwards has been promoted and moved up to the snake pit with you and the other snakes.'
1951 Eric Lambert *The Twenty Thousand Thieves* 314: 'Baxter reckoned the officers and snakes are pinching our beer.'

snake charmer A fettler
1937 A. W. Upfield *Mr Jelly's Business* 16: 'And what are the Snake Charmers?' They are the permanent-way men.'
1969 Patsy Adam Smith *Folklore of the Australian Railwaymen* 279: Fettlers are invariably referred to as 'snake charmers'.

Snake Gully The locale of the radio serial 'Dad and Dave' q.v.
1945 Baker 198: *Woop Woop* and *Snake Gully*, as fictitious names for a remote outback settlement, the home of the most rustic of rustics.
1976 *Nation Review* 16 Jan. 338: South Australia is the quintessential utopia of enlightenment compared with which Valhalla would be thought to resemble Snake Gully.

snake juice Any improvised alcoholic drink; strong liquor generally
1904 E. S. Emerson *A Shanty Entertainment* 70: Then he started them on snake-juice, known as Boot and Blacking Rum.
1916 C. J. Dennis *The Moods of Ginger Mick* 26: 'I've arf a mind to give cold cold tea a go./It's no game pourin' snake-juice in yer face.'
1924 *Truth* 27 Apr. 6: *Snake juice* Strong drink.
1973 Roland Robinson *The Drift of Things* 290: Broke into Eric's hut, threw the 'pickled' specimens out of the jars, and drank the methylated spirits. That must have been the real 'Snake-Juice'. This is a name for the various kinds of beverages some of the alcoholics in the various camps used to concoct.

snake, mad as a cut see **mad**

snake's belly, lower than a Despicable
1932 Leonard Mann *Flesh in Armour* 290: 'It was a dirty trick. He knew about me and her.' 'Dirty! Lower than a snake's belly.'
1951 Dymphna Cusack *Say No to Death* 20: He'd only have to take one look at Jan to be convinced in his honest old heart that his son was lower than a snake's belly.
1957 D'Arcy Niland *Call Me When the Cross Turns Over* 181: My opinion of you is lower than a snake's belly.
1965 John Beede *They Hosed Them Out* 175: I thought, 'if I have to crawl to this illegitimate I'll get lower than a snake's belly.'

snakey Bad-tempered, irritable
1919 W. H. Downing *Digger Dialects* 46: *Snaky* (adj.) (1) Angry (e.g., to turn snaky); (2) Irritable.
1941 Kylie Tennant *The Battlers* 86: 'Don't go snaky on the kid.'
1951 Dymphna Cusack and Florence James *Come in Spinner* 245: 'Snaky?' she asked, looking at him judicially, 'or

just gone troppo?'
1974 David Williamson *Three Plays* 34:
'What are you snaky about this time?'

snarler 'Services no longer required':
applied to a serviceman sent back as a
failure from a theatre of war
1943 Baker 73: *Snarler* A soldier or
flier sent back home from overseas service because of some misdemeanour.
1952 T. A. G. Hungerford *The Ridge
and the River* 49: If he just couldn't
make the grade, then Lovatt would
bundle him back south for a Snarler.

snatch it, snatch one's time To demand
the wages due and leave the job
[1934 J. M. Harcourt *Upsurge* 258:
'Load that barrow or go and take your
time. Any man here who doesn't care
to load his barrow can take his time.']
1944 Alan Marshall *These Are My
People* 158: 'I suppose you struck some
bad bosses in your time?' 'If they're
bad, I snatch it.'
1945 Gavin Casey *Downhill is Easier*
106: There was nothing to do but put
up with it, unless I snatched my time
and left.
1962 Tom Ronan *Deep of the Sky* 55:
'What's more, when we pass Silverton
I'm snatching my time.'
1973 Frank Huelin *Keep Moving* 83:
'What are yous goin' to do? Snatch it
or stay?'

sniper A non-unionist on the wharves,
'sniping' the jobs of unionists
1945 Baker 248: A waterfront term of
fairly recent origin is *sniper*, a non-
union labourer.
1955 John Morrison *Black Cargo* 14:
Plenty of Federation men also know
him by sight, and it will need only one
shout of 'Sniper!' and Lamond will be
lucky to get out without being knocked
down.
1957 Tom Nelson *The Hungry Mile* 72:
The W.W.F. had preference of work,
wharf by wharf. The outsiders (snipers)
would stand back at the gate until the
W.W.F. men were all used.

**sniper, went for a crap and the ~ got
him** Jocular reply to request for anyone's whereabouts
1965 Eric Lambert *The Long White
Night* 94: I looked around me at the
dark figures in the dusk and called
Clancy's name. From behind the tip of
a lighted cigarette an anonymous voice
told me: 'He went for a shit and the
sniper got him.'
1971 David Ireland *The Unknown Industrial Prisoner* 90: 'Where's he gone?'
'Went for a crap and a sniper got him.'
see **he went mad and they shot him,
shot through on the padre's bike,
went through like Speed Gordon**

snob The 'cobbler', the sheep left to the
last as the most difficult to shear [see
quot. 1910]
1910 C. E. W. Bean *On the Wool Track*
The sheep most difficult to shear, which
naturally is left last in the pen, is also
called the 'snob'. As early as in Eliza-
bethan times 'snob' was slang for cobbler (Shakespeare has 'snip and snob'
for tailor and cobbler). The terms have
persisted in old-fashioned English, and
'snob' has added to its several meanings
this peculiarly Australian one.
1975 Les Ryan *The Shearers* 49: 'Get
on to this wrinkled bludger!' he said.
It was the last sheep in the pen . . . 'Real
snob ain't it?'

snodger First rate, excellent, 'nifty':
obsolescent
1919 W. H. Downing *Digger Dialects*
46: *Snodger* (adj.) Excellent.
1924 C. J. Dennis *Rose of Spadgers* 40:
It was a snodger day! . . . The apple
trees / Was white with bloom. All things
seemed good to me.
1946 *Sunday Sun* Suppl. 11 Aug. 15:
There they find the con-ships fitted up
snodger with bulkheads studded with
nails.
1950 *Australian Police Journal* Apr.
119: If something is snodger it is
'mighty' in Queensland, it is 'colossal'
in NSW, and just 'very nice' everywhere else.
1965 Xavier Herbert *Larger than Life*
152: 'They got good stuff. Shirts, pants,
some snodgin' stockwhips, watches.'

snoozer Codger, chap, 'joker': *obsolescent*
1916 *Anzac Book* 99: The chaps of the 16th Battalion / Are not easy snoozers to beat.
1929 K. S. Prichard *Coonardoo* 261: 'Oh, I suppose I'm a cantankerous old snoozer, Bob,' Hugh said.
1932 William Hatfield *Christmastown* 42: Decent sort of snoozer, Allison – no girl stuff about him.
1946 *Sunday Sun* Suppl. 20 Oct. 15: They'd have lamped a snoozer rigged up as an army skipper clop-clopping along on a nag just behind them.
1962 Stuart Gore *Down the Golden Mile* 26: 'Want to watch out for them quiet snoozers. Sometimes they can go the knuckle a bit themselves.'
1964 *Herald* (Melbourne) 12 Dec. 34: Mr Bolte's mates in the local pub near his farm affectionately describe him as a 'real rough old snoozer'. They mean that down on the farm Mr Bolte is just one of the boys.

snork A baby: *rare* [derived by Partridge from *stork*]
1941 Baker 68: *Snork* A baby (2) A sausage.
1944 Lawson Glassop *We Were the Rats* 273: 'Got a scar on his hand, but probably he's had it since he was a little snork.'
1973 Frank Huelin *Keep Moving* 178: *Snork / Bimbo* Young hoboes from 14 to 18 years of age.

snout, have a ~ on As for 'have a nose on' q.v.
1916 C. J. Dennis *The Moods of Ginger Mick* 155: *Snout* To bear a grudge.
1949 Lawson Glassop *Lucky Palmer* 212: 'He's got a snout on the Kid for something.'
1957 Ray Lawler *Summer of the seventeenth Doll* 50: 'You got a snout on that kid the first day you saw him working.'
1966 Tom Ronan *Once There Was a Bagman* 39: 'The reason you blokes have such a snout on him,' I argued, 'is that he's forgotten more Law than you've ever learned.'

snouted Rebuffed, in disfavour
1919 W. H. Downing *Digger Dialects* 46: *Snouted* Under disfavor.
1924 C. J. Dennis *Rose of Spadgers* 117: Don't mind my sulks ... But gittin' snouted ain't wot I expeck.
1943 Margaret Trist *In the Sun* 104: Some of the juniors had him snouted because of it.
1944 Alan Marshall *These Are My People* 155: 'I was sore as a snouted sheila for weeks.'
1970 Richard Beilby *No Medals for Aphrodite* 149: 'That officer happened to have me snouted because I got you across the river, against his orders.'

soak, soakage See quots [f. *soak* a percolation of water; water which has oozed through or out of the ground, strata etc. OED 1707]
1895 *Australasian* 7 Sep. 461: The term soak in Western Australia ... signifies a depression holding moisture after rain. It is also given to damp or swampy spots round the base of granite rocks. [Morris]
1898 D. W. Carnegie *Spinifex and Sand* 80: Round the granite base a belt of grass of no great extent may be found, for the most part dry and yellow, but in places green and fresh. It is in such spots as these that one may hope to tap an underground reservoir in the rock. To these shallow wells has been given the name of 'Soaks'. They seldom exceed fifteen feet in depth.
1931 Vance Palmer *Separate Lives* 189: They had stayed out too long at a time when a bad spell had struck the spinifex, and soaks were drying up.
1937 Ernestine Hill *The Great Australian Loneliness* 330: *Soak* Water beneath the surface of the sand.

soap, not to know someone from a bar of To be completely unacquainted with someone
1938 *Smith's Weekly* 26 Nov. 23: [cartoon caption] 'I don't know you from a bar of soap.'
1945 Kylie Tennant *Ride on Stranger* 309: 'Why doesn't she marry the child's father?' ... 'It's my belief she doesn't

know him from a bar of soap.'
1947 Gavin Casey *The Wits Are Out*
184: 'We can't do that, when we don't
know them from a bar of soap.'
1970 Jon Cleary *Helga's Web* 130:
'I've never met any of his – interests.
Certainly not this girl. I dunno her
from a bar of soap.'

Socceroos Members of a team representing Australia internationally at soccer
(by analogy with the Kangaroos, the
representatives in Rugby League)
1973 *Sydney Morning Herald* 15 Nov.
1: Now that the Australian Soccer team
is basking in honour and glory after
its World Cup victory over South Korea
it can surely do without the name 'Socceroos' which is being increasingly
applied to it.
1976 *Australian* 3 Jun. 20: Socceroos
turn the tide.

sod A damper that has not risen [f. *sod*
ill-raised bread OED 1836]
1900–10 O'Brien and Stephens: *Sod*
badly cooked damper.
1941 Baker 69: *Sod* A damper, esp. a
badly-cooked one.
1957 R. S. Porteous *Brigalow* 206: His
dampers were leaden sods.
1975 Xavier Herbert *Poor Fellow My
Country* 838: 'I want to cook our own
damper, too ... I don't want one of
their sods.'

soda Something easily done, a 'push-
over' [? f. card game U.S. 1843 Mathews]
[1895 Cornelius Crowe *The Australian
Slang Dictionary* 98: Zodiac, or *Soda* the
top card in the box in faro.]
1930 Vance Palmer *The Passage* 83:
'They're getting ready for the long dive
now, and it ought to be a soda for you.'
1943 G. H. Johnston *New Guinea Diary*
151: 'The Middle East was a soda beside
this,' one of them told me.
1955 Alan Marshall *I Can Jump Puddles*
108: 'Swipe him on the knuckles if you
can. If he's like his old man he's a soda.'
1966 Hal Porter *The Paper Chase* 74:
The job, for which I have no really
specialized training, is nevertheless a
soda.

solid Severe, excessive, unreasonable
1916 C. J. Dennis *The Moods of Ginger
Mick* 155: *Solid* Severe; severely.
1948 Ruth Park *The Harp in the South*
62: 'After all, Auntie Josie's got all
them kids to look after. It must be
pretty solid for her with Grandma as
well.'
1951 Frank Hardy *Power Without Glory*
41: 'I got fined fifty quid, Joe twenty-
five.' 'Bit solid, wasn't it?'
1959 Eric Lambert *Glory Thrown In* 66:
'They'll be solid on him for that, won't
they?'

sollicker Something very big, a 'whop-
per' [cf. *sollock* impetus, force (He fell
down with such a sollock) EDD]
1898 Roland Graeme *From England to
the Backblocks* 82: 'Who was it I heard
that in cutting-out some cattle on one
of the Methvin plains, did come down
a soliker and broke his horse's knees?'
1908 *Australian Magazine* 1 Nov. 1251:
sollicker, very big.
1939 Miles Franklin and Dymphna
Cusack *Pioneers on Parade* 168: 'She
gave me a sollicker of a dose out of a
blue bottle.'
1946 Kylie Tennant *Lost Haven* 155:
'It was a great big sollicking stitch if
ever there was one.'
1956 Patrick White *The Tree of Man*
91: 'You can jump down, can't you?
You're quite big, you know.' 'Of course
he can ... he's a sollicker.'

sook A timorous person, a 'softie', a
crybaby (juvenile) [? f. *suck* a 'muff'; a
'duffer'; a stupid fellow EDD]
1941 Baker 69: *Sook* A coward, a timid
person.
1950 Brian James *The Advancement of
Spencer Button* 9: If he nervously declares he can't fight, and shows that
he doesn't want to fight, then he is a
'sook' or a 'sissy'.
1953 Dymphna Cusack *Southern Steel*
328: 'Get along with you: you're getting
real sookey.'
1970 Patrick White *The Vivisector* 11:
He wasn't a sook. He could run, shout,
play, fight, had scabs on his knees, and
twice split Billy Abrams's lip, who was

two years older.

sool To incite someone to a course of action, from the command 'Sool him' to a dog to attack or harass some quarry [f. *sowl* to pull, seize roughly . . . In later use esp. of dogs OED 1607]

1849 Alexander Harris *The Emigrant Family* (1967) 135: 'Hey! hey! sowl her boys!' roared Morgan: and on went the whole pack, seizing the poor beast by the ears, nose, and even eyelids.

1903 Joseph Furphy *Such is Life* (1944) 130: 'Soolim, Pup!' I hissed.

1907 Nathan Spielvogel *The Cocky Farmer* 68: 'Here, Spot. Sool him, s-o-o-l him.' Joe's dog came with a bark, and Bill had to run for it.

1911 Louis Stone *Jonah* 31: The Push gathered round, grinning from ear to ear, sooling the women on as if they were dogs.

1932 L. W. Lower *Here's Another* 89: It followed us to school one day . . . and we sooled it on to the teacher.

1942 Gavin Casey *It's Harder for Girls* 52: 'Sool the dogs after him,' someone called out.

1951 Dal Stivens *Jimmy Brockett* 84: 'I heard McGrath has sooled them on to you. That's all I know.'

1961 Mena Calthorpe *The Dyehouse* 83: Oliver Henery had sooled the Unions on to Renshaw over the loads that the girls were humping about.

1971 Germaine Greer *The Female Eunuch* 190: The hero may either have her on his side and like a lion-tamer sool her on to his enemies, or he may have to battle for his life at her hands.
sooler

1935 H. R. Williams *Comrades of the Great Adventure* 35: Here, as chief 'sooler', he was urging the passing soldiers to patronize the eating-house.

1963 Xavier Herbert *Disturbing Element* 141: She had been sending white feathers round . . . She had become what her former comrades of the I.W.W. called a Sooler.

sooner 1 An idler, a shirker (who would sooner loaf than work, fight, etc.): *obs.*

1892 Karl Lentzner *Dictionary of the Slang-English of Australia* 117: *Sooner* a weak idler, a lazy good-for-nothing.

1919 Edward Dyson *Hello, Soldier!* 31: He slugged a tubby Hun, / Then choked a Fritzie with his dukes, 'n' pinched the sooner's gun!

1931 Vance Palmer *Separate Lives* 17: 'The dirty sooners – they've done me down!'

2 'A jibbing horse (one that would sooner go backward than forward) 1939 NZ.' (Partridge)

1969 Patsy Adam Smith *Folklore of the Australian Railwaymen* 117: This was an old sooner of an engine. She'd had it. On a stiff climb in a tunnel she began to slip.

sore toe (finger), done up like a l Dressed up, and looking uncomfortable

1919 W. H. Downing *Digger Dialects* 46: *Sore finger* An overdressed person (e.g. 'dolled' up like a sore finger).

1939 Kylie Tennant *Foveaux* 430: 'You ought to a seen us in the ole days when we 'ad a procession every year – done up like a sore toe with banners and floats.'

1945 Margaret Trist *Now That We're Laughing* 125: 'Done up like a sore toe, she was, too.'

1958 H. D. Williamson *The Sunlit Plain* 10: 'Get an eyeful of him! Done up like a sore toe.'

1963 Hal Porter *The Watcher on the Cast-Iron Balcony* 81: 'Dressed up like a sore toe, but hasn't had a bath for weeks.'

1965 Patrick White *Four Plays* 168: 'I'm gunna get out of this suit. Dressed up like a sore finger.'

2 Looking conspicuous

1966 Elwyn Wallace *Sydney and the Bush* 69: One young man named Dave whose clean pressed shirt stood out like a sore thumb spoke up at this point.

sorry, you'll be Jocular greeting to new army recruits in World War II

1944 Lawson Glassop *We Were the Rats* 66: Every soldier we passed on the road yelled, 'You'll be sorry.' Every soldier we encountered in camp until we got our issue clothes said, 'You'll be sorry.'

1951 Dymphna Cusack and Florence James *Come in Spinner* 185: A voice called derisively 'You'll be sorry!' Crooked smiles split the soldiers' faces.
1965 Eric Lambert *The Long White Night* 12: Still wearing his civilian clothes, and running the gamut of 'veterans', who had joined camp the day before and achieved uniforms, thereby feeling entitled to call out: 'You'll be sorry!'

sort A girl or woman (at the same level of usage as 'sheila'); applied rarely to men also: *obsolescent*
1933 Frank Clune *Try Anything Once* 93: 'Look here, George,' I said. 'Lend me a suit of civvies. I've got to meet a great little sort, and her father has a dead nark on soldiers.'
1941 Kylie Tennant *The Battlers* 276: 'Hey, Bob!' Dick Tyrell gave a low whistle. 'Take a look at that good sort.'
1949 Ruth Park *Poor Man's Orange* 180: Harry Drummy waited for her, draped mournfully over the rails in the peculiarly filleted manner of his kind, and eyeing off all the good sorts who were pushing and screaming their way on to the Luna Park ferry.
1953 T. A. G. Hungerford *Riverslake* 144: 'Felix came in after tea and said that his sort could come.'
1968 Kit Denton *A Walk Around My Cluttered Mind* 137: They'd told me, 'Don't worry about bringing anything except a bottle. The sorts are laid on.' Even after only ten months I understood this to mean that there would be feminine company.
see **drac**

soul-case, belt (worry, work) the ~ out of To subject to extreme hardship or punishment
1901 F. J. Gillen *Diary* (1968) 34: Fliers were celebrating some festival all night and worried the very soul cases out of us.
1945 Gavin Casey *Downhill is Easier* 146: 'He used t' belt the soulcase out o' her till I come along.'
1951 Dymphna Cusack and Florence James *Come in Spinner* 152: 'If you've

been going in for any of them beach girl competitions, Peggy my girl, I'll belt the soul case out of you.'
1962 Ron Tullipan *March into Morning* 13: 'Then he got the bright idea of bringin' in orphan kids and working the soulcase off them until they turn eighteen and have to be paid more money.'

southerly (buster) The cool, gusty wind that springs up at the end of a hot day, sometimes bringing a shower of rain (originally in Sydney)
1850 B. C. Peck *Recollections of Sydney* 132: It is almost a corollary, that the evening of a hot-wind day brings up a 'southerly buster', as we have heard the vulgar call it, very chill indeed . . . as this wind comes from the southerly region of the Australian Alps.
1859 Frank Fowler *Southern Lights and Shadows* 87–8: The 'Southerly Buster', as this change is called, generally comes . . . early in the evening. A cloud of dust – they call it, in Sydney, a 'brickfielder' – . . . heralds its approach. In a minute the temperature will sink fifty or sixty degrees.
1867 J. R. Houlding *Australian Capers* 137: He left the place as much discomposed as . . . a fashionable belle who had lost her bonnet in a 'southerly burster'.
1880 J. C. Crawford *Travels in New Zealand and Australia* 300: The wind was from the northward when we left Wollongong, but a southerly 'burster' overtook us off Botany Bay.
1896 Nat Gould *Town and Bush* 96: The southerly buster is well named. The wind comes in bursts and whirls the dust about . . . The buster, however, makes up for the inconvenience it causes by clearing the heated atmosphere, and is generally followed by a refreshing shower of rain.
1926 J. Vance Marshall *Timely Tips for New Australians: Southerly buster* A strong, gusty wind peculiar to a section of the East coast of New South Wales.
1935 Kylie Tennant *Tiburon* 229: Complaints from parishioners he blew aside as a southerly wind would blow the

washing on the line.

1949 Ruth Park *Poor Man's Orange* 146: After the unbearably hot day, the old men on the balconies were sniffing the air and saying, 'Here she comes!' The southerly buster, the genie of Sydney, flapped its coarse blusterous wing over the city ... The women undid the fronts of their frocks, and the little children lifted up their shirts and let it blow on their sweaty bottoms.

1956 Patrick White *The Tree of Man* 105: 'They say there'll be a southerly buster later in the afternoon. But no rain.'

1965 Graham McInnes *The Road to Gundagai* 63: The Southerly Buster had blown into town [Melbourne], whooshing up from the high latitudes near Antarctica and covering the suffocating city with a blanket of cool.

see **brickfielder**

souvenir To purloin [listed by Partridge as military slang (1915) obsolescent]

1919 W. H. Downing *Digger Dialects* 46: *Souvenir* To steal, find, capture, etc.

1951 Dymphna Cusack and Florence James *Come in Spinner* 395: Val stared at the cases. 'How on earth did you get those?' 'Souvenired 'em,' said Lofty with a broad wink.

1955 Mary Durack *Keep Him My Country* 298: 'The hides are no good but you might like to souvenir the heads.'

spag An Italian: *derogatory* [abbr. of *spaghetti*]

1966 Baker 344: *spaggie*, an Italian. [as Victorian slang]

1974 *Bulletin* 1 Jun. 39–40: 'And [Al Grassby] brought in all those migrants ... y'know, those coons and spags.'

sparrows (geese) flying out of one's backside An expression for the male orgasm

1959 Gerard Hamilton *Summer Glare* 94: 'What's it like? ... You just wait, son. You'll think a flock of geese are flyin' out yer backside.'

1972 Geoff Morley *Jockey Rides Honest Race* 204: I exploded with feeling and a million sparrows flew out of my backside.

spear, get the To be sacked from a job [variant of the English 'get the bullet']

1912 'Goorianawa' *The Lone Hand* 1 Oct. 27 repr. in *Old Bush Songs* ed. Stewart and Keesing (1957) 273: I've been many years a shearer and I fancied I could shear, /I've shore for Rouse of Guntawang and always missed the spear.

spear To dismiss

1911 Steele Rudd *The Dashwoods* 13: 'If I was the boss here I would. I'd spear him without warnin'.'

special A convict who is educated or well connected, and who is therefore given special treatment

1843 James Backhouse *A Narrative of a Visit to the Australian Colonies* 406: Port Macquarie ... still is a depot for that description of educated prisoners, denominated 'specials'.

1851 John Henderson *Excursions and Adventures in New South Wales* i 111: Port Macquarie, ever since it ceased to be exclusively a penal settlement, has been used as a *dépôt* for what are called 'specials'; that is, special, or *gentlemen –* convicts.

1867 John Morrison *Australia As It Is* 213–14: A laudable consideration was shown by the Government to a class of convicts belonging to what are usually styled 'the upper classes of society', and who were known by the name 'specials'. A settlement was set apart for them, and they were exempted from severe manual labour. One of them made himself very useful ... by teaching in families.

speck To search for gold in small quantities near the surface

1888 Henry Lawson 'His Father's Mate' *Prose* i 4: A pick and shovel, and a gold dish ... with which he used to go 'a-speckin'' and 'fossickin'' amongst the old mullock heaps.

1901 May Vivienne *Travels in Western Australia* 171: Almost everyone in the camp went out for an afternoon's specking (looking on the ground for nuggets).

1932 K. S. Prichard *Kiss on the Lips* 219: Charley Beck and his old woman had specked a thirty-ounce slug.

1936 Ion L. Idriess *The Cattle King* 166: Next morning they picked up gold. In trembling excitement they 'specked' piece after piece.

Speck, the Tasmania [f. size in relation to mainland Australia]

1930 *Bulletin* 11 Jun. 21: N.S.W., V., Q., S.A., W.A. and the Speck.

speedo The odometer (mileage indicator) in a car

1969 Mena Calthorpe *The Defectors* 140: He glanced at the speedo . . . He'd driven almost five miles.

1970 Richard Beilby *No Medals for Aphrodite* 33: We've done just on forty [miles] so far . . . I'm not a complete dill! I can read a speedo!'

Speewa A legendary station used as the locale for tall tales of the outback

1944 Alan Marshall *These Are My People* 144: He suddenly grinned. 'I cooked on Speewa.' I had heard of Speewa, that mythical station used as a setting for all the lies put over on new-chums. I knew many of the tales, so I answered him: 'It's a big place. When I was there they had to get two Chinese to mix the mustard with long-handled shovels. The shearing shed was so long the boss rode up and down the board on horse-back.'

1951 Ernestine Hill *The Territory* 445: On the Speewaa A legendary station of doughty deeds – 'I bet that happened on the Speewaa'. The original Speewaa Station is near Swan Hill on the Murray River, home of great men and tall tales in the very earlies.

1966 Bill Wannan *Crooked Mick of the Speewah and Other Tall Tales* [book title]

spell *n.* A period of rest, interrupting work [f. *spell* a turn of work taken by a person . . . in relief of another OED 1625]

c.**1845** James Tucker *Ralph Rashleigh* (1952) 140: Ralph taking one of their

tools, Bob took another and worked awhile, to give the children a *spell*.

1847 Alexander Harris *Settlers and Convicts* ed. C. M. H. Clark (1954) 137: We were both of us glad of a day's spell. Ibid. 240: We could get our bullocks over it if we gave them a good long spell in the afternoon.

1861 Horace Earle *Ups and Downs* 214: After the dray had departed Tom declared his intention 'to take a bit of a spell, and have a pipe.'

1870 Marcus Clarke *His Natural Life* ed. S. Murray-Smith (1970) 607: 'Take a spell,' says Frere; 'you overwork yourself.'

1886 John Farrell 'My Sundowner' *How He Died* (1913) 65: I proposed that we should take a spell in / The shade of a big tree that stood alone.

1896 Edward Dyson *Rhymes from the Mines* 65: 'Twas good when 'spell-oh' had been said.

1903 William Craig *My Adventures on the Australian Goldfields* 108: With only a small portion of his claim worked out, but unable longer to resist his intense craving for strong drink, he decided to take a 'spell.'

1918 Harley Matthews *Saints and Soldiers* 84: They sat on a hill during a spell in their practice manoeuvres.

1930 Vance Palmer *The Passage* 59: During the days that followed there was little chance of a spell for anyone.

1942 Gavin Casey *It's Harder for Girls* 171: You've worked hard for a long time and ought to be able to afford a spell.

spell *v.* To rest from work

1846 J. L. Stokes *Discoveries in Australia* ii 42: In order to spell the oars, we landed at a point on the east side. [Morris]

1865 Rachel Henning *Letters* ed. David Adams (1963) 199: He went down to Mr Paterson's . . . to 'spell' his horses before starting on a long journey southward.

1892 Harry Morant 'Paddy Magee' *Bulletin* 20 Feb. 14: What are you doing now, Paddy Magee? / Grafting, or spelling now, Paddy Magee?

1908 W. H. Ogilvie *My Life in the Open* 42: The shearers' horses, which have been spelling girth-deep in the river grass, are run up to the yard.
1926 K. S. Prichard *Working Bullocks* 101: When the team had spelled a day Red brought the big whim into action.
1975 Xavier Herbert *Poor Fellow My Country* 1314: By rights the horses should have been spelled for a couple of days before being pushed further.

spider Brandy with lemonade or ginger beer; a fizzy soft drink with icecream added
1854 C. H. Spence *Clara Morison* ii 67: 'I must have a nobbler or a spider to put me to rights.'
1859 Frank Fowler *Southern Lights and Shadows* 52: A *Spider* Lemonade and brandy.
1888 E. Finn *Chronicles of Early Melbourne* ii 548: The favourite tipple of the bushman was mixed brandy and ginger-beer – a 'spider', as it was called – for which 1s. 6d. was charged.
1861 Horace Earle *Ups and Downs* 283: They are neat dancers, good for an hour's polkaing at a stretch, and up to unlimited 'spiders', or lemonade and sherry.
[1920] Graham McInnes *The Road to Gundagai* (1965) 14: She reached for a thick yellow glass and poured in the ginger beer . . . an enormous dollop of ice-cream which she dropped into the ginger beer. 'There's your spider.'
1942 Gavin Casey *It's Harder for Girls* 233, 4: 'You've had your drink, so now you've got to buy us all a spider at Smith's.' . . . I didn't want to go back and sit in Smith's and drink silly coloured muck with ice-cream floating in it.
1962 Criena Rohan *The Delinquents* 122: Mavis had Sharon Faylene, clad only in a damp napkin, on her hip, and both were enjoying a raspberry spider.
1970 *Coast to Coast 1969–1970* 52: 'This calls for a celebration,' Alf said. 'I'll get you another straw and you can suck up the other side of my iniquitous coke-spider.'
1974 *Festival* ed. B. Buckley and J.

Hamilton 127: 'You used to strut into the milk bar as though you owned the place. "A lime spider, Harry." "Harry" you called me!'

spiel *v.* To move quickly (of a horse): *obs.* [E. dial. *speel* to run quickly OED] [**1859** Hotten: *Speel,* to run away, make off.]
1905 'The Broken-down Squatter' in *The Old Bush Songs* ed. A. B. Paterson 56: No more shall we muster the river for fats, / Or spiel on the Fifteen-mile plain.

spiel *n.* 1 The dishonest scheme of a 'spieler'[1]
1932 William Hatfield *Ginger Murdoch* 175: 'I reckon you were thinking you had shaken me off, and could go about your spiel, whatever it is.'
1954 T. A. G. Hungerford *Sowers of the Wind* 174: 'This isn't a spiel, Colonel,' McNaughton said desperately . . .' 'I know this bloke, and he's on the level.'
2 The utterance of a 'spieler'[2], a prepared line of talk
1957 Judah Waten *Shares in Murder* 62: 'I get you Brummel. Go on with your spiel.'
1962 Alan Marshall *This is the Grass* 125: Spruikers in braided uniforms strutted up and down before foyers extolling the virtues of the pictures within . . . I often stood watching them, listening to every word of their spiel.
1971 Robin Miller *Flying Nurse* 69: I delivered my spiel and looked around, feeling as embarrassed as on my first day as a trainee in a Perth hospital ward.
1973 Max Harris *The Angry Eye* 180: 'He must be pretty dim to have fallen for that kind of spiel.'

spieler 1 Someone who lives by his wits; a gambler, 'con-man' [f. G. *spielen* to play U.S. 1891 Mathews]
1885 *The Australasian Printers' Keepsake* 72: Who eyed Bob very suspiciously, muttering 'spieler' and 'Murrumbidgee whaler'.
1896 Henry Lawson 'Stiffner and Jim' *Prose* i 124: He was cracked on the

subject of spielers. He held that the population of the world was divided into two classes – one was the spielers and the other was the mugs.

1901 Rolf Boldrewood *In Bad Company* 7: 'Those larrikins and spielers, that come up partly for work, and more for gambling and stealing.'

1921 K. S. Prichard *Black Opal* 27: 'Which one of us,' George Woods inquired, 'if a mate'd been set on by a spieler in Sydney, would've let him stump his way to Brinarra and foot it out here?'

1935 H. R. Williams *Comrades of the Great Adventure* 234: The spielers worked the three-card trick on the 'mugs'.

1944 Alan Marshall *These Are My People* 81: 'A good spieler can pick his man,' he said. 'It's the greedy bloke they catch; the bunny that wants something for nothing.'

1957 Judah Waten *Shares in Murder* 156: You could match your wits against smart con-men and spielers.

2 A 'barker' for a sideshow; anyone with a plausible tongue [U.S. 1891 Mathews]

1975 Max Williams *The Poor Man's Bean* 33: A spieler calls, 'Come in; come on; come over.'

spill In politics, the declaring of a number of offices in the party vacant as a result of one vacancy occurring

1956 J. T. Lang *I Remember* 311: There had to be an annual election of leader. That made it inevitable that some members would intrigue against the leader hoping for a Cabinet spill.

1975 *Australian* 18 Mar. 1: It will be left to Mr Fraser's supporters to force the issue and move against Mr Snedden through either a spill of leadership positions or a motion of no confidence.

spin 1 A piece of experience (always with an adjective: 'rough spin', 'fair spin', etc.) [? f. *spin* for the toss of a coin OED 1882, or *spin* in various uses implying duration OED 1856, 1875]

1919 W. H. Downing *Digger Dialects* 47: *Spin* See trot. *Trot* An experience

(e.g., 'a rough trot', 'a bad time').

1929 K. S. Prichard *Coonardoo* 188: Mollie had had a crook spin when the children were little.

1934 Vance Palmer *Sea and Spinifex* 247: 'It's about time I had a bit of luck. Me and Mary – we've had a pretty rough spin up till now.'

1942 Leonard Mann *The Go-Getter* 243: 'I had a rough spin during the depression and bad luck since.'

1957 Ray Lawler *Summer of the Seventeenth Doll* 121: 'I know you've 'ad a bad spin and I know you're all on edge.'

1964 H. P. Tritton *Time Means Tucker* 113: When I remarked that he'd had a tough spin he grinned, 'Served me right for being such a blanky fool.'

2 £5, esp. in gambling

1941 Baker 70: *Spin, spinnaker* £5.

1949 Lawson Glassop *Lucky Palmer* 15: 'Not a five bob. A spin,' said the carpenter, fishing a five pound note out.

1953 *Caddie A Sydney Barmaid* 225: 'Yer got a spin,' he said, as I picked up a five-pound note.

1962 Stuart Gore *Down the Golden Mile* 261: 'Backed Sweet Friday for a spin, replied Tug. 'But it never run a drum.'

spine basher, spine bashing A loafer (World War II slang): *obsolescent*

1944 Lawson Glassop *We Were the Rats* 208: 'She's sweet,' I said. 'Go and do some spine bashing.' Ibid. 175: Jim was spine bashing.

1946 Rohan Rivett *Behind Bamboo* 399: *Spinebasher,* one always on his back, always resting.

1946 Kylie Tennant *Lost Haven* 343: 'A bit of drill and a lot of spine-bashing.'

1948 Sumner Locke Elliott *Rusty Bugles* in *Khaki, Bush and Bigotry* ed. Eunice Hanger (1968) 49: 'A man's got to have a rest day, hasn't he?' 'Except of course when he's been spine-bashing the whole week.'

1976 *Sydney Morning Herald* 20 Mar. 14: The elbow-benders, spine-bashers, eternal babblers keep one ear to the loudspeakers, an ear to the ground.

spinifex wire Equivalent of a 'mulga wire' q.v. in the spinifex country

1938 H. Drake-Brockman *Men Without Wives* (1955) 12: 'Whatever's a spinifex wire?' 'That's the way we get our news up here . . . you'd be surprised how quickly it travels sometimes . . . seems like magic. So we say it comes by spinifex wire . . . across on the spinifex grass, you know.'

spinner, come in The cry in two-up that clears the way for the tossing of the coins, all bets having been placed
1945 Tom Ronan *Strangers on the Ophir* 119: Cries of 'Another quid to see him go. Get set on the side. All set, come in Spinner.'
1951 Dymphna Cusack and Florence James *Come In Spinner* [book title]
1965 Leslie Haylen *Big Red* 101: Outside he could hear the gamblers: 'Come on, I want a dollar in the guts.' 'Who'll put a dollar in the guts.' Laughter, shouts, and then silence. 'Come in spinner.'
1975 Les Ryan *The Shearers* 97: 'All set?' Lofty asked. 'Set!' Sandy said. 'Come in, spinner!'

spit, go for the big To vomit (given currency by the Barry McKenzie comic strip)
1967 Frank Hardy *Billy Borker Yarns Again* 40: Don't tell me the Gargler went for the big spit.
1973 Alexander Buzo *Rooted* 43: 'Remember the time he got sick at Davo's twenty-first and went for the big spit? He said to me "Jees I feel crook", and then he raced across the room, shoved his head out of the window and burped a rainbow.'
1975 Richard Beilby *The Brown Land Crying* 225: 'Goin' for the big spit, was I? I don't remember.'

spit chips, to 1 To be extremely thirsty
1901 *The Bulletin Reciter* 108: While you're spitting chips like thunder . . . / And the streams of sweat near blind you.
[1904 Laura M. Palmer-Archer *A Bush Honeymoon* 349: *Spit sixpences* A sign of thirst.]
1946 Alan Marshall *Tell us about the Turkey, Jo* 142: I was spitting chips. God, I was dry!
2 To be in a state of anger and frustration
1947 John Morrison *Sailors Belong Ships* 189: 'Old Mick Doyle's with them. He's spitting chips because they're not using sea water.'
1954 Peter Gladwin *The Long Beat Home* 17: 'It's enough to make you spit chips when you think of Sydney – movies and vaudeville comedies and a decent musician once in two years.'
1965 Ivan Southall *Ash Road* 77: 'Not when I saw Mr Fairhall last. He was spittin' chips because Peter had gone away.'

sport A form of colloquial address
1941 Kylie Tennant *The Battlers* 105: 'Now lay off, sport.'
1943 George Johnston *New Guinea Diary* 186: Before they have been there long they are calling them [the natives] 'sport', which seems to be the second A.I.F.'s equivalent for 'digger'.
1952 Eric Lambert *The Twenty Thousand Thieves* 38: 'Have a swig, sport.' He took the bottle . . . and helped himself to a mouthful. 'Thanks, sport.' He handed the bottle back and idly he noted that he never called a man 'sport' before.
1961 Hugh Atkinson *Low Company* 46: 'Whatyer tryin' to do, sport? Pull me leg?'
1975 Richard Beilby *The Brown Land Crying* 80: 'Come on, sport,' the doorman was saying patiently. 'You can't stop here. You've had a skinful.'

spruik To hold forth like a showman [unexplained]
1915 C. J. Dennis *The Songs of a Sentimental Bloke* 42: 'E'll sigh and spruik, an' 'owl a love-sick vow –/ (The silly cow!)
1916 C. J. Dennis *The Moods of Ginger Mick* 156: *Spruik* To deliver a speech, as a showman.
1934 Vance Palmer *The Swayne Family* 250: 'Wonder you didn't get a job spruiking for the pictures down there in town.'
1941 Kylie Tennant *The Battlers* 181:

316

The ampster's is an easy job. He stands in the front row of the listening crowd registering intense interest and enthusiasm while the showman 'spruiks'.

1951 A. W. Upfield *The Widows of Broome* 31: 'Old Bilge's bound to do a bit of spruiking, but he isn't too bad.'

1975 Hal Porter *The Extra* 244: Hollow-chested men ... who sell agitated toys on street corners or spruik outside strip-tease joints.

spruiker A speaker attracting custom outside a theatre or sideshow; any loquacious person

1924 *Truth* 27 Apr. 6: *Spruiker* A speaker.

1934 Tom Clarke *Marriage at 6 a.m.* 46: *Spruiker* an announcer at the door of a theatre.

1951 Dal Stivens *Jimmy Brockett* 82: A spruiker outside was dressed up like a train conductor and he told you about the tour.

1962 Alan Marshall *This is the Grass* 125: Spruikers in braided uniforms strutted up and down before foyers extolling the virtues of the pictures within.

1964 H. P. Tritton *Time Means Tucker* 33: Madam Cora, a fortune teller, had a long line of people waiting their turn ... Her husband, a pudgy little man, was her spruiker.

1971 Craig McGregor *Don't Talk to me about Love* 159: He declaimed in the voice of a Royal Easter Show spruiker.

spud, not the clean See 'potato'

1925 E. S. Sorenson *Murty Brown* 135: 'He wasn't the clean spud.'

squatter 1 Someone taking up his abode in the bush and living by preying on the flocks of others, dealing in sly grog, etc. [f. *squatter* One who settles upon land, esp. public land, to which he has no legal title U.S. 1788 Mathews]

1830 J. Betts *An Account of the Colony of Van Diemen's Land* 39: The means of rooting out a class of people called 'Squatters'. These were generally emancipated convicts, or ticket-of-leave-men, who, having obtained a small grant, under the old system, or without any grant at all, sat themselves down in remote situations, and maintained large flocks, obtained, generally, in very nefarious ways, by having the run of all the surrounding country.

1833 W. H. Breton *Excursions in New South Wales* 442: There are likewise in the colony certain persons called 'squatters' (the term is American) who are commonly, it may be said always, of the lowest grade. These men establish themselves on some unlocated spot, where they cultivate enough land to supply them with grain, and not unfrequently pilfer whatever else they require, from the neighbouring farms.

1835 *Sydney Gazette* 28 Apr. 2: In every part of the country squatters without any reasonable means of maintaining themselves by honesty, have formed stations, and evidently pursued a predatory warfare against the flocks and herds in the vicinity.

2 A respectable pastoralist; a pastoralist occupying a tract of land with a license from the Crown (from 1836)

1840 Gov. Gipps to Lord Russell *HRA* xxi 130: A very large proportion of the land, which is to form the new district of Port Phillip, is already in the licensed occupation of the Squatters of New South Wales, a class of persons whom it would be wrong to confound with those who bear the same name in America, and who are generally persons of mean repute and small means, who have taken unauthorized possession of patches of land. Among the Squatters of New South Wales are the wealthiest of the Land, occupying with the permission of Government thousands and tens of thousands of acres; Young men of good Family and connexions in England, Officers of the Army and Navy, Graduates of Oxford and Cambridge are also in no small number amongst them.

1848 J. C. Byrne *Twelve Years' Wanderings in the British Colonies* i 186: Squatting in New South Wales, is the occupation without purchase of the Crown lands, within the boundaries of the colony, and of the vast extent of territory beyond the frontiers, or rather old line of demarcation. A squatter obtains his temporary right to what land he requires by procuring a licence from the Crown land Commissioners in the colony, for which he pays annually, the sum of £10; besides being subject to a small annual assessment on his sheep, cattle and horses, for the support of a border police. The squatters are the great producing class of the colony: their vast herds and flocks out-number by many degrees the scanty numbers depastured on the purchased, or granted, land of the country.

1888 H. S. Russell *The Genesis of Queensland* 162–3: The circumstances of the time were combining in 1840 to compel the squatters of the northern district into some more genial climate ... Some who had bought stations there were already seeking, and at times, finding purchasers for what dissatisfied themselves: albeit held under the easy rent of an annual ten pound licence – for ever! as it seemed – with a small assessment upon their stock.... The term 'squatter', as applied to the class it now designates, was not in vogue until two years after this.

3 A pastoral magnate, whether occupying land as tenant of the Crown or as owner, regarded as one of the privileged or affluent

1902 Henry Lawson 'Lord Douglas' *Prose* i 494: 'You're allers findin' excuses for blacklegs an' scabs, Mitchell,' said Barcoo-Rot ... 'Why, you'd find a white spot on a squatter.'

1908 E. S. Sorenson *The Squatter's Ward* 187: Mr Susman was a squatter, and as such to be held above suspicion.

1934 Tom Clarke *Marriage at 6 a.m.* 46: *Squatter* a station owner (corresponds almost to 'squire' in English).

1940 Arnold L. Haskell *Waltzing Matilda* 109: The majority of wealthy squatters (read 'landed gentry') have gained their first experience in this manner as jackaroos (read 'apprentices') on some vast station.

1958 H. D. Williamson *The Sunlit Plain* 42: She might have been a squatter's wife, the way she was dressed, Leo

reflected.

squattocracy The squatters (senses 2 and 3) collectively regarded as a colonial aristocracy, often with a derogatory implication

1846 C. P. Hodgson *Reminiscences of Australia* 118: Throughout the Colony generally English are the most numerous, then the Scotch, then the Irish, amongst the squattocracy.

1852 William Hughes *The Australian Colonies* 124: The aristocracy (or the *squattocracy*) of the colonies.

1865 Henry Kingsley *The Hillyars and the Burtons* iii 265: A miserable and effete Squattocracy (with their wretched aping of the still more miserable and effete aristocracy of the old world).

1888 E. Finn *The Chronicles of Early Melbourne* ii 908: Though presented himself as a Colonial Emissary in England, he was veritably an agent of the 'squattocracy', of which he was one. On the Transportation question he lent himself to promote the interests of the few against the many.

1891 Francis Adams *Fortnightly Review* Sep. 398: One has not endured all these years the rule of the squattocracy, as voiced in a hopelessly subservient and corrupt legislature, for nothing.

1902 Mrs Campbell Praed *My Australian Girlhood* 217: My lady did not enter into effusive social relations with the selectors not specially accredited to her. This was perhaps hardly to be expected in one who, as a representative of the old order, was traditionally opposed to the inroads of agriculturalist upon privileges of the squattocracy.

1919 E. S. Sorenson *Chips and Splinters* 17: He talked like that at his timber-camp meetings, but the timber-getters noticed that he wore a different coat when he was among the squattocracy.

1939 Miles Franklin and Dymphna Cusack *Pioneers on Parade* 2–3: She had canonized anyone who held more than ten thousand acres, and lumped pure merinos and the poorer goats in the one romantic squirearchy known as the squattocracy.

1951 Dymphna Cusack and Florence

James *Come in Spinner* 30: 'She's turning on the dentures for the benefit of some of the squattocracy in the Madrid Lounge.'
1975 Hal Porter *The Extra* 91: Here, you find Petty's Hotel, once the haunt of squattocracy, now a Red Cross Blood Transfusion Centre.

squib *n. & v.* (To act as) a coward [f. *squib* a mean, insignificant or paltry fellow OED 1586–1653 *obs.*]
1924 *Truth* 27 Apr. 6: *Squib* A coward.
1942 Gavin Casey *It's Harder for Girls* 200: 'He shut up, just like th' bloody squib he is.'
1955 D'Arcy Niland *The Shiralee* 50: 'The rough-and-tumble doesn't worry me. I'm not squibbing the issue.'
1966 D. H. Crick *Period of Adjustment* 228: 'You're a squib, like the rest of them.'

squiz An inquisitive look [? f. *squint* + *quiz*]
1916 C. J. Dennis *The Moods of Ginger Mick* 156: *Squiz* A brief glance.
1924 *Truth* 27 Apr. 6: *Squiz* A hurried look.
1946 Dal Stivens *The Courtship of Uncle Henry* 69: He put the chops down and took a squiz at me.
1948 K. S. Prichard *Golden Miles* 97: 'Was jest goin' to send for you to have a squiz at her.'
1975 Don Townshend *Gland Time* 142: He put his hand in his pocket and produced a small box. 'Have a squiz at that.'

staggering bob see **bob**

stand The place allocated to one man on the board of a shearing shed, with the accompanying equipment
1955 'I Don't Go Shearing Now' in *Australian Bush Ballads* ed. Stewart and Keesing 246: You will pay an early visit to the dear old shed, I'll bet – / Perhaps upon your own old stand the oil-rag's lying yet.

stand over *v.* To extort money etc. by intimidation; to domineer over someone

1939 Kylie Tennant *Foveaux* 173: 'I just had Thompson in here and he stood over me for three quid.'
1950 *The Australian Police Journal* Apr. 119: *Stand over* To threaten, menace, or use duress on someone for the purpose of gain.
1952 T. A. G. Hungerford *The Ridge and the River* 209: 'Wilder'll be the poor down-trodden guy that's being stood over.'
1958 Frank Hardy *The Four-Legged Lottery* 192: We'll have to stand over him to get our money.

standover *n. & a.* An intimidatory operation
1939 Kylie Tennant *Foveaux* 180: ''Struth, you earn your money on a stand over,' he told himself.
1954 L. H. Evers *Pattern of Conquest* 198: 'Don't come the stand-over tactics you used with Charlie.'
1957 Judah Waten *Shares in Murder* 63: 'He can't come this standover on me. He's got nothing on me and you know it.'

standover man A criminal using force, or the threat of force, to intimidate or extort
1939 Kylie Tennant *Foveaux* 174: He didn't deserve to be a 'standover man' if he couldn't move quicker.
1951 Dymphna Cusack and Florence James *Come in Spinner* 355–6: It was Joe's bodyguard, Curly – stand-over man as well, they said.
1957 Judah Waten *Shares in Murder* 79: He might end up as a common bully, a standover man.
1962 Alan Marshall *This is the Grass* 60: I guessed he was a stand-over merchant and that he had brought these two men with him like a hunter who goes out with his dogs.
1975 *Bulletin* 26 Apr. 44: The heavies (stand over men) and the bludgers who neither worked nor stole but were simply professional parasites.

Star Hotel See quot. 1941
1905 E. C. Buley *Australian Life in Town and Country* 54: The rags that

serve him for socks are 'Prince Alberts'; he lodges each night in 'The Moon and Stars Hotel, ground floor.'

1941 Baker 71: *Star Hotel, sleep in the* To sleep in the open.

1942 Charles Barrett *From a Bush Hut* 37: Spreading our blankets on stony ground – there wasn't a soft spot within miles – we slept at the Inn of Stars.

starver A saveloy

1941 Baker 71: *Starver* A saveloy.

1959 D'Arcy Niland *The Big Smoke* 211: 'I know what the things I eat cost me. Starvers, crumpets, stale cakes, specked fruit, pies.'

station, there's movement at the Expression for hurried activity, esp. portending some imminent event [f. the opening line of A.B. Paterson's 'The Man from Snowy River' (There was movement at the station, for the word had passed around) 1895]

1966 Tom Ronan *Once There Was A Bagman* 225: There was movement on the station, of course, as soon as old Harry showed over the skyline.

1974 'Ah, now there's movement at the station' (racing broadcaster reporting signs that a race was about to begin.)

1976 *Sun-Herald* 18 Jan. 84: Movement at the Station. Mr Rex Palmer, 2GB's general manager for the past 18 months, left on Friday to head Adelaide's fledgling 'good music' station, 5AA.

steamer Kangaroo meat cooked with pork: *obs.*

1820 C. Jeffreys *Geographical ... Delineations of the Island of Van Diemen's Land* 69: Their meal consisted of the hind-quarters of a kangaroo cut into mince-meat, stewed in its own gravy, with a few rashers of salt pork, this dish is commonly called a steamer.

1834 George Bennett *Wanderings in New South Wales* i 289: The colonial dish called a steamer, consists of the flesh of this animal [kangaroo] dressed, with slices of ham.

1843 Charles Rowcroft *Tales of the Colonies* i 134: The tenderest parts, and those most free from the tendons and

fibres with which the flesh of the kangaroo abounds, were carefully cut out, and chopped up fine; some slices of salt pork were added to this, and the whole put to steam slowly over the fire. This national dish of the Van Diemen's Land bush is called a 'Steamer'.

steer, the red see **red**

sterky As for 'packing them' q.v.: *rare* [abbr. of *stercoraceous*]

1944 Jean Devanny *By Tropic, Sea and Jungle* 162: The croc disappears, and there's Ernest, standing up to his waist in the water, looking for him – scared as hell, but too game to come out. He yells for us to come in ourselves, so my dad goes in. He's a bit sterky too.

1953 Baker 104: *sterky* frightened.

1959 David Forrest *The Last Blue Sea* 24: 'He just gives me the sturks.'

sterling English immigrants, as distinct from the native born [see quot. 1827]

1827 P. Cunningham *Two Years in New South Wales* ii 53: Our colonial-born brethren are best known here by the name of *Currency*, in contradistinction to *Sterling*, or those born in the mother-country.

1844 Louisa Meredith *Notes and Sketches of New South Wales* 50: The natives (not the aborigines, but the 'currency', as they are termed, in distinction from the 'sterling', or British-born residents) are often very good-looking when young.

see **currency**

sticks, the The rural areas generally, or anywhere so regarded [*the sticks* the backwoods U.S. 1905 Mathews]

1958 Christopher Koch *The Boys in the Island* 101: 'Still,' he said with a chuckle, 'what can y' expect, way out here in the sticks? You would pick on a dame from back of beyond.'

1962 Criena Rohan *The Delinquents* 19: Back to that God-awful little town in the sticks.

1971 Frank Hardy *The Outcasts of Foolgarah* 5: A shire clerk's job in the sticks for three years' practice then back to

the big smoke, into the big league.
see **scrub**

sticky Inquisitive [abbr. of *stickybeak*]
1941 Baker 72: *Sticky* (adj.) Curious,
inquisitive.
1974 David Ireland *Burn* 139: 'Have a
gander. Perhaps your mates'd like a bit
of a sticky too.'

sticky-beak *n*. An inquisitive person
(sticking his beak in)
1924 Steele Rudd *Me an' th' Son* 7: 'Did
y' hurt yourself – sticky-beak?' he sez.
1926 J. Vance Marshall *Timely Tips for
New Australians: Sticky-beak* A slang
term denoting an inquistive person.
1938 *Bulletin* 6 Jul. 48: 'Then you'll
spoil your life and hers for what some
old stickybeak and scandalcat has said.'
1947 Margaret Trist *Daddy* 262: 'Well,
if he's not the biggest stickybeak of a
man I've ever met,' Lydia murmured.
1953 *Caddie A Sydney Barmaid* 25: The
stickybeaks were dying to know who
was the father of the baby, but Nellie
wouldn't tell.
1961 Xavier Herbert *Soldier's Women*
471: This clever girl, who had probably
spent her life lying to sticky-beaks
interfering in her affairs, had it all
worked out.

stickybeak *v*. To act as a stickybeak, to
pry into the affairs of others
1935 Kylie Tennant *Tiburon* 111: 'Ain't
I got enough trouble,' he roared, with
them stickybeakin' round 'ere gettin'
me up before the court.'
1945 Margaret Trist *Now That We're
Laughing* 142: 'It's so good of them to
come.' 'Why is it?' demanded Mrs
Henderson. 'They only come to sticky-
beak.'
1957 Judah Waten *Shares in Murder*
83: 'Why don't you stop sticky-
beaking?'
1968 *Coast to Coast 1967–1968* 9: 'I
don't have to put up with you and
your sticky-beaking into my affairs.'
sticky nose As for 'stickybeak'
1966 H. F. Brinsmead *The Beat of the
City* 62: 'At first I followed them in
just to be a sticky nose.'

stiff Out of luck
1919 W. H. Downing *Digger Dialects*
47: *Stiff* Unlucky.
1922 Arthur Wright *A Colt from the
Country* 124: 'On'y just got cut out of
second place,' declared Knocker. 'Ain't
a man stiff?'
1945 Cecil Mann *The River* 137: It's
damn' stiff you can't march this year,
but you will next year.
1955 John Morrison *Black Cargo* 64:
'You're stiff,' cut in Boyd, 'my time's
up at five.'

stiffen the lizards see **lizards**

sting *n*. 1 A strong drink [f. *stingo* strong
ale or beer OED 1635]
1929 K. S. Prichard *Coonardoo* 60: 'I'm
through with prospectin'!' 'Misses his
three square meals a day and sting,'
Bob explained.
1972 John de Hoog *Skid Row Dossier*
4: You can share a bottle of sting
(methylated spirits) down a lane.
2 Dope, esp. in racing
1950 *Australian Police Journal* Apr.
118: *Sting* Dope.
1958 Frank Hardy *The Four-Legged Lottery* 173: The 'smarties' soon found
stings that didn't show on a swab.

sting *v*. 1 To exploit someone by extracting a loan; to overcharge
[1812 Vaux: *Sting* To rob or defraud a
person or place is called *stinging* them,
as, that *cove* is too fly; he has been
stung before; meaning that man is upon
his guard, he has already been trick'd.]
1919 W. H. Downing *Digger Dialects*
47: *Sting* (vb.) Make a request for a
loan or gift. So, also, 'Put in the stings'.
1928 Arthur Wright *A Good Recovery*
161: 'Suppose he wants to put the stings
in for a few quid.'
1941 Baker 72: *Sting, to* To borrow
money from someone.
1945 Kylie Tennant *Ride on Stranger*
63: 'In this world you've got to sting
or get stung,' he pointed out.
1959 D'Arcy Niland *The Big Smoke*
206: 'Pay?' Georgie Barber said, taken
aback. 'What would you sting me?'
1969 Alan O'Toole *The Racing Game*

69: 'I'm being stung for quite a bit of money, at a time when there's none coming in, and there's more bills on the way.'
1970 Patrick White *The Vivisector* 331: 'Who sold you the paintings?' he asked . . . 'Diacono? Then he must have stung you!'
2 (*give the sting*) To dope a racehorse
1949 Lawson Glassop *Lucky Palmer* 36: 'It's a moral. They're going to give it the sting. They'll hit it with enough dope to win a Melbourne Cup.'

stinker An oppressively hot day [f. *stinker* for anything unpleasant]
1941 Baker 72: *Stinker* A disagreeable, highly unpleasant and often humid day.
1950 Jon Cleary *Just Let Me Be* 17: 'Hullo, Mrs Brennan. Stinker of a day, ain't it?'
1959 Dorothy Hewett *Bobbin Up* 170: Already the sky was pale and smoky with the promise of 'another stinker'.
1976 *Sydney Morning Herald* 6 Nov. 11: A thick heat haze is covering the mountains. It's going to be a scorcher. A stinker.

stipe Stipendiary steward (controlling horseracing) [abbr.]
1977 *Australian* 15 Jan. 20: The racing page screamed STIPES PROBE JOCKEY.

stir To act in a way provocative to authority or upholders of the status quo; to create a minor disturbance (juvenile) [? f. *stir the possum* q.v. or the proverb 'The more you stir a turd, the worse it stinks' 1546]
1972 John de Hoog *Skid Row Dossier* 110: Excitement was whipped up over the tiniest incident and when several youths went 'stirring' one day – riding up and down the lifts of large office blocks – conversations dwelt on and enlarged every action.
1973 H. Williams *My Love Had a Black Speed Stripe* 54: It was a pity we couldn't pack this pommy foreman Charlie up to Japan to stir it up with the workers there, where they would soon give him the old samurai treatment.

stirrer Someone given to 'stirring'
1971 Frank Hardy *The Outcasts of Foolgarah* 88: That'd be him, thought the Dean, a shit-stirrer from way back. Ibid. 109: The lurk men and stirrers weren't the only ones burning the midnight oil.
1973 H. Williams *My Love Had a Black Speed Stripe* 55: We were not to be led away by a few stirrers who had no regard for their own union but were just trying to stir it up for their own purposes.

stir the possum see **possum**

stone the crows see **crows**

stonker To defeat, thwart, put out of commission [cf. *stonk* the stake in a game EDD; *stunk* (stonk) to pant, gasp, groan with exertion SND]
1919 W. H. Downing *Digger Dialects* 48: *Stonker* Exterminate; kill; strike out.
1932 A. W. Upfield *A Royal Abduction* 250: 'Why don't they shut off the confounded thing?' 'Too stonkered with surprise, I'll bet.'
1942 Sarah Campion *Bonanza* 42: 'Now you're stonkered all right, if Clancy ever gets on yer track.'
1948 Robert S. Close *Morn of Youth* 99: She threw . . . straight for the target, which suddenly fell down on the road. 'Cripes! You've stonkered it,' I said.
1961 Jon Rose *At the Cross* 79: 'There's nothing I can do . . . I'm stonkered.' Bella began to cry.

stoom, stoomer see **stumer**

stoush *v.* To clout, punch [see *stoush n.*]
1893 J. A. Barry *Steve Brown's Bunyip* 66: 'I'll get stoushed over this job yet. Brombee's got it in for me.'
1896 Henry Lawson 'Shooting the Moon' *Prose* i 150: 'Now look here,' I said, shaking my fist at him, like that, 'if you say a word, I'll stoush yer!'
1900–10 O'Brien and Stephens: *Stoush* to hit or punch.
1911 Louis Stone *Jonah* 50: 'The Push stoushed 'im, an' then cleared.'
1934 'Leslie Parker' *Trooper to the Southern Cross* (1966) 69: 'He had a bit

of turn-up with the military policeman and stoushed him.'
1959 Dorothy Hewett *Bobbin Up* 80: The boys still coming out at playtime in their wrinkled jeans, stoushing each other over the head.
1965 Eric Lambert *The Long White Night* 79: 'Get out of that bloody car while I stoush yer!'

stoush *n*. Fighting, violence [? f. *stashie* (*stash*) an uproar; a commotion, distur-bance, quarrel EDD 1851]
1908 Henry Fletcher *Dads and Dan be-tween Smokes* 32: He looked as though he liked bein' hit an' took stoush fer breakfast every mornin'.'
1916 C. J. Dennis *The Moods of Ginger Mick* 31: The Call of Stoush [poem title]
1939 Kylie Tennant *Foveaux* 247: Strik-ers who pounced into the tram compart-ments and began dealing out 'stouch' to the terrified passengers.
1945 Robert S. Close *Love Me Sailor* 149: It was like the old days when I got Ernie into some stoush ashore just for the hell of fighting him out of it.
1953 T. A. G. Hungerford *Riverslake* 122: 'I'd rather be with him than against him in any stoush.'
1971 Frank Hardy *The Outcasts of Fool-garah* 82: Here they are now with their mob looking for a bit of stoush.

straight wire see **wire**

strength, the ~ of The essential facts about, reliable information upon [? f. *strength* the force, tenor, import (of a document) OED 1425–1602 *obs*]
1908 Henry Fletcher *Dads and Dan be-tween Smokes* 112: 'So yous thinks I'se wore out, Wayback, an' past patchin' an' mendin'?' 'That's about ther strength of it.'
1916 C. J. Dennis *The Moods of Ginger Mick* 157: *Strength of it* The truth of it, the value of it.
1921 Ernest O'Ferrall *Bodger and the Boarders* 52: 'I see that Barnstormer bloke an' got the strength of the whole thing.'
1926 K. S. Prichard *Working Bullocks* 136: 'Now,' she continued ... 'I'll just

give you the strength of Red Burke.'
1939 Kylie Tennant *Foveaux* 154: 'What's the strength of it? Any idea?
1947 Vance Palmer *Hail Tomorrow* 20: 'You've about got the strength of it, Mick.'
1959 K. S. Prichard *N'Goola* 153–4: 'A trapper camped further along the road gave me the strength of them.'
see **strong**

strides Men's trousers, leggings [f. *strides* trousers EDD 1895; also listed by Partridge as theatrical]
1924 *Truth* 27 Apr. 6: *Strides* Trousers.
1932 Leonard Mann *Flesh in Armour* 291: His tunic and light coat were of the ultra fashionable style, and his strides would not have disgraced an officer of the Guards.
1940 Thomas Wood *Cobbers Campaign-ing* 54: 'But if ye'll just wait till I put on me strides I'll get ye there in two-ups.'
1959 D'Arcy Niland *The Big Smoke* 11: It's like taking your strides off and getting into bed, broke and finished.
1975 Don Townshend *Gland Time* 54: Their sex life had come to an abrupt halt and Bluey said he hadn't dropped his strides with Gwenda for weeks.

strike a blow see **blow**

strike paydirt see **paydirt**

string To form a string, move in a string, esp. of cattle [f. *string* to move or progress in a string or disconnected line OED 1824]
1887 W. S. S. Tyrwhitt *The New Chum in the Queensland Bush* 192: He sees through the darkness a line of cattle slowly stringing away across the flat.
1895 A. B. Paterson 'Clancy of the Overflow' *The Man from Snowy River* 21: As the stock are slowly stringing, Clancy rides behind them singing, / For the drover's life has pleasures that the townsfolk never know.
1900 Henry Lawson 'Thin Lips and False Teeth' *Prose* i 242: Brook ... found the road to the school by the children 'stringing' along in the opposite direc-tion.
1905 E. C. Buley *Australian Life in*

Town and Country 26: After the cutting
out is done, the beasts have been sorted
in mobs according to their classes, each
mob is made to 'string' or move in
single file, in order that a count may be
made.

stringy bark An example (like *geebung*)
of the name of the native flora being used
to distinguish some denizen of the outback, as though embodying its uncouth
indigenous qualities
1833 *New South Wales Magazine* Oct.
171: The workmanship of which I beg
you will not scrutinize, as I am but, to
use a colonial expression, 'a stringy-
bark carpenter'. [Morris]
1836 J. F. O'Connell *A Residence of
Eleven Years in New Holland* 49: Let us
suppose the suitor an old 'stringy-bark',
such being the soubriquet in which inland settlers rejoice.
1861 Horace Earle *Ups and Downs* 59:
'She would never have had the bad
taste to prefer a stringy bark like me to
such a fine-looking, first-class fellow
as yourself.'
1865 Henry Kingsley *The Hillyars and
the Burtons* 58: 'Hallo!' said Burton.
'Are *you* Stringy Bark?' [an ex-convict]
'I am from Van Diemen's Land,' said
the old man, quietly. 'But an emigrant.'
The convict gave a grunt of disappointment.
1905 *The Old Bush Songs* ed. A. B.
Paterson 43: 'The Stringy-bark Cockatoo [ballad title]. Ibid. xiii: The stringy-
bark tree is an unfailing sign of poor
land; and the minstrel was much worse
treated when working for 'The Stringy-
bark Cockatoo' than when he was a
'Squatter's man.'

strong, the ~ of As for 'the strength of'
1910 Arthur Wright *Under a Cloud* 31:
'Don't yer want to own up? Some reason for wantin' to preserve yer incog.
I suppose. What's the strong of it?'
1938 Xavier Herbert *Capricornia* 566:
'What's the strong of you? What's the
questioning for? I've done nuthin'.'
1946 K. S. Prichard *The Roaring Nineties* 294: 'What's the strong of it, Mor-
rey?' he asked.

1959 Eric Lambert *Glory Thrown In*
'What's the strong of this joint?' demanded Doc brusquely. 'Not an undertaker's is it?'

stubby 1 A beer bottle containing 370
ml (ceased manufacture in 1977) [f. shape]
1968 Frank Hardy *The Unlucky Australians* 49: He threw an empty stubby
into the box and went to the refrigerator
for a full one.
2 *Stubbies* A brand of men's shorts
1977 *Australian* 7 Apr. 3: Stubbies –
the football shorts with pockets – have
become an international fashion ...
Although the Stubby is a very Australian name – thought of in the context
of short shorts to go with short bottles
of beer – Mr Phillips is confident they
will become as American as apple pie.

stuck into, to get 1 To attack someone,
physically or verbally
1942 Gavin Casey *It's Harder for Girls*
228: 'A bit o' peace after ... you an'
Winch nearly getting stuck into each
other at the pub.'
1953 T. A. G. Hungerford *Riverslake*
120–1: 'What was the trouble, Con? I
saw you stuck into a Balt across the
press as I come down.'
1973 Alexander Buzo *Rooted* 44: 'Then
he tried to job Hammo. Well, Hammo
got stuck into him, I can tell you.'
1977 Jeff Thomson *Sunday Telegraph*
27 Feb. 60: 'They're getting a bit cocky,
the Poms. So I'd like to get stuck into
'em again.'
2 To apply oneself energetically to a task
1955 John Morrison *Black Cargo* 65:
'All right, grab those knives and get
stuck into it.'
1970 Alexander Buzo *The Front Room
Boys* in Penguin *Plays* 29: 'The back
room boys are going to streamline this
department, which means a few heads
are going to roll, so get stuck into it.'
1975 Les Ryan *The Shearers* 124:
'Righto, you blue-tongues!' he bellowed out. 'Get stuck into it!'
3 To consume (food or drink) with gusto
1947 Gavin Casey *The Wits are Out* 89:
'Come on,' Syd said. 'What about getting stuck into it?' They gathered round

the barrel for some serious drinking.
1955 D'Arcy Niland *The Shiralee* 26:
'Never mind that,' he grunted. 'Get
stuck into your tucker.'
1963 D. H. Crick *Martin Place* 218:
'Let's get stuck into them prawns.'
1973 Alexander Buzo *Rooted* 30: 'Davo
got stuck into the grog, didn't he?'

stud See quot. [cf. *bull*²]
1962 *Sydney Morning Herald* 24 Nov.
12: The contractor knows he has four
or five 'stud' shearers (boss's men) on
the board who will vote them dry.

students, the The members of one of the
University sporting teams in N.S.W.
1976 *Sunday Telegraph* 24 Oct. 76: Boycott thrashes Students. Geoff Boycott,
the veteran English test batsman, scored
a casual century for Waverley against
University of NSW yesterday.

stumer, come a To crash financially,
come a cropper: *rare* [? f. *stummer* to
stagger, stumble EDD 1793; or *stumer* a
forged or dishonoured cheque OED 1890]
1898 *Bulletin* 17 Dec. Red Page: *stoomey*
broke; and a *stoomer* or *stumer* is a man
without money.
1900–10 O'Brien and Stephens: *Come
a stoomer* stake a bet and lose everything.
1941 Baker 73: *Stumer, come a* To crash
financially, esp. in a racing bet.
to stoom To knock unconscious, kill:
rare
1908 E. S. Sorenson *Quinton's Rouseabout* 119: 'Seemed plain ter me as Gar-
ron 'ad left 'is team at the station an'
rode 'ome; 'as a kick-up with the ole
gerl over something – God knows wot
– an' she stooms him out – accidental,
as yer might say. Then she hits on the
black stump as an orlright place ter
hide 'im.'
1925 E. S. Sorenson *Murty Brown* 68:
'Might a 'urt yer!' ' 'Urt me!' Charcoal
snorted. 'Might a stoomed me out!'

stump, the black See **black**

stung Drunk, tipsy [f. *sting*¹]
1919 W. H. Downing *Digger Dialects*

48: *Stung* (adj. or p. part.) (1) Drunk;
(2) having been induced to lend.
1941 Baker 74: *Stung* Drunk.
1952 T. A. G. Hungerford *The Ridge
and the River* 62: 'The old bloke's stung
already, and the pubs aren't even
opened yet!'
1965 William Dick *A Bunch of Ratbags*
219: We had arrived at Doreen's sister's
wedding-reception about an hour ago
and by now we were all half stung.
1970 Kenneth Slessor *Bread and Wine*
154: To a total abstainer, the line 'I am
stung, stung to the heart of me' would
convey, I suppose, nothing so coarse
as the associations which I find in it.

style, ball of see **ball**

Such is life An expression given a special Australian currency from being the
supposed last words of Ned Kelly, and
from being adopted by Joseph Furphy
as the title of his famous novel
1880 J. Jenkins *Diary of a Welsh Swagman* (1975) 100: Ned Kelly, the Bushranger was hanged today [9 Nov.] at
8 a.m. His last words at the scaffold
were, 'Such is life'.
c.1897 Joseph Furphy *Such is Life
Being certain extracts from the diary of
Tom Collins* (1903)
1969 *Such Was Life Select Documents
in Australian Social History 1788–1850*
ed. Russel Ward and John Robertson.

sugar bag A nest of wild honey in a
tree; honey [Pidgin]
1830 Robert Dawson *The Present State
of Australia* 136: The strange native
. . . pointed with his tomahawk to the
tree and nodding his head and smiling
at me, repeated the words, 'Choogar-
bag, choogar-bag, choogar-bag!' (sugar-
bag) their English expression for honey,
or anything sweet.
1851 John Henderson *Excursions and
Adventures in New South Wales* 139–
40: There is another mode, however,
of hunting for sugar bags . . . Having
seen a bee alight on any twig or leaf,
the black takes a little bit of the finest
down . . . cautiously steals upon the
bee, and dexterously places the down

upon his back ... Having traced the bee to its retreat ... he then, with his tomahawk, cuts his way up the tree, cuts into the hollow branch where the hive is.
1864 Rachel Henning *Letters* ed. David Adams (1963) 185: The other has been employing his energies in climbing gum-trees after 'sugar-bags', or wild honeycombs.
1901 F. J. Gillen *Diary* (1968) 288: Honey or as the blacks call it 'Sugar bag' appears to be fairly plentiful for the boys cut out two lots yesterday.
1908 E. S. Sorenson *The Squatter's Ward* 32: 'There's allers plenty of 'em pokin' about the bush lookin' for sugar-bags.'
1930 *Bulletin* 8 Jan. 20: The two new hands who were ringbarking on Blade's selection reported gleefully that they had found a bees' nest near the boundary fence. They had heard a lot about 'sugarbags', and had been wasting much of their boss's time looking up trees.
1941 Charles Barrett *Coast of Adventure* 109: Grigalalok already had found 'sugar bag' in a rock cavity, bringing a mass of dripping honeycomb to our conchologist.

sunbeam An item of cutlery or crockery laid on the table but not used, and so not needing to be washed up

sunburnt country, the Australia [f. first line of Dorothea Mackellar's poem: see quot. 1914]
1914 Dorothea Mackellar 'My Country' *The Witch Maid* 29: I love a sunburnt country / A land of sweeping plains.
1953 Ian Bevan ed. *The Sunburnt Country Profile of Australia* [book title]

Sunday too far away An expression given currency by a film of this title (see quot. 1975), but part of the lore of the shearer much earlier
1963 *Sydney Morning Herald* 17 Aug. 11: A lot of greasies (shearers) get hen trouble. Some shearers' wives reckon we shearer blokes are either too tired, too drunk, or too far away.
1975 *Times* (London) 20 May 9: The title [of the film] is from a song, the complaint of a shearer's loveless wife: 'Friday he's too tired, Saturday too drunk, and Sunday too far away.'

sundowner A swagman who arrives at a station at sundown, too late in the day to do any work, but in time to draw rations
[1846 C. P. Hodgson *Reminiscences of Australia* 302: This day's work [climbing a tree to look around] is what is generally though not elegantly termed 'eye-balling' and its duration amounted in colonial phraseology to a 'Sundowner' (? a task requiring no great exertion which lasts until sundown), neither word is to be found I believe in an English dictionary, but both have very expressive meanings.]
1868 'The Song of the Sundowner' *Sydney Punch* 14 Nov. 198 repr. in *Old Bush Songs* ed. Stewart and Keesing (1957) 230: A visit at sundown I manage to pay, / And ask for my evening ration.
1887 W. S. S. Tyrwhitt *The New Chum in the Queensland Bush* 82: There is a class of men in Australia called 'sundowners' from the fact that they always turn up at stations, nominally in search of work, at sundown, never coming in before for fear of having to work for their rations.
1890 Tasma *A Sydney Sovereign* 127: For the chance 'sundowner' who cast his tired eyes upon them, they could not signify much.
1901 Henry Lawson 'A Double Buggy at Lahey's Creek' *Prose* i 596: 'What do you want me to come at sunset for?' asked James. 'Do you want me to camp out in the scrub and turn up like a blooming sundowner?'
1913 John Sadleir *Recollections of a Victorian Police Officer* 109: 'Sundowners', swagmen who travelled without any settled purpose from station to station, obtaining fresh supplies of food at any station where they might chance to find themselves at sunset.

sunny New South see **New South**

sunshine state, the Queensland, in the language of tourist advertising

1962 Criena Rohan *The Delinquents* 128: 'If you ask me, all Brisbane's full of coppers and all of them bastards,' she said, expressing in one concise sentence the full theory of central government of the sunshine state.

1970 *Coast to Coast 1969–1970* 115: 'We had such fun, remember? And somehow it never seemed to rain. Good old sunshine State.'

1974 *Nation Review* 7 Jun. 1117: The recent Queensland Festival of Arts has caused something of a crisis of identity in the Sunshine State. A Queensland festival of arts is, after all, something of a contradiction in terms.

super 1 The superintendent of a station [abbr.]

1857 F. Cooper *Wild Adventures in Australia* 59: 'Scotchy' ... introduced me as a particular friend to Wilder the owner of that run, under the impression that a 'super' was required, as Wilder had from some time spoken of his intention to reside in Brisbane.

1870 Henry Kendall 'Camped by the Creek' *Poetical Works* ed. T. T. Reed (1966) 386: But now let us stop for the 'super'/Will want us tomorrow by noon.

1873 Rolf Boldrewood 'The Fencing of Wanderowna' *A Romance of Canvas Town* (1898) 108: 'I wasn't always a super. I started with a tidy little capital when I first came to Australia, and I lost nine thousand sheep ... within six months.'

1888 'The Jackeroo' *Bulletin* 10 Mar. 14 repr. in *Old Bush Songs* ed. Stewart and Keesing (1957) 79: When I got to the station I saw the super there.

2 Superphosphate

1959 K. S. Prichard *N'Goola* 142: The bottom fell out of the market for wheat. Prices were so low they would not pay for seed and super.

1975 *Australian* 12 Aug. 1: Restore super bounty, says IAC.

3 Petrol with an octane rating above 'standard'

surf, surfie A young habitué of the beaches, long-haired and given to surf-board-riding, seen as a cult figure

1963 *Sun-Herald* 10 Mar. 1: Police will maintain a constant alert today on Sydney's 15 beaches to prevent gang warfare between Rockers and Surfies.

1965 Barry Humphries *Times Literary Supplement* 16 Sep. 812: The Surfies, a repellent breed of sun-bronzed hedonists who actually hold chundering contests on the famed beaches of the Commonwealth.

1975 *National Times* 13 Jan. 40: If you are a 14-year-old schoolgirl and you have just discovered boys are not the same thing as your brothers, what really sends your heart into a turmoil is the sight of a blond, long-haired, blue-eyed, sun-bronzed surf wearing board shorts and bare feet.

Susso Government sustenance for the unemployed during the depression; a man drawing this dole [abbr.]

1942 Leonard Mann *The Go-Getter* 10: Five shillings were five shillings and a handsome help to the sustenance. 'We're on the Susso now.' That was the song they knew and did not sing.

1947 Vance Palmer *Cyclone* 8: 'He thinks it puts hair on his chest knocking about with the sussos.'

1958 Frank Hardy *The Four-Legged Lottery* 44: Some of those who still had work looked down on the unemployed, the 'sussos' as they were contemptuously called.

1969 Patsy Adam Smith *Folklore of the Australian Railwaymen* 190: When war was declared all our big 'susso' camps folded up overnight and the boys went to where they where sure to find work.

1973 Frank Huelin *Keep Moving* 67: 'We want to see the mayor and council about susso.'

swag *n.* 1 Booty, plunder (as in English thieves' slang)

1812 Vaux: *The swag,* is a term used in speaking of any booty you have lately obtained, be it of what kind it may, except money.

2 A collection of legitimate belongings

c. **1845** James Tucker *Ralph Rashleigh* (1952) 125: The cart contained various articles of property of those kinds that generally constitute the bulk of a settler's swag. There were pipes, tobacco, the keg above named, a quantity of tea and sugar, two or three coarse cotton striped shirts, and a pair or two of duck trousers.

1852 G. C. Mundy *Our Antipodes* iii 285: A tall picturesque-looking sprig of the squattocracy has just pitched his 'swag' – a leathern valise – through the open skylight on to the cuddy table.

3 The pack carried by the traveller, usually some essential belongings rolled in a blanket

1853 John Rochfort *Adventures of a Surveyor* 49: Disregarding the state of the roads, on the 24th of August, 1852, we strapped on our 'swags',* consisting of a pair of blankets and a spare pair of trousers, and started for the diggings. *Swags, colonial word for pack.

1855 William Howitt *Land, Labour and Gold* i 297: Those who go up only with their swags, containing their blankets, tea, and sugar, have to buy all their stores all winter at digging prices.

1873 A. Trollope *Australia* ed. Edwards and Joyce (1967) 293: The man who travels on foot in Australia, whether he be miner, shepherd, shearer, or simply beggar, always carries his 'swag' with him, – which consists of his personal properties rolled up in a blanket.

1878 Rolf Boldrewood *An Australian Squire* repr. as *Babes in the Bush* (1901) 134: Dressed in the garb of a bushman and carrying upon his back the ordinary knapsack or 'swag' of the travelling labourer of the period as he strode along the path.

1887 W. S. S. Tyrwhitt *The New Chum in the Queensland Bush* 82: A man came up one evening, 'humping his swag', as the expression is for carrying a bundle.

1896 Henry Lawson 'Enter Mitchell' *Prose* i 132: It was a stout, dumpy swag, with a red blanket outside, and the edge of a blue blanket showing in the inner rings at the end . . . It might have been hooped with decent straps,

instead of bits of clothes-line and greenhide – but otherwise there was nothing the matter with it, as swags go.

1908 W. H. Ogilvie *My Life in the Open* 35: The rouseabouts and shed-hands come in from all quarters on foot, carrying their 'swags', i.e. blankets strapped in bundles across their shoulders.

swag, cigarette see **cigarette**

swaggie A swagman q.v.

1896 Henry Lawson 'She Wouldn't Speak' *Prose* i 115: I thought a damp expression seemed to pass across her face when me and my mate sat down, but she served us and said nothing – we was only two dusty swaggies, you see.

1916 Joseph Furphy *Poems* 28: And across this fenced-in view, like our friend the well-sung Jew, / Goes the swaggy, with a frown upon his brow.

1926 K. S. Prichard *Working Bullocks* 158: He would . . . fraternize with everyone he met, shouting all comers in the hotel bars, pick up any old swaggie and take him home to dinner.

swag it To follow the swagman's life

1870 W. M. Finn *Glimpses of North-Eastern Victoria* (1971) 26: I was much surprised to see two able-bodied men, who informed me that for seventeen years they were swagging it from one place to another; indeed, they had travelled the colony, and had no notion of now abandoning their nomadic way of life . . . They said they were not going to work for any master, and would eke out an existence for their remaining time in the world.

1875 J. Jenkins *Diary of a Welsh Swagman* (1975) 52: It is better than swagging the country . . . searching for work.

1901 *The Bulletin Reciter* 5: And swagging up the long divide that leads to Daybreak Range / We came.

1903 Joseph Furphy *Such is Life* (1944) 198: No man must be allowed to swag the country, ragged and homeless, with the story in his mouth that he had been boundary riding on Avondale for ten

years.
1936 Archer Russell *Gone Nomad* 58: 'Swagging it' to a sheep station on the Queensland border he secured a job as a boundary rider.

swagman A tramp carrying his belongings in a 'swag'. The swagman is sometimes distinguished from the 'traveller', who is regarded as seeking work
1868 Marcus Clarke 'Swagmen' in *A Colonial City* ed. L. T. Hergenhan (1972) 32–3: The Wimmera district is noted for the hordes of vagabond 'loafers' that it supports, and has earned for itself the name of 'The Feeding Track.'
1875 A. J. Boyd *Old Colonials* (1882) 110–11: 'The Swagman' [chapter title]. He tramps across the country ostensibly for work, and at the same time praying Heaven that he may not find it . . . Idleness being the mainspring of the journeys of the Swagman (*anglice*, tramp).
1887 *All the Year Round* 30 Jul. 66: A 'swagman' is a different character. The name is given to any one tramping the country for work, or any other purpose, and carrying his worldly goods slung round him in a bundle, which is always known as his 'swag'.
1893 Henry Lawson 'Some Popular Australian Mistakes' *Prose* ii 24: Men tramping in search of a 'shed' are not called 'sundowners' or 'swaggies'; they are 'trav'lers'.

swamp *v.* To act as an assistant to a bullock-driver; to travel on foot with a bullock-team, giving minor assistance or having one's swag carried; to obtain a lift for oneself and one's swag from any traveller [see *swamper*]
1926 K. S. Prichard *Working Bullocks* 101: Billy Williams the bullocky, and Ern Collins who was swamping for him, turned their team into the yards on the following Monday.
1937 Ernestine Hill *Ports of Sunset* 96: In they came, across the jagged Leopolds, or up from the desert, 'swamping' with a bullocky, staggering behind a pack donkey, or on Shanks' pony.

1944 M. J. O'Reilly *Bowyangs and Boomerangs* 6: My duties were to help to load and unload, bring the horses in the morning, to harness up, help to corduroy bad patches on the track, draw water for the horses at the soaks and wells, hobble out the horses at night, put the bells on, etc. These duties were then known as 'swamping' . . . All this work for the privilege of having one's tucker, tools and swag carried on the waggon. Fortunately the chap I 'swamped' for was an exceptionally good sort.
1946 K. S. Prichard *The Roaring Nineties* 7: He was charging a man five pounds to throw a hundred-pound swag on the wagon and swamp along with the team [to the goldfield].
1951 Ernestine Hill *The Territory* 446: *Swamping* Originally travelling with bullock team to carry the swag, now joining up with the mailman or any regular traveller.
1964 Tom Ronan *Packhorse and Pearling Boat* 170: 'If I broke it for a tenner, I'd roll my swag and swamp my way back to Queensland.'

swamper One engaged in the activities of swamping [f. *swamper* a road-breaker or clearer U.S. 1850; assistant to the driver of a mule team U.S. 1870 Mathews]
1901 May Vivienne *Travels in Western Australia* 284: A 'swamper' is a man tramping without his swag, which he entrusts to a teamster to bring on his waggon. Arrived at the camping-place, . . . the swamper awaits the teamster's coming, recovers his swag and spends the night at the camp. While on foot the swamper will generally leave the track, and prospect.
1900–10 O'Brien and Stephens: *Swamper* West Australian term for a traveller making his way on foot to the goldfields.
1929 Jules Raeside *Golden Days* 380: With many a swamper's swag on / And many a billy black.
1966 Tom Ronan *Once There Was a Bagman* 15: My fellow swamper tossed his swag off [the mailman's truck] here; he was home.

Swans, the The South Melbourne V.F.L. team
1975 *Sunday Telegraph* 7 Sep. 64: Bulldogs race to big Rules win over Swans.

swarm *n.* & *v.* A meeting of shearers, esp. a stop-work meeting
1962 *Sydney Morning Herald* 24 Nov. 12: After seeing them in the yards, the shearers 'swarmed' (held a meeting) and decided to ask the squatter for five bob a ram – away above the award.
1975 Les Ryan *The Shearers* 58–9: 'There's been a swarm. The shearers want to negotiate a complaint.'

sweet All right, in order, 'jake'
1898 *Bulletin* 17 Dec. Red Page: *sweet, roujig* and *not too stinkin'* are good.
1939 Kylie Tennant *Foveaux* 312: 'I brassed a mug yesterday,' he told her, 'and everything's sweet again.' He flashed a roll of notes as big as his fist.
1949 Lawson Glassop *Lucky Palmer* 242: 'Everything jake?' he asked. 'She's sweet,' said Max.
1959 Dorothy Hewett *Bobbin Up* 106: She made certain of her bonus that way and got in sweet with the foreman.
1962 Stuart Gore *Down the Golden Mile* 120: 'Might as well be in it. We'll be sweet for getting back.'
1975 Xavier Herbert *Poor Fellow My Country* 353: Mossie came in ... to say cheerfully, 'She's sweet.'

sweetheart of song Miss Gladys Moncrieff, also known as 'Our Glad' q.v.
1972 Peter Mathers *The Wort Papers* 280: Nor I, sang Gladys Moncrieff, the sweetheart of song.

sweetheart agreement An industrial agreement negotiated directly by employers and employed, without reference to the arbitration court
1974 *Australian* 12 Nov. 3: Miss Martin said Mr Jones' description of the hostesses' and stewards' award as a sweetheart agreement was farcical. The award had been decided by arbitration, not by negotiation between Qantas and the unions.

swifty An act of deception
1953 *Caddie A Sydney Barmaid* 224: 'You didn't work a swiftie on them, did you?' I asked suspiciously. For I was already aware that Bill was collecting three doles for himself.
1962 Ron Tullipan *March into Morning* 43: 'And if these mugs hadn't pulled a swifty they wouldn't have been working for me at all.'
1976 *Sydney Morning Herald* 9 Apr. 6: The Queensland Premier, who thinks there is a centralist under every bed, is now worried that the Federal Treasury may be trying to pull a swiftie.

swill, the six o'clock The last minute rush for drinks in the pubs, occasioned by six o'clock closing (in N.S.W. 1916–55)
1951 A. W. Upfield *The New Shoe* 93: It wanted ten minutes to the fatal hour of six, and the enforced National Swill was in full flood.
1955 Alan Ross *Australia 55* 81: This evening ritual, known amongst Australians as the 'six o'clock swill'.
1961 Frank Hardy *The Hard Way* 73: The [prison] yard was filling steadily, mostly with drunks, and a few victims of the six o'clock swill.
1970 Donald Horne *The Next Australia* 160: The 'six o'clock swill' before the lavatory-tiled bars closed was one of the continuing tests of masculinity.

sword swallower Someone eating from his knife, esp. among shearers
1941 Baker 74: *Sword-swallowing* The practice of eating with one's knife.

system, the bag see **bag**

swy The game of two-up [G. *zwei* two]
1921 *Aussie* 15 Mar. 54: 'Just done me last dollar up at the swi school.'
1924 *Truth* 27 Apr. 6: *Swy* two.
1941 Baker 75: *Swy* The game of two-up (2) A sentence of two years' gaol (3) A florin.
1961 Jack Danvers *The Living Come First* 106: 'Collecting their cut of the local swy-game.'

Sydney or the bush All or nothing (i.e. to make one's fortune, and live in the capital, or lose it all, and seek a livelihood in the bush)

1924 *Truth* 27 Apr. 6: *Sydney or the Bush* All or nothing.

1930 E. Shann *An Economic History of Australia* 365: 'Sydney or the bush!' cries the Australian when he gambles against odds, and the slogan betrays a heart turning ever towards the pleasant coastal capitals.

1945 Cecil Mann *The River* 45: He bet on a Sydney or the Bush basis; and now, to-morrow, it was the Bush.

1953 T. A. G. Hungerford *Riverslake* 127: 'Spin for five,' Murdoch suggested to Novikowsky. 'Sydney or the bush!'

1969 Mr David Fairbairn [challenging Mr Gorton for the leadership of the Liberal Party] *Bulletin* 15 Nov. 27: 'Well, gentlemen, the die is cast. For me it's Sydney or the bush – Kirribilli or Woomargama.'

1970 Richard Beilby *No Medals for Aphrodite* 34: 'Here we go,' Turk murmured grimly, climbing in behind the wheel. 'It's Sydney or the bush! Keep your fingers crossed.'

T

tail To tend and herd stock, esp. on foot; to pursue stock that have strayed

1844 *Port Phillip Patriot* 5 Aug. 3: I know many boys, from the age of nine to sixteen years, tailing cattle. [Morris]

1851 J. Henderson *Excursions and Adventures in New South Wales* ii 2: He was rather old and feeble, and not of much use ... He served, however, for hut-keeper, and did well enough taleing* cattle, or going for rations. *The term used to express looking after cattle on foot.

1852 G. C. Mundy *Our Antipodes* i 314: The stockman, as he who tends cattle and horses is called, despises the shepherd as a grovelling, inferior creature, and considers 'tailing sheep' as an employment too tardigrade for a man of action and spirit.

1861 Horace Earle *Ups and Downs* 10: Cattle require to be tailed, or followed, by the stockman for many months, before they become sufficiently acquainted with each other.

1875 A. J. Boyd *Old Colonials* (1882) 56: See him in some bush township, tailing cattle for a poundkeeper.

1887 W. S. S. Tyrwhitt *The New Chum in the Queensland Bush* 193: 'Tailing' is to cattle what shepherding is to sheep, all you have to do is to keep them together, and let them feed.

1919 W. K. Harris *Outback in Australia* 17: Camels will wander miles away during the night, even though they are hobbled. 'Tailing' horses, bullocks or mules is mere play compared with the task of 'tailing' camels.

1934 Steele Rudd *Green Grey Homestead* 65: You battle on, following the plough and the sun from day to day, tailing the dairy herd.

tailer

1934 Mary Gilmore *Old Days: Old Ways* 242: You must not confuse the stockman with the 'tailer'. The tailer, and, for years the later rouseabout on the sheep-run, were no-account men. They were weaklings; they were menial; and could be asked to cut wood and would do it as part of their lowly, wretched, and good-for-nothing lot.

tailie In two-up, a gambler who habitually backs tails

1919 W. H. Downing *Digger Dialects* 49: *Tailie* A man who backs 'tails' in the game of two-up.

1949 Lawson Glassop *Lucky Palmer* 176: 'Gents', he cried, 'now isn't there a tailie in the school?'

take a look at see **look**

take out To win, esp. in sport

1976 *Australian* 15 Jul. 2: Helen Morse ... takes out the Australian Film Institute's top actress award tomorrow night.

take to the bush see **bush**

talent, the Collective term for those

who stand out in any group, esp. in their own estimation, hence a 'push' q.v.; likely-looking girls (to male observation) [cf. *the talent* the clever ones (racing slang) OED 1883; also *the fancy*]

1870 Rolf Boldrewood 'Shearing in Riverina' *Town and Country Journal* 29 Oct. 10: Upon the 'talent' also, consisting of men who can shear, and shear well, from fifty to seventy sheep more in a day than their fellows, the eye of watchfulness must be kept.

c. 1882 *The Sydney Slang Dictionary* 8: *The Talent* Low gamblers, sharpers, larrikins and their girls, confirmed prostitutes, and 'the fancy' generally who frequent their resorts.

1913 Henry Lawson 'Mateship' *Prose* i 725: Presently the word goes round that Frowsy Sal is stickin' ter Boko Bill, and is received, for the most part, with blasphemous incredulity by the 'talent'.

1950 Jon Cleary *Just Let Me Be* 115: The thick-set detective looked after her, and Harry grinned at him. 'Not bad, eh?' he said, raising his eyebrow. 'That's a bit of the local talent.'

1953 Dymphna Cusack *Southern Steel* 31: He'd learn responsibility quicker married than he would knocking about the ports with the rest of the talent.

1959 Dorothy Hewett *Bobbin Up* 93: The boys hang round the entrance, stamping cigarette butts into the floor, swapping dirty jokes, eyes narrowed to survey the talent.

1968 Geoffrey Dutton *Andy* 222: 'I'll meet you in town at the Salamanca Hotel at 8 p.m. and you can inspect the local talent.'

tall poppy see **poppy**

tall timber, to take to the To decamp, as in 'take to the scrub'

1919 W. H. Downing *Digger Dialects* 49: *Take to the tall timber* Abscond.

1954 T. A. G. Hungerford *Sowers of the Wind* 61: 'Head for the tall timber until the grog runs out.'

Tallarook, things are crook in Catch-phrase for any adverse situation [f. rhyme on place-name]. Other catchphrases include: There's no work at Bourke. Got the arse at Bulli Pass. No lucre at Echuca. In jail at Innisfail. Things are weak at Julia Creek. Things are crook at Muswellbrook. The girls are bandy at Urandangie.

1963 Lawson Glassop *The Rats in New Guinea* 217: 'He says things are crook in Talarook. He's the only soldier on his feet in his weapon pit.'

1969 Leslie Haylen *Twenty Years' Hard Labour* 144: The workers loved it. They cheered hysterically at the glad news that things were crook in Tallarook and likely to remain so until there was a Labor government.

Tambaroora (muster) See quots: *obs*. [f. place-name]

1882 A. J. Boyd *Old Colonials* 63: It may be that the exciting game of Tambaroora is not familiar to all my readers . . . Each man of a party throws a shilling, or whatever sum may be mutually agreed upon, into a hat. Dice are then produced, and each man takes three throws. The Nut who throws highest keeps the whole of the subscribed capital, and out of it pays for the drinks of the rest. The advantage of the proceeding lies in this: Where drinks are charged at sixpence, the subscription is double that amount for each . . . Thus if ten Nuts go in for a Tambaroora, with nobblers at sixpence, the winner pockets five shillings by the transaction.

1895 Cornelius Crowe *The Australian Slang Dictionary* 84: *Tambaroora,* a game of a shilling each in the hat and the winner shouts.

1897 *Bulletin* 18 Dec. Red Page: The essence of a present-day tambaroora is a sweep for the purchase of drinks – frequently on the principle that more liquor can be purchased wholesale for 1s. 6d. than six thirsty people can buy for 3d each. Hence 'tambaroora muster', when the droughty party musters all the coin it's possessed of, and one individual goes and bargains for the beer.

1901 *The Bulletin Reciter* 202: 'Tambaroora' [poem title]

tank A dam, formed by excavation
1903 Joseph Furphy *Such is Life* (1944) 330: On a well-managed station, like Runnymede, a tank is, whenever possible, excavated on the margin of a swamp. The clay extracted is formed into a strong wall, or enclosing embankment, a couple of yards back from the edge of the excavation; and under this wall, an iron pipe connects the swamp with the tank.
1910 C. E. W. Bean *On the Wool Track* 58: The night before last we were making for a tank [added in later editions:] that is to say, a big, low, open reservoir and dam.
1931 Vance Palmer *Separate Lives* 229–30: He had been a mate of Denison's thirty years before, and had helped him sink tanks along the stock-routes from Dawson to the Bree.

tarp A tarpaulin [abbr.]
1919 W. H. Downing *Digger Dialects* 49: *Tarp* A tarpaulin.
1963 Alan Marshall *In Mine Own Heart* 174: 'They were open trucks with no tarps.'
1971 Frank Hardy *The Outcasts of Foolgarah* 183: 'There's plenty of tarps: we'll rig up a tent.'

tarpaulin muster See quots
1904 E. S. Emerson *A Shanty Entertainment* 26: Each one in the room to sing, recite, or shout all round, and if nobody reneged, a tarpaulin muster every half-hour for drinks, or smokes, just as the company cared.
1945 Elisabeth George *Two at Daly Waters* 102: As she had not brought a town outfit, Daly Waters had what we call in the bush a tarpaulin muster (the loan of everybody's best clothes).

tart A girl or woman. Not used in any derogatory sense, although women would not refer to themselves as 'tarts'. The juvenile 'jam tart' is obsolete [abbr. of *sweetheart*]
1899 W. T. Goodge *Hits! Skits! and Jingles!* 150: And his lady-love's his 'donah'/Or his 'clinah' or his 'tart'.
1910 Thomas E. Spencer *Why Doherty*

Died 83: You're a bosker! You're a jewel! You're a tart!/You're the only gel as I was ever sweet on.
1915 C. J. Dennis *The Songs of a Sentimental Bloke* 34: A cove 'as got to think some time in life/An' get some decent tart, 'ere it's too late,/To be 'is wife.
1938 H. Drake-Brockman *Men Without Wives* 15: 'The old tart's impatient, and so'm I. There'll be no peace till she's gone.'
1942 Gavin Casey *It's Harder for Girls* 111: 'She's a stupid sort of tart, anyway.'
1968 Thomas Keneally *Three Cheers for the Paraclete* 114: 'That mortgage office, you've got no idea ... Little tarts with short haircuts running all over the place with folders.'
see **tom, tom tart**

tart, bachelor's see **bachelor**

tartshop, dragged screaming from the Applied to politicians who have come reluctantly to face an election [attributed to W. M. Hughes, but used earlier by Alfred Deakin]
1904 Alfred Deakin *Ballarat Courier* 23 Aug. cit. J. A. La Nauze *Alfred Deakin* (1965) 378: I do not propose to reply to him [W. M. Hughes] except by saying he presents to you as undignified a spectacle as does the ill-bred urchin whom one sees dragged from a tart-shop kicking and screaming as he goes.
1974 *Sydney Morning Herald* 11 Jan. 6: It's time for the Whitlam Government, in Billy Hughes's immortal words, to be dragged screaming from the tart shop.

Tassie (Tassy) Tasmania; a Tasmanian [abbr.]
1894 *The Argus* 26 Jan. 3: Today Tassy – as most Victorian cricketers and footballers familiarly term our neighbour over the straits – will send a team into the field. [Morris]
1898 G. T. Bell *Tales of Australian Adventure* 103: 'I ... am going away to dear old Tassy to see the folks and the girl I left behind me.'
1900–10 O'Brien and Stephens: *Tassy*

slang abbreviation of Tasmania.

1905 *The Old Bush Songs* ed. A. B. Paterson 51: Once more the Maorilander and the Tassey will be seen / Cooking johnny cakes and jimmies on the plains of Riverine.

1915 Henry Lawson 'Fighting Hard' *Verse* iii 154: Fighting hard for little Tassy, where the apple orchards grow.

1934 'Leslie Parker' *Trooper to the Southern Cross* (1966) 2: Coming round the west coast of Tassie we ran into really bad weather.

1963 Bruce Beaver *The Hot Summer* 61: 'Maybe Perth, eh? Or Tassie?'

taxi, black see **black taxi**

tea-and-sugar burglar A swagman who begs or 'borrows' tea and sugar; a minor predator

1900 Henry Lawson 'A Rough Shed' *Prose* i 463: 'Could I explain that I "jabbed trotters" and was a "tea-and-sugar burglar" between sheds.'

1956 Tom Ronan *Moleskin Midas* 165: 'We're pulling off a big job soon ... We'll make these tea-and-sugar bushrangers around this shanty look like a mob of schoolgirls.'

see **frying-pan**

Teddy Bear A show-off, esp. a cricketer given to antics on the field [? rhyming slang for *lair* q.v.]

1953 Baker 135: *teddy bear* A flashily dressed, exhibitionistic person; by rhyme on *lair*.

1965 Wally Grout *My Country's 'Keeper* 55: Umpire Col Egar was so furious at this amateurish attempt at time-wasting that he snapped to the Pakistani bowler: 'Get up you Teddy Bear' (an Australian expression not meant to be complimentary). Ibid. 133: Dave, according to us, was not only a candidate for the Teddy Bear's Picnic, he was driving the bus. In other words, he was inclined to be something rather more than boastful.

1973 Frank Huelin *Keep Moving* 180: *Teddy-bears, Lairs* Brash, vain young hoboes.

1974 Keith Stackpole *Not Just for Openers* 128: When Parfitt made the catch

Greig jumped in the air, and, as he landed, thumped his fist into the pitch ... I said to Greig as I walked past, 'You're nothing but a bloody Teddy Bear.' He returned the pleasantries.

telegraph, bush see **bush**

ten, ten, two, and a quarter A week's rations in the outback: ten pounds of flour, ten of meat, two of sugar, and a quarter-pound of tea (the quantities might vary within this framework)

1867 John Morrison *Australia As It Is* 175: The rations for one man are the well-known weekly allowance of 10 lbs. of flour, 10 lbs. of meat, 2 lbs. of sugar, and a quarter of a pound of tea.

1903 Joseph Furphy *Such is Life* (1944) 104: He [the boundary rider] has some hundreds of pounds lent out (without interest or security) though his pay is only fifteen shillings a week – with ten, ten, two, and a quarter.

1905 *The Old Bush Songs* ed. A. B. Paterson 41: 'But I'll give ten-ten, sugar an' tea; / Ten bob a week, if you'll suit me.'

1937 William Hatfield *I Find Australia* 34: Rations per man per week were eight pounds of flour, ten pounds of meat, two pounds of sugar and a quarter pound of tea. Eight-ten-two-and-quarter, it was known.

1964 H. P. Tritton *Time Means Tucker* 20: Most of the outback stations issued rations. It was not done as a charity ... but as a means of ensuring a plentiful supply of casual labour ... Most of the squatters did not stick strictly to the bare ration laid down by the Pastoralists' Union, which was ten pounds of flour, ten of meat, two of sugar and a quarter pound of tea.

Tench The convict barracks in Hobart: *obs.* [abbr. of *Penitentiary*]

1859 Oliné Keese *The Broad Arrow* ii 432: 'Prisoners' barracks, sir – us calls it Tench.'

1864 J. F. Mortlock *Experiences of a Convict* (1965) 89: The Prisoners' Barracks (commonly called the 'Tench') became the abode of myself and hundreds more, who earned our food and lodging by stone-breaking, or other public labour.

tent, were you born in a Reproach to someone who has come in leaving the door open [Partridge lists *born in a barn* Canadian]

Territorian An inhabitant of the Northern Territory
1941 Charles Barrett *Coast of Adventure* 121: Old Territorians, over a glass of beer at the 'pub', or a pannikin of tea by the campfire, will tell yarns as long as you'll listen.
1968 Frank Hardy *The Unlucky Australians* 11: 'The old Territorian is a good bloke, rough as guts but his heart's in the right place.'
1975 *Australian* 27 Sep. 3: The Territorians – obviously attracted by the commissioners' informality and interest – responded by giving them a good – and welcome – earbashing.

Territory, the The Northern Territory
1933 F. E. Baume *Tragedy Track* 79: They are the rats of the Territory, men who refuse to work.
1951 Ernestine Hill *The Territory* [book title]
1975 *Australian* 27 Sep. 3: Commission gets down to earth on the Territory's troubles.

they were open see **open**

thirds, on See quots
1824 E. Curr *An Account of the Colony of Van Diemen's Land* 77–8: It is common practice for persons who have not sufficient land, or who cannot attend personally to their flocks, to give them in charge to another party, who receives one third of the increase for his trouble . . . In this manner many persons have become possessed of considerable flocks, and if the party taking them for 'the thirds' be careful and trustworthy, it is beneficial to both parties. The same method is adopted with cattle.
1826 *Hobart Town Gazette* 22 Apr. 3: A Gentleman, possessing an extensive Run for Sheep, will have no objection to Run on the Thirds to the Number of 1000 – None need apply but those of respectable Character.
1834 Let. in T. P. Besnard *A Voice from the Bush of Australia* (1839) 14: These sheep I have put out to graze, according to the custom of the country, on *thirds* – that is the person who grazes and takes care of the flock is entitled to $\frac{1}{3}$ of the produce of the wool, and $\frac{1}{3}$ of the lambs that are dropped.
1843 Charles Rowcroft *Tales of the Colonies* ii 109: I had prevailed on him to purchase . . . a hundred ewes heavy with lamb, and to put them out 'on thirds'.
1852 G. C. Mundy *Our Antipodes* i 282: Take stock on the system of 'thirds', in which the working partner gets one third of the wool and of the increase, while the proprietary partner, as he may be called, follows some other profession, or his pleasures, or holds some Government appointment at the capital or elsewhere.

Thommo's A notorious two-up school operating near Sydney [f. Joe Thomas, the organizer]
1959 Dorothy Hewett *Bobbin Up* 69: The show folded up, Kel did all their savings at Thomo's. Ibid. 159: The cockatoos kept watch outside the dirty house in Reservoir Street, where Thomos two-up school did a roaring, open trade.
1966 Elwyn Wallace *Sydney and the Bush* 140: He did his ready at Tommo's game.
1973 *Sydney Morning Herald* 29 Jun. 6: Jack Brown . . . ran a two-up school in the northern suburbs, as popular as Thommo's was in the City.
1976 *Sunday Telegraph* 13 Jun. 12: Police raid Thommo's: 15 charged on two-up Thommo's two-up school, the most famous and longest lasting game in Sydney, was raided by police early yesterday . . . Thommo's two-up school was established during World War II and has flourished ever since. Successive police commissioners have denied the two-up school's existence, claiming it was a 'press myth'.

throat, to have the game by the To be in full control, in a position of advantage
1947 John Morrison *Sailors Belong Ships* 15: 'We're sailors, see? Two sailors. We got the game by the throat.'
1960 Ron Tullipan *Follow the Sun* 105: 'Think we'll get it done to-day?' 'Can't miss . . . We have it by the throat now all right.'
1974 David Ireland *Burn* 58: 'So you got the game by the throat, eh?'

throw a seven see **seven**

throw one's hat in first see **hat**

throw off To deride, ridicule: superseded by *sling off* q.v.
1812 Vaux: *Throw off* to talk in a sarcastical strain, so as to convey offensive allusions under a mask of pleasantry, or innocent freedom; but, perhaps, secretly venting that abuse which you would not dare to give in direct terms.
1935 Kylie Tennant *Tiburon* 190: 'You're not being funny, are you? Sort of throwing off?'
1962 Dymphna Cusack *Picnic Race* 183: 'You're like all the townies. Throwing off at people on the land.'

thumbnail dipped in tar, written with a Catchphrase for rough penmanship, from Paterson's 'Clancy of the Overflow'
1895 A. B. Paterson *The Man from Snowy River* 20: And an answer came directed in a writing unexpected /(And I think the same was written with a thumb-nail dipped in tar); /'Twas his shearing mate who wrote it, and *verbatim* I will quote it: /'Clancy's gone to Queensland droving, and we don't know where he are.'

tickets, to have ~ on oneself To be conceited [? f. sales tickets advertising a high price]
[1915 C. J. Dennis *The Songs of a Sentimental Bloke* 28: 'E's taken tickets on 'is own 'igh worth; /Puffed up wiv pride.]
1941 Kylie Tennant *The Battlers* 20: 'Arr,' the busker said disgustedly, 'you've got tickets all over yourself.'

1953 Gwen Meredith *Beyond Blue Hills* 84: 'I know I'm not in the same class as Danny Marks,' he announced. 'I haven't got any tickets on myself.'
1965 Randolph Stow *The Merry-go-Round in the Sea* 132: 'You've got tickets on yourself,' he finished, lamely.
1970 Jack Hibberd *White with Wire Wheels* in *Plays* 227: 'You're the bastard that's always been smug and had tickets on himself.'

tiger A toiler in a shearing-shed
1897 Henry Lawson 'The Green-hand Rouseabout' *Verse* i 322: Engine whistles. 'Go it, tigers!' and the agony begins.
c. 1910 *Old Bush Songs* ed. Stewart and Keesing (1957) 259: 'A Lot of Lachlan Tigers' [ballad title]
1956 F. B. Vickers *First Place to the Stranger* 135: 'You're going to see something now . . . Those tigers (he meant the shearers) will make you dance.'
tigering Working hard under adverse conditions; roughing it
1880–1904 'The Banks of the Condamine' *Old Bush Songs* ed. Stewart and Keesing (1957) 257: Your delicate constitution /Is not equal unto mine, /To stand the constant tigering /On the banks of the Condamine.
1973 Roland Robinson *The Drift of Things* 385: He was a well-built young man, and a good worker as I was to find out; but then I had done my share of tigering and I reckoned I could hold my own.

tiger country Rough, thickly wooded terrain feared by airmen; any primitive area
1945 Elisabeth George *Two at Daly Waters* 89: The territory a hundred and sixty miles west of Daly Waters and thence to the Western Australian coast is also dreaded by aviators and generally called by them 'tiger country'. Dwellings are from eighty to a hundred miles apart and there are no recognizable landmarks for the flyer who is bushed.
Ibid. 115: What other aviators call tiger country – hills, thick scrub and probably only one chance in a hundred of

landing without disaster.
1961 George Farwell *Vanishing Australians* 20: A Kimberley settler in the undeveloped 'tiger country', away on the wrong side of the rough-shod King Leopold Range.
1968 Patsy Adam Smith *Tiger Country* [book title]
1974 *Australian* 12 Jan. 22: Mr Brown has spent a good part of his tenure as mayor chasing after new industries, urging them to come and settle where there are thousands of acres of Crown land, not wanted for agriculture or housing – 'tiger country', he calls it.

tiger for work (punishment) A 'demon' for work, someone with an insatiable appetite for it
1896 *Bulletin* 24 Oct. Red Page: His father thought a lot of Henry; he used to call him a tiger for work.
1935 William Hatfield *Black Waterlily* 15: 'Tiger for work, aren't you?' he smiled. 'A good fault, of course, if you don't carry it to extremes.'
1953 Dymphna Cusack *Southern Steel* 249: 'I'll hand it to you. You were always a tiger for work.'
1959 Dorothy Hewett *Bobbin Up* 79: 'He's a real tiger for his tucker,' Linnie said, smiling wanly through her tears.
1965 Eric Lambert *The Long White Night* 74: I patted her shoulder. 'Mum, you're a tiger for punishment!'

Tigers, the 1 In N.S.W., the Balmain Rugby League team [f. black and gold colours, and club emblem]
1976 *Sun-Herald* 13 Jun. 52: Tigers' semi-final spot is on the line.
Tigertown Balmain
1976 *Sunday Telegraph* 14 Nov. 160: Sir John Kerr might have moved out of Tigertown, but Kep Enderby has moved in. The former Attorney-General has . . . bought a house in Balmain.
2 In Victoria, the Richmond V.F.L. team
1974 *Sunday Telegraph* 29 Sep. 108: Tigers knock the knockers.

tin-arsed, tin-back, tin-bum, tinny Lucky, a lucky person [? f. being impervious to kicks in the backside. Ap-

parently unrelated to *tin* = money]
1899 W. T. Goodge *Hits! Skits! and Jingles!* 150: And a 'tin-back' is a party / Who's remarkable for luck.
1919 W. H. Downing *Digger Dialects* 50: *Tinny* Lucky.
1950 Jon Cleary *Just Let Me Be* 54: 'Your mother won again, Joe. Six pounds.' 'She's tinny,' Joe said.
1955 D'Arcy Niland *The Shiralee* 142: 'I come up with a stone worth five hundred quid . . . Tin-bum, they call me.'
1962 *Australian One-Act Plays* ed. Eunice Hanger 20: 'Some people are always lucky. So tinny, they must wear tin pants.'
1971 R. F. Brissenden *Winter Matins* 25: This tin-arsed character / Hasn't been there six months before he starts / To fidget, gets to grizzling in his beer.
1975 Les Ryan *The Shearers* 79: 'Good on yer Joe. You always were a tin-arse.'

tin dog An improvised rattle, used when travelling stock: *rare*
1911 L. St Clare Grondona *Collars and Cuffs* 76: I hastily procured a jam tin from the cook, and manufactured what is locally known as a 'tin dog' . . . I put in some gravel, and whenever 'Nigger' fagged, which wasn't seldom, I rattled it for all I was worth.

Tin Hare 1 The mechanical hare used in dog racing
2 Nickname for a train, esp. a rail motor, with a rapid bobbing motion
1941 Kylie Tennant *The Battlers* 159: The 'Tin Hare's' whistle was heard in the distance.

tin, kick the see **kick**

tin-kettle, tin-kettling The beating of dishes etc. to celebrate a wedding or similar event
[1875 A. J. Boyd *Old Colonials* (1882) 49–50: Watch them, when they have scented out a wedding. They collect all the kerosine-tins, pots and pans they can lay their hands on, and in the evening, if the luckless pair have not previously departed on a tour, their ears

are assailed with a most atrocious din. Tins are battered under the windows, stones are thrown on the roof, and yells and cheers make the night hideous ... the maddened benedict rushes out and distributes either money or liquor.]

1892 Barcroft Boake 'Babs Malone' *Bulletin* 20 Feb. 21 repr. in *Where the Dead Men Lie* (1897) 103: What cheering and tin-kettling / Had they after at the 'settling'.

1898 D. W. Carnegie *Spinifex and Sand* 325–6: Christmas Eve is celebrated by a performance known as 'tin-kettling', in which all join. Each arms himself with a dish, or empty tin, which he beats violently with a stick. To the tune of this lovely music the party marches from house to house, and at each demands drink of some kind, which is always forthcoming.

1900 Henry Lawson 'The Songs They Used to Sing' *Prose* i 380: They married on the sly and crept into camp after dark; but the diggers got wind of it and rolled up with gold-dishes, shovels &c. &c., and gave them a real good tin-kettling in the old-fashioned style.

1931 A. W. Upfield *The Sands Of Windee* 39: 'I hope you havn't forgotten that we are to tin-kettle the Fosters tomorrow night.'

1950 Vance Palmer *Coast to Coast 1949 –50* 6: They had missed their chance of tin-kettling the parson on the night he had brought his bride home; it was a ceremony that was organized for couples when there was anything dubious about the marriage.

1964 *Sydney Morning Herald* 25 Apr. 11: At Dalton ... a few weeks back there was a 'tin kettling' (first night after the honeymoon neighbours surround the house and bang tin utensils.)

tin, ring the see **ring**

tinned dog Canned meat
1895 *Bulletin* 17 Aug. 27: We gave him some 'tinned dorg' and a drink.
1898 D. W. Carnegie *Spinifex and Sand* 14: A supply of the staple food of the country, 'Tinned Dog' – as canned provisions are designated.

1901 F. J. Gillen *Diary* (1968) 275: I'm afraid it will take us some days to settle down to damper and tinned dog.
1922 Edward Meryon *At Holland's Tank* 28: The jam stood on the table in its original tin, and the 'tinned dog' or tinned meat, was served likewise.
1946 K. S. Prichard *The Roaring Nineties* 7: Dinny induced the storekeeper to stake him for a few pounds of flour and sugar, tinned dog and tea.
1950 Gavin Casey *City of Men* 326: 'We'll be living in a tent and eating tinned dog. It's no place for a woman.'

tinny see **tin-arsed**

Tin Shed, the Old As for 'the Old Barn' q.v.
1975 *Sun* 4 Dec. 28: The Old Tin Shed, the Stadium, long gone home of boxing heroes, wrestling bums, pop artists and jazz greats.

toastrack A tram with external footboards instead of an internal corridor (discontinued in Sydney by 1960) [f. resemblance]
1941 Baker 77: *Toastrack* One of the old-style footboard trams still used in Sydney.
1966 Peter Mathers *Trap* 190: A tram now, it would be a toast-rack with ten or so compartments with the only physical intercommunication along the outside footboards, and the concertina doors.
1973 *Bulletin* 17 Nov. 44: Visitors there [the Sydney Tram Museum at Loftus] can ride on an authentic toastrack for 15 cents (children 10 cents).

toby 1 A raddle stick for marking sheep not shorn to the employer's satisfaction
1912 'Goorianawa' *The Lone Hand* 1 Oct. 30 repr. in *Old Bush Songs* ed. Stewart and Keesing (1957) 273: I've been shearing on the Goulburn side and down at Douglas Park, / Where every day 'twas 'Wool away!' and toby did his work.
1964 H. P. Tritton *Time Means Tucker* 41: Till the 1902 strike, the owner had the right to raddle any sheep not shorn

to his satisfaction and the shearer would not be paid for it. (Raddle was a stick of blue or yellow ochre, also called 'Toby').

2 A 'dab' at something: *rare*

1941 Baker 77: *Toby* A man silly of mind and clumsy of hand, but willing to do whatever asked.

1944 Alan Marshall *These Are My People* 155: 'I'm not much chop on pies, but I'm a toby on puddin's.'

toe-ragger 1 A swagman, an itinerant down-and-out [also English tramps' slang, as in Orwell's *Down and Out in Paris and London*]

[**1864** J. F. Morlock *Experiences of a Convict* (1965) 83–4: Stockings being unknown, some luxurious men wrapped round their feet a piece of old shirting, called, in language more expressive than elegant, a 'toe-rag'.]

1896 *Truth* 12 Jan. 4: The bushie's favourite term of opprobrium 'a toe-ragger' is also probably from the Maori. [Morris]

1900–10 O'Brien and Stephens: *Toe-ragger* Person of no position, occupation, wealth or attainments.

1903 Joseph Furphy *Such is Life* (1944) 227: 'Come over to the wagon, and have a drink of tea,' says I. 'No, no,' says he, 'none of your toe-rag business.'

1941 Baker 77: *Toe ragger* a person of no position, wealth or attainments.

2 A prisoner with a short sentence.

1918 J. Vance Marshall *Jail from Within* 45: 'Some o' you toeraggers (short-timers) take the cake.'

toey Restive, fractious, touchy [? pawing ground]

1945 Baker 135: *toey* Worried or anxious.

1969 Patsy Adam Smith *Folklore of the Australian Railwaymen* 82–3: We were shunting at Marree and I had a toey crew on. I knew they had booze planted somewhere and they knew I knew.

1974 *Sydney Morning Herald* 1 Jan. 2: 'He's that toey he's got us all nervous, too.'

togs Clothes esp. a bathing costume

[f. thieves' slang OED 1809]

[**1812** Vaux: *Togs* or *Toggery* wearing-apparel in general.]

1857 Charles Thatcher *Colonial Songster* 18: In the colony I've just arrived, / My togs, I know, look rum.

1899 W. T. Goodge *Hits! Skits! and Jingles!* 151: And his clothes he calls his 'clobber' / Or his 'togs'.

1924 Steele Rudd *Me an' th' Son* 9: The storekeeper hands us th' togs – a large set for me, an' a medium lot for th' son.

1945 Baker 183: Swimming costumes are variously known as *togs, bathers*.

1960 John Iggulden *The Storms of Summer* 208: 'Why don't we have a swim?' asked Judy ... 'Get your togs and wake up the others.'

tom, tom-tart A girl or woman. Not derogatory, but not used by women of themselves: *obsolescent* [? f. *tomrig* a strumpet OED 1668]

c. **1882** *The Sydney Slang Dictionary* 8: *Tom-tart* Sydney phrase for a girl or sweetheart.

1906 Edward Dyson *Fact'ry 'Ands* 55: There's a little tom in this flat who'd give er bit t' have you hers for keeps.'

1915 C. J. Dennis *The Songs of a Sentimental Bloke* 20: A squarer tom, I swear, I never seen, / In all me natchril, than this 'ere Doreen.

1933 Norman Lindsay *Saturdee* 181: 'Who's yer tom? She must be yer sweetheart. Why don't yer up an' kiss her?'

1951 Dal Stivens *Jimmy Brockett* 102: 'You did, darling,' one of the little social toms said. She was a nuggety little sheila.

tomahawk To cut sheep while shearing; to shear roughly

1859 Henry Kingsley *Recollections of Geoffry Hamlyn* ii 25 : Shearers were very scarce, and the poor sheep got fearfully 'tomahawked' by the new hands.

1864 James Armour *The Diggings, the Bush, and Melbourne* 17: The latter were often brought to task for 'tomahawking', or leaving ridge-and-furrow shearmarks.

1878 G. H. Gibson *Southerly Busters*

179: I'm able for to shear 'em clean, /
And level as a die; / But I prefers to
'tommy-hawk', / And make the 'daggers' fly.
1898 Roland Graeme *From English to
the Backblocks* 189: 'I don't want small
numbers,' he replied once to a squatter,
who had been boasting of the high
tallies his shearers made, 'but I won't
have my sheep tomahawked.'
1925 E. S. Sorenson *Murty Brown* 105:
'They do a bit o' tommyhawkin' at
shearin' time, an lay up with gammy
wrists about three days a week.'
tomahawker
1964 H. P. Tritton *Time Means Tucker*
40: Tomahawkers were shearers whose
sheep looked as though the wool had
been chopped off with an axe.

Tom Collins see Collins

tom tits, toms, the The shits [rhyming
slang: different from the English use
(Franklyn, Partridge) in being always in
the plural, and in not occurring as a verb]
1944 Lawson Glassop *We Were the Rats*
67: 'Break it down,' said the corporal.
'You'll give these blokes the tomtits
before they get their first lot of C.B.'
1946 Rohan Rivett *Behind Bamboo* 399:
Tomtits dysentery, diarrhoea.
1948 Summer Locke Elliott *Rusty
Bugles* in *Khaki, Bush and Bigotry* ed.
Eunice Hanger (1968) 44: 'You blokes
give me the tom-tits. Always bellyach-
ing about something.'
1964 Thomas Keneally *The Place at
Whitton* 51: 'This place,' Raddles, some
way down the hall, grunted, 'and this
silence business. It gives me the toms.'
1968 Geoffrey Dutton *Andy* 199:
'Yanks? Here? Don't give us the tom
tits.'
1973 Patsy Adam Smith *The Barcoo
Salute* 14: 'What's the matter, got the
tom tits?'

tongs Hand shears [f. shape]
1908 W. H. Ogilvie *My Life in the Open*
36: Most of the . . . sheds in Australia
are now fitted with machinery, but in
many are still to be found the old-
fasioned shears, or 'tongs' as they are

familiarly called.
1910 C. E. W. Bean *On the Wool Track*
195: 'It's the same . . . whether they're
working tongs or machines.'
1955 *Australian Bush Ballads* ed.
Stewart and Keesing 247: There in
crowded huts at night-time, drinking
tea and rigging 'tongs'.
1961 George Farwell *Vanishing Australians* 93: Back in Jackie Howe's day
there were many good men who could
cut their 300 a day 'with the tongs'.

tonk A man with un-masculine characteristics; a male homosexual, esp. in
the passive role: *derogatory* [unexplained]
1941 Baker 77: *Tonk* A simpleton or
fool (2) A dude or fop (3) A general term
of contempt.
1964 George Johnston *My Brother Jack*
65: 'You've got to get rid of those sonky
bloody cobbers of yours,' he said to me
one night. 'The way you lot are heading
you'll end up a bunch of tonks.'
1965 Hal Porter *Stars of Australian
Stage and Screen* 280: During the last ten
years or more, there have been imported
a coterie of *untalented* English homosexuals, English tonks unheard of outside their home country, to dominate
sections of the Australian theatrical
scene.
1968 *Coast to Coast 1967–1968* 2: He
had gone to agricultural college until
he was eighteen, but like most farmers'
sons tended to disguise the fact in his
speech. One taunting cry of 'Tonk!'
and country boys felt they were ruined
for life.
1970 Richard Beilby *No Medals for
Aphrodite* 32: 'You're a good bloke,
Turk, but sometimes you talk like a
tonk,' one of them had told him in a
moment of bibulous candour. And so
he took care not to talk like a tonk . . .
Instead, he had adopted their sloppy,
profanity-riddled speech.

Top End The northern part of the Northern Territory
1933 F. E. Baume *Tragedy Track* 93: She
looked around, stayed one day, and
left again for the more human . . .
regions of the Top End, where at least

one could drink fresh water occasionally.

1941 C. Barrett *Coast of Adventure* 13: He ... asked me casually what had brought me to the Top End of the Territory.

1945 Tom Ronan *Strangers on the Ophir* 37: 'Those Kimberley horse-buyers wouldn't give a fiver for Carbine unless you could show a receipt. And the top-end drovers do their own stealing.'

1951 Ernestine Hill *The Territory* 446: *Top End* The Territory north of Katherine.

1971 *Australian* 10 Oct. 35: The sell-off of Australia's Top End to overseas interests quickened last week with a $US7.6 million offer of shares.

1975 *Bulletin* 30 Aug. 10: May I protest the use of the term 'Top End' ... as applied to parts of North Queensland? This term has long been used to refer to – and only to – that portion of the Northern Territory north of Katherine, including Arnhem Land. Longtime residents of this part of the continent commonly use it with a hint of pride and manage to instil into it some feeling of the remoteness and special character of the region.

Top-ender
1941 C. Barrett *Coast of Adventure* 14: The old Top-ender drank beer, which, to the men up there, is more desirable than iced nectar is to gods.

1961 Tom Ronan *Only a Short Walk* 52: Any 'Top-Ender' who wanted an hotel booking, a tip for the races, or the loan of a fiver ... went to Billy.

top-off *v.* & *n.* To inform to the police; an informer: *derogatory* [? f. *top* to put to death by hanging OED 1812]
1941 Kylie Tennant *The Battlers* 129: 'Who topped off Chigger Adams to the cops?' he shouted angrily.

1944 Lawson Glassop *We Were the Rats* 133: 'I haven't forgot ... how he pooled me with the Q.M. Just a top-off merchant, that's all he is.'

1950 *Australian Police Journal* Apr. 119: *Top-off, A* Informant.

1959 Dorothy Hewett *Bobbin Up* 104: Rosebery was a hybrid mixture of honest workers, top-off men and crawlers.

1966 Betty Collins *The Copper Crucible* 14: 'About four o'clock in the morning some top-off rings the cops.'

1970 Richard Beilby *No Medals for Aphrodite* 177: 'Go on, shout so they can all hear, you top-off bastard.'

Tothersider 1 A person from Van Diemen's Land (Tasmania), from the standpoint of the mainland
[**1855** William Howitt *Land, Labour and Gold* ii 362: Scenery precisely like hundreds of miles which I have seen 'on the other side', as they call Victoria, and as the Victorians call Van Diemen's Land.]

1903 Joseph Furphy *Such is Life* (1944) 276: The ancient t'other-sider [Vandemonian Jack] oscillated his frame-saw.

2 In W.A., a person from the eastern states
1896 Henry Lawson *Letters* 62: W.A. is a fraud ... The old Sand-gropers are the best to work for or have dealings with. The Tothersiders are cutting each other's throats.

1929 Jules Raeside *Golden Days* 224: The population of Hannans, although mostly composed of t'othersiders, included not a small sprinkling of West Australians.

1950 K. S. Prichard *Winged Seeds* 30: 'Unemployed from all over the country swarmin' here, t'other siders as well as W.A. blokes.'

1963 Xavier Herbert *Disturbing Element* 2: My parents ... were what were called T'othersiders, meaning people who had come to West Australia from the other side of the continent.

touch of them, a 1 sc. the 'rats', the d.t.'s
1900 Henry Lawson 'The Hero of Redclay' *Prose* i 302: 'He's boozin' again,' someone whispered. 'He's got a touch of 'em.' 'My oath, he's ratty!' said someone else.

2 sc. the shits
1944 Lawson Glassop *We Were the Rats* 30: 'You tell me you're licked just

because you've taken one on the chin in the first round. You give me a touch of 'em.'
1962 Gavin Casey *Amid the Plenty* 53: 'This place gives me a touch of 'em,' said Lenny.

towel up To give someone a thrashing, verbal or physical
1941 Baker 78: *Towel up, to* To beat, thrash.
1951 Dymphna Cusack and Florence James *Come in Spinner* 372: 'I think you deserve the V.C. for the way you towelled Old Mole up.'
1957 Ray Lawler *Summer of the Seventeenth Doll* 34: 'The kid towelled him up proper.'
1973 Alexander Buzo *Rooted* 42: 'Gary got his big serve working, I chipped in at the net, and we were laughing. Towelled them up in no time.'

Track, the Bridle see **Bridle**

track, on the As for 'on the wallaby track'
1896 Henry Lawson 'Some Day' *Prose* i 138: 'I've been knocking round for five years, and the last two years constant on the track, and no show of getting off it unless I go for good.'
1935 Kylie Tennant *Tiburon* 74: 'See 'ere, Mr Sullivan, I'm on the track, an' I'm down an' out.'
1953 *Caddie A Sydney Barmaid* 255: It would have been impossible for him to maintain the home on a dole ration . . . He was going on the track.* *On the track – Tramping the back country in search of work.
1965 Eric Lambert *The Long White Night* 12: His clothes clearly proclaimed him as a man who had been on the track, one of that tattered, aimless, wandering band which the Depression threw up, who moved from town to town in the bush, drew their dole and then were moved on by the police.

track with To associate with, to cohabit with
1915 C. J. Dennis *The Songs of a Sentimental Bloke* 51: I swear I'll never

track wiv 'er no more; / I'll never look on 'er side o' the street. Ibid. 126: *Track with* To woo; to go 'walking with'.
1924 *Truth* 27 Apr. 6: *Track with* To associate in love affairs.
1926 K. S. Prichard *Working Bullocks* 47: 'Combo's what they call a man tracks round with a gin in the nor'-west.'
1933 Norman Lindsay *Saturdee* 239: 'Who are you trackin' with now?'
1941 Baker 78: *Track with* To pay court to a girl or woman.
1954 T. A. G. Hungerford *Sowers of the Wind* 270: 'I bet it's that cross-eyed harlot he's been tracking with.'
to track square with
1919 W. H. Downing *Digger Dialects* 50: *Track square* To pursue an amorous enterprise with honourable intentions.
1949 Alan Marshall *How Beautiful Are Thy Feet* 64: 'He wants me to track square with him. To look at him you'd never think he could talk seriously. He talked for a long while about tracking square.'
1964 George Johnston *My Brother Jack* 161: 'He's been at me for years about how irresponsible I am, and the first time I come back with a girl I'm tracking square with, I get hoisted!'

trammie A tram conductor or driver [abbr.]
1946 Margaret Trist *What Else is There?* 229: 'A blue uniform, that's air force, isn't it?' 'It depends,' replied Alf cautiously. 'Maybe it was a trammie.'
1959 Dorothy Hewett *Bobbin Up* 1: Shirl had a glimpse of the trammie, swinging on the footboard.
1963 Gunther Bahnemann *Hoodlum* 146: 'There won't be much dough in a trammie's bag, Rob. Shillings, pennies, and so on.'

tramp To give someone the sack: *rare*
1941 Baker 78: *Tramped* Dismissed from employment.
1953 T. A. G. Hungerford *Riverslake* 109: 'If you come in tanked at tea-time, he'll tramp you, sure as your ring points to the ground!'
1975 Les Ryan *The Shearers* 128: 'The

next day I managed to get the pen I was offered, but only after another shearer had been tramped.'

tramper

1950 K. S. Prichard *Winged Seeds* 219: A mate who had been sacked on the trumped-up charge of an underground manager known as 'The Tramper'.

trannie A portable transistor radio

trap for young (amateur) players A hazard for the unwary

1957 R. S. Porteous *Brigalow* 18: I said something about the broken step being dangerous. 'That's right,' he agreed. 'She's a trap for young players.'

1962 Gavin Casey *Amid the Plenty* 80: 'You look out for the hire-purchase, that's a trap for young players, these days.'

1975 Les Ryan *The Shearers* 107: 'Don't be in it,' Lofty advised. 'It's a trap for young players.'

traveller A tramp seeking work in the outback, sometimes distinguished from the 'swagman' and the 'sundowner', and sometimes classified with them; one of the itinerant unemployed in the depression

1868 Marcus Clarke 'Swagmen' in *A Colonial City* ed. L. T. Hergenhan (1972) 33: I remembered at one station, situated on the main road for 'travellers', that the unhappy cook was 'put on the fire' by a crowd of these gentry.

1873 Rolf Boldrewood 'The Fencing of Wanderowna' *A Romance of Canvas Town* (1898) 82: 'They'll lay baits for the swagmen and poor travellers next,' says he with grim, unsmiling visage.

1875 A. J. Boyd *Old Colonials* (1882) 114–15: Before the swagsman became known, a traveller in search of employment was always sure of a hospitable reception at the hands of the squatter. I have lived on a station where it was invariably the custom to serve out two men's rations weekly for the benefit of travellers. All this is now done away with in the more settled parts of the colonies.

1893 Henry Lawson 'Some Popular

Australian Mistakes' *Prose* ii 24: Men tramping in search of a 'shed' are not called 'sundowners' or 'swaggies'; they are 'trav'lers'.

1910 C. E. W. Bean *On the Wool Track* 65: Once a year, for a month or two, on horses, on bicycles, occasionally on foot, come by the 'travellers', shearers on their way from shed to shed.

1919 E. S. Sorenson *Chips and Splinters* 72: 'You seem to think a man's got nothing to do on these stations but cook for travellers.'

1941 Kylie Tennant *The Battlers* 23: Any sergeant will tell you that the 'locals' – that is, the unemployed residing in the town – are bad enough. But the 'travellers – meaning the men with track-cards who wander the country in search of work, getting their food-orders from declared 'dole stations' in towns fifty or sixty miles apart – the travellers are worse.

travelling, a fine day for See quot. 1951

1951 Ernestine Hill *The Territory* 306: 'It's a fine day for travellin',' they told him – the time-honoured phrase that all over the outback is notice to quit.

1953 *Daily Mirror* 18 Mar. 17: Finally, the head stockman told him 'It's a fine day for travellin',' the time-honored phrase that means notice to quit all over the outback.

1962 David Forrest *The Hollow Wood-heap* 214: He was going on a long, long journey, alone and torn in half, and . . . looking out at the morning, decided it was as good a day as any for travelling.

tray (trey) -bit A threepenny piece (before decimal coinage, 1966)

1898 *Bulletin* 1 Oct. 14: 3d. a 'traybit'.

1906 Henry Lawson 'In the Height of Fashion' *Verse* ii 182: Then our country, cold and scornful, / Answered 'Go and get a beer!' / And it threw the tray bit at us / Just to stop our 'silly row'.

1911 Louis Stone *Jonah* 98: 'Well, a tray bit won't break me,' said Chook, producing threepence from his pocket.

1918 Harley Matthews *Saints and Soldiers* 103: Come, join the army, / Make no delay, / Front seats a deener, /

Back seats a tray.
1949 Ruth Park *Poor Man's Orange* 68:
She wanted to say something, to tell
this silly old coot that what she knew
about life could be written on a tray bit.

trays, tray-bits, the The shits [rhyming
slang]
1952 T. A. G. Hungerford *The Ridge and
the River* 24: 'Oscar's got a touch of the
trays.'

treat with ignore see **ignore**

trick, can't take a To be constantly unsuccessful [f. card games]
1944 Lawson Glassop *We Were the Rats*
211: 'He tells us we might be Aussies
but we can't take a trick. He says we
got a canin' in Greece an' had to get
out.'
1963 D. H. Crick *Martin Place* 192–3:
'Looks like curtains for you, pal. Can't
take a trick.'
1977 *Bulletin* 5 Feb. 11: The ACTU
leader can't take a trick.

Tricolours, the The Eastern Suburbs
(N.S.W.) Rugby League team (also the
Roosters)

trizzie A threepenny piece
1942 *Salt* 2 Feb. 18: 3 pence a trey, or
trizzie.
1959 Gerard Hamilton *Summer Glare*
31: My greatest pal now was John
'Trizzie' Peele . . . He always had a
threepeny bit in his pocket which gave
him his nickname.

troppo Mentally or nervously affected
by the privations of war service in the
tropics
1943 George Johnston *New Guinea
Diary* 222: 'A man must be going
troppo,' he remarks quietly.
1946 Rohan Rivett *Behind Bamboo* 399:
Troppo mad, sunstruck, weak-minded,
affected by captivity.
1948 Sumner Locke Elliott *Rusty Bugles*
in *Khaki, Bush and Bigotry* ed. Eunice
Hanger (1968) 88: 'They're taking him
to the psychiatric ward.' . . . 'What's
that?' 'Where they take you when you

go troppo.'
1954 L. H. Evers *Pattern of Conquest*
144: 'Troppo!' said the other man, 'mad
as a hatter.'
1963 Lawson Glassop *The Rats in New
Guinea* 197: Every time I held my hand
out I noticed my fingers shaking . . .
My fingers shook against my lips as I
took a draw at an imaginary cigarette.
My God, I thought, I'm going troppo.
I'm even smoking without cigarettes
now.
1973 Roland Robinson *The Drift of
Things* 266: Cecil tried to give me advice
against the boredom which gripped
everyone in the Territory . . . 'Don't
give way to going "Troppo", as most
of our fellows do.'
1975 *Sun-Herald* 30 Nov. 131: Aunty
Jack . . . could bring a badly-needed
fresh burst of local comedy (in a troppo
way) to our screens.

trot A sequence of chance events, esp.
betokening good or ill fortune ('a good
trot', 'a rough trot') esp. sporting
1911 Louis Stone *Jonah* 216: A trot or
succession of seven tails followed, and
the kip changed hands rapidly.
1919 W. H. Downing *Digger Dialects*
51: *Trot* An experience (e.g. 'a rough
trot'; 'a bad time').
1922 Arthur Wright *A Colt from the
Country* 147: 'Luck? Hang it, no. I'm
having a bad trot. Lost to-day and again
to-night.'
1949 Lawson Glassop *Lucky Palmer*
177: He was 'Lucky' Palmer, having a
bad trot at the moment, admittedly,
but still 'Lucky' Palmer.
1952 T. A. G. Hungerford *The Ridge
and the River* 181: 'We didn't even hope
that she'd last any longer, she had such
a tough trot. But she hung on.'
1965 Wally Grout *My Country's 'Keeper*
166: Most Pressmen I have found to be
good coves who will lay off a player
having a bad trot.
see **spin**

troubles!, my A dismissive expression,
equivalent to 'Don't worry about me!':
obsolescent
1895 Cornelius Crowe *The Australian*

Slang Dictionary 89: *Troubles* 'my troubles' what do I care.
1905 Nathan Spielvogel *A Gumsucker on the Tramp* 90: Off again; round Leuwin Cape; rough seas; My Troubles! I'm coming home.
1911 E. M. Clowes *On the Wallaby through Victoria* 16: A shrug of the shoulders and the 'My troubles' are his response to any advice or sympathy you may offer.
1924 Vance Palmer *The Outpost* 84: 'I never got along with other women. Even the girls at school didn't like me, and weren't slow in showing it. My troubles, though!'
1934 'Leslie Parker' *Trooper to the Southern Cross* (1966) 134: 'I suppose you won't mind if he flirts with Celia,' said Mrs Dicky. 'His troubles,' I said, knowing Celia would turn him down well and truly.
1947 Gavin Casey *The Wits are Out* 44: 'You better lay off Kitty while the old man's about, or there'll be one more out-of-work motor salesman kicking round the city,' Syd suggested. 'My troubles!' Jerry jeered.

try it on, to To seek some advantage to which one is not entitled, esp. by bluff or presumption; to see what one can 'get away with' [f. *try on* to live by thieving OED 1811]
1812 Vaux: *Try it on* To make an attempt, or essay, where success is doubtful. So to *try it on with* a woman, signifies to attempt her chastity.
1845 C. Griffith *The Present State of Port Phillip* 77: Requiring a strict hand to keep them [ex-convicts] in order, as it is part of their system to impose (or as they term it *to try it on*) whenever they have a chance of success, which is of course most likely with new settlers.
1859 Oliné Keese *The Broad Arrow* i 257: 'No, no, Miss Bridget; they [the convict servants] are only trying it on ... When you are more up to their ways, they'll leave you alone.'
1883 R. E. N. Twopeny *Town Life in Australia* 134: The upper forms have a disposition to 'try it on' when a new hand is set over them.

1900 Henry Lawson 'Joe Wilson's Courtship' *Prose* i 547: 'Oh, she tried it on, but it didn't go,' said Romany. 'I've met her sort before.'
1953 Bant Singer *You're Wrong Delaney* 136: 'Nugget caught Martini trying it on with Lily and shot him.'

a try on 'An attempt, esp. an attempt at imposition or deceit' (OED 1874)
1900 Henry Lawson 'A Daughter of Maoriland' *Prose* i 374: The girl's last 'try on' was to come down to the school fence, and ostentatiously sharpen a table-knife on the wires.
1910 C. E. W. Bean *On the Wool Track* 41: There almost always came a time when the boss's authority was at issue; not a continental rebellion, but some mean Anglo-Saxon 'try-on'.

truckie A truck (i.e. lorry) driver [abbr.]
1958 *Coast to Coast 1957–1958* 201: The truckie looked upwards. 'Whaddya want, mate?'
1973 *Australian* 13 Apr. 1: 'Trucking is in my bones; I love being with truckies; I've always thought of myself as a truckie,' he [Mr Ken Thomas] said.

tube 1 The downtube in a shearing shed to which the hand piece is connected
1963 *Sydney Morning Herald* 17 Aug. 11: Get off the tube (out of the game) while you are young enough.
2 A can of beer; given currency by the Barry Mackenzie strip in the 1960s
1971 George Johnston *A Cartload of Clay* 137: 'A beer'd be just the shot,' said the Ocker. 'Never bin known to say no to a tube.'
1974 John Powers *The Last of the Knucklemen* 58: 'We got the old back-slap routine, an 'a few free tubes.'
1975 *Australian* 17 Feb. 3: Meat pies are not the only concession to Ockerism. Should Bazza Mackenzie arrive in Peking seeking a cold tube, Dr Fitzgerald [the ambassador] could cope with that as efficiently as he does the daily round of diplomatic consultations.
1976 *Sydney Morning Herald* 25 Jun. 12: They said 'Good on yer mate. Good on yer. Have a tube.'

tucker, to make To gain an income sufficient only to cover such necessities as food

1861 Horace Earle *Ups and Downs* 336: 'Well, we shall perhaps make tucker* out of it,' was the reply ... for diggers never like to let their neighbours know the extent of their luck. *Food.

1875 A. J. Boyd *Old Colonials* (1882) 127: Patient and plodding ... often months without doing more than earning 'tucker', he [the digger] delves on until he either makes his pile, or is laid up in ordinary.

1880 Rolf Boldrewood *The Miner's Right* (1890) 381: 'I believe you never would have made anything more than tucker – isn't that the expression? – if it hadn't been for your mates and your backers.'

1901 Henry Lawson 'The Golden Graveyard' *Prose* i 344: They 'drove' (tunnelled) inwards at right angles to the fence, and at a point immediately beneath it they were 'making tucker'; a few feet farther and they were making wages.

1933 F. E. Baume *Tragedy Track* 18: During the past year they could not be said to be making more than their tucker.

1944 Brian James *First Furrow* 8: They spoke to Tully and begged him to throw it in. They'd never make tucker, they said, on the job. They'd starve on it.

1954 Miles Franklin *Cockatoos* 120: 'The farms are not big enough to make tucker off.'

tucker dirt, tucker track

1896 Edward Dyson *Rhymes from the Mines* 74: Where gold was getting I was on the job, and early, –/Struck some tucker dirt at Armstrong's, and just lived at Pleasant Creek.

1880–1914 'With My Swag All on My Shoulder' *Old Bush Songs* ed. Stewart and Keesing (1957) 226: It is the best of tucker tracks,/So I'll stay here till I die.

tucker bag, box The bag in which the itinerant carries his rations

1893 Henry Lawson 'Some Popular Australian Mistakes' *Prose* ii 24: The nose (tucker) bag hangs over the other shoulder and balances the load nicely – when there's anything in the bag.

1908 W. H. Ogilvie *My Life in the Open* 52: The 'tucker box' is taken from one of the waggons, and there in the weird silence of the brooding Bush they take their evening meal.

1919 W. K. Harris *Outback in Australia* 143: He 'smoodges' round the cook, and if 'moved on' without his tucker-bags replenished, he does not scruple to do an injury.

1941 Charles Barrett *Coast of Adventure* 36: Old man Rogers enjoyed his supper, and stowed cold roast goose in the tucker-bag, for breakfast.

1968 Walter Gill *Petermann Journey* 82: Squatting on his 'nap', with his back to a tucker box.

Tuesday or Bourke Street see **Bourke Street**

turkey 1 A swag: *rare*

1912 G. H. Gibson *Ironbark Splinters* 6: So you 'pack' your bloomin' turkey,[1] and you take the northern train. [1]'Turkey' – a bushman's slang for 'swag', a bundle of blankets and clothes. The term is sometimes also applied to a pack-horse.

2 In 'plain turkey', 'scrub turkey' etc., a swagman who tramps the plain country, the scrub [f. the birds inhabiting these regions]

1955 D'Arcy Niland *The Shiralee* 27: He had met plenty of these plain-turkeys, as they were known. They zoned themselves on the plains, wandering the roads and the back-tracks among the sheep stations and the wheat farms, doing the rounds year in and year out. They did the rounds from shed to shed at shearing time, ate a couple of good meals, had the tucker-bag filled, and moved on to the next place.

1955 Alan Marshall *I Can Jump Puddles* 152: Father had humped his bluey in Queensland and was familiar with the ways of swagmen. He always called them 'travellers'. The bearded men who kept to the bush he called 'Scrub

Turkeys' and those came down from the plains he called 'Plain Turkeys'.

1964 H. P. Tritton *Time Means Tucker* 15: Many of these men never left the Plains, but between burr cutting and work in the shearing sheds managed to exist. The regulars were known as 'Plain Turkeys' and most of them were well up in years.

1973 Frank Huelin *Keep Moving* 178: *Scrub Turkey* Bagman who has gone Bush. Usually slightly mental or eccentric.

turkey, head over Head over heels [? f. *tuck* the stern of a boat OED 1625]

1906 Edward Dyson *Fact'ry 'Ands* 234: 'One was dumped down two flights, 'ead over tuck, with a fat punch.'

1915 C. J. Dennis *The Songs of a Sentimental Bloke* 43: 'E swallers lysol, throws a fancy fit, / 'Ead over turkey, an' 'is soul 'as flit.

1955 Alan Marshall *I Can Jump Puddles* 46: 'I knock Sir Frederick Salisbury, or whatever his name is, head over turkey into a clump of peacocks.'

turkey, on the 'A fit or spell of intoxication. *Slang. Obs.*' (Mathews 1846)

1903 Joseph Furphy *Such is Life* (1944) 278: 'Gosh! you've been on the turkey; you'll be cutting yourself some of these times.'

turn out To become a bushranger

1875 Rolf Boldrewood *The Squatter's Dream* repr. as *Ups and Downs* (1878) 165: 'I'm not sure that you won't get off light. You have had the good luck not to have killed anybody that I know of since you turned out.'

1899 G. E. Boxall *The Story of the Australian Bushrangers* 274: The reward offered for the capture of Thomas Clarke was raised to £1000, while £500 was offered for his brother John, who had just 'turned out'.

turps Liquor

1962 J. Marshall and R. Drysdale *Journey Among Men* 84: The Sergeant alleged that Ah Fong was a notorious drunkard, forever on the 'turps'. Ibid.

131: 'He likes to hit the turps now and again, and you can't blame him.'

1973 John O'Grady *Survival in the Doghouse* 57: He's humping a dozen cans with him. Ice cold. And he gets a great welcome. Not only because of the turps, but because with him there we can have a four-handed game.

twang Opium [unexplained]

1898 *Bulletin* 1 Oct. 14: Tobacco is 'snout', opium 'twang'.

1900–10 O'Brien and Stephens: *Twang* opium.

1945 Tom Ronan *Strangers on the Ophir* 68: The honest Chinese limits himself to his one pipe of 'Twang' per night.

1961 Ion L. Idriess *Tracks of Destiny* 94: This Chinaman was a 'runner' carrying smuggled 'twang' (opium) from Port Darwin to his compatriots in at the Creek.

two bob The sum of money most often used in derogatory expressions like 'not worth two bob', 'silly as a two bob watch', 'two bob lair' [cf. U.S. 'two-bit']

1944 Lawson Glassop *We Were the Rats* 144: Bert was more the 'two-bob lair' type.

1954 *Coast to Coast 1953–1954* 122: 'Fifty flamin' quid! Why, it's not worth two bob.'

1958 H. D. Williamson *The Sunlit Plain* 257: 'Cunning, too – put it over his own cobbers – sell his wife fer two bob.'

1959 Dorothy Hewett *Bobbin Up* 142: 'One little wizened-up Pommy feller, you wouldn't give a two bob for 'im.'

1966 Elwyn Wallace *Sydney and the Bush* 83: 'There are not too many bloody two bob snobs on the track.'

1974 John Powers *The Last of the Knucklemen* 30: 'I don't get hustled into punch-ups with two-bob lairs.'

two bob each way, to have Not to commit oneself to either of two courses of action; to seek to profit from all contingencies [f. horseracing]

1973 Max Harris *The Angry Eye* 186: I suspect our elegant French trading friends are having two bob each-way in the Australian sex-aid market.

two-tooth A sheep one year old; (as butcher's meat) hogget [? A New Zealandism rather than an Australianism, but reported in Australia]

1863 Samuel Butler *A First Year in Canterbury Settlement* ed. R. A. Streatfeild (1914) 39: Two teeth indicate one year old, four teeth two years, six teeth three years, eight teeth (or full mouthed) four years . . . The above teeth are to be looked for in the lower jaw and not the upper.

1933 Acland 359: After weaning a lamb becomes a (ram, etc.) hogget until shorn. After shearing he is usually called a shorn hogget until the next crop of lambs are weaned about the time he gets his first two-teeth. He is then called a two-tooth. Some people, however, call him a two-tooth as soon as he is shorn, whether his new teeth are up or not.

1935 R. B. Plowman *The Boundary Rider* 66: 'That's a nice young sheep . . . Looks like a well-grown two-tooth.'

two-up A gambling game based on spinning two pennies, and wagering whether they fall as two heads or two tails

1898 W. T. Goodge 'Australia's Pride' *Bulletin* 3 Sep. 32: At 'loo he'd lately scooped the pool; / He'd simply smashed the two-up school.

1926 J. Vance Marshall *Timely Tips for New Australians: Two-up* A prevalent method of gambling by tossing two pennies into the air.

1969 Bobbie Hardy *West of the Darling* 162: 'In 1883 in Silverton I noticed all sorts of games going on outside my Dad's hotel . . . And also around the back you would see a big two up school.'

see **grouter, heading them, kip, spinner, swy**

tyke, tike A Roman Catholic: *derogatory*

1941 Baker 76: *Tike, tyke* A Roman Catholic.

1948 Ruth Park *The Harp in the South* 268: 'I'll do what I like when I like without the interference of any bone-headed tike.'

1961 Patrick White *Riders in the Chariot*

232: 'I would never ever of suspected you Rosetrees of being tykes. Only the civil servants are Roman Catholics here, and the politicians, if they are anything at all.'

1969 Jon Cleary *Remember Jack Hoxie* 86: 'I'm like you, a Tyke. A Catholic.'

tyrants, the last of the Lachlan Macquarie, Governor of New South Wales 1809–22 (in old-fashioned school textbooks)

Tyson, hungry (mean, rich, independent) as Expressions referring to the millionaire pastoralist, James Tyson (1823–98)

[1877 Marcus Clarke *A Colonial City* ed. L. T. Hergenhan (1972) 387: When the stranger hears that the magnificent and park-like lands through which he drives are the property of 'Scabby Moffatt', 'Hungry-man Tyson', and 'Pig-pig Carter', he is apt to understand why a witty barrister called the squattocracy of the colonies the wealthy lower orders.]

1890 *Bulletin* 4 Oct. 11: 'Hungry' Tyson gave £2000 to the Sydney Royal Naval Home.

1898 *Bulletin* 17 Dec. Red Page: 'As mean as Hungry Tyson' (used by people who know nothing of Tyson.)

1928 Arthur Wright *A Good Recovery* 8: 'Th' old bloke's as rich as Tyson.'

1950 *Coast to Coast 1949–1950* 190: 'No more bunging a job in at a minute's notice and walking off with a billycan and a roll of blankets, as independent as Tyson.'

1962 Tom Ronan *Deep of the Sky* 30: He never subscribed to the 'hungry Jimmy Tyson' legend.

U

uey, do a To make a U-turn

1976 *Bulletin* 28 Feb. 27: Ted Heath, like Fraser, began as a professed opponent of big government but was soon 'doing a youee' (U-turn) all over the place.

uncle from Fiji see **Fiji**

underground mutton Rabbit, as an edible meat
1946 A. J. Holt *Wheat Farms of Victoria* 129: 'Underground mutton' (rabbit) is almost always available for those who like it.
1958 H. D. Williamson *The Sunlit Plain* 58: Underground mutton to a rabbit-trapper should be as pig-flesh to a Mohammedan.
1965 Eric Lambert *The Long White Night* 138: 'I thought a feed of underground mutton would go all right for my tea.'
1972 G. C. Bolton *A Fine Country to Starve In* 225: It was apparently a plague season for rabbits, and . . . this may have helped the unemployed and struggling farmers to eke out their diets with 'underground mutton'.

under someone's neck, go see **neck**

uni The university
1962 Alan Seymour *The One Day of the Year* 103: 'I think I might ditch my course. Leave Uni.'
1977 *Sydney Morning Herald* 26 Feb. 21: Sydney Uni spends up to welcome its students.

up the duff see **duff**

up a gum tree see **gumtree**

up there, Cazaly see **Cazaly**

up who, who's (and who's paying the rent) See quot. 1966: World War II slang
1966 Baker 172: *who's up who (and who's paying the rent)?* Just what is happening? Who's in control? e.g. 'Nobody knows who's up who' etc., said of a complete mess-up.
1970 Barry Oakley *Let's Hear it for Prendergast* 66: 'These days you don't know who's up who and who's paying the rent.'
1971 Frank Hardy *The Outcasts of Foolgarah* 162: Finer points, precedents, split straws, who's up who and who's

paying for a strike within the meaning of the act.
1976 Robert Drewe *The Savage Crows* 258: Victor already knew, even here at the end of the world, who was up whom in this life.

upside down, the hut that's The symbol of the strange aspect which Australia presented to the immigrant from the antipodes (Christmas in midsummer, trees losing bark instead of leaves, etc.) with the underlying belief that the inhabitants on the bottom of the world must walk upside down [f. ballad with this refrain]
1957 *Old Bush Songs* ed. Stewart and Keesing 269: 'The Hut That's Upside-down' [ballad title]
1961 Judith Wright *Australian Letters* Jun. 30: The Upside-down Hut [essay title]

upside down, the only river in the world that flows The Yarra river, Melbourne, from its brownish water: *jocular*
1953 Baker 275: *The only river in the world that flows upside down* a reference to the River Yarra which flows through Melbourne.
1965 Frank Hardy *The Yarns of Billy Borker* 43: Melbourne Mick and Sydney Sam might start making sly little jokes about the harbour bridge being an oversized coathanger, or the Yarra the only river in the world that flows upside down.
1966 Jan Smith *An Ornament of Grace* 51: Bet you're from Melbourne, the only city in the world where the river flows upside down with the mud on top. see **Little Muddy**

upter No good at all [abbr. of 'up to putty' or 'up to shit']
1919 W. H. Downing *Digger Dialects* 52: *Upter* A corruption of 'Up to Putty'.
1951 Eric Lambert *The Twenty Thousand Thieves* 169: Go Through slapped Happy's shoulder. 'How are yer, Hap, old feller?' 'Up to shit' ['Upter' in 1963 edn], replied Happy.
1970 Richard Beilby *No Medals for Aphrodite* 174: 'How's the feet, Private Wilkinson?' 'Upta, sir. Can't get me

boots on this mornin'.'

Urandangie, the girls are bandy at see
Tallarook

urger 1 A race tipster who seeks a bonus
from the winnings of others
1924 *Truth* 27 Apr. 6: *Urger* A fraudulent race follower.
1930 L. W. Lower *Here's Luck* 85: Tip-
slingers, urgers and whisperers slunk
like jackals through the crowd.
1946 *Sunday Sun* 18 Aug. Suppl. 15:
Bill's got more nerve than a Randwick
urger.
1950 *Australian Police Journal* Apr.
120: *Urger* A nuisance on a racecourse
who will prevail on a mug to back
something, usually on the pretence that
the urger's brother-in-law trains it,
etc., or something similar, the object
being that the mug might 'sling' if the
horse wins.
1967 Frank Hardy *Billy Borker Yarns
Again* 14: 'An urger is a bloke who
slings out tips and asks for a cut if one
of them wins.'
2 Any parasite or loafer, who incurs no
risk himself
1952 T. A. G. Hungerford *The Ridge and
the River* 155: 'Come on, you urgers!'
he muttered. 'Sooner we get goin', the
sooner we get across.'
1964 George Johnston *My Brother Jack*
325: 'I'm not saying you're an *urger* or
anything like that, but this recruiting
stuff, well, it *is* sort of urging in a way,
don't you think?'

useful A general factotum in a business,
pub etc.
[**1866** Rachel Henning *Letters* ed. David
Adams (1963) 219: There are three
men employed about the place [a
timber-logging business]. The bullock-
driver, the puntman and a 'generally
useful' man.]
1898 Alfred Joyce *A Homestead History* ed. G. F. James (1969) 41: Our
friends had met with a trained carpenter
in town, whom with his wife they had
hired for £20 a year, the man as general
useful, which would include his trade
employment, and his wife as cook for

the proprietors.
1900 Henry Lawson 'Middleton's Peter'
Prose i 261: There were two rooms, of
a sort, attached to the stables – one at
each end. One was occupied by a man
who was 'generally useful'.
1935 Kylie Tennant *Tiburon* 37: Roman
stepped out of the room next to the
laundry of O'Brien's Hotel, where he
was barman, yardman and general useful.
1953 *Caddie A Sydney Barmaid* 6: The
Missus called the useful to take over.
A fight had started in the front parlour
and women were biting and scratching
in one mad mix up.
1962 Criena Rohan *The Delinquents* 31:
'I met Paddy Murphy, you know the
'useful' at your pub, and he had a
look at it.'

ute A utility (vehicle combining the
features of a sedan and a truck) [abbr.]
1951 Eric Lambert *The Twenty Thousand Thieves* 178: 'He gets pissed one
night, pinches a ute from the transport
lines.'
1961 Jack Danvers *The Living Come
First* 17: 'Take the ute and drive in to
Alice. The wire we ordered has arrived.'

V

vag, on the According to the provisions
of the Vagrancy Act
1877 T. E. Argles *The Pilgrim* ii 21:
She had got three months 'on the vag.'
for making a sleeping place of a prominent doorstep.
1896 Edward Dyson *Rhymes from the
Mines* 77: I needed tucker badly, / And
this job, I think, just saved me being
lumbered on the vag.
1916 C. J. Dennis *The Moods of Ginger
Mick* 28: If I don't work they'd pinch
me on the vag.
1951 Dymphna Cusack and Florence
James *Come in Spinner* 300: 'If there's
a police raid the girls are picked up
under the Vag. and that's all there is to
it.'
1959 K. S. Prichard *N'Goola* 148: 'Was

you in the game, love? Or did they get you on the vag?'

vag A vagrant
1895 Cornelius Crowe *The Australian Slang Dictionary* 91: *Vag* a vagrant.
1965 Xavier Herbert *Larger than Life* 40: 'We got a prisoner, eh?' The sergeant grunted. 'Just a vag.'

vagged, to be To be arrested under the provisions of the Vagrancy Act
1930 *Bulletin* 9 Jul. 28: 'We can't have the public's mind polluted by abusive language. You're vagged.'
1941 Kylie Tennant *The Battlers* 11: 'I been vagged,' the Stray mentioned. 'Oh! you have? Well, there you are. If you ain't got any money, they run you in.'
1954 *Coast to Coast 1953–1954* 174: She'd beat that consorting charge now; they couldn't vag her again either.

Vandemonian *n. & a.* 1 Tasmanian [f. Van Diemen's Land, the original name of Tasmania]
1832 *The Currency Lad* 25 Aug. [2]: We are no advocates for the unlimited admission of Vandemonian wheat to our market.
1840 G. Arden *Australia Felix* 9: A shrewd old Vandemonian colonist.
1903 Joseph Furphy *Such is Life* (1944) 273: Vandemonian Jack, aged about a century, was mechanically sawing firewood in the hot, sickly sunshine.
2 An ex-convict from Van Diemen's Land
1855 Raffaello Carboni *The Eureka Stockade* ed. G. Serle (1969) 90: A sulky ruffian . . . [of] the known cast, as called here in this colony, of a 'Vandemonian', made up of low, vulgar manners and hard talk.
1899 G. E. Boxall *The Story of the Australian Bushrangers* 139: It was popularly supposed that these bushrangers were all convicts from 'Van Diemen's Land', hence they were known as 'Van Demonians', 'Derwenters' from the River Derwent, and 'Tother siders'.

Vee-dub A Volkswagen car [f. abbr. VW]
1970 Alexander Buzo *The Front Room*

Boys in Penguin *Plays* 48–9: 'They've got all the defects of the Vee Dub fifteen hundred and none of its virtues'.

velvet, black see **black**

verandah (under the) An exchange market conducted on a city pavement, under an awning, in Victoria; title of a serial column in the Melbourne *Leader* from the 1860s: *obs*.
1868 Marcus Clarke *A Colonial City* ed. L. T. Hergenhan (1972) 18: The Victorian broker . . . begins to be known, he is seen under the 'Verandah' [illustration on facing page], and lunches at the Criterion.
1873 A. Trollope *Australia* ed. Edwards and Joyce (1967) 403: The verandah is a kind of open exchange – some place on the street pavement apparently selected by chance, on which dealers in mining shares congregate. What they do, or how they carry on their business when there, I am unable to explain.
1898 Morris 489: Verandahs . . . are an architectual feature of . . . most city shops, where they render the sidewalks an almost continuous arcade. 'Under the Verandah' has acquired the meaning 'where city men most do congregate.'

Viceroy, the old Lachlan Macquarie, Governor of New South Wales 1809–22, so termed by his supporters after his resignation
1824 Michael Massey Robinson *The Colonist* 5 Feb. 1835 46: 'The Old Viceroy' [song title]

vision splendid, the Any splendid prospect, esp. of the future (from A. B. Paterson's 'Clancy of the Overflow')
1895 A. B. Paterson *The Man from Snowy River* 21: And he sees the vision splendid of the sunlit plains extended, / And at night the wondrous glory of the everlasting stars.
1951 Ernestine Hill *The Territory* 294: Prose and poetry glorify the drover's life into 'vision splendid of the sunlit plains extended.'
1954 Tom Ronan *Vision Splendid* [book

title]
1959 Xavier Herbert *Seven Emus* 110: Such was his acting that he took in his audience along with himself, made them share his optimism, his vision splendid, even ... against their better judgement.
1972 *Sun-Herald* 19 Nov. 11: Scratch the surface of Gough Whitlam's promises of the vision splendid and you quickly run up against some very strange political promises.
1972 Ian Moffitt *The U-Jack Society* 199: I sat obediently and listened, and Sir Phillip spread his vision splendid of electricity extended with nuclear power.

vomit, Burdekin see **Burdekin**

W

waddy A wooden club, often improvised [Ab. 1788 Ramson 126]
1899 Steele Rudd *On Our Selection* 19: We each carried a kerosine tin, slung like a kettle-drum, and belted it with a waddy – Dad's idea.
1930 K. S. Prichard *Haxby's Circus* 236: The men grabbed seats, started to smash them up, and use them as waddies.
1939 Miles Franklin and Dymphna Cusack *Pioneers on Parade* 141: 'No danger,' said William, selecting a waddy.
1947 Vance Palmer *Cyclone* 79: 'They're planning to march out to the camp some night and deal it out to the lot of us with waddies.'
1973 Frank Huelin *Keep Moving* 114: 'The only ones who wait for us are railway demons with boots and waddies.'

wage-plug A worker for wages [cf. *plug* a slow horse U.S. 1860 Mathews; *wage-slave* OED 1886]
1931 Miles Franklin *Back to Bool Bool* 154: 'The Australian working-man is the richest wage-plug on God's earth, and the most leisured.'
1971 Frank Hardy *The Outcasts of*

Foolgarah 22: A grand place to live is Foolgarah, even for wage-plugs.

Wagga (ŏ) blanket, rug A covering made from corn sacks, chaff bags or similar material [f. place-name Wagga Wagga, N.S.W.: otherwise unexplained]
1893 Henry Lawson 'The Darling River' *Prose* i 86–7: The live cinders from the firebox ... fell in showers on deck. Every now and then a spark would burn through the 'Wagga rug' of a sleeping shearer, and he'd wake up suddenly and get up and curse.
1938 Xavier Herbert *Capricornia* 454: The nap ... consisted of two greasy bran-sacks, or, as bushmen call them, Wagga Rugs.
1944 Jean Devanny *By Tropic, Sea and Jungle* 156: When you crawl under your wagga you get in one position and aren't game to move, it hurts so much.
1951 Simon Hickey *Travelled Roads* 52: Any bush worker in the West knows that a Wagga rug is made by top-sewing two cornsacks together, which, with any sort of blanket underneath, would keep out the cold, or even rain, at a pinch.
1962 Ron Tullipan *March into Mroning* 22: A blanket under him, another on top, and over that again a big bush wagga of stitched cornsacks.
1969 Lyndall Hadow *Full Cycle* 248: She went to his camp bed. 'Take your wagga, then.' 'No, it's too heavy.' Besides, he was tired of the prickly cornsacks, half a dozen of them opened out and sewn together that had formed his bedclothes for a long time now.

Wagga grip see **monkey**[2]

waist, lady's see **lady's**

wake up to, to be a To be fully apprised of a situation; to be alert to possible deception [f. thieves' slang: see quot. 1812]
1812 Vaux: *Awake:* an expression used ... as a thief will say to his accomplice, on perceiving the person they are about to rob is aware of their

intention, and up on his guard, *stow it, the cove's awake.* To be awake to any scheme, deception, or design, means, generally, to see through it or comprehend it.

1924 *Truth* 27 Apr. 6: *Awake* To know all.

1932 Leonard Mann *Flesh in Armour* 237: She would see, then, that he was no fool, and take a full wake-up to it.

1945 *Coast to Coast 1944* 85: 'When did you become a wake-up?' 'A wake-up to what?' 'To the papers.'

1957 Ray Lawler *Summer of the Seventeenth Doll* 17: 'She shakes them down for all they're worth the whole time they're here. 'Course they're a wake up, but they don't seem to mind.'

1963 Alan Marshall *In Mine Own Heart* 64: 'The trouble is that Florrie's a wake-up to me. She doesn't believe half the lies I tell her.'

1975 Xavier Herbert *Poor Fellow My Country* 592: 'I got a feelin' he's a wake-up. Still, don't worry. We'll beat him.'

Waler 'An Anglo-Indian name for an Australian horse imported from New South Wales into India, especially for the cavalry. Afterwards used for any horse brought from Australia.' (Morris)

1863 B. A. Heywood *Vacation Tour at the Antipodes* 134: I have heard men from Bengal talk of the 'Walers', meaning horses from New South Wales.

1874 Rolf Boldrewood *My Run Home* (1897) 330: 'I can't imagine any horse but an English thoroughbred worthy to be named in the same day with a high-caste Arab ...' 'I'll show you a "Waler" ["whaler" in 1897] to-morrow that may convert you.'

1900 Henry Lawson 'The Ballad of the Cornstalk' *Verse* i 380: He mounted his waler and rode to the sea.

1964 H. P. Tritton *Time Means Tucker* 90: The horses were bred specially for the Indian Army and known as 'Walers' (because they came from New South Wales).

1966 Tom Ronan *Strangers on the Ophir* 48: That old original waler strain than which no greater or gamer breed of horse ever sniffed the wind.

walk off, do a walk To abandon a rural property through inability to make it pay

1939 Leonard Mann *Mountain Flat* 76–7: 'The one who doesn't get Suttons' will have to walk off.'

1958 E. O. Schlunke *The Village Hampden* 114: 'They're so much in debt that, if the Government Relief Board wasn't carrying them on, they'd all have to walk off their farms tomorrow.'

1959 C. V. Lawlor *All That Humbug* 87: Almost every week one heard of yet another farmer who had 'walked off' in the south-west area of N.S.W. Sad hearts and bitter; moneyless pockets; an obscure future; machinery left behind that could not be paid for.

1970 *Sydney Morning Herald* 21 Jul. 6: The manager of the Bourke Rural Bank can recall four graziers who have 'done a walk', leaving the bank to use the properties as best it could to recover the graziers' debts.

walkabout 1 Temporary migration from one's normal habitat (originally applied to the movements of Aboriginals); any journey away from a home base [Pidgin]

1828 *Sydney Gazette* 2 Jan. 3: When the executioner had adjusted the rope, and was about to pull the cap over his eyes ... he said, in a tone of deep feeling, which it was impossible to bear without strong emotion, 'Bail more walk about', meaning that his wanderings were all over.

1908 Mrs Aeneas Gunn *We of the Never-Never* 218: The day after that was filled in with preparations for a walk-about, and the next again found us camped at Bitter Springs.

1930 Vance Palmer *The Passage* 24: 'Tired of the smell of fish,' he would explain, 'only a cat could stand it so long on end. I'm going for a walkabout – there's plenty doing up in the orchards now the oranges are on.'

1941 Charles Barrett *Coast of Adventure* 14: As an old man whose walkabouts were made in an old-fashioned vehicle, the Doctor understood natives.

1969 William Dick *Naked Prodigal* 10: 'Hold the fort men. I'm going walk-

about,' yelled Arthur, throwing down his trolley with a clang.
1976 *Sydney Morning Herald* 17 May 6: His answers to questions were garbled and grammatically walkabout.
2 A 'meet-the-people' stroll by royalty or other notable (first used of Queen Elizabeth on 12 Mar. 1970 Auckland N.Z.)
1977 *Australian* 24 Mar. 5: A fair-haired 16-year-old girl ... was the other star of the walkabout. She presented the flowers then popped her head up and kissed the Queen on the cheek.

Walla Walla, further behind than Delayed, at a disadvantage [f. place-name, with implication of remoteness]
[1895 Cornelius Crowe *Australian Slang Dictionary* 92: *Walla Walla* going to the country, good bye.]
1953 T. A. G. Hungerford *Riverslake* 161: 'Chuck over that pair of strides, will you – I'm further behind than Walla Walla.'
1967 Frank Hardy *Billy Borker Yarns Again* 19–20: 'Not much use backing a two-to-one winner at this stage. You're further behind than Walla Walla.'

Wallabies, the The Rugby Union team representing Australia internationally [f. analogy with the Kangaroos, the Rugby League team]
1976 *Australian* 22 Oct. 20: Wallabies flop in the wet.

wallaby, on the ~ track Tramping the outback in search of work (as though following the track made by the wallabies)
1861 Horace Earle *Ups and Downs* 208: He had started on the Wallaby track* more than once. *Wallaby track – tramping in search of employment.
1865 E. J. Overbury 'The Wallaby Track' *Old Bush Songs* ed. Stewart and Keesing (1957) 232: There are others who stick during shearing, / Then shoulder their swags on their back; / For the rest of the year they'll be steering / On their well-beloved Wallaby Track.
1870 W. M. Finn *Glimpses of North-Eastern Victoria* (1971) 26: On a sunny day the banks of the river will be covered with clothes of those men who are tramps, and are on what is colonially known as the 'Wallaby Track'.
1887 *All the Year Round* 20 Jul. 66: He perambulates the country, going 'on the Wallaby', as it is strangely termed, nightly receiving the hospitality of the farmers and station-managers whom he honours with his presence.
1891 Henry Lawson *Verse* i 134: 'On the Wallaby' [poem title]
1905 Joseph Furphy *Rigby's Romance* ed. R. G. Howarth (1946) 69: 'I'll live and die on the wallaby. I'm like that character in the Bible ... always going to and fro on the earth, and walking up and down in it.'
1919 W. K. Harris *Outback in Australia* 146: All the ... celebrities of the day were 'on the wallaby', 'humping bluey'.
1961 George Farwell *Vanishing Australians* 107: Since then it has been de rigeur with every bushman on the wallaby.

walloper A policeman [f. *wallop*]
1945 Baker 137: We also call a policeman ... a *walloper*.
1950 *Australian Police Journal* Apr. 120: *Wallopers* Police.
1951 Frank Hardy *Power Without Glory* 33: 'Police! Everyone out! The bloody wallopers are on their way!'
1954 *Coast to Coast 1953–1954* 175: He'd kept pretty clear of courts though ... Always two jumps ahead of the wallopers.
1960 Ron Tullipan *Follow the Sun* 125: 'The wallopers collected him. They got here just as the blue was finished and took him away in the ghost truck.'
1969 Osmar White *Under the Iron Rainbow* 117: 'Brownie never did anything that you wallopers would want him for.'
1972 Alexander Macdonald *The Ukelele Player under the Red Lamp* 237: I saw this enormous walloper leaning affectionately over the driver's window.
1975 *Nation Review* 5 Dec. 212: His

[Ned Kelly's] skull was round for a long while being used as an ashtray by a sensitive and softly spoken walloper.

waltzing Matilda see Matilda

waratah A celebration, festival [? f. the Waratah Festival in N.S.W., for which the waratah is the State flower]
1975 Evonne Goolagong *Evonne* 189: When would they stop clapping? Not for five minutes, according to the journalists who timed it. It was a regular waratah (party) in the stadium.

warb Someone of little acumen, or of disreputable appearance [see *warby*]
1941 Baker 80: *Warb* A low-paid manual worker.
1945 Baker 249: *warb*, a circus labourer.
1953 Baker 135: *warb* A dirty or untidy person; also (by rhyme) *wattle and daub*; whence, *warby*, dirty or untidy.
1967 Kylie Tennant *Tell Morning This* 201: 'But it's a no-hoper's jail – a lot of old warbs and kids mixed up with coves like Amos the Cannibal and chaps that razors bounce off.'

warby Unprepossessing in appearance or disposition; decrepit, unkempt, 'drack' [cf. *warbie* a maggot bred in the skin of cattle EDD]
1941 Kylie Tennant *The Battlers* 264: 'Of all the warby ideas,' he said ... 'the warbiest is you going on your own.'
1949 Ruth Park *Poor Man's Orange* 181: Yeah, there she was, in a warby kind of blue dress, and low-heeled shoes.
1959 D'Arcy Niland *The Big Smoke* 183: A warby unshaven young man in working clothes walked through and right up to him at the back.
1964 Tom Ronan *Packhorse and Pearling Boat* 81: Billy Bunter [in *The Magnet*] was considered worthy neither of dislike nor blame. We had a few similar warby types among ourselves.
1965 Eric Lambert *The Long White Night* 135: 'That was one of the funniest

sights the main street ever saw – my old man's warby old Model A towing Foran's dirty big gleaming new Packard!'
1973 Jim McNeil *The Old Familiar Juice* 74: 'He's down there whackin' up bumpers with a couple of 'is warby mates.'

Warder, Johnny See quot. 1882: *obs.*
1872 *Punch Staff Papers* 218: On the kerbstone sat one of those amiable old ladies who are popularly known as 'Johnny Warders'. She was very drunk.
c. 1882 *The Sydney Slang Dictionary* 5: *Johnny Warder* An idle drunkard who hangs about public-house corners looking for a drink (called after a publican named John Ward who formerly kept a low house in Sydney noted for that species).

warrigal 1 Aboriginal term for dog
1793 J. Hunter *Historical Journal* ed. J. Bach (1968) 274: *Waregal*, A large dog.
2 An untamed creature (e.g. horse, native); an outlaw
1855 'The Cabbage-tree Tile' *The Melbourne Vocalist* 71 repr. in *Old Bush Songs* ed. Stewart and Keesing (1957) 164: I'm a warragle fellow that long hath dwelt / In the wild interior, nor hath felt, / Nor heard, nor seen the pleasures of town.
1875 Rolf Boldrewood *The Squatter's Dream* repr. as *Ups and Downs* (1878) 249: 'He's a good shot, and these warrigal devils [natives] knows it, or they'd have rushed the place long enough before now.'
1892 Gilbert Parker *Round the Compass in Australia* 44: Six wild horses – warrigals or brombies, as they are called – have been driven down, corralled, and caught.'
1903 Joseph Furphy *Such is Life* (1944) 17: 'Well, you know, ole Martin, the head boundary man, he's about as nice a varmin as Warrigal Alf.'
[1916] Oliver Hogue *Trooper Bluegum at the Dardanelles* 25: Some of the kind-hearted station folk in the backblocks had sent down some wild warrigals of

the West . . . old outlaws off the grass that the station hands could never master.

1939 Kylie Tennant *Foveaux* 410: The people of Foveaux were Kingston's 'Warrigals', as he said with a contemptuous affection.

1948 K. S. Prichard *Golden Miles* 244: He was toddling now, a sturdy, obstreperous youngster with a shock of dark hair, and 'the wicked look in his eye of a regular young warrigul,' Dinny said.

washer A face-washer, a 'flannel'

1951 Dymphna Cusack *Say No to Death* 194: Doreen had given her a washer and a drop of warm water to wash the sleep out of her eyes.

1962 *Southerly* 97: We add to *washer* the meaning of *face-cloth*.

1970 Patrick White *The Vivisector* 236: He was reminded of an old face-washer, often grubby, one of the maids had crocheted for him, in wide mesh.

1974 Alexander Buzo *Coralie Lansdowne Says No* 71: 'I'll get you a cold washer.'

watch, silly (crazy) as a two-bob Extremely silly

1954 Peter Gladwin *The Long Beat Home* 72: 'There now, I clean forgot. I'm getting silly as a two-bob watch.'

1964 George Johnston *My Brother Jack* 58: He would describe somebody as being 'as silly as a two-bob watch.'

1972 John de Hoog *Skid Row Dossier* 75: 'Don't buy him a beer, Johnny, he's silly as a two bob watch,' someone advised as he tapped me on the shoulder.

water, over the In Van Diemen's Land (Tasmania), from the standpoint of the mainland: *obs*.

1859 Henry Kingsley *Recollections of Geoffry Hamlyn* ii 23: 'Indeed ' said I; 'and is he in the colony?' 'No, he's over the water, I expect.' 'In Van Diemen's Land, you mean?'

watering-hole A pub or bar regularly resorted to by a particular group

1977 *Australian* 9 Apr. 17: These are the watering-holes where, in the long-lost days of ABC affluence, the Commission's producers, writers, directors and researchers used to dally delightfully with the charming practice known as 'drinking through the script'.

Watsons, to bet like the To wager large amounts [derived by Baker (1966: 73–4) from the Watson brothers, noted bettors]

1945 *Argus* 12 Jun. 15: I have been asked for the origin of the expression 'Betting like the Watsons'. Thinking back, I seem to remember a previous controversy as to who were the Watsons so famous for their betting activities.

1949 Lawson Glassop *Lucky Palmer* 163: 'Bet well? You bet like the Watsons.'

1954 Tom Ronan *Vision Splendid* 76: 'The survey-party is chequed-up to the skies and while they've got it they'll bet like the Watsons.'

1967 Frank Hardy *Billy Borker Yarns Again* 140: 'That Frank Duval must be a game punter, Billy.' 'I'd bet like the Watsons meself if I had a million quid in the bank.'

wayback 1 The regions remote from settlement

1901 F. J. Gillen *Diary* (1968) 277: Like most stock stations in the 'wayback' there has been no attempt made to improve the appearance of the surroundings.

1929 Jules Raeside *Golden Days* 344: The episode reminded me of a boarding-house where I once stayed at in the way-back.

1973 Margaret Carnegie *Friday Mount* 218: No wonder some of the way-back towns had that look.

2 An inhabitant of the 'wayback' regions, unused to city life

1904 Henry Fletcher *Dads Wayback: His Work* [book title]

1912 R. S. Tait *Scotty Mac, Shearer* 125: At a group in front of him a thimble-rigger was expending much eloquence to induce a party of waybacks to relieve him of his surplus cash.

1924 *Truth* 27 Apr. 6: *Wayback* An

Australian resident living far removed from townships and not versed in city customs.

weegie see **widgie**

weekender See quot. 1941
1941 Baker 81: *Weekender* A week-end cottage or shack.
1944 Lawson Glassop *We Were the Rats* 266: It was just a 'week-ender', just like any of the other thousands scattered sparsely around the edge of Lake Carraday.
1951 Dymphna Cusack and Florence James *Come in Spinner* 168: No mere week-ender this, but a house of character and impressive solidity.
1961 Hugh Atkinson *Low Company* 123: 'It used to be so quiet here. Weekenders and holiday cottages, mostly. Now it's a real little suburbia.'
1976 *Australian* 23 Feb. 9: Remember the weekender? They haven't been building too many of them in recent years. It used to be a glorified garage . . . a kilometre from the nearest sealed road, ten kilometres from running water and 100 kilometres from the nearest sewer pipe.

well in Well established financially, prosperous, affluent
1845 Thomas McCombie *Arabin* 241: They had a pretty little farm, and were well in.
1874 Marcus Clarke *A Colonial City* ed. L. T. Hergenhan (1972) 331: When we wished to give a man the highest praise, we spoke of him as being 'well-in', or 'having made his pile'.
1883 Rolf Boldrewood *Robbery Under Arms* (World's Classics 1949) 568: 'My word, he's well in, is the cove' says the horse-driver; 'he's got half-a dozen stations besides this one. He'll be one of the richest men in Australia yet.'
1899 Steele Rudd *On Our Selection* 84: He was reputed to be well-in, though some said that if everybody had their own he wouldn't be worth much.
1922 Arthur Wright *A Colt from the Country* 83: 'Said to be well in, is he not?' queried Mrs Whinston.

1936 H. Drake-Brockman *Sheba Lane* 139–40: 'I told you we were pretty well in. Emily had all the things a girl likes.'
1948 K. S. Prichard *Golden Miles* 15: 'I'm not much to look at, ma'am,' Paddy protested. 'But I'm well in.'
1954 T. A. G. Hungerford *Sowers of the Wind* 35: 'He was an architect before the war, and pretty well in.'
1960 Donald McLean *The Roaring Days* 218: 'I might look up some of my father's people; they're pretty well-in over there, I'm told.'
1976 David Ireland *The Glass Canoe* 180: Someone saw her at the trots with some of the trotting men who were really well in, and she was regarded with awe ever after.

wet Annoyed, irritated
1898 *Bulletin* 17 Dec. Red Page: To get narked is to lose your temper; also expressed by getting dead wet.
1915 C. J. Dennis *The Songs of a Sentimental Bloke* 42: Quite natchril, Romeo gits wet as 'ell. / 'It's me or you ' 'e 'owls, and wiv a yell, / Plunks Tyball through the gizzard wiv 'is sword.
1924 *Truth* 27 Apr. 6: Wet, to get Become annoyed.
1941 Baker 81: *Wet, get* To become angry or irritable.

wet, the The rainy season in N.W. Australia (cf. 'the Dry')
1908 Mrs Aeneas Gunn *We of the Never-Never* 292: 'Not too bad, though,' he said, reviewing the year's work, after fixing up a sleeping-camp for the wet.
1938 Xavier Herbert *Capricornia* 115: People scoffed at O'Cannon's cotton, saying at first that it would never see the Wet through, then that it would never live through the Dry.
1941 Charles Barrett *Coast of Adventure* 14: It was just before The Wet sent over Darwin a reminder that it would take over soon from The Dry: a storm that flooded streets in five minutes.
1953 Nevil Shute *In the Wet* [novel title]
1969 Christopher Bray *Blossom Like a*

Rose 14: 'Oh, it's the Wet coming on. That's what does it. Makes people edgy as can be.'

whale See quot. 1905
[**1895** A. B. Paterson *The Man from Snowy River* 182: Tramping along in the dust and sand, / Humping his well-worn swag. / He would camp for days in the river-bed, / And loiter and 'fish for whales'.]
1905 'Flash Jack from Gundagai' *The Old Bush Songs* ed. A. B. Paterson 27 and note: I've been whalin' up the Lachlan, and I've dossed on Cooper's Creek. 'Whalin' up the Lachlan' – In the old days there was an army of 'sundowners' or professional loafers who walked from station to station, ostensibly to look for work, but without any idea of accepting it. These nomads often followed up and down certain rivers, and would camp for days and fish for cod in the bends of the river. Hence whaling up the Lachlan.
1911 E. J. Brady *River Rovers* 90: Seven years had he 'whaled' the Darling and the Lower Murray, and now he was trekking upstream with his dog for companion.

whaler A bush nomad, managing to subsist without work
1883 R. E. N. Twopeny *Town Life in Australia* 244–5: A 'waler' is a bushman who is 'on the loaf'. He 'humps his drum', or 'swag', and 'starts on the wallaby track'.
1886 Frank Cowan *Australia: A Charcoal Sketch* 31: The Whalers of the Murrumbidgee and the Darling: when it suits his pleasure and convenience, a dolce-far-niente outcast in the fertile valleys of the rivers named, beyond the running of a warrant or a writ; a fisher, hunter, cut-throat, thief or what he will, time, place and circumstance suggesting and determining.
1900 Henry Lawson 'The Darling River' *Prose* i 84: They grow weary of seeing the same old 'whaler' drop his swag on the bank opposite whenever the boat ties up for wood; they get tired of lending him tobacco, and listening to

his ideas, which are limited in number and narrow in conception.
1903 Joseph Furphy *Such is Life* (1944) 4: Willoughby, who was travelling loose with Thompson and Cooper, was a whaler.
1911 E. J. Brady *River Rovers* 90: It was a wrinkled whaler that we camped beside on a sandspit next night . . . A wise old vagabond was this who had bearded many station cooks in his day.
1919 W. K. Harris *Outback in Australia* 144: On the Murrumbidgee we asked several questions of an old 'whaler'* as to roads and grass and water ahead.
*On the Outback rivers sundowners are known as 'whalers'.
1927 R. S. Browne *A Journalist's Memories* 76: In the shearer's huts in the West, on mustering camps and at those little meetings of 'billabong whalers' where two or three were gathered together, the name of 'Billy' Lane was reverenced.
1947 Vance Palmer *Hail Tomorrow* 2: 'There's too many of these billabong whalers, like Tom says, just wandering in for the company and the rations.'
1963 Alan Marshall *In Mine Own Heart* 164: The whaler, a term that had originated from the name given to those swagmen who in the early days spent their time moving up and down the Murrumbidgee River getting handouts from the stations on its banks, now applied to those who walked from town to town in preference to jumping trains. They were generally older men.

whaler, Murrumbidgee see **Murrumbidgee**

wharfie A waterside worker, docker, longshoreman [abbr. of *wharf-labourer*]
1912 *The Lone Hand* 1 May 40: The best testimonial to Hughes' ability is the fact that he has so often swayed the unruly 'wharfies', and controlled their organisation for so long.
1948 K. S. Prichard *Golden Miles* 239: 'The wharfies and returned soldiers have been warned against giving them any excuse for a brawl.'
1955 John Morrison *Black Cargo* 229:

'As long as I'm secretary of the Melbourne Branch of the Waterside Workers I'll continue to put the interests of wharfies first.'
1971 Frank Hardy *The Outcasts of Foolgarah* 7–8: Every job has its perquisites . . . the business executive has the expense account, the wharfie has the busted crate of cigarettes.

wheel, to be on someone's As for 'on someone's hammer' q.v. [? f. cycle racing]
1954 Vince Kelly *The Shadow* 89: 'I'm going back to Melbourne. Down there the cops'll give you a go. Here they're on your wheel all the time.'
1959 A. W. Upfield *Bony and the Mouse* 104: 'I'll be ready for it. I'm going to be right on Tony's wheel when it happens.'
1969 Osmar White *Under the Iron Rainbow* 118: 'The inspector's been on my wheel to trace him.'

wheel, silly as a Extremely silly
1952 T. A. G. Hungerford *The Ridge and the River* 57: Oscar was sound, but silly as a wheel.
1965 William Dick *A Bunch of Ratbags* 124: 'She hasn't changed one bit, she's as silly as a wheel, she's like her mother was.'
1966 *Coast to Coast 1965–1966* 157: 'She was as silly as a wheel, too, but a man's got to do what he can to protect his daughters.'

Whelan the Wrecker Trading-name of a firm of demolition specialists, generalized to any demolition team
1976 W. K. Hancock *Professing History* 124: The government might cut its losses and call in Whelan the Wrecker to clear away the mess on Black Mountain.

whip, a fair crack of the Fair treatment or opportunity, a 'fair go' [listed by Partridge as 'North Country miners': late C.19–20']
1929 K. S. Prichard *Coonardoo* 179: 'I'll see you get a fair crack of the whip now, Mr Watt.'
1944 Lawson Glassop *We Were the Rats* 2: 'I am sorry to have to tell you that

the Lord's had a fair crack of the whip and He's missed the bus.'
1951 Frank Hardy *Power Without Glory* 43: 'I'll give the punters the best crack of the whip.'
1961 Ray Lawler *The Piccadilly Bushman* 72: 'Big slangy stuff like – "Don't come the raw prawn" and "Fair crack of the whip".'
1968 Geoffrey Dutton *Andy* 116: 'Shut up, youse animals,' shouted the sergeant. 'Fair crack of the whip, Sarge.'

whips of An abundance [f. *whips* plenty, lots EDD 1894; cf. *lashings of*]
1905 *The Old Bush Songs* ed. A. B. Paterson 24: We'd whips and whips of Rhino as we meant to push about.
1906 G. M. Smith *Days of Cobb & Co.* 19: I had whips of strength and energy.
1918 Bernard Cronin *The Coastlanders* 123: 'They's whips of feed and the water's not bad.'
1934 Steele Rudd *Green Grey Homestead* 97: 'And tell him I've got whips of room for him.'
1955 Alan Marshall *I Can Jump Puddles* 19: 'There's whips of feed on the creek flats yet.'
1961 George Farwell *Vanishing Australian* 182: 'Then you want capital – whips of it.'

white ants, to have To be eccentric, crazy
1900–10 O'Brien and Stephens: *White ants* silliness, madness. Any person of weak intellect or peculiar in their manner as if insane is said to have white ants.
1908 Henry Fletcher *Dads and Dan between Smokes* 64: It wants a fool or a very sane cove indeed ter live in ther lonely bush an' keep ther white ants out o' his napper.
1926 L. C. E. Gee *Bushtracks and Goldfields* 65: And so he rambles on . . . and in the unsteady glance of his honest, old eyes and his disconnected speech, I read the mark of the Australian solitudes – 'white ants' they call it up north.
1938 H. Drake-Brockman *Men Without Wives* 27: ' "Get the white ants?" What do you mean?' 'Go ratty. Mad.'

1951 Ernestine Hill *The Territory* 446:
White ants in the billy: Crazy.

white lady Methylated spirits, sometimes mixed with something else
1935 Kylie Tennant *Tiburon* 19: Two
old men in the corner lying stupefied
over a mixture of 'white lady' – boiled
methylated spirit with a dash of boot
polish and iodine.
1949 Judith Wright *Woman to Man* 35:
His white and burning girl, his woman
of fire, / creeps to his heart and sets a
candle there.
1962 Ron Tullipan *March into Morning*
57: 'What is it?' Chappie asked, eying
the bottle with suspicion, 'metho?' 'The
white lady.'
1975 Richard Beilby *The Brown Land
Crying* 225: 'Ya was on the White Lady
at the finish, mixin' it with Coke' . . .
'But jees, meths'n Coca Cola.'

white, a ~ man Term of highest commendation, making any other comment
unnecessary [U.S. 1865 Mathews]
1883 Rolf Boldrewood *Robbery Under
Arms* (World's Classics 1949) 503: He
was always the same. The whitest man
I ever knew, or ever shall – that I say
and stick to.
1892 Henry Lawson 'Jack Dunn of
Nevertire' *Verse* i 222: There is no
whiter man than Jack – no straighter
south the line, / There is no hand in all
the land I'd sooner grip in mine.
1911 Louis Stone *Jonah* 190: 'Yous
are a white man, an' I always knew
it.'
1918 Let. in Bill Gammage *The Broken
Years* (1974) 249: One could not find a
whiter man in the whole world. He
would never let a pal down . . . and
would never allow a word to be said
against me, whether I was right or
wrong.
1929 Jules Raeside *Golden Days* 314: I
knew Treffene personally, and found
him every inch a white man.
1939 H. M. Moran *Viewless Winds* 173:
Our commanding officer, who was of
the Irish ascendancy class, a Protestant,
a friend, and, what we call in Australia,
a white man.

white, the man in The referee or umpire
in football [f. dress]
1973 *Sun-Herald* 16 Sep. 63: Refereeing
continued to be a pain in the neck, with
the public asking only one thing from
the men in white – consistency.
1973 Alexander Buzo *The Roy Murphy
Show* 107: 'It's all very well to knock
the men in white, Mike, but you must
bear in mind that referees have many
difficulties confronting them.'

white leghorn See quot.
1975 Les Ryan *The Shearers* 135: *White
leghorn* Colloquial term for a woman
bowler.

Whitely King See quots
1902 *Bulletin* 1 Feb. 16: A billy
fashioned from a fruit tin is universally
known as a 'Whitely King' from the
secretary of the Pastoralists' Union,
who, during the shearing troubles, sent
out bands of non-unionists furnished
with these impromptu utensils. They
are accordingly despised.
1911 E. S. Sorenson *Life in the Australian Backblocks* 278: An improvised
billy made from a fruit-tin, with a bit
of fencing wire for handle . . . is known
as a 'Whitely King' from the fact that
the Secretary of the Pastoralists' Union,
during a shearers' strike, sent out a
bank of non-unionists furnished with
this kind of utensil.

whitewash The overwhelming defeat of
one sporting team by another, esp. when
the losing side fails to score [also U.S.]
1977 *Australian* 24 Jan. 16: Australia
. . . completed a 5–0 whitewash of the
eastern zone semi-final against India
at Royal Kings Park in Perth.

whizz off As for 'race off' q.v.
1963 Lawson Glassop *The Rats in New
Guinea* 87: 'You might have been the
Wizard of Nerridale but I was the
Whizzer of Nerridale.'

**who's up who and who's paying the
rent** see up

Wicks, the The Randwick, N.S.W.,

Rugby Union team [abbr.]

wide brown land, the Australia, from Dorothea Mackellar's 'My Country'
1914 Dorothea Mackellar *The Witch Maid* 29: Her beauty and her terror −/ The wide brown land for me
1934 *The Wide Brown Land: a new Anthology of Australian Verse* chosen by Joan Mackaness and George Mackaness.
1966 Jan Smith *An Ornament of Grace* 33: A nice myth to be dusted off every Anzac Day, about bronzed heroes of the wide brown land.
1970 *Sunnday Telegraph* 9 Aug. 30: The wide brown land is up for sale.
1973 *Australian* 4 May 11: Migrants are staying away in droves from the widest and brownest part of this wide, brown land.

widgie Female counterpart of the 'bodgie' q.v.
1950 *Sun* 5 Jul. 19: A benefit dance will be held on Friday at the Gaiety Ballroom, Oxford Street . . . There'll be competitions for jitterbugging, Charleston, and prizes for the most colorfully dressed 'bodgy' and 'weegie'. Mo and Hal Lashwood will be the judges.
1951 *Sydney Morning Herald* 1 Feb. 1: What with 'bodgies' growing their hair long and getting round in satin shirts, and 'weegies' cutting their hair short and wearing jeans, confusion seems to be arising about the sex of some Australian adolescents.
1963 Gunther Bahnemann *Hoodlum* 48: His milk bar was the biggest assembling place for the bodgies and widgies in town, particularly after the pictures were out.
1965 William Dick *A Bunch of Ratbags* 248: I had never seen so many bodgies and widgies all together at one time before.

wild colonial boy see **colonial**

wild white man, the William Buckley (1780–1856), the convict who escaped and lived for thirty-two years with the natives, being eventually returned to the white community

1856 James Bonwick *William Buckley, the Wild White Man* [book title]
1871 Marcus Clarke *Old Tales of a Young Country* 18: William Buckley, The 'Wild White Man' [essay title]

Wilcannia shower see **shower**

willy willy On land, a spiralling dusty wind; at sea, a minor cyclone: esp. N.W. Australia
1894 *The Age* 20 Jan. 13: The willy willy is the name given to these periodical storms by the natives of the northwest. [Morris]
1898 D. W. Carnegie *Spinifex and Sand* 254: Large tracts of burnt country had to be crossed from which clouds of dust and ashes were continually rising, blown up by 'Willy-Willies' (spiral winds).
1929 Sir Hal Colebatch *A Story of a Hundred Years* 168: The [pearling] industry requires that capital be risked; it takes its toll of life even in ordinary working, and in cyclones or 'willy willys' many lives and much property have been lost.
1942 Gavin Casey *It's Harder for Girls* 113: A corkscrew of sand, the beginning of a willy-willy, danced through the yard, tugging at her skirts as it went and making her drop the wood as she grabbed at the garment with both hands.
1962 J. Marshall and R. Drysdale *Journey Among Men* 114: A willy-willy is what is called a dust devil in many countries. It is a rotary vortex of air that appears suddenly when a gentle breeze is blowing across a blazing desert. A willy-willy can dump a man on to the ground; it can tear through a camp . . . it can carry dust and other debris more than a thousand feet in the air.

Windies, the The West Indies cricket team
1965 Wally Grout *My Country's 'Keeper* 69: The Australian public was enchanted and took the 'Windies' to their hearts from that moment.
1976 *Sunday Telegraph* 4 Jan. 52:

Windies roll with brutal pace beating.

wingy Nickname for someone who has lost an arm [f. *wing* to wound ... in the arm or shoulder OED 1802]

[1895 Cornelius Crowe *The Australian Slang Dictionary* 96 : *Winged* one-armed, or wounded.]

1910 Henry Lawson 'The Rising of the Court' *Prose* i 660: Wingy, by the way, is a ratty little one-armed man, whose case is usually described in the headline, 'A 'Armless Case', by one of our great dailies.

1932 Leonard Mann *Flesh in Armour* 8 : The figure of Nelson ... on the top of the column, was hardly discernible in the dirty mist ... Bill Potter waved a nonchalant greeting with 'Good-day, Nelson.' 'Eh?' asked his companion. 'Just passing the day to old Wingie.'

1945 *Coast to Coast 1944* 32: The only thing I haven't is a left arm ... they can call me Wingy now.

1964 Tom Ronan *Packhorse and Pearling Boat* 129: As Dad later referred to him as 'Wingy' Collins I presume that he had one arm amputated, or some similar disability.

1971 Keith Willey *Boss Drover* 150: One of the most unlikely fighters I knew in the bush was Wingy Collins. He was a big fellow and he took his name from the fact that one arm was twisted, although it still had plenty of strength in it.

wipe To dismiss from consideration, wash one's hands of [f. *to wipe one's hands of* OED 1785]

1941 Kylie Tennant *The Battlers* 196: Giving her money ... in the casual manner that wiped her from all consideration as a human being.

1946 *Coast to Coast 1945* 123: 'Listen pal – your girl wiped you, didn't she?'

1948 Ruth Park *The Harp in the South* 269: 'From now on he's wiped. I never want to see him again.'

1954 T. A. G. Hungerford *Sowers of the Wind* 162: 'She dumped me, wiped me like a dirty nose.'

1962 David Forrest *The Hollow Woodheap* 149: 'She wiped you like last week's bath mat.'

1965 Eric Lambert *The Long White Night* 64: 'We'll have a drink,' I told them. 'Then I'm wiping you two like a dirty floor.'

1975 Richard Beilby *The Brown Land Crying* 295 : 'You can wipe that idea, if that's what you're thinking.'

wire, mulga, spinifex see **mulga, spinifex**

wire, straight Fair dinkum, on the level: *obs.*

1892 William Lane *The Workingman's Paradise* 203 : 'When it's all over you'll remember what I say and know it's the straight wire.'

1909 Arthur Wright *A Rogue's Luck* 70: 'Now, no kid, Harry,' said Ned anxiously. 'Straight wire, did you beat him?'

1915 C. J. Dennis *The Songs of a Sentimental Bloke* 59: Say, ain't it bonzer makin' up agen?/Straight wire, it's almost worth ... Ar, I'm a cow!

1936 Miles Franklin *All That Swagger* 394: 'Straight wire, I will.'

Wollongong Races See quot.

1849 J. P. Townsend *Rambles and Observations in New South Wales* 152: He is bound for the 'Wollongong Races', otherwise the Court of Requests, which bears this name by reason of the numbers who hurry to it from all quarters.

Wolseley The name of the shearing machine which came into use in the late 1880s and the 1890s, patented 1877 [f. F. Y. Wolseley the inventor]

1897 Henry Lawson 'The Boss's Boots' *Verse* i 321: Bogan laid his 'Wolseley' down and knocked the rouser out.

1905 'Flash Jack from Gundagai' *The Old Bush Songs* ed. A. B. Paterson 27 and note: I've pinked 'em with the Wolseleys and I've rushed with B-bows, too. Wolseleys and B-bows are respectively machines and hand shears.

wombat Used in expressions suggesting torpor or stupidity

1896 Edward Dyson *Rhymes from the Mines* 124: I was sullen as a wombat on such still, wan days as these.
1917 A. B. Paterson *Three Elephant Power* 31: Dooley, better known as The Wombat because of his sleepy disposition, was a man of great strength.

wongi A friendly yarn, esp. in N.W. Australia [Ab.]
1916 Arthur Wilson *Mining, Lays, Tales and Folk Lore* (1944) 78: I gave them a 'good luck greeting', and then, somehow, we all fell to a wongi.
1938 Xavier Herbert *Capricornia* 386: 'By cripes, Andy, that was a great wongi.'
1948 K. S. Prichard *Golden Miles* 91: 'All he wanted to do was to go home to his missus, or have a pot and a wongie with his mates.'
1957 Randolph Stow *The Bystander* 186: 'I just wanted a bit of a wongi with you. You know how it is, a joker gets the urge to talk sometimes.'
1969 Lyndall Hadow *Full Cycle* 178: 'If he asks you to have one ... well, he's out for a wongi.'

wonk 1 Aboriginal term for a white: *derogatory*
1938 Xavier Herbert *Capricornia* 252: He went to the Dagoes and Roughs of second-class and won their friendship by buying them liquor and telling them how he had been cast out by the Wonks of the saloon.
1958 Elizabeth Webb *Into the Morning* 116: I began remembering dirty words the boys at the River Camp used to call whites. I said aloud: 'A lot of bloody wonks – I don't care. I don't bloody well care ... a lot of dirty wonks.'
2 A male homosexual
1945 Baker 123: An effeminate male is a ... *wonk*.
1970 Patrick White *The Vivisector* 213: 'I'd have to have a chauffeur to drive me about – with a good body – just for show, though. I wouldn't mind if the chauffeur was a wonk.'

wood, have the ~ on To hold an advantage

1941 S. J. Baker *New Zealand Slang* 53: *to have the wood on a person* to have an advantage over someone.
1949 Lawson Glassop *Lucky Palmer* 156: 'She's got you taped, too, kid. She's got the wood on all of us.'
1954 T. A. G. Hungerford *Sowers of the Wind* 264: 'Can't you realize I've got the wood on you? You've got two minutes.'
1965 Leslie Haylen *Big Red* 55: It was another of his occasions of fear: she liked having the wood on you.
1973 *Sunday Telegraph* 16 Sep. 47: The Swans hold the wood on the Magpies in finals matches.

wood-and-water joey Someone given the menial tasks on a station, etc., having no special skills of his own [f. 'hewers of wood and drawers of water' *Joshua* 9:21]
1882 Rolf Boldrewood *Robbery Under Arms* (World's Classics 1949) 313: 'It's all devilish fine for you ... to go flashin' about the country and sporting your figure on horse-back, while I'm left alone to do the housekeepin' in the Hollow. I'm not going to be wood-and-water Joey, I can tell ye, not for you nor no other men.'
1887 *All the Year Round* 30 Jul. 67: A 'wood-and-water Joey' is a hanger about hotels, and a doer of odd jobs.
1901 *The Bulletin Reciter* 15: Next, the wood-and-water joey fell a victim to his bowie, / And the boss's weeping widow got a gash from ear to ear.
1906 T. E. Spencer *How M'Dougal Topped the Score* 128: He was wood-and-water Joey at the 'Star' / Where she waited, and assisted at the bar.
c. 1926 Alpha *Reminiscences of the Goldfields* 58: She was the only single girl on the creek – sweet seventeen at that – for whom I sometimes acted as wood and water 'joey'.
1935 A. B. Paterson *The World of 'Banjo' Paterson* ed. C. Semmler (1967) 24: 'I'm a fireman,' he says, 'not a wood-and-water joey'.
1955 E. O. Schlunke *The Man in the Silo* 205: A Furphy water-cart, with the wood-and-water Joey sitting unhappily

on the shaft.

wooden To fell, knock out [cf. *stiffen*]
[1908 Henry Fletcher *Dads and Dan between Smokes* 39: When misfochin' as yous can't prevent lands yer a woodener, take it smilin'.]
1911 Steele Rudd *The Dashwoods* 25: 'I never saw him any more till I see you going to wooden him with the furniture.'
1957 A. W. Upfield *Boney Buys a Woman* 124: 'We're all stonkered by now, but that fool Jimmy Wall Eye makes a swipe at Arnold and Arnold woodens him.'
1974 *Southerly* 145: 'If you can't wooden 'em [kangaroos] at a 'undred yards with one I.C.I. bullet, you're not tryin'!'

Woods, the 1 In N.S.W., the Eastwood Rugby Union team [abbr.]
1975 *Sunday Telegraph* 17 Aug. 57: Woods as premiers? Forget it.
2 In Victoria, the Collingwood V.F.L. team (more often 'the Magpies')

Woodser, Jimmy A person drinking alone at a bar; a drink taken alone [see quot. 1933]
1892 Barcroft Boake 'Jimmy Wood' *Bulletin* 7 May 17: Who drinks alone, drinks toast to Jimmy Wood, sir.* *A man drinks by himself is said to take a 'Jimmy Woodser'.
1895 Cornelius Crowe *Australian Slang Dictionary* 40: *Johnnie Woodser* taking a solitary drink at the bar.
1898 *Bulletin* 17 Dec. Red Page: *Jimmy-Woodser* a solitary drinker.
1900 Henry Lawson 'They Wait on the Wharf in Black' *Prose* i 286: 'I wanted to score a drink!' he said. 'I thought he wanted one and wouldn't like to be a Jimmy Woodser.'
1924 *Truth* 27 Apr. 6: *Jimmy Woodser* One who drinks alone.
1933 Acland: *Jimmy* or *Johnny Woodser* Slang. A drink by yourself . . . A correspondent tells me that James Woods was a shearer on the Darling River, New South Wales, in the 'eighties. He spent the off season in

Bourke. He was fond of a glass of beer but was never known to shout. He always drank on his own, so that when the shearers saw any one go to the bar by himself they always said he was having a *J.W.* Hence the saying.
1963 Frank Hardy *Legends from Benson's Valley* 150: The fact that his unexpected wealth purchased a welcome in our school instead of drinking Jimmy Woodsers' pleased him no end.
1971 Hal Porter *The Right Thing* 34: 'I had three with Pauline Ashburn before she whizzed off, and a Jimmy Woodser after. No – two Jimmy Woodsers!'

Woop Woop Imaginary place which is a byword for backwardness and remoteness. Sometimes defined as 'where the crows fly backward, to keep the dust out of their eyes'
1926 J. Vance Marshall *Timely Tips for New Australians: Woop Woop* A humorous method of alluding to the country districts, used most frequently in New South Wales.
1928 Arthur Wright *A Good Recovery* 34: 'They're chasin' Murraba out along the Woop Woop Road, or somewhere.'
1949 Lawson Glassop *Lucky Palmer* 94: 'I don't come from Woop Woop. Harry Hughes is known on every racecourse in New South Wales.'
1959 Hal Porter 'Country Town' *A Bachelor's Children* (1962) 281: Oh, a local, a yokel, a hick, a peasant, a simple boy from Woop Woop! Had I heard of wireless?
1970 Sumner Locke Elliott *Edens Lost* 90: 'I was all over the country. You could drive hundreds of miles back of the beyond out into Woop-Woop or Buggeryville and there I was.'
woop Someone from the remote regions
1939 Miles Franklin and Dymphna Cusack *Pioneers on Parade* 31: 'A glorified woop.' Ibid. 155: 'Every woop from woop-woop.'
1950 *Coast to Coast* 1949–50 201: 'I'll make a fair dinkum woop-woop out of you in no time.'
see **Snake Gully**

word To inform someone privately, tip

1915 C. J. Dennis *The Songs of a Senti-mental Bloke* 50: I met 'im on the quite, / 'An worded 'im about a small affair.
1928 Arthur Wright *A Good Recovery* 26: 'Here's a few bob to go on with. I'll word the landlord to look after y'.'
1939 Kylie Tennant *Foveaux* 349–50: 'You word the paper-boy to send your paper up to Central.'
1941 Baker 83: *Word up, to* To advise, 'tip off' a person.
1951 Dymphna Cusack and Florence James *Come In Spinner* 306: 'Somebody worded me you was round here in the side lift.'
1967 K. S. Prichard *Subtle Flame* 234: 'Ted worded a mate of his on the *Western Star*.'

working off a dead horse see **dead horse**

workingman's paradise, the Australia
1859 Henry Kingsley *Recollections of Geoffry Hamlyn* i 103–4: That was what they saw, and what any man may see to-day for himself in his own village, whether in England or Australia, that working man's paradise.
1892 William Lane *The Workingman's Paradise: An Australian Labour Novel* 38: In Sydney, in 1889, in the working-man's paradise, she stood on the kerb, this blind girl, and begged.
1901 Rolf Boldrewood *In Bad Company* 288: This Australian land of ours. The workman's Paradise!
1911 E. M. Clowes *On the Wallaby through Victoria* 253: Victoria, and, indeed, Australia as a whole, has been spoken of as the 'paradise of the work-ingman'.
1962 *Australian Civilization* ed. Peter Coleman 58: The nineteenth-century conviction that Australia was to be a 'working man's paradise'.

worries, my As for 'My troubles' q.v.
1949 Alan Marshall *How Beautiful Are Thy Feet* 50: 'My worries,' said Correll, contemptuously gesturing, 'She's got nothing on me.'
1953 T. A. G. Hungerford *Riverslake*

174: 'And you're on the outer for sticking up for him?' 'My worries.'
1963 A. W. Upfield *Madman's Bend* 83: 'It's going to be another fine day, isn't it?' 'My worries if it's fine or wet.'

wouldn't it? Expression of exasperation [see quot. 1945 and *root v.*[2]]
1941 Baker 83: *Wouldn't it!* Abbrevia-tion of 'Wouldn't it make you sick?' or 'Wouldn't it make you mad?' etc.
1944 Lawson Glassop *We Were the Rats* 162: 'Do you know our divisions have even got a mobile laundry, decontami-nation unit? Wouldn't it rip you?' Ibid. 135: 'Well wouldn't it rotate you?' said Eddie.
1945 Baker 152n: The authentic digger form is *Wouldn't it root you!*
1951 Dymphna Cusack and Florence James *Come in Spinner* 382: Guinea kicked a hassock across the room. 'Wouldn't it!' she muttered furiously, 'wouldn't it!'
1955 Mary Durack *Keep Him My Coun-try* 161: 'Hell,' Tex groaned. 'Wouldn't it, eh? You can just imagine how this makes me feel.'

wouldn't read about it see **read**

wowser A censorious person; a killjoy [? f. *wow* To whine; to grumble, make complaint EDD 1876]
1899 *Truth* 8 Oct. 5: The Parraween Push / A Partisan Protest / Willoughby 'Wowsers' Worried / The 'Talent' get a 'Turn' On Thursday week at the North Sydney Police Court . . . ten young men were fined sums varying from £2 with costs to 7 / 6 with costs . . . for having behaved in a riotous manner on the Military Rd.
1911 Henry Lawson 'The Song of the Heathen' *Verse* iii 65: O this is the Wowsers' land, / And the laughing days are o'er, / For most of the things that we used to do / We must not do any more!
1916 Joseph Furphy *Poems* 13: The gnats at which the Wowsers strain, / The camels that they entertain / Sec-tarian bigotry insane.
1925 Seymour Hicks *Hullo Australians*

93: 'I am a teetotaller at meals. It looks better in front of the wowzers.'

1936 H. Drake-Brockman *Sheba Lane* 41: 'He drinks, doesn't he?' 'Used to ... But he's apparently chucked it now. Quite a wowser, in fact.'

1942 Leonard Mann *The Go-Getter* 201: 'A few years ago the age [of consent] was seventeen, but some old women got a wowser government to increase the age.'

1955 E. O. Schlunke *The Man in the Silo* 168: 'I'll buy a nine-gallon keg with my bonus and get that old wowser Weismann drunk!'

1965 Hal Porter *The Cats of Venice* 59: 'A sawn-off little wowser. No confidence.'

1976 *Sydney Morning Herald* 14 Aug. 10: Mr Nile does not see the Festival of Light as a puritanical neo-wowser movement.

wowserish, wowserism
1933 Frank Clune *Try Anything Once* 122: They looked much the same although it seemed to me they had lost their dash and grown wowserish.

1976 *Australian* 14 Aug. 20: Australia does not need to battle for the restoration of its image as one of the most wowserish nations on earth.

wrap (up) *n.* A flattering account (interchangeable with *rap (up)* q.v.)
1949 Lawson Glassop *Lucky Palmer* 54: 'Do you want a cigarette paper?' 'Cigarette paper? No, I've got the makings.' 'I thought you wanted to give yourself another wrap up?'

1958 Frank Hardy *The Four-Legged Lottery* 177: Ronnie Hutchison, a specialist in long distance races, getting the wrap up from his mates, Des Hoysted and Frank O'Brien – 'ridden in copybook style by Hutchie.'

1963 Criena Rohan *Down by the Dockside* 155: 'I've got to have a job and a respectable address and someone to give me the big wrap-up.'

1973 *Australian* 7 Aug. 22: When I was at Ipswich I thought it was a great 'wrap' to be picked to play for Queensland.

1975 Xavier Herbert *Poor Fellow My Country* 324: 'Quite a wrap-up, isn't it ... only much more what I'd like to be than what I am.'

wrap (up) *v.* To praise (interchangeable with *rap (up)* q.v.)
1973 *Sun* 1 May 78: Last week I wrapped him over his display of whistle blowing in the Easts-Manly game. This was virtually the 'kiss of death'. Anytime referees get a wrap they seem to get banished to the suburbs.

1975 Xavier Herbert *Poor Fellow My Country* 875: 'Does she wrap you up! Look ... "This sweet and lovely creature".'

wrapped Overjoyed with something (interchangeable with *rapt* q.v.)
1963 Criena Rohan *Down by the Dockside* 212: 'She gave me a quid now and then. I never stood over her for it. She's wrapped in me, see?

1976 *Sydney Morning Herald* 21 Jan. 1: $1,210 a week to play cricket 'I'm just wrapped,' Thomson said. 'The offer is a fantastic one which never in my wildest dreams did I expect.'

wrapper, plain see **plain wrapper**

Y

yabber *n.* Talk [Ab.]
1855 Raffaello Carboni *The Eureka Stockade* ed. G. Serle (1969) 7: There was further a great waste of yabber-yabber about the diggers not being represented in the Legislative Council.

1885 *The Australasian Printers' Keepsake* 71: This was argued out ... with much vehemence, if not rancour, till I got throughly sick of their yabber.

1901 *Bulletin Reciter* 37: Here's the landlord for orders – I'm dry with this yabber.

1908 *The Australian Magazine* 1 Nov. 1252; Others [aboriginal words] have remained, and are likely to remain in the category of slang, such as ... yabber (yabba) talk.

1975 Les Ryan *The Shearers* 155: Yabber Unnecessary talk.

yabber *v.* To talk

1848 H. W. Haygarth *Recollections of Bush Life in Australia* 102: The most loquacious of them all would bear little comparison with an Australian 'gin' when fairly moved to 'yabber'.
1877 Rolf Boldrewood *A Colonial Reformer* (1890) 334: 'Well, what did you see?' pursued his master. 'You can yabber fast enough when you like.'
1903 Joseph Furphy *Such is Life* (1944) 238: 'Nobody could yabber with her but Bob.'
1917 A. B. Paterson *Three Elephant Power* 24: 'Now let's hear him yabber.'

yabber, paper A letter

1888 Overlander *Australian Sketches* 24: I determined to send him [a native] off first with a paper yabber to the other stockman, telling him where we had gone.
1901 F. J. Gillen *Diary* (1968) 303: The letter is carried securely tied in a cleft stick . . . The blacks regard messengers of this sort as sacred; they probably have an idea that if they interfered with a 'paper yabber' some evil magic would result.
1908 Mrs Aeneas Gunn *We of the Never-Never* 195: 'Paper yabber!' he added curtly, passing a letter to the Maluka.
1933 R. B. Plowman *The Man from Oodnadatta* 131: 'I said to tell Billy to send a paper-yabber (letter) by the boy that comes for the flour.'
1935 H. H. Finlayson *The Red Centre* 74: In the bad old days of early settlement undesirable bucks were got rid of by giving them 'paper yabbers' to deliver to distant neighbours.

yabbie, yabby A small freshwater crayfish (*Parachaeraps bicarinatus*) used as bait [Ab.]

1894 *Argus* 6 Oct. 11: Small crayfish, called 'yabbies' . . . may be found all over Australia, both in large and small lagoons. These creatures, whilst nearing a drought, and as the supply of water is about to fail, burrow deeply in the beds of the lagoons, water-holes, or swamps. [Morris]

1941 Baker 83: *Yabbie* A small freshwater crayfish.
1960 John Iggulden *The Storms of Summer* 182: 'We used to catch yabbies this way when I was a kid.'
1965 Graham McInnes *The Road to Gundagai* 142: Down the hill came running McLachlan kids ready to go fishing for yabbies. These small fresh water crayfish, which inhabited every muddy pool in the bush, were the easiest ones to catch in the world.

yabbying

1962 Dymphna Cusack *Picnic Races* 12–13: In the old days he used to go birds-nesting on the hill-side and yabbying in the creek.

see **crabhole, gilgie**

yack, yacker (yakitty-yak) *n. & v.* Talk [*yack* a syllable imitative of a snapping sound; hence as vb. OED 1861]

c. 1882 *Sydney Slang Dictionary* 9: *Yacker* Talk.
1941 Baker 83: *Yacker* Talk.
1959 *Daily Telegraph* 7 Mar. 2: He was a travelling yakitty-yak man in the ubiquitous presence of Mr Graham Webb.
1969 William Dick *Naked Prodigal* 16: All the girls . . . yacking about clothes or some woman who'd just had her twentieth kid.
1971 Frank Hardy *The Outcasts of Foolgarah* 198: Borky yakked on.
1976 Gwen Kelly *The Middle-Aged Maidens* 110: He got up. 'Can't spend any more time yacketing away with women,' he said.

yakker (yakka, yacker) Work [Ab.]

1866 W. Ridley *Kamilaroi* 171: work *yakka*.
1908 *The Australian Magazine* 1 Nov. 1251: Others [aboriginal words] . . . are likely to remain in the category of slang, such as . . . yacker (yakka), work.
1914 Edward Dyson *Spats' Fact'ry* 124: 'But iv yeh don't do yeh fair share iv yacker this after, I'll punt the slacks off yeh.'
1924 *Truth* 27 Apr. 6: *Yacker* Hard work.
1936 Archer Russell *Gone Nomad* 74:

Two days later Adams packed his blanket and his Shakespeare and left for the South . . . No more 'bush yacker' for him.

1946 A. W. Upfield *Death of a Swagman* 87: 'Give us the shovel, Mr Jason,' suggested Harry Hudson. 'I'm used to hard yakka.'

1953 T. A. G. Hungerford *Riverslake* 89: 'One week, maybe twelve pounds. But hard yakka. Still . . . I am young.'

1962 Stuart Gore *Down the Golden Mile* 127: 'I'm not scared of a bit of hard yakka.'

yamidgee An Aboriginal: W.A.

1965 Randolph Stow *The Merry-go-Round in the Sea* 186: 'What's yamidgees?' said the boy. 'Boongs. Noogs. Coloured folk.'

yandy To winnow, now in a tin-mining process [Ab.]

1944 M. J. O'Reilly *Bowyangs and Boomerangs* 48: Yandying, in blackfellow language, means shake-about. It is the natives' method of separating the grass seeds from the husks.

1959 Donald Stuart *Yandy* 158: *Yandy, tjardoo:* Long shallow oval dish, of wood sometimes, but now almost always of sheet-iron, in which mineral is separated from the alluvial rubbish by means of a complicated rocking action. A skill, the working of a yandy, which is almost exclusively aboriginal.

1971 Robin Miller *Flying Nurse* 76: They all lived by collecting tin from the creek beds. The pieces of metal were separated from extraneous matter by a process known as 'yandying', which entailed placing the material in a curved sheet iron container and shaking it expertly until the metal was at one end and the discard at the other.

yarra Insane [f. mental asylum at Yarra Bend, Victoria]

1973 Jim McNeil *The Chocolate Frog* 50: 'Whats'er matter? You gone yarra, or somethin'?'

Yarra-banker A soapbox orator [f. Yarra River, Victoria]

[**1895** Cornelius Crowe *The Australian Slang Dictionary* 98: *Yarra Bankers* vagrants living on the banks of the Yarra.]

1912 Louis Esson *The Time is not Yet Ripe* ed. P. Parsons (1973) 32: 'The man's an agitator, a red-flagger, a Yarra-banker.'

[**1913**] Turner O. Lingo *The Australian Comic Dictionary* 6: *Yarra Banker* Usually a man who stands on a soap box telling the great unwashed how 'dirty' the rich man is.

1973 Dr J. Cairns *Bulletin* 8 Dec. 13: I think that Parliament is a sort of elevated Yarra bank.

yarraman Aboriginal term for horse, used also by whites: *obs.*

1860 Mrs A. Macpherson *My Experiences of Australia* 50: [He] was told by his black guide 'Bail yarraman (no horse) only white fellow.'

1866 W. Ridley *Kamilaroi* 20: *Horse* yarāman * *All the Australians use this name – probably from the neighing of the horse.

1875 A. J. Boyd *Old Colonials* (1882) 69: 'Then there's seventeen yarramen – call 'em thirty pounds a head.'

1891 H. Patchett Martin *Coo-ee: Tales of Australian Life* 280: He just clapped spurs to his old yarraman (horse), and never pulled up out of a gallop till he had got over the range.

1905 Joseph Furphy *Rigby's Romance* ed. R. G. Howarth (1946) 21: 'He needn't be frightened o' these yarramans. I got 'em like lambs.'

1908 Giles Seagram *Bushmen All* 20: 'You accuse me of taking the yarramen. Of course I did. It was our only hope.'

yeller feller Male half-caste in N.W. Australia [f. colour]

1938 Xavier Herbert *Capricornia* 37: What if people found out? . . . A half-caste – a yeller-feller!

1959 Donald Stuart *Yandy* 12: No future in being a yeller feller, down this end, or further north.

1971 Keith Willey *Boss Drover* 29: Part-Aborigines, or yeller-fellers as we called them in the old days, had a hard life.

Yellow Monday A variety of cicada
[f. colouring]
1951 Dymphna Cusack and Florence
James *Come in Spinner* 163: She un-
curled her fingers and showed the
jewelled head of a cicada. 'He's a
Yellow Mundy.'
1959 Anne von Bertouch *February Dark*
124: Through the shimmer of heat and
the drilling song Helen saw the beautiful
cicadas of childhood, the Black Prince,
the Greengrocer, the Yellow Monday,
held on a child's small hand.
1976 Douglas Stewart *Southerly* 177:
They have caught a Yellow Monday/
Slipped it down Anita's blouse.

yike A heated argument, a disturbance
[unexplained]
1941 Baker 84: *Yike* A row or argument
(2) A fight.
1945 Roy Rene *Mo's Memoirs* 186:
'There's that tram connie having a yike
with a drunk.'
1951 Dal Stivens *Jimmy Brockett* 86:
It was a pretty good yike while it
lasted.
1960 Ron Tullipan *Follow the Sun* 32:
'Chow doesn't need that much of an
excuse to put on a yike, even on his
most peaceful days.'
1964 George Johnston *My Brother Jack*
244: 'Sorry your party ended up in a
yike.'
yike To argue, fight
1952 T. A. G. Hungerford *The Ridge
and the River* 213: 'Don't let's yike about
it, Jim.'

yolk Suint, the natural grease in sheep's
wool (OED 1607)
1824 R. S. Macarthur-Onslow *Some
Early Records of the Macarthurs of
Camden* (1914) 405: Send home the
fleeces for the future in much brighter
condition and nearly free from yolk.
1853 S. Mossman and T. Banister *Australia, Visited and Revisited* 76: Here
they [the sheep] remained until the
fleece dried, and the yolk or natural oil
of the wool began to rise, after which
they were considered to be ready for

shearing.
1897 Henry Lawson 'The Green-hand
Rouseabout' *Verse* i 321: Blinded by
the yolk of wool, and shirt and trousers
stiff with grease.
1912 G. H. Gibson *Ironbark Splinters*
43: While we was grimed from top to
toe / With blood, an' yolk, an' tar.
1921 K. S. Prichard *Black Opal* 116:
Grey flannel shirts and dungarees,
blood-splashed, grimy, and greasy with
the 'yolk' of fleeces they had been
handling.

you beaut see **beaut**

you'll be sorry see **sorry**

young and old, it was on for see **on**

Z

zack Sixpence: *obsolescent* [? Yiddish
(G. *sechs* six)]
1898 *Bulletin* 1 Oct. 14: 6d. a 'zack'
1928 A. W. Upfield *The House of Cain*
89: 'When I throw a seven (die), I
won't have a zac on me.'
1949 Ruth Park *Poor Man's Orange* 105:
Miserable grey sausage, which could be
sold at a 'frippence-worf' and a 'zack's
worf', filled the glass window of the
refrigerator.
1958 Frank Hardy *The Four-Legged
Lottery* 215: 'It's mortgaged, Jim. Not
worth a zac.'
1961 George Farwell *Vanishing Australians* 94: 'He never spent more than a
zac on a feed in his life.'

zambuck Ambulance or first aid man,
esp. at a sporting fixture: *obsolescent*
[f. brand name of an ointment]
1943 Baker 90: *Zambuck* A first-aid
man in attendance at a sporting contest.
1956 Ruth Park and D'Arcy Niland *The
Drums Go Bang* 146-7: 'I might have
come home just in time to see the
zambucks carting you two off in the
ambulance.'
1972 Peter Mathers *The Wort Papers*
95: They even supplied the zambuck,

a priest with brown attaché case containing oils and waters for extreme unction.
1976 *Sun-Herald* 5 Sep. 70: If you asked the kids of to-day what a zambuck was, they would probably tell you that he was some type of South African antelope.

ziff A beard [unexplained]
1919 W. H. Downing *Digger Dialects* 54: *Ziff* A beard.
1924 C. J. Dennis *Rose of Spadgers* 137: 'E lobbed in on us sudden, ziff an' all.
1939 Miles Franklin and Dymphna Cusack *Pioneers on Parade* 88: Lord Cravenburn regretted his ziff.
1947 John Morrison *Sailors Belong Ships* 97: 'We all called him The Prophet. He had a long ziff.'
1961 Robert Close *Hooves of Brass* 22:

He was glad now that he'd let his mates kid him into growing a ziff.

zoo, feeding-time at the An undisciplined assault on food and drink; any disorderly but excited scene
1951 Dymphna Cusack and Florence James *Come in Spinner* 33: 'The Public Bar gets more like Taronga Zoo at feeding time every day.'
1970 Richard Beilby *No Medals for Aphrodite* 68–9: 'Gawd, you should get on that crowd . . . It's like feeding time at the zoo.'
1975 *Sydney Morning Herald* 23 Oct. 6: At question time, the Prime Minister gives a daily performance. It's the highlight of the day – feeding time at the zoo. Just about every question thrown at him he appears to greet with relish.